CSWE's Core Competencies and Dimension Examples in this Text

SOCIAL WORK COMPETENCIES FROM EPAS 2015	1. Ethics and Professional Behavior	2. Diversity and Difference	3. Human Rights	4. Research	5. Policy Practice	6. Engagement	7. Assessment	8. Intervention	9. Evaluation
Dimension: Knowledge	CH 4, p. 97	CH 8, p. 239	CH 2, p. 47	CH 5, p. 153	CH 2, p. 36	CH 8, p. 225	CH 13, p. 421	CH 6, p. 182	CH 11, p. 358 CH 9, p. 289
Dimension: Values	CH 9, p. 267 CH 1, p. 6	CH 3, p. 67	CH 10, p. 319	CH 8, p. 243	CH 10, p. 323	CH 6, p. 165	CH 2, p. 39	CH 4, p. 109	CH 13, p. 445
Dimension: Skills	CH 8, p. 235 CH 10, p. 296	CH 12, p. 400	CH 11, p. 364 CH 3, p. 64	CH 10, p. 307	CH 4, p. 92	CH 5, p. 120	CH 3, p. 63	CH 5, p. 132	CH 12, p. 378
Dimension: Cognitive and Affective Reactions	CH 6, p. 166	CH 7, p. 195	CH 1, p. 13	CH 9, p. 279	CH 13, p. 430	CH 11, p. 338	CH 7, p. 199	CH 12, p. 376	CH 7, p. 205

SEVENTH EDITION

The Social Work Experience

A Case-Based Introduction to Social Work and Social Welfare

Mary Ann Suppes
Mount Mary University, Milwaukee, WI

Carolyn Cressy Wells
University of Wisconsin, Oshkosh, WI

Melinda Lee Kiltz, *Contributing Author*
Mount Mary University, Milwaukee, WI

330 Hudson Street, NY, NY 10013

Director, Teacher Education & the Helping Professions: Kevin M. Davis
Portfolio Manager: Rebecca Fox-Gieg
Content Producer: Pamela D. Bennett
Portfolio Management Assistant: Anne McAlpine
Executive Field Marketing Manager: Krista Clark
Executive Product Marketing Manager: Christopher Berry
Procurement Specialist: Deidra Smith
Cover Designer: Melissa Welch
Cover Photo: Rory McDonald/Getty Images
Full-Service Project Management: Udaya Harisudan, Lumina Datamatics, Inc.
Composition: Lumina Datamatics, Inc.
Printer/Binder: LSC Communications
Cover Printer: Phoenix Color
Text Font: Dante MT Pro Regular 10.5/13 pt.

Copyright © 2018, 2013, 2009 by Pearson Education, Inc. or its affiliates. All Rights Reserved. Printed in the United States of America. This publication is protected by copyright, and permission should be obtained from the publisher prior to any prohibited reproduction, storage in a retrieval system, or transmission in any form or by any means, electronic, mechanical, photocopying, recording, or otherwise. To obtain permission(s) to use material from this work, please visit http://www.pearsoned.com/permissions/.

Acknowledgements of third party content appear on the page within the text or page 484, which constitute an extension of this copyright page.

Unless otherwise indicated herein, any third-party trademarks that may appear in this work are the property of their respective owners and any references to third-party trademarks, logos or other trade dress are for demonstrative or descriptive purposes only. Such references are not intended to imply any sponsorship, endorsement, authorization, or promotion of Pearson's products by the owners of such marks, or any relationship between the owner and Pearson Education, Inc. or its affiliates, authors, licensees or distributors.

Library of Congress Cataloging-in-Publication Data
Names: Suppes, Mary Ann, author. | Wells, Carolyn Cressy, author.
Title: The social work experience : a case-based introduction to social work and social welfare / Mary Ann Suppes,
  Mount Mary University, Milwaukee, WI,
  Carolyn Cressy Wells, University of Wisconsin, Oshkosh, WI.
Description: Seventh Edition. | New York : Pearson, [2018] | Revised edition of the authors' The social work experience,
  c2013. | Includes bibliographical references and index.
Identifiers: LCCN 2016055300 | ISBN 9780134544854 (pbk. : alk. paper)
Subjects: LCSH: Social service—United States. | Social service--Vocational
  guidance—United States.
  States—History—Sources.
Classification: LCC HV10.5 .S97 2018 | DDC 361.3/202373--dc23 LC record available at https://lccn.loc.gov/2016055300

2 17

ISBN 10:   0-13-454485-4
ISBN 13: 978-0-13-454485-4

Preface

Developing this text has been an absorbing project for its two authors for many years. The venture began one beautiful, crisp fall day in Wisconsin when two friends, both experienced social work educators, set off by car for a conference 200 miles to the north. We were those friends, and our conversation during that drive sparked the ideas that resulted in the first edition of *The Social Work Experience*. We were both teaching introductory courses in social work that semester and, because our roots were in social work practice, we were frustrated by the lack of well-developed, contemporary case study materials. Authentic, current case material, we were convinced, would help students to identify with the real people who are served by social workers across the United States and with the social workers themselves.

It occurred to us that we could create those materials from our own professional practice experiences and from the field learning experiences of our students. Our case studies could portray diverse populations in both client and social worker roles. Some could illustrate baccalaureate social work students in field practicum settings. We could synthesize real-life situations of people we had known and thus avoid exact duplication of any actual cases. With these ideas and commitments, the book emerged.

In the seventh edition, the primary focus remains entry-level generalist social work practice, but the linkage between generalist and specialist practice is presented as well. The generalist professional practice competencies as revised in the Council on Social Work Education's *2015 Educational Policy and Accreditation Standards* are highlighted throughout the text. The CSWE's nine revised competencies and four new competency *dimensions* (by which attainment of competencies are measured) are introduced: knowledge, values, skills, and cognitive and affective reactions. The competencies are well integrated into the seventh edition of the text, and critical thinking questions in every chapter challenge readers to think about how the competencies and their dimensions apply to chapter content.

The common themes of previous editions remain integrated into every chapter: generalist practice, social research, ethics and values, and human diversity. Augmenting the human diversity theme, we have integrated discussions of poverty, populations most vulnerable to experiencing poverty, and significant social, economic, and environmental justice issues throughout the book. Many chapters include historical information pertaining to different cultural groups, especially those reflected in the chapter-opening case studies.

Every chapter begins with a well-developed case study. Didactic content in the chapter flows from the case study. The seventh edition, as the name of the text suggests, draws readers into the text content through the addition of short case studies within the chapters. Throughout the text, case studies continue to reflect our concern for special issues relevant to women and other vulnerable populations in the United States plus issues and concerns in the international community.

New to This Edition

The seventh edition is available as an enhanced Pearson eText—a rich, interactive learning environment designed to improve the reader's mastery of content with the following multimedia features[1]:

- **Design:** The overall design fosters the reader's understanding with learning outcomes, clear explanations, rich case studies, applications, and feedback.
- **Video Examples:** Our new digital format allows us to build on our case-based approach by directly linking to videos introducing readers to public policy, the history of the profession, social justice issues, and real social work professionals and clients in a variety of settings.
- **Self-Checks:** Embedded assessment questions align with learning outcomes and appear as a link at the end of each major chapter section in the Pearson eText. Using multiple-choice questions, the self-checks allow readers to assess how well they have mastered the content.
- **Chapter Quizzes:** At the end of each chapter, short-answer questions encourage readers to reflect on chapter concepts. We have provided feedback to support the development of thoughtful responses.

As with every revision of this text, we have carefully edited and updated the content, references, and statistics from the previous edition. Beyond that, however, the seventh edition has gone through even more extensive revisions that include the following:

- CSWE 2015 revised competencies, with examples in every chapter
- CSWE's four new competency *dimensions*, with examples in every chapter
- Revised case studies plus new, additional case studies provided in every chapter
- Summaries with major points aligned with learning outcomes and section headings in every chapter
- New instructive photos provided in every chapter

Ancillaries

The following resources are available for instructors to download at **www.pearsonhighered.com/educators**. Instructors enter the author or title of this book, select the seventh edition of the book, and then click the "Resources" tab to log in and download instructor resources.

Instructor's Resource Manual and Test Bank (0-13-454491-9)

This updated manual includes chapter summaries, lecture guides, discussion prompts, classroom activities, out-of-class assignments, and additional resources for each chapter. Test items in multiple-choice and essay format are also available.

---

[1]Please note that eText enhancements are only available in the Pearson eText and are not available in third-party eTexts such as VitalSource and Kindle.

TestGen (0-13-454488-9)

TestGen is a powerful test generator program containing the same items included in the test bank. You install TestGen on your personal computer (Windows or Mac) and create your own tests for classroom testing and for other specialized delivery options. Assessments may be created for both print and testing online.

Tests can be downloaded in the following formats:

TestGen Testbank file – PC

TestGen Testbank file – Mac

TestGen Testbank – Blackboard 9 TIF

TestGen Testbank – Blackboard CE/Vista (WebCT) TIF

Angel Test Bank (zip)

D2L Test Bank (zip)

Moodle Test Bank

Sakai Test Bank (zip)

Online PowerPoint® Slides (0-13-454490-0)

PowerPoint slides of key concepts from the text are organized by chapter. Colorful, simple, and straightforward, the slides may be customized to fit instructors' needs.

Acknowledgments

Today, as we put the finishing touches on the seventh edition, we wish to express appreciation to some of the many people who have assisted us with this project. We wish to thank our editors, originally Julie Peters and later Kevin Davis, for assisting us throughout the publication process. We wish to thank Andrea Hall, editorial assistant, for coordinating initial correspondence among members of the publication team, including reviewers. We are grateful to Rebecca Fox-Gieg, Portfolio Manager, and and Pamela D. Bennett, Content Producer, from Pearson for their leadership and assistance in the production of this text. We wish to thank our project managers from Lumina Datamatics, initially Jenny Vittorioso, later Kristy Zamagni, Saraswathi Muraldihar, and finally Udaya Harisudan, for their invaluable feedback and guidance. We owe special thanks to Christina Robb, for her encouragement and her careful instruction in preparing our manuscript for the Enhanced eText. Lastly, we wish to thank Frances Bernard Kominkiewicz, Ph.D., Saint Mary's College (IN) for the exceptional quality of the ancillaries that she developed for this text.

We are indebted to the reviewers who provided valuable insight for the seventh edition of the text: Margaret A. Seime, Middle Tennessee State University and Nathaniel Worley Jr., Norfolk State University.

We would also like to express our gratitude to those who provided materials for or helped to design our composite case studies: Isaac Christie, Maria DeMaio, Jason Dietenberger, Joe Dooley, Linda Ketcher Goodrich, David Kucej, Julie Kudick, Maureen Martin, Melissa Monsoor, Malcolm Montgomery, Dolores Poole, Wanda Priddy, Colleen Prividera, David Schneider, Nicholaus P. Smiar, Sara Stites, Victor Sudo, Delores Sumner, Jody Searl Wnorowski, and Ellen Zonka. In addition, we are grateful to Elisha Branch, and Heidi Walter for their technical assistance.

We both owe enormous gratitude to our husbands, Dennis Loeffler and Fritz (Fred) Suppes, for their patience, support, and contributions to our research and resource exploration and for stimulating and nurturing our thinking on social issues.

We continue to be indebted to two prominent theorists, Betty L. Baer and Ronald C. Federico, whose vision of generalist social work practice remains alive today in baccalaureate social work education and within the pages of this book. It is our sincere hope that faculty and students alike will find our book helpful in their professional journeys.

Brief Contents

1. The Social Work Profession   1
2. Theoretical Perspectives for Social Workers   34
3. Social Justice, Poverty, and Diversity: The Intersectionality of Multiple Factors   59
4. Social Welfare Policy: Historical Perspectives   88
5. Family and Children's Services   118
6. Social Work in Mental Health   160
7. Social Work in Health Care   190
8. Social Work in the Schools   223
9. Social Work with Alcohol and Substance Use Disorders   261
10. Social Work with Older Adults   294
11. Social Work in the Criminal Justice System   336
12. Developmental Disabilities and Social Work   373
13. The Social Work Profession Looks to the Future   411

Contents

1. The Social Work Profession   1

CASE STUDY: Susan Dunn   1

Understanding the Social Work Profession   5
- Defining and Differentiating Social Work from Other Professions   5
- A Profession Based on Values and Ethics   6
- A Brief History of the Social Work Profession   8
- Social Work and Social Workers: BSWs, MSWs, and PhDs   10

The Context and Work Environment of Social Workers   12
- Social Work Practice Settings   12
- A Broader Ecological/Environmental Perspective   13

Education for Social Work and Career Opportunities   14
- The Baccalaureate Social Work Curriculum   14
- Selecting a Career in Social Work   16
- Employment Opportunities and Employment Patterns   18
- Salaries and Demand for Social Workers   20
- Employment Projections   23

Licensure and Professional Credentialing   24
- State Licensure and Certification   24
- NASW Credentialing of Advanced Professional Practice   25

Professional Social Work Organizations   26
- The National Association of Social Workers   26
- The Council on Social Work Education   27
- The National Association of Black Social Workers   28
- The National Association of Puerto Rican and Hispanic Social Workers   28
- Other Professional Organizations   29
- International Social Work Organizations   29

Comparing Related Professions   30
- Psychology   30
- Counseling   30
- Psychiatry   31
- Human Services   31
- Inter-Professional Collaboration   31

Summary   32

2. Theoretical Perspectives for Social Workers   34

CASE STUDY: The Several Roles of Stephanie Hermann, BSW   34

Systems Theory and the Ecosystems Perspective   38
    Social Work and Systems Theory   38
    The Ecosystems Perspective   40

The Generalist Approach   41
    Levels of Intervention   42
    Environmental Challenges and Spiritual Responses   44
    The Intervention Process   47

Social Justice, Poverty, and the Intersectionality of Multiple Factors   49
    Values, Ethics, and Human Diversity   49
    Intersectionality of Multiple Factors   49
    The Strengths Perspective: Resilience and Empowerment   50

Political Perspectives   51
    The Political Spectrum   51
    Conservative Perspectives   52
    Liberal or Progressive Perspectives   53
    Neoliberalism and Neoconservatism   54
    Radical Perspectives   55

Turning to Each Other: Margaret Wheatley's Perspectives   56

Summary   57

3. Social Justice, Poverty, and Diversity: The Intersectionality of Multiple Factors   59

CASE STUDY: Meet Juanita Chavez   59

Social and Economic Justice   64
    Concepts in Social and Economic Justice   64
    The Impact of Poverty   66

Poverty, Diversity, and the Intersectionality of Multiple Factors   66
    Diversity and the Intersectionality of Multiple Factors   66
    Children   67
    Women   68
    Older Adults   69
    Racial and Ethnic Minority Groups   70
    People with Disabilities   74
    Gay, Lesbian, and Bisexual Persons   75
    Transgender Persons   76

Potent Forms of Prejudice in the United States   77
    Racism   78
    Sexism   78
    Ageism   79
    Heterosexism, Homophobia, and Transphobia   79

Social Justice Issues in the Twenty-First Century   80
    Poverty Programs That Maintain Poverty   80
    Poverty Line Determination Method   81
    Poverty and the Minimum Wage   81
    Affirmative Action Policies: Under Attack   83
    Social Policy and the Growing Gap Between Rich and Poor   84
    Health Insurance Accessibility   85
    Administrative Barriers to Aid   86
    Social Welfare Policy and Social Justice   86
Summary   87

4. Social Welfare Policy: Historical Perspectives   88
CASE STUDY: The Resourcefulness of Donna Rudnitski   88

Concepts in American Social Welfare Policy and Their Historical Roots   91
    Social Welfare Concepts: Residual vs. Institutional   91
    Old World Historical Roots   92
    The Elizabethan Poor Law and the Act of Settlement   94
    New Concepts in Poor Law   94

Poor Relief in the United States   96
    Values   96
    The Charity Organization Society and the Settlement House Movement   97

Social Welfare in the United States in the Twentieth Century   98
    The Progressive Years, 1900–1930   100
    Federal Initiatives, 1930–1968   101
    Cutting Back the Welfare State, 1968 to the Present   104

Social Welfare Policy in the Twenty-First Century   107
    Temporary Assistance for Needy Families   107
    The Working Poor and the Earned Income Tax Credit   107
    Privatization   109
    The Faith-Based Trend   109

An International Perspective   110
    Sweden   113
    Japan   114
    Progress of Social Justice Today   115
    NASW and Ongoing Human Rights Efforts   116

Summary   117

5. Family and Children's Services   118
CASE STUDY: LaTanya Tracy, Child in Need of Protection   118

Historical Perspectives on Family and Children's Services   121
    Historical Perspectives   121
    The Child Welfare Movement and Protective Services Programs   124

Children's Rights as International Law 126
Challenges of African American Families 127

Services and Their Providers: A Continuum of Care 128
Least Restrictive Environment 128
In-Home Services 129
Out-of-Home Services 133
Client Self-Determination and Professional Decision-making 136

Important Family Issues and Family Types 137
Attachment Theory and Emotional Bonding 139
Reproductive Rights and Single Parenting 140
Ecological Concerns 142
The Child Care Conundrum 144
Gay and Lesbian Families 144
Multi-Racial Families 146
Immigrant Families 147
Military Families 148

Cultural Competence 150
Diverse Family Structures 150
Spirituality and Religion 151

Family Policy 153
Research Raises Questions 153
How Family Friendly Is the American Workplace? 154
The Family and Medical Leave Act 156
Assisting Families Around the World 156
Current Trends in the United States 157

Summary 159

6. Social Work in Mental Health 160

CASE STUDY: Meet David Deerinwater 160

Social Work Competencies for Mental Health Practice 163
Basic Competencies: Knowledge and Skills 163
Values and Ethics 166
Knowledge Related to Mental Health Practice 167

Generalist Practice in Mental Health 172
Case Management 172
Working with Groups 174
Community Practice 176
Disaster Services 176
Practice with Diverse Populations 178
Native American History and the Cherokee Experience 179

Social, Economic, and Environmental Justice Issues 181

Social Policy and Mental Health   182
   Historical Perspectives   183
   The Social Work Profession Emerges   184
   Evolving Social Policy Affects Service in Mental Health   185
   Policy and Practice: Future Issues   187

Summary   189

7. Social Work in Health Care   190

CASE STUDY: Meet Katherine Lewandowski   190

Applying Social Work Competencies in Health Care   193
   Building a Knowledge Base for Health Care Practice   193
   Values and Ethics in Health Care Social Work   194
   Focusing on the Community and Populations at Risk   195
   Achieving Competence for Practice in Health Care   196

Selected Health Care Services   197
   Acute Care   197
   Long-Term Care   198
   Home Health Care   200
   Hospice and Palliative Care   200
   Emergency Department: Trauma and Crisis Amid Human Diversity   201
   Health Care for Veterans   203
   Health Care in Rural Areas   205
   Public Health and Health Departments   206

Historical Perspectives   208
   Early History: Caring for the Poor and Sick   208
   Origins of Health Care Social Work   208
   The Emergence of Health Care Social Work in the United States   209

Social Justice: Politics and Economics in Health Care   209
   Medicare   211
   Medicaid   212
   Health Care Reform   213
   The Patient Protection and Affordable Care Act   214
   Cost-Benefit Analysis   215
   Future Health Care Policy in the United States   218
   Human Rights and Health: Global Perspectives   220

Summary   222

8. Social Work in the Schools   223

CASE STUDY: Understanding Lisa and Loretta Santiago   223

A Brief History of Social Work in the Schools   227
   People of Latino or Hispanic Heritage: A Brief History   227
   Historical Highlights of Social Work in the Schools   229
   School Social Worker Certification   233

Social Work Roles in the Schools   233
- Working with Individuals   233
- Family Work   234
- Group Work   234
- Working with Organizations and Communities   234
- Teamwork   235
- School-Linked, Integrated Services   235

The Impact of Diversity in the Schools   236
- Cultural Diversity   236
- Alternative Schools and Charter Schools   239
- Special Needs   240
- Educational Evaluations as Applied Research   242
- School Social Work with Other Special-Needs Children: The Ordeal of Two Gay Brothers   243
- Student Rights and the Law   246

Social Work Values in the School Setting: Policy Implications   247
- The Santiago Sisters   247
- The Larkin Case   248
- Bullying and Violence in the Schools   249
- The Environment and Early Sexual Development   251
- Nutrition and Achievement   253
- No Child Left Behind and the Every Student Succeeds Act   253
- Student Achievement: International Rankings   254
- Spiritual Development and Empowerment   255
- Current Trends   256

An International Comparison: School Social Work in Ghana   257

Summary   260

9. Social Work with Alcohol and Substance Use Disorders   261

CASE STUDY: Meet Dan Graves   261

The Profession's History in the Substance Use Disorders Field   264
- Early History of Social Work Involvement: Mary Richmond   264
- Social Work Contributions and Leadership Evolve   265

Critical Components of Professional Practice   266
- Values and Ethical Issues in the Alcohol and Drug Use Disorders Field   266
- Problem Solving: Use of Engagement, Assessment, Intervention, and Evaluation   267
- Diversity: Gender, Age, Culture and Ethnicity, Gay/Lesbian/Transgender, Disability   275
- Persons with Disabilities   281

The Classes of Substances Used   282

Global and Environmental Models of Prevention and Treatment   286
   A European Prevention and Treatment Approach: The Harm Reduction Model   286
   U.S. Model: Alcoholics Anonymous   287
   Environmental Perspectives   289

U.S. Social Welfare Policy   290
   Shifts in U.S. Social Welfare Policy   290
   Social Justice and Human Rights vs. Criminalization and Incarceration   291

Summary   293

10. Social Work with Older Adults   294

CASE STUDY: Caring for Abbie Heinrich   294

Social Work with Older Adults: A Brief History   299
   The Importance of Generalist Social Work   300
   Gerontological or Geriatric Social Work   302
   Empowerment Practice   303

Who Are Our Older Adults?   303
   Geographical Distribution   303
   Marital Status   304
   Education   304
   Employment   304
   Economic Status   305
   Housing   306
   Health: Physical and Mental   307
   Alzheimer's Disease and Related Dementias   308
   Ethnicity   309
   The Environment and Older Adults   310

Older Adults and Their Families   311
   Daily Life in Later Years   311
   Research on Family Strengths   311
   Ethnic and Cultural Minorities   312
   Gay and Lesbian Older Adults   313
   Older Adults as Caregivers; Grandparent-Headed Families   313
   Caregiver Stress and the "Sandwich Generation"   314
   Elder Abuse and Self Neglect   315

Social Policy and Older Adults: Past to Present   316
   Family Care   316
   Early Pension Plans   316
   Trends in American Private Pensions   317
   Social Security Today   317
   Supplemental Security Income   319
   Housing Assistance   319
   Medicare and Medicaid   320

Food Stamps, or the Supplemental Nutrition Assistance Program 321
The Older Americans Act 322
The Social Services Block Grant 322
Values and Public Policy 323
The "Continuum of Care": Prolonging Independence 324
Emerging Lifestyle Trends and Innovative Programs 328
An International Perspective: The Netherlands 329

End of Life Issues: Care Needs, Religion, and Spirituality 331
Coming to Terms with Long-Term Care 331
Death and Dying 331
Spirituality and Religion 331
Hospice Services, Palliative Care, and Complementary Therapies 333
Social Work with Older Adults: A Growing Future 333

Summary 334

11. Social Work in the Criminal Justice System 336
CASE STUDY: Alan Martin's Social Work Identity Crisis 336

History of the Criminal Justice System 339
European Historical Roots of Criminal Justice Systems 339
History of Criminal Justice Systems in the United States 340
Social Work Emerges: Progressive Contributions of Jane Addams and Hull House Staff 340

Components of the Criminal Justice System 341
Law Enforcement 342
The Courts 344
The Correctional System 345
The Juvenile Justice System 351

Social Work Practice in the Criminal Justice System 354
Value Dilemmas for Social Workers 354
Forensic Social Work 355
Social Work with Groups and Organizations 357

Social, Economic, and Environmental Justice 358
Environmental Perspective: Communities at Risk 359
Environmental Perspective: Community Strength, Restoration, Spirituality, and Resilience 359
Global Context 360
Promoting Human Rights and Social Justice 362
The Death Penalty 365
Reforming Juvenile and Adult Criminal Justice Systems 367

Summary 372

12. Developmental Disabilities and Social Work 373

CASE STUDY: Mary and Lea Perkins 373

Services for People with Disabilities: A Brief History 378
- *Pioneering Efforts* 378
- *Training Schools* 379
- *Protective Asylums* 379
- *The Eugenics Movement* 380
- *New Research, New Attitudes* 381
- *Normalization and the Deinstitutionalization Movement* 382
- *Deinstitutionalization as a Goal* 382

Types of Developmental Disabilities 384
- *Developmental Disabilities: What Are They?* 384
- *Difference Between Disability and Developmental Disability* 384
- *Categorical vs. Functional Definitions of Developmental Disability* 384
- *Intellectual Disability* 384
- *Cerebral Palsy* 386
- *Autism Spectrum Disorders* 386
- *Orthopedic Problems* 388
- *Hearing Problems* 389
- *Epilepsy* 390
- *Traumatic Brain Injury* 390
- *Learning Disabilities* 391
- *Emotional Disturbance* 392
- *Fetal Alcohol Spectrum Disorders; Cocaine-Exposed and Other Drug-Exposed Babies* 392
- *Overall Prevalence and Co-Occurrence of Disabilities* 393
- *The Continuum of Care* 394

Social Work Practice with People Who Have Disabilities 395
- *Education for Work with People Who Have Disabilities: CSWE Educational Policy* 395
- *NASW Code of Ethics* 395
- *Institutional Settings* 396
- *Community Settings* 396
- *Genetic Counseling* 397
- *Spirituality Dimensions* 397

Human Diversity and Social Justice 398
- *Providing Supportive Services to Diverse Families: A Chinese Illustration* 399
- *Asian Americans: A Brief History* 400
- *Social Justice Issues and Disability* 401
- *Mismatch between Person and Environment* 401
- *Discrimination* 401
- *Empowerment, Self-Determination, and Self-Advocacy* 402

The Disability Rights Movement, Social Policy, and Appropriate Terminology 403
- *The Americans with Disabilities Act of 1990 and the Civil Rights Act of 1991* 404

Global Efforts on Behalf of People with Disabilities   406
Value Dilemmas and Ethical Implications   406
Current Trends   407

Summary   409

13. The Social Work Profession Looks to the Future   411

CASE STUDY: Rachel Fox: Student Social Worker in an International Field Placement   411

Social Work: A Profession at the Edge of Change   415
National and International Strategic Planning   417
Globalization: Relevance to Social Work   418

The Major Forces Driving Transformation of the World   420
Demographic Trends   421
The Changing Immigrant and Refugee Population   425
Political Forces   428
Economic Trends   433
Technological Trends and Biomedical Advances   435
Environmental Sustainability   440

The Future of the Social Work Profession   442
The Social Work Workforce: Employment Projections, Social Worker Shortages   442
The Grand Challenges and Contributions of Social Work   443

Summary   445

Glossary   447
References   461
Photo Credits   484
Index   485

1

The Social Work Profession

LEARNING OUTCOMES

- Describe the social work profession.
- Explain the context and work environment of social workers.
- Discuss the professional curriculum of social work and the career opportunities available to social workers.
- Explain how the social work profession is legally regulated through licensure and credentialing.
- Describe the major professional social work organizations.
- Compare and contrast the roles and responsibilities of social workers and those of professionals that social workers frequently work with.

CHAPTER OUTLINE

CASE STUDY: Susan Dunn 1

Understanding the Social Work Profession 5
   Defining and Differentiating Social Work from Other Professions 5
   A Profession Based on Values and Ethics 6
   A Brief History of the Social Work Profession 8
   Social Work and Social Workers: BSWs, MSWs, and PhDs 10

The Context and Work Environment of Social Workers 12
   Social Work Practice Settings 12
   A Broader Ecological/Environmental Perspective 13

CASE STUDY: Susan Dunn

The telephone rang shrilly at the women's shelter at about 6:15 in the evening. The caller's voice was urgent, frightened, and intense, although little louder than a whisper. "I just called the crisis telephone line that was advertised on the radio," the woman began, "and the person who answered told me to try you. I need a safe place to stay, right now. Can you take me?"

"We may be able to," the social worker replied. "It depends on your situation. Our agency has been set up to help women who have been physically abused. Can you tell me something about yourself? What makes you need a place to stay just now?"

"I can't talk very long because I'm so afraid he'll come back soon," the caller responded, her voice slightly louder this time. "My

1

CHAPTER OUTLINE *(Continued)*

Education for Social Work and Career Opportunities 14
- The Baccalaureate Social Work Curriculum 14
- Selecting a Career in Social Work 16
- Employment Opportunities and Employment Patterns 18
- Salaries and Demand for Social Workers 20
- Employment Projections 23

Licensure and Professional Credentialing 24
- State Licensure and Certification 24
- NASW Credentialing of Advanced Professional Practice 25

Professional Social Work Organizations 26
- The National Association of Social Workers 26
- The Council on Social Work Education 27
- The National Association of Black Social Workers 28
- The National Association of Puerto Rican and Hispanic Social Workers 28
- Other Professional Organizations 29
- International Social Work Organizations 29

Comparing Related Professions 30
- Psychology 30
- Counseling 30
- Psychiatry 31
- Human Services 31
- Inter-Professional Collaboration 31

Summary 32

---

husband just beat me up again, but he ran out when I threatened to call the police. The children saw the whole thing. I've decided I've had enough. But I don't know where to go. My friends are afraid to get involved. I've got two kids who have to go with me. I don't have any money of my own."

"Sounds like you're in a tough spot. My name is Pamela Wright. I'm a social worker here. Tell me if you need to stop talking. Call me back if you have to hang up. If you're in danger right at this moment, I can take your name and address and call the police for you."

"Oh, no," the woman said. "The reason I didn't call the police in the first place is that I don't want to get my husband in trouble. I make him upset. Calling the police would embarrass the whole family. I couldn't possibly do that."

"You said your husband hurt you. Do you have injuries that may need immediate medical attention?"

"When he hit my face, I tried to defend myself. I didn't want my face covered with bruises again. I put my hands up to my face. My right arm and shoulder hurt pretty badly now. I don't think I need to see a doctor or go to the hospital. I just need to get away from here."

"Do you feel it is safe for you to talk with me for a few minutes now?"

"Yes. The last time my husband got mad at me and left, he stayed away for a couple of hours. I'm pretty sure he'll do that again this time."

"Well," Pamela Wright said gently, "from what you say, this isn't the first time your husband has physically abused you. I take it that you want to be gone this time when he gets home?"

"Yes. He might come home drunk and hit me again. That's what happened last time. If it weren't for the children, I might take a chance and wait for him because he might come home sorry and ready to make up. But the kids are awfully upset and scared. I want to get out of here this time."

"Have you any relatives who might be able to take you and the children tonight? You might feel a lot better if you had some family members around you to support you and help with the kids this evening. We'd be happy to help you here even if you were staying somewhere else. You could come in tomorrow, in fact, to talk with one of our counselors about things you could think about doing to deal with the physical abuse by your husband."

"I haven't got any family of my own around here. My parents live in another state, and so does my sister. My in-laws live near here, and they're good to me, but they would break down and tell my husband where I was. Then he'd come and he might beat me up again. So I don't want anybody to know where I am."

Recognizing that this was an emergency situation, Pamela Wright said quickly, "We do have a room available in our shelter right now. I think that it is important for you to leave your home as quickly as possible. Will you be able to get yourself over here on your own if I give you the address?"

"Oh, I don't think I can. I don't have a car. My arm really hurts. I don't think I can carry anything. My 6-year-old can make it on her own, but the 2-year-old is too much trouble to take on the bus the way my arm hurts. And I'll need to bring some clothes and things."

"Have you any money at all right now?" Pamela asked. "We do have some special funds to send a cab in emergency situations, but those funds are very tight. Could you pay for a cab to get yourself and the kids over here?"

"Well, I have about $15 in my purse. My husband always keeps the checkbook with him, and he just gives me cash a little bit at a time. But if I spend what I have on a cab, I won't have any money at all to pay for my stay with you, or for anything else, for that matter."

"Our services are free. We can supply you with a small room for yourself and your children. We also provide meals. You can stay with us for up to a month. We will help you to decide what to do next. There will be rules about sharing household tasks and some other things, but I can explain more when you get here. You need to know, though, that we may want you to get checked out by a doctor. Sometimes people are more seriously injured than they initially think they are. Do you think you want to come?"

After a moment's hesitation the caller whispered, "Yes, I do. Can I come with the kids right away?"

"Certainly," Pamela said. "But how bad is your arm? Will you be able to manage?"

"I think I can. I'll just have to pack with one hand. My 6-year-old can help. Is there anything in particular that we should bring?"

"Just bring the routine stuff—you know, toothbrushes, pajamas, toys, extra clothes, anything to keep you and the children as comfortable as possible."

"Okay. Thank you very much. I hope I'll be there soon."

"Fine. I'll give you our address. You are asked to tell it to no one but the cab driver because, for safety reasons, we need to keep it secret." Pamela gave the woman the address of the shelter. "Now," she continued, "if your husband comes home before you get a chance to leave in the cab, do call the police right away, the minute you see him approaching. Or call us, and we'll call the police. Don't take the chance of another beating. Now, what is your name and address? I need to take your phone number, too, just in case." The address that the caller, Susan Dunn, gave turned out to be from a rather affluent suburban subdivision.

When Susan Dunn and her two children arrived at the shelter, their appearance betrayed some of their trouble. Susan's left eye was swollen and turning black. She held her sore right arm awkwardly, and several fingers were bleeding and discolored. The eyes of both children were red from crying. Susan's clothes were rumpled and torn. She carried a small suitcase, and her 6-year-old daughter was wearing a backpack full of school supplies.

The newcomers entered the shelter, a crowded house in a busy city neighborhood, quite hesitantly and looked anxiously about the first-floor hallway with its worn brown rug and cheerful, hopeful posters. A dark-eyed child of 5 or 6 ran up to greet them. Pamela Wright introduced herself and the child, waiting for Susan to introduce herself in turn along with her own children, Martha and Todd.

As Pamela Wright completed the introductions, Susan slumped into a chair and tears streamed down her face. She apologized, saying how grateful she was to be there. Pamela asked again about her injuries, and this time Susan replied, "Maybe I do need to see a doctor. My arm and my fingers hurt so much. Maybe something really is broken."

Pamela immediately unloaded the children's and Susan's few belongings. "Would it be okay if Sara, our student social worker, helped the children get settled in with something to eat while I take you over to the emergency room to get checked out?"

Susan reached for 2-year-old Todd and hugged him to her. She brushed away her tears and said, "I'd really like to get the children comfortable first. Then I think it would be a good idea to get my arm checked out."

An hour later, with the children in Sara's gentle care, Pamela drove Susan to the hospital. In the car, Susan talked more about her husband, Jason, a recent college graduate who was building his future in the business world but with increasing stress and a growing reliance on alcohol. X-rays demonstrated that Susan's right arm and two fingers were fractured. Pamela stayed at Susan's side as the medical staff attended to her fractures. The hospital staff contacted the police, and reports were filed. The ride back to the shelter was a quiet one. As they approached the shelter, Pamela told Susan, "You have had a really difficult day, but you have made some really important decisions for yourself and for your family. You have been amazingly strong today. Please remember that we are here to help you." Susan smiled weakly through her pain and tears and then hugged herself gently and nodded her head in agreement.

The Susan Dunn case was designed to introduce readers to this book and also to the profession of social work. As a reader, you will quickly discover that the entire text is case-based. Every chapter begins with a well-developed case study, and brief case scenarios in the chapters further illustrate text content. The case-based design of this book illustrates the wide range of social problems social workers address, the diversity of both the social workers and the people they serve, and the values and ethics that permeate this profession.

This text is entitled *The Social Work Experience* because it provides a glimpse of what it would be like to practice social work. Chapter 1 gives you a basic understanding of the profession, professional values, the educational preparation for practice, and employment opportunities. In Chapter 2, readers learn about the theories that guide social work thinking. Chapter 3 describes the social justice issues that impact the populations that social workers serve. Chapter 4 explains how social welfare programs of today evolved over time, along with the social work profession. Building on this understanding, Chapters 5 through 12 depict social work practice in mental health, schools, health care, child and family services, and other interesting fields of practice. Chapter 13, the final chapter, considers demographic trends, environmental sustainability, and other social forces that create opportunities and challenges for the future.

The Council on Social Work Education, which is the national accrediting organization for social work in the United States, has mandated a set of competencies that must be attained by students in schools of social work. These competencies are frequently referred to in the book and, because of their importance to social work education, they appear along with critical thinking questions in each chapter. Notice, too, the terms that appear in bold print throughout the book. Because you should understand these terms, their definitions appear at the end of each chapter. Video clips of interest are another special feature of this text. And, last but not least, in order to help you quickly assess how well you understand the material, quizzes appear at the end of each chapter's major topical sections. Short-answer review questions at the end of chapters further enable you to check your understanding.

UNDERSTANDING THE SOCIAL WORK PROFESSION

As the case study of Susan Dunn begins, you can probably imagine Pamela Wright's quick glance at Susan and her observation of the painful way Susan was moving her body and the grim, anxious expression on Susan's face. In her professional practice, this social worker had come to know well the terror and panic that threatened to overwhelm the women that arrived at the door of the shelter. Pamela's heart went out to Susan. She looked so frightened, so unsure of her decision. But, as a social worker, Pamela also had a good intellectual understanding of the dynamics of domestic abuse and the vulnerability faced by adults and children in at-risk situations. Pamela would review quickly in her mind the information she would need to obtain from Susan and the decisions that might need to be made quickly. She would prepare to use her social work expertise to listen to Susan's story and to offer Susan emotional support. Pamela, a baccalaureate-level social worker (BSW), was proud of her profession and confident in her ability to work with the people served by the shelter.

> As you watch this video interview regarding domestic violence, please note how the information shared by Dr. Carolann Peterson is borne out in the case of Susan Dunn and her children.
> https://www.youtube.com/watch?v=nJXwuW0F8Ac

Defining and Differentiating Social Work from Other Professions

We begin our exploration of this profession with a definition of **social work**:

> The major profession worldwide that helps individual people, families, groups, organizations, and communities to prevent or resolve problems in social and psychological functioning, meet basic human needs, achieve life-enhancing goals, and create a just society.

This definition underscores several important aspects of the profession that may not be readily apparent in the definition. First, in conjunction with its focus on preventing and resolving problems in psychosocial functioning and ensuring that basic human needs are met for all people, the social work profession seeks to empower people and to identify and build on the strengths that exist in people and within families, groups, organizations, and communities. In addition, social and economic justice emerges as a focus of social work that is distinctive among the professions. Finally, because the profession of social work delivers social services within governmental and private organizations of nations, it is grounded in the human social welfare systems of countries.

While there are areas of overlap between social work and other professions, there are several ways in which social work is unique. Its dual focus on both the social environment and the psychological functioning of people differentiates social work from

Chapter 1

professions such as teaching, psychology, and psychiatry. The social work approach of building on strengths within people and their communities further differentiates social work from most health care, legal, and criminal justice professions. Nonetheless, this text will demonstrate how all of these professions work collaboratively to achieve the goals of individual people and society.

A Profession Based on Values and Ethics

A characteristic that sets true professions apart from occupations is that professions have a formal code of ethics that is recognized by courts and state licensing bodies for determining the parameters of appropriate professional practice. The *National Association of Social Workers (NASW) Code of Ethics*, initially developed in 1960, has been revised many times, most recently in 2008. The current NASW Code of Ethics consists of four parts: a preamble, which identifies the core values of the profession; a statement of purpose; identification of ethical principles; and the ethical standards (NASW, 2015c). A brief summary of the NASW Code of Ethics follows, but the entire document can be readily reviewed at the National Association of Social Workers website. The code is referred to frequently throughout this book because it is so essential to social work practice.

The NASW Code of Ethics begins with the key (core) values. In general, **values** can be thought of as the philosophical concepts that we cherish as individuals, within our families, and as a nation. The NASW Code of Ethics discusses the profession's core values, which are taught in social work classes. Why are values important pieces of the social work curriculum? To begin, society in the United States and in many other countries holds contradictory values concerning the needy. Some values found in society guide people toward helping the poor; others guide people away from helping the poor, either because poor people are viewed as unworthy or because they are viewed as potential competitors. Because we are all products of our society, an honest assessment of our own personal values may reveal that we have absorbed some quite negative values about certain people—the poor, for example. Yet that clearly conflicts with the profession's valuing of social justice.

Demonstrate Ethical and Professional Behavior

Dimension of Competency Values: Social workers recognize personal values and the distinction between personal and professional values.

Critical Thinking Question: What might the outcome be if the NASW Social Work Code of Ethics did not contain a set of values?

Few other professional ethical codes actually incorporate a set of values. Often, when people have difficulty understanding the profession of social work or why it is that someone would want to be a social worker, they do not know about the values of social work. The core values guide and define the ethical practice of social workers; they are the basic building blocks of the code of ethics. These six core values are as follows:

- service
- social justice
- dignity and worth of all persons
- importance of human relationships
- integrity
- competence (NASW, 2015c, p. 2).

The next section of the NASW Code of Ethics explains how the ethical code is used. A primary purpose of the code is to help social workers determine appropriate actions when questions or dilemmas arise about potential violations or conflicts among different sections of the code. The NASW Code of Ethics also provides a basis for adjudication of malpractice or ethical complaints by courts of law and insurance companies, and it also helps the general public understand appropriate professional conduct by social workers.

The social work values form the basis for the third part of the NASW Code of Ethics, the ethical principles. Like the ethical code of the social work profession, some other professional ethical codes (the law profession, for example) incorporate aspirations—the ideals that members should strive for but are not held accountable to perform. Like the law profession, the NASW Code of Ethics' value of service encourages social workers to provide free, volunteer services and to make service to their clients their primary priority. (Volunteer services, when provided, are often offered outside the place of employment and do not decrease the social worker's salary.) The social work value of social justice instructs social workers to pursue social and economic justice on behalf of people who are poor, discriminated against, unemployed, and subject to other forms of oppression. The next ethical principle calls for social workers to value the dignity and worth of people in ways such as honoring clients' self-determination. In recognizing the importance and value of human relationships in human well-being, social workers are expected to help individuals, families, groups, and communities to develop, promote, and restore relationships. The final principle mirrors the core social work value of competence: It states that social workers should continually develop their professional knowledge and skills (NASW, 2015c).

The heart of the NASW Code of Ethics consists of six ethical standards, each of which has many distinct sub-standards. Each standard relates to an area of ethical professional responsibility. While the six standards are unique to social work, the format of the NASW Code of Ethics and even some of the specific items, are also found in other professions' ethical codes. The six areas identified for social workers involve their responsibilities to clients, to colleagues, within their practice settings, as professional persons, to the profession of social work, and to the broader society. The social work core values are readily identified within the six standards. The first standard, for example, reflects the value of service when it states that social workers' primary responsibility is to their clients. This is the first item in Standard 1. The only exception to this commitment to clients is if there are legal obligations (such as reporting child abuse) or if clients are a danger to themselves or others. Not surprisingly, some of the sub-standards address confidentiality, the prohibition of sexual contact or sexual harassment, and the use of derogatory language in communications with or about clients (NASW, 2015c).

The second standard focuses on the nature of relationships between colleagues (either other social workers or other persons that are also involved in serving clients). This standard also promotes respect of colleagues and development of collaborative interdisciplinary relationships, but the standard also provides clear guidelines when colleagues exhibit serious personal problems, incompetence, or unethical conduct that interferes with their practice or endangers clients. The third standard discusses responsibilities within social workers' practice settings (places of employment). Timely and accurate documentation of client service is a necessity as well as a commitment to employers (except when an employing organization has policies or procedures that are inconsistent with the NASW Code of Ethics). For social workers who are administrators, supervisors, or students' field instructors, clear expectations for performance evaluation and interpersonal relationships with staff are identified (NASW, 2015c).

Standard 4 clarifies the responsibilities of social workers as professionals. These responsibilities include acquiring the necessary competence before applying for a job or having a clear plan to obtain the needed competence. The standard is very clear that social workers must not discriminate and it lists race, religion, sexual orientation, age, immigration status, and disability, among other areas of potential bias. Standard 4 also requires social workers to take responsibility in the event that they, themselves, develop personal problems that could interfere with their professional performance. This standard also explicitly addresses the need to take credit only for written work that social workers have authored; plagiarism, when students fail to cite the correct authors in their term papers, would be a violation of this standard. Standard 5 cites areas in which social workers hold responsibility to their profession such as upholding the integrity of the profession by advancing the knowledge, values, and ethics of the profession. Sustaining high standards for social work research and evaluation is a central concern of Standard 5.

 Standard 6 concludes the NASW Code of Ethics. It points to social workers' ethical responsibilities to the broader society. The standard calls for promoting social, political, and economic justice for all people from local to global communities. Preventing exploitation of and discrimination toward people is expected of social workers. In public emergencies, social workers are expected to provide professional services as needed (NASW, 2015c).

A Brief History of the Social Work Profession

Social work is an evolving, relatively young profession, but it has a longer history than some related fields, such as counseling. As Morales and Sheafor (2002) point out, the profession of social work grew out of and has sustained commitment to a threefold mission: caring, curing, and changing society. All three components are intrinsically related to social justice. From its earliest beginnings, the predecessors of social work have cared for the most vulnerable groups of people in society. Sometimes society's caring was (and still is) prompted by humanitarian concerns; at other times it was mixed with less noble objectives. Persons who were not valued by society because they were too ill, too old or too young, too disabled, or otherwise not productive tended to be the very persons that social workers recognized as needing services and assistance. Social workers have a strong history of helping people change, grow, and develop new skills. Some of the earliest social workers also were reformers who advocated for human rights through labor laws, political action, and community development.

The Civil War in the United States is probably responsible for the first paid social work–type positions. These jobs were created in 1863 by the Special Relief Department of the U.S. Sanitary Commission to assist Union Army soldiers or their families with health and social problems related to the war. The impact of these workers and other humanitarians such as Clara Barton, who later founded the American Red Cross, helped pave the way of the future social work profession. Three subsequent social movements arising in the late 1800s significantly contributed to the development of the profession.

One major movement was the Charity Organization Society (COS); it began in England and took hold in Buffalo, New York, in 1877. Its most famous leader was Mary Richmond. Volunteers for the COS, usually wealthy women who were not permitted by social norms of the time to be employed, visited people in their homes to provide food, clothing, and other needs.

A second major movement contributed a strong social justice thrust to the developing young social work profession. This was the settlement house movement, which, like the COS, began in England. In the United States, Jane Addams was its most famous leader. Addams established Hull House in Chicago in 1889. Settlement workers believed that poverty resulted from unjust and unfortunate social conditions. Settlement workers often chose to live among the poor. They assisted in developing needed services such as day care for children of factory workers through mutual aid. They also advocated for better working conditions and protective legislation through various governmental bodies.

> Watch this video clip. Take note of the variety of services offered by Hull House. Consider how different each service/program was, and yet how there was a central mission among all of the work: social justice.
> https://www.youtube.com/watch?v=NiVsH9ICfVk

A third movement, more diffuse and often not recognized for its historical impact on the development of the profession, was the child welfare movement. This began with the Children's Aid Society, founded in New York in 1853, and was strengthened by the Society for the Prevention of Cruelty to Children, founded in 1875, also in New York City. The child welfare movement, over time, evolved into the entire area of foster care, adoptions, child protective services, and juvenile court services.

A growing desire for professionalization emerged by the late 1890s. Charity organization work and settlement house work were increasingly salaried, but as yet there was no name for this profession. By the early 1900s, the broad field of applied philanthropy began to be called social work or social casework. The New York School of Philanthropy, established in 1904, was the first professional education program. Mary Richmond, leader of the COS, was among the original faculty. The school is now known as the Columbia University School of Social Work.

Gradually, the theory base of the profession was developed, and research began to be published. Freudian theory was widely adopted in the 1920s. The Great Depression turned public attention to the economic and social forces causing poverty. The result was the passage of the Social Security Act in 1935, legislation in which social workers played a prominent role. From its earliest days, the profession of social work embodied focus on social reform and the psychosocial problems of individuals, families, and communities.

World Wars I and II further increased social workers' involvement in mental health as psychiatric casualties of the wars brought large numbers of social workers into military social work. Social workers with master's degrees dominated the profession by the early 1950s, but they tended to work in specialization areas such as child welfare, medical social work, or psychiatric social work. In a remarkable move toward unity, seven specialty areas merged to found the NASW in 1955. Until 1970, when BSWs were added, NASW membership was exclusively limited to MSWs. The founding of NASW and the enactment of the NASW Code of Ethics to ground the practice of all social workers firmly established social work as a profession.

In the years since the birth of the profession, social work has grown dramatically in numbers, in areas of practice, in the people it serves, and in status. It has achieved legal regulation (licensure or certification) in every state. The profession retains its social reform legacy by lobbying against discriminatory legislation and by supporting social policies that promote human welfare and well-being. Social work and social welfare, therefore, remain intertwined today. Because of its commitment to social and economic justice and its mission to work on behalf of people who are discriminated against, the profession of social work is sometimes not well understood or even well accepted. Its values make social work a truly unique profession.

Social Work and Social Workers: BSWs, MSWs, and PhDs

Building on this basic understanding of the history of social work, we will next explore the different levels of professional practice in social work. We begin with the baccalaureate level, the **BSW**. This book will emphasize social work at the baccalaureate level; therefore, more substantial information will be provided about BSW practice than the two more advanced areas, the master's (**MSW**) and doctorate degree levels of the profession (**PhD**).

The BSW is the first, or entry, level into the profession. The degree is generally referred to in conversation as a BSW, but the actual degree awarded by colleges and universities ranges from a BA, BS, BSSW, to the BSW degree. All of these baccalaureate degrees are of equal value, assuming that the social work educational program in which the degree is earned is accredited by the Council on Social Work Education (CSWE). The BSW can be completed in four years of college or university work, longer if the student is enrolled on a part-time basis. The BSW social worker, like Pamela Wright in the chapter case study, is professionally prepared as a generalist to provide services to people in a broad range of circumstances. (Generalist practice will be defined and explained in Chapter 2.)

Advanced, specialized social work practice usually requires additional education. The MSW is designed as a two-year degree following completion of a baccalaureate degree. In actuality, an MSW can be completed in as little as one year for students who are awarded advanced standing because they have already completed a BSW. The MSW prepares social workers for an area of specialization. Although they differ among MSW programs, specializations include various methods of practice (such as group work and administration), fields of practice (clinical social work or health care), social problem areas (poverty and substance abuse), special populations (older adults and a cultural groups such as Hispanic Americans), or even advanced generalist practice.

The domestic violence shelter in the case study employed an MSW social worker as well as Pamela Wright, BSW. Amy Sacks, MSW, received specialized training in working with individuals, families, and groups. This specialization at the graduate level may be called direct practice or clinical social work. Amy's work is rather narrowly defined. It is structured by appointments for individual and family therapy, regularly scheduled group sessions, and staff meetings. Amy is responsible for overseeing the shelter's program in crisis couples' counseling and for the batterers' intervention program, where she works with groups designed specifically for people like Susan Dunn's husband who abuse their

> **Box 1.1 Amy Sacks's Domestic Violence Group**
>
> Amy Sacks, MSW, was the facilitator for a group of men who had been involved in domestic abuse. Susan Dunn's husband, Jason, was not under court order to attend this group, as were several other participants, but Jason was referred to the group by his pastor after Susan and the children had not returned home in two weeks.
>
> Jason initially resented the approach of the groups and he often found the group meetings confrontational and difficult. Amy's weekly group sessions were based on a curriculum that required focus on topics like alternatives to physical confrontation and shared decision-making, including family financial planning. On more than one night after returning home to any empty house following the group meeting, Jason found himself in tears, both angry and desperately wanting Susan back. In his loneliness, he became terribly aware of how badly he had treated her and how much he needed to change.
>
> In time, Amy Sacks and the group helped Jason to understand that it would take time to replace harmful behaviors and be alone at home safely with his family. Jason did not know how he could ever recreate his relationship with Susan, but he realized that he wanted very much to become a nurturing father for his children. This became Jason's goal when the first group series ended and he voluntarily signed up for another group on fathering.

partners. (The Box 1.1 scenario illustrates how Susan Dunn's husband might respond in one of Amy's groups.)

Pamela Wright's BSW role at the shelter is broader and more flexible than Amy's. She too counsels individuals, families, and groups, but usually in a less formal manner and not necessarily by appointment. In addition, she responds to crisis calls, intervenes in problems among the residents, trains volunteers, and supervises the myriad tasks involved in running a residential facility. She does not live at the shelter, but coordinates the schedules of evening staff and occasionally receives calls at night from staff for help during emergencies.

The fact that the BSW is educated to be a generalist does not mean that on occasion she or he does not develop or learn specialized skills in a particular field of practice (or, for that matter, that an MSW cannot be a generalist). In the real world, where funding may not provide the means to hire enough professionals to do a given job, both BSWs and MSWs may carry similar responsibility, but the MSW is able to work at an advanced practice level. MSWs are also more likely to be promoted to administrative positions, especially in larger organizations. The work of the BSW is usually more diverse and it usually involves mobilizing a wide variety of skills and resources.

Doctorate degrees are also offered in social work. Doctorates are the highest degrees awarded in higher education. In social work, a doctorate could take three to five years to complete beyond the master's degree. The doctoral degree in social work, usually a PhD or a DSW, prepares people for teaching in colleges and universities, for advanced specialized practice, or for research and organizational administrative positions.

> **?** Assess your understanding of the social work profession by taking this brief quiz.

THE CONTEXT AND WORK ENVIRONMENT OF SOCIAL WORKERS

Social Work Practice Settings

Regardless of the degree they receive—BSW, MSW, or PhD—social workers practice their profession in a remarkably wide array of settings. By contrast, teachers tend to be employed in schools, physical therapists and nurses in health care organizations, and psychologists in mental health settings. A misconception about social work, held by some people, is that all social workers are employed by governmental organizations and work with the poor or in child welfare, where they take children away from their parents. Social workers do have special concerns about poverty and social injustice, but people of all income levels are clients of social workers. Social workers do not work only in governmental offices, and social workers do make every possible effort to keep families together.

There are so many misunderstandings about the profession of social work! Many people would be surprised to learn about the range of settings in which social workers are found. To begin with, while most social workers are employed by organizations, some social workers are in private practice similar to the private practice of doctors. Like many other professionals (e.g., teachers, lawyers, rehabilitation therapists), some social workers are government employees; however, a declining number of social workers are employed in federal, state, or local tax-supported organizations. Increasingly, social workers are likely to be employed by nonprofit private agencies (such as the American Red Cross), denominational (church-sponsored) organizations, or for-profit businesses (most nursing homes fall into this category). A sampling of the amazing variety of social work practice environments is shown in Box 1.2.

New environments for social work practice constantly evolve. Genetic counseling, for example, has grown in recent years. Social workers who once specialized in child adoption placement now find themselves helping people locate their birth parents. War, terrorism, natural disasters, and even home or apartment building fires have resulted in a need for social workers, who can help people get their basic needs met and deal with physical as well as psychological trauma.

Box 1.2 Social Work Practice Settings: Selected Examples

- Hospitals, emergency rooms, nursing homes, home health care, hospices
- Police departments, probation and parole offices, juvenile detention facilities
- Child welfare: foster care, adoptions, child safety services
- Group homes or residential facilities that care for runaway children, persons with disabilities, or frail elderly persons
- Legislative offices at all levels of government
- Employee assistance programs, victim/witness programs
- Senior centers, older adult day care, planning councils for older adult programs
- Immigrant and refugee centers, disaster relief services
- Schools, after-school group and counseling programs, gang prevention programs
- Mental health hospital and outpatient services, substance abuse programs

Where do most social workers spend the majority of their working hours? Social work is an active profession. Many social workers go wherever people are experiencing problems—to the places where people live, work, study, and play. Social workers who make home visits know that entering into the natural environment of people—entering into their world—often makes people more comfortable and may be much less frightening than an office visit. Sometimes social workers meet their clients in a coffee shop, in a school or hospital, or even on the streets if they are doing outreach work to persons who are homeless. When working with children in foster care, detention, or contested custody cases, social workers may spend hours in court. Meetings in the community occur frequently as groups of professional people, including social workers, come together to advocate for new legislation, fundraising, or for professional education.

Regardless of their settings, social workers have offices where, generally, some clients, family members, or other professionals meet with them. Here, too, social workers have access to computers, telephones, fax machines, files, and other staff including administrative assistants and supervisors. Even those social workers who primarily do outreach work or home visits need to spend time in their offices. Students doing an internship or field placement would also use the office as a home base.

A Broader Ecological/Environmental Perspective

Today the profession is beginning to awaken to the significance of our global physical environment. Natural disasters such as earthquakes, floods, and hurricanes destroy homes and communities, and they seem to be occurring with increased frequency throughout the world. War and industrial pollution claim victims in many parts of the world. Our asthma-infected children and health threats from toxic contamination of the produce being sold in our supermarkets have given many Americans a renewed concern about the physical environment.

Social workers and social work students are increasingly interested in the relationship between human social welfare and ecology. As early as 2009, the National Association of Social Workers' publication, *Social Work Speaks*, pointed to growing ecological concerns for American social workers. These included rural areas where resident farmers and migrant workers alike expose themselves and their families to the hazards of agricultural pesticides. The land along the Mexican-United States border, where Mexican workers live in unsanitary, badly constructed housing, was of special concern. Urban low-income neighborhoods were identified as so polluted by industrial waste, in some cases, that asthma occurs in high rates, especially among children of color. As this article points out, environmental degradation is clearly linked to poverty and health disparities (p. 122).

What this means is that social workers need to be invested in building a healthy environment for all people. Social workers need to develop an understanding of the relationship between poverty and the risks emanating from degraded environments. In their daily practice, social workers have to take special care not to further endanger people by placing them in unsafe housing. We can work with landlords, volunteer groups, neighborhoods,

---

Human Rights and Social, Economic, and Environmental Justice

Dimension of Competency **Cognitive and Affective Reactions: Social workers understand that civil, political, environmental, economic, social, and cultural human rights are protected.**

Critical Thinking Question: When you think about your home or campus community, what environmental hazards, especially in areas occupied by poor people, cry out for advocacy? What should be done? By whom?

> Assess your understanding of the context and of the work environment of social workers by taking this brief quiz.

and communities to clean up degraded areas and create environments that will nurture children, families, and older adults. Of great importance is the advocacy that we engage in together with other environmental activists. Whether we are students or full-fledged social workers, whether we are working with individual clients, families, or groups, or within organizations or communities, our professional behaviors must reflect a sense of responsibility for environmental concerns.

EDUCATION FOR SOCIAL WORK AND CAREER OPPORTUNITIES

The Baccalaureate Social Work Curriculum

When Pamela Dunn, the BSW social worker in this chapter's opening case study, was a sophomore student in college, she declared social work as her major. At that time, she did not realize that the course of study for the major had been designed to be consistent with the standards of the CSWE. In fact, since 1974 CSWE has required BSW programs to design a professional curriculum, one that is built on a liberal arts base. If a college or university's program is to be accredited, it must adhere to the educational policies set by CSWE.

Generally, students begin the social work major with just a few social work courses in the freshman and sophomore years. These courses usually introduce the social work profession and focus on social welfare, its history, current policies, and the impact of political decisions on the people whom social workers seek to help. The first and second years of the social work major are primarily taken up with liberal arts courses, which may include introductory courses in psychology, sociology, biology, college writing, philosophy, literature, and the arts—all courses that provide content that will be used later as professional courses unfold.

Important concepts for professional development appear in the introductory social work and social welfare courses generally taken in the first year or two of college. Professional ethics and values are among these concepts. Probably persons who do not relate to those values identified earlier in this chapter will drop out of social work courses or will leave the profession early in their careers. By contrast, persons who value human diversity and respect the dignity of others are more likely to be good candidates for a career in social work.

In the junior and senior years, the focus on ethics and values becomes deeper. This is when the professional curriculum dominates the courses students are enrolled in. Building on earlier liberal arts and social work courses, students in their junior and senior years develop their knowledge of human behavior. Studying the phases of human development promotes understanding of why people behave as they do. Learning about social systems and how they interact to promote or deter human well-being adds other important dimensions to the social worker's knowledge base.

To work effectively on behalf of the people they serve, social workers also need to understand the basic structures of local, state, national, and even international social welfare systems. Social workers are social change agents and they want to be able to influence the evolution that is constantly underway in the social welfare system. **Policy practice** is the term used for the conscious effort to effect change in the laws, regulations, and provisions of services of governmental and nongovernmental policies and programs.

In junior- and senior-year courses, social work majors also study practice theory. In these courses, they learn how to interview effectively; how to develop respectful, effective relationships with the people they serve; and how to use the social work intervention process that is at the heart of social work practice. Students learn how to uncover strengths in people and their environments. They learn how to assess problem situations and work collaboratively with clients, not imposing their own solutions but engaging people in discovering new and more effective means for dealing with difficult situations. Research is interwoven in the curriculum, often in practice courses that help social work majors learn how to use systematic approaches for gathering data from interviews (**qualitative research**) and/or to use statistical, numerical data gathering and analysis to arrive at valid, reliable conclusions (**quantitative research**). Research skills will help students evaluate the effectiveness of their own practice and also the effectiveness of social programs. Students learn to appreciate the necessity of using research findings to inform their practice and, as they achieve practice skills, they increasingly see how their understanding of social work practice can make them better as researchers.

Respect for human diversity and growing understanding of the amazing diversity of the people they serve is another thread that weaves its way through social work courses. Students learn about cultures, lifestyles, physical and mental health factors, socioeconomic differences, gender identity and expression, age-related issues, and spiritual values and practices that differ from their own. Understanding and valuing differences is not enough, however. Social workers must learn how to actively explore diversity in practice because it affects every phase of the intervention process. Because social justice is the ultimate goal of the profession, social work education provides special attention to populations that are most at risk of poverty, discrimination, and oppression. These are the unloved people of our society. Social work students learn strategies that will be effective in assisting individuals, families, and often whole communities of people. Advocacy strategies can be learned to attain social and economic justice for an individual (**case advocacy**) or whole groups of people (**cause advocacy**).

Field education generally occurs in the junior and/or senior year, when most, if not all, of the other required social work courses have been completed. This is the part of the curriculum that students look forward to most eagerly. BSW students spend a minimum of 400 hours working with clients in one or more supervised field placements. The settings for field placements range widely but may include courts; child or adult protection settings; health care organizations such as hospitals, home health care, or nursing homes; adoption or foster care agencies; community centers; youth-serving organizations; domestic violence shelters; or mental health facilities. Field education is closely monitored and evaluated by social work faculty. By the time students complete field education, they have demonstrated all of the competencies and required practice behaviors of the generalist social worker. In other words, they are ready to begin professional practice!

Selecting a Career in Social Work

College students typically experience a great deal of pressure to select a major and begin a career path. Selecting a career is surely one of life's most exciting and most difficult challenges. Fortunately, many resources are available to help with decisions about the choice of career. Career counseling centers in colleges and universities offer a variety of aptitude and interest tests. The Internet and libraries offer resources such as the *Occupational Outlook Handbook* of the Bureau of Labor Statistics. Professors and advisers are yet another source of career advice and information. In the end, however, the choice is a very personal one.

> ▶ After watching this video focusing on one person's journey to the social work profession, identify what resonates with you about social work. Consider the ways in which you hope to facilitate change and pursue social justice.
>
> https://www.youtube.com/watch?v=fLsFkK0dHd0

Many college students know little about the profession of social work, yet some might think that social work could potentially be a career that would enable them to accomplish their desire of helping others. This book seeks to help you determine if a social work career is right for you.

You will find that every chapter in this book begins with a case study describing social workers in action. The case studies introduce some social workers who struggled with career decisions, just as readers of this book may be struggling. "I want to help people. Which profession should I pursue? Am I in the right major?" These questions are asked over and over again by college students. Social work is an exciting career. There are few "dull moments" in a day for social workers. It is a career that enables people to make a difference in the lives of others. It offers opportunities to transform the world. But it isn't the right profession for all people. Students are encouraged to talk with social workers, do volunteer work, or perhaps test their ability to work with others through a part-time job in the broad area of human services. Taking an introductory course in social work or social welfare is a very useful way for students to further explore their suitability for a career in social work. We hope this book will increase our readers' understanding of social work as a profession. We hope, too, that it will provide a sense of the remarkable opportunities this profession offers to people who sincerely want to make a difference in our world.

In selecting a career, it is helpful for college students to understand the concept of the career ladder, which includes a progression of career advancement opportunities within a single, recognized profession. A **career ladder** is constructed of the steps one must take to progress upward and therefore to advance in a profession or occupation. The notion of a career ladder is based on the assumption that it is possible to begin at a low level and then to move from one position to another, continuously progressing toward the top of the ladder. In some occupations or professions, obtaining an entry degree enables a person to progress up the ladder without returning to school for graduate or postgraduate degrees, advancing based primarily on performance. In other professions, the career-ladder concept is viable only if additional academic credentials are obtained. Social work reflects an interesting mix. Academic credentials are a significant component of the social work career ladder. Experience alone does not necessarily provide access to the next rung of the career ladder in social work. As Figure 1.1 shows, there are multiple educational levels within the profession. We will explain each level, along with typical responsibilities.

At the lowest rung of the ladder is the **preprofessional** (also referred to as paraprofessional) or **human service aide**. Although they do not have access to membership in

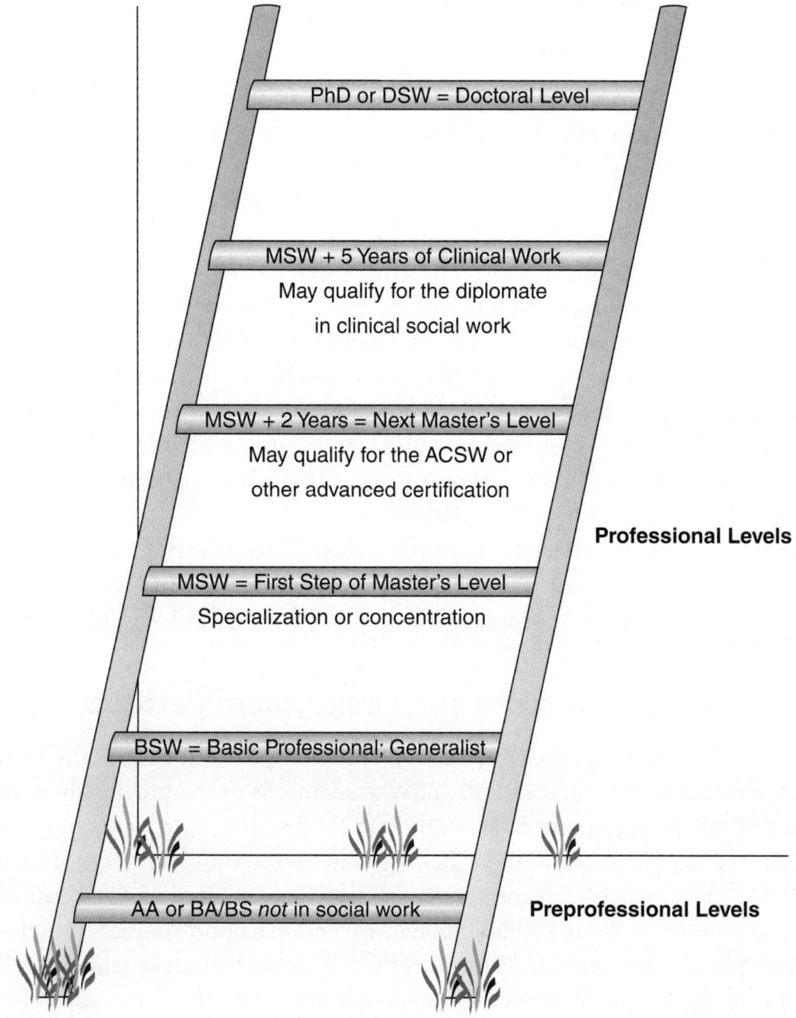
PhD or DSW = Doctoral Level
MSW + 5 Years of Clinical Work
May qualify for the diplomate
in clinical social work
MSW + 2 Years = Next Master's Level
May qualify for the ACSW or
other advanced certification
Professional Levels
MSW = First Step of Master's Level
Specialization or concentration
BSW = Basic Professional; Generalist
AA or BA/BS *not* in social work
Preprofessional Levels

Figure 1.1 The Social Work Career Ladder and Professional Education

NASW or to professional status, persons with bachelor's degrees in areas related to social work (e.g., human services, psychology, and sociology majors) and persons with associate degrees are employed in human services. They assist clients by helping with complicated paperwork or performing tasks such as assisting chronically mentally ill persons, frail elderly people, or persons with disabilities to obtain needed resources. Some preprofessional staff members are hired without regard for their academic credentials but, instead, for their extensive, firsthand knowledge of the community served by the agency.

The BSW is the basic entry level. The academic credential for this category is precisely defined: a bachelor's degree from a college or university social work program that is accredited by the CSWE. The **basic professional level** social worker has been prepared as a generalist and is able to engage in practice with individuals, families, groups, organizations, and communities. In this chapter's case illustration, a distinction is made between the responsibilities of Pamela Wright, the BSW, and those of Amy Sacks, who has an MSW degree. Pamela conducted intake interviews for the domestic violence shelter, worked with the children as well as the mothers, and ran group sessions with all the women in the shelter. As a recognized professional person, Pamela was able to engage clients, do an assessment of strengths as well as the problem situations, design and carry out an intervention plan, and then terminate the intervention. Amy Sacks, in contrast, functioned at the MSW professional level.

The master's degree in social work, the MSW, must also be from a program accredited by the CSWE. The curriculum of master's degree programs builds on generalist content to develop specialization in a practice method or social problem area; some master's degrees focus on advanced generalist practice. The MSW social worker should be able to engage in generalist social work practice and also function as a specialist in more complex tasks. Amy Sacks, the MSW social worker at the shelter in the case study, received specialized graduate training in clinical social work. At the shelter, Amy's role is more focused, and the service she provides is in greater depth than Pamela Wright's. Amy does individual, family, and group therapy, usually by appointment. In addition, Amy is the executive director of the shelter.

At the top of the professional education classification system is the social work doctorate. Some doctoral programs have a teaching focus, whereas others prepare for advanced clinical practice or for careers in research, planning, and administration.

Employment Opportunities and Employment Patterns

Testing out and exploring career and employment opportunities actually begin with social work students' field placements. BSW students, as noted previously, complete a minimum of 400 hours in one or two different field settings just prior to graduation. MSW students complete 900 hours of fieldwork in two settings, although students who enter MSW programs with advanced standing may have as little as 450 hours of MSW fieldwork in a single location. Fieldwork offers exceptional opportunities to explore areas of interest. Social work organizations benefit, too, as they observe students' ability to provide meaningful, ethical service to the people served by the organization. Not surprisingly, BSW and MSW students are often hired by their field placement agency or by an organization in the same field of practice that they connected with during their field placements.

The CSWE's annual field placement data (see Box 1.3) provide insight into the array of BSW and MSW students' field placements. These data do not represent students' actual employment following graduation, but they do reflect the areas of career interest and potential employment opportunities for new graduates. While considerable overlap exists, it is interesting to note the differences that emerge. BSW students are more likely to be in child welfare field placements than MSW students. This is consistent with employment data; historically, child welfare has been the primary field of BSW employment following graduation. By contrast, Box 1.3 lists mental health as the primary field placement for MSW students. This clinical area tends to be the most frequently selected specialization of MSW students and, not surprisingly, mental health is prominent among the employment areas of MSW practice following graduation. The family services provided by BSW students include counseling as well as provision of basic needs such as food, referral services, and case management. Family services are third on the list of field

> **Box 1.3 Primary Practice Areas for BSW and MSW Student Field Placements (In order of priorty)**
>
> | BSW Student Field Placements | MSW Student Field Placements |
> |---|---|
> | Child Welfare | Mental Health |
> | School Social Work | Health |
> | Family Services | School Social Work |
> | Aging | Child Welfare |
> | Health & Mental Health | Family Services |
> | Criminal Justice | Aging |
> | Substance Abuse/Addictions | Substance Abuse/Addictions |
> | Homelessness | Community Development |
> | Domestic Violence | Criminal Justice |
> | Developmental Disabilities | Domestic Violence |
> | Other | Other |
>
> Source: Based on the *2014 Annual Statistics on Social Work Education in the United States*, Field Education section, Tables 29 & 36, pp. 26 and 32. Alexandria, VA: Council on Social Work Education.

placements of BSW students, but it is in fifth place among the field placements of MSW students. School social work is rapidly emerging as a field placement of BSW social workers. Until recently, the MSW was the required credential for all school social workers. The field of aging, also known as gerontological social work, has recently been promoted by the CSWE; increasingly, schools are providing field placements in this area and more graduates are selecting the field of aging for employment. In the remaining prioritized list of field placements, the field of homelessness emerges for BSW student field placements, but it is not among the top 10 field placements for MSW students. Community development, similarly, does not appear among the top 10 BSW field placements in the CSWE field placement data.

Unfortunately, it is rather difficult to find current research data that accurately describe the full scope of employment of social workers once they have received their diplomas. One very plausible reason for this is that social workers are so often employed by other titles. In a few states, too, it is still possible for persons without degrees from accredited social work programs to obtain licensure or certification as social workers; research that included these persons would not provide a true picture of social work employment in that state. Researching the NASW membership base also fails to provide a clear picture of social work employment because not all social workers, whether BSWs, MSWs, or PhDs, hold membership in that social work national organization. While not providing a truly comprehensive survey of the profession, selected past and current studies can demonstrate patterns in social work employment for BSWs and MSWs.

Several past social work employment studies offer information that is still relevant. Quite consistent trends, for example, were established across many years of annual data gathering of post-BSW degree graduates by the Baccalaureate Education Assessment Project (BEAP) sponsored by the Association of Baccalaureate Social Work Program Directors. The prioritized fields of BSW graduates' employment reported in 2010, for example, included child welfare, followed by mental health, aging, family services, health, plus others with smaller frequencies (Buchan, Hamilton, Christenson, Rodenhiser, Gerritsen-McKane, & Smith, 2010). Notice the similarities between these data and the Box 1.3 report of BSW students' field placement sites.

A 2009 NASW membership workforce survey provides a picture of social work practice of persons holding primarily the MSW degree (Whitaker, Wilson, & Arrington). In this study, mental health was the employment category with the greatest number of employed social workers. Health care (combined inpatient and outpatient) was also well represented among MSWs as was private practice. In this study, private practice emerges as a strong area for MSWs, especially solo practice where social workers work independently out of their own offices. Psychotherapy is likely to be the service provided by most of these practitioners. The private practice of social work requires advanced expertise; therefore, it does not show up in Box 1.3, where MSW student field placements are shown, nor does it appear in the listing of BSW social workers' employment.

Salaries and Demand for Social Workers

In recent years, there has been a somewhat uneven job market for social workers. In some urban areas of the United States, it has been difficult for social workers to find employment. At the same time, however, states such as Texas, Iowa, and Arkansas were seeking social workers. Rural areas were so desperate for social work staff that they employed uncredentialed people because they were unable to attract professionally trained social workers.

The job search experiences reported in the BEAP studies previously referred to, however, were quite positive. Although some BSW respondents elected to go to graduate school after receiving their degrees and a small number sought employment in another field or were not successful in finding social work jobs, more than 75 percent consistently obtained social work employment (Buchan, Hamilton, Christenson, et al., 2010).

One of the most stable and reliable sources of employment information regarding social work employment and salaries comes from the Bureau of Labor Statistics (BLS). It is the primary source of information we will provide for salaries and future employment projections. When looking at salary data, however, it is important to consider several factors. First, it is essential to keep in mind that social work salaries tend to increase every year. In other words, the salary information that we provide in this chapter is outdated as soon as the book is published. The salary information we provide here is very likely to be *less* than the salary that social workers in the field are earning when you read this chapter. The salaries today's students are likely to earn when they graduate are expected to be *higher*. Social work salaries vary immensely by region of the country, years of experience, field of practice and auspice, and highest degree earned. Another important factor to remember is that commitment to vulnerable populations is a stronger motivation for some social workers than salary, and many accept employment with seriously underfunded organizations that pay small salaries. This factor tends to skew the earnings data on social work employment and to give an impression of lower salaries than the salaries that, in fact, may be available from other organizations.

The BLS tracks salaries for social workers according to their field of practice, as shown in Box 1.4. This makes it possible to compare salaries according to areas of

Box 1.4 U.S. Bureau of Labor Statistics: Social Work Employment and Mean Annual Wages, for Selected Areas of Practice, 2015

Practice Areas of Social Work Employment	Numbers Employed	Mean Annual Wages
Child, Family, and School Social Workers, Total Category	294,080	$46,610
Elementary and Secondary Schools	37,030	$60,750
Local Government	51,380	$52,810
State Government	66,180	$45,730
Social Advocacy Organizations	4,250	$40,600
Individual and Family Services	69,820	$40,660
Community Food, Housing, Emergency, and Other Relief Services	8,670	$37,160
Medical and Public Health Social Workers, Total Category	155,590	$54,020
General Medical and Surgical Hospitals	45,070	$59,650
Home Health Care	17,270	$58,580
Outpatient Care Centers	9,850	$55,170
Skilled Nursing Care Facilities	15,960	$48,760
Mental Health and Substance Abuse Social Workers, Total Category	110,070	$47,190
Offices of Other Health Practitioners	6,450	$66,730
Individual and Family Services	15,770	$43,930
Psychiatric and Substance Abuse Hospitals	9,130	$53,520
Local Government	11,140	$49,560
Outpatient Care Centers	24,430	$43,420
Residential Facilities	15,130	$41,450
Social Workers, All Other, Total Category	59,570	$57,970
Federal Executive Branch	13,890	$72,840
Insurance Carriers	490	$68,600
Local Government	16,370	$59,220
State Government	11,470	$47,540

Source: Based on "21-1021 Child, Family, and School Social Workers," "21-1022 Healthcare Social Workers," "21-1023 Mental Health and Substance Abuse Social Workers," and "21-1029 Social Workers, All others." Occupational Employment Statistics: Occupational Employment and Wages, May 2015. Bureau of Labor Statistics, U.S. Department of Labor. Retrieved from http:data.bls.gov/cgi-bin/print.pl/oes/current/oes211021.htm; 211022.htm; 211023.htm; and 211029.htm

particular interest to students or beginning social workers. Notice, however, that the BLS places all of the very large number of diverse social work positions into only four categories: (1) child, family, and school, (2) medical and public health, (3) mental health and substance abuse, and (4) all others (BLS, 2015c&d). This provides valuable introductory information, but it requires the reader to do independent research to learn more about specific social work positions of interest, especially within specific regions or localities. The BLS does not differentiate BSW and MSW social workers; all are encompassed in their data. Keep in mind that this BLS information comes from 2015, not from the year that you are reading Box 1.4. Also, only selected information is provided in Box 1.4 from the larger BLS report. For further information, see the website for the U.S. Bureau of Labor Statistics.

Compare the wages reported for social workers employed by governmental to those of non-governmental organizations; next, note whether differences exist between the different levels of governmental employers. In past years, governmental organizations fairly consistently paid higher salaries than non-governmental organizations, many of which were small, poorly funded denominational agencies. That pattern has not been sustained in recent years. Look at the data on numbers of social workers employed in each of the four major practice areas and notice the variation in salaries. Sometimes the mission of the employing organization is more important for job-seekers than what they can pay. Salary may be a more significant need for others.

The BLS offers a vast amount of information on social work employment and salaries. Another perspective that BLS data provide that is not addressed in Box 1.4 is data that reflect the identity of states that provide the highest social work wages. Staying with the four categories that the BLS used in Box 1.4, the states with highest mean wages in 2015 were the following:

- Child, Family, and School Social Workers:
  Connecticut $65,380; New Jersey $61,630; Rhode Island $61,190
- Medical and Public Health Social Workers:
  California $69,970; District of Columbia $67,450; Connecticut $64,450
- Mental Health and Substance Abuse Social Workers:
  New Jersey $66,590; Connecticut $60,920; California $60,620
- All Other Social Workers:
  Rhode Island $74,080; Massachusetts $72,200, District of Columbia $70,940 (BLS, 21-1021, 21-1022, 21-1023, & 21-1029; 2015d)

An earlier 2010 NASW study reported by Whitaker and Wilson provided additional interesting data about social work salaries. In their survey, the median income for the study group (comprised primarily of MSWs but including some BSWs) was $55,000; this may seem low, but remember this was salary data from 2010. It was not surprising that there were some fairly low salaries reported, even among MSWs, as the study group included some social workers who chose to work in underfunded organizations because of the vulnerable populations they wished to serve. What was surprising to readers who assumed that social workers never earned high salaries was the fact that some salaries, even in 2010, exceeded $100,000.

The BLS 2015 data in Box 1.4 identified mean (average) wages, but if the upper limits of social work wages had been shown, it is very likely that figures over $100,000 would emerge. If it was possible to provide social work salary data for the time that you are reading this chapter, you could expect to see upper limits in excess of $100,000.

The annual salary data that we have reviewed serves as a reminder: Both MSW and BSW salaries tend to increase each year, so the salary information presented here won't be a true representation of social work salaries when you read them, and they will be even less representative of social work salaries by the time you graduate from college. In addition, salaries also vary considerably across the different geographic regions of the United States.

Employment Projections

Economic conditions, the political climate, social welfare policy decisions made by the U.S. government, even changing demographics, and technological advances—all of these factors affect employment prospects in social work and other fields. Replacement needs as some social workers retire or leave for other reasons also influence the number of positions available. There tends to be more competition in cities for social work jobs. This is especially likely in cities where professional educational programs are present. In rural areas, however, the need for social workers is often very great and shortages of social workers are very apparent. In fact, rural areas sometimes have great difficulty attracting and retaining social workers.

The BLS prediction for social work is very favorable: It projects social work employment to grow remarkably fast! The projected growth for all occupations combined is 7 percent, while social work projected growth is expected to be 12 percent. Within social work, however, there is variation among the different fields of practice. Box 1.5 illustrates the projected total growth of the social work profession from 2014 to 2024, with breakdowns for the fields of practice, by numbers of social workers employed. The total number of social workers employed in 2014 was 649,300 and by 2024 that number is expected to increase to 724,100. Within the Child, Family, and School Social Work category, an increase of 6 percent (19,000 new social workers) is anticipated by 2024. This social work category, though, is the largest of all, so the number is expected to increase from 305,200 to 324,200 by 2024. A far larger increase of 19 percent is expected for the Health Care

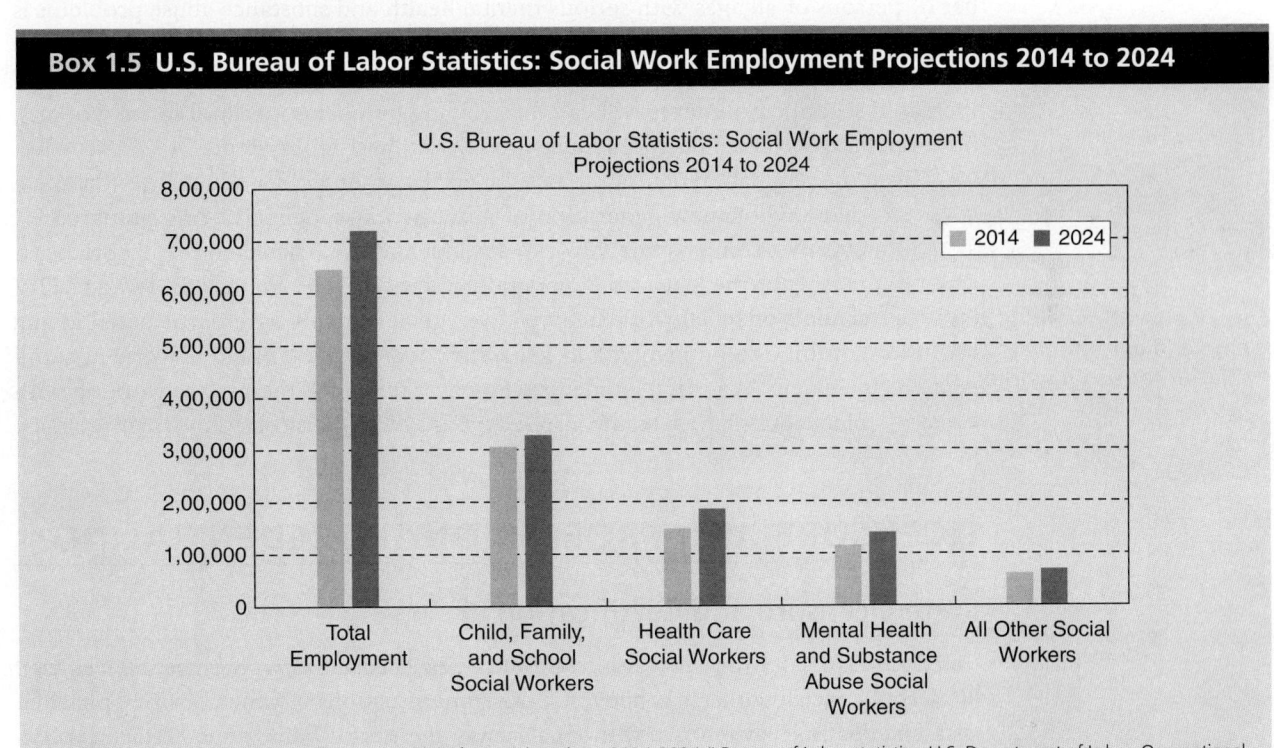

Box 1.5 U.S. Bureau of Labor Statistics: Social Work Employment Projections 2014 to 2024

Source: Based on "Employment projections data for social workers, 2014-2024." Bureau of Labor statistics, U.S. Department of Labor, Occupational Outlook Handbook. 2016-2017 Edition, Social Workers. Retrieved from http:www.bls.gov/ooh/community-and-socialservice/social-workers.htm

social work category, but that increases social work employment from 160,00 in 2014 to 191,000 by 2024 (an increase of 30,900). The 19 percent increase expected among Mental Health and Substance Abuse social workers is also impressive. The 117,800 social workers of 2014 are expected to increase to 140,000 by 2024 (22,300 new social workers) (BLS, Job Outlook, 2015c).

The employment outlook for some professions similar to social work is not quite as positive as that for others. Employment positions in psychology, for example, are expected to increase from 173,900 in 2014 to 206,400 in 2024) (BLS, 2015a) compared with an increase from 649,300 in 2014 to 724,000 by 2024 for social workers (BLS, 2015c). The BLS also notes that in psychology, a doctorate degree is required for most clinical work, although the master's degree is acceptable for some positions in schools and industry. Few opportunities are projected for persons holding only a bachelor's degree in psychology. In rehabilitation counseling, where a master's degree is usually required, 2014 employment of 120,000 counselors is anticipated to increase to 130,900 by 2024 (BLS, 2015b).

Why will social work positions increase in the future? The increasing population of older persons is one compelling reason. Job prospects are expected to be especially favorable in areas involving social work with older adults. A rapidly growing aging population plus the aging baby-boomer generation will require services—services to assist with the stresses that accompany midlife crises related to health, career, and personal issues. Increased demand for social workers is also likely in home health care, hospice programs, assisted living, adult protective services, and adult day care centers. The number of persons of all ages with serious mental health and substance abuse problems is expected to increase as well. Child, family, and school social workers will be needed to work with issues of child abuse, domestic violence, and family relationship problems. Increased school enrollments will call for growing numbers of school social workers; however, budget constraints may reduce growth within school systems.

Given the population demographics, especially among older adults, it is fortunate that a whole new generation of social work students is being prepared for effective, compassionate work with older adults. Thanks to the historic partnership of the Hartford Foundation and the CSWE, over 200 BSW and MSW schools of social work and well over 1,000 students have participated in and continue to be involved in gero-enriched curricula, field placements, and research. As a result, students who never imagined themselves working with older adults have become inspired by this field of practice (Hooyman, 2009).

> **?** Assess your understanding of the requirements of a social work education and of the employment opportunities and salaries for social workers by taking this brief quiz.

LICENSURE AND PROFESSIONAL CREDENTIALING

State Licensure and Certification

Can doctors practice their profession without being licensed? Can pharmacists? Dentists? How about social workers? While there are some situations in which doctors, pharmacists, and dentists may practice without a license, these are relatively few. Medicine, pharmacy, and dentistry were among the first professions to be legally regulated in the United States. The term **legal regulation** refers to governmental authority for the practice of selected professions and occupations. Today doctors, pharmacists, and dentists are licensed by the states in which they practice.

Social workers, too, are legally regulated in all states in the United States. The first statute providing for the legal regulation of social workers was passed in Puerto Rico in 1934 (Thyer & Biggerstaff, 1989). There are several different forms of legal regulation governing social work. In most states, social workers are licensed, generally at both the BSW and MSW levels. In a few states, social workers are certified, not licensed. Canadian provinces generally use the term *registration* instead of licensure or certification for their legal regulation.

Licensure and certification in the United States are very similar. Both are created through the passage of state law, so they are born out of the political process. State boards of regulation and licensing are responsible for administering licensing and certification of all professions. Only persons with appropriate credentials (usually degrees from CSWE-accredited schools) are permitted to take the social work examinations that are required. A national organization, the Association of Social Work Boards, provides examinations to the states; each state determines its own passing score. There is one important difference between **certification** and **licensure**. While certification protects the title *social worker*, it doesn't prohibit uncertified people from practicing social work. Uncertified people simply may not legally call themselves social workers. Certification is not considered to be as strong a form of legal regulation as licensure, which legally restricts the practice of social work to persons who meet the state requirements.

Although states determine the categories of social workers they will license or certify, the four categories most commonly seen and the academic degree and practice experience required are as follows:

Bachelor's: a baccalaureate degree in social work
Master's: an MSW degree; no experience required
Advanced generalist: an MSW degree plus two years of supervised experience
Clinical: an MSW degree plus two years of clinical practice (Association of Social Work Boards, 2013)

Renewal of a state license or certification, which may occur every two years, usually requires documentation of completed continuing education. Earning a degree in social work is truly not the end of a social worker's education!

NASW Credentialing of Advanced Professional Practice

There is a growing demand by consumers and insurance companies for the affirmation of experienced professionals beyond the entry level and even beyond state licensure. NASW has met this challenge by creating specified credentials for social workers. NASW sustains authority over their credentialing process; it is not a form of governmental regulation such as licensing, although it often incorporates requirements for state licensing.

The ACSW was the first advanced practice credential offered by NASW. Developed in 1960, it is still the most respected and recognized social work credential. The Academy of Certified Social Workers (**ACSW**) designates membership into its organization. It is available to members of NASW who have an MSW degree, two years of additional MSW-supervised social work practice, professional evaluations that confirm their practice skills and values, and 20 hours of related continuing education (NASW, 2015b). In 1986, following the development and broad acceptance of the ACSW, NASW created the **Diplomate in Clinical Social Work (DCSW)**. Among other requirements, the diplomate calls for 4,500 hours plus an additional three years of post-MSW or post doctorate clinical practice. The DCSW is the highest level of clinical practice authorized by NASW (NASW, 2015d).

NASW continued to expand its recognition across a range of specific areas of practice expertise, adding advanced practice credentials for several areas of BSW practice. In the area of military practice, NASW now offers recognition of advanced BSW practice with the credential of MVF-SW, Military Service Members, Veterans, and Their Families—Social Worker. Also offered is the MVG-ASW, the credential designating advanced practice at the MSW level with military families. The MVF-CSW is a credential related to MSW clinical practice with military families. There are three clinical practice credentials for advanced MSW practice: the QCSW (Qualified Clinical Social Worker); the CSW-G (Clinical Social Worker in Gerontology); and the C-CATODSW (Certified Clinical Alcohol, Tobacco, and Other Drugs Social Worker). There are three additional credentials in gerontological practice (one at the BSW level), two for hospice and/or palliative care social work (one BSW credential), two credentials in youth and family practice (one BSW), one MSW level health care and a school social worker credential, and two case management (a BSW and an MSW) credentials (NASW, 2015e). The specific requirements for all of these certificates can be accessed online in the "Practice & Professional Development/Social Work Credentials" area at the NASW website.

Credentials that testify to expertise in specialized areas of practice can provide a considerable competitive advantage in the job market. They are also a way of alerting potential clients or referral sources to the knowledge and practice expertise of the social worker.

> Assess your understanding of licensure and professional credentialing for social workers by taking this brief quiz.

PROFESSIONAL SOCIAL WORK ORGANIZATIONS

This chapter has already referred to NASW and CSWE numerous times. Hopefully, this signifies the remarkable importance of these two national social work organizations in the leadership of the profession. NASW and CSWE are undoubtedly the most prominent, but many other professional social work organizations also exist.

The National Association of Social Workers

NASW, located in Washington, D.C., is the major social work professional membership organization in the United States. There are approximately 132,000 members of NASW (NASW, 2015a). It was founded in 1955 when seven existing but quite separate social work organizations (such as the American Association of Medical Social Workers) joined together. The NASW has four major functions:

1. Professional development
2. Professional action
3. Professional standards
4. Membership services

Many social work organizations hold conferences for social work students and professionals that allow them to stay current on social welfare issues and to share challenges and successes with others in the field

Graduates of schools of social work that are accredited by the CSWE are eligible for full membership in the NASW. Students in CSWE-accredited programs are eligible for student membership at reduced rates. NASW's journal, *Social Work*, is a respected source for research findings in various fields of practice (useful for writing term papers). The monthly publication of the national office, *NASW News*, provides information regarding new developments, social policy discussions, and updates on legislation of interest to social workers and their clients; it also advertises social work professional positions. All state chapters publish newsletters, keeping chapter members abreast of statewide developments. At the national level, NASW employs a lobbyist to represent members' views on policy issues known to Congress. Through the Political Action for Candidate Election (PACE) wing of NASW, candidates for national as well as state offices are endorsed, and information about their positions is disseminated. Political action on behalf of the people we serve is identified in the NASW Code of Ethics as a responsibility of all social workers.

NASW's strong commitment to service is dramatically evident in its online resource, *Help Starts Here*. This beautifully designed website provides stories of people who have experienced very difficult times but discovered organizations, experts (sometimes social workers), or even their own inner strength that enabled them to get through a problem or crisis. Helpful, readable, current information on subjects as varied as health and wellness, family problems, and issues facing older adults is offered. Readers are invited to share their own story about how a social worker helped them or a loved one. Under the heading of "Find a Social Worker," a link is provided that provides an anonymous electronic connection with a social worker.

The Council on Social Work Education

Like NASW, the CSWE is a private, non-governmental organization. It is located in Alexandria, Virginia; it has a membership of more than 2,500 individuals as well as institutional memberships of colleges and universities. CSWE is the only organization in the United States that is authorized to accredit social work educational programs. CSWE's mission is to provide and sustain high quality in social work education through developing and maintaining standards for social work education in the United States. CSWE also encourages faculty development, advocates on behalf of social work education, and engages in global social work education collaboratives (CSWE, 2015).

CSWE has accredited MSW programs since its creation in 1952. In 1974, accreditation was expanded to include baccalaureate programs. Currently, 235 MSW programs and 504 BSW programs are accredited (CSWE, 2015). To date, doctoral programs in social work are not accredited by CSWE.

CSWE conducts a number of other activities in addition to accreditation. An annual conference, for example, showcases presentations of scholarly papers and current research. CSWE also publishes a scholarly journal (*Journal of Social Work Education*). A recent and ongoing project aims at strengthening the competence of social workers for work with the growing population of older adults. Through its members, CSWE also seeks to influence social policy and funding, both governmental and private, to support social work education.

The National Association of Black Social Workers

The National Association of Black Social Workers (NABSW) is a membership organization located in Washington, D.C. Its membership is open to any black person who is employed in social work or human services; unlike NASW, it does not specify academic credentials. NABSW was created in 1968 to address issues pertaining to racism and the delivery of social services to black people (NABSW, n.d., History section). The code of ethics speaks eloquently to the mission and purpose of this organization by asking that members promote the welfare of black people and the protection of black persons and communities from unethical practice. Members are also expected to work for improved social conditions and to provide volunteer service in support of black people and black organizations (NABSW, n.d., Code of Ethics section).

More than 100 chapters of NABSW exist throughout the United States. Student units exist on some college and university campuses. National conferences are held annually in key cities in the United States. Summer international conferences offer exciting opportunities to visit and experience the culture and heritage of Ghana, South Africa, and other global African communities (NABSW, n.d., History section).

The National Association of Puerto Rican and Hispanic Social Workers

Founded in 1983, the National Association of Puerto Rican and Hispanic Social Workers (NAPRHSW) offers membership to social workers, students, and other professionals in the field of human services. Like the NABSW, it does not restrict membership to credentialed social workers. It seeks to organize social workers and others to enhance the general welfare of Puerto Rican and Hispanic families and communities. The organization's objectives call for members to advocate for and promote the interests of Latinos and Hispanics, to connect with resources that support Latino people and communities, to provide for professional development of members, and to encourage and recruit students (NAPRHSW, 2015, Mission).

Members of the NAPRHSW have opportunities to attend conferences dealing with issues such as strengths and diversity of the Latino family, immigration reform, and ethnic sensitive practice. The organization also shares information on employment opportunities and engages members in political, educational, and social activities.

Other Professional Organizations

A wealth of other professional organizations exists for social workers. In addition to the NAPRHSW, there is the Latino Social Workers Organization, which sponsors annual conferences and offers committee membership to students as well as professional social workers. Some of the emphases of this organization are training in cultural competency and recruitment and retention strategies. Founded in 1970, the National Indian Social Workers Association seeks to support Native American people, including Alaska Natives. It also provides consultation to tribal and other organizations. Still other groups exist for gay and lesbian social workers, Asian American social workers, and American social workers who live and work in other countries. In addition, there are practice-related organizations such as the National Association of Oncology Social Workers, the National Federation of Societies of Clinical Social Workers, and the North American Association of Christians in Social Work.

International Social Work Organizations

Social workers in countries outside the United States also have professional organizations. Some examples are the Australian Association of Social Workers; the Canadian Association of Social Workers; the Nederlands Instituut voor Zorg en Welzijn (The Netherlands); the Chinese Association of Social Workers; and national associations of social workers in Ghana, Nigeria, and Israel, among others.

One social work organization, the International Federation of Social Workers (IFSW), was initiated in 1956 to help social workers learn about the experience of their counterparts in other countries. Currently, the IFSW represents 116 countries and half a million social workers around the world. Although membership in the IFSW is limited to national social work organizations, individuals may join the Friends of IFSW. This organization provides a global voice for the social work profession. It has achieved so much international respect that it

- has been provided special consulting status by two UN organizations, the United Nations Children's Fund (UNICEF), and the UN's Economic and Social Council (ECOSOC).
- works with the World Health Organization (WHO).
- assists the Office of the UN's High Commissioner for Refugees (UNHCR).
- provides services to the primary human rights office of the UN, the UN High Commissioner for Human Rights (OHCHR) (IFSW, 2015).

The IFSW promotes the use of social development efforts and encourages international cooperation in its effort to seek global social justice.

> Assess your understanding of social work professional organizations by taking this brief quiz.

Just as international trade has developed globally at a rapid pace so, too, have international efforts to improve the health and welfare of all people. Hopefully, the future will bring increasing cross-national and international social welfare development and advocacy efforts, especially to war-torn and economically devastated areas. What a challenge for the next generation of social workers!

COMPARING RELATED PROFESSIONS

To meet the challenges of the present as well as the future, social workers need to understand and develop cooperative working relationships with the professions and occupational groups that work alongside us. Currently, a great deal of overlap exists in the responsibilities and tasks of professions. In hospitals, for example, nurses as well as social workers assist patients with discharge planning. In mental health, the overlap appears even greater. Psychiatrists, psychologists, social workers, and professional counselors all engage in psychotherapy with individuals, groups, and families. Each profession, however, has its own area of expertise. This can be confusing. In the paragraphs that follow, we will try to identify and compare roles and responsibilities across a few professions that social workers frequently work with.

Psychology

Psychology is a field closely related to social work. Psychologists study individuals and try to understand how they develop over the human lifespan. Many psychologists study perception and learning in the laboratory setting and try to understand the inner workings of the mind through experimental means. Other psychologists spend their careers researching, testing theory, and teaching. One branch of psychology is applied; these psychologists counsel individuals and families and conduct IQ tests, personality tests, and the like. Psychologists who wish to specialize in psychotherapy usually earn a doctorate degree.

Social workers take psychology courses and they utilize information from psychology to assess their clients' problems appropriately and to develop workable intervention plans. Social workers cannot focus solely on the individual, as psychologists tend to do; instead, they also work with other persons involved in clients' lives and with groups and community organizations, as needed, to help solve clients' problems.

The BLS lists multiple specializations for psychology. The primary ones are licensed clinical psychologist and counseling psychologist. Both require a doctorate degree. These are the psychologists that social workers often work with, especially in mental health settings. Other specialization areas are school psychology; industrial–organizational psychology; and developmental, social, and experimental or research psychology (BLS, 2014a). School psychologists may need only a master's degree.

Counseling

Counseling is another profession that overlaps social work in many ways: counselors, too, serve the social and emotional needs of people in schools, mental health settings, and other settings where social workers are employed. Most counselors hold master's degrees from university programs in education or psychology, although some doctorates are also available in counseling. There is an array of areas in this field including mental health counseling, school and career counseling, rehabilitation counseling, substance abuse and behavioral disorder counseling, and gerontological counseling. The vast majority of counselors, 273,400, are employed as school and career counselors (BLS, 2015b). Like social workers, counselors work with people who have personal, family, or mental health problems; however, many counselors have special expertise in helping people with educational or career planning.

Psychiatry

Psychiatry is related to social work, but psychiatry is a specialization of medicine. An M.D. (doctorate of medicine) must first be earned, and then the aspiring psychiatrist must complete a postdoctoral internship. Psychiatrists' primary focus on the inner person is grounded in their knowledge of physiology and medical practice. They may practice psychotherapy, but more frequently see patients to prescribe and monitor medications such as antidepressants and the drugs used to treat psychoses (severe forms of mental illness). Psychiatrists frequently see people for 15-minute medication monitoring sessions. They also serve in leadership roles in mental health organizations.

Human Services

In its broadest definition, human services include all occupations and professions seeking to promote the health and well-being of society: lawyers, firefighters, social workers, teachers, and so on. The narrower definition includes only those people who have completed an educational program with a major in human services or people who have been hired to work in the broad human services area without academic credentials. Human service academic programs range from two-year associate, four-year baccalaureate, master's, to doctoral degrees. While knowledge development is not ignored, associate and baccalaureate degree programs in the human service field often emphasize task completion and skill development. Graduates seek employment across multiple paraprofessional and professional job areas; these positions sometimes offer only minimal opportunities for advancement. The authority to accredit human service programs was obtained by the Council for Standards in Human Service Education in 2014.

Inter-Professional Collaboration

If social workers are to be truly effective, it is imperative that they achieve skill in inter-professional relationships. Future case studies in this text will illustrate social work practice involving other professions. Sometimes, especially in advocacy situations, these can be challenging relationships, but they may significantly impact the outcome for the client. Inter-professional relationships can also be a highly satisfying component of professional life.

> Watch this video about interdisciplinary teams working in a hospice setting. In what ways does this setting mirror what you've learned about collaboration among professions?
> https://www.youtube.com/watch?v=KKwyxnouVEI

How might some of the professions described in this chapter become involved in a case such as that of the Dunn family? In one potential scenario, the counseling they receive from the shelter social worker results in Susan Dunn and her husband deciding there is hope for change. They make the decision to begin living together again. With encouragement, they follow up on the social worker's recommendation that they attend longer-term marriage and family counseling with a family service agency. The shelter social worker's professional relationship with the family service agency staff helped Susan Dunn and her husband trust their new counselor at the agency. The Dunn's counselor at the family service agency might be an MSW social worker, a PhD psychologist, or possibly a counselor. A consulting psychiatrist, also retained on the staff of the agency, would become involved if the primary counselor felt medication might be needed if one of the Dunns began to have serious depression. A collaborative working relationship between the Dunns' family service agency counselor and the psychiatrist could increase the Dunns' comfort in seeing the psychiatrist and could help the psychiatrist consider more carefully the need for medication.

But what would happen if, instead, Susan Dunn remained in clear physical danger? Let us say, for example, that while she was at the shelter, her husband refused to attend any kind of counseling with her and openly threatened future abuse. Susan might still choose to go home, believing that, if she behaved more carefully, she would be able to avoid causing her husband to physically abuse her. At some point, however, another crisis could require her to flee again to the shelter. If her husband was drinking or became violent at work and lost his job, Susan may find herself becoming involved with the government's financial assistance program called Temporary Assistance for Needy Families (TANF). The staff she encounters with this program would probably not have professional training in social work as their role is a more clerical one. The shelter social worker may need to accompany Susan to the TANF organization and assertively advocate with agency staff on behalf of Susan.

Once Susan leaves her husband, she is at risk of poverty. Almost overnight, she could become a poor, single mother. The shelter social worker might work with attorneys to help Susan file a legal restraining order through the district attorney's office, thus prohibiting her husband from threatening or even contacting her. If she wanted to file for divorce and child support, Susan's social worker could advocate with attorneys at a legal aid society to obtain inexpensive legal assistance. As Susan's social worker helps her assess her evolving situation, other professional persons might be involved: A career counselor could help plan for employment or further education, a psychologist might become involved if Susan became seriously depressed and needed psychological testing for additional assessment, and a human services worker from the shelter might help Susan with the maze of paperwork needed as Susan's new life begins to unfold. In any event, the shelter social worker might work collaboratively with many other professional persons as she takes whatever steps are necessary to ensure that Susan and her children are safe from harm. Consistent with the NASW Code of Ethics, the social worker would respect whatever decisions Susan made.

> Assess your understanding of professions related to social work by taking this brief quiz.

SUMMARY

- The social work profession is described. Social work is defined, as it is a profession that is often misunderstood. It is a profession that has clearly identified values and a code of ethics that flows from those values. The history of social work evolved out of a sense of caring and concern for individuals and families as well

as need for social reform. Today the professional degrees in social work include the BSW, MSW, and PhD.
- The context and work environments of social workers are explained. Social workers work within private organizations like the American Red Cross and denominational agencies as well as governmental organizations. They are employed by hospitals, police departments, foster care and adoptions agencies, and senior centers, among numerous other locations.
- The professional curriculum of social work and the career opportunities available to social workers are discussed. The career ladder depicts progression upward from lower, entry levels of the profession to the highest levels of advanced practice. Employment opportunities and social work salaries are somewhat dependent on professional education and credentials. Salaries for social work vary considerably but tend to be higher than is generally suspected.
- The social work profession as a profession legally regulated through licensure and credentialing is explained. Social work, like most other professions, is legally regulated by state licensing boards to protect consumers from unethical and uncredentialed practice. In addition, advanced practice credentials are provided under the auspices of the NASW.
- The major professional social work organizations are described. Two primary national social work professional organizations are the National Association of Social Workers (NASW) and the Council on Social Work Education (CSWE). Other national and local social work organizations also exist as well as international organizations.
- Roles and responsibilities of social workers and those of professionals that social workers frequently work with are compared and contrasted. Psychiatrists, psychologists, social workers, and professional counselors all engage in psychotherapy with individuals, groups, and families. Each profession, however, has its own area of expertise.

Recall what you learned from this chapter by completing the Chapter Review.

2

Theoretical Perspectives for Social Workers

LEARNING OUTCOMES

- Discuss the relationship between systems theory and the ecosystems perspective.
- Explain how ecosystems theory guides generalist social work practice.
- Identify several intersecting factors spawning social justice concerns, challenging social work values.
- Discuss the likelihood of support for social programs across the political spectrum.
- Explain Social Darwinism and discuss how Wheatley believes it impacts global economic systems.

CHAPTER OUTLINE

CASE STUDY: The Several Roles of Stephanie Hermann, BSW   34

Systems Theory and the Ecosystems Perspective   38
   Social Work and Systems Theory   38
   The Ecosystems Perspective   40

The Generalist Approach   41
   Levels of Intervention   42
   Environmental Challenges and Spiritual Responses   44
   The Intervention Process   47

Social Justice, Poverty, and the Intersectionality of Multiple Factors   49
   Values, Ethics, and Human Diversity   49
   Intersectionality of Multiple Factors   49
   The Strengths Perspective: Resilience and Empowerment   50

CASE STUDY: The Several Roles of Stephanie Hermann, BSW

Stephanie Hermann, BSW, waited impatiently for the mail that morning since her boss had told her to expect an important memo. Stephanie worked as an assistant administrator in a regional office of the Division of Community Services, a part of her state's Department of Health and Social Services (DHSS). The office interpreted new DHSS policies pertaining to health and social service agencies in the region, both public and private. Stephanie consulted with agency administrators to clarify state policies and to document agency compliance.

Recently, the state DHSS office had received notice from the Federal Health Care Administration that people with developmental disabilities would soon lose eligibility for Medicaid funding in nursing homes. The intent of this policy was to encourage the development of community-based living settings for people with disabilities. A survey had been conducted around the state, and 2,025 adults with disabilities were found to be living in nursing homes. Among them was Sandra McLean, whose story will be a focus of this chapter.

This large number worried DHSS officials. They did not believe there were existing alternative community placement options that could care for anywhere near this number of people. Stephanie's boss had described the memo that was on its way as "at least trying to head us off from a bigger problem later."

The expected memo arrived: "The Department of Health and Social Services finds that an emergency exists.... This order amends the department's rules for nursing homes ... to prohibit the admission of any person with a developmental disability, including cognitive disability, to a nursing home for intermediate nursing care unless the nursing home is certified ... as an intermediate care facility for the cognitively disabled (ICF/CD)."

The memo explained that to obtain certification as an ICF/CD, a nursing home must identify staff skilled in working with persons with developmental disabilities and describe specific internal programs, supplementary services from other agencies, admission policies, and individual care plans for each resident. The DHSS memo defined developmental disability as follows: "cognitive disability or a related condition such as cerebral palsy, epilepsy, or autism, but excluding mental illness and the infirmities of aging."

Stephanie was excited by the new policy. She had long believed that most persons with disabilities should be placed in family-like settings, but few such places of residence currently existed. Adult family care homes (foster homes for adults) required families willing to take in persons with disabilities; small group homes required paid staff. Apartment living required monitoring and support. All required funding and neighbors willing to accept persons with disabilities.

Brockton Manor. When Stephanie received the emergency order from the state DHSS, she decided to consult with every county in her region. At this point, only new clients with developmental disabilities were prohibited from receiving Medicaid funding for nursing home care, so Stephanie believed that new placement options could be developed gradually. She also consulted with nursing homes that were currently caring for persons with disabilities to assist them in developing state-certified ICF/CD programs.

However, only two weeks after the state's emergency ruling, Brockton Manor, a large nursing home in Stephanie's region, decided to phase out its services for people with disabilities. Administrators believed they could easily fill their beds with elderly people, who are less costly to serve. Brockton Manor offered to cooperate with county and state officials in developing alternative living arrangements so that each of its 49 residents with developmental disabilities would have a place to go.

Now Stephanie had an immediate situation to deal with. The worst-case scenario would be that 49 people were displaced to the street, but, fortunately, Medicaid regulations required individual assessments and specific discharge plans, including places to live and **active treatment**. Active treatment involved individualized plans for training, therapy, and services to help achieve the highest possible level of functioning. But how did one find or develop such resources?

Stephanie determined that she would need to play several roles. The first would involve coordinating the efforts of various community agencies. Brockton Manor's major responsibility would be to provide individual plans of care for each resident with developmental disabilities; each county's primary responsibility would be to develop

---

CHAPTER OUTLINE *(Continued)*

Political Perspectives 51
    The Political Spectrum 51
    Conservative Perspectives 52
    Liberal or Progressive
        Perspectives 53
    Neoliberalism and
        Neoconservatism 54
    Radical Perspectives 55

Turning to Each Other: Margaret Wheatley's Perspectives 56

Summary 57

alternative living arrangements, and the state's responsibility would be to provide funding, with federal assistance through Medicaid.

A second community-organizing role would be to involve private voluntary organizations, such as the Association for Citizens with Disabilities (ACD), in planning efforts on behalf of Brockton Manor's clients. For example, the ACD might organize informational meetings and help locate alternative living settings.

Third, Stephanie knew she would have to mediate disputes among various county and state offices. Thirty-five of the 49 residents with developmental disabilities at Brockton Manor originally came from different counties. Their counties of origin were likely to refuse to resume responsibility because of the cost. Fourth, Stephanie planned to help assess the needs of residents of Brockton Manor about to be displaced and to help develop appropriate discharge plans.

Stephanie began to carry out her organizing role immediately. She arranged a meeting of representatives from all the key agencies that would be involved in relocating the residents, including Brockton Manor staff, county officials responsible for finding new living arrangements, administrators from the state DHSS offices, and members of Stephanie's own regional office. A Subcommittee on Relocation was established that met biweekly for more than a year. The subcommittee set up teams to assess all residents with disabilities at Brockton Manor. It also conducted a study to determine the probable cost of **community placement** for each resident.

Engage in Policy Practice

Dimension of Competency **Knowledge:** Social workers are knowledgeable about policy formulation, analysis, implementation, and evaluation.

Critical Thinking Question: In what ways does Stephanie Hermann use her knowledge of policy formulation at federal, state, and local levels in determining how to implement her state's emergency ruling?

Funding complications soon became apparent. Besides encouraging development of more family-like settings, community placement was intended to cut costs. Medicaid thus funded community care at only 60 percent of the institutional-care reimbursement rate for the same person with a disability. Yet the money was supposed to cover active treatment as well as room, board, and assistance in daily living tasks. Many of the people at Brockton Manor required 24-hour care and supervision.

Still, the subcommittee pressed on. It organized a large stakeholders' meeting for all agencies and individuals who might be willing to get involved. Videotapes of several residents were prepared to educate the community and to enhance the human-interest side of the story. The meeting spearheaded a flurry of community activity. Several voluntary organizations collected supplies for new apartments, the Kiwanis Club developed a proposal for public housing for people with disabilities, county departments of social service advertised for adult **family care homes**, and Brockton Manor solicited foster parents from its own staff. Two private social service agencies developed small group homes. Funding for these homes required creative planning; half the residents had to be taken from costly state institutions because the Medicaid funding available for community placement for these persons was higher.

Through the development of small group homes and new **family care homes**, 15 of Brockton Manor's residents were soon placed into the community. One of these persons was Sandra McLean.

Sandra McLean: The Effects of Institutionalization. Sandra McLean's mother had a long and difficult labor, and finally forceps were used in delivery. The forceps injured Sandra's skull. The result was cognitive disability and grand mal epileptic seizures, commonly known as convulsions.

Mr. and Mrs. McLean raised Sandra at home until she was about 8 years old, by which time she was toilet trained, could walk, and could say "Mama" and "Papa." Then they sent her to public school. This was before the days of special education, however, and they soon decided they could educate her better at home. They were able to teach Sandra to bathe, dress, and feed herself.

When Sandra was about 10, her parents had a second daughter—a normal, healthy infant named Susan. After Susan's arrival, the McLeans did not have quite so much time for Sandra, but by then she was more independent. When Sandra was in her late teens, an activity center for people with disabilities was established in a nearby community. Her middle-class parents could afford the moderate fee, so she was enrolled. To the McLeans' delight, Sandra blossomed. She began to talk and smile more. She was a favorite among the staff.

The blow struck when Sandra was 27 years old. First, her father died of a heart attack. Shortly thereafter, her mother had a stroke. Partially paralyzed, Sandra's mother was no longer able to care for Sandra. Susan was ready to go to college, and Mrs. McLean did not want to hold her back. The family doctor suggested that Sandra be placed in a state institution. Mrs. McLean, seeing no other option, reluctantly agreed. At the institution, Sandra was medicated heavily to control her seizures. There wasn't enough staff to provide her with the compassionate care she had received at home or to respond immediately if she were to have a seizure. She spent her days strapped into a wheelchair, eyes glazed, drooling.

Several years later, Sandra was transferred to Brockton Manor, and several years after that, she was referred for community placement by Stephanie Hermann's team. Stephanie arranged for Sandra's mother, then very frail, to visit. The team listened with amazement as Mrs. McLean described Sandra as a young girl, able to walk and talk. Stephanie contacted Sandra's sister, Susan, and heard the same story. Mrs. McLean talked about the activity center Sandra had participated in years before, so staff members there were contacted as well. A therapist who had known Sandra visited and was shocked to see her current condition. The therapist described the smiling person she used to know, who enjoyed socializing and who could walk, talk, feed, and toilet herself. Stephanie and the assessment team called in a physician skilled in working with people with disabilities. The physician was willing to prescribe different medications. The assessment team then held a joint meeting with all the professional staff at Brockton Manor involved with Sandra's care. They explained that Sandra might begin to have seizures again, and they discussed how to deal with them. They suggested that occasional grand mal seizures might not be too high a price to pay if the young woman were able to learn to walk again and to communicate with people, at least in a limited way. The nursing home staff agreed.

The plan worked. Sandra did begin to have seizures again, but they were not too difficult to handle. With physical therapy she learned to walk again, and with occupational therapy she relearned to dress and feed herself. The nurses taught her how to toilet herself again. Sandra became a social person once more and began to use limited words. She clearly recognized her mother and sister. Everyone felt deeply rewarded. Now the time had come to develop community-based living arrangements.

Although Mrs. McLean would have loved to have her daughter return home, she was not physically able to care for her. Sandra's sister, Susan, explained to Stephanie Hermann, with obvious distress, that she worked full-time and had two children to care for. She frequently helped her mother with routine household chores. She did not feel able to take on her sister's care as well. But both mother and daughter welcomed the idea of a family care home for Sandra.

A potential home was located and licensed by social workers from the county Department of Social Services. The foster parents, a childless couple in their mid-30s, had learned of the need through newspaper advertisements. They visited Sandra several times at Brockton Manor and took her home for a trial overnight visit before making a final decision. The Brockton Manor staff taught them about Sandra's special needs, especially about what to do during seizures. Arrangements were made for Sandra to attend the local activity center for people with disabilities during the day, once she was living in her foster home. She enjoyed the social and recreational opportunities, such as exercise classes, educational games, and other small group activities, very much. The placement worked out so well that her foster family took in a second adult with a disability.

Ongoing Challenges of Community Placement. An adult family care home was provided for Sandra McLean by the Department of Social Services because federal funding through Medicaid and Supplemental Security Income (to be discussed in Chapter 4) was sufficient to pay all her bills, including foster care and active treatment at the local activity center. However, funding was not sufficient to permit community placement of residents who needed more care, and eventually many of them had to be transferred to different nursing homes that met the new federal requirements.

SYSTEMS THEORY AND THE ECOSYSTEMS PERSPECTIVE

The case study you have just read introduces a community-level problem requiring social work intervention and describes how a particular person, Sandra McLean, is affected. It illustrates how persons and environments interact and how social welfare policy influences social work practice. You will read more about Sandra and others in this case throughout this chapter. So that you understand why certain theories are important to social workers, we will first discuss theoretical approaches guiding their efforts. Then we will discuss intersecting factors that place certain groups of people in jeopardy of discrimination and other social ills, describe how political perspectives impact social policies, and consider effects of Social Darwinism. For over a century, Social Darwinism has provided a major justification for limiting or denying assistance to persons in need.

Social Work and Systems Theory

Social work is a profession that requires working with systems of many sizes. For example, Stephanie Hermann was employed by a large state organization, the Department of Health and Social Services. The DHSS was, in turn, strongly affected by the policies of an even larger organization, the federal government. Stephanie, by publicizing and interpreting new federal and state policies, affected the operations of the social service organizations and agencies in her entire region, both public and private. She provided professional assistance to help these organizations and agencies meet changing requirements. She educated citizens' groups about new regulations and solicited their aid in developing new resources to meet community needs.

Besides working with larger systems, Stephanie worked with smaller ones. For example, she helped establish a formal task group, the Sub-committee on Relocation, which managed the job of finding and developing alternative living arrangements for residents of Brockton Manor who had disabilities. She met with this group for more than a year. She also worked with a team of staff at Brockton Manor to assess the needs of each resident with a disability.

As part of her work in assessing the needs of individual residents at Brockton Manor, Stephanie worked with a yet smaller system, the individual named Sandra McLean. To help gain a better understanding of Sandra's potential capabilities and needs, Stephanie met with part of Sandra's family system as well, Mrs. McLean and Susan. These family meetings led Stephanie to contact another system or organization, the activity center that Sandra had attended many years before.

Improving the life of a single person can involve skills in working with systems of many sizes. For this reason, social work is a complex practice. It requires the guidance of a broad theoretical framework to help organize and analyze large amounts of information. For many social workers, systems theory provides that theoretical framework. Systems theory helps the social worker attend to and understand the dynamic interactions among the many biological and social systems that affect ongoing practice (Sheafor, Horejsi, & Horejsi, 2000).

> **Assessment**
>
> *Dimension of Competency* **Values: Social workers recognize the implications of the larger practice context in the assessment process and value the importance of interprofessional collaboration in this process.**
>
> **Critical Thinking Question:** How does Stephanie demonstrate that she values interprofessional collaboration in the process of assessing Sandra Mclean's potential capabilities and needs?

Applying systems theory requires familiarity with certain basic concepts. A few will be introduced here. The term **system** has been defined in many ways, but perhaps the simplest is that a system is a whole consisting of interacting parts. These parts are so interrelated that a change in any one part affects all the others.

Let us consider an example of a biological system, the human body. The body is composed of many interrelated, interacting parts, including the skeleton, muscles, blood, and so on. What happens when one part is disturbed in some way? Let's say a piece of the skeleton is broken. Every other part of the system is affected. Muscles tighten and blood circulation increases in the area of the broken bone. Nerves carry impulses to the brain that are translated as pain, which affects every other part of the body.

Each of the major parts of the system called the human body can itself be considered a system: skeletal system, muscle system, blood system, and nervous system, for example. These smaller systems are themselves made up of parts even smaller: organs, molecules, atoms, and particles of atoms. Sometimes smaller systems within larger systems are called *subsystems*. Whether something is considered a system or a subsystem depends only on where the observer decides to focus attention. The important point to keep in mind with respect to systems theory is the concept of interrelationships: A change in one part of a system affects all the other parts in some way. Smaller systems that are parts of larger systems affect each other and the larger system as a whole. Any change in the larger system (or *suprasystem*) affects all the systems and subsystems within.

The human body is an example of a biological system, and humans, as biological organisms, are part of a larger physical environment. But people are also social systems and parts of larger social environments. Both physical and social environments are made up of systems of various sizes to which people must adapt.

Consider the human family. The family constitutes a social system—a whole consisting of interacting parts, so that while its form may vary, family members know who belongs and who does not. A change in one part affects all others: People cannot join or withdraw without other family members responding in some way. In the McLean case, having to send Sandra to an institution undoubtedly affected her mother's well-being in a negative way. Research has even shown that if one family member is physically injured in the presence of another, the physical body of the observer will be affected (stress hormones will be released, muscles will tighten, and so on). For this reason, systems theory has been adapted for use in medicine, social science, social work, and other professions (Wells, 1998).

The Ecosystems Perspective

Social workers have long promoted a holistic, person-in-environment perspective. General systems theory, proposed by biologist Ludwig Von Bertalanffy in the late 1960s, was adopted by many social workers as an overall framework for practice very much because it was congruent with their ongoing experience. The theory helped social workers remember and pay attention to the interactions between larger and smaller systems. However, according to Germain and Gitterman (1995), some social workers felt that systems theory was too abstract for practical use. They adopted instead the closely related ecological or **ecosystems perspective** (Sommer, 1995).

The ecosystems perspective encourages social workers to maintain simultaneous focus on person and environment. The concept of *environment* is virtually synonymous with the concept of a large system in systems theory; *person* is simply an example of a small or sub-system (see Box 2.1).

Box 2.1 The Ecosystems Perspective

Person and environment
Interacting continually
Mutually affecting one another

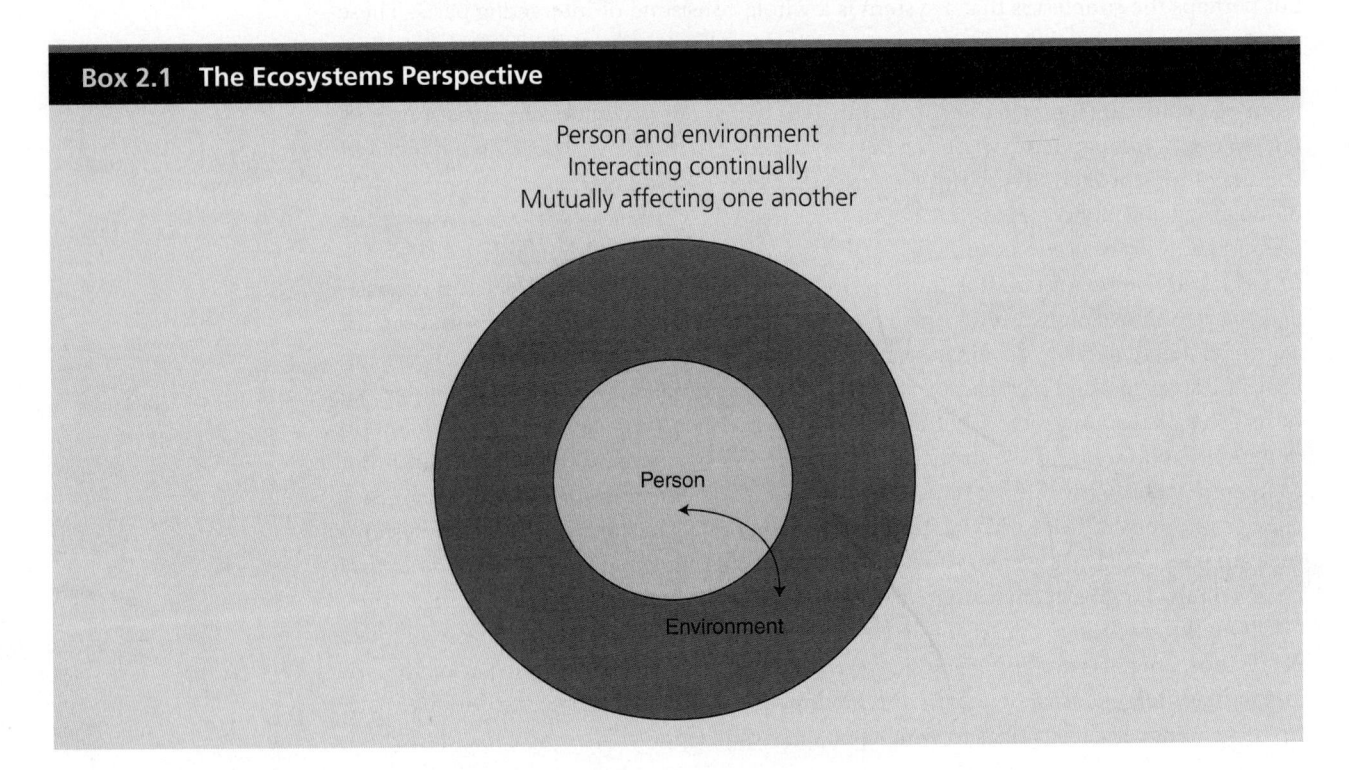

(Diagram: outer circle labeled "Environment" containing inner circle labeled "Person," with a curved arrow between them.)

Guided by the ecosystems perspective, the social worker assesses whether environmental resources meet the needs of a particular client (the person/environment fit). The worker also determines whether the client is experiencing issues or needs that exceed environmental resources (life stressors) and, if so, assists the client to find constructive adaptations to improve the "fit" between person and environment (Johnson & Rhodes, 2005).

To apply ecosystems concepts to the situation of Sandra McLean, consider how Sandra's environment affected her personally. Her experience and behavior became so changed in the state institution that she might as well have been a different person. The heavy dose of drugs that was administered to control her seizures acted as a physiological stressor that suppressed her capacity to adapt, and she essentially became a human vegetable. Only when federal policy changed, requiring changes in state policy, could she have a chance to live a more normal life. Sandra couldn't live a fulfilling personal life until new opportunities were created in the wider environment.

Changes in Sandra also affected her environment. For example, her new abilities affected various medical professionals, who were astounded at what she could accomplish and were then willing to consider modifying medications for other people with disabilities. Sandra's new opportunities also affected the people who became her foster parents and those whom they later took in with her. Sandra's good fortune affected staff at the activity center, who rejoiced for her and were inspired to develop new activities to assist in her recovery. Her mother and sister rejoiced also: A family tragedy had been transformed by what seemed like a miracle (see Box 2.2).

> Watch this video and note how the social worker engages both the client and her son. Consider how the worker applies the ecosystems perspective to the client's situation in identifying the variety of systems affected by the recent Medicaid policy change and how the changes will affect this individual client and her family.

> Assess your understanding of systems theory and ecosystems by taking this brief quiz.

THE GENERALIST APPROACH

The **generalist approach** to social work practice is strongly rooted in systems theory and its descendant, the ecosystems perspective. As described earlier, systems theory and its attention to systems interactions served as a useful guide for social work practice soon after biologist Von Bertalanffy published his ideas in the 1960s. The ecosystems perspective that developed out of systems theory provided the conceptual framework for the development of the generalist approach to social work practice. Thus, the generalist approach involves attention to multiple **levels of intervention** (discussed in the next section); the term *level*, as used in this context, is virtually synonymous with the term *system*.

The ecosystems perspective helps the social worker recognize that intervening on one systems level will prompt all other systems levels to adapt in some way. The worker must assess these adaptations because she or he may then have to intervene on multiple levels (individual, family, group, organization, community, etc.) to achieve the desired result. A generalist practitioner such as Stephanie Hermann, as she begins to intervene at a large system level (the community), is guided by the ecosystems perspective to attend to changes occurring on smaller systems levels due to adaptation processes (Brockton Manor, the McLean family, Sandra McLean as an individual, etc.).

While each CSWE-accredited baccalaureate social work program is encouraged to develop its own definition of generalist practice, the program's definition must be

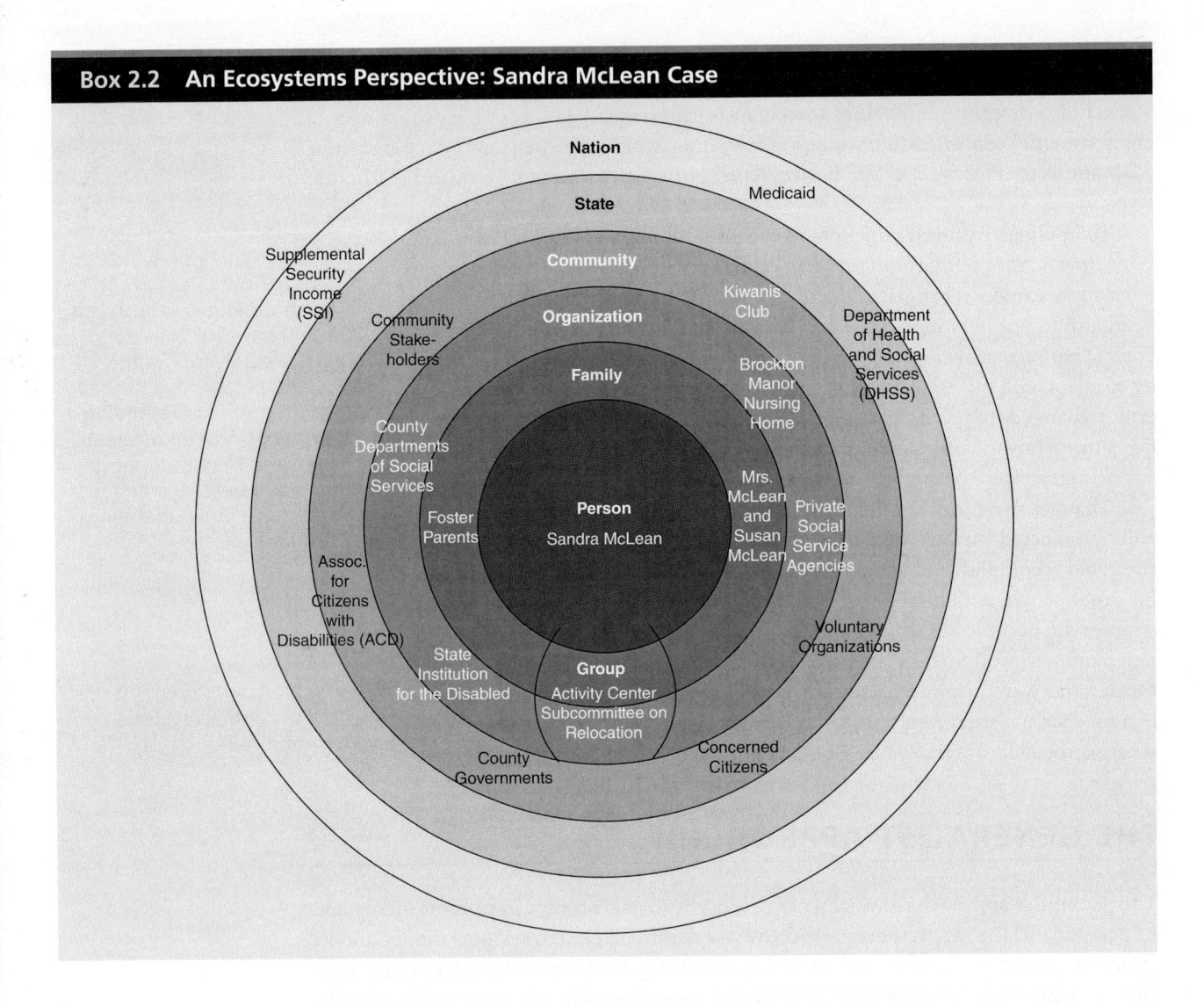

Box 2.2 An Ecosystems Perspective: Sandra McLean Case

Concentric circles from innermost to outermost: Person (Sandra McLean); Group (Activity Center Subcommittee on Relocation); Family (Mrs. McLean and Susan McLean); Organization (Brockton Manor Nursing Home, Kiwanis Club, Foster Parents, Private Social Service Agencies); Community (Community Stakeholders, County Departments of Social Services, Assoc. for Citizens with Disabilities (ACD), State Institution for the Disabled, County Governments, Concerned Citizens, Voluntary Organizations, Department of Health and Social Services (DHSS)); State (Medicaid); Nation (Supplemental Security Income (SSI)).

---

compatible with that provided by the Council on Social Work Education (CSWE). The CSWE's definition is complex, including several important parts: (a) generalist practice is based on a person-in-environment perspective and guided by research; (b) generalist practitioners work with systems of various sizes including individuals, families, groups, organizations, and communities; (c) practitioners identify with the social work profession and abide by the ethical principles of the profession; (d) practitioners work with diverse constituencies, pursuing human rights and social justice; (e) practitioners recognize human resiliency and utilize a strengths perspective.

Levels of Intervention

Note that the preceding definition explains that generalist social work practice involves not only an ecological perspective but the use of an intervention process involving multiple levels of intervention. These levels are described below.

Individual

Intervening at the individual level involves working one-on-one, either to help a person better adapt to his or her environment or to modify the environment so it better meets the needs of the person. In this chapter's case study, Stephanie Hermann worked with Sandra McLean individually to help assess her abilities and needs.

Family

Intervening at the family level may involve working with whole families or parts of a family, such as a mother and child or a pair of parents. Stephanie Hermann worked with members of Sandra's family in planning for her care. Some types of family work can be much more intensive. Family therapy, for example, assists families in overcoming interpersonal conflicts and power imbalances among members.

Group

Intervening at the small group level may involve working with many different types of groups. Stephanie Hermann developed and worked with a task group, the Subcommittee on Relocation, at Brockton Manor. The activity center where Sandra received services ran activity groups and support groups for its clients.

Organization

Intervening at the organizational level involves assessing needs within an organization and planning and coordinating efforts to meet those needs. For example, Stephanie alerted Brockton Manor about new federal regulations regarding care for residents with disabilities. When the nursing home administration decided not to serve these clients any longer, Stephanie helped coordinate the organization's efforts to develop responsible discharge plans.

Community

Intervening at the community level involves evaluating community needs and planning and coordinating efforts to meet those needs. Stephanie Hermann helped her region of the state to evaluate its capacity to provide family-like care for citizens with disabilities and coordinated the efforts to expand resources and options (please review Box 2.2).

Some social workers prefer to speak about micro-, mezzo-, and macro-levels of practice rather than practice with individuals, families, groups, organizations, and communities (Zastrow, 2007). However, professionals may differ in their understanding of which levels of intervention these terms include. For example, the micro-level is sometimes viewed as comprising individuals only, but it is sometimes conceived as comprising families as well. The mezzo-level is sometimes viewed as comprising groups only, but is sometimes conceived as comprising families as well. The macro-level is usually conceived as comprising organizational and community levels.

This text, to simplify, will usually refer to specific levels of intervention: individual, family, group, organization, and community. It is important to remember, however, that as our world seems to shrink and we all become more interdependent, our concept of community must extend to include the whole planet (see Box 2.3).

Box 2.3 Social Work Levels of Intervention

Community	Macro
Organization	
Group	Mezzo
Family	
Individual	Micro

Environmental Challenges and Spiritual Responses

While the generalist approach to social work practice traditionally encompasses individual, family, group, organization, and community levels of intervention, the profession is awakening to the increasing impact of wider environmental issues. These issues extend beyond any particular community—they are global, affecting everyone on Earth today and future generations as well. Social workers need to be aware of global and environmental issues because they affect everyone, not just ourselves and our clients. Spiritual strength can help empower people as they struggle to save planet Earth, currently under siege.

According to the United Nation's Intergovernmental Panel on Climate Change, climate change is occurring worldwide at rapid rates, affecting every continent and every ocean. Its report, titled *Climate Change 2014: Synthesis Report and Summary for Policy Makers*, included the work of over 309 lead authors who consulted over 1,700 additional experts (United Nations Intergovernmental Panel, 2014). The report concludes that climate change is occurring everywhere and already affects human health, the health of the oceans, agricultural production, water supplies, and people's livelihoods. In North America, increased wildfires are predicted, along with increased damages from river and coastal floods. Heat-related human mortality is expected to increase. In Europe and Asia, predictions are similar. Water resources will be gravely stressed in Africa, resulting in decreased food production and increased disease. Central and South America will experience reduced water availability and increased flooding, along with reduced food production and increased water-borne disease. Around the world, oceans will swamp many small island nations.

While risk levels differ, severe stresses on human populations are predicted in many areas of the world, some of which lack even minimal resources to help displaced people. The UN report asserts that without increased efforts to reduce climate change beyond the measures in place today, severe and irreversible global affects will occur by the end of this century.

For students who are socially and politically aware, looking toward the future can be frightening. Preceding generations have been exceedingly short-sighted, and many economic institutions today have built-in pressures to remain short-sighted. (For example, the stock market responds to short-term profits, regardless of how those profits are made. Most corporations, therefore, do whatever they can to increase short-term profits, regardless of the affect on planet Earth. Few investors are willing to invest in a company that does not show a profit, so that clearly we are all culpable at some level.)

Progress will not come easily. The Kyoto Protocol, adopted in Japan in 1997, was a beginning international agreement to cut carbon emissions (carbon is a "greenhouse"

Danger, Air Pollution

gas that traps heat in the Earth's atmosphere). The Kyoto Protocol was accomplished through the efforts of the United Nations, but it did not come into force until 2005, and neither the United States nor China signed it. The United Nations Climate Change Conference in Copenhagen, Denmark, in December 2009 made only slight further progress. In 2012, the Kyoto Protocol was amended and included a revised and expanded list of greenhouse gasses. However, under the Kyoto plan, China and other developing nations were exempt from target emissions, while developed nations were to slash their pollutants since they were the primary producers. Again, the United States continued to refuse to ratify the treaty. China soon became the greatest carbon polluter in the world (followed closely by the United States and India).

Optimism about the easing of climate change was revived in November 2014, with President Obama's historic announcement, along with China's President Xi Jinping, that China and the United States would commit to cuts in carbon emissions. Experts caution, however, that the emissions reductions targets currently proposed will not be enough to prevent an overall rise in global atmospheric temperature of 3.6 degrees Fahrenheit, the point at which irreversible global warming will occur, causing rapid melting of ice in the arctic, rising sea levels, worldwide coastal flooding, extreme storms, extreme droughts, and loss of vast tracts of farmland (Davenport, 2014).

Where is the resolve to come from that might prevent this looming catastrophe? Perhaps nowhere because the political sphere is complicated and stymied by economic greed and the power of the polluters. But there is a move among some in the religious community that could possibly harness the strong resolve that spearheaded the civil rights movement in the United States and the movement for independence in India.

Harvard Divinity School, for example, hosted a conference in November 2014 called "Spiritual and Sustainable: Religion Responds to Climate Change." The conference convened activists from many different religious traditions for the purpose of finding ways religious organizations could address environmental issues. The intent was to sound an alarm among the faithful, to awaken religious people to address what was described as the primary challenge of our age. The president of the Massachusetts Conference of the United Church of Christ, Reverend Jim Antal, proclaimed that it was time for church leaders to take risks, to preach the kind of sermons about climate change that could make their congregations uncomfortable, uncomfortable enough to send the ministers packing (Naughton, 2014).

Even some members of the conservative evangelical Christian movement have called for awareness of the dangers of environmental degradation, particularly global warming. For example, Reverend Richard Cizik, former Washington spokesperson for the National Association of Evangelicals, has urged national action toward reducing global warming based on the biblical demand for "creation care" or stewardship of the land provided by the Creator (Lampman, 2006). Cizik developed his concern after talking with an Evangelical scientist based at Oxford University who laid out the scientific consensus on the issue.

In addition, there is evidence that even some of the most serious polluters on the planet, American corporations, now understand that climate change is increasing at such a rapid rate and is so hazardous to human life that government regulation is necessary. General Motors, for example, in 2007 joined a list of companies urging federal policies to tighten standards on vehicle emissions (Trumbull, 2007). Since then, the Obama administration has done so, although experts fear the requirements are not sufficient. Even so, a conservative Congress is trying to reduce or repeal the upgraded standards as this chapter is being revised.

In December 2015, a hopeful development took place in Paris—the United Nations Framework Convention on Climate Change. This agreement was facilitated greatly by the 2014 agreement noted above, between President Obama and China's President Xi Jinping, to cut carbon emissions. After two weeks of intensive negotiations, accompanied by demonstrations around the world, 195 nations pledged to curb carbon emissions, implement a transparency system in which compliance can be monitored, and assist developing nations financially to help them recover from climate change damage and build cleaner futures. The United States and China, the world's two largest polluters, formally ratified the Paris agreement in September, 2016 (Wernick, 2016).

Unfortunately for the environment, in November 2016, Americans elected as president a man who claims that climate change is a hoax perpetrated by the Chinese: Donald Trump. Mr. Trump did not win the majority vote of Americans—that went to Hillary Clinton—but he won the election according to the rules of the Electoral College as stipulated in the Constitution. Thus, the cooperation of the United States with other nations in working toward ameliorating climate change according to the Paris agreement is in serious jeopardy.

The outcome of the 2016 election highlights how important it is for young people, including students, to exercise their right to vote. In 2016, young people, women, and minorities voted in lower numbers than in previous elections. When elections result in a low voter turnout, the result is sometimes unanticipated. In 2016, conservatives took control of the U.S. government. This resulted in mass protests in the United States and abroad, and a growing liberal progressive movement was energized by young people who became increasingly aware of the need to participate in the electoral process.

Hopefully, social workers and students today will recognize that their work must extend beyond traditional forms of service to include efforts toward achieving global and ecological sanity so that plants, animals, and people (including ourselves and our clients) can survive on this earth.

The Intervention Process

To continue our more mundane discussion of the generalist approach to social work practice, another major component (besides the ecosystems perspective and the use of multiple levels of intervention, as previously described) is the **intervention process**. It is sometimes referred to as the problem-solving or planned change process, but in this text we will use the terminology *intervention process*.

In social work practice, a careful, step-by-step process must be employed. It is all too easy for a caring person to hear about a situation that needs to change and immediately jump in to try to "do something," unintentionally causing serious complications. For example, acting after hearing just one person's side of a story neglects other people's experience and points of view.

Advance Human Rights

Dimension of Competency **Knowledge:** Social workers understand strategies designed to ensure that civil, political, environmental, economic, social, and cultural human rights are protected.

Critical Thinking Question: How can knowledge of environmental policies and possible strategies to improve them help social workers as well as their clients?

Thus the CSWE has identified nine specific competencies the organization has determined must be mastered in order for the social worker to practice in a professional manner. A social work **competency** is the ability to integrate and apply the profession's knowledge, values, and skills to practice situations in a purposeful, intentional, and professional manner to promote human and community well-being (CSWE, 2015). The nine required competencies are identified in the 2015 CSWE Educational Policy (see Box 2.4). The first five establish a necessary context for competent generalist practice; the last four outline the four major steps required in conducting competent practice itself: engaging, assessing, intervening, and evaluating at multiple levels of intervention.

Box 2.4 Social Work Competencies as Identified by the CSWE 2015 Educational Policy Statement

Social Workers:
- Practice in a professional, ethical manner
- Practice with diverse populations
- Pursue social and environmental justice
- Utilize research-informed practice and practice-informed research
- Demonstrate policy practice
- Seek to develop effective relationships in order to engage in practice with individuals, families, groups, organizations, and communities
- Assess the needs of individuals, families, groups, organizations, and communities
- Intervene effectively with individuals, families, groups, organizations, and communities
- Evaluate their practice with individuals, families, groups, organizations, and communities

Generalist practice involves the exercise of professional ethics, a respect for diversity, and a commitment to social and economic justice. It requires ongoing involvement in research and social policy analysis. With these competencies constantly in operation, the social worker undertakes the careful steps of the intervention process itself: engagement, assessment, intervention, and evaluation, all at multiple systems levels.

Obviously, this process is complicated and requires expertise. To translate for beginning students, the generalist social worker usually begins with a *situation in which change is desired*. Let us use this chapter's case study as an example. Government officials in the state where Stephanie Hermann worked desired to change the situation in which people with developmental disabilities were routinely placed in nursing homes. Stephanie's job as a social worker in her regional government office was to assist the desired change to come about. She entered into *engagement* processes with her client system, in this case the social service providers in her region, by alerting them to the coming policy changes. She used her interpersonal skills to help prepare them for action.

As part of *assessment* processes, Stephanie helped her clients collect and organize relevant data: for example, how many nursing home clients would be affected? What alternative placements might be available for them? How could new placements be financed? When Brockton Manor announced that it wanted to seek alternative placements for all its residents with developmental disabilities, Stephanie, in collaboration with the nursing home and various other community agencies and organizations, helped develop goals, objectives, and strategies to implement this plan. The work involved developing mutually agreed-on responsibilities and roles for a number of community stakeholders.

As part of *intervention* processes, Stephanie helped implement the mutually determined plans of action using the best knowledge and technological advances available (involving, e.g., medical evaluations and video services). She displayed leadership in developing new resources (e.g., new group homes and family care homes). She also advocated for individual clients with developmental disabilities (such as Sandra McLean) to assure that their needs were met.

Stephanie used *evaluation* processes on an ongoing basis, continually monitoring outcomes throughout her intervention efforts. When circumstances improved to her clients' satisfaction, she facilitated the transition of leadership from herself to the community organizations and regional social service providers involved.

The intervention process helps the generalist social worker determine which level or levels of intervention to involve in resolving the issue or concern at hand. In Stephanie's case, resolving the issue included working at every level of intervention: the community (Stephanie's region of the state); the social service agencies and voluntary organizations within that region; and several families, small groups, and individuals like Sandra McLean. On the other hand, generalist intervention may involve working only with a single individual or a particular family, group, or organization. The important point is that the plan of action determined by the generalist worker depends on the nature of the circumstances and careful implementation of the planned change process. The plan of action is not determined according to a method that simply happens to be preferred by the worker—for example, one-on-one counseling or group work.

▶ As you watch this video clip, take note of how suggestions of a team approach by the social worker (woman with dark hair) and specific ideas of social work interventions on behalf of clients lead to potential policy changes.

? Assess your understanding of generalist practice by taking this brief quiz.

SOCIAL JUSTICE, POVERTY, AND THE INTERSECTIONALITY OF MULTIPLE FACTORS

Values, Ethics, and Human Diversity

The trend toward community placement of people with developmental disabilities was a welcome one for the social work profession. Social work values, as identified in Chapter 1, include the dignity and worth of each person. It is easy to recognize the dignity and worth of fortunate individuals with no apparent disabilities, who can live independently as expected in our society. But what about persons like Sandra McLean, who, no matter how hard they may try, will require ongoing assistance throughout their lives? A basic ethical principle in social work requires that social workers respect the inherent worth and dignity of all. Sandra, despite her disabilities, was a whole person who deserved respectful treatment designed to meet her special needs, treatment that would help her maximize her potential.

Sandra was a member of a vulnerable population: people with disabilities. The dignity and worth of people with disabilities is frequently overlooked, as is their right to self-determination (another basic social work value). In fact, **ableism** is identified by Berg-Weger (2005, p. 104) as a practice in which people who do not have disabilities exclude and/or oppress those who do. Sadly, the worth and dignity of the person with a disability may be overlooked by the wider community because that community simply wants to spend the least amount of money for care possible. Self-determination may never even be considered, so many people with disabilities are drugged to unconsciousness to make them easier to manage, as was Sandra McLean. Yet in many instances, people with disabilities are able to make many decisions for themselves, and in all cases, worth and dignity should be honored. Fortunately, respectful care often leads to skilled, professional treatment, which can turn out to be less expensive than warehousing in institutions, as in this chapter's case example.

Intersectionality of Multiple Factors

As will be discussed in more detail in Chapter 3, certain populations in this society are in more danger of experiencing poverty, discrimination, and oppression than others. Risk factors include gender, age, race, class, sexual orientation, religion, immigration status, and many others. Disability is a risk factor, and its affects may be compounded if the person with the disability shares other characteristics that also may lead to discrimination and oppression. For example, Sandra McLean was not only a person with a disability but a female, two intersecting risk factors, and she was rapidly becoming an older female by the time she was assessed for community placement, another intersecting risk factor. The **intersectionality** of multiple factors impacting poverty can greatly increase the overall risk.

Social workers can serve as advocates to assist vulnerable persons such as Sandra to live happy, productive lives. A major professional value promoted by the National Association of Social Workers is **social justice**, with the related ethical principle of challenging social injustice. Social workers can assist persons with disabilities to determine and achieve their own goals, which can be as varied as the goals of people without disabilities, instead of being warehoused in impersonal institutions.

> Watch this video and observe the client's explanation of the various intersecting risk factors he is experiencing and how the social worker demonstrates empathy regarding each issue and offers resource options appropriate to meet the client's needs.

The Strengths Perspective: Resilience and Empowerment

Dennis Saleebey pioneered what has become known as the strengths-based approach to social work practice. He reminds us that it is of great importance to seek and identify strengths in all client systems. Focusing only on problems and deficits tends to discourage workers and clients alike. Saleebey (2006) notes that despite the difficulties our clients may have experienced, they have also developed many skills and attributes that have helped them to meet and overcome difficult challenges. People often exhibit remarkable resiliency in the face of adversity.

Glicken (2004) points out that the strengths perspective always views clients in a hopeful and optimistic way, regardless of the complexity of their issues. Like Saleebey, Glicken believes that all clients have innate strengths and abilities. Social workers can enhance these strengths when they focus on positive and successful client behaviors, which can be found in even the most difficult situations. Glicken counsels social workers to do a conscious asset review of a client's many positive behaviors and qualities.

The strengths-based approach is especially appropriate in working with clients with disabilities. The focus can and should be on strengths and abilities, not on deficits. Consider the example of Sandra McLean. Despite being strapped into a wheelchair and drugged for many years, this remarkable woman rebounded courageously when given a chance. She turned out to be an amazingly resilient human being. She relearned how to walk, talk, feed, and toilet herself, and she was especially talented in the area of social relations.

Assisting clients to discover and honor their own strengths and powers of **resilience** may be our very best service to them as individuals. In addition, many external environments, even seemingly the poorest and most harsh, offer important resources that can make a difference in our clients' lives. The practitioner's challenge is to help find these resources and assist clients to utilize them.

Young woman in wheelchair working with a male colleague

The **strengths perspective** leads naturally to the idea of empowering clients; recognizing and honoring strengths is a firm foundation for **empowerment**. According to Dubois and Miley (2011), empowerment involves both personal and political aspects. *Personal empowerment* involves one's sense of competence, control, mastery, socioeconomic security, and the like. *Political empowerment* involves resource accessibility and the power to make choices. Genuine options must be available in the wider environment, and people need the power to choose them (or not) to have political empowerment.

> **?** Assess your understanding of social justice and risk by taking this brief quiz.

POLITICAL PERSPECTIVES

The concept of empowerment leads to a discussion of political perspectives and their importance to social workers and their clients. Remember that the impetus for Stephanie's region to provide community placements for people with disabilities came from changing *government policies* at the *federal* level. These policy changes were a result of political action by various groups of people with disabilities and their advocates, including social workers. It was a positive result of long years of work by those who wanted people with disabilities to have the option to live in family-like settings in order to lead more fulfilling lives. It was an achievement that helped empower many people with disabilities. However, even if enough family care and small group homes were available to care for all, many disabled people would be unable to pay for them. That is because people with disabilities are especially at risk of poverty and discrimination. Without government help, many people with disabilities are simply unable to secure the financial resources to pay for community care.

Helping people with challenges such as poverty achieve their needs and goals is considered a legitimate government function by some people in the United States today, but not by others. The political parties differ markedly in their views on this matter. Thus, it makes sense for students considering the social work profession to become informed voters. Social work clients frequently belong to vulnerable populations who are likely to experience poverty and other ongoing challenges. Government assistance can be crucial in allowing them to obtain the resources necessary to improve their lives. One way social workers can help their clients is by voting for the candidates whose policies will genuinely assist the poor and disadvantaged. Even better, professional social workers can develop active political careers themselves.

To help students make thoughtful choices in the voting booth, this chapter will discuss political perspectives known as **conservative, liberal, or progressive**, and **radical**. It will also briefly describe **neoconservative** and **neoliberal** views. The discussion here will be very basic; students are encouraged to read as much as possible from additional sources and to examine Box 2.5, "Up for Debate."

The Political Spectrum

Political parties in the United States today fall along a political spectrum, described as *right* to *left*. Those on the right are considered relatively conservative; those on the left are considered relatively liberal or progressive. The major conservative political party in the

> **Box 2.5 Up for Debate**
>
> *Proposition: Should the federal government develop programs designed to assist poor people?*
>
> | Yes | No |
> | --- | --- |
> | People are naturally industrious and will use government assistance responsibly to better their lives. | People are naturally lazy, and government assistance will only make them lazier and more irresponsible. |
> | Environmental conditions such as discrimination may hold a person back unless government assists to "level the playing field." | Individuals are autonomous and achieve according to their inborn talents; they have complete free will and achieve according to their efforts. |
> | Government programs are necessary to help meet basic human needs for all. | The free market economy is the best way to fulfill individual needs. |
> | A free market economy needs intervention and regulation by government to ensure that competition is fair. | Government's role should be to support, not regulate, the free market. |

United States today is the Republican Party, and the major liberal or progressive party is the Democratic Party. There are parties even further right (or more conservative) than the Republican Party, however, and parties further left than the Democratic Party.

The term *liberal* implies favoring reform in social institutions such as education, religion, and politics so as to strengthen democracy and personal freedom. *Liberal* is sometimes described as *progressive*, or the quality of favoring change to bring about improvement, especially in significant social institutions such as education, religion, or politics. By contrast, the term *conservative* implies favoring preservation of established traditions and opposing any changes in them. Thus there are important differences in perspective between liberals (or progressives) and conservatives in the United States.

People who find themselves on different ends of the political spectrum tend to have very different attitudes regarding the proper role of government with respect to the economic market (Popple & Leighninger, 2005; Karger & Stoesz, 2010). We will discuss some of these differences next.

Conservative Perspectives

The term *conservative* is derived from the verb to *conserve* or to *save*, so it should come as no surprise that people who are conservative want to preserve traditions; preserving traditions for conservatives particularly necessitates preserving and/or restoring the traditional free market economic system. Conservative persons tend to be "haves" and believe not only that the free market system got them where they are, but also that it is the system that can best keep them at the top. Additionally, conservatives tend to be people who believe the traditional free market system is the one that can best take them where they want to go if they are not yet one of the "haves." Given these perspectives, it follows that conservatives do not believe that government should use its powers to help poor people. They worry that government assistance might increase what they perceive as a tendency to be lazy. Thus, most conservatives would answer "No" to the question posed in "Up for Debate," Box 2.5.

Conservatives believe that rather than developing programs to assist poor people, government should, instead, provide tax breaks for the rich because wealthy people invest money in the economic market. New investment theoretically could lead to new jobs for poor people, who would be better off with more work. This perspective is popularly known as the *trickle-down theory* or, more formally, as *supply-side economics*. Donald Trump promised to cut taxes on the rich during his campaign for the U.S. presidency. Conservatives do not oppose all help to the poor, but they believe aid should be offered only through the private sector as charity (Karger & Stoesz, 2010).

The conservative orientation goes beyond economics. Preservation of social traditions such as the nuclear family is also strongly promoted (as long as a marriage is heterosexual). Thus, political conservatives generally oppose potential public services such as government day care programs because, from this perspective, childcare should be provided only by a wife within a nuclear family household. Conservatives also generally oppose single parenthood, gay marriage, sex outside of marriage, abortion, and homosexuality because these practices are not considered traditional.

This type of conservatism, sometimes called **cultural conservatism**, results in major contradictions. While conservatives insist that government take a hands-off (laissez-faire) position with respect to intervention in the economic market, many conservatives push hard for government intervention restricting reproductive choice, access to sex education in the schools, gay marriage, and the like.

The major conservative political party in the United States today is the Republican Party, as mentioned earlier: that of Presidents Nixon, Ford, Reagan, George H.W. Bush, George W. Bush, and Trump. Within the Republican Party is a powerful faction known as the Tea Party, even further to the right (more conservative) than the general membership.

Other conservative parties include the Traditionalists, who believe that Christian doctrine should become the law of the nation, and the Libertarians, who oppose virtually all government regulation (including taxation), except when one individual threatens the physical safety of another (Karger & Stoesz, 2005, 2010).

Liberal or Progressive Perspectives

The liberal or progressive **worldview** is quite different from that of the conservative. First of all, the conception of human nature is more optimistic. Liberals believe that people are naturally good and do not need to be controlled or forced to work. Rather, they need to be protected from corrupting influences in the wider environment (Popple & Leighninger, 2005). Liberals believe that people are industrious by nature and will take pleasure in hard work and personal accomplishment if opportunity exists and conditions are humane.

Liberals believe that conditions in the social environment strongly affect people's chances to develop their talents and achieve a fulfilling life. From this viewpoint, if people are poor, it is in large part due to lack of opportunity, societal discrimination, oppression, and the like—problems that lie in the external environment. Thus liberals would tend to answer "Yes" to the question in "Up for Debate," Box 2.5.

> **Box 2.6 The Political Spectrum**
>
> | Liberal or Progressive Perspectives | Conservative Perspectives |
> |---|---|
> | Change can help make the world a healthier, happier place. | Change should be avoided; tradition is best. |
> | People are naturally industrious and of good moral character. | People are naturally lazy, careless, and corrupt. |
> | The environment strongly affects a person's ability to succeed. | People have complete free will and their accomplishments are not affected by their environment. |
> | Family forms may change in order to adapt to external conditions. | The traditional family should be upheld; programs designed to help non-traditional families should be opposed. |
> | The social system presents an uneven "playing field"; government should intervene in the economic market to assist disadvantaged populations. | Government regulation threatens individual liberty and smooth functioning of the economic market; the social system functions correctly as is. |
>
> Source: Popple, Philip R., & Leighninger, Leslie. (2011). *Social Work, Social Welfare, and American Society*, 8th Edition. Pearson Education, Inc.: Upper Saddle River, NJ.

Liberals or progressives support government intervention in the workings of the economic market to try to level the playing field for groups they believe are disadvantaged. For example, they tend to support government social welfare programs that provide monetary assistance to poor children and their families. They tend to support affirmative action programs to provide better access to jobs for women and racial minorities. They support national programs such as Head Start, which provides early environmental and educational enrichment for poor children to give them a better chance to fully develop their talents (see Box 2.6).

The major political party in the United States today that supports a liberal or progressive perspective is the Democratic Party, that of Presidents Kennedy, Johnson, Carter, Clinton, and Obama. There are other parties more liberal than the Democratic Party in the United States; they are much smaller, however. The Green Party is an example. It promotes environmental sustainability, community-based economics, grassroots democracy, nonviolence, respect for diversity, feminism, and social justice, among other progressive policies. The party began in Germany and is now a worldwide movement (Karger & Stoesz, 2005, 2010).

Neoliberalism and Neoconservatism

Confusing to many students is the fact that there are *neoconservative* and *neoliberal* perspectives, which are also important forces on the political scene. While a great deal could be said about them, it will be stated here only that both are to the *right* of their parent movements, the conservative and the liberal. American politics in general shifted greatly to the right toward the end of the twentieth century, and the shift intensified in the twenty-first. The momentum has been strong enough that many liberals have tried to distance themselves from the term *liberal*, using the term *progressive* instead. For neoconservatives, the shift to the right has involved adopting stands that are strongly culturally conservative, such as opposing reproductive choice for women, banning gay people from the military, and banning gay marriage. Their stance could be described as *reactionary*, opposing any policy empowering minorities. For neoliberals, the shift to the right has involved adopting favorable policies toward big business.

Bill Clinton was among the founders of the neoliberal movement, believing that a more favorable attitude toward big business would help him get elected. This attitude may have been what persuaded him, as president, to sign the bill (to be discussed in a later chapter) known as the Personal Responsibility and Work Opportunity Act, which, in 1996, ended the entitlement of all poor children in the United States to public welfare assistance under the Social Security Act. To be sure, the bill was passed by a Congress largely composed of Republican neoconservatives.

Radical Perspectives

The radical perspective, which may be described as *left* of the liberal, is held by a much smaller number of people in the United States than either the conservative or liberal perspective, but is still influential. The radical view of human nature parallels that of the liberal or progressive—that people are inherently good and naturally industrious, and that environmental influences may prevent people from achieving their full potential. However, while liberals believe that enlightened reform is possible *within* the capitalist system, radicals believe that capitalism itself is the problem because a wealthy and powerful elite make decisions that further their own interests at the expense of others (Popple & Leighninger, 2008; Karger & Stoesz, 2011).

Probably the major party in the United States today that most nearly reflects the radical perspective is the Socialist party, although it is very small (see Box 2.7).

Liberal and conservative positions fall toward opposite ends of the political spectrum, as described earlier. Conservatives oppose government intervention in the workings of the free market, except to bolster big business, and liberals support intervention to correct power imbalances and empower citizens who fall outside the mainstream. By the late twentieth century, these positions had polarized. A Democratic majority elected

Box 2.7 The Political Spectrum

Left				Right
Radical	Liberal	Neoliberal	Conservative	Neoconservative
Socialist	Green	Democratic		Republican Libertarian

This exhibit portrays where the author believes certain political parties lie today along the "left-right" political spectrum. Other people's views may differ. In some ways, it is incorrect to place Libertarian to the "right" of Republican, as Libertarians strongly promote individual liberties, including those of the less powerful, so they do not promote legislation limiting women's right to reproductive choice or gay marriage, etc.

to both houses of Congress in 2006 helped limit the power of the then-neoconservative executive branch, but discourse continued to be strident.

When President Obama was elected in 2008 along with a strongly Democratic Congress, the new President clearly hoped to work collaboratively across party lines. However, not a single Republican would support any bill proposed by Democrats. Republicans opposed the health care bill intended to assist millions of Americans lacking health insurance. President Obama was finally able to get the Affordable Health Care Act passed in 2010 by personally leading the effort, but he was unable to save a "public option" component that would have provided a government-run health insurance plan to compete with the huge private insurance industry which continues to drive up health care costs today.

Not content to let the Affordable Health Care Act be put into practice, conservatives immediately challenged the bill and took the challenge as far as the Supreme Court. Most of its provisions were upheld, but, unfortunately, not the part important to America's poorest citizens. The act had called for states to extend Title 19, Medicaid (to be discussed in Chapters 4 and 7) to all poor families, but the Supreme Court removed this requirement and left implementation to the option of the states. Many states opted out. Thus, many poor citizens in the United States remain without health insurance. Donald Trump, elected president in 2016, pledged, during his campaign, to repeal and replace the Affordable Care Act (Kiefer, 2016).

While the Obama administration worked hard to provide average Americans more opportunities—for example, programs to assist homebuyers nearing foreclosure, a stimulus bill to help retain and restore jobs, increases in college student loans, restoration of family planning funds lost under G.W. Bush, new protections for women against pay discrimination (to be discussed in Chapter 3)—still, the military budget remained massive, draining public funds that might otherwise have been available to assist American citizens.

To return to our chapter's case study regarding a politically powerless but personally plucky individual like Sandra McLean, would there be any condition in which people from both ends of the political spectrum might be willing to assist her? Remember that it was a policy change at the *national* level that prompted reassessment of her care in the *local* nursing home. Which political perspective, the liberal or the conservative, would be more likely to support developing programs to help Sandra and other people in need? Why? Students are requested to keep such questions in mind as they read further in this text and others.

> Assess your understanding of political perspectives by taking this brief quiz.

TURNING TO EACH OTHER: MARGARET WHEATLEY'S PERSPECTIVES

Dr. Margaret Wheatley, an organizational consultant, author, and international speaker with a strong orientation toward systems theory (described earlier in this chapter) believes that Americans may ultimately have to turn to each other to meet today's challenges. Wheatley, who works with organizations all over the world, including the United Nations, believes that the recession that became worldwide in 2008 was *not* a financial crisis. It was, instead, a global crisis that occurred because the world has become organized according to economic values. These values place cost-cutting, not service provision to persons in need, as the primary goal. Economic values are espoused by virtually every corporation, organization, and nation on earth today. The result has been a disaster for millions who have lost their means of support or who work for wages too low to support themselves and their families.

Wheatley asserts that we live in a culture that is still based on Social Darwinism, a powerful theory that arose out of Charles Darwin's 1859 book *On the Origin of Species*. The theory presents life as a struggle for survival in which each individual must compete against every other, and only the fittest can survive. This perspective leads to the belief that if you "make it" in this world you are "fit," but if you don't, you are defective and should be allowed to perish. (Social Darwinism will be discussed in more detail in Chapter 4.)

To the contrary, Wheatley notes life's building blocks are relationships, not competitive struggles. People survive only in community. She describes healthy communities as ones that identify themselves as community, preserve and learn from their histories, involve their youth in significant ways, invite a diversity of voices into conversation, and expect leadership from everyone.

Wheatley notes that relationships are crucial not only for physical survival but also for emotional and spiritual well-being. Due to the intense competitiveness of our times, many people rush about without time for meaningful relationships. Wheatley reports that sadly, loneliness and alienation have resulted in suicide being the second leading cause of death among adolescents in the United States. Clearly, many young Americans do not have a sense of belonging.

Wheatley believes that the best hope for the world rests on people turning to one another and pulling together. She observes that anyone can be a leader. All it takes is genuine caring and a willingness to help. In times of great need, she finds, communities respond; people help each other. Wheatley has learned through her work that there is no power greater than a community discovering what it cares about (Wheatley, 2009, 2010).

Fortunately, the profession of social work is made up of a remarkable number of people such as those Wheatley describes—people who care about and will assist others in times of need. They work with individuals, families, groups, organizations, and communities, depending on where the need or opportunity arises. Not only professional practitioners, but social work students are helping all over the world today, making a difference.

> **?** Assess your understanding of Wheatley's perspectives by taking this brief quiz.

SUMMARY

- The relationship between systems theory and the ecosystems perspective are discussed. Systems theory's influence on the development of the ecosystems perspective adopted by most generalist social workers, given its focus on interactional effects, is discussed.
- The way in which ecosystems theory guides generalist social work practice is explained. Ecosystems theory, with its emphasis on continuing interactions between person and environment, guides the generalist approach to practice by influencing the social worker to pay attention to relationships among multiple levels of intervention. The perspective also suggests the importance of

- a systematic intervention process that can be facilitated by the nine social work competencies identified by the CSWE's 2015 Educational Policy.
- Several intersecting factors spawning social justice concerns, challenging social work values, are identified. Several factors that intersect to increase a client's vulnerability to discrimination and poverty are identified, spawning social justice concerns for the social worker. The importance of a strengths-based orientation and recognition of client resilience is discussed. Appropriate levels of social work intervention today may extend beyond former notions of community to include global, ecological, and environmental considerations.
- The likelihood of support for social programs across the political spectrum is discussed. Basic political theory is introduced to help social work students understand different views on government action that can strongly affect their practice with clients. Conservative perspectives are contrasted with the liberal or progressive, and neoconservative and neoliberal points of view are discussed. Social work students are challenged to think about which political perspective might best assist in their work with clients.
- Margaret Wheatley's insights as to the effects of Social Darwinism on global economic systems today are explained and discussed, along with her assertion that if people are to thrive, they must turn to one another. Social workers can provide role models for this endeavor.

> ✓ Recall what you learned in this chapter by completing the Chapter Review.

3

Social Justice, Poverty, and Diversity: The Intersectionality of Multiple Factors

LEARNING OUTCOMES

- Define social justice, describe how economic justice relates to social justice, and explain how prejudice and discrimination can interfere with their achievement.
- Discuss how the intersectionality of multiple factors increases the likelihood that certain populations will experience discrimination and poverty.
- Describe four potent forms of prejudice in the United States.
- Identify and discuss seven major social justice issues in the twenty-first century.

CHAPTER OUTLINE

CASE STUDY: Meet Juanita Chavez 59

Social and Economic Justice 64
    Concepts in Social and Economic Justice 64
    The Impact of Poverty 66

Poverty, Diversity, and the Intersectionality of Multiple Factors 66
    Diversity and the Intersectionality of Multiple Factors 66
    Children 67
    Women 68
    Older Adults 69
    Racial and Ethnic Minority Groups 70
    People with Disabilities 74
    Gay, Lesbian, and Bisexual Persons 75
    Transgender Persons 76

Potent Forms of Prejudice in the United States 77
    Racism 78
    Sexism 78

CASE STUDY: Meet Juanita Chavez

Juanita cheered when she was offered the job as a social worker at Urban Neighborhood Center. A recent BSW graduate, Juanita knew she was competing for the position with more experienced workers. But she had an important skill: She spoke both Spanish and English fluently. Moreover, as part of the requirements of her social work major, she had served her senior-year field placement in an alternative school where Spanish was the first language of many of the students. Urban Neighborhood Center was located in an area where many residents were of Hispanic origin. Juanita hoped her bilingual abilities would help her get the job. They did.

Juanita had now been working for several months. She felt she was developing a broad understanding of the needs of the neighborhood as a whole that surrounded the agency. As part of her job,

CHAPTER OUTLINE *(Continued)*

Ageism 79
Heterosexism, Homophobia, and Transphobia 79

Social Justice Issues in the Twenty-First Century 80
Poverty Programs That Maintain Poverty 80
Poverty Line Determination Method 81
Poverty and the Minimum Wage 81
Affirmative Action Policies: Under Attack 83
Social Policy and the Growing Gap Between Rich and Poor 84
Health Insurance Accessibility 85
Administrative Barriers to Aid 86
Social Welfare Policy and Social Justice 86

Summary 87

she was expected to help identify major needs of community residents, to inform residents about the services available at the center, and to provide them with information concerning community resources that might help meet their needs. The center provided after-school recreational programs for school-age children, limited tutoring services, and a food pantry staffed by volunteers. Lately, however, the food pantry had been short on supplies, and hungry people had been sent home empty-handed. That bothered Juanita very much. While she liked the fact that her position gave her a broad perspective of the neighborhood in which she worked—indeed of the midsized city of which the neighborhood was a part—the knowledge she gained could be disturbing. She now knew that resources needed by many of the poorer residents were frequently not available.

Juanita's first crisis call on the job related to Temporary Assistance for Needy Families (TANF, a cash-benefit program requiring work or work training. It is run by the county, but it was established under state law according to federal guidelines). Juanita remembered the phone call well. A volunteer helping supervise a recreational program had called her just as the new social worker was trying to organize her tiny office. Two children much too young for the agency's after-school programs and much too young to be out on the streets alone, had been brought in by a school-age child who regularly came to the agency. The child said she had found the toddlers on the sidewalk, crying and apparently lost. Juanita soon encountered the young children, ages approximately 2 and 3, who said their names were Tomas and Tomacita. They could not provide an address or last name. They said they had been put to bed for a nap by their mother, but when they awakened, she was gone. Frightened, they began to search for her.

Juanita decided that she would have to call Protective Services to report abandoned children. Because the situation was not perceived as an emergency by the city's overburdened department, however, no worker arrived at Urban Neighborhood Center for several hours. Toward the end of the day, one of the longtime agency social workers returned after having made some home visits. By good fortune, this worker recognized Tomas and Tomacita and knew that they were siblings of a teenage girl who sometimes attended tutoring programs at the agency. There was a family telephone number on file. A call was made immediately, and a distraught mother answered. She had had to report to job training that day under the rules of the TANF program, she explained. Her older daughter, who usually babysat, was involved in a field trip with her school class, and the mother had not wanted her to miss it. The neighbor who had promised to substitute had been unavailable at the last minute. The children's mother didn't dare miss her job training as she could then be eliminated from the TANF program. That would take away her only source of money for food and rent. She knew people who had missed a single day of training due to lack of child care and had already been dismissed. So Tomas and Tomacita's mother had opted to take a serious risk, leaving her children alone after putting them to bed for a nap, hoping against hope that they would remain asleep.

The children's mother and the Protective Services worker arrived at Urban Neighborhood Center at almost the same moment. Only the advocacy of the agency social worker who knew the mother prevented the children from being taken into the foster care system then and there. Had that happened, months might have passed before Tomas and Tomacita were returned home. Their mother promised, of course, never to leave the children again without a babysitter. The Protective Services worker scolded her for not taking advantage of child care that was supposed to be provided by the TANF program. The mother explained that she had applied for child care months before, but that it hadn't come through yet.

Juanita learned later that child care, while theoretically available to poor mothers enrolled in TANF in her city, in reality involved a long waiting list. While her state permitted child care assistance for poor mothers under an option allowed by federal TANF legislation, funding was inadequate to meet the need. Tomas and Tomacita's older sister missed school regularly so that the mother could attend job training. The ability to secure a pay check to purchase food and shelter was naturally perceived by this family as more important than education.

Juanita soon became aware that many other families who lived near Urban Neighborhood Center were in the same situation. Many parents, languishing somewhere on TANF waiting lists for child care, depended on older children to babysit so they could go to work. Others with regular jobs earned wages too low to afford child care and also depended on their older children, especially teenage girls, to babysit. These helpful teens risked truancy proceedings, adding to family difficulties.

Juanita began to collect data on a number of high school girls in her area who were routinely missing school to babysit for younger siblings. She hoped eventually to influence legislators to appropriate more funds for child care. Juanita also hoped to see a Spanish-speaking day care center established by her agency because none yet existed in the city. She even made an appointment to speak with her agency's board of directors about establishing such a service. She was excited when the board appointed a special committee to study the situation and appointed Juanita a member. The committee then authorized Juanita to conduct a door-to-door survey to find out how many families would take part in a Spanish-speaking day care center if one were available. In this way, the social worker became engaged in community organization work, along with her other responsibilities at the neighborhood center.

As Juanita walked up the steps of a tiny, single-family cottage one day collecting data for her survey, she noticed that one of the special school vans that transport students with disabilities was pulling up to the door. The driver honked and then asked Juanita to knock, since he needed to deliver a child. No one answered the door, however, and the driver explained that he would have to take the child back to school. Juanita could see the sad face of a little girl peering out of the side window of the bus. Her head was misshapen and too large for her features. The driver muttered something about irresponsible mothers, shook his head, and drove away.

Juanita returned to the cottage later that day. This time her knock was answered by a young woman who appeared to be in her early 20s. Juanita explained who she was and why she had dropped by earlier. The woman looked blank, and then said haltingly, with a heavy accent, "I no speak English." Juanita then greeted the young woman in Spanish.

Her reward was an enormous, engaging smile. When Juanita mentioned the incident with the bus, however, the young woman's face took on an alarmed expression. She invited Juanita inside. She introduced herself as Carla Romero. "You say you are a social worker from Neighborhood Center?" she asked in Spanish. Juanita nodded. "Maybe you can help me, then," Carla continued.

"Tell me how I can assist," Juanita replied in Spanish, and the young woman began her story.

Carla told Juanita that her young daughter, Maria, was physically and cognitively disabled due to complications of birth that had resulted in permanent swelling of the brain. Now 6 years old, Maria functioned at a 12-month level. She had to be constantly supervised. But Carla had to work to support herself and the child. Her ex-husband, father of the child, kept in touch but had returned to Puerto Rico from where the couple had come. Child support checks were few and far between. Carla went to work when Maria began public school at the age of 3. The little girl received skilled service at school: occupational, physical, and speech therapy. Lately, however, there had been an embarrassing problem. The school nurse had sent Maria home with head lice. Carla had bought a number of products from the neighborhood pharmacy and used them carefully, but a few nits, or eggs, seemed to persist no matter what Carla did. The child continued to be sent home.

Carla, since she could not speak English, had already had a neighbor call the school to explain that she was doing all she could. The neighbor asked politely if the child could remain in school in spite of a few nits because her mother, Carla, had to work to provide food and shelter for the family. But the school nurse insisted that Maria could not attend school unless she was nit-free. The next day, Juanita called the nurse. She got the same story: no exceptions. Juanita called the health department for assistance. There she learned that certain strains of lice were currently resisting all remedies available in the store. The health department had effective treatments, a nurse there told her, but due to funding cuts, the staff could no longer provide services to help with this problem. Lice were no longer considered a "communicable disease" under current funding definitions! The nurse suggested taking the child to a doctor and fumigating the house.

Carla was fortunate in that, while her job paid very low wages and did not provide health insurance, she was nevertheless able to take her daughter to the doctor and to save enough money to pay for fumigating the house. That was because Maria qualified for Medicaid and Supplemental Security Income (SSI), (programs authorized under the Social Security Act, both of which require a "means test," or income below a certain level, to be eligible) as a child with a disability. The doctor told the young mother, however, that he did not know of any better treatment for lice or nits than the over-the-counter remedies she was already purchasing in the local stores. Carla then bought another standard treatment at the neighborhood pharmacy. She also had the house fumigated. But the problem continued.

Carla called Juanita at Urban Neighborhood Center in desperation after her daughter was sent home from school for the third month in a row. Her neighbor was babysitting regularly now, but she was not happy about it, and the cost was taking up most of Carla's food budget. The young mother frequently had to turn to Neighborhood Center's food pantry, but sometimes even the pantry was out of supplies. Juanita called the health department again, explaining that Carla had done everything she could, but still her child was being sent home from school. The department continued to insist that it had no staff to deal with the problem. In desperation, Carla shaved Maria's head. Even that did not work! Tiny nits persisted, and Maria continued to be sent home. Juanita had angry words with the school nurse, explaining that the little girl, through no fault of her own, was missing out on valuable therapies at school and that her physical condition was deteriorating as a result. But the nurse, perhaps understandably, was unmovable.

Then Juanita had an inspiration. She called the social worker at the school Maria attended. That worker was aware of the problem and had already tried to intervene with the school nurse, but to no avail. But this worker and Juanita agreed that both of them would make impassioned pleas to the health department. The health department refused once more, pleading budget cuts. Finally, the school social worker had her supervisor call the supervisor at the health department. That worked. At last, a public health nurse visited the Romero home. Juanita was present at the appointment, serving as translator and family advocate. The nurse promptly diagnosed Maria's strain of lice precisely and provided an effective remedy. Little Maria went back to school. But she had lost out on four months of education and therapy at an important developmental stage.

The Romero family's problem was not unique, of course. In Juanita's rounds of the neighborhood to collect information for her survey, she found that little Maria was not the only child missing school because of resistant strains of head lice. She also found several teenage girls at home taking care of babies, sometimes their younger siblings but sometimes their own children. Unable to afford the child care that would have enabled them to stay in school and lacking any hope of reaching the top of the TANF waiting list for child care, they dropped out. The teen mothers were lucky if their parents let them continue to live at home because most jobs available to people without high school degrees paid too low a wage to cover rent, food, clothing, and child care.

In addition, Juanita found several children in the neighborhood who stayed out on the streets after school because their parents had to work long hours and could not be home to supervise. Local schools offered a few sports programs for boys, but similar programs for girls were lacking. She also learned to her surprise that many of the families who used the agency's food pantry included full-time workers; some of the larger families included two full-time working adults, yet they still could not make ends meet. Wages were simply too low to cover expenses for a family, so cupboards stood empty at times.

Juanita decided to take the results of her survey back to the committee who had appointed her and to the full Urban Neighborhood Center board of directors as well. Now, besides a Spanish-speaking day care center for young children, she was interested in developing an after-school sports program for girls, as none currently existed in the area. Perhaps she could work with neighborhood schools to this end. Juanita also wondered if there might be a way to increase the supplies in her agency's food pantry.

Assessment

Dimension of Competency Skills: Social workers understand methods of assessment with diverse clients and constituencies to advance practice effectiveness.

Critical Thinking Question: How did Juanita's assessment skills enhance her practice effectiveness with her client population?

Juanita hoped that, with a number of caring minds working on the problems she documented, effective solutions might be generated, including ways to raise funds to finance new programs. The agency's budget was limited, she knew. But as a social work professional, Juanita believed she could make a difference, especially if she could combine her problem-solving efforts and energies with those of other dedicated people committed to the agency and the surrounding community.

This chapter examines social and economic justice concerns that place certain population groups at particular risk of discrimination and poverty. We describe diverse groups that are especially vulnerable. You will learn about potent forms of discrimination in the United States, as well as seven major social justice issues prevalent today.

SOCIAL AND ECONOMIC JUSTICE

Concepts in Social and Economic Justice

Little Tomas and Tomacita, and Carla and Maria Romero, each belonged to a population group especially vulnerable to experiencing poverty in the United States. In fact, each belonged to several. Tomas, Tomacita, and Maria were children; Tomacita, Carla, and Maria were female; all were members of the ethnic minority group known as Hispanic or Latino. Children, women, and ethnic minorities are all populations especially likely to experience poverty in this country. **Prejudice** (preconceived negative judgment) against certain groups of people, such as ethnic minorities and women, is common. Prejudice often results in **discrimination**, or unfair treatment, toward members of these groups. **Poverty**, a basic issue of social and economic justice, is a common result. *Poverty* may be defined broadly as the lack of resources to achieve a reasonably comfortable standard of living.

Because of the suffering imposed by poverty, social welfare policies and programs have been developed in many times and many places to help promote social and economic justice, to help improve the lives of people mired in poverty. Sometimes these efforts have been successful, sometimes not. Some programs, unfortunately, seem to have been designed more to control people who are poor than to alleviate poverty or promote other forms of social or economic justice. The TANF program, for example, forces poor mothers to work outside the home for low wages rather than remain at home caring for their children. The program does not lift poor women and children out of poverty.

If **social and economic justice** were to be realized, members of diverse population groups would have an equal chance to achieve a reasonably comfortable standard of living. There would be fairness among people so that one's gender, race, ethnicity, sexual preference, and so on, would not act as handicapping conditions getting in the way of obtaining a good education, rewarding employment, fulfilling leisure opportunities, quality medical care, and other aspects of a comfortable standard of living. This is an ideal condition, of course, which would require vision and social cooperation to accomplish. Economic justice is part of

---

Human Rights and Justice

Dimension of Competency **Skills:** Social workers understand that every person in society has fundamental rights such as freedom, safety, privacy, an adequate standard of living, health care, and education.

Critical Thinking Question: In what ways did Juanita's skills as a social work practitioner effectively promote an adequate standard of living, health care, and education for Carla and Maria Romero?

the larger concept of social justice, relating specifically to people's right to an adequate income to secure the basic necessities of life (food, shelter, clothing, medical care, etc.).

The United Nations' Universal Declaration of Human Rights, adopted in 1948, is an inspirational document comprising 30 articles that outline important elements of social justice. Hodge (2007) notes that this is still the most widely accepted human rights declaration in the world today. Article 1 affirms that "all human beings are born free and equal in dignity and rights. They are endowed with reason and conscience and should act towards one another in a spirit of brotherhood." Many other articles specify conditions necessary for the attainment of social justice as an overall ideal. Article 25 relates most specifically to economic justice and includes the following (UN, 1948):

- All people have a right to an adequate standard of living including sufficient food, clothing, shelter, medical care, and social services.
- All people have a right to assistance providing security in circumstances of unemployment, illness, disability, old age, or other circumstance beyond one's control.
- Motherhood and childhood require special assistance. All children should receive equal protection whether born within or outside of wedlock.

Cynthia Rocha and Andrea McCarter (2003/2004) note that students need assistance to understand how social and economic justice relates to trends in the economy and social welfare policies and programs. This text will try to further that understanding. This chapter's case study, for example, illustrates how poverty can result in young children left without parental supervision, lost educational opportunities, entire families experiencing hunger, and mothers forced to work outside the home although badly needed within. It introduces some of our national poverty programs purporting to ease the plight of the poor. But do our current policies and programs advance social and economic justice? Do they provide adequate "special care and assistance" to poor mothers and children as advocated by the United Nations' Universal Declaration of Human Rights?

Although the United States is the wealthiest nation in the world today, poverty is widespread. More than one child in five lives in poverty. More than 49 million Americans

Hungry child seeks food in a dumpster

suffer **food insecurity** (not enough food for healthful living; hunger), and nearly 16 million of them are children. The United States, to its shame, has the second highest child poverty rate among 35 industrialized nations, even though it has the largest economy in the world ("Ending Child Poverty Now," 2015; "Hunger and Poverty Fact Sheet," 2013). What does it say about a nation's commitment to social and economic justice when so many people, especially children, suffer poverty and malnutrition?

The Impact of Poverty

What is the matter with being poor? After all, some believe that poverty is beneficial, motivating family members to work hard, pull together, and practice frugality. Indeed, self-help efforts have assisted many poor people to survive. However, poverty is almost always harmful because it substantially limits people's choices. Where it is severe, the means for securing necessities such as food and shelter are lacking so that poverty can literally steal people's lives.

The Children's Defense Fund, an advocacy organization for children, explains that poverty results in poor health of children and adults alike, lowers high school graduation rates, and increases involvement with the criminal justice system. It costs the nation billions of dollars a year in lost productivity and increased crime. Not only do children suffer disproportionately with respect to other groups, but their experiences in childhood influence their adult lives; childhood lays the foundation for adult abilities, interests, and motivations ("Ending Child Poverty Now," 2015).

A nation's social policies, if that nation so wills, can prevent child poverty and lay the foundations for a fulfilling, competent adulthood. This has been proven by the experiences of other countries, particularly the Scandinavian and some of the other European nations. But policies that create social and economic justice and eliminate poverty require an aware populace with the value base, political savvy, and determination to bring them about.

> **?** Assess your understanding of social and economic justice by taking this brief quiz.

POVERTY, DIVERSITY, AND THE INTERSECTIONALITY OF MULTIPLE FACTORS

Diversity and the Intersectionality of Multiple Factors

Everyone in the world is, to some degree, vulnerable to experiencing poverty and other hazards. But not everyone is vulnerable to the same degree. Research has clearly demonstrated that members of certain diverse groups in the United States, those groups whose members are different from white and male, are more likely to experience poverty than others, for reasons beyond their own control and not due to chance or laziness.

Members of diverse vulnerable populations make up the clientele with whom social workers do most of their work. For example, Susan and Martha Dunn of Chapter 1 are members of a population vulnerable to poverty because they are female; Martha and Todd Dunn are vulnerable because they are children. Sandra McLean of Chapter 2 is vulnerable because she is female and further at risk because she has a disability. Tomas, Tomacita, and Maria of this chapter's case study are vulnerable because they are children; Carla, Tomacita, and Maria are vulnerable because they are female. Members of two or more intersecting categories of vulnerability, such as children who are female or members of ethnic minorities, suffer even more risk of poverty because the intersectionality of multiple factors (e.g., age, gender, disability, ethnicity) seriously increases the risk of poverty and other perils.

It should be recognized here that intersectionality of multiple factors does not necessarily increase a person's risk of poverty—for example, the intersectionality of factors such as white male status, adulthood, higher education, and excellent health increases a person's chance to achieve economic comfort. But in this chapter we are identifying factors that undermine one's chance of such success.

> **Diversity and Difference**
>
> *Dimension of Competency* **Values: Social workers understand that, as a consequence of differences, a person's life experiences may include oppression, poverty, marginalization, and alienation.**
>
> **Critical Thinking Question:** In what ways did social worker Juanita Chavez demonstrate her social work values that Carla and Maria Romero deserved assistance despite the marginalization and alienation resulting from their minority heritage and Maria's cognitive disability?

Children

Sadly, children in the United States' are especially likely to be poor. During the 1980s, growth in child poverty rates led to the coining of the term **juvenilization of poverty**. The child poverty rate today is higher than it was 50 years ago. As noted above, more than one child in five is poor, and approximately 16 million children live in homes that are food insecure. A third of all persons living in poverty in the United States today are children ("Hunger and Poverty Fact Sheet," 2013). These statistics have remained stagnant for decades. The formal figures, serious as they are, belittle the problem because the United States' formula for determining the poverty line (to be discussed later in the chapter) severely underestimates the number of people who actually experience poverty.

Children who have come to this country as undocumented immigrants comprise a group especially in peril of poverty. Many children were brought by their parents when very young, but in recent years hundreds of thousands more have risked their lives to escape violence in their countries of origin (especially Guatemala, El Salvador, and Honduras, but also Mexico). President Obama's Deferred Action for Childhood Arrivals (DACA) program, initiated in June 2012, provides undocumented immigrant children with some protection as this chapter is being written. The program allows deportation to be deferred for a temporary period of time on a case-by-case basis for those who have met specific eligibility criteria. President Obama tried to expand the program to cover more categories of children in November 2014 (e.g., expand the DACA age cap of 16, reduce the number of years a child must have lived continuously in the United States), but in February 2015, a federal district court in Texas put the expanded DACA program on hold (Restrepo and Garcia, 2014; "The Obama Administration's Deferred Action for Childhood Arrivals [DACA]," 2015).

In 2016 Donald Trump, a political conservative, was elected president. Trump made a campaign promise to build a wall between the United States and Mexico with the intent of halting all immigration by undocumented persons, children or adults. During his campaign he also made many unfavorable comments regarding persons of minority status. With his election, therefore, continuation of the DACA program looked unlikely.

Clearly, in the United States, we do not enjoy the situation often piously described as "women and children first." Children especially frequently come last, and sadly, they

> **Box 3.1 Poverty Harms People**
>
> Poverty harms people. It leads to hunger and homelessness. It destroys dreams. Sadly, poor people in the United States are worse off than those of almost any other country in the developed world even though this nation has the strongest economy on earth. While American politicians, especially conservative politicians, piously mouth the importance of "family values," they consistently vote in Congress to reduce or eliminate public benefits that would help poor children and their families.
>
> Poverty in America is a political problem, caused not by a lack of resources but by a refusal to respond with generosity by those in positions of power (and by the people who elect them). While it is universally understood that food, shelter, health care, and other basics are crucial to the well-being of children and families, what is largely ignored in the United States is the fact that millions of families do not have enough income to provide these necessities. Therefore, members of far too many families suffer ongoing hardship and face futures that are bleak.

often know it. They may feel unappreciated and unloved as well as poor and deprived. However, the situation is not necessary or inevitable, but rather the result of choices our electorate and our elected representatives have made (see Box 3.1).

Women

Women compose another population at risk. Although progress has been made over the past two decades, that progress, unfortunately, may be less than what most people believe. Women's limited ability to earn is shown by the disparity in average earnings between female and male full-time workers in the United States. The average woman worker in 2015 earned only 78 cents for every dollar earned by a man. Education can be an important tool for women to increase their earnings, but it does not close the pay gap: Women earn less than men at every level of academic achievement and, in some cases, experience a higher pay gap at higher levels of education. Women experience a pay gap in virtually every occupation, and the gap increases with age, even for women without children. The disparity is even greater for women of color (Hill, 2015).

According to an analysis by TIME magazine, between the ages of 22 and 25 women earn 15 percent less than men on average, and a horrifying 38 percent less between the ages of 51 and 64. They lose an average of $435,049 over the course of their careers, according to a 2015 study by the National Women's Law Center (Wilson, 2016).

Achieving equality for women through legal action is difficult. For example, in May 2007, the U.S. Supreme Court ruled against a female employee, Lilly Ledbetter, of Goodyear Tire and Rubber Company. After being employed by Goodyear for many years, Ledbetter learned via an anonymous letter that she was earning several thousand dollars per year less than her male counterparts. She filed a legal challenge within a month of receiving the letter, but the Supreme Court ruled against her on the grounds that she had not filed within 180 days of *original employment*.

Ruth Bader Ginsburg, the only woman then on the Court, wrote a powerful dissent to the conservative Ledbetter ruling, calling on Congress to enact legislation to correct the "high court's parsimonious reading of pay inequity claims" (Terzieff, 2007). One of the bright spots in progress toward gender equity for American women took place in the fall of 2008 when a Democratic Congress passed the Lilly Ledbetter Fair Pay Act. This was the first act President Obama signed into law, on January 29, 2009. It stipulates that pay discrimination claims accrue with every discriminatory paycheck an employee receives, not only when a discriminatory pay decision or practice is adopted ("Lilly Ledbetter Fair Pay Act," 2009). However, in another regressive conservative decision in 2011, the U.S. Supreme Court ruled against women employees in their class action suit against Walmart.

While, as mentioned above, women experience a pay gap in almost every occupation, part of the gender-based wage gap can be attributed to women workers clustering in industries related to service and caregiving, occupations which tend to be low paying. In addition, women provide the bulk of unpaid caregiving for their children, older family members, and other dependent persons. Thus, they may be forced to work only part-time outside the home, or require flexible schedules, which can cut back substantially on their earnings (Baxter, 2015).

Unfortunately, the American economic system undervalues caregiving work. It completely overlooks the fact that caregiving *is* work when provided in the home. Because wages are not involved, caregiving work at home does not qualify a woman for her own Social Security benefits or for unemployment insurance if she is "fired" by her husband. It no longer entitles her to public assistance under the Social Security Act when she is a single parent with dependent children, even though women shoulder most of the burden of child rearing in cases of divorce or birth out of wedlock.

Outside the home, caregiving is poorly paid, exposing even full-time female wage earners to poverty. It is not surprising that in 2012, nearly 31 percent of female-headed families lived in poverty, over six times the poverty rate of a family headed by a married couple ("Poverty in the United States: A Snapshot," 2013). The substantial poverty of women has led to the coining of the term **feminization of poverty**.

There was some good news for women when Obama was elected—the Obama administration appointed over 1,000 women to government positions within its first year; it continued to appoint women to positions of authority throughout Obama's second term as President. Empowerment of women can be significantly enhanced through such visible government action.

> ▶ Watch this video about a young single mother. Please note how the policies discussed in Chapter 3 affect this young woman and her ability to provide for herself and her family.
> https://www.youtube.com/watch?v=F6HJUF2aH5k

Older Adults

Older adults comprise another population at risk. There is some good news, however, for this group. Social Security amendments passed in the 1960s and 1970s (primarily Medicare and SSI, to be discussed later in the chapter) helped reduce poverty rates for people over age 65 from more than a third to 9.1 percent in 2012, the lowest rate among all age groups. While this rate stayed the same as the previous year, the absolute number of older Americans living in poverty rose from 3.6 million to 3.9 million ("Poverty in the United States: A Snapshot," 2013).

If older adults enjoy a poverty rate lower than that for the population as a whole, how can they be considered a vulnerable population? The fact is that the overall figures hide wide discrepancies among older people. Older women and ethnic minorities have a much higher poverty rate than the average. Nearly three-quarters of unmarried older adults receive at least half of their income from Social Security, and nearly half of them rely on Social Security for an astounding 90 percent or more of their income. Over half of married couples receive over half of their income from Social Security ("Fact Sheet, Social Security," 2013). The G.W. Bush administration tried to privatize Social Security, but fortunately this effort failed as privatization most likely would have resulted in reduced benefits for many recipients.

Older adults in financial need frequently face discrimination in the workplace, and elderly women and members of ethnic minority groups are even more likely to face it. For those fortunate enough to receive a pension upon retirement, the pension is almost always less than the wage earned previously. Many people do not receive a pension at all. Companies are not legally required to offer pension plans, and those that do may go bankrupt and be unable to honor their commitments. Some older adults lose their pensions because they are intentionally laid off just before reaching retirement age. Today, huge numbers of pension plans have been replaced by tax-sheltered annuity options, which involve substantial employee contributions and financial risk. People are more and more left on their own by their employers to finance their own retirement so that a strong Social Security program is more important than ever.

The percentage of older adults who are considered to live in poverty would rise significantly if the standard for measuring poverty were updated. The poverty line used as today's standard was established in the early 1960s. It resulted from surveys taken from 1955 through 1961 that indicated that the ratio of food consumption to all other household expenditures was 1:3. A basic food budget was then generated by the Department of Agriculture and was multiplied by three to determine the **poverty line**. The food budget developed for the elderly was lower than that for younger people, so the official poverty line for the elderly was also lower. In 2015, it was $11,367 for a single person 65 and over as compared with $12,331 for a younger person ("Poverty Thresholds for 2015," 2016). The percentage of older adults who are recognized to be poor today would go up considerably if the poverty line used were the same as that for younger people. Moreover, the formula for determining the poverty line has not changed since the 1960s except to account for inflation, even though food now comprises a much smaller percentage of the average family budget.

Racial and Ethnic Minority Groups

Racial and **ethnic minority groups**, those with distinct biological or cultural characteristics different from the majority, are other major populations at risk of poverty. Groups that are considered minorities differ from country to country and from region to region. For example, although Hispanics are a minority group in the United States, that is not the case in Mexico or Latin America. The term *race* usually refers to physical or biological characteristics.

In the United States, four racial **minority groups** are usually distinguished: Native Americans, African Americans, Hispanics, and Asian Americans. This can be confusing because these four categories do not comprise all persons of racial minority status, and many are of mixed heritage. It can also be confusing because not all members of minority groups are people of color. Persons who consider themselves Hispanic, for example, include both whites and non-whites. Thus, Hispanics can more accurately be considered an ethnic group rather than a race. In addition, the four major racial classifications listed above include populations with enormously varied physical characteristics: for example, the category "Asian" includes populations as diverse as Chinese, Indians from India, Tibetans, and Pacific Islanders such as Hawaiians.

Ethnic groups, as contrasted with **racial groups**, share certain cultural characteristics that distinguish them from others, such as customs, values, language, and a common history. An ethnic group may contain members of different races, as in the example given above of Hispanics, or it may differ culturally from the race it most resembles physically.

Racial and ethnic minority groups, earlier in U.S. history, were expected to become part of a national melting pot. Minority groups were thus pressured toward giving up cherished aspects of their cultural identities. Today, however, a new paradigm, or model for understanding, is emerging: **cultural pluralism** and ethnic diversity, in which difference is expected, acknowledged, tolerated, and even celebrated. This paradigm is increasingly embraced by social workers, and **cultural competence**, or the skill of communicating competently with people of contrasting cultures, is becoming an increasingly important expertise in social work practice (Lum, 2007). One simple reason: Fewer than two-thirds of Americans today are "white alone" (a census category that includes Hispanic persons who are white)—62.6 percent in 2013 ("People Quick Facts," 2015).

What minority groups have in common in the United States is that they have less power than the majority group. Lack of power renders minority group members vulnerable to discrimination and devaluation. (In this sense, females are considered a minority group even though they constitute a numerical majority.) Discrimination in the United States influences the amount minorities are likely to earn so that they suffer a greater risk of poverty. For example, in 2012, while the poverty rate for whites was 11 percent, the rate for Asian Americans was 13 percent. The rate for Hispanics was 25 percent and

Homeless man begging on the street

for Native Americans 26 percent. The poverty rate for African Americans was 28 percent (Krogstad, 2014).

Sometimes a person's racial or ethnic heritage affects where he or she can live more directly than income alone. Those who succeed financially despite discrimination may find themselves unwelcome and may be actively harassed in areas predominantly inhabited by persons of European background. Fortunately, due to civil rights activism and legislation in the 1960s, such harassment is no longer legal (see Box 3.2).

Arizona passed a law in 2010 that seems to reinstitute legal harassment of ethnic minorities. This law allows police to stop anyone "reasonably" suspected of being an illegal immigrant. Arizona has a large number of undocumented immigrants living in the state, and most are Hispanic. Darker-skinned people are usually the ones suspected of being illegal and, thus, are much more likely to be stopped by police. The Supreme Court struck down a part of Arizona's law, which would have criminalized immigrants not carrying their federal registration cards, but upheld the provision allowing police to stop and question anyone suspected. Following Arizona, the states of Utah, Indiana, and Georgia passed similar laws and, in 2011, Alabama passed one that was even harsher, making it illegal for anyone even to assist an undocumented immigrant (Whitehead, 2012). Laws such as these endanger the civil liberties of everyone.

In some cases, the cultural heritage of a minority group has been actively suppressed, not only in historical times but also in the present. In the worst-case scenario, sometimes members of majority groups try to exterminate others entirely. The example of the Holocaust against Jewish people, Gypsies, homosexuals, and persons with disabilities under Germany's Nazi regime during World War II is a case in point. In the

---

Box 3.2 The Segregation Challenge

The election of an African-American president in 2008 seemed to hail a new era of racial equality in the United States, but sadly, segregation persists. Major sections of cities, particularly in the North, still house mainly whites, while other sections, usually poorer ones, house African Americans. Such segregation occurs even given the passage of important civil rights legislation over many years and the widespread passage of open housing laws.

While custom alone probably accounts for a certain amount of the segregation, prejudice is clearly also an issue. The frustration experienced by residents of poorer African-American neighborhoods became clear in the widespread rioting that took place in 2014 and 2015 in Ferguson, Missouri, and Baltimore, Maryland, when police shot unarmed African Americans. It was also evident in Charleston, South Carolina, and Madison, Wisconsin, when police in those cities also shot unarmed African Americans. Even though the latter two cities avoided riots, peaceful protests made it clear that many African Americans do not feel valued in America and do not trust the police officers who are supposed to protect them.

Sadly, the killing of unarmed African Americans by police continues today, although certain cities have been required by the federal government to provide diversity training for police officers. Even more sadly, white citizens themselves sometimes deliberately kill African Americans, as occurred in Charleston in 2015 when a young white male shot and killed nine African Americans in church. Whites also all too often set fire to the churches in which African Americans worship. Racial biases and tensions dehumanize all persons, majority and minority alike.

United States, hundreds of thousands of Native Americans were exterminated during the migration of white people across the continent. The Chinese massacred millions of people in Tibet in the 1960s and 1970s. The ethnic cleansings in Bosnia, Rwanda, Kosovo, Darfur, Iraq, Syria, and other areas of the world in recent times provide chilling evidence that people have not learned that the example we set today plants seeds for the future.

Since the terrorist attacks in New York City and Washington, D.C., in the fall of 2001, the United States has experienced a powerful new challenge relating to minority ethnic groups. Because the men who hijacked the planes crashing into the World Trade Center and the Pentagon were of Middle Eastern origin, people of that ethnic group immediately became suspect. Thousands, including students, were arrested without delay. Congress soon passed the USA Patriot Act, legislation that diminished many cherished American civil liberties. For example, student records could be subpoenaed if a judge agreed they might obtain information pertinent to terrorist investigations, and any person's residence could be searched without that person's knowledge or consent. All phone records were routed and stored in a national data bank for possible review.

On June 1, 2015, the provision in the Patriot Act allowing the government to carry out its sweeping phone records surveillance program expired, due to an unusual coalition of progressives and libertarians. The unusual alliance, known as the Civil Liberties Coalition, was formed due to the concern of many members on both left and right ends of the political spectrum regarding government intrusion into American privacy. The coalition's efforts resulted in the passage of the USA Freedom Act, outlawing the surveillance of phone records by the federal government (although these records will now be kept by telephone companies); the coalition plans to pursue a multi-year strategy to push Congress to continue further reforms of the Patriot Act (Sorcher, 2015).

The fear that understandably arose from the 2001 attacks was used by President G.W. Bush to declare war on Afghanistan and then Iraq, despite strongly expressed disagreement by the United Nations and most other nations of the world. Bush then declared, as America's commander-in-chief, that people captured in these wars were enemy combatants without any legal rights, as opposed to prisoners of war protected under the Geneva Convention.

Torture was used against the prisoners at Guantanamo Bay, and other terrorist suspects were kidnapped all over the world and taken to nations where torture was widespread, a practice called *extraordinary rendition* ("Anti-torture Efforts on Capitol Hill," 2006). The purpose was to extract information from prisoners in ways that would not normally be legal in the United States under its Constitution. The U.S. Supreme Court overturned certain aspects of the Bush administration's policies (Civil liberties and human rights, 2004), and the United Nations Committee Against Torture called upon the United States to close the detention camp at Guantanamo Bay (Richey & Feldman, 2006).

President Obama ordered torture to be halted immediately after his inauguration in 2009, and his administration began releasing carefully screened prisoners from Guantanamo Bay. The camp, however, remained open at the end of his administration. President Obama had searched for ways to close it but his efforts were continually blocked by Congress. There were other challenges as well: e.g., certain prisoners had no country willing to take them, and some were considered (at least by a vocal minority) too dangerous to release even to prisons in the United States.

Information was leaked to the press in 2006 that the federal government under G.W. Bush was routinely tapping, without judicial warrants, the telephone conversations of all persons suspected of communicating with suspected terrorists (translation: the federal government under G.W. Bush was tapping all telephone conversations with all persons overseas). Like the federal government's collecting and storing of all telephone records, this routine phone tapping may also be challenged at some point by the Civil Liberties Coalition.

Many Americans agree that national security concerns should trump human rights, but legal and humanitarian protections lost to one are lost to all. If a U.S. President can now remove legal protections from anyone by simply declaring that person an "enemy combatant" and have the person imprisoned indefinitely without charge, who among us is "free"?

As noted by Grier (2001), government officials in situations of war or imminent war must determine, under severe time pressure, how to respond. They must determine how much danger the nation is in and whether cherished individual rights must be sacrificed in order to protect it. Grier notes that officials can make mistakes—the internment of Japanese-American citizens during World War II is a serious case in point, today considered a blot on the nation's honor.

People with Disabilities

People with disabilities are another population vulnerable to discrimination and poverty since people who do not have disabilities may hold negative attitudes toward those who do. An extreme example of the inhumane treatment that may result took place in Nazi Germany, where many people with disabilities were sent to concentration camps and exterminated. In the United States, historically, many people with disabilities were sent to public institutions and sterilized so they could not reproduce.

Today, persons with disabilities may find themselves subject to social ostracism, ridicule, job discrimination, and the like. The civil rights movement in the United States in the 1950s and 1960s helped develop an awareness of social justice issues for persons with disabilities, and they and their families began to advocate for legal rights and protections. Legislation important to persons with disabilities in the United States will be discussed in Chapter 12.

Societal definitions of disability differ with time and are hotly debated; the consequences are serious because certain protected populations can benefit from legislation from which others are excluded. For example, tens of thousands of poor children lost their federal disability benefits as part of 1996 welfare reform legislation simply because of changes in the legal definition of disability.

Persons with disabilities experience many barriers, both social and economic, to full participation in today's world. Many suffer unemployment or underemployment. For this reason, many qualify for SSI, as did little Maria in this chapter's case example, but SSI rarely lifts a person with a disability above the poverty line. The Americans with Disabilities Act of 1990 was designed to help people with disabilities improve their chances of escaping poverty. It has had mixed results and will be discussed in more detail in Chapter 12.

Today, as is well known, the wars in Iraq, Afghanistan, and elsewhere in the Middle East have produced a new cadre of people with disabilities, including veterans who have had the misfortune of losing limbs and/or their mental stability due to combat conditions. They and their families suffer ongoing issues that the U.S. government has been challenged to address. These will also be discussed in more detail in Chapter 12.

Gay, Lesbian, and Bisexual Persons

Gay and lesbian persons are those who are sexually attracted to members of their own gender. Bisexual persons are those who are attracted both to members of their own gender and to members of the opposite gender. If a bisexual person decides to marry someone of the opposite gender, probably no problems with prejudice will ensue. But if the bisexual person falls in love with a member of the same sex, he or she may encounter the same issues as those suffered by gay and lesbian persons: prejudice, discrimination, and, until 2015, an inability to marry in many states due to state law. This section will focus on the issues faced by gay and lesbian persons, but these issues also pertain to bisexuals who wish to marry someone of the same gender.

> ▶ Watch this short video about one young woman's struggle to survive on her small monthly employment income and SSI cash benefit. How does her situation resonate with what you know about poverty and marginalized groups of people, such as those with disabilities? How likely is it that Kira will be able to lift herself out of poverty and feel financially secure?
>
> https://www.youtube.com/watch?v=vglkPCV7h5w

Gay and lesbian persons have been fighting for the right to marry for decades, and the fight finally came to fruition in June 2015, when, in a 5–4 decision, the Supreme Court finally legalized gay marriage in the *Obergefell v. Hodge* ruling. Discrimination, however, is still a fact of life for many gays, lesbians, and bisexuals. Unlike other groups who suffer discrimination, federal civil rights protections do not include them, at least as this chapter is being written. One can marry one's same-sex partner legally today but be fired from his or her job for doing so tomorrow. The reason seems to be that many people, because of their personal or religious values, do not accept those whose sexual orientation is toward persons of the same gender. A poll taken several days after the *Obergefell v. Hodge* decision found that only 39 percent of Americans approved of the Court's decision (Crary & Swanson, 2015). Two major Republican candidates for the then-approaching 2016 presidential election, Ted Cruz and Mike Huckabee, urged states to ignore the new law.

The history of the struggle of gay and lesbian persons to obtain equal rights under the law in the United States has been a long one, and is not over. Without civil rights protections, people who are perceived as gay or lesbian can be fired from their jobs, denied home mortgages, refused apartment rentals, and so on, without legal recourse. To protest these and other discriminatory practices, decades ago in 1993, hundreds of thousands of gays, lesbians, and other civil rights activists marched on Washington, seeking to obtain civil rights protection under the law.

The 1993 march on Washington failed to obtain its immediate objective, but gay rights did gain recognition as a national issue. But in 1994, another set-back occurred. A Republican Congress was elected, slowing and progress toward equality. Concerned that the state of Hawaii was about to legalize gay marriages, Congress responded by passing the Defense of Marriage Act of 1996. This act permitted states not to accept as legal gay marriages performed in other states.

The issue of gay marriage survived, nevertheless, and then gained a kind of critical mass beginning in the year 2000. In that year, gays and lesbians won a joyful victory in Vermont; the state legislature approved civil unions for same-sex couples, legally equivalent to marriage (Marks, 2000). Another step forward took place when the Massachusetts Supreme Court ruled in 2003 that barring persons to marry solely because those persons wanted to marry persons of the same sex violated the Massachusetts constitution (Paulson & Stern, 2003).

Following these significant court decisions, a surge of legalization of same-sex marriage began to take place, and, by 2015, 37 states had legalized it—26 by court decision, 8 by state legislature, and 3 by popular vote. Thirteen states still banned gay marriage, however (Farrell, 2010; "State by State," 2009; "37 States Have Legal Same Sex Marriage," 2015).

This progress occurred despite the fact that Republican President G.W. Bush proposed constitutional amendments to ban gay marriage throughout the country virtually every year of his administration. When President Obama was elected in 2008, he had not yet made a decision regarding his personal position on gay marriage, but he did want to help protect gay and lesbian persons from violence. In 2009, he signed into law federal legislation that includes, under the list of federal hate crimes, acts of violence against gay and lesbian persons. He then began working to modify the "don't ask, don't tell" policy requiring gays in the military to remain "in the closet" if they wanted to remain in military service. President Obama was successful: In late 2010, with his urging, a lame-duck Congress (a Congress whose term was ending) passed legislation permitting gays and lesbians to serve openly in the military.

The Obama administration then made the important decision to support gay marriage. In 2011, it instructed the Department of Justice to cease defending the Defense of Marriage Act. And as a further boost to the progress of gay marriage, the Supreme Court, in 2013, in the *Windsor v. United States* case, ruled that the federal government could not deny married same-sex couples the protections of federal policies and programs that pertain to all other married couples. The ruling did not go so far as to require states still banning gay marriage to recognize gay marriages performed in other states, but it was a huge victory for gay rights nevertheless ("The Defense of Marriage Act," 2015).

Then, finally, on June 26, 2015, the Supreme Court ruled that states could not refuse gay and lesbian couples the right to marry. However, these couples still do not enjoy all the civil protections granted to heterosexual couples.

A step forward in marriage equality for gays and lesbians took place in Utah in October, 2015. State laws normally recognize that the spouse of a woman having a baby is a legal parent of that baby, but Utah refused to recognize the parental rights of Angie Roe to baby Lucy, although Angie was legally married to Lucy's mother. The American Civil Liberties Union sued, and Angie was granted her parental rights (Dumesnil, 2016).

Transgender Persons

Transgender persons have come into wider public awareness in recent years, perhaps due to celebrities such as Olympic athlete Bruce Jenner courageously publicizing that he was transitioning from male to female. He let it be known that he had always felt female despite his male genitalia and that he had become ready to make the transition. When physiological changes became sufficiently visible due to surgery and hormonal treatments, she chose to be called by a new, feminine name, Caitlyn.

Transgender persons are those who feel that the gender represented by their genitalia at birth and, thus, the gender identity assigned to them at birth, does not match the gender identity they feel inside. Like other people, they may identify as heterosexual, gay, lesbian, bisexual, or something else. Transgender persons have historically been forced to remain quiet about their internal gender identity because of fear of prejudice and discrimination. However, today more and more people are making the serious decision to change their gender physically through surgical or hormonal treatment, or both, to the gender that feels right to them. Such decisions, of course, result in changes visible to other people, which expose them to prejudice and discrimination, sometimes violent. The National Coalition of Anti-Violence Programs reported in 2013 that 344 transgender people had been victimized that year, with 13 of them murdered. In 2011, 41 percent attempted suicide, indicating the condition is stressful for many people (Terry, 2015).

Many transgender persons wish to use restroom facilities in accordance with their gender identity rather than the gender suggested by their birth genitalia. In 2015, President Obama, to assist schools struggling with the matter, issued a directive to allow transgender students to use the bathroom in accordance with their gender identity. This set off something like a firestorm of complaints, particularly in southern states. Myriad lawsuits immediately challenged the directive (Davis, 2015). Yet states with less public prejudice against transgender persons simply developed private unisex bathrooms available to all that have resolved any concerns.

LGBTQ

The initials LGBTQ are often used to designate the population of persons who are lesbian, gay, bisexual, and transgender. Lesbian, gay, bisexual, and transgender persons have been discussed above. But what does the "Q" in LGBTQ stand for? It usually has either of two meanings: "questioning," or "queer." "Questioning" refers to those persons who are not sure of their gender identity and are seeking answers. "Queer" is an umbrella term for all sexual and gender minorities that are not heterosexual. Originally it was a pejorative term, but more recently it has been reclaimed by activists to help establish community and assert a politicized identity.

Many LGBTQ persons became exceedingly nervous at the election of Donald Trump in 2016, a man who made many derogatory remarks against minorities during his campaign.

> **?** Assess your understanding of the intersectionality of multiple factors by taking this brief quiz.

POTENT FORMS OF PREJUDICE IN THE UNITED STATES

Although Americans proclaim an overall belief in equal justice for all and although various social movements have produced important legislation to protect the rights of minority groups, a marked discrepancy still exists between principle and practice today. Certain potent societal isms are clearly still in evidence.

Isms are prejudices common to large segments of society that relegate people who are perceived as different to a lower social status. Isms in the United States stem from cultural teachings such as white is better, male is better, young is better, and heterosexual is better. Isms have many consequences, including the fact that members of minority populations face more barriers than other people. These barriers can vary from milder forms of social discrimination such as lack of access to certain jobs and lower pay to intentional attempted extermination. Sadly, people who suffer prejudice and discrimination often take their poor treatment to heart, so they suffer loss of self-esteem as well.

Racism

Racism is the belief that one race is superior to others, a belief that tends to justify exploiting members of other races. In the United States, the majority race includes a variety of white-skinned ethnic groups of European origin who tend to consider themselves superior to people with darker skin. Racism leads to discrimination against people of color perpetrated by both individuals and social institutions such as governmental bodies and private organizations. Institutional racism, or patterns of racial discrimination entrenched in law and custom, lives on in many subtle forms today. It was far more blatant, of course, before the civil rights movement of the 1960s and early 1970s. The civil rights movement was sparked in 1955 by Mrs. Rosa Parks' refusal to obey a white man's demand that she give up her seat to him on a Montgomery, Alabama, bus, as required by racist laws. (It should be noted that Mrs. Parks had trained diligently in nonviolent action prior to her courageous deed and subsequent arrest.)

Today, overtly racist laws have been ruled unconstitutional, but subtler institutional racism and personal affronts continue. Ongoing racism is clearly illustrated in the United States today by the residential segregation visible throughout most of the nation, and sadly, it still leads to violence against members of minority populations. For example, in 2011 three teenaged white boys beat and then killed a 47 year old African American man in Jackson, Mississippi. They shouted "White power" as they attacked, and one teen later bragged to a friend, "I just runned that nigger over" ("Racist Hate Crimes," 2015). Equally or perhaps even more horrendous, in 2015 a White male in his twenties shot and killed 9 African Americans attending a church service in Charleston, South Carolina. Since that time many additional atrocities have occurred, many immediately after the election of Donald Trump, who personally demeaned members of various minorities during his campaign, affectively "normalizing" such abuse.

Sexism

Sexism is the belief that one sex is superior to the other, usually that males are superior to females. This belief tends to justify exploiting females economically and sexually. Sexism is undergirded, unfortunately, by various organized religions that cite ancient texts alleging the superiority of the male. However, modern scholars have found substantial evidence indicating that these texts were selectively edited over time to conceal the value of female roles and to stifle women's leadership potential. Whole books have been written about this fascinating subject, including *The Gnostic Gospels* by Elaine Pagels (1979), *Beyond Belief* by the same author (2003), and *The Chalice and the Blade* by Riane Eisler (1987).

Although numerous laws have been adopted in recent times to help create equal opportunity for females, a constitutional amendment, stating simply, "Equal rights under law shall not be denied or abridged by the United States or by any State on account of sex," was never ratified. Many women helped fight to *maintain* gender inequality, fearing loss of certain legal protections such as exemption from military draft. However, more and more women are already serving voluntarily in the military, so that it is unlikely that the draft, if reinstated in the future, would exclude women. Women's contributions to the paid labor force, including the military, are simply too important to ignore today.

Discrimination against females has important effects. Girls and young women tend to limit their aspirations to the types of positions they perceive they can get. Unskilled women, for example, tend to fill service positions, while educated women disproportionately select service professions like nursing, teaching, and social work. As discussed above, women are characteristically paid less than men, even with the same education, the same job position, and the same number of years of paid work experience. This injustice forces many women to remain economically dependent on men (Navetta, 2005; Baxter, 2015).

Ageism

Ageism is the belief that youth is superior to age, that old people have outlived their usefulness and therefore are of little value. Ageism involves stereotypes such as that the majority of old people are senile, old-fashioned, and different. These stereotypes tend to justify discrimination against the elderly.

Robert Butler (1994), the social scientist who originally coined the term *ageism*, pointed out a peculiar irony many years ago that is still true today. Most people dream of a long life, and in general this hope is being realized. However, instead of celebrating the possibility of longer years for themselves, younger people view the elderly as potential economic burdens. They resent older adults' access to Social Security benefits at the same time that they fear that the Social Security system will be bankrupt by the time they are old enough to collect. Butler pointed out that this fear is greatly exaggerated because, due to the falling birthrate, the total dependency–support ratio (ratio including dependents both below 18 and over 64 to working adults in a given family) has been steadily declining since 1900. It will continue to do so until 2050.

Myths that most older adults are senile and physically debilitated are simply that: myths. Most older people describe their health as reasonably good. Memory loss is associated more with stress than with age, and it is usually reversible. The exception is memory loss caused by medical factors, such as Alzheimer's disease (see Chapter 10). Younger people, however, can also be victims of this disease. Various studies have shown that what appear to be characteristics of aging, such as decreased mobility and memory loss, can also afflict younger people. These difficulties can often be reversed even among the very old with proper health and mental health care.

Heterosexism, Homophobia, and Transphobia

Heterosexism is the belief that heterosexuals are superior to homosexuals. **Homophobia** is the fear, dread, or hatred of people who are homosexual. **Transphobia** is the fear, dread, or hatred of people who are transgender. All lead to social and economic discrimination against fellow human beings.

There was a time when homosexuality was viewed as a mental disorder. However, research has led to the knowledge that sexual orientation has nothing to do with one's mental health (except, of course, that discrimination can result in fear and depression). For this reason, homosexuality is no longer listed as a pathology in the *Diagnostic and Statistical Manual of Mental Disorders* used by mental health professionals. Gays and lesbians are similar to other people in every way except their **sexual orientation**. No one understands the causes of homosexuality, but it generally is not considered a personal choice; hence, most gays and lesbians prefer to speak of "sexual orientation" rather than "sexual preference."

No one understands the reason why some people feel strongly they have been born into the body of the wrong sex, or why some are people are sexually attracted to members of the same gender. These are mysteries, and there are no clear explanations on the horizon today, except that diversity is a fact and it exists within and among members of all species on earth.

> **?** Assess your understanding of potent forms of prejudice by taking this brief quiz.

SOCIAL JUSTICE ISSUES IN THE TWENTY-FIRST CENTURY

Discriminatory treatment, as discussed earlier, tends to result in ongoing poverty by a disproportionate percentage of populations that are at risk. Poverty directly causes many other problems, such as hunger and homelessness. These remain important social justice concerns in the twenty-first century. The following issues are of great concern to the profession of social work.

Poverty Programs That Maintain Poverty

Most U.S. financial assistance programs leave beneficiaries far below the poverty level. For example, consider the poverty suffered by Tomas and Tomacita and their mother in our chapter's case example. The mother worked hard, albeit in a state Temporary Assistance to Needy Families (TANF) program. But she was not paid even the equivalent of the federal minimum wage—rather, she received a stipend of $755.00 per month, or about $13,860 per year counting food stamp assistance. Her budget looked roughly like this:

Income:	$ 755	Income from TANF
	400	Food stamps
Total	$1,155	
Expenses:	$ 495	Rent (heat included)
	425	Food for three
	65	Electricity
	25	Laundry
	45	Transportation to TANF program
	60	Clothes (including diapers)
	40	Telephone
Total	$1,155	

By comparison, the 2015 Federal Poverty Threshold lists $19,096 as the poverty line for a family of three that includes two children under 18 ("Poverty Thresholds for 2015," 2016), many thousands of dollars more per year than what this family was trying to survive on. No wonder the mother couldn't afford a babysitter. No wonder she and many other TANF participants in her neighborhood frequently relied on Urban Neighborhood Center's food pantry to help keep body and soul together. Note that there was no room in this budget for child care, miscellaneous items, emergencies, or recreation. It seems as if we like to punish the poor just for being poor, as if they have no right to enjoyment or security of any kind.

While states have wide discretion under the federal TANF law to set their own eligibility criteria and benefit levels, benefit levels are below 30 percent of the poverty line in 33 states and the District of Columbia ("Temporary Cash Assistance for the Poor," 2015). Tomas and Tomacita's mother received her stipend in a state with an unusually high benefit level, even though it was well below the poverty line.

Poverty Line Determination Method

As mentioned earlier, the method of determining the nation's poverty line has not been revised or updated for many years, except for inflation. When developed in the 1960s, it was based on the price of food. The Department of Agriculture's least expensive food plan was multiplied by three because an earlier study showed that the average family at that time spent about one-third of its income on food (Fisher, 1998). Today, however, housing, utilities, child care, and medical care make up a much higher proportion of the average family's budget. Many experts believe that a true analysis of modern costs of living would require a much higher poverty line.

Poverty and the Minimum Wage

U.S. social policy seems to be based on the idea that anyone can find a job and that, by working, people can pull themselves and their families out of poverty. The problem is that this idea does not represent reality for large numbers of Americans today. Many people simply do not possess the educational qualifications or the technical skills required to get the jobs that are available. And, in many places today, especially in rural areas, jobs paying wages that can lift a family out of poverty simply do not exist.

Many people who work full-time remain in poverty. This problem is rooted in government policy. The federal minimum wage in 1968 was set so that a worker employed full-time at that wage could maintain a family of three (husband, wife, and child) at 120 percent of the poverty line. The minimum wage, however, has never been indexed to inflation. It remained at $5.15 per hour for a full 10 years, from 1997 until early 2007, when a new Democratic Congress was able to pressure President Bush, a Republican, into signing an increased minimum wage law. The minimum wage rose to $5.85 in the summer of 2007, to $6.55 in the summer of 2008, and to $7.25 in the summer of 2009. The minimum wage remains at $7.25 as this chapter is being revised, although several states have raised their own minimum wages slightly and President Obama tried for years to persuade Congress to raise it nationally to $10.10 per hour.

> **Box 3.3 Judy and George Emerson: A Case of Rural Poverty**
>
> Judy had an automobile accident on her way home from her job as a caregiver to homebound seniors. It had snowed during the day, and the rural roads were slippery. She hit a patch of ice, spun out, and smashed into one of the huge trees lining the road. Judy slumped unconscious over the steering wheel; a concerned driver passing by fortunately stopped and dialed 911.
>
> When Judy awakened in the hospital, she found she had broken both ankles and her left wrist, but worse, she had suffered a small stroke, which partially paralyzed her left side. She had received good medical care, however, involving multiple stitches and casts. Nurses checked in on her frequently.
>
> Judy was frightened, and not only because of her serious physical condition. She remembered she had never purchased health insurance—she had opted not to buy it under the Affordable Health Care Act because her income was too low to pay income taxes, so she had been sure she would not have to pay a penalty. But her job did not provide health insurance and gave her only part time hours of work; her income was only about $800.00 per month. Judy's husband, George, was a veteran with a partial disability; between his small disability check from the Veteran's Administration and Judy's small pay check, the two were usually able to make ends meet. But they would not be able to pay huge medical bills. And now Judy was temporarily unable to earn any income at all.
>
> Judy expressed her fears to a nurse, and not long afterward a hospital social worker came to her room. The first visit was short as Judy was still in a state of confusion due to a concussion from the accident. But the following day the social worker, with great understanding and tact, discussed Judy's financial situation with her. Judy learned that she could qualify for Title 19, Medicaid, due to her limited income. The social worker explained that the state where she lived had fortunately opted to expand Medicaid to adults with limited income under the Affordable Care Act.
>
> What a relief! Soon Judy was medically stable enough to leave the hospital, but she could not go home. Her husband, with his disability, would be unable to care for her. The social worker again came to her aid, contacting every nursing home within 20 miles of her house that had a rehabilitation facility. But not one would accept Judy because Medicaid payments were so low, well below the usual charge. Judy had to spend a few extra days in the hospital before the social worker could track down a new facility, quite a distance away, which still had empty beds to fill so that it was willing to accept Medicaid's low reimbursement rate.
>
> A different problem arose then—Judy's husband, George, could not drive due to his disability, and he wanted to visit Judy in the nursing home. The rural county where the couple lived had no public transportation, and George could not afford to hire a taxi. Fortunately, however, the social worker knew of a volunteer organization that provided drivers for seniors needing transportation to medical appointments; while Judy and George did not fit that scenario, the social worker advocated persistently for them, and at last a volunteer driver was found.
>
> Both Judy and George were extremely grateful for the assistance of the social worker; they wondered what they would have done without her.

Even when the minimum wage finally reached $7.25 per hour in 2009, a full-time employee earning that wage still took home less than a poverty level income for a family of three. Thus, many working families today turn to food pantries and/or the federal Supplemental Nutrition Assistance Program (SNAP, formerly known as the food stamp program) to feed their children.

One federal program has provided particularly important assistance to low-wage workers—the Earned Income Tax Credit (EITC), which will be discussed in more detail in Chapter 4. Low-wage working families can receive an earnings supplement through the federal income tax program as a tax credit. Interestingly, this program was instituted under a Republican President, Gerald Ford. As discussed in Chapter 2, Republican policy (at least as it has evolved over the past century or so) generally does not favor government programs that help the poor, but this one was different because the EITC helps boost business earnings. It allows businesses to keep their workers' wages very low, thus boosting profits. Taxpayer-provided supplements help the workers keep body and soul together.

Affirmative Action Policies: Under Attack

Affirmative action policies are designed to try to "level the playing field" for populations at risk. Due to historical exploitation, prejudice, discrimination, and the isms discussed earlier in this chapter, members of vulnerable populations suffer economic hardships through no fault of their own. There are two main approaches in the United States to address this injustice: **nondiscrimination** and **affirmative action**. Nondiscrimination laws simply ban discrimination. The Civil Rights Act of 1964 was the first powerful national legislation to bar discrimination, carrying with it the power of the courts. Title VII of this act, as amended in 1972, prohibits employment discrimination on the basis of race, color, religion, sex, or national origin. Today, age and disability are also protected categories.

Despite the Civil Rights Act, discrimination remained widespread, so courts began to require companies who lost discrimination cases to engage in affirmative action efforts to improve compliance with the law. Affirmative action required targeted outreach toward minorities.

This approach has always been controversial because a member of a protected minority might be recruited ahead of an equally qualified member of a non-protected category. Such instances have led to accusations of *reverse discrimination*. Court decisions since 1978 have been inconsistent, sometimes upholding affirmative action efforts and sometimes not. Today, with conservative political trends, affirmative action is under attack and policies have become weaker. A major assault on affirmative action came with the Supreme Court decision in 2007 not to allow race as a deciding factor in assigning students to certain schools. Many public school systems had used race as a factor in school assignment to maintain racially integrated school populations. The decision was 5–4; had Sandra Day O'Connor not left the Court, to be replaced by President Bush's choice of an ideologically extremely conservative justice, Samuel Alito, the decision would likely have gone 5–4 the other way (Richey, 2007) (see Box 3.4).

Further undermining affirmative action, the Supreme Court in *Fisher v. University of Texas* ruled in 2013 that lower courts must re-examine whether a race-conscious affirmative action program at the University of Texas at Austin should be allowed to continue. The implication seemed to be that the university admissions formulas including race should be re-examined. Then, in 2014, in the *Schuette v. Coalition to Defend Affirmative Action* case, the Court upheld Michigan's voter initiative that banned affirmative action in Michigan in public education and in state employment and contracting. Six of the judges agreed that states may end racial preferences without violating the U.S. Constitution (Palazzolo, 2014).

Box 3.4 Up for Debate

Proposition: Affirmative action programs should be maintained to assist in provision of equal opportunity for all.

Yes	No
Affirmative action programs help correct past discriminatory hiring practices by seeking qualified applicants of color and women.	Affirmative action programs may discriminate against people who are white, especially white males.
Affirmative action programs help ensure that jobs are genuinely and equally accessible to qualified persons without regard to sex, race, or ethnicity.	Affirmative action programs may hire women and people of color rather than others who are equally or sometimes more qualified.
Affirmative action programs help ensure that qualified persons of merit gain employment, even if minority or female, rather than applicants who simply happen to be white and male.	Affirmative action programs may help qualified minorities and females gain employment, but at the expense of white males who may be equally or more qualified.
In a democratic, multiracial society, integrated institutions can provide higher levels of service than agencies run entirely by one sex and race.	The most qualified applicants should always be hired, even if they all happen to be white and male.

Watch this video from The Wall Street Journal explaining the recent U.S. Supreme Court decision regarding affirmative action and public colleges and universities. How will this decision affect YOUR institution's admissions policies and practices?

https://www.youtube.com/watch?v=6oCoHGfzzos

With the above rulings, affirmative action seemed to be on its deathbed. But then, in a most unexpected turn of events, the Supreme Court affirmed the race-conscious admissions program at the University of Texas at Austin in a re-hearing of the *Fisher v. University of Texas* case in June, 2016. Supporters of affirmative action applauded the decision, which was 4–3 with Justice Anthony Kennedy writing the majority opinion (Liptak, 2016). Affirmative action was still alive, very probably due to the death of conservative justice Antonin Scalia in February, 2016, leaving a vacancy on the court (a conservative Senate had refused to consider then-President Obama's nominee to fill the vacancy). With conservative president Donald Trump's likely conservative nominee(s) for the Supreme Court, affirmative action is unlikely to be upheld.

Social Policy and the Growing Gap Between Rich and Poor

The old saying "the rich get richer and the poor get poorer" has been the reality for the United States over the past several decades. Wealth in America (the value of everything a family owns, minus debts) has increasingly been concentrating in the hands of a privileged few. Today the top 1 percent owns more than 35 percent of all private wealth, and their take is growing at the same time that the median household wealth of the average American has been declining. In 2012, a member of the 1 percent had 288 times the wealth of the median U.S. household. Globally, the situation is even worse. The richest 1 percent of the world's population owns 40 percent of the wealth. A quarter of that wealth is held by Americans (Kavoussi, 2012; Mishel and Bivens, 2011; Amadeo, 2014; Karimi, 2015).

With respect to income, one-quarter of American workers today earn less than $10 per hour, relegating families even with full-time workers to life below the poverty line. The top 10 percent of American earners secured half of all income in 2013, and the top 1 percent took in 20 percent (Amadeo, 2014). Americans in the top 1 percent amass 58 percent of *new* American income. The gap between this super-rich 1 percent and the rest of Americans has become wider than at any point since 1928, the year before the Great Depression (Scherer, 2015).

In protest of the growing inequality in America, a movement known as Occupy Wall Street began in New York City in 2011 and spread to other cities throughout the nation for a short time. Concerned people camped out in public parks and delivered speech after speech to draw national attention to the issue of inequality in America. Except for publicity, however, little was accomplished. Congress neither raised the minimum wage nor changed the tax structure.

The gap between the rich and the poor in America is growing in large part due to deliberate social policies at the national level justified by conservative ideology. The shamefully low minimum wage is one such policy. The G.W. Bush administration's personal income tax reduction tremendously favoring the rich is another. Also devastating is a tax policy that has led to the decrease of manufacturing jobs in the United States, a policy that allows U.S.-owned multi-national corporations to avoid paying taxes on profits earned in other countries (Rocha & McCarter, 2003/2004). As a result, large numbers of these companies have moved their operations abroad, and thousands upon thousands of Americans have lost jobs that paid union wages. New jobs have primarily been available in the service and retail sectors of the economy, in which wages are much lower (and benefits much poorer, if available at all).

The huge wealth and income disparities in this nation could be prevented and relative fairness to all re-established if the tax structure were restored to the progressive policies implemented after the Great Depression of the 1930s, if the minimum wage were raised significantly, and if family-supporting programs such as government-subsidized child care were available to all families. But such policy changes that could make this nation a model for the world would require the insistence of our citizens and the action of our representatives.

After several years of Obama administration policies, which helped create new jobs, some progress was achieved—middle and low income families in 2015 saw an increase in their household income. The upward trend occurred for all racial groups and across all regions of the country. It was the first single-year increase in family income since 2007, although the improvement did not bring most Americans back to their pre-recession income levels (Shekhtman, 2016).

Health Insurance Accessibility

A huge number of Americans under the age of 65—nearly 47 million in 2005—lacked health insurance, and the number was continuing to grow at a frightening rate when President Obama was elected in 2008. More than 8 in 10 of the uninsured came from working families with jobs that did not provide benefits (National Coalition on Health Care, 2007). Nine million of the uninsured were children, and millions more children were underinsured ("Nine Million Uninsured Children," 2007).

Good news arrived in 2010—after a full year of squabbling in Congress, where Republicans refused all support, the Obama administration was finally able to pass the Affordable Health Care Act (ACA). Many compromises had to be made in order to secure the Democratic votes needed (no Republican would vote for the bill). Its provisions allow students to remain on their parents' health insurance policies up to the age of 26. It denies insurance companies the right to exclude children with pre-existing conditions, and, beginning in 2014, it denied them the right to exclude adults with pre-existing conditions. The act mandates adults to purchase health insurance or pay a penalty. It forbids insurance companies to place lifetime caps on benefits. As the law was originally passed, states were required to set up insurance exchanges so people could investigate their options. Poor adults with incomes at or below 138 percent of the poverty line were to be covered through an expansion of Title 19, Medicaid.

The law was immediately challenged before the Supreme Court in the *National Federation of Independent Business v. Sebelius* case. The Court ruled that the "individual mandate" was lawful (the law requires a penalty for those who do not purchase health insurance; it also provides tax credits according to income, a type of subsidy, for those who do). However, the Court also ruled that states could not be required to expand Medicaid benefits or set up their own insurance exchanges.

Data indicate that the ACA helped expand health insurance coverage to millions of previously uninsured Americans, including nearly all poor adults in states that opted to expand Medicaid. However, millions remained uninsured. These included many poor adults in states that refused to expand Medicaid. People of color, people living in the South, and people living in rural areas were especially likely to lack health insurance ("Key Facts About the Uninsured Population," 2014). Donald Trump, elected president in 2016, pledged during his campaign to "repeal and replace" the Affordable Care Act.

Administrative Barriers to Aid

A different type of concern is that the U.S. welfare system often discourages even eligible categories of people from applying for aid. Forms are lengthy and complicated; they are especially confusing to people with limited education or whose first language is other than English. Work requirements under TANF programs can be confusing and discouraging to people who lack child care provisions, adequate clothing for work, and/or transportation. Even if needy people decide to apply anyway, they may end up languishing on waiting lists, like Tomas and Tomacita's mother in this chapter's case example, who was still waiting for child care assistance. Such complications are known as administrative barriers to aid.

Social Welfare Policy and Social Justice

Social justice remains a major, even a growing, issue today. However, many organized attempts have been made to alleviate the suffering of poor people over the past centuries. Assistance is sometimes informal: For example, individuals, families, and religious groups from time immemorial have carried out private acts of charity. But in recent centuries, social justice issues have also led to government legislation creating formal public social welfare policies and programs designed to assist at least some of the poor.

Social welfare policy establishes the goals and procedures that enable social welfare programs to commence and to operate. Such policy is often established by government legislation. For a glimpse of public social welfare programs sanctioned by government social welfare policy in the United States today, let us consider this chapter's introductory case example.

While many families living near the Urban Neighborhood Center were very poor, a few public programs were available that assisted them to some degree, even though these programs did not lift the families out of poverty. As discussed earlier, Tomas and Tomacita's mother was enrolled in the TANF program. Maria Romero was assisted by SSI and Medicaid because she was a severely disabled child. TANF, as explained earlier, is a cash benefit program (requiring work or work training) run by the county but established under state law according to federal guidelines. SSI is a cash benefit program for certain categories of poor people administered by the federal government, and Medicaid is a federal program administered by the state that provides medical care for certain categories of poor people.

These programs are all part of the U.S. system or institution of social welfare. They help families survive, but, sadly, are not designed to lift poor people out of poverty. Hence, efforts by voluntary organizations and private charities to help poor Americans remain essential for basic survival. The next chapter will focus on the development of social welfare policies and programs in the United States today, both public and private.

> **?** Assess your understanding of social justice issues in the twenty-first century by taking this brief quiz.

SUMMARY

- Social justice is defined, how economic justice relates to social justice is described, and how prejudice and discrimination can interfere with their achievement is explained. Negative effects of prejudice and discrimination on social and economic justice are discussed. The cases of Tomas and Tomacita and of Carla and Maria Romero dramatize the predicament of people who are dependent on a variety of income maintenance and social service programs in the United States.
- The intersectionality of multiple factors involving diversity that increase people's vulnerability to poverty and other perils is discussed. Populations particularly vulnerable to poverty are identified: children, women, older adults, racial and ethnic minorities, people with disabilities, and gays, lesbians, bisexuals, and transgender persons. These are the populations usually in most need of assistance from the social work profession.
- Four potent forms of prejudice are described: racism; sexism; ageism; and heterosexism, homophobia, and transphobia.
- Seven major social justice issues facing the nation today are identified and discussed: poverty programs that maintain poverty, the poverty-line determination method, poverty and the minimum wage, affirmative action, the growing gap between the rich and the poor, health insurance accessibility, and administrative barriers to aid.

> **✓** Recall what you learned from this chapter by completing the Chapter Review.

4

Social Welfare Policy: Historical Perspectives

LEARNING OUTCOMES

- Describe how residual and institutional concepts of social welfare shaped welfare policy in the Old World and the New.
- Discuss contrasting societal values and their effect on poor relief programs in the United States.
- Identify and describe three contrasting periods of American social welfare policy in the twentieth century.
- Discuss American social welfare policy in the twenty-first century and identify the societal values it reflects.
- Compare and contrast social welfare policies in the United States, Sweden, and Japan.

CHAPTER OUTLINE

CASE STUDY: The Resourcefulness of Donna Rudnitski 88

Concepts in American Social Welfare Policy and Their Historical Roots 91
    Social Welfare Concepts: Residual vs. Institutional 91
    Old World Historical Roots 92
    The Elizabethan Poor Law and the Act of Settlement 94
    New Concepts in Poor Law 94

Poor Relief in the United States 96
    Values 96
    The Charity Organization Society and the Settlement House Movement 97

Social Welfare in the United States in the Twentieth Century 98
    The Progressive Years, 1900–1930 100
    Federal Initiatives, 1930–1968 101

CASE STUDY: The Resourcefulness of Donna Rudnitski

Donna Rudnitski, BSW, put down her local newspaper with a sigh and turned to her husband. "Ray," she said, "things are getting hard for families around here. The newspaper says that our county's unemployment rate is the highest in the state. "I didn't know it was that bad," Ray replied, "but with the furniture factory closing down two years ago and the sports equipment store going bankrupt last year, I'm not surprised. The cutlery factory moved to China last year, too, and that sure didn't leave much work for people around here."

"Most people who are laid off can get unemployment benefits for a while," Donna mused, "and usually some food stamps. Food pantries can help a little also, but when people lose their homes because they can't pay the mortgage, they have no place to go in this county."

"I thought people who got foreclosed on by the banks here were getting sent down to the city," Ray replied, "so they could stay in shelters there."

"True," Donna responded, "they are. But the city shelters are overflowing, from what I hear at work."

Donna worked in the foster care section of her local human services department. She had already placed children in foster care because the parents had lost their homes and didn't want the children living on the streets. Donna hated this part of her job because she felt something should be done to help these families stay together.

Her concern growing, Donna made an appointment to talk with the director of her human services department. She found that the director, too, was alarmed about the local homeless situation. He had already spoken with the mayor of the town to see if there were any funds available for emergency housing, but no money was accessible. Tax revenues were down not only because of high unemployment, but because many jobs paid very low wages. The taxes they generated were minimal or non-existent.

Donna and Ray talked the problem over again a few days later, when they read in the newspaper that another local business, a building supply store, was going under. That would mean more breadwinners would lose their jobs. What would happen to them and their families?

"If public agencies can't help, what about our church?" Ray asked. "We have a parish hall that could house a few homeless families."

"But that would get in the way of the Sunday school, the women's club meetings, the scout meetings, 4-H—I don't think our pastor would allow it," Donna said slowly. "But it couldn't hurt to find out."

The next Sunday morning Donna asked her pastor, Reverend Jonas, if she could talk with him privately after church. The pastor readily agreed, thinking that Donna wanted to consult about a family problem. What he heard, of course, was about a multiple-family problem. Reverend Jonas was already aware of the serious issue of local families losing their homes. Some of the newly homeless belonged to his church.

"Well," the man said thoughtfully, "we could probably take several families in for a short while, but a few will need shelter for months—we can't give up church space for that long." He looked sympathetic but started to shake his head.

Donna had an idea. "What if other churches in town would join us?" she asked. "Maybe the churches could take turns so that each one would only have to give up space for a short time?"

And so the Compassionate Council of Churches was born. Eight local churches plus four more in nearby towns agreed to shelter homeless families for one week each on a rotating basis. Each church agreed to find volunteers to help with cooking, cleaning, and transporting children to school.

One of the churches donated an old, unused parsonage to serve as a day center for adults. The Council decided to hire a social worker to run the day center and to assist adults in finding work and more permanent shelter. Donna Rudnitski applied for the job even though she knew it would involve a cut in pay.

The Rutherford Family. Katherine and George Rutherford considered themselves comfortably middle class. Now in their mid-40s, they were proudly helping their two children, Tina, 20, and Anthony, 19, attend college. To help with the college expenses, they had recently taken out a second mortgage on their home. Two mortgage payments were

CHAPTER OUTLINE (Continued)

Cutting Back the Welfare State, 1968 to the Present 104

Social Welfare Policy in the Twenty-First Century 107
  Temporary Assistance for Needy Families 107
  The Working Poor and the Earned Income Tax Credit 107
  Privatization 109
  The Faith-Based Trend 109

An International Perspective 110
  Sweden 113
  Japan 114
  Progress of Social Justice Today 115
  NASW and Ongoing Human Rights Efforts 116

Summary 117

a stretch, but the parents paid every month on time. Kathy worked part-time on the cleaning staff of a nearby motel, and George worked for a local building supply store.

Then disaster struck: George was laid off from his job. The changing economy had harmed the local building supply business. Now, besides loss of most of the family income, the family lost the health insurance plan formerly provided by George's employer. Kathy's job provided no benefits, and her wage was only $8.50 per hour. Furthermore, she was given only 20 hours of work per week, even though to keep her job she was expected to be available 24/7, a common business practice in her area. She could not work elsewhere without jeopardizing her current employment. The family's finances immediately plunged into a danger zone.

Kathy and George had a small savings account, which would help them cover their normal bills for about two months, once George began collecting unemployment insurance. George applied right away. But even after his timely qualification, no money was left over to cover unexpected expenses. The couple knew they should probably replace their health insurance via the Affordable Care Act (ACA), but they learned that their income was so low, given George's lay off, that they would not encounter a tax penalty if they didn't purchase it. In fact, if their state had opted to provide health insurance coverage for low income families through Medicaid, a provision of the ACA, the couple would have qualified. But by this time, the Supreme Court had struck down the act's requirement for states to provide health insurance for low income families. The Rutherford's state was one of many that opted out.

Because their family budget was stretched tightly, Kathy and George decided not to purchase health insurance on their own. They considered themselves fortunate in that they had no current health concerns, and neither did Tina or Anthony. They decided it was more important to try to save some money.

This decision, however, turned out to be a very bad one. Only a few weeks after George's layoff, he developed a pain on the right side of his abdomen. He believed he had probably eaten too much dessert at dinner, so at first he wasn't worried. But by midnight, he was bent over in pain. Still, George determined to wait until morning before deciding what to do; he didn't want to incur the high cost of going to an emergency room without insurance. He hoped fervently he would feel better by morning. But instead, by morning George was in agony. Kathy, terribly worried, insisted he let her take him to the local hospital. Soon George was in an operating room. His appendix had burst, flooding his abdomen with toxic substances. Surgery and subsequent hospitalization saved his life, but the process generated staggering medical bills.

Soon Kathy and George were struggling to pay those medical bills. The result was getting behind on both their mortgages. Kathy's small pay check helped, and George's unemployment benefits helped also, but their combined income totaled far too little to cover massive medical expenses. They tried to negotiate with the hospital for relief and met with some success, but even with the discount the hospital granted, the remaining medical debt was far beyond their ability to pay. With two mortgages, there was no equity left in their house to call on to help with a financial emergency such as this. Embarrassed, the couple found themselves applying for food stamps and seeking additional help at a local food pantry.

Desperate, Kathy and George advised their son and daughter that they could no longer help with college costs, but they urged Tina and Anthony to do whatever possible to continue their education. The resourceful students applied for loans and work study funds and were able to stay in school, but they were not able to help their parents financially. They grieved for their parents and for themselves as well because they knew they might lose their childhood home.

Soon, Kathy and George decided that they had to file for bankruptcy. The procedure allowed them to keep their house, but even after this traumatic process they found they still could not meet their mortgage payments. George could not find a new job, and Kathy was unable to obtain more hours at the motel where she worked. The unfortunate couple fell further and further behind with their mortgage payments, and after several months, the bank foreclosed.

What to do? Where to go? It was the Rutherford's pastor, Reverend Jonas, who urged the couple to consider staying temporarily in the shelter organized by the Compassionate Council of Churches. He apologized that they would have to share space with many other people, including young children, and would have to move sleeping quarters every week. He was glad to be able to tell them, however, that there was a day center that stayed in one place.

In better times, the Rutherfords had contributed to the shelter fund through their church, never dreaming that they would need to make use of it themselves. Fearful but grateful, they moved in. The next morning, at the day center, they met social worker Donna Rudnitski, who had recently been hired for the new position. Donna welcomed them warmly and offered support by listening with empathy to the Rutherford's ongoing ordeal.

Donna soon realized that the couple had several pressing needs. Among them was supportive counseling because both people were thoroughly discouraged and demoralized by now. Another was appropriate housing. Donna hoped she could help the couple find rental housing they could afford even with their limited income. In addition, both George and Kathy needed help finding suitable work. Donna hoped she could help Kathy find an employer that would not require 24/7 availability while providing only half-time work, and she hoped to help George find work that could utilize his skills in the building trade. She wasn't sure she could meet all these challenges, but she knew she would do her best. Last but not least, Donna hoped to persuade the Rutherfords to buy health insurance once they regained financial solvency.

This chapter describes poor relief in Old World England, especially Elizabethan Poor Law, and the ways in which it set the stage for poor law in the American colonies. We discuss three important periods of American social welfare policy in the twentieth century, as well as social welfare policies in the twenty-first century. The welfare policies of two other nations, Sweden and Japan, are described in order for you to compare them with the American.

CONCEPTS IN AMERICAN SOCIAL WELFARE POLICY AND THEIR HISTORICAL ROOTS

Social Welfare Concepts: Residual vs. Institutional

What is **social welfare**? Social welfare is a system, sometimes referred to as an institution, comprising a wide variety of policies, programs, and services that help people meet their basic needs. These needs may be economic, social, health related, and/or educational. The institution of social welfare not only helps individuals to survive, but ideally promotes harmony and stability in the wider society. Is social welfare the same as social work? Not exactly, although the two are certainly related. Social work, as described in Chapter 1, is a profession with the purpose of assisting people to improve their lives. The profession frequently makes use of the programs and services provided by the social welfare system. Social work is really only one profession among many that can be considered part of the U.S. institution of social welfare. Other professions that also contribute to helping people meet social, economic, educational, and health needs are medicine, education, library science, and law, to name only a few.

Because many of the decisions and referrals a social worker makes rely on familiarity with the various programs available within the social welfare system, we will focus on them before turning to the fields of practice explored in the coming chapters.

Wilensky and Lebeaux (1965) pointed out many years ago that the United States holds two dominant conceptions of social welfare: residual and institutional. These distinctions are valid today. Those who endorse the residual approach to social welfare believe that people should normally be able to meet all their needs through their own family or through the job market. Only after the family and the job market have failed should the formal social welfare system get involved. Under these circumstances, the assistance is considered *residual*; it is activated only as a temporary, emergency measure. Services are accompanied by the stigma of charity, as they imply personal failure. The intent is that they be short-term, lasting only for the duration of the emergency.

Under the institutional conception, social welfare services are viewed as "normal, first line functions of modern industrial society" (Wilensky & Lebeaux, 1965, p. 138). According to the institutional view, social welfare services should be offered routinely as part of normal, non-emergency, problem-solving processes; they should be available without stigma to help prevent further problems. This approach assumes that in a complex society, everyone needs assistance at times. For example, even the best workers may lose their jobs when a company downsizes.

The social welfare system in the United States today reflects both the residual and the institutional approaches. Historically, the residual approach is older. Developments during and after the Great Depression of the 1930s pulled the social welfare system strongly toward the institutional concept, however. Then, during the 1970s, conservative politicians and presidential administrations began to pull it back toward the residual approach. This pull is extremely powerful today. The two concepts of social welfare are outlined in Box 4.1.

Now, let us examine historical roots of the social welfare system in the United States because what happened in the past has shaped what the system looks like today.

Policy Practice

Dimension of Competency Skills: Social workers understand that social welfare services are mediated by policy and its implementation at the federal, state, and local levels.

Critical Thinking Question: Which approach to social policy, the residual or the institutional, do you think would best allow social workers to exercise their practice skills in meeting current human needs? Why?

Old World Historical Roots

Social welfare policy is controversial today, and perhaps it always has been. Questions inevitably arise about whom to help and how much. We may think we want to help our neighbor, but how much? And are we interested in helping a stranger at all?

Box 4.1 Residual and Institutional Concepts of Social Welfare

Residual Approach
- Needs are to be met through family and job market.
- Aid from welfare system is considered abnormal.
- Aid is offered after family and job market have failed.
- Aid is temporary, emergency, and as little as possible.
- Stigma is attached.

Institutional Approach
- Social welfare system is viewed as part of first line of defense.
- Aid from government welfare system is considered normal.
- Aid is offered before family breakdown, for preventive purposes.
- Aid is preventive, ongoing, and adequate to meet needs.
- No stigma is attached.

The earliest form of assistance for the needy was probably mothers caring for children. Mutual aid among adults familiar with each other would be another example of help for the needy in early times, when reciprocal helping was provided by extended family members or members of one's tribe.

Only when more formal institutions had developed could a concept like *aid to the stranger* arise. Religious groups provided one of the earliest known forms of aid to the stranger. The idea that services to the poor should be provided by **faith-based organizations** clearly goes back a long way! In Judeo-Christian tradition, almsgiving was commonly practiced. The commandment "Love thy neighbor," accentuated in the New Testament but based on early Scripture, motivated people to give of what they had. Many believed that aiding the needy would provide a means of salvation in the next world. Some religious groups established formal tithes, with a portion of the money raised being used for assistance to the poor. Such assistance was residual in nature because it was offered as temporary charity in times of emergency.

England provided the model for social welfare provisions in its colonies in America, so we will focus on the social welfare history of that country. Responsibility for the poor in England remained primarily a function of the church until the arrival of the Black Death (bubonic plague) from continental Europe in 1348. So many people died at that time that a labor shortage resulted. In 1349, a law was passed called the Statute of Laborers, which forbade able-bodied people to leave their parishes and required them to accept any work available. Alms were forbidden to the able-bodied (Karger & Stoesz, 2010). Such a law clearly reflected the interests of the ruling class. Since the time of the plague, many secular laws relating to the poor have been designed to control the labor supply at least as much as to relieve the suffering of the destitute.

Throughout the 1500s, the Commercial Revolution grew and feudalism declined. Tenants were evicted from the land, sometimes to make room for sheep, whose wool was increasingly valuable in the manufacture of cloth. Large numbers of destitute people went looking for work in the cities, where they found themselves crowding into urban slums. The resulting poverty and social need led to government assumption of more responsibility for social welfare. In England, legislation culminated in the famous Elizabethan Poor Law of 1601 (Whitaker & Federico, 1997). The Elizabethan Poor Law was brought by the first colonists to America. Its concepts still influence current thinking about provisions for the poor in the United States and, hence, affect current law.

The Elizabethan Poor Law and the Act of Settlement

The Elizabethan Poor Law of 1601 was the first public legislation establishing a governmental system to meet the needs of the poor. The law established which unit was responsible to assist whom. By establishing which categories of people were eligible for what kind of assistance, the law was also geared toward social control (Segal & Brzuzy, 1998).

The local governmental unit, usually the parish (a geographic area similar to a county), was to maintain its own poor, and taxes could be levied for this purpose. An overseer of the poor—a public official, not a member of the clergy—was to be appointed. Families were to take care of their own members (reflecting the residual concept of social welfare). Whenever possible, grandparents were responsible for the care of children and grandchildren, and similarly, children and grandchildren were responsible for parents and grandparents.

Poor people were divided into categories, and relief was provided according to the category. Two of the categories, the "impotent" poor and dependent children, were considered *deserving* and so were offered aid. Children were to be indentured or placed in the service of whoever would charge the parish the least amount of money for their care (the *lowest bidder*). The impotent poor (the old, the blind, and people with disabilities) were to be either put into an **almshouse** (**indoor relief**) or offered aid in their own homes (**outdoor relief**), depending on which plan would be least expensive to the parish.

The category of able-bodied poor was not considered deserving. These people were treated punitively. Alms were prohibited. People who came from outside the parish (**vagrants**) were to be sent away. Able-bodied poor who were residents were to be forced to go to a **workhouse**, where living conditions were hard and work was long and tedious. If they refused, they were to be whipped or jailed or put in stocks (Trattner, 1999; Federico, 1984).

The intent of the Elizabethan Poor Law of 1601 was that almshouses and workhouses should be separate institutions, with the almshouses meeting the special needs of the deserving sick and infirm. In practice, most communities that built such facilities combined them into one building for the sake of expense. Records indicate that people dreaded going into such places (see Box 4.2).

Jill Quadagno (1982) writes that Elizabethan taxpayers (much like taxpayers today) did not want to support poor people, so that overseers of the poor tried hard to prevent people from qualifying for help. The Settlement Act of 1662 required every person to be enrolled as a resident in some parish somewhere. Procedures establishing residency were complex. Persons who could not prove legal residence in the parish where they were living could be declared vagrants and sent away. Minor adjustments to the law were made over the years, but the Settlement Act of 1662 increased parish control over poor people.

New Concepts in Poor Law

Two acts were passed in England in 1795 that temporarily improved the condition of the poor. One act forbade parishes to drive nonresidents away unless they actually applied for relief. The other, the Speenhamland Act, introduced new concepts into poor law.

> ### Box 4.2 A Workhouse Experience
>
> **Q:** And, in your opinion, many of the old people in your union would rather die than go to the workhouse?
> **A:** Very many of them; they would rather, sir...
> **Q:** Did you find that work severe?
> **A:** No, not severe; monotonous. You did not know what to do. You could not go out to write a letter, or to read, or to do anything: you had no time of your own; in fact, it was a place of punishment, and not relief...
> **Q:** Would you state any other objections you have to the treatment of the aged poor?
> **A:** I think the taskmaster is very much more severe than he should be.
> **Q:** In what way?
> **A:** Well, when you go to dine, or to breakfast, or anything like that, he says, "come quicker," and pushes you partly into the seat; that is a very trifling thing. I had a sore throat, and he objected to my wearing a scarf around my throat and he said, "I will pull those rags off you when you come back here again." That is, if I went back again. "You must not wear things such as this." I said, "I have a sore throat," and he says, "I don't care whether you and your father and your grandfather had sore throats." My father died of starvation through his throat growing together, and he suffered with sore throat. I suffered with sore throat, but not much; still, sufficient.
> **Q:** Did you complain to the master of the workhouse of the language and treatment by the man you call the taskmaster?
> **A:** No, my lord, not the slightest good in doing that.
> **Q:** Why?
> **A:** Whatever the taskmaster wished the master to say, the master would say. They were all under one control, even the doctor, and everybody was the same.
>
> Source: Quoted from Jill Quadagno. (1982). *Aging in early industrial society: Work, family, and social policy in nineteenth century England.* New York: Academic Press, pp. 107–110.

This act was a humane response to the rising price of wheat. Rather than force poor able-bodied people into workhouses after they were destitute, the law established a wage supplement to help prevent destitution. The size of the supplement was determined according to both the number of children in a family and the price of bread.

Improvement of the condition of the poor was temporary under this act because the law did not include a requirement for a minimum wage. The gentry tended to lower the wages they paid, and the difference was picked up through the wage supplement that was financed by taxes paid by small farmers. Hence, before long, taxpayers strongly opposed the law (Quadagno, 1982).

In 1834, the New Poor Law reinstated most of the provisions of the Elizabethan Poor Law and introduced a new principle known as **less eligibility**. This was based on the idea that "pauperism was willful and the condition of the pauper who was relieved should be worse than the condition of the poorest, independent, self-supporting laborer" (Quadagno, 1982, pp. 97–98).

Today, as a similar example, the United States has a minimum wage law, but the minimum wage in 2016 was the same as that which began in summer 2009 ($7.25 per hour). It leaves a family of three (e.g., husband, wife, and child) that includes a full-time bread winner with an income well below the poverty level. A full-time worker with a family thus may qualify for public relief such as **food stamps** and/or the **Earned Income Tax Credit**

> **?** Assess your understanding of the historical roots of American social welfare policy by taking this brief quiz.

(EITC—a wage supplement administered through the federal income tax system). Taxpayers' anger tends to focus on people who receive such assistance rather than on employers who increase their profits by providing very low wages.

POOR RELIEF IN THE UNITED STATES

Each colony in America enacted its own version of the Elizabethan Poor Law of 1601; Plymouth Colony was the first, in 1642. Ideas such as settlement and less eligibility, although codified under English law after the original colonization of America, continued to influence colonial attitudes.

After the American Revolution, the U.S. Constitution separated functions of state and federal governments, and assistance to the poor became a state prerogative. The federal government did not become involved until the end of the Civil War, in 1865, when the first national agency for social welfare was established: the Freedmen's Bureau. Through the Freedmen's Bureau, federal taxes supported free educational programs and financial assistance for former slaves for a few short years (Lieby, 1987). The bureau was disbanded in 1872 as a result of political infighting.

Values

Values strongly affected American poor law, and like the law itself, the major religious and cultural values of the United States originated in the Old World. Religious doctrines of various traditions taught that rich and poor alike should give what they could for others, motivated by love and compassion, not fear.

During the Protestant Reformation of the sixteenth century, many of these teachings were questioned. A Protestant ethic of salvation by hard work challenged the older notion of salvation by helping people in need. Puritan Calvinists believed that God Himself decided whether a person was to be a member of the elect or else damned, and that charitable works would not alter God's judgment. While no one could know for sure, many people came to believe that prosperity indicated one was among the elect and that poverty meant one was not (Tropman, 1989). From this point of view, why help the poor?

Also in conflict with older religious and **humanitarian** ideals to help the unfortunate were new ideas from philosophy and economics. In *The Wealth of Nations* (1776), Adam Smith argued in favor of the principle that became known as **laissez-faire**: Government should not interfere in the "natural functioning" of the market by imposing interference such as taxes. The market should be allowed to perform solely according to the influences of supply and demand. Taxation to support poor people interfered with the rights of the wealthy and only created dependency among the poor, according to Smith's argument.

Thomas Malthus, an economic philosopher and clergyman, published *An Essay on the Principle of Population* in 1798. In it, he argued that relief for the poor contributed to overpopulation and that surplus population would result in disaster. Also contributing to reluctance to help poor people was Herbert Spencer's philosophy known as *social Darwinism*. Influenced by biological theories of evolution discussed in Charles Darwin's book *On the Origin of Species* (1859), Spencer preached that only the fittest people should survive. Poor people should be allowed to perish as they have demonstrated they are unable to compete (Karger & Stoesz, 2010). Such an argument overlooked the fact that

Darwin studied survival patterns *between and among* species, not individuals *within* species. He clearly recognized that no individual member of the human species could survive without the cooperation, as opposed to the competition, of others. Obviously, no one can survive infancy or early childhood without the care and assistance of others.

Do any of these arguments for or against aid to poor people sound familiar? Although some are centuries old, these ideas and values still affect societal responses to poor people today. Obviously, the value base underlying the social welfare system is complicated and conflicting. Conflicting values in social and political arenas affect what happens in social welfare legislation; social welfare legislation affects the resources available to social workers and their clients.

The Charity Organization Society and the Settlement House Movement

The effects of values on approaches to social welfare in the United States are seen particularly clearly in two movements in private charity that strongly affected relief measures beginning in the 1880s. These movements, the Charity Organization Society and the settlement house movement, were introduced in Chapter 1 and are discussed more fully here because they, along with a more scattered child welfare movement, led to the birth of the social work profession. The two movements differed markedly in philosophy and methods.

The Charity Organization Society (COS) began in England in 1869; its first office in the United States opened in Buffalo, New York, in 1877 (Popple, 1995). Leaders of the COS believed that many poor people were unworthy, so applicants for aid should be carefully investigated. Records were to be kept about each case, and a central registry was developed to ensure that no person received aid from more than one source. The principal form of help to be offered should be "moral uplift," which was to be provided by "friendly visitors." Most of the visitors were women recruited from the upper class. Not only were these the persons who had the most time to volunteer, but, due to the patriarchal nature of the era, church-related, unpaid work was among the few outlets for these women's talents.

The methods developed by the COS were used as models for local public agencies; organization, investigation, and written records proved very useful in welfare work. Mary Richmond, a well-known leader of the COS movement in the United States, taught in the first social work training school, the New York School of Philanthropy (now the Columbia University School of Social Work), begun in 1898. The COS replaced most friendly visitors with paid staff by the early 1900s, partly because there were not enough volunteers and partly because volunteers were found to lack appropriate expertise (Popple, 1995). The settlement movement, in contrast, involved concepts of self-help and mutual aid rather than moral uplift. Jane Addams, one of the movement's most famous leaders, established Hull House in Chicago in 1889. Settlement work arose in response to continuing pressures of the Industrial Revolution, which brought large numbers of immigrants to American cities, where they were forced to work long hours in factories under dangerous, unhealthful conditions.

Ethics and Professional Behavior

Dimension of Competency Knowledge: Social workers understand the profession's history, its mission, and the roles and responsibilities of the profession.

Critical Thinking Question: How can knowledge of the profession's history and mission assist social workers today to best carry out contemporary roles and responsibilities of the profession?

> **Box 4.3 Comparison of Charity Organization Society and Settlement House Movement**
>
> | Charity Organization Society | Settlement House Movement |
> |---|---|
> | **LEADER** ||
> | Mary Richmond | Jane Addams |
> | **TYPE OF WORKER** ||
> | Friendly visitors | Volunteers who lived among poor |
> | **TYPE OF AID OFFERED** ||
> | Central registry of poor | Mutual aid |
> | Short-term charity | Self-help |
> | Moral uplift | Social and political action |
> | **PRIMARY LEVEL OF INTERVENTION** ||
> | Casework with individuals and families | Group work; work with families, organizations, and communities |

Settlement houses brought idealistic young people, including many women of upper-class backgrounds, into the slums to live and work with less fortunate people. Settlement staff assisted immigrants in organizing into self-help groups and established **mutual aid** services ranging from day nurseries to garbage collection to organization of cultural events. In addition, settlement house staff and neighborhood participants became involved in political processes, advocating for better working conditions in the factories, better sanitation in the cities, and protective legislation for women and children (see Box 4.3).

While most settlement houses were established and staffed by white women, Minneapolis boasted a settlement that, while founded by local women in 1924, was directed from its inception by Gertrude Brown, an African American woman who traveled to Minneapolis from Charlotte, North Carolina, to take the position. The settlement house was founded to assist a growing African American population in Minneapolis. Ms. Brown served as director from 1924 to 1937. The settlement house was named the Phyllis Wheatley Community Center after Phyllis Wheatley, an African American woman who became a published poet despite being enslaved ("W. Gertrude Brown Placed a Premium on Education," 1993).

> **?** Assess your understanding of poor relief in the United States by taking this brief quiz.

SOCIAL WELFARE IN THE UNITED STATES IN THE TWENTIETH CENTURY

The history of social welfare in the United States in the twentieth century revealed, according to James Lieby (1987), an increasing role over time for both public and private non-sectarian agencies (agencies not affiliated with particular religious groups). Lieby also found that there were three major trends in social welfare policy during the twentieth century:

- 1900–1930: Action at the level of state and local governments, including action by local agencies organized by the Community Chest.
- 1930–1968: Major initiatives by the federal government prompted by the Great Depression.
- 1968 and onward: The stopping or turning back of the progress of the "welfare state."

Lieby made these observations many years ago; it is clear today that he was right—progress toward the welfare state has indeed turned back. That trend was highlighted by the passage of the Personal Responsibility and Work Opportunity Act (PRWOA) in 1996, which will be discussed later. Then, in the early twenty-first century, the Republican administration of President George W. Bush engaged in an attack on the poor that was not limited to mothers and their children, but targeted at the elderly and persons with disabilities as well, via a push to privatize Social Security. See the time line in Box 4.4.

Box 4.4 Time Line: Major Historical Events in Social Welfare and Social Work

1348	Black death. Feudal system begins to break down
1349	Statute of Laborers (England)
1500s	Accelerated breakdown of feudal system (Commercial Revolution)
1601	Elizabethan Poor Law (England)
1642	Plymouth Colony enacts first colonial poor law, based on English Poor Law
1662	Settlement Act (England; idea migrates to colonies)
1795	Speenhamland Act (England)
1834	New Poor Law (England)
1865	Freedmen's Bureau (the United States—ends in 1872)
1869	First Charity Organization Society (COS), London, England
1877	First COS in the United States, Buffalo, New York
1884	First settlement house (Toynbee Hall, London)
1886	First settlement house in the United States (Neighborhood Guild, New York City)
1889	Hull House, Chicago
1898	First formal social work education program (summer training by COS in New York City; evolves into New York School of Philanthropy, later Columbia School of Social Work)
1915	Flexner's report concluding social work is not a full profession
1917	First organization for social workers, National Social Workers Exchange
1919	American Association of Schools of Social Work (AASSW) formed
1921	American Association of Social Workers formed (from National Social Workers Exchange)
1928	Milford Conference; determines social work is a single profession

(continued)

Box 4.4	**(continued)**
1929	Stock market crash leads to Great Depression. International Council on Social Welfare (ICSW) founded in Paris
1933	President Franklin D. Roosevelt launches "New Deal" program
1935	Social Security Act signed into law
1936	National Association of Schools of Social Administration (NASSA) established
1952	Council on Social Work Education (CSWE) forms, merging AASSW and NASSA; accredits MSW programs
1955	National Association of Social Workers (NASW) forms, merging seven separate social work organizations; accepts MSW only
1956	International Federation of Social Workers (IFSW) established; membership consists of national social work organizations
1957	Greenwood article declares social work a full profession
1964	President Lyndon Johnson launches the War on Poverty
1967	The Work Incentive Program (WIN) established under the Social Security Act
1970	NASW admits baccalaureate social workers as members
1974	CSWE begins accreditation of baccalaureate social work education programs; Supplementary Security Income program established under the Social Security Act for the aged, blind, and disabled; category of poor children omitted
1975	Earned Income Tax Credit established under President Ford
1981	WIN program eliminated under the Reagan administration
1988	Family Support Act; parents receiving aid for dependent children under the Social Security Act must work when child is 3 years old
1996	Personal Responsibility and Work Opportunity Act signed into law by President Bill Clinton; eliminates entitlement of poor children and parents to aid under Social Security Act; establishes Temporary Assistance to Needy Families (TANF) program
2000	Push by President George W. Bush to privatize formerly public assistance programs and provide federal funding to "faith-based" programs
2004	Medicare Part D signed into law by President George W. Bush, providing limited assistance to older adults in purchasing prescription drugs; law prohibits government from negotiating drug prices
2010	Affordable Health Care Act (ACA) signed into law by President Obama, providing access to affordable health insurance to the majority of Americans beginning in 2014, including those with pre-existing conditions
2016	Donald Trump elected president; promised to "repeal and replace" the ACA. Post-election he vowed to privatize Medicare and Social Security

The Progressive Years, 1900–1930

The early 1900s were a time of reform in the United States. World War I slowed down reform efforts but did not entirely eliminate them. Women, for example, first gained the vote after the war, in 1920. A few women began to go to college, and some started to use ways to plan their pregnancies. Magazines designed to appeal to women appeared, such as *Good Housekeeping*, helping women begin to relate to other women. Activists such as those involved in the settlement house movement advocated, and in many cases secured, laws for the protection of women and dependent children, for better sanitation and for better safety conditions in the factories. Forty states enacted mother's pensions, although only for those considered fit: the widowed mothers (Bartkowski & Regis, 2003). By 1920, 43 states had passed workers' compensation laws. Federal guidelines were soon established; today all states have workers' compensation laws that meet federal guidelines. National leadership in protective legislation for children was provided by the Children's Bureau, established in 1909 as part of the U.S. Department of Labor.

Voluntary organizations also expanded during this period. Examples include the establishment or significant growth of the Boy Scouts and the Girl Scouts, the American Cancer Society, the National Association for the Advancement of Colored People, the National Urban League, and the Red Cross.

Federal Initiatives, 1930–1968

A great economic depression followed the stock market crash of 1929. Voluntary organizations and state and local governments did what they could to meet what seemed like unending financial need. But soon local treasuries were empty, including both private charities and relief-giving units of local government. People turned to the federal government for help. President Herbert Hoover was a proponent of laissez-faire economic theory and a political conservative. He believed that the federal government should not interfere with the economic market. Desperate Americans, however, began to perceive the widespread and rapidly increasing poverty as a **public issue** (an issue affecting so many people that it is considered beyond the fault of each affected individual) rather than a **private trouble**. Franklin D. Roosevelt was elected president in 1932 because he promised to involve the federal government in solving the crisis.

Roosevelt ushered in a series of emergency programs on the federal level to meet immediate needs for **income maintenance** and employment. His overall program was known as the New Deal. The New Deal offered temporary cash assistance and work-relief programs to needy people regardless of race. Roosevelt's major long-term proposal was the Social Security Act, passed by Congress in 1935. Since 1935, almost all additional federal social welfare policies have been adopted as part of this act (Segal & Brzuzy, 1998).

The Social Security Act established the concept of **entitlement** to government aid. Entitlement means that if one meets specific eligibility criteria, one has a legal right (one is *entitled*) to assistance. The Social Security Act is a complex piece of legislation that has been amended many times. The 1935 law established three types of federal provisions: (1) **social insurance**, (2) **public assistance**, and (3) health and welfare services.

Social insurance and public assistance are quite different. Insurance programs require the payment of taxes (in this case, the Social Security, or FICA, tax) earmarked for a special fund available only to the insured. Following rules relating to the amount of money contributed, benefits cover the expected problems of a modern industrial society, such as the death of a breadwinner.

Public assistance programs, on the other hand, are funded out of general tax revenues, usually income tax revenues, and people may receive benefits even if they have never paid taxes themselves. One qualifies according to whether one fits a specified category (e.g., elderly person) and in addition meets a **means test** or has an income below

Frustrated single mother with baby forced to work for pay

a certain level specified by law. A stigma is often attached to public assistance benefits because they are considered unearned.

The social insurance provisions of the original Social Security Act were Old Age and Survivors Insurance (OASI) and unemployment insurance. OASI was intended to provide income for retired workers, widows, and minor children of deceased workers. Later, in 1957, coverage was extended to include persons with disabilities. In 1965, Title XVIII, Medicare was added to the act. (Medicare and Medicaid, Title XIX, will be examined in detail in Chapter 7.)

Three categories of people were originally eligible for aid under public assistance: the blind, the aged, and dependent children. Later, Aid to Dependent Children was expanded to include the mother and in some cases the father; the program became known as **Aid to Families with Dependent Children (AFDC)**. A fourth category of people eligible for aid, the permanently and totally disabled, was added in 1950 (McSteen, 1989). In 1965, Title XIX, Medicaid was added to the act.

Initially, most African Americans were barred from Social Security benefits because of the power of southern Democrats, who insisted that domestic and agricultural workers be excluded from the law. They argued that such benefits would undermine the work ethic of their servants and laborers of whom African Americans comprised 50 and 60 percent (Tyuse, 2003). It was not until 1950 that agricultural and domestic workers were finally included.

In 1974, to equalize benefits nationwide and to help remove stigma, public assistance income maintenance programs for the blind, the aged, and persons with disabilities were combined into one program known as **Supplemental Security Income (SSI)**. SSI is funded and administered by the federal government, and people apply for benefits through federal Social Security offices, not local welfare offices. However, benefit levels are so low that some states provide a cash supplement, the **State Supplementary Payment (SSP)**.

Poor dependent children were not included in the SSI program. Why? The answer seems to be that some categories of poor people are still considered undeserving of aid. Political passion can be inflamed by criticizing poor single mothers or men who for whatever reason fail to provide. Their children suffer accordingly. AFDC remained a poor relation of SSI, with benefits that varied from state to state but, on the average, maintained recipients well below the poverty line, until 1996. In August of that year, the Personal Responsibility and Work Opportunity Act (PRWOA) ended the AFDC program and all entitlement of poor children and their mothers to government assistance. The PRWOA will be discussed more fully later in this chapter.

Reflecting the rescinding of all legal right to assistance in the United States for poor children and their mothers, Bartkowski and Regis (2003, p. 58) note: "The compassion of the maternalistic state manifested in the early decades of the 1900s had, by century's end, given way to the discipline and austerity of paternalistic governance."

General Assistance

One category of people has never been eligible for assistance under the Social Security Act, able-bodied adults between the ages of 18 and 65 (age 60 for widows) who have no minor children. Sometimes able-bodied adults in need can receive help from local programs known as general assistance or poor relief. These programs varied widely across localities in the past, but in most places today they have simply been eliminated. Conservative ideologies focus on decreasing taxes rather than helping the poor. General assistance, in those very rare places where it still exists, is strongly residual: Aid is temporary and carries a stigma. Repayment is usually required.

Food Stamps/SNAP and Other Federal Voucher Programs

The food stamp program was established by Congress in 1964; today the program is called SNAP (Supplemental Nutrition Assistance Program). The program is administered by the U.S. Department of Agriculture, but state and local welfare departments process the applicants and provide what used to be the stamps or **vouchers**. Today something similar to a debit card is issued. The program is means-tested, and allotments are based on family size and income.

Originally, many poor adults who qualified for no other aid could receive assistance in the form of food stamps. But in 1996, the Personal Responsibility and Work Opportunity Act (PRWOA) enacted large cuts in food stamp availability, cutting the program's funding by nearly $28 million over the six-year period to follow. Today some states have enacted even more stringent eligibility laws, requiring a significant work record to qualify.

From a high of 27.5 million people in 1994, only 17.3 million received food stamps in 2001. By 2014, however, 46.5 million people were receiving them, indicating a very high level of need. This increase occurred despite complicated application processes and an average per person benefit of only $125.35 ("Supplemental Nutrition Assistance Nutrition Program Participation and Costs," 2015).

> Watch this video from the Maryland WIC program. How does the information provided enhance your understanding of the need for this program as well as the possible pitfalls of this program NOT being an entitlement?
>
> https://www.youtube.com/watch?v=r3RtBW-J5Z4

In addition to food stamps, the federal government offers other voucher programs, such as fuel assistance, rent subsidies, and infant nutritional supplements. The Women, Infants, and Children (WIC) program is one of the best known of the latter. It provides supplemental foods to pregnant and breast-feeding women and their children up to age 5. The program is means-tested; applicants with pre-tax incomes up to 185 percent of the poverty line are eligible. Coupons or vouchers for specific food items are provided for purchases at grocery stores. The program is not an entitlement; funds may not be available to serve every woman who meets eligibility criteria. Yet WIC is very important; it served over 8.2 million children and their mothers every month in early 2015 ("Frequently Asked Questions about WIC," 2015).

Post-Depression Trends

The Great Depression came to an end in the 1940s, when World War II provided full employment. The nation began to look at poor people as unworthy again. The 1950s set the stage for the social activism of the 1960s, however. Women who had worked full-time in paying jobs during World War II were sent back home to make room in the job market for returning veterans. Although returning to the home was more a philosophical idea than a reality for many women (especially for the poor and those from ethnic minorities, who often had no choice but to work outside the home), the 1950s gave rise to feminist activism based on women's loss of status and access to employment equality. The decade also harbored the beginning of the civil rights movement, sparked by Rosa Parks's refusal to give up her seat to a white man on a bus in Montgomery, Alabama, in 1955.

Then in the 1960s came the War on Poverty, under the leadership of Presidents Kennedy and Johnson. This movement was stimulated by Michael Harrington's book, *The Other America*, originally published in 1962, which exploded the myth that people in poverty deserve their own misery. Much liberal legislation was initiated in the 1960s, furthered by the civil rights movement as well as by renewed understanding of societal causes of poverty. The AFDC-UP (Unemployed Parent) program, the food-stamp program, WIC, the Head Start program, educational opportunity programs, college work-study programs, job training programs, Peace Corps, Vista (Volunteers in Service to America), Medicare, and Medicaid all were instigated during this period (Champagne & Harpham, 1984; Karger & Stoesz, 2006).

Increasing welfare rolls led to new public outcry, which led to the passage of the Work Incentive (WIN) program in 1967. The WIN program was designed to encourage welfare recipients to take paid employment. Those who could find jobs were allowed to keep part of their welfare grant up to a certain earnings level. The program was unable to reduce welfare costs, however, as not enough jobs were available, and funds were lacking to provide adequate job training. In addition, day care facilities and inexpensive transportation were lacking (Champagne & Harpham, 1984).

Cutting Back the Welfare State, 1968 to the Present

Earned Income Tax Credit

Major efforts to reform the welfare system were made by Nixon's Republican administration from 1969 to his resignation in 1974 and by the Democratic Carter administration from 1977 to 1981, but Congress did not accept their plans. However, President Gerald

Ford (Republican, 1974 to 1977) signed into law an important provision of the tax code, the Earned Income Tax Credit (EITC), which has become the largest means-tested income transfer in the United States today. Low-income families can receive an earnings supplement of up to 40 percent, to a maximum in 2014 of $6,143 for families with married parents filing jointly (same-sex marriages are recognized), including three or more children, with earned incomes under $52,247. The wage supplement varies according to income and family size. The EITC is popular today because benefits go only to the working poor, perceived as worthy (Bane, 2003; Segal & Brzuzy, 1998; Earned Income and AGI Limits, 2015).

In effect, through this legislation taxpayers supplement wages for employers who increase their profits by paying their workers wages too low to support their families. There is a danger that, as in the time of the Speenhamland Act, the public will eventually instigate a tax revolt and repeal the wage supplement, rather than insist that employers pay a wage sufficient to support the average family (see Box 4.5).

Welfare Reform

The president who was able to get major welfare reform proposals accepted was Ronald Reagan (Republican, 1981 to 1989). President Reagan was elected in 1980 with an apparent public mandate to lower taxes and inflation and to repair the budget deficit. Elected with massive financial support from right-wing conservatives, he and his administration were politically committed to investing in the military. Cutting taxes while building up the military obliged President Reagan to drastically reduce federal expenditures for income maintenance programs. The savings thus incurred were very small compared with the massive amounts of new money being poured into the military. The budget deficit became astronomical during Reagan's two terms of office. (President Reagan did not accomplish these deeds alone, but with the sanction of a Democratic Congress.)

The political agenda of the 1980s involved forcing able-bodied people, including the working poor, off welfare. The concept of aid returned to the old residual idea to assist helpless children on a temporary, emergency basis and only as a last resort (an approach popularly called the *safety net*). The result was the 1981 Omnibus Budget Reconciliation Act. The financial incentive built into the WIN program (described earlier) was eliminated. Most of the working poor opted to keep their jobs despite the loss of welfare benefits, but their financial circumstances were severely hurt, especially as many lost eligibility for Medicaid as well.

Box 4.5 Issues with EITC

The Earned Income Tax Credit (EITC) is a guaranteed income support program for poor families that include a wage earner, established by President Ford in 1975. However, in 1996, Congress passed the Personal Responsibility and Work Opportunity Act (PRWOA) that eliminated the entitlement of all poor children to support from the Aid to Families with Dependent Children program (AFDC) under the provisions of the Social Security Act. Thus since 1996, two categories of children unfortunate enough to be born into low-income families in the United States have become an uncomfortable reality—one category has a public safety net, the EITC; the other one does not.

Does it make sense for this nation to abandon its children when their parents are unable to find paid work? Are these children undeserving of aid? Are they unimportant to America's future?

Source: based on Kim, R. Y. (2001). The effects of the earned income tax credit on children's income and poverty: Who fares better? *Journal of Poverty*, 5(1), 1–22. Copyright © 2001 Routledge.

> Watch this video from The Young Turks. What are the main points made by panelists regarding the recent push by several states to require drug testing for welfare recipients? What is the "demonization" of Temporary Assistance for Needy Families (TANF) recipients? Do you think testing welfare recipients for drug use is a good idea? Why or why not?
>
> https://www.youtube.com/watch?v=xPZQQP47vl8

President Reagan signed another major welfare bill in 1988, the Family Support Act, just before he left office. This one was designed to force mothers who had remained on AFDC into the job market. All parents with children over 3 years old (1 year at states' option) were required to work or enter job-training programs (if available) under this bill. However, it wasn't until 1996 that poor children lost all entitlement to aid under the provisions of the Social Security Act. The Personal Responsibility and Work Opportunity Act (PRWOA) was signed into law by President Clinton, a Democrat, in August of that year, ending six decades of guaranteed government aid for economically deprived children and their families. Clinton's acceptance of this law (proposed and passed several times by a Republican Congress until Clinton finally signed it) was seen by many liberals as a betrayal of the poor. The former AFDC program was totally eliminated by this bill. In its place, a new program called **Temporary Assistance for Needy Families (TANF)** was established. TANF was to be funded by federal block grants to the states. Block grant funding is very different from the former open-ended funding for AFDC; each state receives a fixed sum of money for TANF and no more, regardless of need (Tyuse, 2003).

Under TANF, no family or child is entitled to assistance. Each state is free to determine who can receive assistance and under what circumstances. If a state runs out of money in a given year, it can simply stop providing aid, and poor families will have to wait until the following year for assistance. Besides the fact that assisting needy families is optional for states, regulations are complex and confusing under TANF. Some of the most significant requirements are that states are not allowed to assist anyone for longer than five years in that person's lifetime. States must require parents to work after 24 months of assistance. When parents work, the state may, but is not required to, provide child care assistance. Minor parents may not be assisted unless living at home and attending school. Assistance must be eliminated or reduced if the family is uncooperative with respect to child support–related requirements (e.g., if the mother does not name the father). Assistance may be denied to children born into families already receiving public assistance. Karger and Stoesz (2006) describe TANF legislation as a type of "welfare behaviorism," or social engineering. The law is designed to force poor parents to work outside the home regardless of suitability of jobs available or adequacy of wages. If they do not comply, punishment is severe (hunger, homelessness, loss of children to foster care, etc.).

While this law was touted as a way of ending welfare dependency, no national programs were created to help address the many external factors keeping poor people on the welfare rolls (e.g., lack of affordable day care, lack of a family-supporting minimum wage, lack of educational opportunities, lack of adequate job training programs, lack of jobs in the skill range of many recipients or in the geographic areas where they live, and lack of affordable transportation to places where jobs are available).

Fortunately, Medicaid was not included in the TANF block grant, and poor families who met the previous income guidelines continued to be eligible for this program. Saving eligibility for Medicaid for many poor families required dedication and persistence by many legislators of liberal persuasion.

> **?** Assess your understanding of three major periods of social welfare in the United States in the 20th century by taking this brief quiz.

SOCIAL WELFARE POLICY IN THE TWENTY-FIRST CENTURY

As noted by Goldberg (2002b), if any nation has the means to lift its poor out of poverty, it is the United States. Instead, however, welfare provisions for poor Americans have steadily eroded over recent decades. The trend toward diminishing social welfare policies and programs apparent in the beginning of the twenty-first century began, of course, in the twentieth. Aid for poor families today is work-based and thoroughly residual, forcing mothers to take jobs outside the home at paltry wages, with no attempt on the part of the nation to develop decent employment opportunities. The Elizabethan Poor Law of 1600's England has returned to America.

A few of the major twenty-first century welfare programs are summarized in the following sections.

Temporary Assistance for Needy Families

TANF, as discussed earlier, is not an entitlement program. No needy child or poor parent in the United States has a legal right to aid today, and aid under TANF, where provided, is limited to five years in a given parent's lifetime. Amendments hard-fought by organizations advocating for the poor, such as the National Association of Social Workers (NASW) and the Children's Defense Fund, have resulted in some ameliorating provisions, thankfully. For example, states may now opt to allow battered women to postpone employment for a time. States may also opt to provide child care assistance for longer than five years, since child care is not classified as a cash benefit. However, conservatives in Congress and the White House increased work requirements under this program during the G.W. Bush administration. The amount of cash assistance is terribly low, in 2015 below 30 percent of the poverty line in 33 states and the District of Columbia. In not a single state is it above half the poverty line (see Box 4.6). The cash benefit varies from state to state, from a low in Mississippi of only $170 per month to a "high" in Alaska of $923. TANF cash benefits have been steadily eroding since the inception of the program in 1976 (Temporary Cash Assistance for the Poor, 2015; Floyd & Schott, 2014).

The Working Poor and the Earned Income Tax Credit

The federal government and several of the states provide earned income tax credit programs. The EITC lifts more children and families out of poverty today than any other federal program—far more than TANF. Yet millions of Americans remain poor today. In 2015, the U.S. child poverty rate was nearly 22 percent, virtually unchanged since 2010, and the poverty rate of all Americans in 2015 was a disturbing 14.7 percent, slightly lower than in 2014 but still unsettling (Poverty in the United States: A Snapshot, 2015; Picchi, 2015; Bishaw & Glassman, 2016). While the EITC does help many poor families, it also subsidizes businesses by allowing them to keep wages low and thus reap higher profits at the expense of the average taxpayer.

Box 4.6 Janine Jenkins

When Janine Jenkins was 17, a senior in a small-town high school, she became infatuated with a handsome young man named George. Janine met him at a local dance. George was a private in the army and posted in a different state, but the two met while George was visiting friends during a leave.

George was Janine's first serious boyfriend, and she was very proud to have him in her life. She talked about him constantly with all her friends, and she hoped to marry him. She became concerned, however, when George began to press her for sex during his visits. Janine had had a sex education course in high school the previous year; the teacher in the class had urged all students to abstain from sex both for religious reasons and to avoid pregnancy. The teacher did not discuss any means of contraception because she said sex was simply wrong for unmarried people.

One night during a leave George overcame Janine's objections and had sex with her. Janine was not expecting this and so she took no precautions with respect to pregnancy; she wouldn't have known what to do anyway. George did not take any precautions either. Janine became pregnant. When George learned about the pregnancy, he told Janine to have an abortion. He was not ready to be a father. He never returned to visit her. George was later transferred overseas, and Janine never heard from him again.

When Janine told her parents she was pregnant, they were furious. They forbade her to tell anyone else so as not to bring shame on the family, but they told her not to have an abortion because abortion was against their religion. They told her she could live at home and finish her senior year in high school as long as her condition was hidden. But by the time Janine graduated, she was beginning to show, and her parents told her she was no longer welcome. They were embarrassed by her situation. They told Janine she had made her own bed and now she must lie in it.

For a time, kind parents of Janine's best friend provided her a place to stay, but after the baby, a boy, was born, they told Janine she needed to find somewhere else to live. The baby kept them up at night, and besides, it was too expensive to feed two additional mouths—a hungry young mother and now her baby.

Janine's friends were helpful, however; they did some investigating and told her she could probably stay at a homeless shelter in a neighboring city. Janine was exhausted by now from worry, lack of sleep, and constant care needs of the new baby. She was terrified of leaving her home town, the only place she knew. But with no idea of what else to do, she packed herself and the baby up and traveled to the city. Her friends gave her the address of the shelter and enough money to get there by cab. After that, Janine would be on her own.

Fortunately, there was a social worker at the city shelter, Mary Elliott. Mary welcomed Janine and recognized right away that the teen was physically and emotionally exhausted. Mary gently explained to Janine that there was room for her and the baby to stay for a few days, but that the shelter facilities were not appropriate for a mother and her baby. She talked with Janine to find out if there were a more suitable place for her to stay, but Janine explained she was not welcome at home and had no relatives she could call on. She had already worn out her best friend's welcome. At that, Mary helped Janine find an empty cot in a relatively quiet corner of the shelter and settle in with what belongings she had. Mary let Janine take a much-needed rest while she herself changed the baby into clean diapers and held him close to calm his cries.

As Janine was sleeping, Mary began working out a plan of action. As a social worker, she had excellent knowledge of resources, and she knew of two local programs run by private charities that offered temporary housing for young single mothers. She began making telephone calls and was relieved to find that, by good fortune, there would be an opening at Harriet's Home in a few days. Janine could stay there for up to a year.

Mary decided she needed to explain the TANF program to Janine. She recognized how hard it would be for the young mother to enter a work training program while her baby was still tiny, but in order to receive cash assistance in her state, work was required of a mother when her infant was only

(continued)

> **Box 4.6 (continued)**
>
> a few months old. Janine would need cash to pay the monthly fee to stay at Harriet's Home, money needed to help keep the program operating.
>
> Mary knew Janine would need more material assistance than the tiny payment TANF could provide her. So she telephoned the social worker at Harriet's Home, Rosa Salazar, to suggest referring Janine not only to TANF but to food stamps and WIC. She found that Rosa was planning to do so already. Rosa asked Mary whether Janine and the baby were enrolled in Medicaid. Fortunately, Mary knew from her previous conversation with Janine that she was carrying a Medicaid card—the social worker at the hospital where the baby was born had helped her fill out the forms.
>
> Now Mary knew she had done all she could for Janine, except provide supportive counseling while the young mother was still at the shelter. She also knew, however, that Rosa, the social worker at Harriet's Home, would do all she could to help the girl. Janine and her baby boy had a rough road ahead of them.

Privatization

Privatization involves shifting the provision of social services and financial benefits from publicly operated government programs to private organizations, either nonprofit or for-profit. For example, many states now contract with private agencies and organizations to operate TANF programs.

The political philosophy behind privatization is conservative: Government should have a minimal role in promoting the public welfare especially when it involves provision of economic assistance to the poor, as this might interfere with the economic market. (Workers might be unwilling to labor long hours for low wages if given an alternative.) This philosophy asserts that competition among private businesses is the most economical way to provide services and benefits. Donald Trump, a conservative businessman elected president in 2016, represented this view.

The Faith-Based Trend

"Charitable choice" language first appeared in the 1996 Personal Responsibility and Work Opportunity Act (PRWOA). This legislation permitted public funds to be used for religiously oriented social service programs. While denominationally sponsored social service programs had been eligible for public funds for many years, these earlier faith-based programs separated their social services from religious proselytizing. By contrast, charitable choice language in the PRWOA broadened eligibility to allow public funding for church-sponsored programs that incorporated pervasive religious content. The G.W. Bush administration strongly promoted transferring public social service programs to private, religious organizations.

Promoting the provision of social services by faith-based groups comes at a risk. Religious organizations, for example, are

Intervention

Dimension of Competency Values: Social workers understand that intervention is an ongoing component of the dynamic and interactive process of social work practice with, and on behalf of, diverse individuals, families, groups, organizations, and communities.

Critical Thinking Question: What can social workers do if their employing agency has policies that exclude certain categories of people for service or employment, violating professional values?

exempt from employment nondiscrimination laws. Stoessen (2004, p. 4) noted in the *NASW News* that the Salvation Army "has come under scrutiny due to some of its policies about hiring and providing services to lesbian, gay, and bisexual people."

In other organizations, beneficiaries in great need may find themselves required to espouse certain religious beliefs before they can receive food or shelter. However, in a court case that could served as an important precedent, a federal district judge in Iowa ruled in 2006 that a faith-based prison ministry program that required participating inmates to attend weekly revivals, religion classes, and prayer services where Jesus Christ was presented as the sole means of salvation overstepped the hazy line governing church-state relations (Paulson, 2006).

There is another important concern, however. The provision of social services by faith-based groups can allow the federal government to bow out of any responsibility to care for its poorest and most vulnerable citizens and divert its tax revenue instead to huge increases in military spending. That is exactly what happened under the administration of President George W. Bush. The Democratic Obama administration increased attempts to assist poor Americans (e.g., increased student loans, increased mortgage assistance, extended unemployment benefits for a time), but ongoing military engagements continued to divert funds to for-profit corporations producing weaponry.

Most faith-based organizations are not capable of providing widespread services to large numbers of people in need over long periods of time. It was the inability of faith-based and other voluntary organizations to meet the public need during the Great Depression that led to the passage of the Social Security Act in 1935. Due to the severe recession, charitable giving in America declined by about 6 percent in 2009 (Whittle & Kuraishi, 2009). People strapped by their own financial circumstances simply cannot give as generously as they might like to.

Still, faith-based programs remain an important part of U.S. efforts to help the poor. Consider our chapter's case example. Without the assistance of the churches in their area, Mr. and Mrs. Rutherford would have become street people. And yet the churches could provide only a highly inconvenient form of shelter—the Rutherfords would have to move to a different church every week. The churches themselves suffered as well, having to give up space normally used for religious services and/or religious education for those weeks.

> **?** Assess your understanding of American social welfare policy in the twenty-first century by taking this brief quiz.

AN INTERNATIONAL PERSPECTIVE

Probably most Americans believe that our country ranks first in the world on almost every measure. After all, "proud to be American" is a phrase used so often it even appears on bumper stickers. Perhaps for this reason it makes sense to take a careful look at how our nation actually compares with other countries with respect to issues of importance to ordinary citizens, such as their common welfare.

How does the United States compare with other advanced nations of the world with respect to promoting the common welfare of its citizens? Sadly, a rather sobering assessment has been compiled by the Children's Defense Fund. In its 2015 data sheet "How America Ranks among Industrialized Countries," this committed advocacy organization notes that the United States measures up very poorly with respect to other nations in a number of important areas. For example, while the United States spends more money than any other nation on health care, the infant mortality rate is very high—twenty-seventh highest among world nations at the time of this study. The United States has the highest birth rate among teens 15–19. While the United States has the highest gross domestic product and the highest number of billionaires in the world, this nation also has the largest wealth gap between the rich and the poor. It has the highest child poverty rate among industrialized nations. The United States also has the highest number of people incarcerated. These facts are nothing to be proud of. The same data sheet also notes that the United States is the only major industrialized country in the world that does not guarantee prenatal care to women who are pregnant. Black women in the United States are more likely to die of prenatal and birth complications than mothers in Azerbaijan, Turkmenistan, and Uzbekistan. Over 100 nations have lower percentages of low-birth-weight births, including Algeria, Botswana, and Panama (see Box 4.7). Does this information surprise you? Does it matter?

Americans have always liked to think of themselves as a people who care about human life, especially children. What do the facts presented above suggest about this idea? With fewer tax dollars coming into the federal treasury because of huge tax cuts enacted under the G.W. Bush administration (mainly benefiting our richest citizens) and later because of the recession that struck heavily at the end of that administration, with billions and billions of dollars still going out in military spending, what does that mean for the ordinary citizen?

Box 4.7 Up for Debate

Proposition: Medical care should be provided in a free, single-payer government program.

Yes	No
All Americans need medical care, so it should be freely available to all.	People would abuse the system and demand medical care they didn't need.
Physicians could help all in need, not just those who could purchase insurance or pay out-of-pocket.	Physicians might receive less income than they are accustomed to.
Prenatal care for all pregnant mothers would reduce infant mortality and low birth weights.	Women who cannot afford medical care should not get pregnant.
Hospitals in poor areas would be more financially solvent if they received payment for all their patients.	Hospitals in financial trouble should limit their care to those who have purchased insurance or can pay out of pocket.
In the long run, medical expenditures would be lower in the United States if all Americans could receive treatment when first needed.	Short-run costs for medical care would be too high to justify providing medical care for all.
A single-payer government system would provide more actual health care per dollar spent, since administrative costs of Medicare are under 5 percent, but administrative costs of private insurance are nearly 40 percent.	People are accustomed to private insurance and it meets most needs of those who can afford to purchase it.

> **Box 4.8 Where Our Income Tax Money Goes**
>
> - 37% Pentagon spending for past and current wars
> - 19% Health care
> - 17% General government
> - 15% Dealing with poverty
> - 8% Supporting the economy
> - 3% Energy, science, and the environment
> - 2% Diplomacy, international assistance, and preventing war
>
> Source: Based on "Where Do Our Income Taxes Go," Friends Committee on National Legislation, 245 Second Street, Washington, D.C., 2015.
>
> Note: This allocation does not include moneys gained from Social Security taxes since these are earmarked for Social Security expenditures. Changes in allocation of income tax dollars occurs annually.

While President Obama's budget proposals regularly called for an increase in many important federal initiatives such as child nutrition, Head Start, support for low-income college students, American Indian education and health services, the Peace Corps, housing assistance, and health care, yet due to the values and actions of the Republican Congress that opposed him throughout his administration, most of Obama's aims were thwarted. Then, in 2016, Donald Trump was elected president. He promised to reduce taxes of the wealthy even beyond the cuts enacted under the G.W. Bush administration, thus further diminishing U.S. tax revenues that could support programs to assist Americans in need.

"Guns or butter" is an old saying in U.S. common folk wisdom. Can the United States really be secure when millions of its citizens, especially children, lack access to basic necessities? Are guns a better collective investment than food, shelter, education, and health care for all American citizens? That is perhaps the most crucial question for the future (see Box 4.8).

The United States is not the only nation where welfare has been diminishing in recent years—this unfortunate situation has been occurring even in nations with generous, long-established policies of social provision, such as Sweden. An excellent book examining this phenomenon, *Diminishing Welfare* (2002), by Gertrude Goldberg and Marguerite Rosenthal, finds that wherever governments have failed to defend full employment policies, social welfare programs have been cut back. This is because without full employment, a nation's tax base isn't broad enough to provide adequate resources for a strong social welfare system. At the same time, sadly, without full employment, more people need assistance. So, many must go without.

The trend toward diminishing welfare among industrial nations seems to relate to the increasing power of international corporations. Corporations do not usually favor full employment policies or comprehensive social welfare programs because they prefer cheap labor. Corporations use their considerable assets to lobby against social welfare provisions nation by nation and to convince the general public through advertising that social welfare programs cause budget deficits (obscuring the real culprits: tax cuts favoring rich individuals and rich corporations, along with increased military spending). Donald Trump, a billionaire, paid no income taxes for years and bragged during his campaign that this showed he was "smart." Ordinary citizens without political savvy and without ready access to jobs and/or adequate social welfare provisions do not have the information or clout to fight for better jobs or better wages. And unemployed and underemployed citizens cannot provide the tax base necessary to support a generous social welfare system.

The following sections will describe social welfare programs in two different countries, Sweden and Japan. These have been chosen as useful examples in comparison with the United States because one nation (Sweden) is quite generous by American standards while the other (Japan) is perhaps slightly less generous.

Sweden

While Sweden has cut back its social provisions in recent years, its system is still extremely generous by American standards. This nation invests nearly twice the percentage of gross domestic product in social expenditures as the United States (Goldberg, 2002a). The following are some of the social programs benefiting Swedish citizens that are only a dream for most Americans:

- A universal children's allowance, with extra allocations for single parents not assisted by the non-custodial parent
- Universal parental leave with significant salary replacement—including leave for fathers
- 60 days annual leave for care of sick children, with significant salary replacement
- Highly subsidized child care centers
- Highly subsidized public housing, so that homelessness is rare
- Universal, very low cost health care for all; free health and dental care for children under 20
- Means-tested general assistance programs available to all unemployed adults after unemployment insurance has been used up

Truly, life for a Swede is not nearly as insecure as for an American. Poverty is rare. However, program cuts in recent years mean that poverty is no longer unknown. Pensions for the elderly have been especially weakened in the past decade. They are now based on each individual's lifetime earnings instead of providing a universal amount for everyone (some credit is given for years of study and child care). A 2.5 percent payroll tax is earmarked for investment in private accounts, providing no guarantee of future yield (a policy proposed in the United States by the G.W. Bush administration).

As with most countries in the world, Sweden has experienced growing inequality among its citizens since the economic crisis of 2008. The top fifth of income earners take home a larger proportion of the nation's total income every year. Homelessness is on the rise, reaching 34,000 in 2013 (of Sweden's population of approximately 9,000,000), largely due to unemployment and the fact that landlords hesitate to accept the means-tested general assistance payment, which has been losing value in recent years. The child poverty rate has reached over 12 percent, with children of immigrant families the most vulnerable.

The Swedish welfare system provides lower benefits today than in the past due to income and property tax cuts initiated by a center-right government elected in 2006. According to Mats Olson, professor of economic history, these tax cuts have been financed by cuts to the welfare system (Alfredsson, 2013). Cuts to corporate taxes in 2010 and 2014 have also undermined the tax base that supports the welfare system (Swedish corporate tax rate, 2015).

Thus Sweden's welfare system today is clearly weakened by diminishing resources. Still, its provisions are exceedingly generous compared to those in the United States.

Japan

Japan is the most advanced industrialized country outside of Europe and North America and has the seventh largest population in the world. Yet at the end of the twentieth century, it spent an even smaller proportion of its gross domestic product on social welfare programs than the United States (Goldberg, 2002a).

While Japan does have a few public welfare programs, Nomura and Kimoto (2002) estimate that less than one-tenth of the eligible population actually received benefits at the turn of the century. They list three reasons:

1. Large businesses and government bodies provide medical care, housing, pensions, and other important provisions that promote the common welfare in Japan. These provisions support almost a third of the Japanese workforce. Such generosity was hard-won by workers after World War II, when conditions were so dire labor unions were organized that were strong enough to win many benefits.

2. Persons who are self-employed in Japan, almost a fifth of the labor force, comprise a sector of the population with significant political strength. The Japanese government creates policies that assist this sector, such as regulating competition from large retail chains, in order to maintain loyalty.

3. Farmers and other small businesses in Japan have organized and achieved enough political strength to win government protection from outside competition. Protection allows them to earn sufficient income to maintain a reasonable standard of living. They are expected to support their own members in return.

In Japanese families, the wife of the eldest son is expected to care for his parents for life, and nearly half of Japan's elderly do live with family members. Full-time work among women outside the home is discouraged by a tax policy in which the husband loses a tax deduction if his wife earns over a certain limited amount, and the wife then has to contribute to the public pension system. Full-time homemaking for women is encouraged by a tax policy in which she may receive a basic public pension (described later in this chapter) without contributing any money to the fund.

Government assistance to single mothers involves a severe means test and carries a strong stigma, so most women in this situation must get a job. Japan has had a children's allowance since the early 1970s, but it is not intended to fully support a child. There is so strong a social stigma against single-parent families that they are virtually nonexistent (only 1.3 percent of households). Nearly all pregnant teens get abortions. The divorce rate is very low and the remarriage rate high.

With respect to health care, all Japanese workers must purchase medical insurance, and there are different programs for different categories of workers. Those who work in large businesses receive most of their care from company programs.

Japan's pension system for the elderly has three tiers. The first tier is a basic program for all the insured, partially funded by the state. Full-time housewives are eligible. Beyond the basic program, large employers in both private and governmental sectors fund additional tiers. Benefits relate to a worker's before-retirement income. Despite these programs, fully one-quarter of elderly Japanese over 65 today work out of necessity. Beginning in 2000, all Japanese have contributed to a system of nursing care insurance for the elderly. The program is designed to supplement family care, not replace it.

Japan's unemployment program favors full-time workers and provides short-term benefits. Only about one-third of part-time workers are assisted. As in the United States, when unemployment benefits run out, there is no further assistance offered. Families are expected to provide. In some situations, subsidies for tuition for retraining programs are available.

Japan's tax and protectionist policies for small family firms and farms, however, have assisted families to provide for the basic needs of their members to a much greater extent than their counterparts in the United States. There is a very strong expectation for families to provide for their own.

As can be seen by the above description, Japan had very limited national social welfare programs at the beginning of the twenty-first century (Nomura & Kimoto, 2002). This system depended on long-term, full employment with most needs being met by employers. But in more recent times, Japan's economy has weakened, impacted strongly by the worldwide recession of 2008. In addition, the nation has experienced major earthquakes and a disastrous tsunami, dislocating many parts of the population. Moreover, Japan's population is aging.

For these reasons, poverty is growing in Japan; child poverty reached 14.9 percent by 2015; poverty among women of working age rose to 12.6 percent. Thus, more people have been applying for welfare benefits. These are paid in cash for basic living expenses covering food, clothing, utilities, housing, childbirth, education, medical care, skill training, and funerals. The minister of health and welfare sets a minimum living standard and the government pays the difference between that and verified household income. Benefit amounts vary with geographic location according to the cost of living (Kayama, 2011; Taro, 2015).

However, there is a powerful stigma attached to welfare. The Japanese population as a whole still holds a strong belief that jobs are easy to find, so that anyone who is unemployed is simply lazy. Thus, only around a fifth of those who meet eligibility requirements for welfare actually receive it—the rest are too embarrassed to apply or else are turned away. Welfare fraud is broadcast widely in the media, although almost all applicants are honest. The result is that only about 1.7 percent of the population of Japan receives government welfare benefits. Dozens of poor people choose to starve to death each year at home rather than apply for welfare (Japan and the poor, 2013).

In early 2013, the Japanese government, rather than increasing welfare benefits to meet increasing need, slashed them by 10 percent per household. And in 2014, the Supreme Court ruled that an 82-year-old man originally from China, but a permanent foreign resident of Japan, was not eligible for welfare benefits because he was not a Japanese national. The ruling means that no permanent foreign resident of Japan, including a spouse of a Japanese national, has a right to welfare (Osaki, 2014).

Clearly, in contemporary Japan, much like in the United States, it is becoming more difficult to qualify for welfare benefits, and the benefits themselves are diminishing.

Progress of Social Justice Today

The United Nations' Declaration of Human Rights, parts of which have been quoted in Chapter 3, states that everyone has the right to a decent standard of living, including food, housing, medical care, and security in the event of unemployment, illness, and the like. The declaration asserts that motherhood and childhood should receive special care and assistance.

The U.N. Declaration was made more than a half century ago. Has progress been made toward achieving its goals? The answer varies according to the nation under consideration. Sweden, for example, has achieved a good deal more (despite recent cutbacks) than the United States or Japan.

Unfortunately, overall commitment to social justice seems to have decreased worldwide in recent years. Assistance to poor people has diminished at the very time that economic insecurity has grown. Goldberg and Rosenthal's research (2002) indicates that even the long-established programs of social provision in nations such as Sweden have diminished. This trend continues in the twenty-first century, placing heavy burdens on international organizations such as the United Nations that try to assist the poor. According to the Food and Agricultural Organization of the United Nations, nearly 800 million people in the world were still undernourished in 2015, a decline from the previous year but still far too many ("World hunger falls," 2015).

The National Association of Social Workers (NASW) finds it increasingly important to advocate for poor people in these times. To that end, it has developed guiding principles and programs to advance human rights, some of which are discussed here. It has also allied itself with other organizations committed to achieving social justice in the United States and throughout the world.

NASW and Ongoing Human Rights Efforts

As part of its efforts to help achieve humane social policy in the United States, the NASW has developed several policy statements. One regards the "Role of Government, Social Policy, and Social Work" (see Box 4.9).

The NASW focuses on several issue areas that the organization believes are of special importance in the world today (NASW, Issue Areas, 2015). These currently include gender equality, women's rights, children's rights, foreign assistance, health, immigration, refugee resettlement, psychological support, and peace and social justice.

Box 4.9 Government Social Policy vs. Social Work Values

Professional social work values include honoring the worth and dignity of every person so that persons who seek social work services are understood as worthy, regardless of the various issues that may have brought them to seek help. The social worker will assess clients' underlying problems and seek appropriate resources to assist. Often the issues that bring clients to request assistance are recognized by the worker to reside mostly the wider environment: e.g., racism, sexism, ageism, homophobia, and the like, which can result in severe poverty that is not the fault of the people who endure this condition.

By contrast, government policies today seem to place full responsibility for a given person's problems, such as severe poverty, on that person alone, blaming him or her as undeserving. Worse, policies today seem not only to "blame the victim," but to punish them for their poverty. The category of "undeserving poor" has expanded to include persons considered blameless before, such as children, people with disabilities, and adults in old age. Government policies formerly in place to assist these categories of persons have been cut back, or eligibility to receive them severely restricted, so that few can benefit despite serious, ongoing need.

The National Association of Social Workers asserts that government must play a role in achieving economic justice, eliminating poverty, and improving the lives of all persons, not just those who are poor. Policies that are needed include universal access to comprehensive health care, a minimum wage that can support a family, sufficient affordable housing, and first-rate education for all.

Source: Based on Social Work Speaks: National Association of Social Workers policy statements, 2009–2012 by the National Association of Social Workers.

Social Welfare Policy: Historical Perspectives   117

To help promote social justice, the NASW has established a Human Rights and International Affairs Department. This department houses the organization's efforts on behalf of women, gays and lesbians, and racial and ethnic groups. It addresses issues such as diversity, discrimination, affirmative action, and cultural competence. The NASW has also become part of an alliance of U.S.-based international and humanitarian nongovernmental organizations called InterAction, the American Council for Voluntary International Action. This alliance comprises more than 160 organizations working to advance social justice around the world, and it includes many well-known advocacy organizations such as CARE, Oxfam America, and Save the Children (Association Joins Global Coalition, 2005). The NASW has also established partnerships with several issue-focused groups such as the Child Labor Coalition, the International Family Planning Coalition, and the Campaign for U.S. Ratification of the Convention on the Rights of the Child (NASW, Collaborative Partners, 2015).

Clearly, social justice throughout the world can be achieved only by cooperative, committed, intensive, and long-term efforts.

> **?** Assess your understanding of international perspectives, especially with respect to Sweden and Japan, by taking this brief quiz.

SUMMARY

- The ways in which residual and institutional concepts of social welfare shaped welfare policy in the Old World and the New are described. To help understand why American income maintenance programs operate as they do today, we begin by examining their roots in Old World poor law, especially Elizabethan. Residual and institutional concepts of social welfare are discussed. The Rudnitski case helps illustrate how middle-class American families can fall swiftly into poverty and homelessness.
- Contrasting societal values and their effect on poor relief programs in the United States are discussed. Contrasting values have shaped the American social welfare system. Certain religious values encourage helping the poor, sometimes by suggesting that giving aid might be a means of salvation in the next world. Other religious doctrines, especially Calvinism, teach that one's actions in this world do not affect salvation. Social Darwinism preaches that the poor should not be helped as poverty proves they are unfit to survive.
- Three contrasting periods of American social welfare policy in [the twentieth cen]tury are identified and described: 1900–1930, the Progressive Y[ears; 1930–1968,] Federal Initiatives; and 1968–present, Cutting Back the Welfar[e State].
- American social welfare policy in the twenty-first century is d[iscussed, and] the societal values it reflects identified. American social welfa[re policy in the] twenty-first century is described as embracing residual concep[ts, providing] only minimal, short-term assistance to persons or families in n[eed. Benefits are] low and usually require work outside the home. The result ha[s been an increase] in poverty particularly for children and single parents.
- Social welfare policies in the United States, Sweden, and Japan [are compared] and contrasted. In general, Sweden's policies are more genero[us, while Japan's are] similar to or perhaps even more miserly than America's.

> **✓** Recall what you learned from this chapter by completing the Chapter Review.

5

Family and Children's Services

LEARNING OUTCOMES

- Describe evidence, historical and contemporary, for the need for child protective services.
- List and briefly describe seven in-home social work services for families in need and five out-of-home services.
- Identify and discuss four important family issues and four special family forms or types.
- Explain cultural competence and why it is so important in social work practice.
- Describe several shortcomings of contemporary American family policy and how certain findings of the United Nations pertain to American women.

CHAPTER OUTLINE

CASE STUDY: LaTanya Tracy, Child in Need of Protection 118

Historical Perspectives on Family and Children's Services 121
    Historical Perspectives 121
    The Child Welfare Movement and Protective Services Programs 124
    Children's Rights as International Law 126
    Challenges of African American Families 127

Services and Their Providers: A Continuum of Care 128
    Least Restrictive Environment 128
    In-Home Services 129
    Out-of-Home Services 133
    Client Self-Determination and Professional Decision-Making 136

CASE STUDY: LaTanya Tracy, Child in Need of Protection

LaTanya Tracy's great-grandmother, Ruby Bell Lowe, called Protective Services in a panic early one morning. Ruby had become exhausted from trying to care for LaTanya, an infant of only 9 months. The baby had been crying all night, and Ruby had gotten little sleep. In her mid-80s, the elderly woman had been caring for LaTanya single-handedly for the past 3 weeks, ever since Natasha Tracy (Ruby's granddaughter and LaTanya's mother) had asked her to babysit late one evening. Ruby had felt uneasy accepting at that hour, suspecting that Natasha planned to go out drinking, but she had agreed for the baby's sake.

Natasha had not returned the following morning as promised, and LaTanya was keeping Ruby awake night after night. Natasha did not answer Ruby's frantic telephone calls; the phone had been disconnected. Exhausted and angry, Ruby remembered that a social worker from the County Department of Protective Services had been helpful a few years before when Natasha neglected her parental responsibilities to her son, Martin, because of a drinking habit.

The intake worker with whom Ruby spoke at Protective Services checked the computer files and found that Natasha Tracy, 24 years old, had indeed been referred to the department previously. At that time, Natasha's young son, Martin, had been placed temporarily in foster care due to **neglect**, or failure to provide appropriate care, brought on by Natasha's drinking. (For reasons of confidentiality, the worker did not relay this information to Ruby, although Ruby probably already knew.) Martin had been returned to his mother after 8 months, and the case had been closed. That was because Natasha had entered an alcohol treatment program and had followed all court orders carefully. There had been no further referrals for child neglect until Ruby's anxious telephone call. The intake worker at Protective Services, on consultation with her supervisor, accepted the case for investigation and referred it to the social worker who had worked with Natasha previously, an experienced professional named Lauren White.

Lauren White, BSW, like Natasha, was a woman of African American descent. She knew from personal as well as professional experience that black families have many strengths. In times of difficulty, for example, extended family members such as Ruby frequently pitch in to help care for young children. Grandparents, great-grandparents, aunts, uncles, older siblings, and even neighbors frequently help out when needed. Lauren checked Natasha's files to assist in recalling the facts of the former case. Four years before, the paternal grandmother had called to report neglect of Natasha's then-infant son, Martin. At that time, Natasha was abusing alcohol, marijuana, and cocaine. A single parent, she was trying to cope with a baby with no assistance from that baby's father.

The case with Martin had a satisfactory ending, at least at the time. Once the little boy had been placed in foster care, Natasha had been willing to work hard to meet the conditions required by the court to get him back: regular participation in an alcohol and drug abuse treatment program and in a parenting class. Once court conditions had been met, Martin had been returned home, and the case had been closed shortly thereafter.

Lauren White's first step was to call Ruby Bell Lowe. She remembered the great-grandmother from her previous work with Natasha. Besides, no current telephone number had been given for Natasha, and the number on file was no longer working. From Ruby, Lauren learned that Natasha's telephone had been disconnected. Ruby could not take the bus to visit Natasha to talk with her as she was too frail to climb the vehicle's steep steps with an infant in her arms. She could not afford a cab. Ruby told Lauren that she didn't think she could keep LaTanya much longer. The baby had severe asthma attacks that frightened the old woman and sometimes kept her up many hours of the night. Ruby gave Lauren Natasha's address. She explained that she believed her granddaughter was abusing alcohol and possibly other drugs again. When Lauren asked where Natasha's son, Martin, was currently staying, Ruby didn't know.

CHAPTER OUTLINE (Continued)

Important Family Issues and Family Types 137
  Attachment Theory and Emotional Bonding 139
  Reproductive Rights and Single Parenting 140
  Ecological Concerns 142
  The Child Care Conundrum 144
  Gay and Lesbian Families 144
  Multi-Racial Families 146
  Immigrant Families 147
  Military Families 148

Cultural Competence 150
  Diverse Family Structures 150
  Spirituality and Religion 151

Family Policy 153
  Research Raises Questions 153
  How Family Friendly Is the American Workplace? 154
  The Family and Medical Leave Act 156
  Assisting Families Around the World 156
  Current Trends in the United States 157

Summary 159

Natasha Tracy opened the door of her apartment hesitantly at Lauren's knock, wearing an old bathrobe and smelling of alcohol although it was early in the afternoon. She recognized her former worker and invited her in with an embarrassed smile. She offered Lauren a seat on an ancient sofa and sank into a nearby chair with a sigh. "I know," she said. "I'll bet my grandmother called you."

Lauren replied that the elderly woman had done just that. "Ruby is very worried about you, Natasha," the worker continued sternly, "and LaTanya is hard for her to care for, as you can imagine. What has happened that you felt you had to leave LaTanya with your grandmother?"

Thus began a long, hesitant conversation in which Natasha seemed almost grateful to have someone to talk with, even if that someone was a social worker from Protective Services with the power to take away her children. Natasha explained that things had gone well enough for a couple of years after her son, Martin, had come home. But then she had become involved with an abusive boyfriend, LaTanya's father. This man frequently struck her when he was angry and ridiculed her when she cried. Then, just before LaTanya was born, the boyfriend had been arrested for armed robbery. He was now serving a long prison sentence. That solved the **abuse** problem, at least temporarily, but left Natasha alone with a young son and an infant with severe asthma. After LaTanya's father went to prison, Natasha applied for Temporary Assistance for Needy Families (TANF; see Chapter 4). The TANF program in Natasha's state required her to find a job right away since LaTanya was more than 12 weeks old by then. The young mother complied but soon felt exhausted by her dual responsibilities—sole parent to two young children, one a baby with asthma, and full-time employee at a fast-food restaurant. Even worse, the child care promised by TANF did not come through. There was a substantial waiting list for this service. Most of LaTanya's relatives and friends were also working outside their homes, many of them required to do so by the same TANF program. They could only occasionally help Natasha. Soon, Natasha lost her new job because she was absent caring for LaTanya too often. Discouraged, the young mother began to drink again. Eventually, realizing she was unable to care for her children properly, she took LaTanya to her grandmother's house and Martin to the home of his paternal grandmother. That was 3 weeks earlier. Now, Natasha's drinking was completely out of control, and she was in debt to her landlord for her rent, facing eviction.

Lauren White realized that here was a young woman with multiple problems, but that she and her extended family had many strengths. First, there were two elderly grandmothers willing to help as long as possible. Probably other relatives could also be found to help from time to time. Second, Lauren knew from past experience that Natasha was a good mother when she was not drinking. She had even been responsible enough to find other caretakers for her children when she realized her drinking was getting out of control again.

Gently, Lauren asked the young mother what she wanted for herself and her children. Did Natasha want to continue in the direction she was now heading, addicted to alcohol and in danger of losing her children, or was she willing to accept assistance toward recovery? Lauren *asked* Natasha because self-determination is a core social work value, to be implemented to the greatest extent possible even with involuntary clients. Clients who feel heard and respected will usually work harder to meet their goals.

Engagement

Dimension of Competency Skills: Social workers understand strategies to engage diverse clients and constituencies to advance practice effectiveness.

Critical Thinking Question: What strategies and skills did Lauren White use to engage her client, who was involuntary, in a process that could lead toward needed change?

Natasha's eyes filled with tears as Lauren asked her what she wanted to do with her life. She admitted that she had a substance abuse problem and said she was ashamed that she wasn't caring for her children. She knew she needed help.

Lauren had her work cut out for her to find resources to assist Natasha, but she was successful. An aunt was able to help Ruby Bell Lowe care for LaTanya until Natasha felt ready to take the baby home again. The paternal grandmother was willing to care for Martin a little longer. Family members loaned the young woman enough money to pay her back rent. Lauren was able to arrange counseling for Natasha at the Islamic Family Center. While Natasha was not a Black Muslim, the Islamic Family Center was willing to accept her as a client even though Natasha's only way to pay was through Medicaid, a health insurance program for certain categories of poor people, which has a very low payment schedule (see Chapter 4). Natasha's counselor at the Islamic Family Center connected her with an Alcoholics Anonymous (AA) group that met in her neighborhood. Partly motivated by the provisions of a court order that Lauren White secured, and partly motivated (and increasingly empowered) by the encouragement and support she now received in counseling, Natasha attended her AA group faithfully. She regained control of her drinking.

Within a few weeks, Natasha stopped drinking entirely. After that, she was able to bring her children home under Lauren White's supervision. She found another job and was able to work regularly enough to keep it. She was able to work regularly this time because, as a Protective Services client, she was eligible for immediate child care services through a Protective Services program. Natasha continued counseling at the Islamic Family Center and attending her AA group. After a few months passed, Lauren knew that Natasha was ready for release from supervision from Protective Services. She was worried, however, because once Natasha ceased to be a Protective Services client, funding for childcare through that agency would stop. Lauren realized that she would need to become involved in advocacy for Natasha with the TANF program to assist her in being readmitted and to help ensure continuity in child care. Without that, Natasha would be right back in the situation that precipitated her previous substance abuse. Lauren knew that her task would not be easy, but she was willing to go beyond the call of duty to do what she could to ensure a decent future for LaTanya, Martin, and Natasha Tracy.

This chapter examines family and children's services in the United States from a historical perspective. We examine various social work services to families in need and discuss the importance of cultural competence when working families of diverse cultural and religious backgrounds. Social policy impacting the well-being of families in America is described.

HISTORICAL PERSPECTIVES ON FAMILY AND CHILDREN'S SERVICES

Historical Perspectives

Children and families in need have been helped by family members and other members of their villages or tribes since well before written history. Otherwise, we could not have survived as a species. Given that human infants are born totally helpless, it is cooperation among various members of humankind, not competition, which has enabled humanity to survive. Early human beings foraged for food and shelter at the mercy of an unpredictable environment. Survival was precarious, as it still is today in impoverished areas of the United States and other parts of the world.

Formal services to help those in need are a relatively recent invention. In earlier times, infanticide and abandonment were the primary means available for families to deal with infants they couldn't care for. In the ancient Greek city of Athens, a child's birth was recognized socially only 5 days after the biological event. Before that, he or she could be disposed of.

As recently as the middle of the eighteenth century, nearly half the children born in London died of disease or hunger before they were 2 years old. In eighteenth century France, two-thirds of all children died before they reached age 20 (Kadushin & Martin, 1988). A high death rate is probably a major reason why rates of childbirth were so high in the past and remain high in poorer countries even today: Adults have multiple offspring in the hope that one or two will survive.

Both Jewish law from the Old Testament and early Christian teachings stressed the importance of caring for needy children and families. The Catholic Church, in particular, exhorted the sanctity of all human life and taught (as it still does) that not only infanticide but also abortion and even birth control were unacceptable. By preaching against all methods of regulating family size, the church obligated itself to help needy parents care for mouths they otherwise could not feed. A portion of church revenues was set aside for this purpose as early as the second or third century. Infants were often abandoned at church gates (Kadushin & Martin, 1988).

Under secular law, in early Europe there was no recognition of the rights of the child; the father had absolute control and no obligation to protect or maintain a child. Many babies were abandoned. The first known asylum for abandoned infants was founded in Milan in the year 787. After that, many other orphanages were established, among them the London Foundling Hospital that was opened in 1741 to save newborn babies and very young children who had been abandoned in churchyards or left on the streets (Kadushin & Martin, 1988).

Other mutual aid groups that helped children and families were the guilds (small groups of merchants and craftsmen that generated basic income to meet family economic needs of their members). However, with changes in technology, guilds ceded their function to factories, which were large, impersonal places of work with no sense of obligation to those who labored. Secular law began to provide some assistance to replace or supplement informal charity by church or guild. Life was still very hard, and assistance was extremely limited in kind and form. By the mid-1500s the average human life span was only about 30 years, and children were earning their own living by age 7 or 8. An English statute of 1535 stipulated that children between the ages of 5 and 14 who were begging on the streets could be put to work by city or town governments (Kadushin & Martin, 1988).

The English Poor Law of 1601 codified many previous laws dealing with the needy. As described in Chapter 3, aid was usually offered only in almshouses or workhouses. The death rate in these institutions was extremely high because sick and insane people were usually housed with everyone else. Destitute families were separated, as children were apprenticed out to whoever offered to take them for the least cost to the parish.

English poor laws were brought to the New World in the 1600s, and help for needy children and families in America through the mid-1800s remained roughly the same: the almshouse for most destitute people, with children being apprenticed out as soon as possible. Death rates and sheer human misery were high. Some towns did offer temporary "outdoor relief" (assistance in one's own home), but this practice was rare.

Overcrowding, crop failures, displacement of skilled artisans by the industrial revolution, and religious and political chaos in Europe brought immigrants by the thousands to the United States in the early and mid-1800s. They came looking for freedom and economic opportunity. Some found it, but many ended up crammed into filthy tenement buildings in city slums. Children born into these conditions often had to fend for themselves as soon as they were old enough to navigate the streets ("Early Immigration in the U.S.," n.d.).

By the 1850s, there were an estimated 30,000 homeless children in New York City alone. In 1853, Reverend Charles Loring Brace took an innovative approach to helping these children with the founding of the New York Children's Aid Society. Brace developed training schools, workshops, and living quarters for the city's destitute children, but the magnitude of their needs and the growing problem of juvenile delinquency alarmed him. He responded by devising a plan to ship the children out of the city to farmers in the West who might be able to use their labor. He viewed this as a way of finding foster homes for the children and also to "drain the city" of a serious problem. Beginning in 1854, many thousands of children were sent west on Brace's *orphan trains*. They were generally turned over to anyone who would take them. Many people opposed the plan, including parents who hated to see their children go but were too poor to support them. Charity workers sometimes called the program "the wolf of indentured labor in the sheep's clothing of Christian charity." The westward transport continued, however, through the early 1900s; more than 120,000 children were eventually placed (Trattner, 1999; "The Orphan Trains," n.d.). A positive legacy was a growing public interest in foster care for needy children.

The federal program that assisted African American and destitute white families in the South for a brief period after the Civil War (between 1865 and 1872), the Freedmen's Bureau, was almost revolutionary in concept. It was the first federal program to aid the poor. As discussed earlier, it provided education, work, land, and relief directly to families in the home setting. Unfortunately, this remarkable program fell victim to partisan politics after only 7 years of operation.

In the late 1800s, the settlement house movement, originating in England, came to the United States. Inner-city settlement houses began to offer services to poor families with children by helping to organize cooperative child care and other self-help programs. Jane Addams, as noted in Chapter 4, founded the famous Hull House of Chicago in 1889.

Partly due to activists in the settlement movement, laws began to be passed in the United States in the late 1800s against the use of "mixed almshouses," institutions in which destitute young children were housed with the sick and the elderly. One result was that more orphanages began to be established. Unfortunately, most excluded African American children, so black people were forced to continue to rely on a strong network of extended family, friends, African American churches, and other African American voluntary organizations for basic survival.

Also in the late 1800s, a major organization committed to helping families stay together in times of need, the Charity Organization Society, took shape, first in England

and then in the United States. Mary Richmond was the major leader of the movement in the United States. "Friendly visitors" were sent into poor people's homes to counsel parents toward better ways of living. The distribution of material aid to people's homes was centrally coordinated. Early friendly visitors believed poverty could be relieved by "moral uplift" of the poor. Later on, as workers became more knowledgeable about causes of poverty (such as low wages and poor health), they began to advocate for social reform in collaboration with settlement house workers. (The Charity Organization Society, the forerunner of today's family service agencies, and the settlement house movement were discussed in Chapter 4.)

The Child Welfare Movement and Protective Services Programs

The child welfare movement was a major contributor to the birth of the social work profession. Its roots can probably be traced to Charles Loring Brace's founding of the New York Children's Aid Society in 1853. While the practice of shipping children west became controversial, as it divided families and subjected children to serious trauma, Brace's efforts publicized the plight of poor children and orphans. Many Children's Aid Societies were founded in other cities. By the 1870s, some of these societies began to board impoverished children in family homes instead of sending them west, the beginning of foster care and adoption programs in the United States (Karger & Stoesz, 1998).

Public debate arose around the use of orphanages vs. foster homes for needy children. This question was resolved, at least in theory, with the 1909 White House Conference on Children. The conference was attended by Jane Addams, famous leader of the settlement house movement. It recognized the importance of families and unequivocally recommended foster rather than institutional care. Although many children continued to be placed in large institutions due to funding considerations and lack of available homes, the 1909 conference focused national attention on the plight of poor children. It was so successful that the conference reconvened every 10 years until 1971. The Republican Reagan administration ended the tradition.

The need for **protective services**, the type of social services mobilized in the LaTanya Tracy case described in this chapter, formally came into recognition around 1875. The catalyst for protective services for children was a 10-year-old girl named Mary Ellen Wilson (see Box 5.1).

Because of increased public awareness of abuse to children as a result of the Mary Ellen case, many societies for the prevention of cruelty to children were created throughout the country in the late 1800s. These were private, voluntary agencies. By the 1920s, there were nearly 300 of them scattered throughout the nation. In some parts of the nation, they still exist; in other parts, they have merged with various other social agencies serving children.

Prior to 1935, when the Social Security Act was passed, the federal government played almost no role in child welfare policy or planning. Despite the growing number of voluntary societies for the prevention of cruelty to children, many cities and most rural areas lacked access to these services. Finally, in 1912, the federal Children's Bureau was created. It played a small role, however, until the Great Depression leading to the passage of the Social Security Act. A provision of that act authorized the Children's Bureau to

> **Box 5.1 The Case of Mary Ellen**
>
> Mary Ellen Wilson was badly abused by a woman to whom she had been indentured at 18 months of age. The woman later admitted in court that Mary Ellen was the illegitimate daughter of her deceased first husband. Neighbors tried to help the girl because she was beaten regularly and kept as a virtual prisoner in her home. In 1874, they enlisted the help of a visitor to the poor, who appealed for assistance to the police and various charitable societies. As no assistance was forthcoming, the visitor then appealed to the president of the New York Society for the Prevention of Cruelty to Animals (SPCA), who sent an investigator. Due to conditions documented by the SPCA, a court order was obtained to temporarily remove the child from the home. The president of the SPCA then took Mary Ellen's case to court as a private citizen. He called it to the attention of the *New York Times* as a means of publicizing the problem of cruelty to children. The newspaper story succeeded in arousing widespread public concern. Mary Ellen was removed from the abusive home permanently, and her foster mother was sentenced to a year in prison.
>
> Source: Based on Sallie A. Watkins (1990, Nov.). "The Mary Ellen myth: Correcting child welfare history." *Social Work, 35*(6), 501–503.

work with state public welfare agencies to strengthen child protection services. This was at least a small step toward involving the central government in protecting children from abuse and neglect (Myers, 2008).

Formalized public services to protect children were not mandated by law in the United States until the passage of the Child Abuse Prevention and Treatment Act of 1974. Federal funds were provided to the states for this purpose, and a national Center on Child Abuse was established. Title XX of the Social Security Act was also passed in 1974 and provided block grants to the states, which helped finance child abuse programs (Segal & Brzuzy, 1998; Samantrai, 2004). Some states had provided these services on their own initiative for a number of years, but all states created protective services programs by 1978.

Establishment of protective services programs was accompanied by new laws requiring certain categories of professionals, such as doctors and social workers, to report suspected child abuse to designated authorities, a requirement known as *mandated reporting*. Mandated reporting, not surprisingly, resulted in a great increase in reports of suspected child abuse and neglect. Unfortunately, however, most protective services programs are seriously underfunded and understaffed, so workers generally can provide service only in situations of crisis proportions. In an effort to improve protective services, the Children's Bureau provides a limited number of competitive annual grants to states and Indian tribes each year (Karger & Stoesz, 1998; Samantrai, 2004, "FY 2016 Children's Bureau Discretionary Grant Awards," 2016).

Families who are reported to protective services units are often referred for more intensive counseling to private family service agencies, those connected historically with the Charity Organization Society. These agencies provide remedial services such as counseling to help improve conditions for neglected or abused children. They also usually provide preventive and educational programs. For example, all member agencies of Family Service of America provide family counseling, family life education programs, and family advocacy services. In our case example, Natasha Tracy's protective service worker referred her to the Islamic Family Center, where she received excellent counseling to help resolve her personal troubles and, in addition, a referral to Alcoholics Anonymous.

The Family Preservation and Support Services Act was passed as part of the Omnibus Budget Reconciliation Act of 1993, during the Clinton administration. This law aims to strengthen families by providing funds to states to develop new family support and preservation services. Responsibility for developing plans for specific programs rests with the states, which must target services in areas of greatest need and utilize community-based strategies that involve community groups, residents, and parents in the planning process (Samantrai, 2004).

Children's Rights as International Law

The idea that children have rights is rather new. The United Nations, in November 1954, proclaimed through the General Assembly's Declaration of the Rights of the Child that children all over the world have certain rights (see Box 5.2). These rights became international law in 1990 as the Convention on the Rights of the Child. The United States signed the convention in 1995, but, as of 2015, is the only nation in the world that has refused to ratify it. Signing a treaty means that a country supports its principles, but ratification means the country is legally bound by it. Ratification in the United States requires a two-thirds majority vote in the Senate, and the treaty has never even come to a vote because it is strongly opposed by conservative Republicans. They say it would usurp American sovereignty. There are indeed areas in the treaty that conflict with American law: For example, children under 18 in America can be (and all too often are) jailed for life without parole; despite laws against child abuse, a third of American states allow corporal punishment in the schools and no state prohibits it in the home. Because the convention prohibits cruel and degrading punishment of children, these practices might be challenged in court. In addition, conservatives fear that ratifying the convention might require the government to develop programs assuring that all American children have enough to eat and a place to live. The Democratic Obama administration supported ratification, but its efforts were blocked by Congress ("Why won't America ratify," 2013; Mehta, 2015).

Underscoring the importance of children's rights, the International Federation of Social Workers developed a specific policy supporting the Convention on the Rights

---

Box 5.2 United Nations Declaration on the Rights of the Child

- All children in the world have rights.
- All children have the right to citizenship in a country and the right to a name.
- All children have the right to sufficient food, shelter, and medical care.
- All children with disabilities have the right to special care and treatment.
- All children have the right to grow up in a safe, loving family.
- All children have the right to appropriate education and recreation.
- All children have the right to protection from cruel treatment.
- All children have the right to grow up without fear and hatred.
- All children have the right to grow up in an environment of love, peace, and friendship.

Source: Based on UNICEF (n.d). "Fact Sheet: A summary of the rights under the Convention on the Rights of the Child."

of the Child. Hopefully, the United States will ratify the convention sometime in the foreseeable future, but it is unlikely to happen as long as conservatives control Congress.

Challenges of African American Families

As noted in the chapter-opening case study, both Natasha Tracy and Lauren White were of African American descent—members of a minority group that has suffered immense challenges in the United States both historically and in contemporary times. Many, like Natasha, still struggle to meet basic needs. Others, like Lauren, have secured the education that allows them to enter the professional world. Lauren's path was easier, of course: She did not have two young children to provide and care for.

As is well known, African Americans have endured a history of slavery in the United States, enriching others at terrible cost to themselves. But the first African Americans came to the colonies in 1619 not as slaves but as indentured servants. The institution of slavery did not take firm hold in the United States until the late 1600s, when the South developed an agricultural economy dependent on slave labor (Lum, 1992).

The legacy of slavery is profound and reaches to the present day. Africans were different from other immigrant groups because the vast majority, including most of the indentured servants, were brought to the United States as captives against their will. Unlike other immigrant groups, they had no stable community of free kinsmen or countrymen to turn to for assistance upon arrival. Instead, slave traders systematically separated families and tribal members and sold them apart from one another to reduce chances of coalition and revolt. Native languages and religious traditions were forbidden. Every attempt was made to suppress the spirit of the slaves. Laws denied them the right to marry, to maintain families, to assemble in groups, to learn to read and write, or to sue for redress of grievances. Slaves were legally not persons but property.

Slavery existed at first in both northern and southern states and territories. Rhode Island was the first state to free its slaves, in 1784, a few years after the American Revolution (Quarles, 1987). By the time of the Civil War, there were approximately half a million free blacks in the nation (Logan, Freeman, & McRoy, 1990). They were strictly regulated, however. All had to carry special papers certifying their free status, and they could be sold back into slavery if their papers were lost or stolen. In most states, they were denied the right to vote, hold public office, or testify in court.

The Civil War from 1860 to 1865 freed the slaves, but at great cost. One in four died from disease and deprivation related to the terrible conflict (Logan et al., 1990). The first federal social welfare agency, the Bureau of Refugees, Freedmen, and Abandoned Lands, known as the Freedmen's Bureau, was established 2 months before the end of the war, in anticipation of the enormous human need that would follow. The Freedmen's Bureau distributed food, clothing, and medical supplies to starving blacks and whites alike. It also established 46 hospitals, several orphan asylums, and more than 4,000 schools for African American children. It established institutions of higher learning for African Americans, including Howard, Atlanta, and Fisk Universities (Axinn & Levin, 1992). Unfortunately, the Freedmen's Bureau was terminated in 1872. Had it been allowed to continue, the conditions for African Americans as a whole today would be much improved.

After slavery, all former states of the Confederacy except Tennessee passed *Black Codes* that limited the property rights of African Americans and forbade them to hold skilled jobs such as craftsman or mechanic. In Georgia, unemployed African Americans could be rounded up and put on chain gangs as criminals. State and local welfare programs for blacks were inferior to those for white people. Orphaned black children in Mississippi, for example, were apprenticed, and their former masters were given preference. No guarantees for adequate food, clothing, or education were written into the terms of indenture, as were included for white children (Axinn & Levin, 1992).

Under such difficult conditions, mutual aid and self-help were crucial for the survival of African Americans. The extended family rescued thousands of orphaned children, and churches organized orphanages, day care centers, and kindergartens. Churches also helped care for sick and elderly members and arranged for the adoption of children. African American lodges like the Masons and the Odd Fellows raised funds and provided needed services, as did various women's organizations (Logan et al., 1990).

African Americans make up about 13.3 percent of the U.S. population today ("QuickFacts, United States," 2015). They constitute the second largest minority group, after Hispanics. Among the many strengths of African American people is the fact that mutual aid extends beyond nuclear family boundaries. Aid is routinely offered to extended family members, friends, and neighbors, permitting the survival of many in need. Aid from the extended family network was crucial to the survival of LaTanya Tracy and her family in this chapter's case study.

It is important for social workers to remember that there is no single African American family structure. African American families may be nuclear (including two biological parents or blended in a variety of ways) or single parent; they may be wealthy, middle income, or poor. However, because of the realities of discrimination and limited opportunity, a disproportionate number are poor and single parent, increasing the chances of involvement with the social service system.

? Assess your understanding of historical perspectives on family and children's services by taking this brief quiz.

SERVICES AND THEIR PROVIDERS: A CONTINUUM OF CARE

A significant percentage of child and family services are offered by professional social workers. The 1980 Adoption Assistance and Child Welfare Act recommends a minimum of a baccalaureate-level degree in social work (but unfortunately does not require it). While this important work is often performed by people without appropriate training or experience, the social work degree remains the best professional preparation for the field. Workers with this background can be instrumental in improving the quality of service.

Least Restrictive Environment

Services to children and families should be offered in the **least restrictive environment**, the setting that provides the least interference with normal life patterns yet provides the most important and needed services. The least restrictive environment for children is normally the biological family home.

Box 5.3 A Continuum of Care

Least Restrictive: In Home

- Financial aid
- Family life education
- Homemaker services
- Day care
- Family therapy
- Protective services
- Family-based services
- Foster care
- Group home
- Adoption
- Institutional care
- The judicial system

Most Restrictive: Out of Home

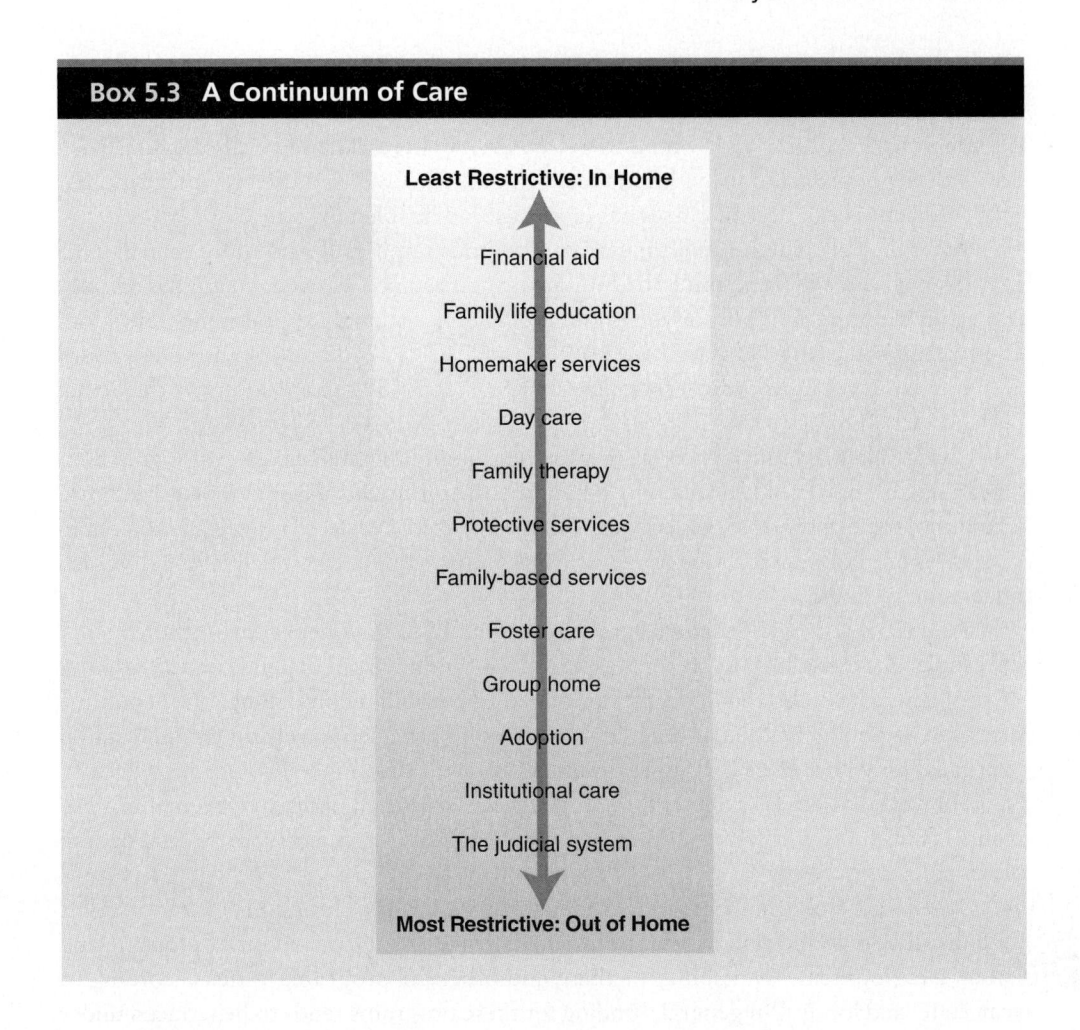

Services offered to children in need can be classified in several ways, but one of the simplest is to divide them into two major categories: in-home (the least restrictive environment) and out-of-home. (Be careful not to confuse these contemporary service categories with *indoor* and *outdoor relief* as offered under historic English poor laws.) A continuum of care from least restrictive environment to most restrictive is illustrated in Box 5.3.

In-Home Services

In-home services (see Box 5.3) are provided to a family to help members live together more safely and harmoniously in their own homes. They are preventive in orientation. Paradoxically, some (like day care) may be offered outside the home, but the goal is to assist families to stay together. In-home services are described in this section. A discussion of out-of-home services appears further on. There is some overlap between in-home and out-of-home services, of course. For example, adoption, while classified here as an out-of-home service because it removes children from their biological homes permanently, also *provides* needy children with homes.

Financial Aid

Many families require financial aid to survive. The major programs available are described in Chapter 4 and will be reviewed briefly here. The federally administered Social Security program provides income to families in which a breadwinner who has paid sufficient Social Security taxes has died, become disabled, or retired.

States *may* provide limited financial aid to poor families for no more than 5 years in a given parent's lifetime under the Temporary Assistance for Needy Families (TANF) program. This option is authorized under the federal Personal Responsibility and Work Opportunity Act (PRWOA) of 1996. TANF replaced Aid to Families with Dependent Children (AFDC), a program previously *entitling* poor children to aid under the Social Security Act.

Medicare and Medicaid programs provide funding for medical care for many families in need. They are authorized by amendments to the Social Security Act. Medicare primarily provides funds for elderly and disabled people. Medicaid is available to certain categories of poor people who pass a means test. Most people who qualify for TANF also qualify for Medicaid.

Food stamps provide financial assistance to families in voucher form (the voucher now looks like a credit or debit card). The amount of aid given depends on the number of people in a household and on the combined household income. Since the economic recession beginning in 2008, more and more families have had to rely on the food stamp program (now known as the Supplemental Nutrition Assistance Program, or SNAP). Sadly, however, to slow enrollment, many states have made eligibility requirements more complex and added work obligations even where work is scarce and sometimes impossible to obtain.

Other forms of financial aid include subsidized school lunch programs, surplus food distributions, and rent assistance provided by the U.S. Department of Housing and Urban Development. Availability of these and other aid programs varies according to year, state, and locality. In general, funding for these programs tends to be reduced under conservative administrations.

Family Life Education

Family life education is an in-home social service intended to prevent as well as to help solve family problems. This type of educational program is often offered at traditional family service agencies and also at family support centers that are found in some areas of the country. Usually family life education classes are held at the sponsoring agencies, but sometimes workers go out into the home setting. Topics covered vary with the setting, but typically they include information about the developmental stages of childhood, weaning and toilet-training issues, building self-esteem, parenting skills, communication skills, and constructive methods of discipline.

Homemaker Services

Homemaker services may be provided to families in which one member is too ill, too old, or too emotionally unstable to carry out normal household tasks. Such services may also be provided on a short-term basis to care for children when a parent is temporarily absent because of physical illness or mental breakdown. Sometimes a homemaker is assigned to a family that has been reported to protective services for neglect, as a temporary corrective measure. In these cases, homemakers assume a teaching or modeling role.

The provision of homemaker services can allow families to stay together in their own homes under circumstances that might otherwise break them up. Services may include cleaning, shopping, cooking, laundry, and childcare. They are offered at low cost to eligible families that meet a means test, through both public and private social service agencies. In most cases, services are provided by aides rather than social workers.

Day Care

Day care is considered an in-home social service, even though it is often provided outside the home. This service permits a working parent who has no partner, or two working parents, to maintain young children as part of the household.

Too common are "latchkey children," who spend part of their day in school and part at home alone, having let themselves in. Even this arrangement, however, is not feasible for families with infants and toddlers; without day care, these very young children would require foster care. For this reason, some states and counties have established programs in which day care is publicly subsidized, and a sliding fee is charged according to the income of the parent(s). The replacement of AFDC by TANF makes subsidized day care programs particularly imperative today since most poor mothers have to work outside the home. Yet there is no national requirement for such a service and no national program on the horizon.

Day care centers that serve special populations of children are probably most likely to have social workers on staff. For example, some centers offer care for children with developmental disabilities or for those adjudicated by the courts as **children at risk**. At-risk children usually come through the recommendation of protective services social workers, who have determined that these children would be reasonably safe at home if their parents were relieved of child care responsibilities during all or part of the day.

Family Therapy

Family therapy is a service available to families experiencing many different kinds of distress. Although it usually is conducted in professional offices, it is considered an in-home service because it assists family members to live together more safely and harmoniously.

Family therapy is a practice concentration within the social work profession, and it requires a master's degree. Family therapy may be provided by members of related professions as well, such as psychologists or psychiatrists. Sometimes family therapists work in teams in which a psychologist administers psychological tests, a psychiatrist administers medication, and both serve as consultants to the social worker, who usually provides the ongoing counseling.

Protective Services

Protective services are designed to shield children from maltreatment, including both abuse and neglect. Lauren White of the LaTanya Tracy case was a protective services worker. While each state develops its own definition of child maltreatment, the Child Abuse Prevention, Adoption, and Family Services Act of 1988 provides a general federal definition of maltreatment specifying that it may be physical, mental (including emotional), or sexual, and entail either neglect or abuse (Gustavsson & Segal, 1994).

Intervention

Dimension of Competency **Skills: Social workers are knowledgeable about evidence-informed interventions to achieve the goals of clients and constituencies.**

Critical Thinking Question: How might well-developed skills in the use of evidence-informed practice help social workers improve the outcome of their work with child protective services clients?

Protective services workers usually begin by investigating and monitoring a referred child's own home. Since the mid-1990's, many states have implemented a "differential response" approach to child protective services: Workers may determine to follow different "pathways" in working with families depending on the type and severity of maltreatment reported. Families perceived to be low risk may be offered a family assessment along with the option to receive services recommended by the worker, while high-risk families receive a full investigation and may be compelled to meet certain legal requirements (as in this chapter's case study, in which protective services worker Lauren White obtained a court order requiring Natasha Tracy to receive counseling and cease drinking before her children would be returned). This approach allows for efficient use of resources ("Differential Response in Child Protective Services," 2014).

In situations of extreme risk (and when such resources exist), protective services workers may mobilize family preservation teams for intensive in-home intervention. Where safety issues remain serious, children may be placed in foster care (Reich, 2005). Children removed from parental homes are ideally placed in homes of relatives, as in the LaTanya Tracy case.

The primary goal of protective services programs under the Adoption Assistance and Child Welfare Act of 1980 was to preserve families while providing safe environments for children at risk. This law emphasized rehabilitation of parents so that children could leave the limbo of foster care and return to their own homes (McKenzie & Lewis, 1998; Reich, 2005). However, despite the good intention of this law, many children then remained in the limbo of foster care awaiting parental rehabilitation, in situations where the parents indicated little or no interest in change. The Adoption and Safe Families Act, signed into law by President Clinton in November 1997, acknowledges the importance of family preservation and support services but also encourages more timely **permanency placement**, recognizing children's developmental need to have a permanent home. The bill authorizes bonuses to states to increase adoptions of children and also speeds up timelines for holding hearings initiating proceedings to terminate parental rights ("Adoption and Safe Families Act," 1997). States receive "report cards" on performance factors such as the number of adoptions completed and the shortness of stay in foster care (Samantrai, 2004).

Family-Based Services

Family-based services were prompted by the federal Adoption Assistance and Child Welfare Act of 1980, which required states to maintain children in the least restrictive environment possible (Smith, 1998). Later, in 1993, additional legislation entitled "Family Preservation and Family Support Services" was added to the Social Security Act. The purpose was to help keep families together, healthy, and safe. In 1997, the program's scope was expanded and reauthorized as the "Promoting Safe and Stable Families Program."

Family support services are generally designed to promote the stability and well-being of families and to prevent family problems from escalating to a crisis point where out-of-home placement might be required. These services are usually targeted toward at-risk families—those where there is increased risk of abuse or neglect—and may include a variety of health, mental health, social, and educational benefits. Usually no time limit is imposed.

Family preservation services are designed specifically to help families that have been reported to public authorities for problems of neglect and abuse, when the children are at immediate risk of placement outside the home. Crisis workers may spend many hours per week in the family home on a short-term basis, focusing on parenting skills. Family preservation services are usually employed only after all other assistance has failed (Samantrai, 2004).

Out-of-Home Services

Sometimes, regardless of the amount of effort invested by protective and other supportive services, family circumstances still remain unsuitable for the upbringing of a child. In these cases, **out-of-home services** must be substituted, short or long term, depending on the circumstances (see Box 5.3).

Foster Care

The type of foster care provided to LaTanya and Martin Tracy was perhaps the very earliest form available: care in a relative's home. Placement may be informal, purely a family matter. However, placement by a government agency such as a department of child welfare involves a foster home licensing process. Requirements for licensing include factors such as the amount of space in a house compared with the number of people living there, the number of bedrooms, and compliance with building codes and fire safety regulations. In addition, prospective foster parents must be investigated with respect to character, reliability, and parenting skills. Usually, social workers are the professionals who conduct foster home studies and recommend acceptance or rejection.

Once a foster home is accepted, social workers supervise the home. They visit on a regular schedule and talk with both foster parents and children to make sure that a constructive relationship is developing. When there is a problem, social workers become involved in solving it. Some foster homes are specialized; they are licensed to care for children who have unusual needs, such as physical or mental disabilities, behavioral disturbances, or emotional illness.

Normally, while a child is in foster care, the social worker works with the biological as well as the foster parents. The purpose of this work is to enable the natural parents to prepare for the successful return of their child, wherever possible.

Group Homes

Group homes are usually licensed to house eight people, a number large enough so that residents can have a variety of others to meet and talk with but small enough so that they can receive individual attention. Homes for children usually have a stable staff of youth care workers, often BSWs, supplemented by a housekeeping staff and childcare aides. The aim is to make the setting as family-like as possible.

This type of out-of-home service meets several needs. First of all, given the shortage of licensed foster homes, group homes can provide shelter when regular foster homes are not available. In some cases, group home care may meet a particular child's needs better than a foster home can. For example, some teenagers cannot make the emotional investment necessary to develop close relationships with foster parents. They may be much more willing to relate to peers in a group home.

Shelters for runaways have emerged in many cities over the past two decades. Originally founded by volunteers, many shelters have become licensed as foster group homes. Runaway shelters usually provide bed, board, and crisis counseling, and their ultimate goal is to reunite families under conditions that are safe for the children.

Shelters for battered women and their children, which were introduced in Chapter 1, can be thought of as another type of group home for family members who are "running away from home." These shelters provide short-term bed and board. In addition, most provide information and referral services and crisis counseling. Usually, shelters are more widely available for battered women than for battered men. This is because women are most often the victims of battery and because women activists (including social workers) have usually been the driving force behind the creation of the shelters.

Adoption

Sometimes out-of-home substitute care goes beyond the temporary and becomes permanent by adoption. Adoption benefits needy children by providing permanent plans of care. It provides children and their adoptive parents the same legal rights and responsibilities with respect to one another as are available to biological parents and their children. Children become available for adoption only when the rights of both natural parents have been terminated.

When children are removed from a home due to severe neglect or abuse, social workers will engage in a practice known as "concurrent planning." They will work hard to help families achieve reunification through improving home conditions and meeting requirements of court orders, but at the same time they will develop alternative permanency plans in case family conditions do not improve. Only when parental rights are terminated by court order do children removed from abusive homes become available for adoption.

The Adoption and Safe Families Act of 1997, as discussed earlier, encourages increased recognition of children's need for permanent homes. To this end, incentives are offered to speed up adoption procedures in situations where evidence is persuasive that the biological parents cannot provide suitable homes.

Social workers often provide counseling for people trying to reach the difficult decision of whether or not to place a child for adoption or even, in recent times, whether or not to continue a problem pregnancy. Termination of pregnancy is potentially an option in many circumstances, although the U.S. Supreme Court's 1989 Webster decision provided states with more regulating power. In recent years, more and more states have used this power to enact restrictive laws, and in early 2006 the U.S. Supreme Court overturned a nationwide injunction aimed at preventing violence at abortion clinics (Roth, 2006). Thus, women can be intimidated by extremist groups from trying to obtain abortions.

Children who have special characteristics or needs (such as those who are older, part of a sibling group, of mixed race, or have a disability) are hard to place and may spend their lives in foster homes. These are the children that single people or older couples are encouraged to adopt. An important task for social service agencies is the recruitment of adoptive placements for children who might otherwise never find permanent homes.

Because a very high number of American Indian children were being removed from their homes and placed for adoption with non-Indian families, a federal law was passed by Congress in 1978 to help keep Indian children with Indian families. This was both for the children's sake and to promote the integrity and stability of Indian tribes as a whole. The law established federal requirements for state child custody proceedings involving Indian children and acknowledged the importance of tribal governments in supporting tribal families. Thus, special procedures apply to the adoption of Indian children; whenever possible, Indian children are placed with Indian families ("Indian Child Welfare Act of 1978," n.d.).

States are authorized under the Adoption Assistance and Child Welfare Act of 1980 to provide adoption subsidies for hard-to-place children. The medical costs of raising physically fragile children, for example, can be exorbitant. Subsidies make adoption a more realistic choice for many families (Gustavsson & Segal, 1994). The law provides financial support for adoptive parents of children with special needs; a portion is federally funded and the remainder comes from states and counties ("Adoption Subsidy Definitions," n.d.).

Adopted children may want to try to find their biological parents at some point in their lives. In recent years, laws have been changed in many states, allowing adopted persons (after becoming adults) to obtain some of their social service agency records or, as in New Hampshire, to obtain copies of their original birth certificates (Collins, 2005). Parents who terminate their rights and place a child for adoption today may opt, in some states, to note in the records that they would be willing for the adult child to contact them.

Institutional Care

Institutional placement is another out-of-home option for the care of minor children. In the recent past, children who lost their parents were often placed in large institutions known as orphanages. Most of these facilities have now been closed, replaced by foster homes and small group homes. Where large childcare institutions still exist, they usually provide specialized treatment or short-term emergency shelter for children awaiting placement in less restrictive environments.

Some children are placed for a year or more at a type of institution known as a residential treatment center. These children usually have been determined by professional evaluation to be seriously emotionally disturbed; they often are referred by courts in an effort to control delinquent behavior. Residential treatment centers often provide a comprehensive range of services that include behavior modification programs (an approach sometimes called milieu therapy), individual counseling, family therapy, and instruction by teachers skilled in working with children who are emotionally and behaviorally disturbed.

The children who are placed in residential treatment facilities usually have been referred first to special education services in their respective community schools. Federally mandated special education policy requires treating children in the least restrictive environment possible. Only if less restrictive interventions fail will a child be referred to a residential treatment center, and only then if the community is willing to accept the expense (or, in rare cases, if parents can afford the expense).

The Judicial System

If a child has committed frequent and/or severe-enough crimes, he or she may be sentenced by the court to what amounts to a jail for minors. Pending a court hearing for an alleged offense, a child may be held temporarily in a detention center. Older teens

> **Box 5.4 Child Welfare in the United States: Milestones**
>
> | | |
> |---|---|
> | 1642 | Plymouth Colony enacts poor law similar to Elizabethan Poor Law of 1601. Destitute children and orphans are apprenticed. |
> | 1790 | First publicly funded orphanage in the United States: Charleston, South Carolina. |
> | 1853 | Reverend Rev. Charles Loring Brace founds Children's Aid Society, New York City. |
> | 1865 | Freedmen's Bureau founded, first federal welfare agency; in action until 1872. |
> | 1877 | Society for Prevention of Cruelty to Children founded in New York City. First Charity Organization Society in the United States founded in Buffalo, New York. |
> | 1886 | First Settlement House in the United States founded in New York City. |
> | 1889 | Hull House founded in Chicago by Jane Addams. |
> | 1909 | White House Conference on Children. |
> | 1912 | U.S. Children's Bureau founded. |
> | 1935 | Social Security Act: Dependent children who are poor receive entitlement to aid. |
> | 1974 | Child Abuse Prevention and Treatment Act. |
> | 1993 | Family Preservation and Support Services Act. Family and Medical Leave Act. |
> | 1996 | Personal Responsibility and Work Opportunity Act ends entitlement of poor children to aid under Social Security Act. Establishes Temporary Assistance for Needy Families (TANF) program *at states' option*. |
> | 1997 | Adoption and Safe Families Act. Promoting Safe and Stable Family Program. |

may be tried and sentenced as adults. This step is truly a last resort, and it usually represents the failure of other services. This is what is likely to happen when a child needed residential or other treatment earlier in life, but the care was not provided because of monetary cost. Attention to short-term budgetary concerns without consideration of long-term costs, both human and monetary, has been tragically characteristic of social planning in the United States (see Box 5.4).

Client Self-Determination and Professional Decision-Making

> Watch this short video of a student explaining the importance of client self-determination. Identify three important reasons for promoting the self-determination of ALL clients and client systems.
>
> https://www.youtube.com/watch?v=ByhAx9cYDO0

The social work profession holds as an important principle the right of clients to make their own decisions. A major principle of the NASW Code of Ethics deals specifically with **self-determination**. It requires social workers to respect clients' right to self-determination unless their actions create a serious risk for themselves or others.

The LaTanya Tracy case is a good example of a situation in which a social worker, Lauren White, in her professional role as a protective services worker, determined that Natasha Tracy's actions were posing a serious risk to herself and her children. Thus, while the principle of self-determination would normally guide a social worker to honor a client's own decisions,

Natasha's substance abuse presented a substantial enough risk to justify Lauren's intervention ethically as well as legally. However, Lauren maximized her profession's ethical principle of self-determination to the greatest extent possible under the circumstances. She listened respectfully to Natasha; helped the young mother identify the many problems in her life that needed addressing; helped her sort out her own goals, which included caring for her children; and assisted in developing a plan of action that would solve many of the problems and permit the children to return home.

> **?** Assess your understanding of services and their providers by taking this brief quiz.

IMPORTANT FAMILY ISSUES AND FAMILY TYPES

In the United States, we are so accustomed to thinking of child rearing as a family responsibility that we forget that the nation as a whole benefits. Their survival is essential to carrying on the fundamental tasks of the economic market. Today's productive adults will grow old and die; they will need replacement. Thus, despite superficial appearances, it is in the national interest, not just the interest of the family, to provide for children so that they can grow up to be emotionally stable, well educated, and capable of contributing to the common good (see Box 5.5).

Box 5.5 Up for Debate

Proposition: Poor children should be entitled to public assistance that provides a decent standard of living and allows a parent to provide child care at home.

Yes	No
Children, especially young children, need a parent to care for them at home for consistent parental bonding, supervision, and a sense of security.	Even in many intact, middle-class families today, both parents have to work to make ends meet.
Day care services affordable to poor parents who have to work outside the home are likely to be unregulated and of poor quality, putting poor children at increased disadvantage.	Day care services may be available in centers offering a sliding fee. Besides, babysitting for other people's children can provide poor mothers a means of earning an income.
Poor parents usually have been disadvantaged with respect to education; they often must accept jobs at or near minimum wage, which is too low to raise their families out of poverty.	If public assistance is offered to poor children, their parents may opt not to work outside the home, thus depriving potential employers of low-wage workers.
Many studies, both national and international, have shown that good welfare programs do not increase birth rates in single-parent families. Besides, regardless of the circumstances of their birth, all children deserve a minimum standard of living even if their biological parents cannot provide.	Assisting poor children may encourage poor, single mothers to have more children whom society does not want.

Because we don't seem able to recognize as a nation the value of raising children—to recognize child rearing as valid work—we do not consider the task worth paying for (if provided by the mother). The Personal Responsibility and Work Opportunity Act (PRWOA) rescinded any national responsibility to assist poor parents in their child rearing job. Thus, as described in our chapter's case example, when the men in Natasha Tracy's life abandoned her to raise their two children alone, so did the nation. She then faced an impossible dilemma. Natasha needed to hold a paying job to feed herself and the two children, but her paycheck wasn't large enough to purchase child care. She needed to purchase child care to keep her paying job. This dilemma is experienced by millions of poor women today. The TANF program (see Chapter 4) can help for a time, if it is offered, but it requires a mother to work outside the home. In many states, even where a TANF program is provided, assistance with child care is not available (see Box 5.6).

Has the PRWOA and its TANF program helped poor people in the United States, as trumpeted enthusiastically by supporters? It was supposed to reduce welfare "dependency," thus producing "proud, self-supporting mothers" previously labeled "too lazy and dependent" to work outside the home. After the PRWOA was passed, welfare caseloads did indeed drop significantly, which was touted as a great national success. Sadly, as McNally (2015) notes, while at one point in our history a program's success was judged according to how many Americans were helped, today, given the conservative perspective, a program's success is judged according to how many people lose that help or are never helped in the first place.

Reduction in welfare caseloads has meant that millions of poor people, mostly women and children, have simply lost access to assistance. Only about 60 percent of the adults initially forced off welfare found jobs when they lost their benefits, and only about half of those earned enough to pull their families above the poverty line. Rarely did the

---

Box 5.6 Single Mothers—Should They Be Forced to Work Outside the Home?

Today, American social policy in the form of TANF forces all single mothers who are poor to work outside the home when their children are very small—only 2 years old according to federal law, and considerably younger in many states. Is this sensible policy? Single mothers already shoulder a double burden—they must perform all the roles usually shared by two parents. They need to prepare meals, clean house, do laundry, empty the garbage, fix things that get broken, mow the lawn (if they have one), provide nurturance and comfort for the children, discipline the children when necessary, and carry out countless other tasks. Is this possible if the mother is constantly forced to leave her home to perform a paid job flipping hamburgers or something similar, usually according to a schedule not tailored to meet the needs of a parent with a young child? When that parent is constantly worried about transportation to her place of employment, transporting her child to day care, plus the high cost of day care itself? What happens if she or her children get sick?

Research shows that young children need to bond with a significant adult in order to develop a secure sense of identity, but how can this happen when that adult is frequently absent at a paid job, exhausted when home, and constantly worried about making ends meet because wages are inadequate to meet living expenses?

Is this a reasonable way for a nation to develop healthy, well-adjusted citizens? Raising healthy children involves emotional investment in their well-being. It takes both quality and quantity time. Is this possible for a single mother when so many other burdens are placed upon her? When she is probably very young herself, inexperienced, and frightened because of her circumstances?

jobs they found provide decent pay or benefits such as health insurance. Only a third of the newly employed were able to work continuously for a full year. Many who enrolled in TANF were forced off the program due to **sanctions** (Hays, 2007). Many were sanctioned as they were unable to meet TANF work or training requirements due to child care needs.

It is true that TANF helped some young parents when it was implemented—perhaps 10 to 15 percent ended up in a better position than they would have been if the PRWOA law had not been passed. Some have been provided with valuable training, work clothes, bus vouchers, childcare subsidies, and income supplements, at least for a time in the more progressive states (Hays, 2007). However, many single mothers have been unable to meet TANF requirements and have experienced what happened to Natasha Tracy and her children—they were "sanctioned:" simply dropped from the program.

States have various options under the PRWOA. For example, they may require a mother to work outside the home before her child reaches the federally mandated age of 24 months. Natasha's state required her to work outside the home when LaTanya was only 12 weeks old. States may institute a lifetime policy benefit shorter than the federal limit of 5 years; they may deny additional benefits to children conceived by women receiving assistance; and they may choose weak, moderate, or strong sanctions for recipient infractions such as missing work due to child care needs.

How are poor people faring since the passage of the PRWOA? Not very well. In 2014, according to a survey by Feeding America, food insecurity (hunger) existed in every county in the United States. Over 48 million people lived in homes that were food insecure, including more than 15 million children. The highest percentages of food-insecure households involved households headed by single women with children (35 percent), households of African Americans (26 percent), and households of Hispanic persons (22 percent). More than 46 million persons lived below the poverty line, including more than 15 million or 21.1 percent of children ("Hunger and poverty fact sheet," 2015).

Many Americans fared much worse than simply living in a food-insecure household. Many had no households at all. The National Coalition to End Homelessness found that in January 2015 there were nearly 580,000 homeless people in the nation, and more than 22 percent were children. Their research indicated that the high cost of housing was a major reason for homelessness. A family with only one full time working person earning minimum wage could not afford the fair-market rent for a two-bedroom apartment anywhere in the United States ("Frequently Asked Questions," 2015).

Attachment Theory and Emotional Bonding

Forcing poor mothers of infants and young children to work outside the home in order to ward off starvation and homelessness can have serious consequences with respect to emotional bonding or attachment between the child and the mother. The first attachment theorist, psychologist John Bowlby, described attachment as a long-term psychological connection between people. He believed that the very earliest bond between an infant and a primary caregiver is of enormous importance, influencing a person's entire life. Attachment theory holds that caregivers who are consistently available and responsive to their infants' needs create secure foundations for their children to begin to explore the world. Such infants are described as having secure attachments. But where caregivers are not dependably responsive to their infants' needs, secure attachments will not be achieved.

Psychologist Mary Ainsworth expanded on Bowlby's theory. In her study of children 12 to 18 months old, she found that those who were "securely attached" exhibited little distress when separated from their caregivers. When frightened, they returned with confidence to their caregivers for comfort and reassurance. However, children who were not securely attached demonstrated very different behaviors. Those with "ambivalent attachment" became exceedingly upset when separated from caregivers. Ainsworth's research data suggested that ambivalent attachment resulted from poor maternal availability. Those with "avoidant attachment" tended to avoid their parents or caregivers; when offered a choice, they showed no preference between caregivers and strangers. Data suggested that abuse or neglect can cause avoidant attachment.

> Watch this video demonstrating different types of attachment. How do these examples support attachment theory as described in the text?
> https://www.youtube.com/watch?v=DH1m_ZMO7GU

What happens to children who do not form secure attachments? Research suggests that their behavior is negatively affected throughout their entire lives. They are frequently diagnosed with oppositional defiant disorder, conduct disorder, and post-traumatic stress disorder (Cherry, 2010). Could these disorders help explain why the United States puts such a high percentage of its population behind bars? Could this be a very costly downstream solution to the problem of poverty?

Can a single mother who is forced to work outside the home be consistently and reliably available to meet her infant's or young child's needs? While parents with a partner may also work outside the home, there are two responsible adults available to share parenting, breadwinning, and housework tasks. Two parents can also provide emotional security for one another. By contrast, the single parent must struggle alone and may need to hold more than one job to make ends meet. Thus, it seems unlikely that such a parent could provide a child with the kind of dependable, ongoing attention required to develop secure attachment. TANF requirements force her to get another job instead, usually one that is unskilled and poorly paid.

Reproductive Rights and Single Parenting

Ironically, at a time when the nation is abandoning its poor children, it continues to deny poor mothers the means to terminate unwanted pregnancies. In 1973, the Supreme Court ruled that women have a constitutional right to safe and legal abortions (*Roe v. Wade*), but the Hyde Amendment of 1976 denied Medicaid funding for abortions to poor women. That amendment remains in force today. Since the 1973 ruling, all women have found it increasingly difficult to get an abortion, poor or not. Many states have passed restrictions such as parental notification for minors and mandatory waiting periods. Hundreds of clinics have been shut down by disruptive demonstrations and threats on people's lives. The National Organization for Women secured a court injunction preventing demonstrators from blocking clinic entrances, but the Supreme Court overturned the injunction in early 2006 (Roth, 2006).

The Supreme Court also made abortions more difficult to obtain by allowing a late-term abortion ban in 2007. It was a 5–4 decision, extremely dangerous to women as it allowed no exception to safeguard a woman's health. Justice Ruth Bader Ginsburg, the only woman then on the court, blasted the majority for using "flimsy and transparent justifications" for upholding the ban (Richey, 2007).

Subsequent to the 2007 Supreme Court decision, several states began passing new laws restricting women's access to abortions. Then, in 2015, Texas passed a law requiring abortion clinics to meet requirements so stringent most would have to close down. The requirements included qualifying as surgical centers and obtaining admitting privileges to hospitals. The latter requirement was a "catch-22" because abortions are so safe clinic physicians very rarely have to refer their patients to hospitals, so that hospitals have no incentive to extend admitting privileges.

The Texas law was immediately challenged, but a circuit court upheld the restrictions. However, on June 27, 2016, the U.S. Supreme Court ruled 5–3 that the Texas law placed undue burdens on women seeking abortions and struck down the law. Legal scholars believe the ruling in this case, *Whole Woman's Health v. Hellerstedt*, will impact abortion law in many other states which have also passed severe restrictions in recent years ("NASW Backs Court," 2016).

As this chapter is being revised in 2016, a Republican Congress is working hard to deny any federal funding to Planned Parenthood, an important organization which, while providing abortions in some places, also offers inexpensive medical care to many thousands of poor people nation-wide. Conservatives seem intent on making abortions impossible to obtain. This seems odd on the face of it because they are the ones who worked hard to deny aid to poor children under the provisions of the Social Security Act once they are born.

The election of Donald Trump in 2016, who, as a conservative, apposes abortion, could reverse any progress toward keeping family planning services and/or abortion available in the future. Young women and men of reproductive age need to realize the importance of exercising their right to vote. Voter turnout in 2016 was at a 20-year low; only about 55 percent of eligible voters cast ballots (Wallace & Yoon, 2016). The result was the election of a president with little sympathy for minority rights, including women's right to self-determination.

The approval granted by the U.S. Food and Drug Administration (FDA) in 2006 allowing non-prescription sale of an emergency contraception pill to women over 18 was an important development. This pill can prevent fertilization of the woman's egg "the morning after" unplanned intercourse. It therefore does *not* cause an abortion; rather, it prevents conception. Initially the "Plan B" pill was available without a prescription only to women 18 and older, but after successful lawsuits by the Center for Reproductive Rights, the FDA, in 2013, announced that it would allow the pill to be available to all women.

While the FDA's decision was an advance for the United States, most other nations are not nearly so conservative. For example, public health clinics across the nation of Chile freely distribute the morning-after pill to women and girls age 14 and older. This policy was instituted by then-President Michelle Bachelet, a woman, because a very high percentage of Chilean girls were becoming pregnant by age 14. Bachelet's policy was strongly opposed by the Catholic Church, but a ruling by Chile's Supreme Court permitted distribution centered on the fact that the pill is not abortive, but works to inhibit ovulation, thus preventing fertilization (Ross, 2006). Interestingly enough, at the end of Bachelet's term in office, her approval rating was over 70 percent in Chile in large part due to her support of mothers and children's education programs (Llana, 2010).

No one knows for certain what the future will bring with respect to reproductive rights in the United States, but conservative judges across the nation appointed by then-President George W. Bush placed abortion rights in jeopardy. The election of Donald Trump placed abortion rights at further risk. Hostility of lawmakers toward women who become pregnant out of wedlock may help explain the government's paradoxical refusal both to fund abortions for poor women who want them and to help them finance raising the children Medicaid policies force them to bear. After all, lawmakers in the United States are overwhelmingly male.

One goal of welfare reform was to encourage single women to marry, in part by making marriage more economically imperative. However, research has found that the number of marriages per year actually declined after the 1996 PRWOA was passed (Campbell, 2004). We have much to learn about factors that lead to marriage. Economic desperation by legislation does not seem to be sufficient incentive.

As noted by Weissman (2014), for the millennial generation, childbirth out of wedlock is "the new normal." Among women under 30, over half of all births take place outside of marriage, although many young single mothers co-habit with partners. While marriage was once seen as the first step of adulthood, many young people today see it as one of the last, after a person attains financial security. Single women who view prospects for marriage or successful careers as very limited may see raising children as something meaningful they can do with their lives, despite the obvious challenges, financial and otherwise.

Ecological Concerns

Ecological research alerts us that not only are poor people at risk on this good earth, but all people are—in large part because the world's population is exploding. The population of the United States reached over 324 million in 2016, and the population of the world reached more than 7.3 *billion*. A net gain of one additional person in the world (births as compared with deaths) takes place approximately every 13 seconds ("U.S. and World Population Clock, 2016").

In addition to the danger of people outgrowing the food supply as farm lands succumb to housing and industry, the natural environment is in grave danger. Climate change is accelerating, due in part to high carbon emissions into the atmosphere from human use of fossil fuels. The average global temperature increased by more than 1.4 degrees Fahrenheit during the last century. The ice caps are melting, glaciers are receding, sea levels are rising, and oceans are becoming warmer and more acidic, threatening marine life.

Change in the average global temperature by even a degree or two has serious consequences. Crop yields are reduced, precipitation tends to occur in torrents causing flooding, and droughts and wildfires increase. The wildfires and flooding experienced to date are in accord with predictions for global warming, and scientists project that Earth's average temperatures will rise between 2 and 12 degrees Fahrenheit by 2100 ("Climate Change Facts," 2015). Major population disruptions will have to take place.

What must be done to save the environment so that the human species can survive? As of the time this chapter is being revised, the conservative-dominated U.S. Congress has continued to avoid the counsel of the vast majority of scientists to take action, but President Obama took up the challenge personally and worked directly with President Xi Jinping of China to try to slow climate change. The United States and China are the two major polluters in the world.

In November 2014, a historic agreement was reached between the two presidents to reduce carbon emissions in both nations. It was reaffirmed in September 2015. The agreement was not legally binding, but the hope was that by announcing specific targets, momentum would increase in worldwide global climate negotiations, hopefully leading to a successful outcome at the UN conference on climate change taking place in Paris in December 2015. And this is exactly what happened. An important agreement among 190 nations was reached in Paris. It was ratified by both the United States and China in September 2016 ("U.S.-China Joint Presidential Statement on Climate Change," 2015; Wernick, 2016).

Alarmingly, however, Donald Trump declared climate change a "hoax" during his campaign and vowed to cancel the Paris agreement, as well as to dismantle the U.S. Environmental Protection Agency "in almost every form" (Davenport, 2016).

Education and family planning services hopefully can allow the world population to stabilize through voluntary means. Population stabilization is desperately needed if our species is to survive (along with every other species). Many studies have shown that women with access to family planning services, educational opportunities, and rewarding careers decrease their family size voluntarily. The alternative has been demonstrated in China, where, beginning in 1980, a burgeoning population led the government to restrict families to a single child. The result was involuntary abortion, increased voluntary abortion, and infanticide. An alarming imbalance in the ratio of males to females was thus created: Chinese families restricted to one child tended to keep the male because the male child is expected to marry a wife who is expected to care for her husband's parents. By 2013, there was a shortage of *30 million* women of marriageable age. This created enough of a crisis that the government began to allow adults who were only children to

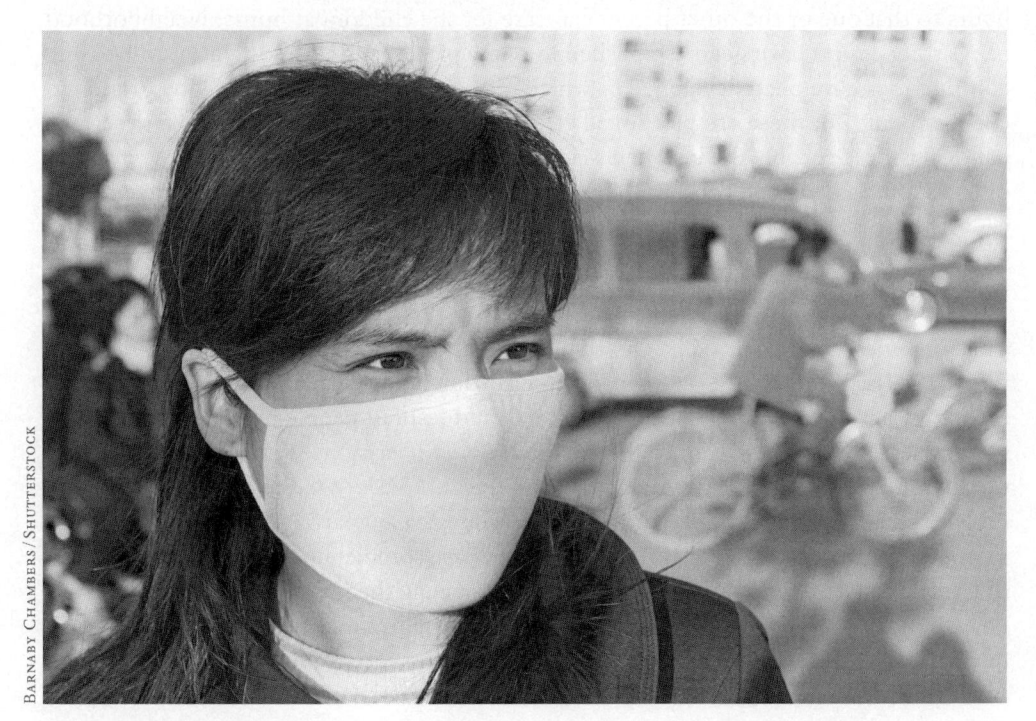

Masks to protect against air pollution are becoming increasingly necessary

have two children. Less than 20 percent of those eligible applied for the privilege soon after it became available, however. If the limited response continues, it will strengthen the data that women with access to education and economic opportunities tend to have fewer children voluntarily (Walsh, 2015).

The Child Care Conundrum

Over 70 percent of American mothers with children under 18 participate in the paid workforce today, and over 60 percent of those with children under 3 do as well. This is a huge change from previous generations. Yet there is no national system of child care in place, or even in the works. The reason relates to the ambivalence Americans still feel about working mothers. The Heritage Foundation and other conservative "think tanks" suggest that child care subsidies might further undermine the traditional family (presumably by making it easier for a mother to work outside the home). Yet conservatives are the very people who forced poor mothers into the paid work force. The contradiction is breathtaking.

Child care is expensive—more costly on average than in-state college tuition. The TANF program provides subsidies for very low-income women forced to work outside the home in some states, but these subsidies are not available in all states. And regardless of income level, the cost of childcare places an enormous strain on family budgets. Low-income workers spend approximately 40 percent of their earnings on child care, and married couples with greater means spend most of one parent's salary on it. Childcare fees for a family with two children are greater than the average cost of rent in all 50 states. Yet childcare workers themselves, usually women, are paid very low wages. Like the 40 percent of women who are their family's sole or major breadwinner, they struggle to make ends meet. The situation is unsatisfactory from every perspective (Hanes, 2015).

Families are creative, of course. Many husbands and wives stagger their working hours so that one or the other parent can care for the children at home. Neighborhood babysitting co-ops have been established in many places, and more than 100 co-housing communities have been developed in which residents share child care. Many grandparents help out. But these are piecemeal attempts to deal with a widespread and serious national issue. Probably the best news is that employers have begun to urge government officials to invest in child care. Employers have found that the most productive employees are those who are not distracted by child care worries (Haynes, 2015).

Gay and Lesbian Families

The Supreme Court legalized gay marriage throughout the United States in the *Obergefell v. Hodge* decision on June 26, 2015, in effect legalizing not only gay marriages but the formation of gay families. Marriage is a right **gay** and **lesbian** people had been fighting for state by state for decades. Prior to the Supreme Court's decision, 36 states and the District of Columbia had legalized gay marriage, and the 2012 *US v. Windsor* decision had previously ruled that the federal government must recognize gay marriages performed in states where they were legal. These new laws combined have completely changed the legal status of gay and lesbian persons in the United States, providing them with essential new rights.

Opponents of gay marriage utilized as part of their arguments against permitting gay marriage that, in their opinion, children of gay parents did not fare well. However, the American Sociological Association provided an amicus curiae ("friend of the court") brief for the *Obergefell v. Hodge* case. The overwhelming conclusion from methodologically sound research was that children being raised by same-sex parents achieved parity with children of heterosexual parents on multiple measures of well-being: cognitive development, academic achievement, psychological health, social development, early sexual activity, and substance abuse ("Same-Sex Marriage and Children's Well-Being," 2015). The NASW and several other organizations also submitted amicus curiae briefs supporting gay marriage. Thus, an important battle was won, but by a 5–4 decision only, indicating strong, mixed feelings around this issue even among Supreme Court Judges.

> How does this young woman's experience reflect and support (or refute) the research discussed in the text regarding the long-term well-being of children raised in same-sex households?
> https://www.youtube.com/watch?v=saD-c9D2zs0

Before-and-after comparison studies in states where legislatures legalized marriage found that among gay and lesbian persons, depression, adjustment disorders, and hypertension—conditions all related to stress—were significantly reduced once marriage was legalized (Novotney, 2014). Perhaps costs of medical and psychological treatment will diminish across the nation now that gay marriage has been legalized!

The legal battle with respect to marriage has been won, but prejudice against gays and lesbians by many fellow citizens will probably continue for a long time. A survey taken immediately after the *Obergefell v. Hodge* decision found that only 39 percent of Americans approved it (Crary & Swanson, 2015). Still, from previous research noted above, stress on families with gay members is likely to be reduced, and this is a very good thing.

How to become parents presents practical problems for both lesbian women and gay men. Adoption is a possibility for some. Those who want to become biological parents face a different challenge. Some women may ask male friends to consider becoming sperm donors, while others may turn to sperm banks. The use of medically administered sperm banks eliminates the potential danger of later court battles for parental rights (donors in medically controlled donor insemination programs waive parental rights and responsibilities), so many women prefer this option. Gay men, on the other hand, unless they or their partners have custody of children from prior heterosexual relationships, must find surrogate mothers. For them, the risk that a surrogate may later sue to gain custody is a real concern.

When the practice of artificial insemination was first begun, secrecy was practiced. Donor records were destroyed to protect the privacy of the adults involved. However, similar to adoptive children, some children conceived through artificial insemination wish to meet their biological fathers. Many sperm banks today provide an option for donors to be contacted by children once they have turned 18. Some require potential donors to grant grown children that right.

Unfortunately, **heterosexism** and **homophobia** are still very much alive in the United States. It is important that social workers maintain not only a broad cultural perspective but an understanding of the conditions in their own communities. While self-disclosure may help many gays and lesbians create a more integrated life, it can expose others to backlash and other dangers. Social workers who counsel gay and lesbian persons and their families need to understand the challenges this minority still faces and consider both empowerment and safety concerns.

The election of Donald Trump created fear and anxiety among gay and lesbian families. Trump, however, declared soon after the 2016 election that gay marriage was law and he had no plans to challenge the law. Trump's vice president, however, Mike Pence, has been a staunch anti-LGBT political crusader. In 2015, as governor of Indiana, Pence signed an anti-LGBT religious liberty law which could, among other concerns, permit a civil servant to refuse to issue a marriage license to a gay couple. When Pence was a member of Congress, he supported "**conversion therapy**." In a speech as a radio host, Pence asserted that marriage equality would lead to societal collapse, and declared that stopping gays from marrying was "God's idea" (Signorile, 2016). The Congress that was also elected in 2016, being even more conservative than the previous one, could ally with Pence to place gay rights at risk.

Fortunately, there are many organizations that fight for the rights of LGBT persons and families. Among them are the Human Rights Watch (HRA), the American Civil Liberties Union (ACLU), the National Black Justice Coalition (NBJC), and the Gay and Lesbian Alliance Against Discrimination (GLAAD). The Election of Donald Trump as president and Mike Pence as vice president alerted these and many other organizations about the serious work lying ahead to protect the rights of the LGBTQ community.

Multi-Racial Families

To the amazement of many today, only in 1967 did the U.S. Supreme Court legalize marriage between persons of different races throughout the nation. It had previously been banned in many states, especially in the South. Multi-racial families are now a growing part of the American scene. For the first time, in 2000, the U.S. census identified 7 percent of married-couple households as being interracial or interethnic, and the number increased to 10 percent by the time of the 2010 census (an inter-ethnic household refers to a household where both partners are of the same race but not of the same ethnic background, for example, where both partners are white but one is of Hispanic heritage). The number of interracial or interethnic households with unmarried partners was even larger according to the 2010 census at 18 percent; and was even higher for unmarried same-sex partners at 21 percent ("2010 Census Shows Interracial and Interethnic Married Couples," 2012). More that 15 percent of new marriages in 2010 were interracial (Yen, 2012).

The percentage of multi-racial children in the United States is growing rapidly; it increased by 32 percent in the 2010 census over the previous census. These children may encounter special challenges: The question "what are you" requires a skillful response. Teens especially may be pushed by peers to adopt part of their racial identity and reject another. Supportive parents can make an important difference in helping interracial children cope with a complex, sometimes hostile world.

On the positive side, multi-racial children are less likely to be subjected to stereotyping. They are resilient, and their mixed racial identity helps them develop empathy for others who are different, along with an appreciation for diversity. Social workers and other counselors can help multi-racial children develop pride in their dual heritage and identity (Grieg, 2013).

Interracial couples face special challenges; at least one set of in-laws may reject the chosen partner. Interracial couples may find themselves socially isolated not only from families of origin but from former friends. In response, many associate mostly with other interracial couples. Moreover, each partner brings different cultural expectations to the marriage, so role expectations may require skillful negotiation. Many couples meet these challenges successfully.

The modern family may be multi-racial

Intercultural adoptions involve a different set of challenges. They are usually opposed by people of color, especially African Americans and Native Americans, who believe that white parents cannot provide minority children appropriate exposure to their cultural heritage or teach them how to cope with discrimination in the wider society. Many children of color adopted by white parents in the United States today are born overseas. Special efforts must be made to help these children learn about their cultural heritage.

Immigrant Families

Immigrant families are growing in number and diversity in the United States and across the globe due to war, famine, poverty, and oppression. According to the United Nations Population Fund, the number of international migrants worldwide reached 232 million in 2013, a 33-percent increase over 2000 and fully 3 percent of the world's population. Their numbers increased substantially in 2014 and 2015, largely due to the war in Syria and climate change-related disruptions in Africa ("International Migration 2013," 2013; "International Migration Outlook 2016," 2016). Most migrants travel to developed countries.

Among the immigrants, people who achieve the legal status of "refugee" are perhaps the luckiest, as they have certain rights under the 1951 Convention relating to the Status of Refugees held in Geneva, Switzerland. The Convention was a response to the enormous displacement of people after World War II. Amended in 1967, it spells out who qualifies as a refugee; it grants legal protections and other assistance and includes a provision that a refugee cannot be forcibly returned to the country of origin ("The 1951 Convention," n.d.).

Unfortunately, those who are labeled "migrant" have no legal protection under international law. Yet many have been forced to leave their homes due to warlike conditions, ecological disasters, and virtual starvation. During 2015 alone, more than one million undocumented people migrated into Europe, almost half of them children, creating a crisis there. All would need to be assessed as to legal status, refugee or migrant. Many were escaping war-torn Syria and many were fleeing war-torn African nations or African regions reduced to starvation partly due to climate change, risking their lives to cross the Mediterranean Sea by means of smugglers. Thousands drowned due to inadequate, leaky, crammed vessels (Vick, 2015).

Today, nearly one-quarter of American children (24 percent) belong to families where at least one parent is foreign-born. Their numbers will inevitably increase in the future given unstable conditions around the world. Along with multi-racial families, immigrant families face myriad challenges although they differ in nature. Fathers often find that the vocational and educational skills they worked so hard to achieve in their nation of origin are not transferable to the United States. Financial need may require the wife to find a job to supplement the family income. In paid work settings, the wife may learn that gender roles in the United States allow more freedom to women and that she has new legal rights. She may begin to challenge the gender roles of her nation of origin, leading to marital strife.

Recent immigrant children, along with their parents, may be traumatized by their journey and tremendously confused by the new cultural mores they encounter. They may learn new languages faster than their parents, but serving as translators for parents can burden children by exposing them to adult issues before they are ready. They are likely to challenge their parents' authority at an early age, leading to family disruption. Family therapy can help family members appreciate each other's strengths, but immigrant families rarely seek out such services. This may be due to lack of information as well as cultural norms that teach that family issues should remain within the family (Delgado, Jones, & Rohani, 2005; "Immigrant Families," 2014).

Immigrant families often suffer poverty in their adopted countries, ironically among the very conditions they were trying to escape. While these families have high employment rates in the United States, their new jobs often provide very low wages. Unfortunately, changes to welfare benefits under the 1996 Personal Responsibility and Work Opportunity Act reduced the access of immigrant families to public assistance. Some states enacted new laws to help fill the gaps, but other states instead passed further restrictions on access to aid ("Immigrant Families," 2014). Thus, many immigrants in the United States struggle on their own.

To add to the struggles of immigrants families, Donald Trump insisted during his campaign that immigration of all Muslim persons be stopped. He pledged to deport all 11 million illegal immigrants already in the United States, and to withhold federal funds from "sanctuary cities" such as New York and Los Angeles (cities that shielded people residing in them illegally). Immigrants braced for trouble ("Sanctuary Mayors Revolt," 2016).

Military Families

Military families suffer special challenges. First and foremost, the family member serving in the military faces the very real risk of death, dismemberment, traumatic brain injury, or other serious physical injury. Anxiety about these possibilities, for both the service member and his or her family, arises even before deployment. Once the service member is deployed, both that member and the family left behind suffer serious stresses including separation anxiety and ongoing worry. The enlisted person may return home apparently uninjured but suffer invisible psychological damage that affects the entire family: post-traumatic stress disorder (PTSD) or other undiagnosed behavioral health disorders (see Box 5.7). According to Carter (2014), more than 50,000 men and women have been seriously wounded in action since 9/11, and an estimated one in five soldiers returns with PTSD or major depression. Given that over 2.5 million men and women have been deployed since 9/11, that is one whole lot of injured men and women.

Not only injured soldiers suffer from visible and invisible war wounds, but their families do as well. Over one million family members, usually young spouses or older parents, bear the burden of ongoing caregiving. Many struggle to manage both unpaid caregiving at home and paid work elsewhere. The burden can lead to strained family

Box 5.7 Coming Home

John Sanchez proudly enlisted in the army when he felt his country needed him, shortly after the attack on the World Trade Center in September 2001. He served two deployments in Iraq and two in Afghanistan. In each deployment, he saw friends blown up, literally, in whole or in part. He became hyper-alert to try to avoid a similar fate. John made it through his assignments without physical injury, and when he returned home after his fourth and final deployment, he was immensely relieved at first. His wife, Loretta, was overjoyed. But John became beset by guilt—why had he survived while several friends had not? He couldn't calm the hyper-alert mental state he had developed during his time overseas. He had difficulty sleeping because of nightmares and flashbacks, and he began to suffer both anxiety and depression so severe he considered suicide. Instead, to cope with his emotional pain, John self-medicated with alcohol and other drugs. Soon, minor habits of his wife that had never bothered him before triggered violent anger. One day, after drinking too much vodka, John got so angry at Loretta that he struck her several times and knocked her down. Loretta called the police as soon as she could get away, and John was arrested on a domestic abuse charge. A few weeks later, in a fit of rage, John beat Loretta severely, and this time she landed in the hospital. Loretta was traumatized, and John faced a possible prison sentence.

Fortunately, the judge who handled John's case was familiar with a condition haunting many returned veterans: post-traumatic stress disorder, or PTSD. John had the major symptoms: hyper-alertness, anxiety, depression, substance abuse, nightmares, flashbacks, and suicidal thoughts. So instead of prison, the judge sent John to a transitional home for veterans suffering from PTSD, established by a non-profit organization on the grounds of a VA hospital. There John received peer counseling from other returned veterans and from a social worker with special credentialing from the National Association of Social Workers for work with military families. The social worker counseled not only with John but Loretta, individually and together. Loretta was understandably afraid of John by now. Whether the marriage could be saved was an open question. A psychiatrist at the nearby VA hospital assessed John and prescribed medication to help relieve his anxiety and depression.

John had a very long road ahead of him for recovery, but he was one of the lucky ones. Transitional homes for veterans are few and far between, the result of private efforts, and peer counselors are the result of an executive order to the VA by President Obama. A combination of peer counseling, professional counseling by social workers and/or psychologists, and psychiatric assessment for medication provides the best possible route to recovery for returned veterans suffering from PTSD.

relationships, poor health for the caregiver as well as the injured veteran, and issues at the workplace (Carter, 2014).

Because of the need for mental health treatment for returned service men and women with PTSD as well as their families, social workers find many opportunities for employment in all branches of the service, the U.S. Department of Veterans Administration, and the U.S. Public Health Service. Social workers assess the needs of service members and their families, provide mental health treatment, crisis-intervention services, and high-risk management. They provide advocacy and education to veterans and their families. For these reasons, the NASW has developed a comprehensive set of standards for practice with service members, veterans, and their families, a free online five-course training module, and BSW and MSW professional credentials for work with military families ("NASW Professional Credentials," n.d.).

> **?** Assess your understanding of important family issues and family types by taking this brief quiz.

CULTURAL COMPETENCE

Diverse Family Structures

Social workers today frequently work with families to help strengthen the relationships among members, foster nonviolent parenting skills, assist in finding financial and material resources, help protect abused and neglected children, help arrange foster care, provide home studies for adoption, and the like. For this reason, it is very important that workers recognize, understand, and respect family diversity, whether ethnic, cultural, lifestyle, socioeconomic, or whatever. The NASW Code of Ethics specifically instructs social workers to learn about differences among people and to recognize that certain groups may suffer oppression through no fault of their own. Advocating for justice for these groups is also an important provision of the code.

The U.S. Census officially recognizes six racial groups: White, American Indian and Alaska Native, Asian, Black or African American, Native Hawaiian and Other Pacific Islander, and Hispanic or Latino. In addition to these groups are many others not recognized on the census form, and many persons belong to two or more races. Racial diversity is rapidly increasing in the United States due to world political and ecological conditions as discussed above, and along with racial diversity, ethnic and cultural diversity is also increasing to such an extent that no social worker can possibly develop expertise in every population group. Therefore, it is increasingly important for social workers to consult members of the populations they serve as expert informants, with the social workers as learners. Cultural competence involves knowledge of a given population's history, values, customs, and language. Since there are variations *within* populations as well, the worker's knowledge must constantly be refined and updated ("Racial and ethnic diversity in the US," 2015).

Carter and McGoldrick point out that diverse groups have very different cultural expectations relating to the family, including the importance attributed to different life-cycle transitions, intergenerational relationships, gender roles, and the like. For example, to consider only those of European background, the Irish place great emphasis on the wake, viewing death as the most important life-cycle transition. But Italian and

Polish families place greatest emphasis on the wedding. Jewish families emphasize the bar mitzvah and bat mitzvah, the transition to adulthood for boys and girls, respectively. With respect to intergenerational relationships, families of British heritage may feel they have failed if their children do *not* move away from the home as adults. Italian families may feel they have failed if their children do move away! Italian and Greek children are taught at an early age that it is their responsibility to care for their parents in old age. But older adults of British heritage tend to consider dependence on adult children a tragic situation (Carter & McGoldrick, 2005).

Diversity in America will continue to increase in the foreseeable future. It is estimated that by 2020, racial minority children combined will comprise a majority of all Americans under 18, and by 2044, racial minorities are predicted to comprise a majority of the overall U.S. population. No single racial or ethnic group is predicted to dominate in terms of size by that time (Chappell, 2015).

Spirituality and Religion

Social work literature has reflected an increasing interest in spiritual issues in recent years, and many social workers on the front lines have felt a growing need for a vision of society and the human person that transcends the material. In the United States, a person's worth is often measured in dollars only, and those who serve the less fortunate may experience a hunger to find a measure of human worth providing more dignity and hope.

Some find solace in traditional religions, but others look toward what can perhaps be a more all-embracing source of strength, **spirituality**. Spirituality can be defined most simply as the universal search for meaning and purpose. It is an aspect of humanity common to all: atheist, Christian, Jew, Buddhist, Muslim, traditional Native American, whomever. It involves a loving appreciation for all that exists, allowing almost mystical new perspectives, increasing one's understanding and ability to cope with human suffering (Lindsay, 2002).

Most Western educational institutions (with the possible exception of theological schools and departments) avoid any discussion of spiritual issues in the classroom. After all, Western science has "proven" that people are material only, that one's life ends at death, that the soul is a fictional concept, and so on. This worldview, espoused by Western science, is known as materialism. Meantime, sadly, traditional religions often battle one another trying to impose their particular non-materialistic interpretations of reality on others.

Spirituality shares much in common with religion, but does not claim any particular truth nor does it try to impose anything on others. Instead, spiritual seekers remain open to new understandings involving human capabilities and our place in the universe. Such seekers may or may not affiliate with a particular religious group.

Oddly enough, new understandings involving human capabilities and spirituality are emerging from an unexpected source: Western science! To be more specific, they are deriving from the work of a few courageous scientists who use Western scientific methods to prove that the Western scientific worldview of materialism is inadequate. These are the researchers into psychic phenomena (a field known as parapsychology). As asserted by psychologist (and parapsychologist) Dr. Charles Tart, one can be both a serious scientist and maintain a strong interest in psychic research. He writes that one can take a scientific stance toward life and, using rigorous kinds of scientific procedures, demonstrate properties of the human mind that underlie what is generally thought of as spiritual (Tart, 2009).

Psychic research has been ignored and/or ridiculed by mainstream science because psychic phenomena are considered impossible according to the Western worldview. Research funding is thus extremely limited. Still, an impressive amount has been accomplished. Tart considers research evidence for what he calls the "basic five" psychic phenomena—telepathy, clairvoyance, precognition, psychokinesis, and psychic healing—so strong that he describes them as "basic possibilities for humans" (Tart, 2009).

A series of books by Dr. Larry Dossey, physician of internal medicine, describes a number of modern, controlled, double-blind research studies that provide highly statistically significant evidence that prayer and/or human intention can promote healing—not only in humans (where a placebo effect, or the power of expectation, might confound these experiments) but in a variety of animals, bacteria, fungi, cancerous tissues, human brain cells, and enzyme preparations. Prayer has even been demonstrated to make plants grow faster. Focused human *intention* has been demonstrated to modify the output of random number generators in numerous research laboratories, and focused human *attention* has been demonstrated to modify the output of random number generators worldwide during major international events, for example during 9/11 (Dossey, 1989, 2003, 2008, 2013; Radin, 2006, 2013). Something demonstrably related to something non-material is happening in all these situations—but what?

Most of the preceding research has been ignored by mainstream scientists as it lies outside the Western scientific paradigm of thought, and no one has the slightest idea how or why the demonstrated effects happen. But regardless, it is important for social workers to understand that even though Western science may denigrate religion as delusion, there is strong evidence from controlled, double-blind research that materialism does not hold all the answers to existence. Moreover, research has demonstrated that people who practice their religion have better health and longer life expectancies than people who do not (Levin, 2001). Why shouldn't social workers then endeavor to understand and work with people's religious beliefs and practices, rather than ignore or, worse, disparage them?

Historically, much of what is considered "social work" today developed out of the work of religious institutions (the church provided the earliest "poor relief," for example), and many church bodies over time have created and/or provided financial support for social service agencies. Religion and social work share many similar goals, such as improving family relationships and promoting the welfare of communities. Therefore, assessing religious or spiritual aspects of a client's life only makes sense. Helping a client clarify religious or spiritual beliefs can assist in decision-making in other areas of a client's life. A salient example would be how to deal with a problem pregnancy. If the client's religious beliefs differ from that of the social worker, the worker can say something like "agency policy does not allow us to share our religious affiliation" in order to avoid conflict. The social worker's personal beliefs need not get in the way of assisting a client to explore his or her own perspectives, or to help the client utilize them in problem solving. Social workers should never attempt to convert a client, but rather help a client explore and clarify his or her own beliefs and values. Thus, it is important for the worker to gain as full an understanding as possible of a given client's beliefs and traditions to be able to best assist in working through the issues bringing the client to the worker. It may be appropriate to recommend spiritual books and / or to refer the client to a religious counselor if, on assessment, such referrals would seem helpful.

> **Assess your understanding** of cultural competence by taking this brief quiz.

FAMILY POLICY

Research Raises Questions

Is the United States meeting the needs of its children and families? While lip service is given to family values, few governmental supports exist to provide assistance to those in need. The result is unfortunate: for example, research data reveal that the United States falls far down the list of comparative infant mortality rates among western industrialized nations—it was twenty-sixth in 2010, below Hungary and Slovakia (MacDorman et al., 2014). There were slight gains by 2013, but infant deaths still registered at 596.1 per 100,000 births, only slightly below the 6.1 registered in 2010 (Kochanek et al., 2014). Since the year 2000, child poverty rates in the United States continued to rise until 2015, when they fell slightly; still, more than one child in five lived below the poverty level in 2015, with poverty rates much higher in families of ethnic minority heritage ("About Poverty-2014 Highlights," 2015; "New American Community Survey Statistics," 2016).

How do other nations help keep their children out of poverty? Many different approaches are taken, but virtually all Western industrialized nations except the United States provide universal health care. Many nations also provide universal, non-means-tested children's allowances to help keep families out of poverty in the first place, recognizing that children bring additional expenses to every family. Some countries provide an additional stipend if a non-custodial parent fails to keep up with child support payments. Many nations provide universal day care, either free or on a sliding scale. Others provide paid maternity and/or paternity leaves for as long as a full year, with the guarantee that one has a job when one is ready to return to work. Unfortunately, however, all these benefits are in jeopardy worldwide and have been diminishing for the past two decades, because of intense international competition among global corporations and trends in privatization of social services.

Research Informed Practice

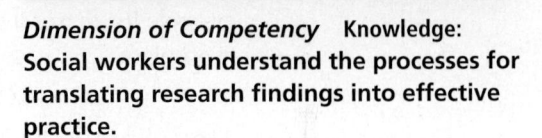

Dimension of Competency **Knowledge: Social workers understand the processes for translating research findings into effective practice.**

Critical Thinking Question: How can social workers utilize their knowledge of international research findings to work for improvements in American social welfare policy?

The good news is that government programs can make a difference to children and can help strengthen families. A distinct low point in U.S. child poverty rates was achieved in 1969, and it was not due to any accident, but rather was the result of the combined effects of important programs in the War on Poverty at that time. The War on Poverty was not lost because it could not be won, but rather because the money was diverted to the military budget and the conflict in Vietnam (Van Wormer, 1997).

The bad news is that the United States continues to use a huge proportion of its tax revenues to support the military and military action. "Guns vs. butter" has been the subject of persistent debate: Which is more important, military action or humanitarian aid at home and abroad? In recent years, guns have clearly trumped butter; the United States spends more on its military than *all* the other nations in the world *combined*. As a result, hunger and homelessness have been growing here, and the refugee population and other displaced persons in the world have also been growing.

In the United States, a network of emergency food providers has arisen to try to meet the ever-increasing need, such as Feeding America, mentioned in an earlier section. Other organizations such as the National Coalition for the Homeless have been trying to provide shelter in many places. Coalitions of churches have been working hard to try to meet hunger and shelter needs also, as described in Chapter 4's case study of the Rutherford family. But while the work of voluntary organizations is impressive, the fact that so many people are so poor today is quite an indictment of the values of the leadership of this country, currently the wealthiest nation in the world.

Research thus indicates a strong need for basics such as food and shelter for poor citizens in the United States. When President Obama was elected along with a Democratic House and Senate in 2008, an opportunity seemed to open for change in our nation's priorities. But with a huge budget deficit inherited from the Republican G.W. Bush administration; declining tax revenues due to the recession; and two ongoing, very expensive wars; the new administration started out with a huge handicap. President Obama was able to pass health care legislation in 2010 to help average Americans, but the country remained mired in war in Afghanistan and Iraq, and Obama later engaged in another war as well, this time in Libya. The frightening civil war in Syria taking place as this chapter is being revised, and continuing atrocities by ISIS (the Islamic State of Iraq and Syria) and other terrorist groups around the world continue to serve as catalysts for increased military spending.

Given the enormous ongoing costs of the military budget, and the promise of Donald Trump to lower taxes of the superrich, less money than ever will be available for social programs. Average Americans will be increasingly be on their own trying to provide for themselves and their families. Will they be able to meet their needs in the workplace?

How Family Friendly Is the American Workplace?

Given that the shrinking of government welfare programs is forcing more and more parents to work outside the home, the question of whether the workplace is family-friendly becomes increasingly important. Studies show, unfortunately, that the workplace in the United States has a long way to go.

Very important, of course, is the fact that the minimum wage is so low in the United States. A full-time worker earning minimum wage cannot support a family above the poverty line, and a low minimum wage tends to serve as an anchor to other wages and salaries. In 2015, the median income in the United States remained below pre-recession (2006) levels, and the middle class continued to shrink. While single mothers had already been forced into the job market by the TANF law, after the great recession many married mothers were forced into the paid job market as well (Trumbull, 2015).

Women in the workplace suffer special challenges. One involves the fact that they earn less than men in every job category; another involves pregnancy. A study by the

Center for WorkLife Law at the University of California–Hastings found that pregnancy discrimination lawsuits in the United States rose from 97 in 1996 to 481 in 2005 (Gardner, 2006). By 2007, they had increased to over 5,500 (Shellenbarger, 2008). Charges filed with the Equal Employment Opportunity Commission (EEOC) claiming employment discrimination against pregnant women increased by 47 percent between 1997 and 2011 (Walton, 2015).

Workplace discrimination lawsuits continue to increase today because a woman is all too likely to be transferred or terminated if she becomes pregnant, especially if she requests family leave. Men have also been terminated for requesting family leave. In addition, employers frequently refuse to consider women for promotion if they are pregnant or have young children. Few firms allow flexible schedules, crucial for parents with young children, or allow a new parent who has taken a leave to phase in the return to work.

The United States is unique in the Western industrialized world in that it does not require employers to provide *paid* parental leave under law. A former president of the NASW, Elvira Craig de Silva, reminded social workers in 2006 that the United Nations adopted two covenants in 1966 involving human rights, the International Covenant on Civil and Political Rights and the Covenant on Economic, Social, and Cultural Rights, that pertain to women and families. They include rights to liberty, health, and education and the right to work, protect one's family, and earn a decent standard of living. Because the United States has not lived up to these covenants, the NASW has become a partner of the ONE Campaign, a worldwide movement to end poverty (de Silva, 2006).

The National Organization of Women (NOW) is also trying to move the United States toward meeting the terms of these UN covenants, trying to achieve a more just nation and a more family-friendly workplace. When the United States filed a report with the United Nations claiming compliance with the International Covenant on Civil and Political Rights in October 2005 (10 years late), circumventing many issues such as prisoner abuse, domestic wiretapping, and infringement of civil liberties in the guise of fighting terrorism, this report asserted that American women have full protection under the law from sex discrimination. Disputing this assertion, NOW Foundation filed a "Gender Shadow Report" with the United Nations in July 2006, asserting the following:

- The U.S. government has failed to adopt effective laws that address persistent pay inequity for women.
- Laws against sexual harassment and discrimination in employment and education in the United States are inadequate and poorly enforced.
- Family support policies are seriously lacking in the United States, and their absence makes it nearly impossible for women to achieve equality in the workforce. Family and medical leave provisions are among the most unfriendly of all developed nations, providing only unpaid leave and requiring only about half of all employers to provide even this.

The effort to highlight U.S. problems such as these to the United Nations was successful: The UN Human Rights Commission's concluding observations on U.S. compliance, after considerable subsequent investigation, was that the commission was "especially concerned about the reported persistence of employment discrimination against women" (Erickson, 2006b, p. 17). The UN has persuasive powers only, however;

it cannot require a nation to reform. So far, the United States has not acted on the UN recommendations regarding its citizens who are women.

The Family and Medical Leave Act

As far back as 1993, during the Democratic Clinton administration, the Family and Medical Leave Act was passed to help families in which a medical condition, including pregnancy, necessitated a leave of absence. The act grants an eligible employee 12 weeks of unpaid leave during a 12-month period to deal with that employee's serious health condition or that of an immediate family member. The unpaid leave can also be granted for birth or adoption of a child.

Many employees and their families have benefited from this act, of course, but there are serious limitations. First, the leave is unpaid, making it an unrealistic option for many families. Moreover, the law only applies to companies with at least 50 employees. To be eligible, employees must have worked for the company for at least 12 months, and for at least 1,250 hours. Employers may require certification of medical need from a health care provider. Thus, many persons in need of a medical leave do not qualify under the Family and Medical Leave Act. Sometimes those who qualify are fired for asking.

There has been some slight movement toward family-supporting policies in a few of the American states: for example, California, New Jersey, and Rhode Island now offer paid family and medical leave. In all three states, the leave is funded through employee-paid payroll taxes and is administered through disability programs. Connecticut requires 40 hours of paid sick leave for private sector employers with 50 or more employees. Massachusetts adopted a paid sick leave law in 2014. Several states provide a limited number of hours for parents to attend school-related events and other activities for their children ("State and Family Medical Leave Laws," 2014) but the great majority do not.

The success of the family supporting policies in the states that have enacted them should provide incentive for other states to do the same, but so far little progress has been made.

Assisting Families Around the World

Fortunately, many of the best minds on earth today are concerned about worldwide issues of grave concern to the family. The United Nations has provided a forum where many of these minds can meet and work together. In 1990, a special committee created the UN Millennium Declaration, which established eight major goals. In 2000, a landmark agreement was achieved among leaders of developed nations to commit to achieving these goals, with 2015 set as the target date. The goals were as follows:

- Eradicate extreme poverty and hunger
- Achieve universal primary education
- Promote gender equality and empower women
- Reduce child mortality
- Improve maternal health
- Combat HIV/AIDS, malaria, and other diseases
- Ensure environmental sustainability
- Develop a global partnership for development

In 2015, the UN released *the Millennium Development Goals Report*. The report provided the encouraging information that progress had been made toward every goal: over one billion people were lifted out of extreme poverty; primary school enrollment in developing regions increased significantly; girls now received as much education as boys in most developing nations; global infant mortality declined by over 50 percent and maternal mortality by 45 percent; over seven million deaths from AIDS were prevented through distribution of anti-viral therapy; access to clean water and sanitation facilities substantially improved in most developing countries; and assistance to developing nations from the developed nations increased by 66 percent, reaching over $135 billion in 2015. Access to the Internet increased from only 6 percent of the developing world's population in 2000 to 43 percent in 2015, and the number of cell phone subscriptions skyrocketed.

As pointed out by then-UN Secretary-General Ban Ki-Moon, all this progress proves that nations working together can make an enormous difference improving conditions in the world. However, the Secretary-General also pointed out that while progress has been made toward reaching the millennium goals, the goals were not fully achieved. In 2015, women continued to endure job discrimination and earned 24 percent less than men globally. Maternal mortality deaths were four times higher than in developed nations. At least 800 million people still endured extreme poverty and hunger. Over 16,000 children died before their fifth birthday, mostly from preventable diseases. Risks of all kinds were much higher for people living in rural areas. Major conflicts worldwide increased: For example, every day in 2015, 42,000 people were forced to leave their homes to seek protection, almost four times higher than the number in 2010. By the end of 2014, conflicts had pushed fully 60 million people out their homes.

While some ecological advances were made—for example, ozone-depleting substances were virtually eliminated and the number of protected marine and terrestrial areas increased significantly—climate change and environmental degradation continued at a dangerous rate. Global emissions of carbon dioxide increased by more than 50 percent between 1990 and 2015.

According to Secretary-General Ban Ki-Moon, unfinished business will not be abandoned. A post-2015 agenda is emerging at the UN and will be discussed in Chapter 13. The new agenda, while addressing many concerns, highlights the importance of preserving the natural environment. Strengthening data production will be crucial to measure ongoing needs and to monitor progress toward unmet goals ("The Millennium Development Goals Report," 2015).

Current Trends in the United States

A major concern of the American family today is the fact that many middle- and working-class families still struggle to make ends meet. While conditions have improved since the Great Recession beginning in 2008, wages have continued to stagnate so that breadwinners lucky enough to find work often need to hold more than one job to support their families. Many families require two full-time earners to meet their needs. However, many families lack two full-time earners—the single-parent family has become almost the norm. In 1970, fully 40 percent of U.S. households were comprised of married partners with a child under 18; by 2012 only 20 percent fit that description (Trumbull, 2015).

National economic policy strongly affects family welfare. For example, when G.W. Bush took office as president in 2001, he had major political obligations to wealthy businessmen, the religious right, and the National Rifle Association, among other conservative constituencies that financed his campaign. Thus, he proposed and was able to pass substantial tax cuts favoring the wealthiest of Americans. His spending on war-related efforts exploded over the years, creating enormous budget deficits.

As a result of G.W. Bush policies favoring big business, income inequality grew at an alarming rate during his administration. The top 1 percent of households tripled their income and gained ownership of one-third of the wealth and 40 percent of all financial assets in the United States (Yule, 2006).

The Obama administration was unable to reverse the Bush tax laws because of conservative opposition in Congress, and Congress refused to raise the minimum wage as well. One sad result: By 2014, according to the most recent figures available, CEOs earned *303 times* the salary of the average, non-management employee. Before the sun rose on Jan. 2, the CEO had already earned his or her average employee's entire annual salary (Bump, 2016).

When President Obama took office in 2009, the Democratic president and Democratic Congress made some immediate important changes to help American families: For example, childcare subsidies were increased for low-income families, emergency aid was made available for struggling homeowners, increased loans were made available to university students, and the *gag rule* was quietly removed from federally funded family service agencies (allowing workers to discuss abortion with pregnant women as a possible option, banned during the Bush administration). Congress passed and Obama signed the Lilly Ledbetter Law, bolstering the possibility of improving pay equity between men and women. The Affordable Health Care Law was passed. Military spending, however, continued to increase due to the aggressions of the Islamic State, limiting the funds available for social programs.

An article by Trumbull (2015) listed several ongoing challenges for American families in 2013, the most recent figures then available. For example, health insurance costs were rising in spite of President Obama's Affordable Care Act. Average working age households had less wealth (assets minus liabilities) than two decades earlier, and they had less than a month's savings to fall back on in case of lay-off. The result was ongoing anxiety for many Americans. This anxiety was perhaps the reason why so many Americans voted for "change" in the 2016 presidential election, regardless of what kind of change they were likely to get. They elected a superrich businessman, a conservative who supported tax reductions for the rich, opposed social programs helping people in need, and frequently expressed disdain for minority populations.

For poor Americans in need, voluntary organizations will still probably provide emergency food and shelter for some. Small privately run programs, such as the one helping the Rutherford family in Chapter 4's case study, can be tailored to meet specific needs of specific communities. They may be supported by grants from governments or private foundations. However, such efforts are fragmented, without dependable funding, and not available to all who need them.

> **?** Assess your understanding of family policy by taking this brief quiz.

SUMMARY

- Evidence, historical and contemporary, for the need for child protective services is described. Children are often abused. The causes are many, including substance abuse by the parents and the ongoing stresses of poverty. Historically, the first efforts to help abused children came from private citizens, later from voluntary organizations, even later from governmental agencies and programs, and finally from international law.
- Seven in-home social work services for families in need and five out-of-home services are listed and described. In-home social work services for families in need include financial services, family life education, homemaker services, day care, family therapy, protective services, and family-based services. Out-of-home services include foster care, group homes, adoption, institutional care, and the judicial system.
- Four important family issues and four special family forms or types are identified and discussed. Important family issues include attachment theory and emotional bonding, reproductive rights and single parenting, ecological concerns, and the childcare conundrum. Special family forms or types include gay and lesbian families, multi-racial families, immigrant families, and military families.
- Cultural competence and why it is so important in social work practice is explained. Cultural competence can be especially challenging for social workers because there is so much diversity in the United States. It involves knowledge of the culture's language, customs, values, and history. Social workers are urged to view themselves as learners and to consult with the people they serve as the experts.
- Several shortcomings of contemporary American family policy and how certain findings of the United Nations pertain to American women are described. Shortcomings of American family policy today include the fact that the minimum wage is not family-supporting, there is little flexibility of hours in the workplace and no national day care program, and the Family and Medical Leave Act can help few families as it is unpaid and applies only to companies with at least 50 employees. The United Nations is working worldwide to reduce poverty and has met with some success. Its findings indicate that the United States has inadequate laws protecting women from employment discrimination.

> ✓ Recall what you learned from this chapter by completing the Chapter Review.

6
Social Work in Mental Health

LEARNING OUTCOMES

- Explain the competencies that are needed by social workers who work in mental health settings.
- Explain how social workers in mental health apply their generalist practice knowledge and skills across social systems.
- Discuss the social, economic, and environmental issues that relate to mental health globally.
- Trace social policy related to mental health from the colonial period of the United States to the present, paying special attention to progress within the last decade and continuing concerns for the future.

CHAPTER OUTLINE

CASE STUDY: Meet David Deerinwater 160

Social Work Competencies for Mental Health Practice 163
 Basic Competencies: Knowledge and Skills 163
 Values and Ethics 166
 Knowledge Related to Mental Health Practice 167

Generalist Practice in Mental Health 172
 Case Management 172
 Working with Groups 174
 Community Practice 176
 Disaster Services 176
 Practice with Diverse Populations 178
 Native American History and the Cherokee Experience 179

CASE STUDY: Meet David Deerinwater

Roberta Sholes, a BSW with several years of experience at the Oklahoma State Mental Health Center, had just returned from vacation in the eastern part of the state, where she had visited Oklahoma Indian country. Now she would be working with a newly admitted Cherokee man who was from that area. Psychiatric staffings (interdisciplinary patient care meetings) always excited Roberta's interest, but today she was especially eager to meet David Deerinwater, her new client.

Sadly, the first of the five persons discussed by the team was a young woman who was critically ill following an aspirin overdose. Next was a 55-year-old attorney who had been readmitted following an episode of frenetic behavior; he had discontinued taking the medication prescribed for his bipolar disorder. Following him were two elderly women who had been admitted with severe depression. Then the psychiatric resident who had admitted David Deerinwater began by sharing what he knew about his case.

David Deerinwater had come to Tulsa from a ranch in the Goingsnake District of Oklahoma about 10 years ago in search of employment. Living in a series of one-room, inner-city apartments, he sustained himself with odd jobs and some janitorial service work; he had few social contacts, although he seemed to identify strongly with his tribal people. David had been living on the streets for at least six months and seemed to have no possessions and no family or friends in the city. Increasingly isolated, his energy seemed to decline, and he lost weight. On admission, speech was of a muttering, incoherent quality, and his gestures suggested that he might be hearing voices. David voluntarily admitted himself to the hospital through the assistance of a social worker from the hot-meal site where he had obtained food for the past six months. The admitting diagnosis was schizophrenia, a severe form of mental illness.

As David Deerinwater was being wheeled into the staff meeting, Roberta was startled to see the cold, distant expression in his dark eyes. He stared straight ahead and was completely unresponsive to the questions that were asked, yet Roberta sensed that he had some awareness of what was happening around him. After he left, it was confirmed that Roberta would be the social worker for David.

When Roberta went to see David later in the day, she found him in his wheelchair on a sunporch, staring at the trees and park area beyond the window. She was pleased when he motioned her to sit down. Remembering the quiet pride of the Cherokee men she had seen, Roberta sat beside him for a time, not speaking. After a while and without turning to her, he asked, "Well, what do you want?" It was a good sign that he acknowledged her presence, and Roberta was pleased. She explained simply that she wanted to help. He replied, "That is not possible." Roberta then introduced herself slowly and said again that she wanted to help. Several minutes passed before he replied, "Then you will help me to get out of here." Roberta told David that she would need his help for that and that she would work with him to accomplish it. She wasn't sure he heard her. He no longer seemed aware of her as he stared into the distance.

The next morning, David Deerinwater greeted Roberta with an almost imperceptible wave of his hand. She again sat quietly beside him. Then, because it was a beautiful, warm day, Roberta asked David if he would like to go outdoors with her for a few minutes. For a moment, his expression appeared to be one of startled disbelief. Then a somber, closed expression again came over his face, but he nodded assent. Roberta wheeled his chair outdoors and across the carefully tended lawn to the shade of the ancient catalpa trees. David inhaled deeply. He was silent, perhaps more peaceful than she had seen him previously. Roberta began telling him about the hospital, its location, its purpose (to help people get well and return to their homes), and the staff and how they worked together. Again, Roberta stressed that she would need his help, adding that she needed to understand about his life, his growing up years, and his family. Again David nodded his head, acknowledging that he understood, but he added, "I am very tired now."

The following morning Roberta was surprised to find David Deerinwater waiting for her at the nurse's station. He was no longer using a wheelchair, she noted. She took him to the sunporch. Once there, he spoke: "You said that you could help me to get out of here." She replied that was just what she aimed to do, but that she wanted to be sure that he was feeling better and that he would have a place to go. He replied, haltingly, that he was eating and sleeping better now, but he was feeling cooped up and

> **CHAPTER OUTLINE** *(Continued)*
>
> **Social, Economic, and Environmental Justice Issues** 181
>
> **Social Policy and Mental Health** 182
>   Historical Perspectives 183
>   The Social Work Profession Emerges 184
>   Evolving Social Policy Affects Service in Mental Health 185
>   Policy and Practice: Future Issues 187
>
> **Summary** 189

didn't think he could stay much longer. Although he was not an easy person to interview, Roberta appreciated the quiet dignity beneath David's cool, distant gaze. She tried not to hurry him as she gently asked about his family and his experiences as a child.

Slowly and somewhat hesitatingly, over the next half hour, David gave Roberta a picture of his youth in the Goingsnake District, including memories of stomp dances (social events centering on spiritual dances), green corn feasts in the fall, and much hard work on the ranch. He spoke, too, of having been sent to boarding school with other Indian children and of the pain he felt when teachers spoke degradingly of Cherokee Indian life and reprimanded the children for speaking in their Cherokee language. He recounted serene times with family as well as hardship and poverty. David's father had been chronically ill with diabetes and had died when David was 16. Joe, three years older than David, had taken on major responsibilities for his mother, David, and three younger girls. The family had relied on help from friends and neighbors and had worked their small ranch and summer garden; that was how they had survived. Roberta realized that David was beginning to develop some trust in her when he willingly signed a form giving Roberta permission to share information about him with his family and with the Health and Social Services Department of the Cherokee Nation.

Roberta had not worked with a Cherokee Indian before, and she realized that she would need to acquire a better understanding of this ethnic group before she could adequately assess David's situation and begin to develop a plan with him for life within and beyond the hospital. She telephoned the Health and Social Services Department of the Cherokee Nation and found that Dorothy White, one of the social workers in the office, knew the Deerinwater family. Dorothy offered to drive to their small ranch and ask David's mother to telephone Roberta the next day from the Cherokee Nation office because the family had no phone. She also volunteered to send Roberta information about the Cherokee Nation's services. She suggested it might be important to David's potential recovery, both physically and mentally, that he return to his home. She said she suspected that he really needed to be back with his people and in his natural environment where he would be understood and cared for by his family. Through the Cherokee Nation clinic, he could receive medical, rehabilitative, and mental health services that incorporated the beliefs and values of the Cherokees. She explained that the clinic offered group services, for example, that helped people come together to achieve harmony with each other, the community, and the natural world.

Dorothy White proved to be extremely helpful. When she called Roberta the next day, she had both David's mother and Joe, David's brother, in her office. David's mother was very eager for news about her son. She was especially concerned about David's weakness and nutritional state, and she concluded by saying, "We will bring him home. He needs to be with his people." Roberta explained that David was not yet well enough to leave the hospital and that he would have to determine for himself whether he wished to return home or remain in Tulsa. For now, however, he needed to gain strength and to continue taking his medication. David's mother replied that she knew what he would eat; she would cook for him. Then Joe Deerinwater came to the phone and said that he and his wife would drive to the city the next day. They would stay with friends and could visit David daily. They would bring food prepared by his mother. Roberta replied that she would be eager to see them.

In the days that followed, David Deerinwater benefited greatly from the visits of family members, and his nutritional status improved considerably. He also seemed to be responding well to his psychotropic medication, the drugs prescribed by doctors to improve his mental functioning. Although increasingly coherent, he remained isolated, interacting minimally with other patients. Roberta explained to the staff that David, like most Native Americans, did not engage readily in frivolous social conversation and would be unlikely to socialize unless he had a reason to do so. He also was probably quite frightened of the institution. Roberta had learned to adjust her own sense of time when speaking with David, and she had learned to respect periods of silence. She worked with other staff, too, to help them communicate more effectively with him. As David became increasingly coherent, Roberta encouraged him to talk with the nurses, dieticians, and medical staff about his home community and the Cherokee culture.

In the next staff meeting, the psychiatric resident described David's response to medication as being very good. The psychologist's summary of the psychological testing he had completed supported the early diagnosis of schizophrenia. The staff were very interested in Roberta's assessment and her recommendations of post-discharge planning. Roberta provided a social history of David within the context of his family, his ethnic community, and his sense of unity with nature. Roberta stated that she was not as convinced as the other team members that David's mental illness was as serious as the diagnostic label, schizophrenia, suggested. He was much more oriented to reality than was usual for persons with schizophrenia. She explained the perspective of the Cherokee Nation Health Center that often behaviors that are appropriate in one culture (such as an Indian's seeing signs in birds or the sky) are considered to be very inappropriate, sometimes even to be indicators of mental illness, in another culture. She agreed to take responsibility for helping David, his family, and his home community to plan for post-hospital care.

Fourteen days after admission, David Deerinwater was released. His discharge diagnosis remained schizophrenia. David wanted to return home to live with his mother, but he would be receiving follow-up care from the Cherokee Nation Health Center, which provided a full range of mental health services, including access to tribal spiritual healers. He could also see the vocational rehabilitation counselor at the Cherokee Nation about future employment and career options. Roberta was satisfied that David would receive social work services and health care that respected his cultural heritage.

As she said farewell to David, Roberta thought about the Cherokee people and the Deerinwater family. She realized how much she had learned from this person, his family, and community and how much they had enriched her life.

SOCIAL WORK COMPETENCIES FOR MENTAL HEALTH PRACTICE

Basic Competencies: Knowledge and Skills

We open this chapter by introducing you to a sample of social work practice in the very broad field of mental health. Just a reminder: Baccalaureate-level generalist practice is the focus of this text, but the text depicts the entire profession as well. In the Chapter 6 case study, the social worker is a BSW, a generalist. If the case study had described an MSW, more advanced counseling, **psychotherapy**, might have been described. You will encounter case studies in other chapters of this book that feature MSW social workers. This chapter begins with an overview of the competencies (the knowledge, values, and skills) needed for work in mental health at all levels of practice. Case management is described as well as work with groups and communities. You will read about issues related to social justice in the mental health field and environmental dimensions of practice. Practice with culturally diverse populations will carry forward the insights gained from the David Deerinwater case study, and you will learn about the historical experiences of Native American people, especially the Cherokee, in the United States. We conclude the chapter with an overview of past and current social policy decisions that have impacted the nature of mental health services within our country.

Roberta Sholes is a good example of a competent generalist BSW social worker. Pay attention to the interviewing skills she demonstrated. Notice how she spoke quietly, gently, and slowly to David Deerinwater, helping him focus on her words. She reassured him yet confronted him with reality. Notice how Roberta's respect for the culture of the Cherokee people and of Cherokee family life were so evident in her interviews with the Deerinwater family and in the action she took to involve the Cherokee community in David's mental health care.

To prepare for a career in mental health, Roberta might have had a field placement in a mental health setting while earning her BSW degree. If she did not, there is a good likelihood that any field placement would present opportunities to work with people who are experiencing mental or emotional problems. BSW social workers are not expected to take responsibility for complex psychotherapy; that is the role of MSWs. If Roberta decided that she would like to become a therapist, she would need to pursue a master's degree. The MSW curriculum also has a generalist practice base, but most MSW programs provide an opportunity to complete a concentration in mental health or clinical social work. State licensure is also required for MSWs to practice psychotherapy. MSWs routinely provide individual, family, and group therapy as well as marriage counseling. They may also be found in administrative positions in mental health hospitals and clinics. In some parts of the United States where MSWs are in short supply, BSWs assist and sometimes even assume major responsibilities for therapeutic work, especially in state hospitals and with persons who have persistent and major **mental disorders**. BSWs, however, do not claim to be psychotherapists, and they are alert to situations that require assistance from or referral to someone with advanced expertise.

In mental health settings, social workers find that, as a professional group, they have certain advantages. Their professional education prepares social workers with competence in practice behaviors and roles such as advocacy, accessing referral resources, treatment, and crisis intervention. Social workers' professional demeanor in their communication skills and interdisciplinary teamwork is respectful of clients and colleagues, and often it affords access to leadership positions in mental health organizations.

Mental health crises or emergencies are not uncommon in social work practice across all possible settings; therefore, BSWs as well as MSWs need to have ability to work with people with a wide range of problems. The BSW curriculum teaches interviewing skills and how to use the problem-solving process. These skills are used when

BSWs in mental health settings provide crisis intervention and as they work with the families of patients and counsel persons individually and in groups. Like Roberta Sholes in the case study, they serve as the hospital's link to the community, teaching its staff about the population while offering preventive mental health education within the community.

In many community-based programs, BSWs carry important responsibilities for people who are chronically mentally ill. Dorothy White, the social worker in the Cherokee Nation's Health and Social Services Department, was also a BSW; she provided advocacy, counseling, and case management services to Cherokee families. After David Deerinwater's discharge from the hospital, Dorothy or another social worker in the department would serve as his case manager. A **case manager** coordinates and ensures that all the services needed by a client (medical, financial, legal, etc.) are, in fact, provided. Case managers must be skilled both in working within the community and in working individually with lonely, isolated, and sometimes resistant persons. The generalist preparation of BSWs—especially their courses in practice methods and field experience—prepares them with the knowledge and skills they need for the diverse and challenging practice responsibilities they can expect to have in the mental health field.

Psychotherapy is the realm of the MSW. In the past, a social worker who was qualified to engage in psychotherapy was called a psychiatric social worker. Today the term used most often is **clinical social worker**. The National Association of Social Workers (NASW) expects social workers who engage in private practice of psychotherapy to be recognized by the Academy of Certified Social Workers (ACSW) at a minimum. As Chapter 1 noted, social workers can also earn the advanced practice NASW credential, the Qualified Clinical Social Worker (QCSW), after 4,500 hours of post-MSW clinical experience. The Diplomate in Clinical Social Work (DCSW) is reserved for social workers who have completed three years of clinical practice beyond the 4,500 hours required by the QCSW (National Association of Social Workers, 2015). State licensure is required for clinical social workers.

> **Engagement**
>
> *Dimension of Competency* Values: Social workers value the importance of human relationships.
>
> **Critical Thinking Question:** What kinds of healing did you see in the social worker's role with David Deerinwater and his family? How will this be sustained following his discharge from the hospital?

All social workers in mental health settings, whether BSWs or MSWs, are responsible for collecting and assessing data that contribute to the mental health team's diagnosis and understanding of individual people in relation to mental health. These social workers are responsible, too, for creating intervention plans in collaboration with people, for implementing the intervention, for monitoring and evaluating the outcomes, and for terminating relationships with clients. Knowledge of the community and its resources is one of social work's unique contributions to the mental health team. The social worker also brings to the team an understanding of social policy and its impact on programs that exist and programs still needed to prevent and treat mental illness. An understanding of and sensitivity to the culture or lifestyle of diverse groups is another contribution made by social workers in mental health settings. In sharing knowledge about cultural practices, evolving social policy issues, or even community resources, social workers continually educate others.

Values and Ethics

Knowledge and skills alone, however, do not make a good social worker. A third dimension is essential: values and ethics. Social workers demonstrate integrity when their personal values and behaviors are compatible with those of the profession. Professional social work values and the NASW Code of Ethics require attention to and respect for the uniqueness and intrinsic worth of each person. The first standard in this code of ethics states that the primary responsibility of social workers is promoting the well-being of the people they serve. This may not be as readily achieved as it initially appears. Clients are not always lovable and their behaviors and appearance may be challenging to us. Chapter 6 will later discuss a form of prejudicial behavior, **stigma**, directed toward people with mental disorders. Although this is clearly not consistent with social work values and ethics, recent research has shown that some social workers, along with other mental health practitioners, are among the professional people that hold negative stereotypes of persons with mental disorders (Sickel, Nabors, & Seacat, 2014).

> Watch this clip of CNN news personality Anderson Cooper as he engages in an exercise to experience the auditory effects of schizophrenia. Although he is not a social worker, how does his experience reflect the social work value of empathy as it relates to working with individuals with mental illness?
> https://www.youtube.com/watch?v=yL9UJVtgPZY

Social workers, instead, should empower clients and encourage them to be as self-directing as possible. They should carefully respect privacy and confidentiality. Their professional ethics compel social workers to go even further. They urge social workers to work to make social institutions more humane and more responsive to people's needs. Because our society tends not to respect the mentally ill, especially those who are chronically ill, social workers often have to advocate on behalf of the mentally ill. Within their communities and within the health care institutions that employ them, social workers attempt to create an environment that deals humanely with persons who are mentally or emotionally ill.

In this chapter's case study, Roberta Sholes demonstrated much sensitivity for David Deerinwater as a client. Her respect for his uniqueness and worth led her to learn more about Native American ethnicity. Even if she believed that returning to his home community was in David's best interests, she did not force this plan on him. Instead, she engaged him in making decisions about his own post-hospital care, thus respecting his right to self-determination. Roberta demonstrated compliance with the NASW Code of Ethic's requirement of confidentiality, which she demonstrated by obtaining his written permission before sharing information with his family or other agencies.

Ethical and Professional Behavior

Dimension of Competency Cognitive & Affective Reactions: Social workers understand how their personal experiences and affective reactions influence their professional judgment and behavior.

Critical Thinking Question: How do social workers balance their personal values and beliefs with professional ethics in the mental health field when, for example, clients are verbally offensive?

Few professions stress values in the way that social work does. This is especially apparent when a social worker practices in a **secondary setting** (one in which social work is not the primary function), such as mental health. Schools and courts are other examples of secondary settings. Not only do social workers in secondary settings need conviction about their values, but they also need to acquire an understanding of the primary function of the setting that they are in. In fieldwork courses and on the job, social workers learn about the organizational context in which they work.

Increasing use of technology raises ethical challenges. Some loss of control over confidentiality can occur when groups meet online. Confidentiality agreements or contracts are useful in clarifying parameters for sharing of private information, but this remains somewhat more challenging than when groups meet in person. Personal, private identifying information can be protected with increasingly effective software safeguard programs; however, the frequency and success of hackers is of concern in protecting client privacy.

Knowledge Related to Mental Health Practice

Interprofessional Collaboration

The settings in which social workers are employed almost always require an additional layer of knowledge and skills. Because social workers are flexible and tend to move from one area to another during their professional careers, they have a splendid opportunity to acquire a rich array of specialized knowledge. In mental health, social workers must learn how to work effectively in multi-disciplinary teamwork relationships. The traditional mental health team consists of a psychiatrist, a psychologist, a psychiatric nurse, and one or more social workers. Roles overlap considerably in mental health. Many of the team members provide psychotherapy, often as co-therapists in family and group therapy. Team members also perform unique functions (see Box 6.1). The traditional team may be supplemented by speech, recreational, art, and occupational therapists. Teachers are an added component in children's mental health programs.

In addition to direct work with the consumers of mental health services, the roles for social workers in mental health have expanded considerably to include administration of mental health programs; discharge planning; case management; and, of course, therapy for individuals, families, and groups. It is not surprising, then, that mental health teams often comprise several social workers but just one psychiatrist, one psychologist, and one or two nurses.

In our case study, the psychiatric facility's mental health team consisted of the following professionals:

Box 6.1   Social Work in Mental Health: The Traditional Mental Health Professional Team

- *Psychiatrists* prescribe medication. They hold the MD (doctor of medicine) degree and have additional training in psychiatry. Some also engage in psychotherapy.
- *Psychologists* administer and interpret psychological tests. They generally hold the PhD degree in clinical psychology. Clinical psychologists may provide psychotherapy as well as testing.
- *Psychiatric nurses* have training in nursing, which enables them to administer prescription medications, give injections, and assist in various other medical procedures. They generally hold a master's degree in nursing; however, in some regions of the country, nurses with a baccalaureate degree in nursing (BSN) serve on mental health teams.
- *Social workers* have specialized knowledge about community resources. They generally obtain the social history of a patient (a chronology of the individual's life events related to a potential mental health problem), which assists the team in arriving at a diagnosis and a treatment plan. Both BSWs and MSWs function as members of the mental health team; MSWs carry primary responsibility for psychotherapy, but both BSWs and MSWs provide counseling, facilitate groups, and provide case management.

- The chief psychiatrist, who served as team leader, conducted staffings, supervised residents, wrote prescriptions, and did some individual therapy.
- Three psychiatric residents, who were assigned for a six-month period. (Because they were students, they carried a limited number of cases and were under the supervision of the chief psychiatrist.)
- Two psychiatric nurses, who administered all nursing and bedside care of patients, participated as co-therapists in group therapy, and supervised student nurses.
- Three MSWs and one BSW, who provided individual, family, and group therapy; obtained social histories; and linked the hospital with the community.
- One clinical psychologist, who administered and analyzed psychological tests and engaged in individual, family, and group therapy.

The mental health team in the case study was fairly typical of the teams in teaching hospitals. In hospitals that are not connected with a university medical school and in community practice, the mental health team often has no medical or nursing students and, hence, is much smaller. Considerable effort is required to keep a team in any setting functioning smoothly, for friction is inevitable when professional roles overlap. Team members learn quickly that they need to understand the perspectives of other professionals who make up the mental health team.

Understanding the DSM

Social workers in mental health settings clearly need a common language that is shared by the other team members when discussing mental disorders. Thus, they need to be able to use the terminology of the current psychiatric mental disorders classification system. Students are generally introduced to the classification system as part of their course work. Becoming truly adept at its use occurs with practice experience in a mental health setting and with advanced study and professional development.

The system widely used in the United States to diagnose and teach about mental disorders was created and published by the American Psychiatric Association (APA) as the *Diagnostic and Statistical Manual of Mental Disorders (DSM)*. The 2013 version of this manual is known as the *DSM-5*. It incorporates a numerical coding system that is used to identify mental disorders. The *International Classification of Diseases (ICD)* is a categorization of mental disorders developed by the World Health Organization that is used by most countries outside the United States. The multi-national, research-based thinking that characterizes *DSM-5* is closely aligned with the *ICD* (American Psychiatric Association, 2013). The *DSM* helps us to understand that it isn't people who are diagnosed; their disorders are. So it is not correct to speak of a *schizophrenic*, but it is appropriate to refer to a *person with schizophrenia*.

In recent years, a great deal has been learned about how the human brain functions physiologically. Building on this knowledge, researchers of multiple disciplines are now exploring the impact of our biological and genetic makeup, our physical and social environments, and also our emotions and our thinking as these evolve into the human behavior that is seen by others as mental health or mental illness. DSM-5 is refreshing in its understanding that mental disorders are not entirely distinct and discrete but, instead, often share behaviors and may evolve over time even within the same person. That makes diagnosis more complex than in the past, but it explains why a person's diagnoses may change over time or be different across mental health professionals. Psychiatrists, psychologists, counselors, social workers, rehabilitation therapists, nurses, art therapists, and physical therapists are among the professions that utilize the *DSM* to understand the nature of mental disorders. The *DSM* does not determine how to treat mental disorders, but research pertaining to treatment is closely linked to the *DSM*.

In this chapter's case study, David Deerinwater was diagnosed as having schizophrenia because he seemed to be experiencing hallucinations. Because cultural factors related to David's behaviors complicated the diagnosis, neither the social worker nor the Cherokee community mental health center staff was convinced that this was the correct diagnosis for David; however, they recognized that he did need treatment, especially treatment that was culturally sensitive in the way it was delivered. **Schizophrenia** is described in the *DSM* as a mental disorder that is serious, one that is characterized by hallucinations and delusions. Schizophrenia often makes its appearance in young adulthood. It can be treated, but it may require treatment for the remainder of the person's life. There are many misconceptions about this mental disorder—most commonly, that it entails one personality that has split into two or that multiple personalities have emerged out of a single personality. Such symptoms can occur, but they are not usual or necessary in order for a diagnosis of schizophrenia to be made. In fact, the characteristic symptoms of schizophrenia include disorganized thinking (sometimes involving **delusions**, a strong belief that one is being persecuted, for example) or **hallucinations** (hearing voices or seeing apparitions). Risk of suicide is relatively high with schizophrenia. Persons with schizophrenia may have good intellectual capacity, but their thinking disorder may limit their social skills and ability to sustain employment (American Psychiatric Association, 2013).

The *DSM-5* is a hefty volume consisting of 947 pages describing 22 categories of mental disorders. Social workers across most fields of practice do encounter people with mental disorders; therefore, they tend to use the *DSM* as a resource. Social workers in the mental health field work in an environment with other professions that depend heavily on the *DSM*. Consequently, although social workers tend to assess client situations from a much broader ecological systems perspective, they do need competence in working with the *DSM*. A small sampling of mental disorders beyond schizophrenia that social workers in mental health need to be aware of include bipolar, depressive, and anxiety disorders.

Bipolar disorders are characterized by episodes of excessive mood—either of exceptional energy, happiness, and self-confidence or serious depression, inability to sleep, and suicidal thoughts. In its most severe form, people with this disorder are at high risk of suicide, financial difficulty resulting from purchase of excessively expensive items, and an inability to sustain employment. Milder forms of bipolar disorder occur as sustained periods of low mood and high mood, but never reach the levels or risks of serious bipolar disorders. Genetic factors are common with bipolar disorders (American Psychiatric Association, 2013).

Depressive disorders, too, range in severity. Recurrent thoughts of suicide, insomnia, and an inability to function in terms of self-care or employment may be brief but intense with a major depressive disorder. In a persistent depressive disorder, the behaviors may vary in intensity, but they persist for two or more years at a time. In the less severe disorder, friends and family members may not even be aware of the presence of depression. Suicide may be a very high risk with a major depressive disorder (American Psychiatric Association, 2013).

Anxiety disorders include phobias (excessive fear of specific objects), generalized anxiety, separation anxiety, panic disorders, and obsessive-compulsive disorder. The fear and anxiety of these disorders vary in intensity and may impact the person's quality of life (American Psychiatric Association, 2013). The primary characteristic of **trauma- and stressor-related disorders** (which are also considered one of the anxiety disorders) is exposure to an event that produced fear and stress. Examples include accident, injury, sexual abuse, military combat, or death of a loved person. Responses typically include recurrent memories and/or dreams of the event, flashbacks, and intense psychological distress. Post-traumatic stress disorder may not occur for months after the event but may persist for years. Acute stress disorder typically lasts less than one month. Adjustment disorders may involve significant distress and impairment of functioning; they typically occur within three months of the stressful event, but they discontinue within six months following the event (American Psychiatric Association, 2013).

Diagnosis of these and a wide range of other mental disorders remains an imprecise procedure. Mental health professionals, MSW social workers included, who are responsible for diagnosing mental disorders must exercise great care in their assessments. BSW social workers who are employed in mental health settings, like Roberta Sholes in the case study, learn a great deal about the specific mental disorders in the course of their professional work. BSWs do not diagnose, but they are responsible for gathering data that will be combined with the information obtained by other members of the interdisciplinary mental health teams in their diagnostic work.

Psychotropic Medications

Diagnosis, of course, is just the beginning. Treatment of mental disorders is complex. In mental health care today, medication is widely utilized in the treatment of many of the mental disorders. Social workers need to learn about some of these psychotropic medications, their uses, and their side effects so that they can be alert to possible complications in their clients. Some side effects of psychotropic medications include loss of sense of balance, sexual dysfunction, and even severe emotional reactions. When unpleasant side effects occur, people sometimes discontinue taking their prescribed medication, and this may result in reoccurrence of the mental illness. The medications that have come on the market in recent years have fewer side effects than drugs previously used to treat mental disorders. They have been of significant benefit to large numbers of people. With the newer drugs, though, some people feel so well that they discontinue taking their medications. They are then at high risk of relapse. Today's medications are helpful, but symptom control still remains elusive for some persons with schizophrenia (O'Hare, 2016). Other people are unable to afford the extraordinarily high cost of some of the newer psychotropic drugs—costs may be as much as $6,000 per month!

Among the medications used to treat some forms of mental illness are tranquilizers. Tranquilizers can be dangerous, even life-threatening, if taken with alcohol. They can also create lethargy and such overwhelming sleepiness that the person has considerable difficulty holding a job or studying. The opposite effect, hyperactivity, can occur with drugs prescribed for depression. Weight gain is a less-threatening side effect. These are just a few examples of the complexities of psychotropic medication treatment. Social workers monitor medication use by their clients and often educate clients and family members regarding the use of medications. Ongoing communication with the professional who prescribed the client's medication is an important part of the social worker's monitoring function.

Social workers, too, have ethical questions related to the use of psychotropic medications, especially when they are prescribed for children. Concerns relate to the appropriateness of drugs (e.g., use of amphetamines for children), possibility for negative side effects, and the potential development of psychological dependence on drugs. There is concern that children could begin to cope with normal stresses by taking medication rather than learning healthy adaptive behaviors. When children are in foster and institutional care and in the custody of the state, there are times when social workers must make decisions on the child's behalf about medical care. These are not easy decisions, as Box 6.2 suggests. Social workers often know their clients and family members more intimately and communicate with them more openly than other members of the treatment team. As a result, social workers are frequently in the unique position of being able to make clear to the physician the preferences and circumstances of the child's parents or the client, if the client is an adult, and to help clients understand the medical situation and available options.

Today treatment of mental disorders often consists of a combination of medication, monitoring, various forms of psychotherapy, and patient education. The treatment programs that deliver these services have come to be known as **behavioral health care**. They may be provided during hospitalization or on an outpatient basis. Hospitalization, when needed, tends to be much briefer than it was in the past, in part due to psychotropic medications but also due to curtailed length of stay dictated by insurance or managed-care corporations. Many patients (like David Deerinwater) now remain hospitalized for only a matter of days, followed by outpatient treatment to continue psychotherapy and to monitor the medication.

Box 6.2 Up for Debate

Proposed: Medications should be used routinely to help children with attention-deficit/hyperactivity disorder (ADHD).

Yes	No
Research has shown that medications such as Ritalin have a quieting effect on hyperactive children.	There are numerous known side effects of medication, especially Ritalin, including decreased blood flow to the brain, insomnia, and disruption of normal growth in the body, including the brain.
Medication can increase the alertness of hyper- active children at the same time it is decreasing over-activity.	The long-term effects of medicating hyperactive children are not well researched or well known.
With medication, many children with ADHD can function at an acceptable level in the classroom and progress in learning.	Medication does not cure hyperactivity.
The aggressiveness of hyperactive children is lowered through the use of medication, making them less of a threat to their siblings and classmates.	The chemical composition of Ritalin is similar to that of cocaine, and there are instances of recreational use and abuse of Ritalin by college students.

> Assess your understanding of the competencies needed for social work practice in mental health by taking this brief quiz.

Hospitalization and, for that matter, even medication are not necessary for all persons who are experiencing mental health problems. Social workers are among the professionals who provide counseling and psychotherapy for individuals, families, and groups with the objective of preventing and treating mental and emotional disorders. The many ways in which social workers, including BSWs, contribute to the prevention and treatment of mental disorders are described in the next section.

GENERALIST PRACTICE IN MENTAL HEALTH

The David Deerinwater case study is an example of generalist social work intervention occurring simultaneously at several different systems levels: the individual client, the family, the mental health team, and the community. The primary focus of Roberta Sholes's social work service, however, was the individual client, David Deerinwater. We now examine social work in other types of mental health settings and with groups and communities as well as with individuals.

Case Management

Case management generally focuses on individual clients, many of whom have serious, persistent mental disorders. Services are provided to people in the community, most often where they live, shop, visit a doctor or dentist, work, or go to school. The same generalist practice, multiple-phased change process, is used as described in Chapter 2 of this book. The process begins when the social worker reaches out and seeks to engage the client, establishing a sound working relationship. At the same time, information is gathered about the nature of the mental health problem and the client's needs and strengths. Then, with the collaboration of the client, a plan is developed and the case management intervention is implemented. Good quality services are located to address client needs, and monitoring is established to ensure that they are delivered in a respectful manner; often clients need help to learn how to utilize the services. The case management relationship may be terminated because the client no longer needs this service, because the social worker leaves the agency and a new case manager is assigned, or because the client chooses to end the service.

Case management often, although not always, involves long-term work with people who have multiple and complex problems. Some clients may be resistant. Some may have been or currently are homeless and living on the streets. At times, strong advocacy is needed to convince an organization or a professional person to provide needed care. Finding a dentist who will see a 45-year-old man who has not had dental care in 25 years may not be easy. Helping the client agree to accept the needed service and keep follow-up appointments may be no easier, but accomplishing these challenges can be very rewarding.

Box 6.3 provides an example of case management involving a 55-year-old Asian woman. Social workers have noted that case management is a more comfortable fit with many Asian people than the traditional clinical service model of American outpatient mental health care. Asian people tend to view health and well-being holistically, with

Box 6.3 A Case Management Case Study: Kai Lee

Kai Lee (not the client's real name) was brought to the Manhattan Community Services (MCS) organization by an outreach social worker from the Salvation Army after finding her confused and apparently homeless on the street. Kai was asleep in a corner of the waiting room when an MCS social worker, Lori Chang, approached her. Initially, she appeared to be very elderly, but when the social worker began to talk with her in the small interview room, Kai said that she was 55 years old, a widow who was Hmong and had come to the United States in 1975 from a refugee camp in Thailand. The young social worker explained that she was Hmong, too, but she had only limited ability to speak the Hmong language, which was obviously Kai's primary means of communication. It quickly became apparent, though, that the social worker and Kai were able, with some effort, to understand each other. Lori learned that Kai had been on the streets for the past week following the death and funeral of her husband. Having no money to pay the rent, she was forced out of her apartment. She was lost, had little food, no clothing, and had left her medication behind. She and her husband were childless and had no family members in the United States. The social worker learned that Kai needed medication for diabetes as well as depression. It was late in the day, but Lori Chang was able to convince a nearby women's shelter to take Kai in.

Kai was fearful and clung to Lori Chang's arm during the admission procedure at the shelter. She hungrily ate an entire bowl of peaches offered to her. At Lori Chang's insistence, the shelter's nurse was called in. Lori helped her obtain some medical history from Kai, which surprisingly revealed the name of Kai's doctor. In short order, the nurse was able to get a new prescription for Kai's diabetic and anti-depressant medication. The doctor asked to see Kai and the social worker agreed to accompany her to the doctor's office in two days. The nurse was gentle and respectful with Kai and together they helped Kai to get settled into a small room. Kai was still reluctant to see the social worker go, but Lori promised to be back in the morning.

When Lori Chang returned to her office and reported her interaction with Kai to her supervisor, the supervisor immediately assigned Lori responsibility for providing case management services to Kai. The next morning, Kai greeted Lori with a small but warm smile. She cried, however, as she told Lori that she was lost and had nowhere to go. She didn't know how long she could stay at the shelter. Lori explained that her agency had given her permission to work with Kai on a continuing basis. This would mean helping her to find housing, obtain financial assistance, and return to her doctor for health care. The older woman now cried in relief. Before she left, Lori confirmed with the shelter staff that her agency would provide services to Kai and it was agreed that Kai could remain at the shelter for at least two weeks while housing was located for her.

In the weeks that followed, Lori met with Kai daily. She was able to locate a single room for Kai in an apartment building close to the local Southeast Asian community. She obtained financial assistance for Kai as well as medical care. Initially, Kai wanted only to sleep. She ate poorly and would not have taken her medication without Lori's encouragement and monitoring. After three weeks, Lori was able to reduce her visits with Kai to twice weekly as Kai was gradually beginning to respond to Southeast Asian neighbors that she met on walks in the nearby park with Lori. Slowly, Kai shared her past history in a refugee camp, her arranged marriage to her husband in the camp, her resettlement in Manhattan, the long years of her lonely life without her family, and the months spent with her dying husband. Lori found that quiet, attentive listening helped Kai to work through some of her grief, but depression remained a feature of Kai's life. The anti-depressant medication, however, was helpful. Lori planned to continue to provide case management services on an ongoing basis. She hoped that in time Kai would agree to become involved with a group of women, many of them Asian, who were members of the Grand Avenue Club, which met regularly at a mall several blocks from Kai's home. This informal "club" served as a support group for people with mental health and other problems. Lori was pleased that Kai was gradually achieving increased comfort with other people and confidence in her ability to care for herself.

mental, physical, emotional, and spiritual elements inseparable. Family relationships are highly valued, and a person's self-concept is intrinsically related to her or his involvement with family. When refugees have endured war, separation from family, and political persecution before coming to the United States, they may transfer their sense of family obligation to others, especially people of their same culture, but they may be very guarded and reluctant to trust professional people or service providers. They may appreciate home visits, however, and may gradually accept help from a social worker who sustains contacts and demonstrates concretely his or her willingness to help (Eng & Balancio, 1997).

Case management incorporates a great deal of counseling, advocacy, and monitoring. Social workers at many different educational levels are involved in case management. Doctoral-level social workers may provide consultation and expert backup for case managers. MSW social workers may supervise case management programs or may provide clinical case management themselves. BSW social workers like Lori Chang provide extensive case management services. Other professionals—such as nurses, psychologists, and professional counselors–also provide case management services. Some organizations use persons with no academic credentials beyond a high school degree to assist professional staff or to provide case management with special populations.

Working with Groups

Social workers in mental health settings use groups extensively. Groups are used with people of all ages for providing therapy, counseling, teaching skill development as well as for psychoeducational purposes such as raising self-esteem, and teaching problem-solving skills of many kinds. Insurance companies find group work to be less costly than individual counseling, so they are sometimes more likely to authorize group sessions for continuing care, which has encouraged the growth of groups in recent years. Group workers tend to be flexible, creative, and open to involving pets, arts, poetry, and community field trips to offer growth-enhancing and corrective experiences for people with painful, frightening mental disorders.

Therapy groups, sometimes known as treatment groups, have existed in mental health settings for many years. Inpatient mental health facilities today initiate patients to group therapy with the expectation that individual or group therapy will be continued following discharge. Therapy groups focus on helping people to change their behavior or thinking or improve their coping skills. Generally, a combination of psychotropic medication and psychotherapy (possibly both group and individual therapy) begins the treatment process. Although not all persons can benefit from group therapy, it is used successfully to treat people with a wide range of mental disorders, including depression, schizophrenia, and bipolar disorders, and persons that are dually diagnosed (co-occurrence of substance abuse and mental illness), among others. Children and adolescents with behavioral and mental health disorders are often treated in residential treatment centers, so called because they live in the facility for several months while attending school and receiving psychotherapy individually and in groups. In these facilities, social workers tend to comprise the majority of the treatment staff. Many people today, with serious as well as milder forms of mental health disorders, are never hospitalized or institutionalized but instead receive all of their mental health treatment in the community

Traumatized child responds to animal assisted therapy

through private practitioners, clinics, and various community organizations. Group therapy tends to be intensive and often involves confrontation, but group members are encouraged to assist and support each other, too. Social workers well trained in clinical social work, along with psychologists and counselors, tend to be the facilitators of therapy groups. BSWs and MSWs without clinical training often co-facilitate therapy groups.

Community organizations of many kinds also provide mental health services. The clubhouse model, as described by Martin (2016), employs social workers (often BSWs) to serve a multiplicity of needs for their "members" (the term they prefer to "clients"). Kai Lee, the Hmong woman with depression from the Box 6.3 case study, would potentially become involved in a support group of women in a clubhouse. The clubhouse model serves people with chronic mental health problems across the United States. It utilizes a strengths approach, focusing more on the diverse needs and strengths of the persons who utilize services. Diagnostic mental disorder labels are of much less importance than the personhood of members. Like the settlement house movement of the past, group services are central, but members are also engaged in classes, job searches, and employment referrals, among other forms of assistance. All staff and members work together to care for the clubhouse. Groups offer encouragement and emotional support, sharing personal experiences and offering advice. The clubhouse provides socialization, transitional housing and employment, and monitoring of members who are in crisis or who are functioning at a borderline level.

Therapy groups and the clubhouse model of support and socialization groups are presented as contrasting approaches to group work. Other models of group work are used by social workers in the mental health field. Educational groups focus on providing information on psychotropic medications, for example. Two other types of groups are self-help groups, which may be facilitated by social workers but provide considerable input and direction from group members and computer-mediated social networking groups—a growing trend in which group treatment is provided using computer technology (Kirst-Ashman & Hull, 2015).

Community Practice

In addition to individuals and groups, social workers seek to assist communities, at-risk populations, and organizations to promote mental health or to design programs for people with mental health problems. Examples of social work community practice behaviors often appear in *NASW News*, the monthly publication of the NASW.

Allison Gould, a clinical social worker from New York, used technology to reach out to other mothers who, like herself, had experienced the loss of a baby. She developed a blog to introduce yoga as a tool to help grieving mothers and fathers to deal with the post-traumatic stress that can take the form of flashbacks, high levels of anxiety, and insomnia ("social work in the public eye," 2015).

Sarah Hamil, a social worker who works in the field of child, adolescent, and family therapy, provided community education about the dynamics of bullying in an article in the *Jackson Sun*, a Tennessee newspaper. The newspaper story enabled her to explain bullying as hazardous both to the bully and to the child who is victimized. She pointed out that bullying is not normal behavior, but that this aggressive behavior may occur when children do not have other means of getting their needs met. She explained how parents can better understand and learn to deal with bullying in their child ("social work in the public eye," 2006).

Strong motivation to educate the community about suicide and decrease the stigma related to depression and suicide led Chris Gilchrist to organize a walk, the annual Out of the Darkness Walk, for Hampton Roads, VA. Gilchrist is one of many social workers who perform leadership roles in annual walks that occur across the country. Focusing on depression, especially untreated depression, is a key function of the walks. A memory wall is provided for people to post pictures of a lost loved one and that person's name is read, too, during the Hampton Roads walk. Recognizing the increasing suicide rate of active duty military personnel as well as veterans, Gilchrist ensures that there is a strong military presence at the community walk (Pace, 2014).

Disaster Services

When disaster strikes, generalist practice skills enable social workers to intervene immediately to solve problems and address crises. According to Ken Lee, social workers may be the best equipped of all mental health professionals to respond to disasters. Lee, a social worker from Hawaii and member of the American Red Cross Air Incident Response Team, is also a mental health trainer for the Red Cross. He was one of countless mental health professionals who assisted at the Ground Zero site following the terrorist attack on the World Trade Center in New York in 2001 ("social work in the public eye," 2002). This remains one of the most significant community disasters in U.S. history.

Both the American Red Cross and the federal Substance Abuse and Mental Health Services Administration (SAMHSA) recommend group treatment for survivors of disasters and for volunteers. The focus is present-centered, avoiding vivid details of the actual trauma but listening to the pain of the emotions and helping group members to support and bond with each other. Effort is made to prevent people from re-traumatization through exposure to the grim details of their own or others' detailed accounts of the event, but the emotions, pain, and consequences of the experience are thoroughly validated. Energy is directed to helping people reconnect with missing family members and access medical care, as well as providing food and housing (Johnstone, 2007). Whether disasters are caused by terrorist attacks, shootings at a school, or natural events such as hurricanes, earthquakes, tornadoes, floods, or forest fires, social workers respond.

During and immediately following disasters, people may be subjected to overwhelming physical and psychological distress, often known as **acute traumatic stress**. Normal reactions cover a wide spectrum of behaviors. Emotionally, people may experience shock, feeling as though they are in a fog, an unreal world. They may feel numbness and have no physical pain even in the presence of profound injuries. Or they may react with terror, panic, anger and hostility, grief, or a marked sense of isolation. They may be confused and disoriented, have difficulty making decisions, experience racing thoughts, or replay the experience over and over again in their minds. Withdrawal and difficulty communicating is a common behavioral response to traumatic exposure. So is pacing, aimless walking, or an exaggerated startle response. Immediate mental health intervention at the time of the disaster or traumatic experience may prevent or minimize the development of an enduring stress disorder.

People recover from trauma in their own time, using their own strengths and with the support of their family, friends, and community. Life may never be the same again, especially if there has been a death or permanent disability. Many people, however, do survive disasters, and there are even people who actually grow and thrive as a result of their experience. In the weeks that follow the traumatic experience, there is first a period of disorganization with depression and anger and then a period of reorganization when new patterns for functioning evolve and new relationships are built.

Post-traumatic stress disorder (PTSD), if it occurs, can be treated through individual or family counseling or with group therapy. Some therapeutic models focus on helping the person cognitively, by increasing their intellectual comprehension of the experience and their reaction to it. Behavioral methods seek to change ineffective responses to behaviors that strengthen the person's ability to cope. Medication is sometimes used in conjunction with counseling. Social workers tend to use a holistic approach that identifies strengths in the person and connects people with others who can help: family members, friends, and co-workers. Spiritual beliefs are another source of support that is valued. Referrals are made to community resources if appropriate.

Practice with Diverse Populations

Commitment to social justice and increasing appreciation of both the physical and social environment has enriched social workers' valuing of human diversity. Unfortunately, in the past, social workers and other mental health professionals have not always been very sensitive to ethnic differences in the people they serve. Today, however, social work education is seeking to prepare students to work with an increasingly wide range of populations in ways that will empower individuals and their communities and will safeguard the integrity of family life, as it is defined by diverse populations.

Building knowledge and sensitivity to diverse cultures is a career-long process. As social workers, we sometimes come from very complex and diverse backgrounds that we have never really examined. Yet our appearance, the way we talk, and the way we present ourselves immediately convey messages more powerful than we know to clients of contrasting cultures and backgrounds. If we are to develop skill in utilizing culturally appropriate interventions, we must build self-awareness and appreciate our own uniqueness as well as that of each individual client. Social work researchers such as John Red Horse provide guidelines that aid our understanding of the intensity and the differences in our own and our clients' identification with cultural roots.

Many years ago, John Red Horse (1988) classified Native American families along a continuum. Family members in a traditional family, he explained, use their native language at home and in the community, practice the native religion, and sustain tribal beliefs regarding disease. These families rely on traditional rituals and ceremonies to rid them of mental and physical illness and to bring their minds and bodies back into harmony with the spiritual world and the universe. One step from traditional families is *neo-traditional* families, in which some members use the English language and have adopted new rituals and spiritual healers; most family members, however, retain traditional beliefs. *Transitional* families use English in the community but speak the native language at home. They retain some traditional spiritual beliefs and practices, but they are beginning to use contemporary American health care. *Acculturated* families have lost their native language, religion, and often even their extended kinship system; they rely on American contemporary health care systems. Finally, *pan-renaissance* families seek to renew their native language fluency and to revitalize some aspects of the traditional religion. Consideration of this continuum can help social workers to be more sensitive to the differences within groups as well as the differences between groups.

Incorporating these understandings into interviews—along with warmth, empathy, and respect—takes time to learn but will become a part of professional preparation for a career in social work. Classroom role plays of interviews plus actual experience in fieldwork are just the beginning of cultural competence, which is acquired over a professional lifetime.

In the David Deerinwater case, Roberta Sholes demonstrated sensitivity throughout her work with the client, his family, and the Cherokee community. The result was that Mr. Deerinwater was reunited with his family, and he gained access to a whole set of support cultural networks that would perhaps otherwise not have been available to him. Roberta's newly gained knowledge of Cherokee history, beliefs, traditions, and even food preferences helped other members of the hospital's mental health team to understand this client and others like him. Hopefully, it also helped to humanize the institution, resulting in increased respect and social justice for future Native American clients.

Native American History and the Cherokee Experience

Recognizing that Native American history and culture have not been well represented in the social work literature spurred the authors of this text to feature a case study involving Native American people. The text authors also realized that the rich cultural components of this case and its implications for mental health practice would be better understood with further background information on the history of Native American people in the United States, with special attention to the Cherokee Nation.

We begin with a basic awareness that Native Americans, also known as **First Nations People**, were the first Americans. Scientists now believe that the ancestors of today's Native Americans probably migrated across the Bering Strait from Asia. By the time the first Europeans arrived, there were approximately 1.5 million native people thriving in North America, representing a wide variety of tribal groups, customs, and languages (Lum, 1992).

For Native Americans, the coming of the Europeans was a catastrophe. Europeans immigrated in massive numbers, dangerously armed with the power of the gun while bringing new diseases that decimated many Indian populations. They drove the Indians from their lands and frequently massacred those who resisted. This genocide is depicted in the story of the Cherokee's Trail of Tears, written by Wilma Mankiller (Mankiller & Wallis, 1993), a social worker and also the first woman to hold the position of principal chief of the Cherokee Nation. According to Mankiller, Cherokee people had long been living in the Great Smoky Mountain region when European settlers arrived on the coast of the United States. The Cherokees developed remarkably advanced communities, attaining wealth through their farms and plantations as well as commercial trading contracts with merchants in European countries. The discovery of gold on Cherokee land in Georgia ultimately led to broken treaties with the U.S. government and to President Andrew Jackson's order for removal of the Cherokee people to western lands. In 1835, 7,000 federal soldiers arrived; they rounded up Cherokee families, held them in stockades, and then forced them westward at gunpoint for the historic Trail of Tears. It is believed that of the 18,000 persons forcibly removed, approximately 4,000 died.

The first winter in Oklahoma resulted in additional deaths from starvation and freezing. By 1839, however, a new constitution was written, and Tahlequah was established as the Cherokee capital. By 1851, the Cherokee Nation had created a comprehensive school system including schools of higher education. The strong work ethic and tribal pride of the Cherokees resulted in the rapid development of commerce, farms, government, and a judicial system. In 1862, during the Civil War, Cherokee land was invaded and taken by the Union Army. War destroyed ranches, homes, and the Cherokee economy. When the Civil War ended in 1865, Congress decreed that all Indians were wards of the government; no prior treaties were honored. Native Americans were then confined to reservations. In the 1870s, railroad expansion brought homesteaders from the East. Despite the protest of Indians, the federal government sold previously protected Indian Territory to white settlers.

The General Allotment Act (the Dawes Act) of 1887 dealt a severe blow to Indian territories across the United States. The act provided private ownership of parcels of former reservation land—allotments—to individual Indians, with the remaining lands reverting to the U.S. government for homesteading or other purposes. Many Cherokees unknowingly sold their parcels of land for little or nothing and were left destitute. The Dawes Act dispossessed Indians in Oklahoma and across the country of nearly all their holdings. The next blow to Indian independence and self-rule came in 1898 with passage of the Curtis Act, which ended tribal courts as of that year and tribal government by 1906.

Beginning in the early 1900s, additional efforts were made to destroy Native American culture. Children were forced to attend white boarding schools far from their reservations. They were forbidden to speak their own languages or to honor their own religious traditions. It only in 1924 that Native Americans were finally granted full U.S. citizenship.

In 1934, the Indian Reorganization Act signaled a change in U.S. policy. Providing for the re-establishment of tribal governments, it was strongly supported by John Collier, a social worker and President Franklin D. Roosevelt's appointee as head of the Bureau of Indian Affairs. Collier was a crusader for the welfare of Native Americans. The Cherokee and many other Indian tribes were able to regroup and rebuild their governmental structures and communities under the provisions of the Indian Reorganization Act.

> Watch this video clip from Rich Heape Films about the experience of Andrew Windyboy and the Native American boarding schools. How could the trauma suffered by Native American children in these schools lead to mental illness? How have Native Americans dealt with the trauma of forced separation from family and the attempted stripping of their Native American culture?
>
> https://www.youtube.com/watch?v=qDshQTBh5d4

The history of the Cherokee nation reflects the history of Native American people generally. All shared common experiences of broken treaties and harsh treatment from the U.S. government. All tribes today continue to struggle with poverty; discrimination by the majority society persists. Despite this, there are vast differences among Native American peoples today. Of 500 different Indian nations or tribes, some include fewer than 100 members, while others may have in excess of 100,000 members. Some have very large land holdings, with families often living in isolated rural areas, while others, such as the Cayuga of New York, have no actual land holdings at all. There are many differences in religion, language, and culture among the tribes.

While Indian leaders such as Wilma Mankiller have engendered increasing self-respect and pride among native people, the historical tearing of family structures that resulted from the Trail of Tears and all other Indian removal programs is only now beginning to be addressed. Treatment programs—especially in Indian mental health and substance abuse programs—promote Native American intergenerational healing by focusing on both the strong survival skills and the unhealthy coping behaviors that people used when faced with a hostile environment. Although the history of broken treaties and oppression of Native American people goes back many years, it has links to our time. Maria Yellow Horse Brave Heart, a social work practitioner and educator, is another respected authority on Native American history of trauma. Writing as a Native person herself, she reports that almost all Indian families today include someone who was humiliated and traumatized by boarding schools or who lost family members—generally children—taken by Indian agents or social workers, sometimes even given over by parents for adoption into non-Indian homes to avoid overwhelming poverty (2004). In her work, she frequently

> ? Assess your understanding of generalist practice in mental health by taking this brief quiz.

deals with the unresolved grief and historical trauma of native people. Clearly, much healing remains to be done. The scars remain deep and painful.

SOCIAL, ECONOMIC, AND ENVIRONMENTAL JUSTICE ISSUES

Human rights and social justice concerns abound in the field of mental health. The very diagnostic labels described earlier may cause damage. To label someone as schizophrenic, for example, can be very damaging; a person so labeled is expected to perform (or not to perform) in a specific, predetermined manner. When hospital or clinic staff, schools, correctional facilities, employers, or other organizations know this label, other people are likely to assume or to anticipate the expected behaviors. Political careers or administrative promotions have been jeopardized when it is discovered that a person was labeled, correctly or incorrectly, with a psychiatric diagnosis. Diagnostic labels can follow a person for life with devastating results. Although medical information is supposedly confidential, private, and protected by law, in reality it is remarkably available to a large number of persons the client has never even seen. A child's school record, for example, is passed from one teacher to another, complete with psychological evaluations. Medical records are handled not only by doctors, nurses, and therapists of many kinds but also by clerks, aides, medical records personnel, and insurance staff.

Persons with psychiatric labels may be stereotyped or subjected to stigma by others, but something even more debilitating occurs when people begin to define themselves by a label. Tragically, stigma occurs internally as well as externally. Even when people do not know their diagnosis, they do understand that they have been labeled with some kind of mental problem. Because of the stereotyping and discriminatory attitudes of society, this knowledge may deprive people of their dignity, their human rights!

It is also not difficult to imagine how unsafe and hazardous environments put mentally ill persons living on the streets at great risk of physical health problems, rape, and criminal victimization. While untreated mental health problems may create behaviors that alienate people from their families and leave them homeless, the sometimes toxic environmental context of homelessness can exacerbate existing mental health problems.

In a 2007 report, *Quantifying Environmental Health Impacts*, the World Health Organization described mental health and behavioral risks that are specifically linked globally to environment. Suicide, for example, was shown to be linked to work-related stress and stress stemming from degraded environments. Environmental factors varying from country to country were shown to affect access to the means used by people to commit suicide. These ranged from the ingestion of pesticides in Trinidad, Sri Lanka, and Malaysia to the use of charcoal fumes in China and gunshot in the United States. Approximately 30 percent of suicides globally were attributed to the environment. The report noted that improving chemical safety and limiting access to guns could save lives. In the United States, legislation to put sensible limits on gun purchase has been consistently blocked by the powerful National Rifle Association (the NRA). The unrestricted right to gun ownership has been highly valued and protected by political conservatives who are unlikely to advance restrictive gun ownership legislation as long as they control the federal and many state legislative bodies.

The World Health Organization's Mental Health Action Plan 2013–2020 required all United Nations member countries to take action to improve mental health, recognizing that nations differ and each country would need to adapt the plan individually. The plan identified specific groups of people as at special risk of mental disorder internationally including people in poverty, those experiencing human rights violations, and people exposed to homelessness or incarceration. Unhygienic living conditions as well as physical and sexual abuse were identified as human rights violations of people with mental disorders in some health facilities globally (World Health Organization, 2013).

Social workers with an environmental perspective could not ignore the physical surroundings of the people they served. The environmental context became increasingly a focus for mental health practitioners. Today, globally, environmental degradation is witnessed in slums with deteriorating housing and uncollected garbage, hazardous-waste landfills, crops heavily treated with toxins that run off into rivers, and destruction of forests. Degraded environments sap peoples' energy and destroy motivation, leaving people feeling isolated and trapped (Dominelli, 2012). Mental health practitioners must be prepared to respond to the long-term emotional needs of victims of trauma created by toxic physical and social environments as well as natural disasters, terrorist attacks, and war.

If social workers are committed to advocating for change, fairness, and an end to discrimination and inequality, then environmental issues must become more central to their work in the mental health field. Counseling and psychotherapy for individuals, families, and groups are basic to social work practice in mental health, but we must also focus our skills on changing the societal factors that affect access to care, quality of care, and nature of the environment in which we live. To do this will require knowledge about and active involvement in the social policies and legislation that affect mental health.

> **Intervention**
>
> *Dimension of Competency* **Knowledge:** Social workers understand theories of human behavior and the social environment, and critically evaluate and apply this knowledge to effectively intervene with clients and constituencies.
>
> **Critical Thinking Question:** How might social workers use their understanding of human behavior and social environments to identify and change the factors that exacerbate mental illness and sometimes lead to suicide in the United States?

> **?** Assess your understanding of the social, economic, and environmental justice issues in mental health by taking this brief quiz.

SOCIAL POLICY AND MENTAL HEALTH

As social workers today attempt to help people heal from many kinds of traumatic experiences and provide services to diverse populations with complex mental health needs, they do so within the context of governmental policy that creates or limits access to mental health programs. Sometimes it is really difficult to understand government policy and a societal climate that fails to provide care. Unfortunately, attitudes toward mental illness today still reflect the mixture of repulsion, fear, and even amusement with which the mentally ill were regarded for centuries. But progress has been made both in our understanding of and attitudes toward mental illness and in our professional technologies for treating it.

Historical Perspectives

To understand the mental health system in the United States today, we must look back to its roots. The colonists who came to the United States from Europe brought attitudes that were harsh and notions about caring for people with mentally disorders that stressed containment and coercion, whips, and chains. The first state hospital for the mentally ill in the United States was opened in Williamsburg, Virginia, in 1773. Before this, the mentally ill were cared for by their families or in poorhouses that also provided for people with tuberculosis, syphilis, and other contagious diseases as well as persons with physical or cognitive disabilities.

Social reform began almost simultaneously in the United States and Europe during the late 1700s and early 1800s. Leaders emerged whose reform activities produced a shift in societal attitudes toward mentally ill persons. In Paris, Dr. Philipe Pinel, a physician, attracted public attention in 1779 when he struck off the chains of the mentally ill men at Bicêtre, a "lunatic asylum." A Quaker religious community in York, England, provided funds to William Tuke to develop an institution for the humane treatment of mentally ill persons (no chains were permitted). In the United States, Dr. Benjamin Rush, a physician and one of the signers of the Declaration of Independence, instituted many reforms at Pennsylvania Hospital; he also wrote the first American text on psychiatry.

The most famous reformer, however, was Dorothea Lynde Dix, an activist and reformer whose work in the mid-1800s brought attention to the inhumane treatment of the mentally ill in the United States. A schoolteacher, Dix, volunteered to teach a Sunday school class at the East Cambridge women's jail near Boston in 1841. Here she discovered mentally ill poor people in prisons. She was horrified by the inhumane conditions in which they were kept, and she felt compelled to do something about it. Dix's well-trained mind told her that only carefully conducted research to document the conditions of the mentally ill would elicit the attention of public officials. Accordingly, she set about visiting every jail, prison, and almshouse in Massachusetts. She systematically recorded her findings. People, barely recognizable, were in boxes, cages, and dank cellars, their bodies malnourished and their limbs permanently contracted from confinement in tiny areas. Some had frostbite. Some were chained. Many mentally ill persons were kept in woodsheds without light, heat, or sanitation. The dates, places, and details of her investigations were all documented in a 30-page report that was presented to the Massachusetts legislature in January 1843. Legislation authorizing the building of hospitals to treat persons with mental illness was quickly passed in Massachusetts. Her work came to be regarded as one of the first pieces of social research in the United States (Wilson, 1975).

Dix continued her efforts until her death. The results included construction of mental health facilities in Canada and several states in the United States. Because many states were either unwilling or unable to finance hospitals for the mentally ill, Dorothea Dix decided to go to the federal government for help. A bill was passed by Congress that would have permitted funds from the federal government's sale of western lands to be used to care for the mentally ill, but President Franklin Pierce vetoed the bill in 1854.

Unfortunately, the new state hospitals—founded on the principle of humane treatment—soon deteriorated, causing alarm for Dix and her followers. Mental hospitals became dumping grounds for society's problems. The foreign-born were housed separately from non-immigrants and often in inferior quarters. African-American people—in those states that even admitted them to state hospitals—were also segregated. By 1900, conditions in state hospitals were investigated and were vividly described in news articles. Across the country, reformers demanded strict guidelines for the proper care of the mentally ill.

In 1908 Clifford Beers's book, *A Mind That Found Itself,* captured a more receptive public. The book told the author's personal story. Beers, a Yale University graduate, suffered a mental breakdown and endured years of inhumane treatment in both private and state facilities. He eloquently described what he saw and heard from attendants and others, even when he was seriously mentally ill. The book captured the attention of the public as well as professionals. Beers subsequently founded the Connecticut Society for Mental Hygiene and assisted in the development of the national and international mental hygiene movement, which advocated for federal government intervention in the problem of mental illness.

> ▶ Watch this short video done by Boston History about the life and work of Dorothea Dix. How did her reform efforts pave the way for the national spotlight to be put onto the experiences of those suffering from mental illness?
>
> https://www.youtube.com/watch?v=FmkX9s9EH1Q

The Social Work Profession Emerges

Even in the earliest days of the profession, the early 1900s, social work pioneers were involved in mental health work. In 1907, Mary Antoinette Cannon was hired by Massachusetts General Hospital to work with mentally ill patients. She was the first social worker to enter this field of practice. Mary Jarrett was employed in 1913 as the first director of social services at the Boston Psychopathic Hospital, where she is said to have coined the term *psychiatric social worker.* Soon social workers began to be routinely hired by hospitals and clinics to provide therapy.

Social casework, emerging from the work of the Charity Organization Society, was the primary social work method in the mental health field. The pivotal work done by Mary Richmond, the founder of social casework, in her seminal texts *Social Diagnosis* (1917) and *What Is Social Casework?* (1922), demonstrated the strong relationship between poverty and the mental health, personality development, and well-being of social work clients.

World War I, which lasted from 1914 to 1918, resulted in battle casualties that were psychological as well as physical. *Shell shock* was the term used to describe psychiatric problems created by war experiences. Mental health staff, including social workers, was needed. Recognizing the need for social workers trained to work with mental disorders, Mary Jarrett initiated a specialized psychiatric social work training program in 1918 at what is now the Smith College School for Social Work.

Sigmund Freud's writings were introduced into the United States from Germany in the early 1900s and had become well accepted by the 1920s. Freud's psychoanalytic theory taught that because mental illness derived from unresolved conflicts, patients could best be helped by remembering and discussing early events, even dreams, with a trained person. As Freudian theory was popularized in the 1920s and 1930s, public and private mental clinics began hiring many social workers to provide psychotherapy. These were still the early years of the profession, and the mental health movement gave the profession of social work a real boost. Social workers became valued parts of mental health treatment teams.

The demand for social workers to staff the clinics and hospitals spurred growth of the profession. The American Association of Psychiatric Social Workers, founded in

1926, became a strong force within the profession. In 1955, it merged with other specialized social work organizations to form the NASW. Bertha Capen Reynolds was one of many social workers who provided leadership in the field of mental health practice. This feisty, intellectual clinical social worker and educator is also remembered for her social activism, strong support for labor unions, and critique of capitalism. Reynolds was committed to fighting against wars, oppression, and human degradation. Her books *Between Client and Community* (1934), *Learning and Teaching in the Practice of Social Work* (1942), and *Social Work and Social Living* (1935) helped social workers to build unique skills in meeting psychological and emotional needs of clients and families, at the same time undertaking social change efforts in communities and society. Bertha Capen Reynolds is celebrated as a leader in progressive social work.

The first book on child psychotherapy, *The Dynamics of Therapy in a Controlled Relationship* (1933), written by Jessie Taft, a psychologist, was based on her experiences with a social work agency, the Children's Aid Society in Pennsylvania. Taft and Virginia Robinson, a social work professor at the Pennsylvania School of Social Work, developed what came to be known as the functional school of social work. Use of time and time-limited casework was a major focus of functional theory, thus making the functional school a precursor of modern-day brief, or time-limited, therapy.

When World War II began in 1939, the army created officer-level positions for mental health social workers, and social workers functioned on military neuropsychiatric teams. The one million persons with neuropsychiatric disorders admitted to U.S. Army hospitals during the war resulted in an expansion of mental health social services, especially group work, for the military and their families. By the end of the war, in 1945, the military services and the Veterans Administration hospitals had become the largest employers of professional social workers, and they remain so today.

Evolving Social Policy Affects Service in Mental Health

The first major piece of mental health legislation passed by the U.S. government was the National Mental Health Act of 1946. The act provided federal funding for research, training, and demonstration projects to help the states develop programs for the prevention and treatment of mental illness. The act set the stage for the creation of the National Institute of Mental Health (NIMH) in 1949. The leadership and authority of this federal organization came to be well recognized, and it had a major impact on the development of state mental health programs.

During the 1950s, social work continued its growth in the mental health field. Prominent among the theorists and writers were Helen Harris Perlman (*Social Casework: A Problem-Solving Process*, 1957) and Florence Hollis (*Casework: A Psychosocial Therapy*, 1964). Hollis's work has been described as the springboard for the clinical social work movement (Meyer, 1987).

The Community Mental Health Centers Construction Act of 1963 was the next major piece of federal legislation related to mental health policy. With the strong support of President John F. Kennedy, this act gave credibility to the leadership and commitment of the federal government in mental health. It provided grants for the construction of community mental health facilities to provide care for the persons released from hospitals for the chronically mentally ill. It defined the concept of continuum of care and required that care be provided even to those who could not afford to pay for it. Many historians believe that this legislation revolutionized the mental health system in the United States because it resulted in large-scale development of community mental health programs as well as the de-institutionalization of patients.

Over the next decade, as the effectiveness of psychotropic medication grew, the length of inpatient stay declined and the shift to outpatient services dramatically expanded. Decisions in the 1970s by the U.S. Supreme Court *(O'Connor v. Donaldson)* and the U.S. Court of Appeals for the Fifth Circuit *(Wyatt v. Stickney*, an Alabama case) set precedents in the areas of mental health and developmental disability. These rulings directed that persons who had been committed to a hospital had a right to release (assuming they were not dangerous to themselves or others) if they were not receiving treatment. Care for people with mental disorders or "retarded persons" was to be provided in the least restrictive (i.e., the least confined and most homelike) setting possible. The plan to provide people released from institutions with well-integrated, publicly funded community mental health services, however, did not materialize. The numbers of chronically mentally ill persons living on the streets increased dramatically, calling public attention to the inadequacies of the community mental health centers.

In response, the NIMH, for the first time, introduced new forms of service delivery, many of which incorporated case management. Private insurance corporations began to cover mental health services for employed persons, although not at the same level as other health care. With insurance money increasingly available, private general hospitals expanded their inpatient and outpatient facilities. States began to gradually turn over their mental health programs to private enterprise to administer. A system that had once been largely a governmental operation was slowly transformed to a non-profit and then, increasingly, to a for-profit economy.

A consumer movement emerged at this time and grew remarkably quickly. The **National Alliance on Mental Illness (NAMI)** was founded in 1979 by consumers (this term is preferred to patients), family members, and concerned professionals. Today NAMI continues to support research, education, and social policy and political activity that will enhance access to community-based services. The organization is supported by members and now has affiliate offices in all 50 states (National Alliance on Mental Illness, 2010).

The federal Mental Health Systems Act of 1980 finally attempted to address the ramifications of de-institutionalization. To meet the basic needs of thousands of persons who were homeless and needing follow-up care, the act formally authorized the use of case management. Almost immediately, many new programs for persons with persistent and serious mental illness were put into place. Social workers committed to work with persons with mental disorders were quickly employed in administering and serving these programs.

Sadly, the Omnibus Budget Reconciliation Act of 1981 significantly shifted the federal government away from its leadership role in mental health services. This legislation, supported by President Ronald Reagan but opposed by social workers and many people in the mental health field, effectively repealed the Mental Health Systems Act and shifted responsibility for funding and future development of mental health programs to the individual states in the form of block grants. Most states, however, had already closed or substantially reduced their mental health facilities. As a result, many states developed contractual arrangements with counties and with private organizations to provide community-based services. This led to fragmentation and reduction of services.

The election of President Bill Clinton in 1992 signaled a readiness for new approaches to health care financing and, indeed, numerous Americans supported some form of national health care, as proposed by Clinton. But the Clinton Administration's plan met with a great deal of opposition, and eventually it was withdrawn. Clinton then responded by spearheading a Mental Health Bill of Rights, a set of principles to ensure that basic consumer rights would be met. The bill addressed rights to information about health care plans, the professionals who delivered the services, choice of providers, participation in treatment decisions, respectful care, confidentiality, and the right to appeal decisions of the health care plan (KEN Publications/Catalog, n.d.). NASW was one of the sponsors of the first Mental Health Parity Act, which was passed in 1996.

Finally, in 2008, a strong federal Mental Health Parity and Addiction Equity Act was passed that extended coverage to care for mental health and addiction disorders. The law required that health insurance plans provide equivalence between mental health and physical health coverage. Co-payments, deductibles, out-of-pocket payments, and even limitations on the number or frequency of visits were all addressed in the law. In 2010, in conjunction with the Affordable Health Care Act, additional rules to the 2008 law were written to further close some of the loopholes remaining that left employees of some companies without parity in health care coverage.

The 2010 health care reform law, officially the **Affordable Health Care for America Act (ACA)**, was written to be fully implemented by 2019. Portions of the law that affected access to mental health care were implemented in 2014. In 2016 the provisions of the 2008 Mental Health Parity and Addiction Equity Act were finally applied to persons enrolled in the Medicaid and Children's Health Insurance Program (CHIP), thus closing a loophole in the ACA (Federal Register, 2016).

Policy and Practice: Future Issues

The ACA contained some loopholes related to mental health that were anticipated to be addressed prior to full implementation by 2019. By 2020 it was expected that 32 million people would have gained access to mental health and addiction care under the ACA. This would include people not covered earlier under the ACA because 19 states had opted not to work with the ACA. The election of Donald Trump and Republican majority control of both houses of Congress in 2016, however, cast doom on the future of the ACA (Norris, 2016).

The Trump administration and many conservative members of Congress had a clear mandate to dismantle the revolutionary health care reform law. Nonetheless, portions of the law such as the requirement that insurers could not deny access to coverage based on a previously existing health condition continued to receive support. There was also support for mandatory coverage of adult children up to age 26 still living in their parents' home. It became apparent that the ACA could not be dismantled immediately. A plan evolved for Congress to vote for repeal of the ACA but leave it in place for two years in order to have time to design a health care plan that would have the support of the President as well as the Congress. Concern soon emerged, though, that millions of people enrolled in the ACA would find themselves without insurance if insurance companies discontinued coverage in anticipation of change to federal law.

The future of health care, including mental health care policy in the United States may well be unsettled for years. The goal of achieving a national health care plan that would establish health care access to all Americans, which was the essence of the ACA, seems to have gotten lost in the politics of the United States in recent years. All of the behavioral health care professions including social work, plus consumer groups will advocate vigorously to ensure that mental health care will remain available and will be affordable for all people in the United States. These groups will surely closely monitor all policy changes affecting future mental health care. Hopefully the public will also be galvanized into action and offer powerful support for federal legislation that will truly ensure that our country will be strong and healthy into the future.

In addition to access, the quality of mental health care will also continue to be an issue for the future as the financing of all health care continues to evolve. The traditional, open-ended therapies used in the past by social work psychotherapists and the long-term involvement so characteristic of many BSW caseloads have given way to brief, highly focused approaches to practice. In many settings, intermittent services have replaced long-term client contact. Managed care has encouraged the use of groups, often with a psychoeducational focus instead of individualized psychosocial therapy, for inpatient as well as community-based practice. The use of standardized protocols, sometimes referred to as **preferred practices**, is another response to the demand for short-term, highly focused, cost-conscious intervention. These protocols are directives that determine the treatment plan to be followed for specific client problems. They may have benefit for some people and for cost containment, but persons with persistent, serious mental health problems often fall between the cracks of this system. More research studies are needed to provide a strong base of evidence on the effectiveness of treatment strategies. Fortunately, long-term case management has emerged as beneficial for some persons with persistent and severe mental disorders. Case management seems to have been accepted as a cost-containment form of practice.

Mental health social and economic policies will continue to influence social work practice in the future, and new forms of practice are likely to evolve. Strategic or solution-oriented approaches are used to help clients focus narrowly on ineffective behaviors and achieve new perspectives that enable the efficient achievement of goals. Time-limited family and group interventions, even single-session treatment approaches, continue to evolve. Social workers are increasingly using computerized Internet groups and computer-assisted therapy, enabling people to benefit from cost-effective groups, in privacy and without leaving their homes.

Future trends in mental health social work practice will surely continue to be strongly influenced by the evolution of technology as well as evolving health care policy. Cost containment is likely to remain a pressing issue. Social workers of the future will be challenged to research and design new practice approaches and to provide evidence that they are achieving their goals in meeting client needs. Is this a big job? Yes! Clearly it calls for well-educated and prepared professionals who are strongly grounded in compassion for clients and commitment to professional values and who are equipped with advocacy skills to seek the kind of social change that will lead to increased health and well-being for all people.

> **?** Assess your understanding of social policy and mental health by taking this brief quiz.

SUMMARY

- The competencies that are needed by social workers who work in mental health settings are explained. The case of David Deerinwater, a Native American man, introduces readers to the basic competencies needed for generalist practice in the mental health field and the profession's values and ethics related to mental health practice. Areas of knowledge especially relevant to mental health practice are identified: interprofessional collaboration, the *DSM-5*, selected mental disorders, and psychotropic medications.
- The way social workers in mental health apply their generalist practice knowledge and skills across social systems is explained. Generalist practice in mental health is explored through examples of case management, work with groups, community practice, disaster services, and practice with diverse populations.
- The social, economic, and environmental issues that relate to mental health globally are discussed. Social justice issues include discrimination that results from diagnostic labeling and the stigma of persons with mental disorders. Poverty is an economic justice issue that has serious impact on access to mental health care. Hazardous environments put people at risk of mental and behavioral disorders globally. Environmental factors affect access to the means used to commit suicide.
- Social policy related to mental health from the colonial period of the United States to the present, is traced, paying special attention to progress within the last decade and continuing concerns for the future. Social policy related to mental health is traced from the early colonial days of the United States to more contemporary times. The historical development of the social work profession is reviewed. Recent significant legislation related to efforts to attain parity for mental health care is presented. The passage of health care reform is described as well as the struggle to implement the Affordable Care Act (including mental health care) and the health care policies that will be implemented in the future. Future social policy and mental health practice issues are discussed.

Recall what you learned from this chapter by completing the Chapter Review.

7
Social Work in Health Care

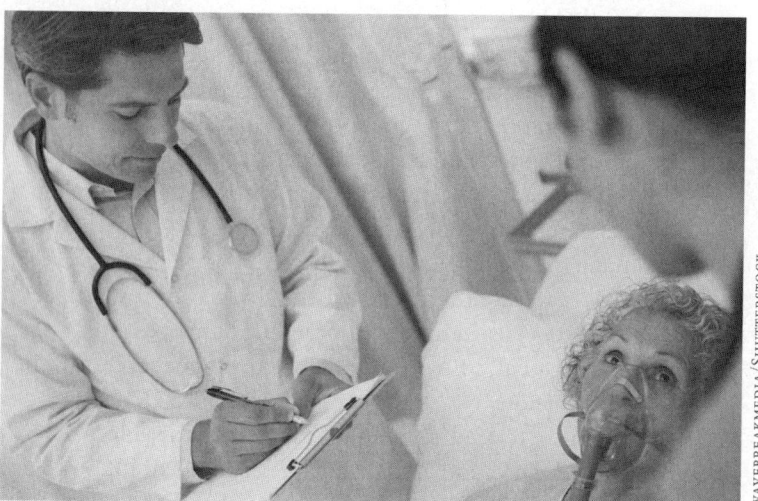

LEARNING OUTCOMES

- Explain how the knowledge, values, and skills of their profession prepare social workers to be effective in the health care field.
- Identify and describe the work that social workers do in four of the eight selected health care services presented in this chapter.
- Trace the historical development of the social work profession within health care from the time of the lady almoners to the present.
- Explain the politics and economics surrounding the drive to ensure access to health care for all people in the United States.

CHAPTER OUTLINE

CASE STUDY: Meet Katherine Lewandowski 190

Applying Social Work Competencies in Health Care 193
   Building a Knowledge Base for Health Care Practice 193
   Values and Ethics in Health Care Social Work 194
   Focusing on the Community and Populations at Risk 195
   Achieving Competence for Practice in Health Care 196

Selected Health Care Services 197
   Acute Care 197
   Long-Term Care 198
   Home Health Care 200
   Hospice and Palliative Care 200
   Emergency Department: Trauma and Crisis Amid Human Diversity 201
   Health Care for Veterans 203

CASE STUDY: Meet Katherine Lewandowski

As Linda Sanders walked down the corridor on the third floor of St. Anne's Hospital, she smiled at some of the nurses she passed. She was just beginning to know the staff, now that she was entering the second month of her senior-year social work field placement at this community general hospital. After all the years of classroom courses, it felt really good to finally be in a program that permitted her to do fieldwork and apply what she had learned.

    Linda was thinking now about Katherine Lewandowski, the person she was about to visit. Katherine, an 86-year-old widow, had been placed in a nursing home two months ago because she had suffered several minor fractures as a result of **osteoporosis**, a bone-thinning disease most commonly found in women over 50. Linda liked the silver-haired, frail woman who spoke both Polish and English. Katherine had a hearty sense of humor, but it was revealed infrequently during her hospitalization, for she was frightened of the medical setting and of staff in white uniforms. Fortunately, she had related well to Linda from the start.

    As she approached the hospital room, Linda recalled her two previous visits with Katherine. She had provided emotional support, which the elderly woman badly needed at the time of her arrival at St. Anne's. In the days that followed her admission to the hospital—necessitated by a fall at the nursing home, which had fractured her hip—Linda had tried to help Katherine understand and accept the recommended surgical procedure to repair the break. The surgery, performed three days ago, had gone well.

Linda tapped lightly on the door and entered the room. She glanced at Katherine and was startled by her appearance. Katherine's eyes were closed, but there were tears on her cheeks. Her color was poor. From her movements, it was clear she was in pain. When Linda spoke a quiet, gentle greeting, Katherine opened her eyes. Linda delivered the message she had come with: The doctors felt Katherine could return now to her nursing home; an ambulance would take her there in the morning. Linda had spoken with Katherine's daughter, Donna, who had said that she would visit her mother at the nursing home the next evening. Katherine's response to this message was to turn her head toward the wall. Linda asked if Katherine had any questions, if there was anything she could do. Katherine closed her eyes; then, after a silence, she said, "No." Gently, Linda asked, "Katherine, are you okay? You seem to be upset. Can we talk about whatever is troubling you?" Katherine turned her face even more toward the wall. When she said, "I am all right," her tone was one of dismissal.

Linda was troubled as she left the room. She wondered whether Katherine was really ready to be discharged from the hospital. Katherine was in pain, and she was weak and obviously distressed. Linda immediately discussed her concerns with Katherine's nurse, but the nurse said that she had already been in the hospital more than five days, and that most patients with hip fractures were able to leave in that period of time. Linda then spoke with her field instructor, who advised her to contact Katherine's doctor. The physician seemed somewhat annoyed with Linda's call and indicated that Katherine had used all the days of hospital care allowed by Medicare. She could recuperate just as readily in the nursing home.

Again Linda sought clarification from her field instructor, an experienced social worker whom Linda admired and respected. Marge O'Brien helped Linda review carefully what she had observed in Katherine's behavior. Then Marge explained that Medicare paid the hospital based on diagnosis, and this determined the length of stay. The business office had notified the doctor that Katherine was reaching the end of her predetermined hospital stay. The doctor's discharge plan for Katherine was final unless it was clearly inappropriate or threatened the patient's well-being. Linda had already alerted the doctor to her concerns, which was a very important form of advocacy, because the doctor would continue to be responsible for Katherine in the nursing home. Marge was very sensitive to Linda's concerns about Katherine. Premature hospital discharges were increasing, she said, because of efforts to reduce the high cost of medical care. Hospital social workers were increasingly alarmed about the risk to patients. Marge directed Linda to report her concerns to Katherine's daughter immediately and also to the social worker at the nursing home.

CHAPTER OUTLINE (Continued)

Health Care in Rural Areas 205
Public Health and Health Departments 206

Historical Perspectives 208
Early History: Caring for the Poor and Sick 208
Origins of Health Care Social Work 208
The Emergence of Health Care Social Work in the United States 209

Social Justice: Politics and Economics in Health Care 209
Medicare 211
Medicaid 212
Health Care Reform 213
The Patient Protection and Affordable Care Act 214
Cost-Benefit Analysis 215
Future Health Care Policy in the United States 218
Human Rights and Health: Global Perspectives 220

Summary 222

When Linda telephoned Katherine's daughter, Donna said she was concerned, too, but she felt the doctor must surely know what was best. Linda encouraged Donna to remain in close contact with the doctor and to advise him of any change in her mother's condition. Then, as she made ambulance arrangements and gathered medical information for the nursing home, Linda was alert to any additional data that she could possibly use to seek a delay in Katherine's discharge. There were none. Linda faxed the necessary forms and medical records to the nursing home; then she telephoned the social worker there to report her observations and her concerns about Katherine.

Two days later, when Linda returned to the hospital for her next field placement day, she asked about Katherine. The nursing staff reported that Katherine had been discharged and returned to the nursing home without incident. Linda continued to think about Katherine, however, knowing that the discharge to the nursing home—which was still not *home* for her—and the uncomfortable ambulance ride might have been quite difficult.

On Sunday evening, Linda picked up the section of the Sunday paper that contained the classified ads and the obituary column. She thought she would check the advertised social work positions. Suddenly the obituary column caught her attention. There was Katherine! She had died three days after returning to the nursing home. Linda was stunned. She reviewed her telephone call with Katherine's daughter, her last conversation with Katherine, and her phone call to the doctor. Could Katherine's death have been prevented? Had she given up too quickly? What else could she have done? As she thought about it, Linda realized that it was possible that Katherine might have had additional health complications after returning to the nursing home. She turned back to the newspaper. Then she recognized the name of another patient who had been discharged recently, and then she saw another name she knew. Reading on, she counted five recently discharged elderly patients' obituaries. Feeling very troubled, Linda put the newspaper down. She knew that she would have many more questions to ask her field instructor.

Still troubled by Katherine's death, Linda noted some especially interesting research findings as she worked on a term paper for one of her classes. A *Mayo Clinic Proceedings* article (Lee, 2015) reported an increased risk of osteoporosis among persons with depression. Similar findings were reported in earlier medical journals (Bab & Yirmiya, 2010; Cizza, Primma, Coyle, Gourgiotis, & Csaka, 2010). When she turned to the website of the National Osteoporosis Foundation (n.d.), she learned that while studies are showing a link between depression and osteoporosis, it was not clear which came first: the osteoporosis or the depression. The National Institute of Mental Health website (n.d.) called for assessment of persons with depression for potential risk of osteoporosis and careful management of depression in persons who already had osteoporosis. Linda found a *Social Work in Public Health* article (Lawrence & Azhar, 2010) that identified social work efforts to prevent osteoporosis in women. Linda reported her research review at the next staff meeting of the hospital social work department.

The staff had not seen this research, but the social workers were very interested, especially when Linda proposed the development of a study group to initiate an osteoporosis prevention program that incorporated assessment for depression. Linda suggested that community outreach and education could be a component of the program. Dietitians, nurses, physical therapists, and doctors could all participate. Social workers could take leadership roles in creating this change in the way that the hospital as an organization dealt with both inpatient and outpatient osteoporosis prevention and treatment. Linda advocated for new procedures to ensure that older adults with existing osteoporosis, like Katherine Lewandowski, would no longer be sent to nursing homes following surgery without careful assessment of their psychological and emotional well-being.

This case study has introduced one component of health care social work: hospital-based practice. A student social worker was intentionally chosen so that our readers could begin to look at how social work knowledge and skills are developed to provide a basis for practice in health care. The chapter will also describe some of the rapidly growing and diverse health-related areas in which you will find social workers. You will learn that the historical development of health care social work grew out of a commitment to advocacy for people denied access to health care. Then you will see how social justice issues continue to dominate the politics and economics of health care.

APPLYING SOCIAL WORK COMPETENCIES IN HEALTH CARE

Building a Knowledge Base for Health Care Practice

Social work students begin their education with liberal arts courses in areas such as literature, writing, biology, sociology, and psychology. In the case study, Linda's liberal arts courses ensured that she had the knowledge and skill to engage in research and to be involved in an action plan that would potentially improve the well-being of persons served by the hospital. The sophomore and junior years of most schools of social work include professional courses in generalist practice, research, human behavior in the social environment, cultural diversity, and social policy. Courses in generalist practice concentrate on building the skill base as well as knowledge of social work practice theory that prepares students for competent social work practice in health care or other settings. Beginning in the second semester of the junior year or in the senior year, baccalaureate students spend a minimum of 400 hours participating in fieldwork. It is in fieldwork that all the theory is applied and that students demonstrate that they have the competence needed to practice social work when they graduate.

In the case study, Linda's fieldwork practice experience included seeing patients on a one-on-one basis to counsel, intervene in crises, and help families with discharge plans. Often, too, Linda referred patients and their families to other community resources, such as nutrition or hot-meal programs, mental health, and substance abuse treatment. Generally, Linda and the other hospital social workers did not engage in long-term counseling; therefore, people who needed ongoing, intensive counseling were referred to local social service agencies or to private practitioners in social work, psychology, or psychiatry. Linda might also assist the hospital social workers who provided educational and support groups for persons who were newly diagnosed with cancer or who were dependent on alcohol or drugs. One of the social workers had developed a support group for people who had had transplants. Linda's field placement gave her a strong sense of growing professional competence.

Births and deaths, accidents and injuries, and acute illnesses and chronic diseases—these are the concerns in health care settings. Social workers must have a solid knowledge base if they are to further other health care team members' understanding of the emotional factors in illness. Coursework in the liberal arts provides a basic understanding of the biological sciences as well as the social, psychological, and cultural sciences. As we saw in Chapter 1, unlike the training of other health care providers, the social worker's professional education stresses the person within his or her environment. The generalist social worker is prepared to intervene with individual persons (like Katherine Lewandowski); with entire families or selected family members (e.g., Katherine's daughter); with small groups; with organizations (like St. Anne's Hospital); and with large groups, neighborhoods, and communities.

Hospitals like St. Anne's generally employ MSW as well as BSW social workers. MSWs generally work within specialized services such as cardiac intensive care and neonatal nurseries because of their complex nature and the immediacy of the services needed by patients and families. Especially fast-paced areas such as the emergency room (ER) also require very skilled, experienced social workers; except in small hospitals and sometimes in rural areas, MSWs are given these responsibilities. The MSW curriculum is also based on liberal arts preparation and a generalist perspective, but it provides advanced, specialized class and field courses.

Values and Ethics in Health Care Social Work

Hospitals and other health care settings work daily with frightened, hurting, vulnerable people. As organizational systems, health care facilities often deliver services in ways that seem cruel and heartless. Social workers in health care, guided by the values of the profession, can help humanize the health care environment for people and teach staff how to individualize the people they serve. Among the values that the profession holds are regard for individual worth and dignity, the right of people to participate in the helping process, and the right of clients to make decisions that will affect them.

These values and the NASW Code of Ethics were introduced in Chapter 1. The code of ethics is strongly emphasized in social work courses, and students are required to demonstrate ability to engage in ethical social work practice. Health care, however, is a field of practice that often challenges social workers to sustain their commitment to professional values and ethics. The health care environment itself sometimes contradicts social work values. This is especially true when health care organizations make huge profits but deny some people access to health care and when salaries range from hundreds of thousands of dollars for some and barely minimum wage for other health care employees.

Linda Sanders, the student social worker, was shocked by Katherine Lewandowski's death and by the depression that she saw in many other persons who were discharged to nursing homes or back to their families following treatment for fractures caused by osteoporosis. She began to think about the ethical questions related to the care of these people. Was it possible that people were being discharged from the hospital prematurely, without adequate assessment and treatment for depression? If so, was this happening because the professional staff was not aware of the high rate not only of depression but also of death following osteoporosis-related fractures? Was it instead possible that the health insurance companies who sought to expedite discharge to contain costs encourage premature discharge?

Biomedical ethics is not a concern for physicians alone. Social workers, too, especially those in the health care field, encounter ethical and value-laden issues in daily practice. Often social workers assist families with decisions about continued use of life-support systems for terminally ill persons or for infants with profound disabilities. Social workers frequently serve as the conscience of institutions as they challenge policies and procedures that have negative impacts on people. Students preparing for careers in social work develop an understanding of moral and ethical problems through liberal arts courses, such as philosophy and theology, and through content regarding ethics and values in their social work courses.

Focusing on the Community and Populations at Risk

The health care social worker is the essential link between people, health care facilities (whether hospitals, clinics, health departments, or nursing homes), and the community and its resources. Knowledge of the community means more than a mere listing of community resources, which would be available to any hospital employee. Truly understanding the community means understanding the diverse racial and ethnic groups that make up that community, their traditional beliefs about illness and health care, and any special healers that people might turn to. The faith and spiritual values of people in the community must be understood and respected by social workers. Often such values are the one vital, sustaining source of strength for a person or a family. In health settings, social work has traditionally been the professional discipline that interprets the ethnic, class, or cultural roots of beliefs and behaviors that influence responses to illness. Armed with the knowledge of cultural diversity and the community, social workers sometimes help families design remarkably creative plans for post-hospital care or as an alternative to nursing home placement.

There has been a long history of disparity of health services in the United States. Of serious concern to social workers are the poor (especially members of racial and ethnic minority groups), people with disabilities, persons without legal documents, and those who are HIV-positive. These are among the populations that are seriously at risk when some health care professionals avoid or even refuse to treat them. Sometimes it is extremely difficult for social workers to locate health services for persons in poverty and those who fall between the cracks of health insurance programs. Sustaining contact with culturally diverse persons whose needs have not been met or whose health care has been delivered in an insensitive, disrespectful manner may also be difficult.

Diversity and Difference

Dimension of Competency Skills: Social workers understand that, as a consequence of difference, a person's life experiences may include oppression, poverty, marginalization, and alienation as well as privilege, power, and acclaim.

Critical Thinking Question: When a hospital social worker discovers that a person's inpatient care is not being delivered in a culturally respectful manner, what creative means can the social worker use with the hospital staff, and how might the social worker reach out to assist the patient during and following the hospitalization?

For social work students, awareness and appreciation of human diversity and community norms is built gradually. This learning starts with the liberal arts courses taken in the freshman and sophomore years. Courses in literature, history, political science, and sociology help prepare social work students to understand the influences of class, gender, race, and ethnicity. Students begin to understand such concepts as social norms and roles and to appreciate the rich contributions of many cultures to contemporary society. Social work courses taken in the junior and senior years further prepare students for practice within the community and with a variety of populations. The field practice that concludes the baccalaureate-degree program enables students to demonstrate competent social work practice, not in a classroom but out in the community.

Achieving Competence for Practice in Health Care

Accidents, injury, and illness all have impact. Pain, often both psychological and physical, occurs. There may be days lost from work or school. This can mean getting behind on schoolwork or projects on the job. It could even mean loss of a job and loss of income. Competence for practice begins with an understanding of the social systems and ecosystems perspectives (as described in Chapter 2). In health care, social workers must anticipate that there will almost always be consequences for persons beyond the patient. There may be impact on the job site, for example, if a person is hurt at work. If a parent is ill or injured, there are consequences for the family. Loss of income could have devastating results for the family, potentially even homelessness. Young children don't understand illness or disability well; they may be very upset emotionally by the events unfolding in their family. In a single-parent family, severe or prolonged illness of the parent may require placement of the children with a relative or even in foster care if relatives are not available. In any event, health care problems of the parents often change the quality of nurturing that is so necessary to the healthy development of young children. In some cases, too, older children must take on greater family responsibility, which may include staying home from school to care for younger brothers and sisters.

The generalist practice theory that social work students acquire, based on social systems theory and the ecosystems perspective, provides a basis for understanding the impact of illness and injury on individuals and families as well as larger social systems. In generalist practice courses, students acquire the interviewing techniques and communication skills that are needed in health care social work practice, and they learn to apply the problem-solving process with individuals and families. They also learn how organizations and communities function as systems and how to help organizations, like St. Anne's Hospital in this chapter's case study, change procedures and initiate programs or engage in efforts to prevent illness and injuries.

Whole communities suffer when there are epidemics of flu or much more serious contagious diseases, so social work efforts in prevention are important. Every day social workers help young parents understand the preventive care needed by new babies or young children. Illnesses threaten masses of people in society when the health care system of our country does not ensure that everyone has access to health care. Vigorous political advocacy for health care reform engaged social workers along with other professions and citizens in an effort to create a national health care policy in the United States. This resulted in the 2010 Patient Protection and Affordable Care Act (ACA). Today social workers continue to use critical thinking to analyze and monitor health care reform as it evolves. Students often have exciting opportunities to become involved in policy practice within their fieldwork.

> **?** Assess your understanding of the competencies needed for social work practice in health care by taking this brief quiz.

SELECTED HEALTH CARE SERVICES

Linda Sanders's social work field placement was in a community general hospital, but hospitals are not the only health care settings that employ social workers. The U.S. health care system, fueled by a desire to sustain profitability while controlling rapid increases in health care costs, has created a wide variety of health care ventures. Mergers and acquisitions of hospitals, nursing homes, rehabilitation centers, HMOs, pharmacies, and diagnostic testing centers created giant, profitable, and, in some cases, multi-national health care corporations. The implementation of the Health Care Act brought more social workers and nurses into newly created prevention and outreach programs. Users of health care and all of the health care professions have been and probably will continue to be impacted by the changes to the American health care system.

The result of ongoing change throughout the system is that social workers may now be found in a very wide variety of health care settings (see Box 7.1 for a sampling of settings). As the list of settings suggests, social work is a viable profession in a growing number of health-related community organizations.

Acute Care

The majority of health care social workers today are employed in **acute care** (facilities that provide immediate, short-term care): hospitals, inpatient and outpatient clinics, rehabilitation centers, and specialized services such as sexual assault treatment centers. Rehabilitation centers provide intensive medical services for people who do not need to remain in the hospital but also may not need, or hopefully can avoid, long-term care. While lengthier and somewhat less expensive than hospitalization, care in a rehabilitation facility is fast-paced. Social workers collaborate with patients and families to plan for

---

Box 7.1 Examples of Health Care Settings that Employ Social Workers

General hospitals	Sexual assault treatment centers
Children's hospitals	Health planning boards
Physicians' offices	Specialized health organizations (American Cancer Society, National Kidney Foundation)
Public health clinics	
Health maintenance organizations (HMOs)	Hospice and palliative-care programs
Veterans Administration hospitals/clinics	Insurance companies
Rehabilitation services	Private social work practice
Nursing homes and residential care facilities	Homeless shelter health clinics
Home health care organizations	Outpatient clinics

the physical therapy and ongoing medical services and appliances that are often needed when people are discharged home. While short-term, these social work services often involve intensive emotional exchanges with patients and family members. Advocacy with staff or with outside community organizations may be involved. Service functions in acute care also include social support assessments, discharge planning, psychosocial counseling, case consultation, health education, information and referral, program interdisciplinary consultation, and community planning.

Hospital social work is changing dramatically, as hospitals themselves are changing. Once there were hospital social work departments administered by MSW social workers. Now social workers are employed by hospitals, but they often work out of designated units such as cardiac intensive care, the spinal cord injury area, or the unit that cares for high-risk newborns (neonatal intensive care). Social work service in hospital emergency departments is taking on increased importance. Twenty-four-hour social work staffing is now provided in busy metropolitan hospitals. Nonetheless, there has been a shift away from hospitals toward increased use of outpatient, community-based, and in-home health services.

> Watch this video about a day in the life of a health care social worker, Maureen. Identify at least three primary roles that the social worker must use on a regular basis.
> https://www.youtube.com/watch?v=g1Vo-SIG2no

Long-Term Care

Although most people think of a nursing home when they think about long-term care, a growing number of services are, in fact, included within the purview of long-term care. In addition to nursing homes, some of the community-based services include home health care, assisted-living facilities, home-delivered meals, and adult day care. **Long-term care** consists of any combination of nursing, personal care, volunteer, and social services provided intermittently or on a sustained basis over a span of time to help persons with chronic illness or disability to maintain maximum quality of life.

Not all users of long-term care are people who are elderly, but with the population of older persons increasing, a growing segment of long-term care consumers are likely to be older persons. The 1999 U.S. Supreme Court Olmstead decision encouraged states to develop programs to ensure that older adults and persons with disabilities could live in the least restrictive environment possible. The result was pressure from the federal government for states to evolve programs that enabled elderly persons to avoid nursing home placement or return to community living if they had been placed in a nursing home. However, over time, **cost-containment** concerns—concerns about the need to control rising health care costs—have limited the funding available for home-based care from both Medicare and private insurance. Currently, these programs and Medicaid are more likely to provide for nursing home than in-home care.

Nursing homes remain one of the most common forms of long-term care. In the United States, a large number of nursing homes is owned by proprietary (for-profit) corporations. There are also private, non-profit homes (some operated by religious denominations) plus federal (Veterans Administration), state, and county public facilities. Nursing homes are licensed by the state. Nursing services are provided 24 hours per day, augmented by physical, occupational, and activity therapists; dieticians; and social workers.

Transitional living and assisted living are less restricted and more homelike facilities for older adults who are fairly independent. Both are designed as small apartments, and they are often located on the same property as or attached to existing nursing homes, thus providing for a range of care, depending on need. The residents of these facilities have intellectual, social, political, and spiritual interests and considerable capacity to enjoy them, thus making field trips, even travel, a possibility. Groups and activities of many kinds can be used by creative social workers to meet the social, intellectual, and emotional needs of residents.

Federal law requires that nursing homes provide social services to help residents obtain the highest possible physical and psychological functioning. Large facilities with over 100 residents are required to have at least one full-time social worker, but other homes must make social work services available. Although each long-term care facility is unique, social workers in long-term care are likely to assume most of the following responsibilities:

- Admission planning with the potential resident and family (including evaluating need for care and other options, providing emotional support for the incoming resident and family, and psychosocial assessment of strengths and needs)
- Assistance with adaptation to the facility, transfers within the facility, and discharge planning
- Ongoing individual, family, and group services, as needed, to assist residents with evolving needs, developing supportive interpersonal relationships, and dealing with loss
- Facilitating interprofessional collaboration to ensure that residents' needs are met—advocating, when necessary
- Discussing advance directives, financial power of attorney, and other significant legal decisions with residents and families

In thinking about the ways in which social workers might utilize all available biopsychosocial information to assist nursing home residents, we can recall the case study from the beginning of this chapter. We might ask, "What could a nursing home social worker do to help an elderly woman like Katherine Lewandowski?" As in all social work practice, assessment will be crucial. Social history information obtained at the time of admission could tell the social worker that Katherine Lewandowski had a very strong sense of family and that her Polish ethnicity and faith in the Catholic religion were all very important to her. The social worker would quickly understand that Katherine's despair was heightened by significant losses: the death of her husband five years ago, the death of a son from cancer 18 months ago, and the loss of control over her own body as she became increasingly frail and handicapped by osteoporosis.

Like social workers in all fields of practice, nursing home social workers can advocate for and assist people best when they understand the previous life experiences of that person and the intersectionality (the coming together) of the client's unique characteristics. A resident like Katherine Lewandowski could benefit from encouragement and reassurance provided by a culturally sensitive social worker during frequent visits to her room and also to the hospital when Katherine had surgery. The social

Assessment

Dimension of Competency **Cognitive and Affective Reactions: Social workers understand how their personal experiences and affective reactions may affect their assessment and decision-making.**

Critical Thinking Question: How would a social worker's ability to complete an initial assessment on a new resident be affected by the resident's striking resemblance to the social worker's grandmother, who she loved dearly (or who she had difficulty relating to)?

worker could educate and advocate with other nursing home staff so that they could be more sensitive to her needs. The activities staff, for example, could be encouraged to engage Katherine in socialization activities with other Polish women in the nursing home, thereby helping her to re-establish her sense of identity and linkage to a familiar community. The Catholic chaplain or a priest from Katherine's parish might have been a significant resource, helping her find comfort in her faith and thereby engaging another source of strength. Too often the spiritual life of clients is ignored in hospitals and nursing homes.

Nursing home social work offers unique opportunities for long-term involvement with people during a phase in their lives when many crises may occur. This area of social work practice also offers opportunities to work with families and with groups, to provide education for resident care staff, and to be one of the decision-makers that influence the organization's policies and procedures. Nursing home social workers have remarkable opportunities to become very strong advocates for their clients.

Home Health Care

Home health care is the provision of health care services, including social services, to people in their own homes. Home health services are provided by organizations such as the Visiting Nurse Association, by hospitals, by public health departments, and by proprietary (for-profit) corporations. Social workers are key members of the home care team today. Through counseling, they help family members, especially those in caregiver roles, to work through their feelings of frustration, anger, grief, and pain. Supporting the family and preventing personal and family breakdown during the care-giving time is an objective of the social workers. They also locate needed resources, such as financial aid and bedside nursing equipment. Much rewarding interprofessional collaboration is done with others routinely on the team, primarily physicians and nurses. Ancillary staff often include homemakers, physical therapists, and dieticians.

With their professional colleagues, home care social workers increasingly deal with ethical dilemmas related to questions about how much autonomy and self-determination to support with older persons who have significant physical or cognitive disabilities or when family caregivers become overburdened. Home health hospice programs—which now serve children and adults of all ages with cancer, heart disease, and Alzheimer's disease—raise similar ethical questions. Nonetheless, this is a rapidly growing field of service and one that offers considerable satisfaction as well as challenges.

Hospice and Palliative Care

Hospice refers to a specialized approach in caring for terminally ill persons. As previously noted, hospice care is a program that can be provided at home as well as in a hospital, or in a facility designed specifically for the purpose of serving persons who are dying. Some nursing homes are now adding hospice-care units. Hospice settings are designed to be as comfortable and homelike as possible. Some of the newest designs include an outdoor healing terrace; pets are also welcomed in some hospice programs. The treatment approach used by hospices is **palliative care**. This means that treatment efforts are directed at controlling pain and providing the best quality of life possible for people when there is no longer any curative treatment. The philosophy underlying hospice care is one of a profound respect for life and for death as a normal part of human life.

The term *hospice* originated in medieval times when hospices were way stations, generally run by religious orders that provided rescue, shelter, and assistance to travelers. A member of the Irish Sisters of Charity, Sister Mary Aikenhead, established Our Lady's Hospice in her Dublin home to care for dying persons in 1846. Her concept of caring for terminally ill people was carried forward in Ireland but remained unknown elsewhere until Cicely Saunders, a nurse and social worker who worked at a hospice in Ireland, founded the famed St. Christopher's Hospice in London in 1967. Cicely Saunders's commitment to humane care of the dying led her to obtain a medical degree, and St. Christopher's Hospice incorporated the practice of medicine and the development of research (Richman, 1995). The first hospice programs in the United States emerged around 1970 and were patterned after the model for humane care established by Cicely Saunders.

Hospice care today is provided by an interdisciplinary team comprised of doctors, nurses, social workers, and clergy, often supplemented by a core of volunteers. Many insurance programs, including Medicare, cover hospice care because it is less costly than hospital or nursing home care. Insurance policies require a physician's certification that the potential hospice patient is within six months of death. Persons who apply for hospice care must agree to forego curative treatment. Hospice programs provide care to infants and children as well as young and older adults, although older adults comprise the largest cohort of people in hospice.

> Watch this video on Cicely Saunders. How is hospice care today reflective of her early work?
> https://www.youtube.com/watch?v=mAU2p5bN4II

The NASW policy statement on hospice care affirms that compassionate care for the dying is consistent with the values and with the code of ethics of the social work profession (Kelly & Clark, 2009). The NASW policy statement also affirms that persons who are dying should have the right to self-determination regarding how they live the remainder of their lives, which is basic to the philosophy of hospice care. Social workers in hospice programs are an integral part of the health care team. Social workers

- provide counseling and emotional support to dying persons and their families;
- assist dying people to deal with physical as well as emotional pain;
- advocate with other staff to ensure that clients' and families' needs are met;
- provide crisis intervention;
- assist with anticipatory grieving (Dziegielewski, 2004).

Following death, hospice social workers continue to assist family members and friends with bereavement.

Emergency Department: Trauma and Crisis Amid Human Diversity

Hospitals that operate large, active emergency care facilities employ social workers on all shifts, seven days a week. In smaller facilities, social workers staff the emergency department during periods of high demand and they function on an on-call basis during less busy periods. Every television viewer knows well the life-and-death drama of the hospital emergency room, as the emergency department was once called. For the social worker, emergency department practice means fast-paced crisis intervention work and brief contact with clients. For example, the 17-year-old who took an overdose of aspirin when her boyfriend threatened to end their relationship needs someone to help her sort out her embarrassment and shame, after the aspirin has been removed from her stomach. The social worker makes a rapid assessment of the young woman's psychosocial situation and determines that referral for counseling is needed both for the young woman and for her family.

When a community disaster occurs, hospital emergency departments receive injured and psychologically traumatized patients. All hospitals have disaster plans, so social workers and other staff know their roles in advance. Emergency care of medical needs must take priority, of course. Social workers are important members of the team. They assess and comfort children and adults whose injuries do not appear to require

---

Box 7.2   Emergency Department Case Examples

Miguel, a 5-year-old boy, is admitted to the emergency department (ED) with multiple fractures suffered in a car accident. Dr. Hastings asks the ED social worker to stand by to help the parents while he and the nursing staff work with Miguel. Dr. Hastings anticipates that Miguel will have to be admitted to the hospital after receiving initial care in the emergency room. Every 15 minutes, Sarah, the social worker, provides information to the parents—information obtained from Dr. Hastings or the nurses who are with the boy. The parents, a young Puerto Rican couple, show their immense concern about their son very openly. The wife, who is pregnant, is extremely nervous and is breathing irregularly, and she appears to be on the verge of having an *ataque* (an episode similar to a seizure; *ataques* are sometimes experienced during periods of severe emotional stress and are recognized in the Puerto Rican culture as a cry for help). The husband's anger with the hit-and-run driver who injured his son takes the form of angry threats, loudly voiced, and of demands that the hospital staff do something to save his son.

The social worker provides emotional support to the parents and helps them to a room where they have more privacy and where additional family members can be with them as soon as the social worker is able to contact them. She provides them with Kleenex and offers water. With the social worker's help, the mother's sister is reached and she immediately agrees to come to the hospital. The parents become calmer with the care and emotional support of the social worker. Within 30 minutes, the mother's sister arrives and shortly afterwards Dr. Hastings asks the social worker and family to come to Miguel's bedside. Miguel's bloody clothing has been removed; he is pale but smiles sweetly as he tries to reach out to his mother. The doctor explains that Miguel has been given medication for his pain and he is increasingly sleepy. He will recover, but he will need surgery in the morning for his fractures. His kindly, careful explanation enables the parents to understand. Miguel's father signs the consent for surgery forms.

Sarah then helps the parents gather their things and the social worker and family members accompany Miguel's cart as he is taken to his third-floor hospital room. When the social worker is sure that the family is comfortable, she leaves the room but not before Miguel's mother smiles for the first time and gives her a hug to thank her.

Before the evening ends, the social worker will also have helped a 55-year-old, white, middle-class woman whose husband's life could not be saved following his third heart attack; an elderly Catholic nun who required admission to the hospital because of pneumonia; and a poor, inner-city African-American mother and infant who were hungry and whose heat had been turned off by the landlord for non-payment of rent. The social worker interpreted medical information to waiting families, offered psychological strength, demonstrated concern and caring, confronted inappropriate behavior, used crisis counseling techniques, and connected people with needed community resources. In addition, the social worker helped the doctors and caregivers understand and appreciate the cultural dimensions that influenced patients' responses to pain and their families' responses to crisis.

immediate care if all medical staff members are needed for more seriously injured persons. They provide emotional assistance to persons whose trauma is threatening their mental health status. All of this is done with appreciation for the diversity of the people involved and for the community environment.

Social workers' well-developed interprofessional teamwork relationships are extremely valuable when serious emergencies strike. The experience and expertise hospital social workers develop in their day-to-day work with persons who are ill, injured, dying, or recovering from surgery and facing a bright new future—all of this serves the social worker, the health care team, and the traumatized persons who are helped during times of personal or community disaster.

Health Care for Veterans

The Veterans Health Administration (VHA), a U.S. federal government program, is one of the largest health care systems in the world, and it is the largest employer of social workers in the United States. Its history goes all the way back to 1636 when the Pilgrims of Plymouth Colony enacted legislation requiring their government to become responsible for disabled soldiers. Veterans' homes, known as **domiciliaries**, were established following the Civil War. World War I resulted in massive numbers of military personnel needing medical care. As the war was drawing to closure in 1918, Congress hurried to address the rush of injured returning troops. Hundreds of private hospitals and even hotels were initially leased; subsequently, new hospitals were built that offered outpatient as well as inpatient care for veterans (Department of Veterans Affairs, n.d.).

The health care needs of military personnel grew substantially during World War II and in subsequent military actions. The VHA responded. Today there are 152 hospitals, 800 clinics, 126 nursing home units, plus 35 domiciliaries (Department of Veterans Affairs, n.d.). Considerable change in the nature of health services provided has taken place. The injuries resulting from more technologically advanced weapons and warfare became a catalyst for the evolution of medical treatment and technology. Now, for example, more sophisticated treatment has been developed for the care of amputations. Many new programs have been initiated or expanded to work with post-traumatic stress and suicide prevention. While males continue to comprise the greatest cohort of military personnel, increasingly women are entering the military services in larger numbers, which means that new programs have been developed to focus on the medical, surgical, rehabilitation, and mental health needs of women veterans.

Speaking at a national NASW health care conference, Carol Sheets, of the Care Management Social Work Services at the VA in Washington, D.C., reported that a transformation is currently taking place within the Department of Veterans Affairs. She described the new patient-centered approach to health care that systematically draws patients into discussions and thinking about their personal health care needs and future plans. New programs are evolving to address health care needs of women veterans. Increasing attention is also being given to meeting the needs of veterans in rural areas. Sheets anticipated that the VA would be leveraging computer technology in the future including video conferencing, telemedicine, and possibly social media. She noted that the transformations underway in the system might require the social work workforce at the VA to expand (Pace, 2013).

Box 7.3 Social Work Class Field Trip: VA Spinal Cord Injury Center

During a social work class field trip to the Clement J. Zablocki VA Medical Center in Milwaukee, WI, one of this text's authors found that their new spinal cord injury center (SCI Center) facility had already implemented many of the transformations that Carol Sheets described previously. This self-contained facility on the vast hospital grounds receives persons with combat injuries from almost anywhere in the world where U.S. military forces are located, and from the local Midwest area of veterans whose injuries were sustained in their civilian life, in car or motorcycle accidents, for example. **Spinal cord injuries** represent damage to the spinal cord that result most frequently from a traumatic blow to the spine, gunshot wound, car accident, sports injury, or a fall (Mayo Clinic, 2015). The SCI Center also treats diseases of the spine such as cancer, stroke, multiple sclerosis, and **ALS** (amyotrophic lateral sclerosis).

The Veterans Administration provides spinal cord injury care through a network of services. Newly injured active-duty service members or veterans are first stabilized at a military treatment or trauma facility. Then they are referred to one of 24 regional SCI Centers in the United States for specialty care, referred to as "hubs." The "spokes" in this "hub-and-spoke system" are the 134 primary care teams at local VA hospitals where care is provided by multi-disciplinary teams comprised of a doctor, nurse, and social worker (Veterans Health Administration, n.d.).

Persons who receive their initial treatment following injury at the SCI Center in Milwaukee are expected to continue subsequent care at the SCI Center. The veterans' ages range from very young adults to persons in their 90s. The SCI Center's multi-disciplinary staff that met with the social work students explained that the work of the center was organized on the basis of team decision-making. It quickly became apparent that the social work staff served a prominent role within the health care team, working closely with psychologists, doctors, nurses, and therapists. Social workers carried primary responsibility for admissions and for discharge planning, while also being involved with persons during and following hospitalization. The SCI Center's teamwork model emphasized patient-centered care. The students involved with this field trip were quick to observe the collaboration and quick communication among team members and the ready access they had to each other. It was explained that the professional staff teams met regularly, have well-developed procedures for ensuring input from all disciplines, and thoroughly involved patients and their family members, as that is an important part of the SCI Center's concept for planning and decision-making. Women, although fewer in number than the male veterans, also received care from the SPI Center's inpatient and outpatient programs.

New approaches to patient care were evident everywhere in the facility from efforts at major re-design of exercise activity equipment to re-configuring kitchen space to make it more possible to view food cooking on the stoves in the small apartments used by entire families in preparation for veterans' discharge from the SCI Center. The class observed high-tech conference rooms that enabled the professional team to provide health and social services via **telemedicine** to discharged veterans who had returned to their home communities hundreds of miles from the facility. The ongoing and evolving needs of discharged veterans with spinal cord injuries and their families in rural areas require considerable creative thinking and effort from the social work staff, especially when crises occur. Veterans with spinal cord injuries often have exceptionally complex needs during their hospitalization but also in anticipation of discharge. Alcohol and substance abuse, mental health issues, complicated family relationships, and dramatically changed mobility are among the problems that social workers encounter in their work within this Veterans Health Administration facility. This field trip encouraged many of the students to consider health care social work as a potential career.

Health Care in Rural Areas

Health care facilities in rural areas often require considerable community involvement from the social worker. In rural settings, social workers call on all their generalist practice skills as they work with families and communities to help people obtain health care and to provide care following hospitalization. Long distances between health centers, isolated dwellings, poverty, and lack of transportation make it difficult for many rural people to obtain high-quality health care. Pregnant rural women, for example, are at increased risk because they often have inadequate access to prenatal care. Poor overall health and considerable chronic illness are common in many rural areas. The exodus of young people to metropolitan areas leaves rural areas with an aging population. Hospitals in rural areas or small towns generally have no more than 50 to 100 beds. Complex and expensive medical services such as **hemodialysis** (a procedure to cleanse the blood of persons with chronic kidney disease) are often not provided. Severe financial pressure is often experienced by small hospitals, and many have closed in the past 15 years.

> Watch this video from the U.S. Department of Veterans Affairs regarding one of their spinal cord injury programs. Although social work is not the focus of the video content, how would a health care social worker interact with this multi-disciplinary team? What unique skills would a social worker bring to the environment?
> https://www.youtube.com/watch?v=iMvavOXLEe8

Usually a small hospital employs only one or two social workers. Generalist practice skills are vital. Social workers in small health care facilities have to be very knowledgeable about the local community and its resources. In rural areas when needed resources such as home health care are not available, the social worker helps to create them or calls on clergy, police, or neighbors for assistance. In small towns, friends, neighbors, and co-workers sometimes provide exceptional help.

Rural communities sometimes lack information about medical conditions such as AIDS and mental disorders. This may exacerbate stigma and existing lack of tolerance for diversity and difference of all kinds. Sometimes negative responses to people who are HIV-positive stem from concerns about contagion or from moral judgments that derive from very strongly held religious values. Social work support for the people and their families may be needed to deal with the emotional burden and with social isolation. Providing counseling and psychotherapy for mental health needs becomes especially challenging in rural areas for social workers since people tend to know their neighbors and confidentiality is often threatened. Social workers provide community education and also advocate for needed community resources.

The rural health care facility—a rehabilitation center, hospital, or nursing home—often serves people from a very large geographical area. The social worker must have a good understanding of several counties' welfare and human service resources. One county may have a Meals on Wheels program, for example, while another does not or can provide only general nutrition but no special diets (such as a diabetic diet). A large geographical area may also mean long-distance travel for the social worker when a home visit is needed. Telemedicine, however, is a bright spot in the rural social work environment, and it is already narrowing the gap electronically between people needing service and regional service providers in hospitals, private practices, and increasingly in government agencies (Battista-Frazee, 2015).

Evaluation

Dimensions of Competency Cognitive and Affective Reactions: Social workers recognize the importance of evaluating processes and outcomes to advance practice, policy, and service delivery effectiveness.

Critical Thinking Question: In order to continually improve services to people, how can social workers conduct evaluations that capture their own and their clients' experiences with new methods of service delivery such as telemedicine?

Public Health and Health Departments

Public health is not a single profession; instead, it is a field that engages numerous professions in a common goal of prevention of illness and disability while promoting health and well-being. We can think of public health on two levels: work within communities and larger social systems to promote health, and direct work with individuals and families to teach infant and child care, provide family planning information, and advocate for the resources needed for people. Some of the professions employed in public health are physicians, epidemiologists, lawyers, engineers, teachers, social workers, and nurses.

Concern about threats to public health actually goes back to the mid- to late 1900s, when social reformers in England came to believe that overcrowding in urban areas was toxic to the physical and mental health of the population (Susser & Morabia, 2006). The social reformers perceived that the rapid urbanization, poor sanitation, overcrowding, and stark inequalities of the Industrial Revolution were responsible for the concurrent spread of disease. Awareness that environmental toxins such as mercury and lead could contribute to specific physical and mental illnesses, however, has evolved steadily over the years until today; a great deal is known about the relationship between environmental issues and health.

Historically, social work and public health emerged at about the same time in the United States. The legacy of social work pioneers dramatically displays their aggressive and systematic work to achieve social, economic, and environmental justice. Indeed, Jane Addams, who is revered as a social work pioneer, was personally involved in political action to secure proper sanitation for the city of Chicago. She and the staff of Hull House exposed the "sweating" (sweatshop) system as a primary factor in Chicago's typhoid epidemic. Hull House and other settlement houses of the early 1900s engaged people from the communities they served, primarily poor immigrant people, in political action for justice. When they achieved passage of child labor legislation, the quality of life for children was forever improved. Substandard housing, industrial accidents, poverty, and domestic abuse were among the other issues the settlement house workers took on, in part because they understood the linkage between these issues. The Hull House residents of Chicago and the persons involved with settlement houses in other parts of the United States were teachers, doctors, nurses, lawyers, and others. These early pioneers understood that health and well-being for people were significantly related to and dependent on the state of the environment (Sable, Schild, & Hipp, 2012).

Today some public health social workers, like the early pioneers, are primarily employed in policymaking, program planning, community organizing, research, and administrative positions. Others work in the community directly with groups, individuals, and families. Public health services are offered through private organizations such as YWCAs and community neighborhood centers, but local health departments are the primary providers and are sometimes described as the "work horses" of the public health system. Most hire social workers for a wide range of programs including violence prevention, safe housing, woman and child health, and refugee programs. The Family and Community Health Program unit of the public health department in many cities teams social workers and nurses to do home visiting to high-risk families.

This mother received prenatal care and the family is now happily expecting a new baby that will not be born prematurely like their first child

An example of risk would be pregnant women who have previously had one or more premature or complicated births. They receive services, generally in their homes, on an ongoing basis through the prenatal period up to their child's third birthday. Together the social worker and nurse monitor the mother's and child's health and try to ensure that babies receive immunizations that protect them from communicable diseases. Fathers as well as mothers are taught how to keep babies safe (including safe sleeping), how to create attachment and bonding, and how to ensure proper nutrition for their baby. Sexually transmitted diseases, contraception, and family planning are often discussed. Referrals are made when families need infant formula, cribs, diapers, and other supplies. Housing and sanitation is assessed. Care is taken to ensure that lead and other hazards are not present and that the home is properly heated and ventilated. Health inspectors are involved and action is taken if landlords fail to keep rental properties safe and consistent with housing codes. Since many families receiving care through this program are in poverty, special attention is given to employment search skills, and referrals are made

> Assess your understanding of selected health settings by taking this brief quiz.

to educational resources. Immigrant and refugee family needs are assessed and basic resources are often provided. Assessment may be done, too, when concern emerges about potential domestic abuse, depression, and substance abuse.

HISTORICAL PERSPECTIVES

The chapter content now shifts to history. We begin with a quick look at the origin of hospitals and then trace the history of social work within the broader field of health care. Of special interest here is the proud history of health care social work as one of the earliest developments in the social work profession. This is also a field of practice that has become quite agile in adapting to changing times.

Early History: Caring for the Poor and Sick

It is not clear when health care institutions were developed, but archaeologists have uncovered ruins of what may have been such facilities dating from the 6th century B.C. The tithing of the early Christians produced funds that churches could use for the care of the poor and the sick. Around the 3rd century A.D., monks of the Roman Catholic Church began to provide rescue service and health care to avalanche victims in shelters known as hospices. The victims were mostly southern Europeans who were fleeing from famine and economic hardship and were trying to reach northern regions in search of a better life. They were unfamiliar with and unprepared for the harsh weather of the mountains. Gradually, the term *hospice* came to be used for institutions that cared for ill persons. In Western Europe, hospices housed not only the sick but, until almshouses were organized, the poor as well. Gradually, hospices developed into larger institutions that were run primarily by religious orders of priests or sisters. (Even today, in most of Europe, a nurse is called *sister*.) In England during the mid-1500s, the Crown confiscated monasteries in the historic dispute between Henry VIII and the Roman Catholic Church. With the seizure of religious holdings, the settings that cared for the sick were gradually converted into publicly held institutions.

Origins of Health Care Social Work

The English forerunners of today's health care social workers were the **lady almoners**, persons who provided food and donations to the poor. In 1895, a lady almoner was stationed at the Royal Free Hospital with the understanding that she was to interview patients to determine who would receive free, or partly free, medical service and who to exclude from free care. But soon the lady almoner realized that many, probably the majority of the people she interviewed, were in serious financial straits (Cannon, 1952). This early social worker, like many today, preferred to define the nature of her professional practice herself, rather than permitting hospital authorities, physicians, or others to govern how she understood and carried out her professional responsibilities. Therefore, she became an advocate for patients, fighting for the rights and needs of the poor and underserved, the persons that the Royal Free Hospital saw as unsuitable. The use of almoners, later known as social workers, spread throughout British Commonwealth hospitals, and their role soon broadened to include counseling, referral to other community resources, patient education, and advocacy.

The Emergence of Health Care Social Work in the United States

The person who is generally considered the originator of medical social work in the United States is Ida Cannon. As a young woman, Ida Cannon had worked as a visiting nurse in the slum areas along the Mississippi River in St. Paul, Minnesota. Inspired by Jane Addams, the great settlement house worker, Cannon became interested in social work and went to Boston to pursue her studies at the Boston School of Social Work. In 1905, Dr. Richard Cabot, whose concerns about poverty and its impact on illness paralleled her own, asked Cannon to join the staff of Massachusetts General Hospital.

In her professional practice, Cannon was not only a competent social worker but also a dynamic leader, a teacher of medical as well as social work students, and an articulate author. Health care social workers were the first among the various social work specialty groups to organize professionally. Cannon was among the founders of the American Association of Hospital Social Workers in 1918. This organization, later known as the American Association of Medical Social Workers (AAMSW), published its own journal, *Medical Social Work*. The AAMSW eventually merged with other independent social work organizations to become the NASW in 1955. Cannon's 1952 text, *On the Social Frontier of Medicine: Pioneering in Medical Social Service*, describes the early years of hospital social work.

Soon after Cannon developed the social service department at Massachusetts General Hospital, Bellevue Hospital in New York hired a social worker. Slowly hospitals across the country began hiring social workers. Soon public health concerns about patients with tuberculosis and venereal disease resulted in the employment of social workers by state health departments and tuberculosis sanatoriums. The passage of the Social Security Act in 1935 resulted in entitlements that further encouraged the expansion of social work in health care settings. Both the American Hospital Association (AHA) and the American Public Health Association developed standards and requirements for social workers in the facilities they regulated.

One of the most influential persons in shaping health care social work over ensuing years was Helen Rehr. For more than 30 years, she provided leadership, creating many innovative programs within the social work department at Mount Sinai Medical Center in New York. A prolific author, she published many works related to health care social work, among them were *Medicine and Social Work: An Exploration in Interprofessionalism* (1994) and *Advancing Social Work Practice in the Health Care Field* (1982). Even in her retirement, this health care social work pioneer continued to consult, to contribute to her community, and to publish; her most recent book was *The Social Work–Medicine Relationship: 100 Years at Mount Sinai* (2006).

> **?** Assess your understanding of the history of health care social work by taking this brief quiz.

SOCIAL JUSTICE: POLITICS AND ECONOMICS IN HEALTH CARE

By 1905, when Ida Cannon initiated the first hospital social work department, the U.S. health care system had evolved from one delivered by women within their own households, relying primarily on homemade medical preparations, to an industry dominated by specialized professionals, pharmaceutical corporations, and institutions. Massive hospitals, first built during the Civil War, utilized new techniques of hygiene and, by the early 1900s, vastly increased the number of surgical procedures performed, thanks to the development of diagnostic X-rays and anesthesia.

By the early 1900s, many European countries (England, Germany, Austria, and others) and Russia had initiated **compulsory health insurance programs** (where all citizens were required to purchase insurance), thereby ensuring access to health care for all citizens of their countries. (Compulsory health insurance was a key feature of the United States' 2010 Affordable Health Care Act.) Interest in such programs was emerging in the United States. In 1912, Jane Addams and social workers in the settlement house movement, well aware of unmet health needs—especially of women and children–threw their support behind presidential candidate Theodore Roosevelt when he advocated compulsory health insurance for the United States. With the advent of World War I (1914–1918) and the Bolshevik Revolution in Russia, however, the U.S. public began to perceive anything that appeared German (such as compulsory health insurance) as negative and threatening and anything Russian as Communistic. Jane Addams and other proponents of compulsory health insurance were branded as traitors to the United States. Even the Federation for Social Service of the Methodist Church faced extremely adverse publicity. The American Medical Association (AMA) shifted from supporting compulsory insurance and began what was to become a lengthy history of opposition to any form of what they called "socialized medicine" (Moniz & Gorin, 2010).

Social workers and other health care policy reformers did not give up, however. Julia Lathrop and Grace Abbott, both former colleagues of Jane Addams and former residents of Chicago's Hull House, disseminated research findings showing that the exceptionally high rate of infant mortality in the United States was related to inadequate prenatal care and poverty (Trattner, 1999, as cited in Moniz & Gorin, 2010). Another social worker, Jeanette Rankin, serving as the first woman elected to the U.S. Congress, introduced and achieved the passage of the Sheppard–Towner Infancy and Maternity Act of 1921. This legislation provided funding to states for numerous public health programs aimed at improving the health of women and children. With the advent of the Great Depression and concerted opposition from the AMA, which saw public health services as interfering with its right to free enterprise, the Sheppard–Towner Act was terminated in 1929. The establishment of Blue Cross and Blue Shield insurance programs in the 1930s created a **third-party payment system** (where insurance companies provided reimbursement for some insured members' health care costs). This changed health care financing in the United States, and soon employment-based insurance emerged (Moniz & Gorin, 2010).

In the 1930s, social workers provided courageous leadership in health care reform efforts. Harry L. Hopkins, a social worker who had worked with Franklin D. Roosevelt in New York when Roosevelt was governor, became a trusted adviser of Roosevelt when he was elected U.S. president. Hopkins and Frances Perkins, another social worker and Roosevelt's Secretary of Labor (the first woman to occupy a cabinet position), both supported compulsory health care and hoped to have it included in the Social Security Act of 1935. As a result of a flood of opposition orchestrated by the AMA, compulsory national health insurance was removed from the final version of the Social Security Act.

By the 1940s, former charity hospitals had become profit-making businesses, with income generated by cash-paying customers and insurance companies. Public health services, which had served the nation through several waves of infectious diseases and provided health care to low-income populations, were politically crushed by the increasingly powerful entrepreneurial, for-profit, health care industry. By the 1960s, it became clear that the private health insurance industry was not able to provide for the total population needing health care, nor was it able to contain the increasing costs of health care. At the same time, nationwide pressure was building for national health insurance (Weiss, 1997).

Medicare

The federal government's involvement in health care financing became a reality in the 1960s with the enactment of the programs known as Medicare and Medicaid. **Medicare** was created in 1965 with an amendment, Title XVIII, to the Social Security Act. Labor unions strongly supported this legislation while the AMA, the AHA, and the insurance industry battled hard to keep government out of health care. Some of the compromises won by the AMA and the AHA included limiting government control over the size of reimbursements for services and, a major victory, allowing for the numerous insurance companies that comprised this industry to be the conduit for payments made to providers.

Medicare currently covers 55 million Americans who meet the following criteria:

- People who are 65 years old
- People with disabilities
- People with permanent kidney failure (The Medicare Blog, 2015)

Although the 2010 Affordable Health Care Act (ACA) changed Medicare, it continues to have four parts. Part A provides insurance for hospital care and 100 days in a nursing home. Medicare comes from payroll taxes paid while people are working; however, it is definitely not free. It requires substantial co-payments. Hospice care is provided for terminally ill persons, but only if they are expected to die within six months. Many qualifications must be met before a person may receive home health care under Medicare.

Part B is different from Part A. It closely resembles a private health insurance program. It is entirely voluntary, but it is vital to most people because it pays for some of the health care expenses not covered by Part A. Like private insurance, there are monthly payments of approximately $134 in 2017 (Medicare.gov, 2016). The payment amount is almost always increased when there is a raise in Social Security. Part B is often thought of as outpatient insurance since it provides payment for physicians, laboratory services, medical equipment such as wheelchairs or walkers, and outpatient surgeries.

To the surprise of some people, Medicare does not cover all medical expenses of the elderly. Sometimes social workers must explain the limitations of Medicare to disbelieving elderly persons who have trusted that the money they paid into Social Security would take care of all of their medical needs in old age. Services not provided by Parts A or B include the following:

- Long-term nursing or custodial care
- Dentures and dental care
- Eyeglasses
- Most prescription drugs

Several options to Medicare Parts A and B were initiated in 1997 as Part C. These plans are obtained through private insurance corporations. Also known as the Medicare

Advantage Plan, this option includes a variety of managed-care plans plus Medical Savings Accounts. The Medical Savings Accounts require a very high deductible payment plus monthly premiums. If illness occurs, the deductible has to be paid before the plan takes over, but when it does, it pays all remaining medical expenses.

An advantage of the Medicare Part C programs was that many included prescription drug coverage. The failure of Medicare Parts A and B to provide coverage for prescriptions became so volatile that, in 2003, a prescription drug benefit plan, Part D, was created. This complex plan is administered by private health insurance companies and requires the following payments:

- The Medicare Part B premium deducted from the monthly Social Security check, $134 for 2017
- A monthly premium set by the private insurance company, possibly around $80, but varies
- Co-payment: the insurance carrier's charge, a percentage of the drug cost (could not exceed $400 in 2017)
- Coverage gap cost ("donut hole") (Medicare.gov, 2016)

Medicare's Part B premium must be paid for Part D's prescription plan to be activated. An additional monthly premium (which is competitively priced and varies considerably) is paid to the private insurance carrier, but persons whose income exceeded $85,000 in 2017 paid up to $76.20 additionally, per month, directly to Medicare. The monthly premium, co-payments, and coverage gap costs are determined by and paid to the insurance company.(Medicare.gov, 2016).

Medicare was improved by the ACA, which called for termination of the extremely problematic "donut hole" in 2020. While the ACA remains in place, when the predetermined coverage gap level is reached (at $3,700 in 2017), the insured person must pay a designated percentage of prescription (less for brand-name drugs) that was not previously required. The ACA scaled back the personal responsibility from 65 percent for generic drugs in 2015 to 25 percent in 2020. The ACA also reformed Medicare by covering preventive services such as mammograms, colonoscopies, and annual wellness exams that were not previously included in Medicare. Brand-name drugs, sometimes required for certain medical problems, are discounted for persons in the coverage gap period, until it is terminated.

Medicare, despite its failings, is a remarkable program. It provides health care to millions of people, many of whom could otherwise not afford it. It is expensive, and it has problems, one of which is the millions of dollars lost each year in fraud that is perpetrated by laboratories, managed-care plans, physicians, hospitals, nursing homes, and others, sometimes including patients.

Medicaid

Social work as a profession has a special commitment to people who are poor or vulnerable. Of course, this includes people who are at risk of or who have existing physical and mental health problems. Because **Medicaid** is the largest U.S. financial aid program for poor people, it is obvious that social workers need to know something about Medicaid. Most social workers, however, will not need to know all of the intricate details;

they do need to know where they can find information about Medicaid. One of the best sources is the Medicaid website. Some very basic information about the Medicaid program follows.

Medicaid, also known as Medical Assistance, was enacted in 1965 as Title XIX of the Social Security Act. The federal government and states jointly fund the program, but the states administer the program. It now covers over 60 million people, including people who receive Supplemental Security Income because they are blind, aged, or have disabilities. Pregnant women and children with a family income below 133 percent of the poverty line, in general, are also eligible. Medicaid is a lifeline for poor people because it pays for prescriptions, laboratory tests and X-rays, inpatient and outpatient hospital care, skilled nursing home care, and home health care. Medicaid expanded in 2014 when two new groups of people became eligible: adults under the age of 65 whose incomes were below 133 percent of the poverty line, and children aging out of the foster care system (up to age 26) (Medicaid.gov, Keeping America Healthy, 2016).

Medicaid is a means-tested program, which means that applicants must provide proof of poverty according to their state's definition. Many people find the application procedure humiliating. Medicare, by contrast, is automatically available to people who are 65 or older, who are disabled, or who have permanent kidney failure. Like Medicare, the Affordable Care Act has created changes to Medicaid, including broadening the eligibility requirements so that more people will have access to health care.

Health Care Reform

The quest to secure access to health care for all Americans has been slow, but health care reform has been pushing its way toward the top of the political agenda since the early 1900s. The first proposed large-scale health care reform proposal was President Bill Clinton's Health Security Act of 1993, which would have created a national health insurance plan for the United States if it had become law. **National health insurance plans** are those systems within a given country that ensure participation in comprehensive, generally compulsory, health care insurance, thus giving all citizens access to health care services.

In the 1990s, when Hillary Clinton campaigned vigorously across the country seeking support for the Clinton Health Security Act, her message that health care was a basic human right and represented social justice, was not well received (Barnes, 1994). Opponents argued that national health care was so expensive that it would destroy the country's economy. Liberals, who wanted national health care, failed to support the Clinton proposal because many believed that without a **single-payer system** to administer the program, the assortment of private for-profit insurance corporations would produce excessive administrative costs and would be too expensive. (A single-payer system exists when either the government or a single selected corporation administers an insurance program.) The Clinton Health Security Act was defeated in 1994.

Change, however, was inevitable. Massive numbers of persons were uninsured. As health care costs skyrocketed, employers began to shift more of their health insurance costs to their employees through increased deductibles or co-pays. Doctors' authority over hospital admission and discharge was increasingly taken over by insurance corporations' managed-care policies. The political winds began to shift as dissatisfaction with the health care financing system grew.

Between 2006 and 2007, Massachusetts and Vermont passed health care reform laws, and additional states had similar legislation pending. Lack of action on the part of the federal government resulted in state action to deal with growing numbers of uninsured persons, mostly young adults and children. Some of the states' bills required all citizens to purchase health care insurance through their employers or a variety of other programs, and they incorporated disincentives for employers who failed to provide insurance coverage. Other states moved more slowly and incrementally, with plans focusing on only portions of their uninsured citizens. Interestingly, some of the leadership in health care reform came from Republican state governors such as Arnold Schwarzenegger of California and Mitt Romney, the former governor of Massachusetts. Political action groups emerged ranging from community or state citizens' groups such as Health Care for All to physicians' groups dedicated to health care policy reform.

But, others asked, how could health care financing be changed for the entire country? It became apparent that health care reform could be initiated with small, incremental steps, or through a major overhaul of the existing health care system. Would the United States create a **national health service system** similar to that of England and Germany, where citizens receive health care through government-owned and operated hospitals? That option was not likely to win much support in the United States. Reform could also mean federal funding to states to develop programs that would ensure quality health insurance for all citizens, with most existing systems remaining in place. Or it could require a single-payer program such as the Canadian system, where each state negotiates with a single insurance corporation to handle all claims, thereby dramatically reducing bureaucracy as well as billing, marketing, and other health care administrative costs. Some public citizen health advocacy groups were convinced that the single-payer approach was the only option that would make **universal coverage** affordable (Wolfe, 2006). Elimination of the profit motive currently driving the U.S. health care industry, they believed, would put a stop to growing health care costs and would inevitably be more humane and much less expensive than the current free market, for-profit system (Karger & Stoez, 2010). It was clear, though, that the private enterprise health care industry in the United States would vigorously oppose government-administered health care, preferring that individual citizens be required by law to purchase insurance from private insurance providers whose plans met prescribed requirements. With skyrocketing costs in health care, change became inevitable.

The Patient Protection and Affordable Care Act

There was no landslide majority that won passage of this 2010 federal legislation; indeed, it was passed by a narrow majority. It was, however, a political victory for the president, Barack Obama, who made health care finance reform a central priority of his administration. The Affordable Care Act (ACA), which came to be known as Obamacare, was revolutionary for it created the first nearly **universal health care system** for the United States. It was breakthrough legislation in that it ensured access to health insurance, thus to health care, for the 32 million Americans who had no health insurance. It was not a major overhaul of the system but, instead, sustained current providers, employment-based insurance programs, Medicare and Medicaid, and a familiar system of hospitals, doctors, and government as well as private providers. Built into the law was a plan for incremental implementation.

The authors of this text have tried to simplify this very complex piece of legislation somewhat by focusing on its basic goals and the mechanisms for their achievement. The plan's basic goals, as seen by the text authors, were to

- provide access to affordable health insurance to all Americans;
- prevent disease and improve the health outcome for Americans;
- bring health care costs under control;
- retain with only minimal change in the existing American health care system.

The primary mechanisms to accomplish these goals were to

- require all Americans to obtain some form of approved health insurance;
- sustain employer-provided health insurance;
- sustain the existing system of private as well as public hospitals, clinics, and health care services;
- expand Medicaid eligibility;
- create insurance exchanges in each state offering insurance plans to low-income individuals who did not qualify for Medicaid and for small businesses;
- incorporate Medicare as an approved insurance;
- encourage use of preventive health care to improve the well-being of people and to decrease health care spending.

Portions of the ACA were implemented immediately, but much of the law remained to be gradually implemented. Some of the major provisions of the law and their completed or scheduled implementation dates are shown in Box 7.4.

Although the law was passed by a narrow majority, the Henry J. Kaiser Family Foundation reported that its poll, taken several months following enactment of the law, showed general support for many provisions of the ACA. The least-favored provision of the law was the requirement that individuals must obtain health insurance (2010). The mandate to purchase insurance became a rallying point for ongoing opposition to the ACA. Conservatives opposed the law, even calling for its repeal, while political liberals tended to support the law. Some changes were made to the ACA by Congress, President Obama, and even by the U.S. Supreme Court. The Supreme Court redefined the ACA as, essentially, an option and a voluntary decision, but one that would result in payment of a tax if government-approved health insurance was not obtained (Turner, 2015).

Cost–Benefit Analysis

Now, with health care policy in turmoil, it is useful to do a brief cost-benefit analysis of the ACA. We can begin by looking at the first goal of the ACA: to provide access to affordable health insurance to all Americans. Data collected by the U.S. Census Bureau suggests that the ACA has demonstrated improvements in the rate of uninsured Americans. For several years prior to the ACA, the rate of insured persons had been fairly stable around 86.7 percent. In 2014, the year that was targeted as the first year for all Americans to purchase insurance, the rate of insured increased to 89.6 percent: the number of uninsured fell to 33 million (U.S. Census Bureau, 2015). By mid-2016 the rate of uninsured fell to a record low of 8.6 percent, a decline to 27.3 million. Following the elections in 2016, enrollments suddenly began to increase rapidly as uninsured people became increasingly

Box 7.4 The Patient Protection and Affordable Care Act

The Affordable Care Act sought to reform health care through incremental changes to the health insurance and health care delivery system in the United States. Some of the major provisions of this law are listed here according to the time line for their implementation.

2010

- Provided immediate access to insurance for uninsured persons with pre-existing conditions
- Eliminated lifetime limits on coverage and restricted annual limits
- Included preventive health services insurance coverage in all new plans
- Extended dependent coverage up to age 26 for young people not covered by their own employer-provided coverage
- Gave states the option of covering parents and childless couples up to 133 percent of the federal poverty level through Medicaid

2011

- Increased Medicare reimbursement to primary care physicians and general surgeons by 10 percent
- Provided Medicare beneficiaries with a free annual wellness visit and personalized prevention plan
- Initiated a 50-percent discount on all brand-name drugs during the donut hole for Medicare Part D enrollees prior to completely closing the donut hole by 2020

2013

- Required health plans to implement uniform standards and electronic patient records to reduce paperwork and administrative costs

2014

- Required individuals who could afford it to obtain health insurance coverage or pay a penalty of $95, with the penalty scheduled to increase annually
- Established health insurance exchanges where individuals and small employers could comparison-shop for insurance, and persons with minimal income exceeding Medicaid levels could obtain tax credits in order to prevent bankruptcy due to medical expenses
- Medicaid was expanded to cover childless adults under age 65 with an income up to 133 percent of the poverty line

2015

- Established an independent advisory board to submit proposals to Congress aimed at extending the solvency of Medicare and lowering health care costs
- Created a value-based, as opposed to volume-based, physician payment program for Medicare patients

2018

- A 40 percent excise tax on employer-provided health plans exceeding $10,200 for individuals or $27,500 for families is implemented

2020

- Medicare's "donut hole" prescription benefit gap is terminated

Source: Based on Affordable Health Care for America: Health insurance reform at a glance, Implementation timeline (Publication No. 8082), *HealthCare.gov*. (2010). Retrieved from www.healthcare.gov/law/introduction/index.html; Turner, G. (2015, June 9). *Health policy matters posts: 51 changes to ObamaCare... so far*. Retrieved from http://www.galen.org/newsletters/changes-toobamacare-so-far/; U.S. Department of Health and Human Services. (2014). *HHS.gov/HealthCare: Key features of the Affordable Care Act by year*. Retrieved from http://www.hhs.gov/healthcare/facts/timeline/timeline-text.html#2014. Obamacare facts: A timeline of health care reforms 20-10-2022. Retrieved from http://obamacarefacts.com/health-care-reform-timeline/

anxious about the uncertain future of health care policy under the new Trump administration (Obama Care Facts: Enrollment, 2016).

Improving the health of Americans was the second goal of the ACA. A prominent measure traditionally used to evaluate health systems' performance is life expectancy. The data that follow were published in 2016 by the Organisation for Economic Co-operation and Development, an international organization. The countries with the 10 highest life expectancy levels (in years) follows:

- Japan   83.4
- Spain   83.2
- Switzerland   82.9
- Italy   82.9
- France   82.3
- Australia   82.2
- Iceland   82.1
- Israel   82.1
- Sweden   82.0
- Luxemberg   81.9

Countries with the lowest reported life expectancy were South Africa with 56.8 and India with 67.7 years of life expectancy. The United States, which had held the 10th highest life expectancy of 76 years in 2013 had improved its life expectancy to 78.8 years in 2016 but numerous other countries had improved to life expectancies well above those of the United States.

Life expectancy is just one health indicator. Others that were captured from multiple sources for an *Atlantic* magazine report indicated that of the developed nations, America's health indicators were shockingly low at all stages of life and across income levels. The United States, for example, had the highest rates of the developed nations for death from violence and from car accidents, and the greatest likelihood of children dying before their fifth birthday. Americans had some of the highest rates of death related to alcohol and drug use. Americans also had some of the highest rates of chronic disease such as heart disease and diabetes (Rubenstein, 2013). If one considers that the United States spends nearly twice the amount on health care of other industrialized countries, would it not seem likely that the United States could achieve better life expectancy and infant mortality rates than it currently does? So the critical question for the future will be if our country's evolving health care policy will be able to improve these health indicators. What could be the effect if all Americans actually had access to health care for at least several years? Will U.S. health indicators begin to demonstrate improvement?

As citizens seek answers to the health care dilemmas in the United States, some look to the Canadian system. Enacted in 1971 and known as Medicare, it is of considerable interest because Canadians share many of the values and beliefs of Americans. A primary difference between U.S. and Canada health care is the sharp distinction in their approach to financing health care. Canadian health care is publicly funded through income taxes, but health care services are provided through mostly private physicians, hospitals, and other health services. Canada has a single-payer system, where each province (similar to a U.S. state) manages the entire insurance program. The simplicity of the system results in minimal expenses for administration, compared with the multiplicity of private and governmental health payers in the United States. It is estimated that approximately half of the difference in cost between Canadian and U.S. health care relates to administrative expenses. Canadians are free to choose their own doctors and health care providers. They merely present their provincial health identification card. Hospitalization or other services are immediately covered, so they are not billed. All Canadian citizens are covered; all receive the same insurance benefits. Benefits are comprehensive for hospitalization, medical care, and mental health care. Long-term care is covered somewhat differently by the provinces, but it is covered. Prescriptions are provided for individuals over age 65 and those with catastrophic illnesses. All others must pay for their own prescriptions; however, the Canadian government has negotiated such low prices for prescriptions that Americans living along the Canadian border often find ways to purchase their prescriptions in Canada. A principle of the Canadian system is that of portability: Each province's insurance can be used across all provinces. The Canadian system does not link health insurance to employment, thus eliminating considerable administrative work and cost for employers, too (Health Care in Canada, 2015; Khazan, 2014; Mizrahi, Fasano, & Dooha, 1993).

Although no Canadian is denied health care based on financial ability, many uninsured or underinsured Americans in the recent past postponed preventive or diagnostic care. The result has been more expensive care, debilitation, and even premature death from preventable serious illness. A criticism of the 2010 Affordable Care Act is that it focused on ensuring access to health care, but it kept in place an array of public and private insurance programs with varying levels of coverage and with bloated administrative costs. Now, with health care policy in turmoil in the United States, it might be time to revisit the goals of the ACA and also to recognize that the progress of this health care reform had been unmatched in prior U.S. history.

Future Health Care Policy in the United States

Americans are highly suspicious of bureaucracy. There has been reluctance to consider a single-payer system. This suspicion generates fear about government regulation and centralized authority. It is a mistake, though, for Americans to think that the U.S. health care system is not bureaucratized and regulated: It is thoroughly regulated by thousands of insurance and managed care corporations. The U.S. system isn't centralized. Sometimes that is an advantage, but when it leads to fragmentation and lack of access to needed care, it can be a serious limitation. The Canadian system is also not managed by a single federal government bureaucracy; instead, the 10 Canadian provinces each administer their own services.

The inequity and huge administrative costs of the present U.S. system make change inevitable. Box 7.5 offers arguments for and against a national health plan for the United States that would be based on the Canadian single-payer system. In this plan, private as well as public hospitals would continue to exist and doctors could be employed in public health or could operate private practices. Their health care system, with a public rather than a for-profit base, is generally well liked by Canadians. As one doctor stated: "Today a politician in Canada is more likely to get away with canceling Christmas than canceling Canada's health insurance program" (New Rules Project, n.d.). Canadians, however,

> **Box 7.5 Up for Debate**
>
> *Proposition: The United States should implement a single-payer system of health care financing.*
>
> | Yes | No |
> |---|---|
> | Use of a single, public system to process claims based on standardized forms would be cost-efficient, saving billions of dollars. | If desired, it would be possible for the U.S. insurance industry to standardize all billing forms. |
> | The health insurance industry should not be where the U.S. health care dollar is invested. | The nation's economy would be adversely affected by the demise of the health insurance industry. |
> | A single-payer system would eliminate duplication of information and reduce the frequency of misinformation. | A single-payer system with standardized billing forms would tend to stagnate the development of technological advances in billing procedures. |
> | Co-payment by patients is non-existent in most Canadian provinces. | Even in the Canadian system, co-pays are used in some provinces, so some limited billing to patients still takes place. |
> | Equal access and the same level of care, which is inherent within a single-payer health financing program, is a moral right of all citizens. | There is no constitutionally defined right of citizens to health care. |

do report frustration with waiting for emergency room care or waiting for elective hip replacement or similar surgeries (Khazan, 2014).

A single-payer system (where one insurance plan selected by the state or federal government pays hospitals and providers directly) would eliminate the multiplicity of insurance carriers and administrative overhead that inflate health care costs. This design has not been acceptable to Congress, but it could remain an option for the future.

Health care financing remains a volatile political topic of discussion in the United States following the election of President Donald Trump and a majority of conservative Republicans in both the U.S. House of Representatives and the Senate. As "TrumpCare" began to replace "ObamaCare," some portions of the ACA seemed likely to survive. This included coverage for preexisting conditions and extended coverage for young people with no access to insurance. Both of these provisions existed in the ACA when it came into existence in 2010.

The Trump administration is committed to creating a system embedded in free market principles (using as little government programming as possible). The ACA clearly accomplished improved access for millions of previously uninsured Americans, but it had not yet achieved the goal of coverage for all Americans. With both the Congress and President Trump opposed to mandating that every American carry health insurance, a significant portion of the population will elect not to have coverage. Whether children aging out of foster care and uninsured young adults under 26 years of age will be provided with coverage in the future remains uncertain. Undocumented immigrants, fearful of deportation, could have access to health care markedly cut back. The population of uninsured persons in the United States is projected to increase in coming years.

Donald Trump, however, may be able to accomplish a feat that previous administrations have not even attempted: successfully negotiating reduced prices from pharmaceutical companies. The power of the pharmaceutical industry in the United States has rarely been significantly challenged. Donald Trump, however, seems confident that he can deal successfully with this sector. He has also expressed interest in opening up access to drugs from other countries and changing laws that currently inhibit sale of insurance policies across state lines. Thus he could potentially meet another of his goals: to reduce the cost of healthcare, at least for the portion of the population that is insured (donaldjtrump.com, 2016).

The shaping of health care policy for the United States will constitute a considerable political battle. It will be essential that people, including social workers and social work students, become much more engaged in the political process. Ensuring that all people do have access to health care is a value that is worth fighting for! Hopefully, the outcome of an energized political process will be a system that provides excellent quality, dignified health care to all Americans. If we have the political will to do so, we can accomplish this social justice goal.

Human Rights and Health: Global Perspectives

The World Health Organization (WHO) once noted that if a girl was born today, she could anticipate living to 80 years if she was born within one of the more advantaged countries, but she might live to only 45 if her birth occurred elsewhere. Dramatic differences in health care resources clearly exist between countries, but even within some countries disparities in health care could result in enormous consequences. The data collected by WHO over many years demonstrate serious inequities in health care resources between developing countries and industrialized nations and inequities as well in access to care even within some of the wealthiest nations.

War, famine, and poverty—all facets of social injustice—carry negative implications for health and human rights. In rich nations as well as poor nations, children are at much higher risk of dying if they live in poverty and are malnourished. In the world's poorest nations, social, political, and economic instability contributes to deteriorating rates of adult survival, too. Violations of human rights that potentially threaten the health and well-being of people include such current practices as trafficking in women and children. **Trafficking** refers to the use of physical or psychological coercion in transporting persons, often for financial gain; women may be trafficked for commercial sex or domestic labor purposes, while children may be transported for sexual purposes, low cost labor, or illicit adoption. Human rights violations put both children and adults at great risk of ill health, injury, and sexually transmitted disease (including HIV/AIDS), regardless of the country in which the exploitation occurs. When people are transported from one country to another, diseases of many kinds travel with them, thus placing other populations at risk.

In 2000, the WHO created a set of somewhat lofty goals to be achieved by the nations of the world by 2015. Not all goals were, in fact, met by 2015, but a few of the health goals truly did demonstrate remarkable progress! Global epidemics of tuberculosis, malaria, and HIV were dramatically reduced or eradicated. Child mortality rates worldwide declined 53 percent and maternal mortality rates fell by 40 percent in those 15 years (World Health Organization, Media Centre, 2015). One of the lessons learned by the world community has been the critical nature of strong health systems. The tragedy of the Ebola epidemic in West African countries was blamed, in part, on those countries' weak basic health systems that were unable to respond to the severity of the Ebola outbreak and its contagious qualities. Even after Ebola came under reasonable control, the weak and depleted health systems of these countries left them unable to provide basic needs such as immunizations and maternal and child health care. Gradually, the concept of universal health care became increasingly recognized and valued. With encouragement and some assistance from WHO, the 5 "BRICS countries" that hold about half of the world population (Brazil, China, India, the Russian Federation, and South Africa) have begun health system reform aimed at strengthening and improving access to health care for their people. Unlike most of the developed nations, these countries had minimal or no universal health care system (World Health Organization, Bringing UHC into Focus, 2015).

The progress achieved in meeting important components of its Millennium Development Goals of 2015 and the hope of achieving previously unmet goals inspired the development of the UN's plan of action for the next 15 years. The UN announced its 2030 Agenda for Sustainable Development in September 2015. The document lists 17 Sustainable Development Goals; the third goal focuses on health. It calls for the promotion of health and well-being for people of all ages. A feature of the 2030 Sustainable Development Goals is its identification of implementation targets for each goal. The targets guide action as well as the evaluation of achievement of each goal. The third goal's first target is the reduction of maternal mortality and the second seeks to reduce the preventable deaths of children, especially newborns and children below the age of 5. Other targets include ending epidemics such as AIDS and tropical diseases, reducing mortality from traffic accidents, hazardous chemicals, and pollution and contamination of various kinds. Improving prevention and treatment of alcoholism and narcotic drug abuse is another target. Actions to accomplish Goal 3 include supporting the development of vaccines and access to medication especially needed to control diseases that impact developing countries. Development of early warning systems and risk reduction efforts for all countries is another action to be implemented. A target of Goal 3 is the achievement of universal health coverage that ensures access to good quality health care, vaccines, and affordable medication. Interestingly, the Sustainable Development Goals statement emphasizes that all of the goals are equal in value and also that they are often interdependent. The health goal, for example, is interrelated with Goal 1 of ending poverty and with Goal 2 of ending hunger and improving nutrition (United Nations, Sustainable Knowledge Platform, 2015).

This chapter ends with the bright hope that comes with the goals developed by the United Nations for 2030. The goal related to health, while ambitious, seems every bit as achievable as were many of the former Millennium Development Goals of 2015. When achieved, the global health and human rights of people will have progressed remarkably!

> **?** Assess your understanding of the politics and economics related to health care by taking this brief quiz.

SUMMARY

- The ways in which the knowledge, values, and skills of their profession prepare social workers to be effective in the health care field are described.
- The work that social workers do in four of the eight selected health care services presented in this chapter is identified and described. A sampling of the wide array of health care settings in which social workers practice are identified and described, including acute care, long-term care, home health care, hospice and palliative care, the emergency room, health care services for veterans, public health departments, and the unique challenges in providing health care within rural environments.
- The historical development of the social work profession within health care from the time of the lady almoners to the present is traced. The history of social work in health care is traced back to the lady almoners of the Royal Free Hospital in London, England, who in 1895 advocated fiercely on behalf of impoverished people desperately needing health care. Thus began a lengthy and proud history of social work efforts to provide counseling and link people to needed services as well as to make health care organizations and social policy more responsive and more sensitive to the needs of people.
- The politics and economics surrounding the drive to ensure access to health care for all people in the United States are explained. Complex political and economic challenges that are encountered in the effort to strengthen and reform the health care system are explained. Policies and programs like Medicare, Medicaid, and the Patient Protection and Affordable Care Act were significant victories, but now there are major challenges to the achievement of social justice in U.S. health care. Social workers of the future will be called upon to continue their advocacy to ensure truly excellent quality health care for all.

✓ Recall what you learned from this chapter by completing the Chapter Review.

8

Social Work in the Schools

LEARNING OUTCOMES

- Describe the history of social work in the schools.
- Identify and discuss major social work roles in the schools.
- Explain the impact of different types of diversity in the schools.
- Discuss social work values in the school setting and their policy implications.
- Describe similarities and differences in school social work as practiced in the United States and Ghana.

CHAPTER OUTLINE

CASE STUDY: Understanding Lisa and Loretta Santiago 223

A Brief History of Social Work in the Schools 227
- People of Latino or Hispanic Heritage: A Brief History 227
- Historical Highlights of Social Work in the Schools 229
- School Social Worker Certification 233

Social Work Roles in the Schools 233
- Working with Individuals 233
- Family Work 234
- Group Work 234
- Working with Organizations and Communities 234
- Teamwork 235
- School-Linked, Integrated Services 235

The Impact of Diversity in the Schools 236
- Cultural Diversity 236
- Alternative Schools and Charter Schools 239

CASE STUDY: Understanding Lisa and Loretta Santiago

Frank Haines, social worker for the Valdez Middle School, checked the memos in his mailbox as he did every weekday morning. Sure enough, there was a new referral concerning **truancy**. Two sisters, Lisa and Loretta Santiago, had been absent for nearly two weeks.

Children whose primary language was Spanish, such as Lisa and Loretta, could learn basic subjects like math and reading in their native language at this school, enrolling at the same time in English as a Second Language (ESL). Other Spanish-speaking children who had a better grasp of English could take most classes in English, and a bilingual teacher would assist them in Spanish as needed. Frank Haines, the social worker, was not Latino, but he spoke a fair amount of Spanish. In his former training to be a Catholic priest, Frank had traveled to two Latin American countries and had also served as a street worker among Latino youth. He recognized that there were great differences as well as similarities among Latino families and that linguistic dialects and cultural norms differed

CHAPTER OUTLINE *(Continued)*

Special Needs 240
Educational Evaluations as Applied Research 242
School Social Work with Other Special-Needs Children: The Ordeal of Two Gay Brothers 243
Student Rights and the Law 246

Social Work Values in the School Setting: Policy Implications 247

The Santiago Sisters 247
The Larkin Case 248
Bullying and Violence in the Schools 249
The Environment and Early Sexual Development 251
Nutrition and Achievement 253
No Child Left Behind and the Every Student Succeeds Act 253
Student Achievement: International Rankings 254
Spiritual Development and Empowerment 255
Current Trends 256

An International Comparison: School Social Work in Ghana 257

Summary 260

significantly among Spanish speakers from Mexico, Puerto Rico, Cuba, South America, and the southwestern United States.

Frank had eventually changed his career goals to social work because he wanted to have a family of his own. He then earned an MSW, the degree most commonly required for this type of employment in the public schools. He also took courses in education to obtain certification in school social work, as required by his state's department of public instruction.

To begin his work with the Santiago sisters' case, Frank examined the girls' school files for records of attendance, conduct, and grades. He found that the two sisters had transferred from a school in Texas three years before. Their attendance had been regular until recently. The younger girl, Loretta, a seventh-grader, had good grades up to the most recent report. Lisa, an eighth-grader, had only fair grades the previous year, but her grades for the first quarter of this year were absolutely terrible. Frank wondered if something might have happened recently to upset the children, especially Lisa.

Frank then checked with the children's teachers. Loretta's teachers expressed concern for the girl and worried about her absence, but otherwise reported that she was a good student. Her homeroom teacher had sent the parents a note about attendance, but there had been no response.

Lisa's teachers reported that ever since summer vacation, the girl had seemed "different." The mathematics teacher and the ESL teacher said that Lisa stared at the classroom walls for long periods of time. Sometimes she would cry or chew on her knuckles. Teachers had sent notes home, asking for a conference with the parents, but so far, no one had responded.

Frank's next step in his investigation was to try to talk with the parents. No one answered his first several telephone calls. Finally, a young woman answered who said she was the children's stepmother. She told Frank the girls had run away two weeks before. Frank made an appointment for a home visit late the next day, when Mr. Santiago would be home from work. He mentally crossed his fingers, hoping he would get his work done in time to have supper with his family. All too frequently, Frank's work hours conflicted with his precious time at home.

Fortunately, both Mr. and Mrs. Santiago were present when Frank arrived for his appointment. In the Latino **culture**, it is often considered improper for an unrelated man to visit alone with a woman, even on official school business. Frank greeted the couple in Spanish, which warmed the atmosphere immediately. Mrs. Santiago served the two men coffee and then withdrew to manage several small children. Frank began the interview with Mr. Santiago in his best halting Spanish, but the latter, with a broad smile, responded in imperfect but much better English. "Spanish is a beautiful language," he said, "but I think perhaps it will be easier for you to speak in English. I understand you are here because of my two older daughters, Lisa and Loretta. You see," he said, "they come from my first wife, who still lives in Texas, and sometimes they cause me a great deal of trouble."

Frank soon learned that Mr. Santiago had been battling with his former wife over custody of Lisa and Loretta for years. The court had awarded him custody because his second marriage was intact, whereas the biological mother was not legally married to her live-in boyfriend in Texas. Mr. Santiago loved Lisa and Loretta as well as his five younger children by his second marriage, but, like many urban men of Mexican descent, he translated his love for his daughters into powerful protectiveness and control.

> **Engagement**
>
> *Dimension of Competency* knowledge: Social workers understand that engagement is an ongoing component of the dynamic and interactive process of social work practice with, and on behalf of, diverse individuals, families, groups, organizations, and communities.
>
> **Critical Thinking Question:** How do you think Frank's knowledge of the Spanish language and culture helped him engage with Mr. Santiago?

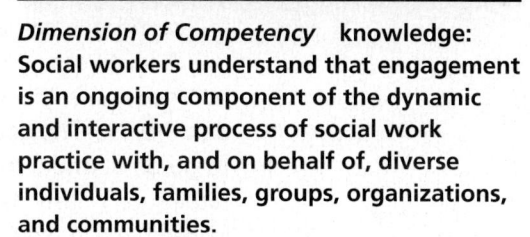

The girls had run away, he said, because Lisa broke his rule against dating. Lisa had taken Loretta with her on the date as a family chaperone, but that was not enough to satisfy the father. When he learned what had happened, he became very angry, gave them both a severe lecture, and grounded them for two weeks. Then he locked them in their bedroom, but they broke out and ran away. Mr. Santiago knew where they were, he said: with his current wife's sister. They were afraid to come home, he said, because they knew he was so angry he "might be tempted to use the belt."

"How will the girls learn that you are ready to let them come home without that kind of punishment?" Frank said. "Fear of that belt certainly might keep them away."

"Oh," Mr. Santiago replied breezily, "if I tell my wife it's OK, they'll be home soon enough."

Frank suspected that the father might be ready for an excuse to let his daughters come home, as he cared enough about them to let them stay in a safe place until he calmed down. The social worker seized the moment to tell Mr. Santiago he was very worried; the father was breaking the law by allowing his daughters to remain truant. If they stayed out of school much longer, a parental conference would have to be set up with the principal. That would mean Mr. Santiago would miss work and could lose hours of pay.

After a few minutes, Mr. Santiago said he had decided it was time. He would speak to his wife, and she would bring the children home. Two days later, Lisa and Loretta were back in school. Frank called them into his office for a conference. Both girls moaned to Frank that they would never be able to lead a normal life. All their friends were allowed to go out with boys when they were in junior high, they said.

"All of them?" asked Frank. "You know, I've heard that girls from Latino families are often not allowed to date, at least without a brother or sister along."

"But I took my little sister," Lisa wailed, "even though I know lots of girls who don't have to. None of the Anglo kids have to do that."

Frank empathized with the girls, but he pointed out that because they lived with their parents, they would have to obey their parents' rules.

"But we don't live with our parents," Lisa wailed again, "and these aren't our parents' rules. We live with our father, and they are our father's rules. And I hate him," Lisa said suddenly in a much different tone, intense and furious. "He was mean to my mother, very mean. Last summer I was visiting her in Texas, and he was staying with my grandparents there. I was walking with my mother when my father saw us on the street. He came up and stood in her way and wouldn't let her by. He called her horrible names and shoved her until she nearly fell. I thought he was going to hit her. My mother was shaking all over. He made her cry, and I heard every terrible word he said. I hate him."

Now Frank understood why Lisa was acting so troubled and defiant. She had been through an emotionally traumatic experience. He let both girls talk at length. He wondered out loud if they might want to see a counselor either by themselves or with their father and stepmother. But they insisted a counselor wouldn't help.

A few weeks later, Lisa and Loretta violated their father's curfew again. When they returned home, Mr. Santiago lost his temper and began shouting at his daughters, yelling that they were no good and would be grounded for a month. They would not be allowed to go on a school trip they had been counting on. The girls retaliated by calling their father every nasty name they could think of, in both English and Spanish. Mr. Santiago locked them in their room, but they left through the window.

Soon afterward, the girls showed up at Frank's office door at school, sobbing angrily. Fortunately, no one else was there, so he invited them in right away. Before Frank could find out what was wrong, however, Mr. Santiago himself arrived, clearly in a rage. Lisa immediately began to scream and curse. Mr. Santiago shouted for her to be quiet and then yelled at Frank that he had had all the disrespect and disobedience from his daughters that he could take. "Listen to that!" Mr. Santiago shouted, jabbing at Lisa and Loretta with a powerful forefinger. "Listen to how my daughters defy me! Listen to the kind of language they use with their own father! These girls are runaways, Mr. Haines! I want you to call the police! They are no longer welcome in my home!"

Lisa and Loretta continued to cry and yell. The more they carried on, the angrier Mr. Santiago became. Suddenly, he turned abruptly and began to stalk out of the office.

Frank stopped him. "Obviously, Mr. Santiago," he said quietly, "you have had a very difficult time. But I think we need to talk a little longer to decide what to do now."

"I will not talk anymore!" Mr. Santiago shouted. "I have had all the disrespect I can take from these children! They must be punished! I want you to call the police. I will not allow these girls to darken my door again." He stormed out of the office and was gone.

After calming Lisa and Loretta as best he could and finding out what had happened at home, Frank determined that it would not be safe for the girls to return there. He called the Protective Services unit of the county social services department. No one was free to come to the school. Underfunding and understaffing are perennial problems of Protective Services programs. Frank, therefore, took the girls to Protective Services in his own car, a personal risk for him, beyond his professional obligation. If he had had an accident, his automobile insurance company might not cover him because he was doing work-related driving.

The social worker on duty tried to place Lisa and Loretta temporarily with their stepaunt, the person they requested. But the woman declined a formal arrangement, saying it might ruin her relationship with her brother-in-law. So the girls were placed with strangers. And unfortunately, soon afterward, their foster father was charged with sexually molesting a former ward. The girls could not be left in that home. The Protective Services worker consulted with Frank. Should Lisa and Loretta be transferred to a different foster home, enduring another major adjustment, or should Mr. Santiago be approached about taking the girls back again? The worker said she had already looked into sending the girls to their mother in Texas, but lengthy court action would be required because of the prior custody battle and interstate regulations. Additional time in foster care would be required during that process.

Frank felt compassion for the children. They had been through a great deal. But he thought that Mr. Santiago and his second wife basically meant well. The problem was that Mr. Santiago set rigid rules that drove his daughters to disobey. The rules were within the bounds of his cultural norms but different from those of many of the girls' Anglo friends. The father verbally assaulted Lisa and Loretta when they disobeyed and gave them lengthy punishments, but the girls provoked him further with their own harsh words. If the cycle of provocation could be stopped, Frank believed that this family could learn to live together more peacefully and happily. As the discovery of sexual abuse in the foster home illustrated, life elsewhere was no bed of roses either.

Frank felt the best plan for the girls would be to go back home, with family counseling to help improve communication and understanding among the generations. He knew, however, that the girls should be consulted first and that the father would need some persuading. The Protective Services worker was more than willing to let Frank take on those tasks.

Frank talked with the girls the following day and learned they were ready to return to their father and stepmother. They were lonely and afraid in the foster home. Frank made an appointment with Mr. Santiago through the stepmother. When he arrived, he was not surprised to hear Mr. Santiago announce that the girls were no longer welcome in his home. Frank called on his former training for the priesthood to help accomplish his goal of having the children return. Given Mr. Santiago's cultural heritage, he expected that the man would be a devout Catholic. So he told the story of the Prodigal Son in somber, measured tones, inviting this father to forgive like the father in the Bible. Eventually, Mr. Santiago was persuaded to take his daughters back and to participate in family counseling if a Latino counselor could be found. Mr. Santiago's job provided very limited insurance benefits, so a very low-cost provider would have to be found. Frank took on the challenge. He soon found a Latino social worker with expertise in family counseling, Ramon Garcia, who was willing to see the family free of charge providing that he could use the opportunity to train two graduate students in field placement. Mr. Santiago agreed, and Frank arranged the first session personally.

A week passed, and then another. Lisa and Loretta both attended school regularly. There were no more incidents of truancy. At a meeting with Frank, they explained that Ramon had helped family members talk to each other without fighting so much. At a follow-up home visit, Frank learned that the parents were also pleased with the counseling experience. They believed they understood the girls better. They had become a little more flexible with their rules, and the children no longer tested them so severely. Life for the family was much happier.

A BRIEF HISTORY OF SOCIAL WORK IN THE SCHOOLS

People of Latino or Hispanic Heritage: A Brief History

Lisa and Loretta Santiago and their parents were members of the largest minority group represented in the United States—Latinos. Latinos are classified as Hispanics by the U.S. Bureau of the Census, but *Latino* is the term more commonly used. Including people from 26 countries, Latinos form a rapidly growing, diverse minority group comprising almost 57 million people in 2015. They constitute approximately 18 percent of the U.S. population, overtaking African Americans in 2003 to become the nation's largest minority group. Approximately 64 percent are of Mexican origin, 9.5 percent are Puerto Rican, 3.7 percent are Cuban, 3.7 percent are Salvadorian, 3.3 percent are from the Dominican Republic, and 2.4 percent are from Guatemala. Of the remaining Latino population, no other single country of origin accounts for more than two percent. Over a quarter of all Latinos live in California and Texas, but Florida, New York, Illinois, Arizona, New Jersey, Colorado, and New Mexico also have prominent Latino communities. Eight states, California, Texas, Florida, New York, Illinois, Arizona, New Jersey, and Colorado each have over one million Latino residents. Nearly half of New Mexico's population is Latino. The Hispanic population is growing rapidly in many other states including Arkansas, Kentucky, Mississippi, North and South Carolina, and Tennessee (Bernstein, 2007; "USA Quick Facts," 2011; Brown and Lopez, 2013; Brown, A., 2015).

Texas, California, Arizona, and New Mexico originally belonged to Mexico. There were border disputes in Texas and California between white settlers and Mexicans, however. Texas declared its independence from Mexico in 1836, and the United States admitted it as a state in 1845. President Polk accepted the boundary claimed by Texas rather than that claimed by Mexico and ordered General Zachary Taylor to enter the eastern bank of the Rio Grande to defend the disputed territories, thus precipitating the Mexican–American War. Mexico City was captured in 1848, resulting in the Treaty of Guadalupe Hidalgo. Under this treaty, the United States took ownership of the disputed territories.

Mexicans who lived in the formerly disputed territories (lands that became Texas, California, Arizona, and New Mexico) were allowed to stay, with American citizenship, or to leave for what remained of Mexico. Those who chose to stay in the United States were supposed to keep ownership of the lands they held before the war. However, the burden of proof of ownership was placed on the Mexicans, and many legal records were deliberately destroyed during and after the war. Gradually, people of Mexican heritage who stayed in the United States lost their land, becoming second-class citizens (Lum, 1992).

After losing their land, Mexican Americans resorted to work as laborers, primarily in agriculture. And because economic conditions in Mexico were poor, other Mexicans crossed the border to seek work in the United States. These immigrants, legal and illegal, formed the backbone of the migrant laborers who traveled the nation to harvest crops according to the season. Low wages, poor housing, and lack of sanitation and health care greeted them in many places. As a result, strong efforts were made to win the right for farmworkers to form unions and engage in collective bargaining. In the late 1980s, the work of self-advocacy organizations such as La Raza resulted in amnesty being offered to many illegal immigrants who had lived in the United States for a significant period of time.

Today, the challenge continues as poor people from Mexico continue to enter the United States as undocumented immigrants looking for work, even though, due to the recession that began in 2008, many have returned to Mexico. Between 2009 and 2014, in fact, nearly 140,000 more Mexicans left the United States than entered it ("More Mexicans Leaving than Coming to the U.S.," 2015). This fact, of course, is directly contrary to the claim made by Donald Trump who alleged, while he campaigned for the presidency, that Mexicans were streaming over the border into the United States in vast numbers. Trump promised to build a wall to stop this fictional hoard.

Mexican immigrants, documented or undocumented, are viewed by many industries as a good source of cheap labor, so, where available, they are often hired—angering many American workers who view them as competitors. The status of undocumented laborers continues to be debated across the nation today. Arizona's 2010 law, allowing any person to be stopped, interrogated, and jailed or deported if lacking proof of citizenship or legal immigration status indicates the level of tension surrounding this issue.

Puerto Ricans form another major group of Hispanic or Latino people in the United States. Puerto Rico became part of a commonwealth of the United States in 1917. Many Puerto Ricans later migrated to the mainland to pursue economic opportunity, usually settling in New York City. Today most still live in the northeastern region of the country. Unfortunately, many subsist in inner-city neighborhoods and suffer high rates of unemployment.

Cubans migrated to the United States in large numbers in the early 1960s to escape Fidel Castro's government. They settled primarily in Florida. Early immigrants from Cuba were usually professionals and businesspeople who were economically advantaged. Later, however, many of the immigrants arrived destitute and required numerous services for basic survival. Latino immigrants from Central America have also come primarily as refugees. In particular, wars in Nicaragua and El Salvador forced many to seek asylum in the 1970s and 1980s. Numerous people were denied entry and returned forcibly to dangerous situations. The needs of those who were allowed to stay strained the resources of agencies and programs designed to assist them (Lum, 1992).

An important concern today involves the immigration of undocumented children. Between October 2013 and July 2014 alone over 52,000 children, aged 17 and younger, attempted to cross into the United States and were detained at the border between the United States and Mexico. This was double the number of undocumented children trying to enter the United States during the entire prior year. The majority came from Honduras, El Salvador, and Guatemala, escaping drug-related and gang violence as well as limited economic opportunity (Brody, 2014).

Given such multiple origins, it is easy to understand that Hispanic peoples are racially as well as ethnically diverse. When asked to describe their cultural heritage, most Latinos refer to their national identity (e.g., Mexican or Puerto Rican). Not all speak Spanish, and not all have surnames that appear Spanish in origin.

In recent years, there has been widespread pressure in the United States to modify immigration policy. President Obama enacted the Deferred Action for Childhood Arrivals (DACA) program that provided temporary amnesty and two-year work permits allowing undocumented children who met certain qualifications to stay. But this program has been widely opposed by conservatives and most likely will terminate under conservative President Donald Trump, who campaigned with an anti-immigrant platform. Immigration reform in general has become a touchstone of partisan politics in recent years.

Like other minority groups, Latino Americans face discrimination and limited economic opportunity in the United States. A sad result is that a large percentage lives below the poverty line: 25 percent in 2013 ("Poverty Rate Among Hispanic Origin Groups," 2015). However, after many years of President Obama's policies, by 2015 the rate had fallen to 21.4 % ("People in Poverty," 2016).

Historical Highlights of Social Work in the Schools

School social workers do what they can to assist all students, including Latinos, to succeed in school. Frank Haines, the social worker who assisted Lisa and Loretta Santiago, came from the proud but relatively short tradition of school social work. The history of this field is described in this section. It is important to realize, however, that even today many schools lack social workers. In many other schools, these hardworking professionals may have to educate administrators and teachers as to their potential roles.

Early Years

As with many of the fields of professional social work today, social work in American public schools began with the far-sighted efforts of voluntary organizations. In 1906, two New York City settlement houses, Hartley House and Greenwich House, assigned "visitors" to do liaison work with three school districts. One of these visitors, Mary Marot, was a teacher and a resident of Hartley House. A natural leader, she formed a visiting teacher committee at the settlement house. The Public Education Association of New York became interested in her work and asked her if she would make her committee part of its organization. She agreed, and the association publicized the concept of "visiting teacher." At about the same time, the Women's Education Association in Boston established a "home and school visitor" to improve communication between the home and school settings. In Connecticut, the director of the Psychological Clinic of Hartford hired a "special teacher" to assist him in making home visits and to act as a liaison between the clinic and the school (Hancock, 1982). In Chicago, the Chicago Women's Club engaged Louise Montgomery to work at Hamline School in the Stockyards District (See Box 8.1). Because of the poverty of the area, populated mostly by immigrant families, Louise Montgomery developed programs bringing school and community together in an effort to enrich the social environment for the children (Constable, 2009).

The fact that the concept of visiting teacher took hold at about the same time in four separate cities indicates that this was an idea whose time had come. Initially, visiting teachers were financed by settlement houses or other private associations or agencies. But from about 1913 to 1921, various school boards began hiring them, beginning with Rochester, New York, in 1913 (Dupper, 2003). The movement gradually expanded from the eastern to the midwestern states. The early focus of these workers was community based; settlement houses in particular lent an orientation toward finding ways to alter the environment to improve individual lives. Visiting teachers tried to find ways to intervene in the school and community settings to help prevent delinquency, improve attendance, and develop scholarship.

In 1916, a working definition of school social work was presented by Jane Culbert at the National Conference of Charities and Corrections. As was characteristic of the time, Culbert's definition focused on the environment surrounding the child, rather than on the characteristics of the individual child. She described the social worker's role as helping teachers and the school understand life in the neighborhood so as to prepare children for a successful life and to interpret to parents the demands of the school (Constable, 2009).

The passage of compulsory attendance laws during this time reflected growing societal awareness of the importance of education and that every child had not only a right but an obligation to go to school. Compulsory education laws increased the employment of visiting teachers (Costin, 1987). Increasing numbers of visiting teachers led to the establishment of the National Committee of Visiting Teachers in 1921 (Freeman, 1995).

During the 1920s, the initial emphasis on community liaison and environmental change gradually shifted toward concentration on adjustment of the individual child. Attention was focused on reducing delinquency and improving mental health, not so

> **Box 8.1   Timeline: History of School Social Work**
>
> | | |
> |---|---|
> | 1906–1907 | School social work services begin independently in New York City, Boston, Hartford, and Chicago. |
> | 1913 | Rochester, New York, becomes the first school system to finance school social work services. |
> | 1921 | National Association of Visiting Teachers is established. |
> | 1923 | Commonwealth fund of New York increases the visibility of school social workers by providing financial support for a program to prevent juvenile delinquency that includes the hiring of 30 school social workers in 20 rural and urban communities across the United States. |
> | 1943 | The U.S. Office of Education recommends that a professional school social work certificate be a master's degree in social work (MSW). |
> | 1955 | NASW by-laws provide for the establishment of a school social work specialty. |
> | 1959 | Specialist position in school social work is established by the U.S. Office of Education. |
> | 1969 | "Social Change and School Social Work" is the national workshop held at the University of Pennsylvania, and its proceedings resulted in the publication of the book entitled *The School in the Community* (1972). |
> | 1973 | NASW Council on Social Work in the Schools meets for the first time. |
> | 1975 | Costin's school–community–pupil relations model of a school social work practice is published. |
> | 1976 | The first set of standards for school social work services are developed by NASW. These standards emphasize prevention as an important theme. |
> | 1985 | NASW National School Social Work Conference "Educational Excellence in Transitional Times" is held in New Orleans, Louisiana, and results in the publication of *Achieving Educational Excellence for Children at Risk*, which contains papers from this conference. |
> | 1992 | The school social work credentialing exam, developed by NASW, the Educational Testing Service, and Allen-Meares is administered for the first time. |
> | 1994 | NASW launches school social work as its first practice section. |
> | 1994 | The School Social Work Association of America (SSWAA) is formed, independent of NASW. |
>
> Source: *School Social Work: Skills and Interventions for Effective Practice*, by David Dupper. Copyright © 2003 by John Wiley & Sons, Inc.

much through improving school and community conditions as through helping the child personally to adjust. This shift in emphasis paralleled the growth in popularity of Freudian psychology, which strongly focused on individual treatment rather than social change.

The Great Depression of the 1930s drastically reduced employment for social workers in the schools. Early in this period, those who retained their jobs tended to become heavily involved in locating and distributing food, shelter, and clothing. When the federal government began to provide these necessities, social workers gradually resumed their trend toward becoming caseworkers with individual students and their families. This orientation was well in place by the 1940s.

Middle Period

Throughout the 1940s and 1950s, with the federal government providing many basic financial and material needs to American families, social workers tended to maintain a clinical orientation, which increased their prestige in the school setting. Refinement of practice techniques to help individual students adjust to their environments then became the primary goal. Florence Poole, however, helped shift the focus from the "problem pupil" alone to a perspective that pupils and schools need to mutually adapt to each other, using the rationale that children had a right to an education. As early as 1949, Poole wrote that it was the responsibility of the school to offer its students something that would help them benefit from an education (Constable, 2006).

The l960s brought a number of social protest movements. With them came a shift in emphasis again to changing the school environment to help better meet the needs of diverse students. Social workers were to pursue this goal in collaboration with other school personnel. In the 1970s, development of systems theory and the ecological perspective helped focus social workers' attention on the complex problems of schools and communities, including racism and students' rights. Not all workers made the transition, however (Freeman, 1995). During this time, the term *visiting teacher* gradually changed to *school social worker*.

Employment of school social workers expanded in the 1960s and continued to expand in the 1970s. One reason was that legislation provided a variety of new employment settings. For example, the Economic Opportunity Act of 1964 created Head Start programs, which often employed social workers full- or part-time. Money appropriated under the Elementary and Secondary Education Act of 1965, an act that sought to improve educational opportunities for disadvantaged children, sometimes was used to employ social workers. In 1975, the Education for All Handicapped Children Act created new roles for social workers as part of a **special education** team. This act later evolved to become the Individuals with Disabilities Education Act (IDEA) (Dupper, 2003).

In 1973, Lela Costin developed an important model for school social work practice, which she named the school-community-pupil relations model. It was grounded in systems theory and focused on interactions among the school, the community, and the students. Social workers were to serve as negotiators, mediators, and consultants. Costin's model strongly influenced the field (Constable, 2009).

In the mid-1970s, the National Association of Social Workers (NASW) developed standards for school social work. This project was initiated by the NASW Task Force on Social Work Services in the Schools and completed by its successor, the Committee on Social Work Services in the Schools. The basic purpose of these standards was "to provide a model or measurement that school social workers can use to assess their scope of practice and their practice skills" (Hancock, 1982). The standards specifically identify three major targets of service: pupils and parents, school personnel, and the community. Clearly, the intent of the standards is that school social work services maintain a strong preventive, ecological perspective.

Recent Times

In the 1980s, school social workers began to pay more attention to students' rights, cultural diversity, parental involvement in the schools, and school–community–family partnerships. The impact of IDEA legislation in particular encouraged active parental involvement in educational planning for their children. The 1997 IDEA amendments established the **Individualized Education Program (IEP)** as the major tool in assisting every student to progress; every IEP requires parental input. Social workers have assumed much of the responsibility to make the goals of the act a reality. They frequently provide information to parents about programs and services, serve as mediators in conflicts regarding educational decisions, and provide mental health services in the classroom (Freeman, 1995; Dupper, 2003).

The growth of child poverty and homelessness over the past several decades has presented school social workers with increasing challenges, given the associated negative impact on attendance, achievement, and graduation rates. The impact of poverty on school performance will be discussed in more detail in a later section. Sadly, the recession beginning in 2008 accelerated these problems at the same time that social work positions were being cut in many schools due to budget shortfalls.

School Social Worker Certification

Various states have developed certification requirements for school social workers. Many require the MSW; others require the MSW plus a certain number of credit hours in education courses. There are several states that require the BSW only (alternative and charter schools provide the best opportunity for BSWs). As noted in Chapter 1, BSW student social work field placements in schools are currently of high priority, second only to child welfare placements. Students interested in becoming school social workers would do well to check into the particular requirements of the state where they hope to practice.

The School Social Work Association of America recommends one school social worker with the MSW degree per 400 students; this recommendation is a beacon that is rarely followed.

> **?** Assess your understanding of the history of social work in the schools by taking this brief quiz.

SOCIAL WORK ROLES IN THE SCHOOLS

Roles of school social workers vary from community to community and are constantly changing to meet shifting school, community, and societal needs. Social workers must be creative, innovative, and proactive in developing, implementing, and interpreting potential new roles in this challenging setting. Nevertheless, like all social workers, they utilize a variety of levels of intervention, as discussed in the rest of this section.

Working with Individuals

Social workers perform a variety of roles in the schools. First of all, as illustrated in the Santiago case, social workers frequently counsel with individual students. Students may be referred for a variety of reasons, among them truancy, undesirable behavior, and pregnancy. In schools where there is a guidance counselor, such cases may be assigned either to the counselor or to the social worker, depending on who has more time available.

School social workers today work with individual school personnel in a variety of ways as well: consulting with teachers about the needs of particular children, sharing with teachers and each other knowledge about cultural factors in the educational process, informing staff about important community resources, consulting with teachers about classroom relationships, and so on.

Some school social workers become involved in screening individual students for material aid, such as free or reduced-fee lunch programs. Some schools also distribute donated books, clothing, writing materials, and the like, to needy children. Often it is the social worker who identifies the children who need this material help.

Family Work

Another type of social work service in the school setting involves working with parents and families. The social worker is the main link between the family and the school; as in the Santiago case, the worker is often the *only* person from the school who makes home visits. Parents are contacted to gain information that may help teachers work more effectively with particular children. The worker may also make suggestions about parenting techniques in the home.

When a student is referred to **special education** for evaluation, especially for suspected **emotional or behavioral disturbance**, the school social worker usually interviews the parents to learn more about that child's early development and about how he or she currently behaves in the home and community settings. This responsibility will be discussed in more detail in a later section of this chapter. When appropriate, school social workers refer families to community agencies for material assistance, counseling, or other services.

Group Work

> Watch this video created by Oxford Academic (Oxford University Press) at Archbishop Molloy High School. What are three social work values demonstrated by school social worker Chris Dougherty?
> https://www.youtube.com/watch?v=J4WeHHQPMrE

School social workers also often develop and lead groups of students. Group work utilizes peer processes and other motivational techniques to help resolve attendance, academic, and social difficulties (Pawlak, Wozniak, & McGowen, 2006). Topics are sometimes controversial, such as pregnancy prevention, sexual orientation, preventing sexually transmitted diseases, and coping with parents who are drug abusers. Groups can become the focus of heated community debate because some parents want these topics to be discussed only at home.

School social workers may also become involved in leading groups of parents and/or teachers, with topics depending on circumstance and need. Some school social workers become involved in leading groups to promote change in the school system or the wider community.

Working with Organizations and Communities

In accord with the generalist approach, educating and organizing school personnel and the wider community is an important part of school social work. The social worker is often the major link between the school and the wider community. This role is increasingly important today as children's problems grow and school resources shrink. For example, more and more children today find themselves without a parent to go home to after school because, in many families, both parents must work outside the home to support their families. Social workers increasingly find themselves doing community assessments to find resources for after-school programs, only to end up organizing these programs themselves within the school setting using laboriously recruited volunteer staff.

Involvement with school-linked, integrated services (discussed later) is another undertaking that requires skill in working with organizations and communities.

Teamwork

Perhaps the most important thing to note about teamwork in the schools is that the school presents the social worker with a **secondary social work setting**, or host setting, for employment. The primary purpose of the school system is educational. The position of the social worker within the school setting is to support the educational function of the institution. In contrast, a family service agency is an example of a **primary social work setting** for a social worker. The primary purpose of the family service agency is to enhance social functioning, which is also the primary purpose of the social work profession; thus, the majority of the staff members are social workers (see Box 8.2).

Social workers almost always function as part of a team in school social work. That team might consist only of the social worker and a referring teacher, working together to meet the educational needs of a particular child. It might be a multi-disciplinary team assessing a student referred for special education evaluation. In the latter situation, the team might include the regular classroom teacher; a special education teacher; the school principal, guidance counselor, and school nurse; a county social worker; and one or more parents. Teams are constructed by their members according to the need at hand; decision making is collaborative, implying shared ownership of problems and solutions. Teamwork is an important element in planning and carrying out change in the wider school environment as well. Because social workers value cooperation and are trained to communicate well across disciplinary boundaries, they are often assigned to work as team coordinators and leaders (Constable & Thomas, 2006).

> **Ethics and Professional Behavior**
>
> *Dimension of Competency* **Skills:** Social workers understand the role of other professions when engaged in interprofessional teams.
>
> **Critical Thinking Question:** How did well-developed skills in understanding the roles of other professionals assist Frank Haines in his work with the Santiago sisters?

School-Linked, Integrated Services

Many American children enter school with so many needs that they are unable to learn—they are poor, undernourished, and come from deprived environments. Many have health care needs that have not been met, and many suffer from mental health

---

Box 8.2 The Secondary Social Work Setting

The social work job function is affected in major ways when it is performed in a secondary, or host, setting. For example, most of the employees in a school are teachers; if there is a social worker, usually there is only one employed in that setting. This can be a lonely position because nobody else is likely to have the same knowledge, values, and skills. In addition, many social workers are assigned to several schools. They may not have private offices but instead must share space with other staff, holding interviews in temporarily empty classrooms or even empty utility closets. Private telephones may be unavailable, so scheduling home visits or discussing family problems by phone can be difficult if not impossible. Organizing the political support required to secure needed changes is not easy in a secondary setting where the social worker may be the sole representative of his or her profession.

problems as well. For these reasons, a movement toward school-linked, integrated services has been under way in many communities across the United States. The intent is to make schools "hubs" for the delivery of a full range of services, involving various health, mental health, and social service agencies from the wider community (Franklin, 2000; Kronick, 2005). Sometimes these services are provided at the schools themselves, and sometimes they are simply coordinated by school personnel.

Schools where coordinated community services are actually delivered on site are sometimes called "full-service" schools. They have been developed in several states to help children at risk: those who arrive unprepared for the educational process and are unable to concentrate on school work due to abuse, neglect, homelessness, poverty, and poor health. Services such as counseling, family intervention, and group work may be targeted toward children displaying specific at-risk behaviors. Some full-service schools also offer comprehensive health and mental health services. Other, more broadly based services may also be available, such as case management, advocacy, child care, and transportation.

Only a few schools have achieved full-service status. One interesting example is a middle school in the Washington Heights section of New York City, which has teamed with the Children's Aid Society to create a settlement house right in the school facility. Other New York City schools are less comprehensive but are working toward the full-service model. Located in low-income areas, they describe themselves as "community schools" and seek to serve as nerve centers for comprehensive neighborhood revitalization (Constable & Kordesh, 2006).

The Affordable Care Act

The Affordable Care Act (ACA), passed in 2010 through intense efforts by the Obama Administration, strongly supports services to students in the schools, especially health services. The act provided $50 million for four years (2010–2013) to construct or renovate and equip school-based health centers. It continued to provide competitive grants to states and tribes to institute school-based dental services and to support the Prevention and Public Health Fund (PPHF), which invests in community health initiatives, throughout the years of the Obama administration. The ACA also offered, throughout the Obama years, a Pregnancy Assistance Fund, a competitive grant program providing supportive services to teen and adult parents to help them complete high school and to help improve services for victims sexual assault, stalking, and domestic violence (Vaughn & Princiotta, 2013).

However, Donald Trump, elected president in 2016, stated during his campaign that he planned to repeal and replace the ACA. Soon after election, Trump stated that repealing the ACA would be an immediate priority for his administration.

> **?** Assess your understanding of social work roles in the schools by taking this brief quiz.

THE IMPACT OF DIVERSITY IN THE SCHOOLS

Cultural Diversity

Cultural diversity has been increasing rapidly in the United States over the past few decades. The impact of cultural diversity on the city school system where Lisa and Loretta Santiago attended was considerable. When Latino children first began attending the public schools, they were a small minority and were placed in classrooms where only English was spoken; some of these children swam, but many of them sank. No help was offered to those who could not handle the experience. This is still the situation in many schools in the United States today. Rural school systems are particularly devoid of resources for children whose native language is other than English.

Birth rates (which of course affect diversity in the schools) have been falling for every racial group in the United States since the beginning of the great recession in 2008. It is unclear if this trend will continue, but recent data indicate that there will be fewer U.S. citizens in every racial group than was projected a few years earlier. The Latino fertility rate in 2013 was only slightly above 2.1 children in a given mother's lifetime (2.1 children is considered the number required to replace the parents, factoring in mortality). The perception that the Latino fertility rate is vastly above that of whites and blacks is incorrect. In 2013, the black fertility rate, also down from 2008, was 1.88 births per mother; that of non-Hispanic whites was 1.75. Thus, while Latino women had the highest fertility rate, that rate was barely above replacement, and women in every racial group were modifying their family size (Reed, 2015).

The American cultural myth of the melting pot has lulled many people into assuming that children who are not native speakers of English can assimilate the language effortlessly. Yet many children struggle and cannot keep up in basic subjects like math and history. Crucial early learning time, the foundation for more advanced study, is lost (see Box 8.3).

Many schools have devised innovative programs to meet the needs of children from diverse backgrounds. The primary thrust came from educators, but social workers provided strong support. Two models for teaching children whose native language is not English have emerged. The **bilingual** model allows students to take courses like math and history in their native languages, while studying English in specialized **English as a Second Language (ESL)** courses. The other model plunges students immediately into intensive **Sheltered English Immersion (SEI)** to get them up to grade level in English and into regular classrooms as quickly as possible (Llana & Paulson, 2006). The SEI model may be required in schools where multiple languages are spoken, but in schools where only English plus one non-English language is spoken, the bilingual model may be preferred.

The model used at the Valdez Middle School that Lisa and Loretta Santiago attended was bilingual. Hispanic children could take all their classes in Spanish, if desired, enrolling

---

Box 8.3 Children with Limited or No English

An astonishing number of children in the United States live in homes where a language other than English is spoken—over 20 percent and growing. They often begin their educational experience bewildered by the school environment because they do not understand the language in which they are being taught. Their parents may not be able to help them because the parents themselves do not speak English very well, if at all. The cultural background of these homes may be worlds away from that of the school, so that communication gaps between children, parents, and teachers go well beyond language. Another confounding condition concerns economic deprivation—children who come from non-English speaking homes are much more likely to be poor, so they lack the family resources that otherwise might help them overcome language barriers. Tutors, for example, may be economically out of reach. Thus, the likelihood of successful achievement in school for these children is limited.

Box 8.4   Up for Debate

Proposition: Bilingual education should be provided in the public schools.

Yes	No
Children learn more easily in their native language, especially complex concepts.	Children need to learn the language of the majority culture as quickly as possible.
Children feel more comfortable in an environment where their native language is spoken.	Children need to learn to feel comfortable in an English-speaking environment in the United States.
Teaching in one's own language affirms children's cultural identity and thus enhances self-esteem.	Pride in one's cultural heritage should be taught outside of the school.
Some children simply fail when they must learn in a language that is not their own.	Some children will fail regardless of the language in which they are taught.
The United States needs bilingual citizens to maintain an enlightened place in the world.	All Americans should speak English as their primary language.

concurrently in ESL courses. Students with more understanding of the English language were **mainstreamed**, or educated in English in as normal a fashion for an American child as possible, while still having bilingual teachers available who could assist them in Spanish when needed (see Box 8.4).

California passed a law in 1998 eliminating bilingual education from its public schools, followed by Arizona and Massachusetts. The rationale was that students would learn English faster in an "immersion" type program and that they would be able to join their English-speaking peers in less than a year. However, a careful study in Massachusetts found that 83 percent of its SEI students were unable to join regular classrooms after a year, and more than half had not achieved fluency in English after three years in an SEI classroom. No study has actually shown that students learn faster in an English immersion classroom; many educators today believe that the most effective programs are "dual language," or programs where children learn in their native language for part of the day and study in English for part of the day. These educators also argue that in today's shrinking world, it is important for at least some Americans to be fluent in more than one language and knowledgeable about more than one culture, so that maintaining bilingual education is good for the nation as a whole (Llana & Paulson, 2006). In 2016, California voters repealed the 1998 law so that English-only classes are no longer required in that state's public schools (Sanburn, 2016).

Bilingual teachers, social workers, and other staff are needed in schools where a large proportion of children speak languages other than English; however, these professionals need to know about the cultural backgrounds of their students as well as the language. Frank Haines, for example, secured his job at the Valdez Middle School partly because he spoke basic Spanish, but also because he had direct experience working with various Hispanic peoples in his prior training for the priesthood. To work effectively at the Valdez school, for example, Frank needed to know about dating customs constraining young Hispanic girls and to understand normal disciplinary practices among Hispanic families

Box 8.5 Exploring Cultural Diversity in Today's Schools

Cultural diversity in today's schools is so extensive that it would be impossible for any social worker to be knowledgeable about all of them. Hence, it is important for workers to view themselves as learners and consult with members of the groups with whom they work. Cultural diversity involves not only race and ethnicity but also religion (among other components). Today, for example, Muslim children may experience severe **bullying** at school, especially girls who wear head scarves and Sikhs who wear turbans and are mistaken for Muslims. Social workers can develop innovative school-based programs teaching tolerance and fostering empathy for those who are different.

Cultural diversity also involves disciplinary practices. Physical punishment of children, for example, is viewed very differently according to class, race, and religion. No state forbids parents to administer physical punishment, and while the majority of states do forbid teachers to administer such punishment in the schools, 19 states allow it (Hanes, 2014). Hence, it is particularly important for social workers to be knowledgeable about disciplinary practices among the populations they serve and the values that underlie them. Intervening to create change in this area can require great delicacy.

Social workers can learn what behavior is appropriate in a given culture or **subculture** by talking with other workers who are knowledgeable, by observing behavior directly, talking with members of the subculture in question, taking classes, and reading. Many sources of information are available, but they must be conscientiously pursued.

---

living near the school. He needed to understand sex-role behaviors and authority patterns (see Box 8.5).

Another important impact of cultural diversity in the schools involves the fact that the children learn from each other. **Norms** that might go unquestioned within a single culture may be questioned as the children learn that there are other ways of doing things. On the positive side, this can lead to flexible, informed, tolerant citizens later on in life. On the negative side (as in the case of the Santiago sisters), it may lead to rebellion against family norms and expectations because other alternatives are readily in evidence.

Particularly during the teenage years, most children enter a period of rebellion as they attempt to define who they are. A major developmental task of adolescence is to differentiate the emerging self from parents and other family members. Cross-cultural issues complicate this normal process. Social workers may need to reach out to contact children who are experiencing difficulty because some cultural norms do not promote a tendency to seek professional help. On the whole, the value of exposure to differences and the learning that children must undertake to deal with conflicting information probably far outweigh the discomfort of temporary confusion or rebellious behavior.

Diversity and Difference

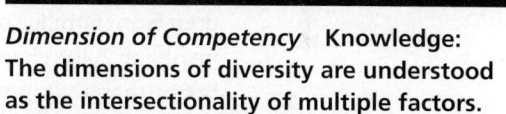

Dimension of Competency Knowledge: The dimensions of diversity are understood as the intersectionality of multiple factors.

Critical Thinking Question: How did social worker Frank Haines's knowledge of the intersectionality of multiple factors in the Santiago case (age, gender, ethnicity, religion, etc.) help him to resolve the truancy issue?

Watch this video published by the National Education Association (NEA). Although it is geared toward the teaching profession, how can a school social worker use the skills discussed to help meet the cultural and linguistic needs of English Language Learners?
https://www.youtube.com/watch?v=5HU80AxmP-U

Alternative Schools and Charter Schools

Another impact of cultural diversity in the schools is a proliferation of what are known as **alternative schools**, schools that operate outside the regular public system. These schools are usually privately run, although a few cities provide taxpayer money to poor parents to help finance tuition. Alternative schools may develop formal agreements with public schools and even share staff. Alternative schools are not limited to children of ethnic minority background, but in many places minority parents have become strong advocates because they tend to have small classes and may include cultural and/or religious teachings in the curriculum. A problem, however, is that most lack the resources to provide special education services.

Charter schools are a type of alternative school growing rapidly in states that permit them. They are tuition-free public schools (financed through tax revenues like regular public schools) that are operated independently. They are regulated at the state level and deal with complex financial and management challenges. Most emphasize the particular academic philosophy that motivated their creation (Hare, Rome, & Massat, 2006).

President Obama made charter schools a primary ingredient of his educational reform policies, probably due to the success of the charter school movement in Chicago, where he lived for many years. As part of a $4.35 billion initiative, President Obama encouraged states to make it easier to start these schools. As a result, several states lifted their restrictions on charter schools. Charter schools experienced a 100-percent growth between 2007 and 2014, comprising an enrollment of 2.57 million students in 2014. These schools are very likely to continue to grow because, with the passage of the Every Student Succeeds Act (ESSA) in 2015, funds were provided to replicate and expand the ones that were high-performing. The ESSA provided additional grants to states for start-up funds as well ("What are Charter Schools," 2015).

The first charter school was opened in Minnesota in 1991 to meet the needs of children from families mired in poverty. Results have been mixed—according to a large study involving 2,403 charter schools performed several years ago, student achievement was no better than that in regular public schools. A more recent study, however, by the Center for Research on Education Outcomes at Stanford University, found that these schools do particularly well teaching minority students, low-income students, and those learning English. ("What are Charter Schools," 2015).

Special Needs

Since 1975, many social workers have been hired by schools to work with special education programs. Before that time, many students with special needs were simply refused admission to public school. In 1975, however, landmark federal legislation—Public Law 94-142, the Education for All Handicapped Children Act—changed public education forever. This law is now known as the Individuals with Disabilities Education Act, or IDEA, promising free and appropriate public education to all children with disabilities (Dupper, 2003). It was amended in 1997 and then reauthorized as the Individuals with Disabilities Education Improvement Act of 2004 (Constable & Kordesh, 2006).

While a great boon for the students and families it helps, the law has placed a strain on state and local community financing. That is because educating a child with disabilities costs approximately twice as much as educating the average child. IDEA law requires the federal government to pay up to 40 percent of the "excess cost" of serving special needs children, but Congress has never authorized sufficient funding. To help the situation, President Obama promoted and signed the American Recovery and Reinvestment Act of 2009, which included $12.2 billion in additional funds for IDEA ("Idea Funding

Gap, 2010). In 2016, however, the federal budget included plans to cover only 16 percent of the cost of special education, approximately $17.85 billion less than the original commitment promised under the IDEA law (Heasley, 2016).

IDEA requires that social workers be part of a **multidisciplinary team** (sometimes called an **M-team, pupil planning team,** etc.) that evaluates referrals. Students are referred to special education services for a variety of reasons: speech or language impairment, physical disability (including visual or hearing impairment), learning disability, cognitive or other developmental disability, emotional or behavioral disturbance, pregnancy or health impairment, autism, and traumatic brain injury. Many children who never would have received an education, or completed one, now have a much better chance.

Part C of IDEA, as reauthorized in 2004, reinforces federal legislation originally passed in 1986, extending the right of special education services to infants and toddlers with disabilities. Part C has a strong focus on family; it signals a change in philosophy for early childhood intervention from child-centered to family-centered services. The family-centered model guides social workers toward family–professional collaboration whether they are working directly with families or developing policy, programs, or evaluation strategies (Bishop, 2006).

Social workers in special education programs assume many roles, but a prominent one involves evaluating children who are referred because of suspected "emotional disturbance" (sometimes labeled "behavioral disturbance"). Essentially, these are the children who are identified by teachers as behaving in harmful or inappropriate ways. School social workers often need to become involved before evaluation of a referral can take place because, under special education law, all parents must consent in writing. Usually a child's referring teacher contacts the parents about a referral and the reasons it was made. Then a permission slip is sent for the parents to sign. If the parents do not return the form, the social worker usually makes a home visit to explain the situation further and try to obtain permission.

Once permission to do an evaluation has been obtained, the social worker's next responsibility is to interview the parents to determine whether a referred child exhibits disturbance in the home or community environment. If a referred child misbehaves at school but gets along well in the home and community settings, then perhaps the problem lies with the school and not with the child.

A multidisciplinary team (M-Team) will meet to determine whether a referred child qualifies for special education services. Social workers serve on many of these teams, particularly if a child is referred for emotional disturbance. The M-team will comprise a variety of professionals depending on the nature of the referral (e.g., regular education teacher, special education teacher, psychologist, nurse, guidance counselor, social worker, school principal, etc.). The referred child's parents are also invited to be part of the team.

Once a child has been accepted into special education, the law requires that the educational program be provided in the **least restrictive environment** and in an environment tailored to each child's special needs; an **Individualized Education Program** (**IEP**) must be developed for each child. The IEP is a formal, written document developed by the multi-disciplinary team that has evaluated the child's special needs. If the child is evaluated as eligible for special education services, the IEP specifies what services are appropriate. The document must detail the child's present levels of educational performance, the goals of any special services, and a description of how the child's progress toward these goals will be measured. The document specifies the extent to which the child will be educated along with children who do not have disabilities. Today, many, if not most, special needs children are **mainstreamed**, or educated in the regular classroom, with supplementary services provided as needed.

An important role for social workers is to mobilize a variety of services to help attain IEP goals. Social workers may provide direct services themselves to assist these children, such as individual or group counseling, and they may assist teachers and parents in developing behavior management programs (Dupper, 2003).

Educational Evaluations as Applied Research

What the evaluation team does when activated by a school special education referral is an example of applied research. Each member of the multi-disciplinary team seeks information about the referred child in his or her area of expertise. Results of these research efforts are used in joint decision-making. Within 90 days of a referral, the M-team must meet to determine whether the child is indeed qualified to receive special services and, if so, what kind. This type of applied research has serious, immediate consequences for a given child.

The social worker researches the child's developmental history and also investigates his or her current behavior at home and in the community. When researching the child's developmental history, the social worker gathers information that will help determine if the child has developed "normally" or not. How did the parents feel about the child's birth? Did the child walk and talk at about the same age as most children? How has the child related to the parents? How does he or she behave at home? Has the child been in

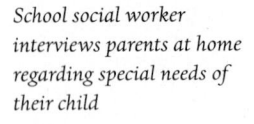

School social worker interviews parents at home regarding special needs of their child

any sort of trouble in the community? If so, what kind? What concerns do the parents have about the child today? About the school? These are only a few of the questions a social worker might ask. Assurances of confidentiality can help concerned parents to provide detailed information.

While the social worker is conducting his or her part of the investigation, other members of the evaluation team will also be at work. The psychologist may be conducting a battery of psychological tests designed to indicate evidence of emotional disturbance and may also administer an IQ test. The teacher will observe the child in the regular classroom, taking detailed notes to document the percentage of the time the child is doing assigned work ("on task"), as opposed to how much time the child spends misbehaving, wandering around, daydreaming, and the like.

Unfortunately, the beliefs and actions of some people in the wider society can *create* clients for social workers in special education. In an ideal society, special education evaluation would be a waste of time for these children because, given acceptance by others, there would be no problems to evaluate. The following is an example.

> **Research Informed Practice**
>
> *Dimension of Competency* **Values:** Social workers use and translate research evidence to inform service delivery.
>
> **Critical Thinking Question:** What professional values do you think underlie the type of research questions asked by school social workers employed in special education programs?

School Social Work with Other Special-Needs Children: The Ordeal of Two Gay Brothers

Todd Larkin was about 11 years old when he began to sense he was different. As early as the sixth grade, he sometimes felt very alone. His buddies made cracks and catcalls at the girls, and the girls flirted in return. Everyone seemed to share some sort of secret. Todd, who had many friends who were girls, couldn't grasp what it was all about. He liked girls as people, but the flirting and catcalls left him bewildered. However, he didn't talk to anyone about his confusion because he was afraid there might be something wrong with him. Since he was handsome, athletic, and gregarious, nobody noticed his pain.

When Todd was in his early teens, he noticed a strong attraction to his male friends. No other boy mentioned such an attraction, so he felt confused and scared. Other boys were starting to date, but they dated only girls. Todd felt a desire to date boys. Increasingly, he wondered if something was wrong with him. He was afraid to talk with anyone about his fears, however. He didn't even have the vocabulary to help him name his difference from other children.

Then, by chance, Todd saw an old movie replayed on television at home. The movie was called *The Truth about Alex*. The movie's hero, Alex, was handsome, athletic, and outgoing, just like Todd. And also like Todd, he was physically attracted to boys, not girls. Alex kept his difference a secret for a long time, but eventually he told a close friend in high school. As a result, Alex was labeled **homosexual** and ostracized by all his former friends.

Todd began to believe that he was homosexual, too, but given Alex's experience in the movie, he was determined to remain absolutely silent. He even began to date girls to make sure no one would ever suspect. He "passed" very successfully. He was popular among the young ladies, but he graduated from high school with the whole burden of worry about his sexuality on his own shoulders. He didn't even talk with his parents about it.

Because Todd felt so lonely and misunderstood in high school in his small, rural town, he decided to go away to college in a large city. He hoped he might be able to talk with someone there about his concerns. Being extremely bright and an academic achiever, he was admitted to a prestigious private urban university. But his first days at college were disappointing. Right across the hall from his dorm room, for example, a large poster was displayed making fun of **gay** and **lesbian** people. And in theology class, Old Testament scriptures were quoted that rebuked gay people. Again, the boy felt lonely and afraid.

One day, a hall director found Todd staring at the poster on the door across from his room. The director, a sensitive young woman who also served on the Campus Ministry staff, asked Todd if the poster offended him. Todd admitted that it did. The director agreed and suggested that Todd talk with a certain priest at the university, who felt the same way.

Todd made an appointment. When he arrived at the priest's office, he felt sick to his stomach, not sure what to say. However, Father Healy's gentle sense of humor broke the ice. "Hello, son," the man began with a smile. "Come on in and let's talk." Todd did just that. By the time he left Father Healy's office, he had been invited to attend a group of gay and lesbian students run by Campus Ministry, co-led by the priest and Todd's own hall director.

In the nurturing environment provided by the Campus Ministry gathering, Todd began to understand that his worth and dignity as a spiritual being were not diminished by his sexual orientation. He began to open up and tell his story. Six months into the school year, Todd decided that he was, indeed, gay and that it was time to come out of the closet.

Encouraged by his support group, Todd began by telling his mother about his sexuality. To his shock, Todd's mother told him that she had suspected he was gay for some time and that she was glad he was finally able to tell her. Todd's mother eased the boy's way toward acceptance in the family by telling his father and stepfather for him. Todd's stepfather accepted the news fairly well; his biological father was more ambivalent. Neither man, however, totally rejected Todd, as he had feared they would.

The one person Todd pledged his mother not to tell was his younger brother, Tim. Todd felt that Tim, having weathered his mother's divorce and remarriage, needed a stable male role model in his life. Todd believed he was that role model and feared Tim would be upset at a critical time in his life if he learned that Todd was gay. The mother consented.

Ironically, Tim was struggling with questions about his own sexuality. Like his brother before him, he was afraid to talk to anyone. At age 11, the boy began to abuse drugs, perhaps to mask his worries and confusion about his sexuality. At age 13, Tim took a major overdose and had to be hospitalized to save his life. It was there, by Tim's bedside at the hospital, that Todd learned what his brother had been going through. As Todd sat in the visitor's chair and asked Tim what was wrong and why he had tried to kill himself, he heard the younger boy say things like "I'm all alone" and "No one understands me."

Suddenly, Todd recognized his own feelings and experiences in high school. Was it possible that Tim too had doubts about his sexuality? Finally, he asked. Tim began to cry, and then Todd cried, and the two brothers shared as they never had before.

Something entirely unexpected happened shortly after Tim's hospital stay, and it looked as if the brothers' ordeal were about to be over. The United States Supreme Court legalized gay marriage. Todd and Tim were ecstatic. Now, at last, they believed they could reveal their sexual orientation, at least to a few trusted people. After all, amazing progress had just been achieved nation-wide for the rights of gay people.

It would be nice if the story ended happily there, but sadly, it didn't. Shortly after the historic Supreme Court decision, Tim decided to confide in a close friend at his junior high school. He chose the friend carefully and hoped for the best.

But Tim's friend turned out not to be trustworthy. A terrible replay of *The Truth about Alex* began to take place in this small, rural town. Within a week, bullies at school began taunting him. The boy felt betrayed, angry, confused, ashamed, and scared. His family's house was pelted with eggs. When the family appealed for help from the police, the police did nothing. "A few eggs never hurt nobody," one of them sneered to Tim's mother.

A couple of weeks after that, a boy in Tim's eighth-grade class pointed at him rudely and jeered loudly, "You're a fag, Tim Larkin! You're a fag!"

Tim's teacher should have protected him. But, instead, the man pointed a long finger at the boy. "Well, Tim," the man said, looking down his considerable nose, "is it true?"

Tim couldn't speak at first. Then he took a deep, slow breath. "I don't know, Mr. Humphrey," he replied bravely. "I'm not sure yet."

The class roared with laughter. The teacher glared and said, "I thought so. I thought so."

Mr. Humphrey's tone was so harsh and the laughter in the classroom so derisive that Tim couldn't bear to stay in his seat. He leaped up and ran home, shut the window shades, and locked the door. He refused to go back to school. When his mother and stepfather were able to persuade him to go back a few days later, Tim found himself thrown against lockers and spat upon. The school principal refused to help. "We aren't in the business of protecting queer kids around here," he said, when Tim's parents went to the school to complain. "Maybe the Supreme Court likes gays, but the folks around here sure don't."

Tim stopped going to school again, and the principal soon threatened to prosecute for truancy. At this point, Tim's mother appealed for help at the state level, wanting to know her and her son's rights. She also took Tim to a social worker in private practice, an MSW who specialized in family counseling.

The social worker helped Tim and his mother understand that confusion about sexual orientation was a normal part of adolescence. She helped the mother provide Tim with much-needed understanding and support so that despite the harsh daily reality of rejection from outside his family, Tim did not attempt suicide again. Instead, he brought his troubles and frustrations to the safe haven of home or a counseling session.

On the suggestion of the state office of public instruction, Tim's mother referred the boy for special education services at the school. The social worker who was counseling privately with the family wrote a powerful letter to the evaluation team describing the school as an environment hazardous to Tim's physical and mental health. The team then determined that Tim was a student at risk and authorized homebound instruction.

At about this time, hoping to help create positive social change, Tim's mother courageously agreed to take part in a public radio program discussing challenges for parents with homosexual children. When she returned to her job (she had been a caretaker for an elderly woman for more than 15 years), she found her belongings piled on the front porch, the door of the house locked, and a note telling her she was fired. She was never allowed to speak with her former client, a shut-in, again.

With such truly depressing experiences, one could hardly blame this family for becoming bitter and giving up. But instead, they maintained hope and overcame the odds. Tim eventually passed his high school equivalency exam with the help of a dedicated tutor. Tim's family, excited and relieved, gave him a formal graduation ceremony along with Todd's new partner, who had completed his GED at approximately the same time. Many friends and family members attended the ceremony. Tim was accepted into college. Todd later graduated from the prestigious university he attended and went on to earn the MSW degree. He married his partner. Today he works with gay and **lesbian** youth.

Tim's mother explains that she is still careful to maintain a safe haven for her two sons at home. She declares that anti-gay people, even long-term family friends, are not allowed in the house when her sons are present. This impressive woman has also paid attention to her own needs. Not only has she survived being fired from her caretaking job, but she has updated her nursing credentials and developed entrepreneurial skills. Today she runs her own bridal shop.

Student Rights and the Law

Many court rulings have affected students in the public schools, and the public schools themselves, in important ways. The following is a brief list of notable cases decided by the U.S. Supreme Court, some pertaining to public elementary and secondary schools, some to public universities (Jacobs, 2008; "After Decades of Action," 2014):

- 1948: *McCollum v. Board of Education of School District No. 71*. This decision struck down release time for religious instruction in public school classrooms.
- 1954: *Brown v. Board of Education of Topeka*. The doctrine of "Separate but Equal" in public education was struck down. School segregation by race was no longer legal.
- 1969: *Tinker v. Des Moines Independent School District*. Students have a right to express themselves in school as long as they don't disrupt classes or invade the rights of others. (This case involved a student disciplined for wearing a black armband in protest of the Vietnam War.)
- 1977: *Ingraham v. Wright*. Teachers can use corporal punishment if their state and school district allows it.
- 1985: *New Jersey v. T.L.O.* School officials may search a student's property if they have "reasonable suspicion" the student is committing a crime or breaking a school rule.
- 1988: *Hazelwood School District v. Kuhlmeier*. Schools may censor student newspapers and other forms of student expression, such as yearbooks and theatrical productions.
- 1990: *West Side Community Schools v. Mergens* If a school allows any student-interest clubs to meet on school grounds (e.g., a chess club), it must also allow students to meet on campus to discuss religion or politics.
- 1995: *Veronia School District v. Acton*. Schools may require athletes to submit to drug testing.
- 2000: *Santa Fe Independent School District v. Jane Doe*. Public schools cannot sponsor religious activity, but student-initiated group prayer may be allowed on school grounds if not sponsored by the school.

- 2003: *Grutter v. Bollinger*. Colleges can use race as a factor in admissions as long as no quota is set and the school conducts a thorough review of each applicant's qualifications.
- 2007: *Parents v. Seattle & Meredith v. Jefferson*. Public schools cannot use racial classifications in making public school assignments to achieve racial balance.
- 2007: *Morse v. Frederick*. A student can be disciplined by the school for raising an offensive banner at a school event (in this case, "Bong Hits 4 Jesus").
- 2009: *Safford Unified School District v. Redding*. Search of student undergarments for prescription painkillers violates the Fourth Amendment.
- 2013: *Fisher v. University of Texas*. Lower courts must re-examine whether a race-conscious affirmative action program at the University of Texas should be permitted.
- 2014: *Shuette v. Coalition to Defend Affirmative Action*. Michigan's voter initiative banning affirmative action in public education and state contracting is upheld.
- 2016: *Fisher v. University of Texas*. Admissions officials may continue to use race as one factor among many in determining student admissions to ensure a diverse student body.

As can be seen from these rulings, some overturn or at least seem to conflict with others. Despite the grounding of U.S. law in the Constitution, human beings determine how to interpret the Constitution. Perspectives and, thus, interpretations can change over time. The political leanings of the litigants influence the nature of the cases they bring before the court, and the political leanings of the judges may influence their rulings.

> **?** Assess your understanding of the impact of diversity in the schools by taking this brief quiz.

SOCIAL WORK VALUES IN THE SCHOOL SETTING: POLICY IMPLICATIONS

Social work professional values strongly affect the policies social workers promote in the school setting. The Santiago and Larkin cases will be used as illustrations followed by a discussion of other serious school issues that tend to be addressed in very different ways depending on value orientation.

The Santiago Sisters

Let us begin with the Santiago sisters. Years ago, truancy would have been viewed simply as bad behavior, and the response of the school system would have been punitive. However, over the years, more enlightened values in the fields of education and social work together have led to the development of a more individualized approach to truancy. Today, many schools have a policy of assigning a social worker to approach the investigation not as an effort at social control but as a fact-finding task. The uniqueness of each child's personal circumstance is recognized, and the worth and dignity of each child is respected. Usually the truant child needs assistance with some underlying problem.

The very existence of bilingual education illustrates how values have affected policy in the schools. The primary thrust for the development of bilingual education came from the profession of education, of course, but social work values such as self-determination strongly support it if that is what minority people request. Recognition of minority languages and cultures in public schools not only helps children learn but also shows respect for the worth and dignity of all persons. Such attention helps children gain self-esteem and pride in their own heritage.

Values also were the fuel for the development of special education programs in the public schools. Certainly it is easier for a school system simply to refuse admission or to expel children who bring with them special problems and needs. But over time, the values of fairness and individual worth and dignity have led to the recognition that children don't have much of a chance to make it in this society without an education. Even children with special problems should have a right to public education. Committed organizing and political strength were required to translate these values into public law, however.

The Larkin Case

The Larkin case is an example of what happens when conformity rather than diversity is valued by a school administration. Social work values, by contrast, honor the worth and dignity of all persons, and they teach respect for diversity. If social work values had been activated in Tim's school during his ordeal, new school policy would have been proposed, at the very least, to protect the rights of minorities. However, no one on the staff stepped forward to organize for change. Ideally, such a task would have been taken on by a school social worker (see Box 8.6). Unfortunately, even today, some social workers may be **homophobic**, or at least **heterosexist**, themselves.

The NASW strongly supports full equality and civil rights for gay and lesbian persons. How different life for gay and lesbian students would be if all school personnel, including social workers, took a serious interest in this issue and worked hard to solve it! Schools can be ideal settings to provide education about sexual orientation because almost all children and families become involved in them. School programs can help teach understanding and acceptance of diversity to students and parents alike, given the commitment to do so.

Beyond the school setting, social work values support protective laws and full civil rights for people with same-sex orientation and their families. The Supreme Court's decision legalizing gay marriage nationwide is a huge step forward, but as of 2015 only 21 states and the District of Columbia had laws protecting gay and lesbian persons from

---

Box 8.6 Challenges of Gay Youth

While conditions for gay and lesbian students are somewhat improved in many schools today, especially since the Supreme Court ruling legalizing gay marriage, challenges remain. Gay and lesbian students are frequently bullied, and it is important that school policies against such bullying are in place and enforced. Positive role models, such as respected gay and lesbian teachers, should be part of the school staff. Sex education curriculum should include accurate information regarding sexual orientation. Social workers should challenge negative stereotypes and discrimination against gay and lesbian youth, and they should serve as positive role models for respect and appreciation of diversity in all its many forms. They should provide in-service training for teachers and other staff to help improve the school's climate for gays and lesbians.

discrimination in employment, housing, and public accommodations (Rottmann, 2015). The result for many people is likely to be the same thing that happened to Todd Larkin's mother, fired from a job she had performed faithfully for many years. Moreover, progress toward full civil rights for this population was probably halted by the conservative sweep that took place in the 2016 election, placing a conservative in the White House and maintaining a conservative majority in Congress.

Bullying and Violence in the Schools

Bullying involves unwanted aggressive behavior directed toward another person in situations where there is an imbalance of power and an intent to cause harm. It is likely to be repeated. It may take many forms: verbal, physical, social, and cyber-bullying (an indirect form of bullying accomplished via Internet, texting, and email).

Bullying can take extreme forms. The mass shooting at Columbine High School in Littleton, Colorado, in April 1999 awakened everyone to its frightening reality. The massacre at Virginia Tech in April 2007 reawakened considerable fear. The Sandy Hook Elementary School killing of 20 young children and six teachers in Newtown, Connecticut, in December, 2012, greatly magnified the fear and horror surrounding such events.

How can such horrors be prevented? As far back as 1994, the federal government mandated **zero-tolerance** policies in the public schools under President Bill Clinton's Gun-Free Schools Act. Zero tolerance means that a student *must* be expelled from school for a calendar year if caught carrying a weapon (administrators are given some slight latitude according to the circumstance). After the mass shootings at Columbine, many schools began bringing in police, hall monitors, metal detectors and surveillance cameras, and they began requiring student ID badges. Students began being disciplined for very minor infractions.

Is zero tolerance and strict disciplinary action the best way to prevent violence? Many social workers disagree. Professional values stress the worth and dignity of every person and the provision of options and choices, not repression. Many other professions also advise that preventing attacks involves far more than punitive measures. Many school shootings over the past several years have been carried out not by the bullies, but rather by the victims of bullying (Openshaw, 2008). Surveillance measures may only make victimized students more afraid.

While mass shootings are by far the most publicized and extreme forms of bullying, bullying can take many other forms, less lethal but seriously oppressive to the average student: physical threats (pushing, kicking, unwanted sexual contact, etc.) and verbal intimidation such as ridicule, rumor-spreading, name-calling, and insults. Today the Internet can spread bullying rumors to hundreds of students at the click of a mouse. A 2013 study by the national Center for Disease Control (CDC) found that nearly 20 percent of students in its representative sample reported being bullied on school property in the previous 12 months, and nearly 15 percent reported being bullied over the Internet ("Understanding School Violence," 2015). The CDC noted that bullying can lead to many negative health and behavioral outcomes: physical injuries, fear, anxiety, depression, substance abuse, and even suicide. Several characteristics have been identified as risk factors for victimization (see Box 8.7).

Twemlow and Sacco (2008) assert that in order to successfully address bullying, the entire school *system* and the climate surrounding the school system must be addressed. For

Box 8.7 Bullying: Risk Factors and Signs

Children at risk for bullying often exhibit certain traits that place them at higher risk for bullying at school. These traits include having a disability; having some type of minority status including race, religion, or sexual orientation; having a family background mired in poverty and/or a family background that involves poor family functioning; achieving poor grades; associating with peers who have a history of delinquency; having a history of prior violence; and using unhealthy substances including tobacco, alcohol, and other drugs.

Signs parents can look for to learn whether their children are being bullied at school include trouble sleeping, changes in eating habits, loss of friends and or/belongings, making excuses not to go to school, and returning home with unexplained injuries and torn clothes. Bullied children may talk of suicide.

example, they note that in many high-achieving schools, there is such strong emphasis on achievement that the environment is extremely coercive, encouraging competition to the point that students are dehumanized. These authors point out that school systems must also address the "undiscussables" if they are to reduce bullying and other forms of violence: teachers who bully students, nonteaching staff who bully students, administrators who bully teachers and staff, coaches who bully athletes by pressuring them too hard to succeed, parents who bully teachers, and prejudice (usually denied but exhibited through bullying) against various minorities. When authorities model bullying, students follow suit.

Unfortunately, the man elected president in 2016, Donald Trump, modeled bullying and intimidation of various persons and populations throughout his campaign, including women, ethnic minorities, people he considered physically unattractive, Muslims, and persons with disabilities. Immediately after Trump's election, reports of bullying began spreading from college campuses down through secondary and even elementary schools.

Young girl suffers from bullying at school

As reported by a mother whose young son was bullied at his elementary school, children now believed it was OK "to be mean to others because the president is doing it." ("Post-Trump Victory Bullying," (2016).

In order to reduce bullying and other forms of school violence, the Center for Disease Control recommends that universal, school-based programs should be delivered to all students: programs that teach positive social skills, emotional self-awareness, conflict resolution skills, teamwork, and non-violent problem solving. The CDC also recommends family-based programs to improve parenting skills and family relations. Information about child development, communication skills, and non-violent problem resolution should be included. In addition, street outreach programs are recommended that can reduce youth violence by connecting trained staff with young people to help mediate conflict and provide appropriate referrals to community resources ("Prevention at School," n.d.).

> Watch this Comedy Central video by Key and Peele. What information is the aggressor sharing with viewers about his bullying behavior? How might this information assist social work practice?
> https://www.youtube.com/watch?v=CUvFeyGxaaU

The Environment and Early Sexual Development

Early sexual development is particularly hazardous for young children today because it leads to a greater risk of early pregnancy. The consequences are serious, impacting educational achievement, particularly for young girls.

No one is certain why girls are maturing physically earlier than in previous times, but many scientists believe that environmental pollution is a major culprit. The CYGNET study (Cohort Study of Young Girls' Nutrition, Environment, and Transitions) of over 1,200 girls residing in San Francisco, Cincinnati, and New York has found that Caucasian girls are entering puberty four months earlier on average than their counterparts in 1997. African-American girls are developing several months earlier on average than Caucasian girls (with nearly 20 percent showing signs in first grade), and the first signs of puberty for Latina girls falls somewhere between.

The trend toward early puberty is dangerous as early puberty is associated with increased risk of breast cancer. The CYGNET study, being longitudinal, will follow these girls for many years to learn about how early puberty affects their cohort. Researchers suspect endocrine disrupting chemicals probably cause the onset of early puberty, including Bisphenol A (BPA), parabens and phthalates (both widely used in personal care products), flame retardants, heavy metals including lead and cadmium, pesticides, and tobacco compounds. Researchers describe the situation as "a perfect storm" because the same chemicals that affect estrogen metabolism also cause girls to develop more fat tissue, and fat cells secrete more estrogen, creating a positive feedback loop. The CYGNET study is also investigating other factors possibly influencing early puberty such as stress, nutrition, family structure, and physical activity (Dayton, 2014).

Regardless of the reasons young girls are maturing sexually at earlier ages, whether schools should get involved in sex education has been controversial for decades. Many people insist that sex education should take place in the home only. However, sadly, comprehensive sex education is rather uncommon in the home. For this reason, school social workers frequently advocate for sex education in the schools. They may work in teams with school nurses, guidance counselors, physical education teachers, and others. Social workers are likely to take on the difficult but important task of developing parental support for these programs (see Box 8.8).

> **Box 8.8 Sex Education in the Schools?**
>
> Teaching sex education can be extremely controversial in the public schools because many parents oppose any discussion of the topic outside the home. In one situation known to this author, a young health education teacher included information on contraception in her health class and was ordered by the school administration to stop immediately due to multiple complaints from parents. Yet what subject is of more direct importance to the average teen? Ironically, it seems that those parents who most oppose having sex education taught in the classroom are the very ones who also avoid any discussion of the topic at home.
>
> Even when the biology of sex is taught in the schools, often myriad important related issues are overlooked, (e.g., the many emotions involved, the impact of sexual experience on one's inner life, and the impact of sexual experience on one's relationships). Associated issues are virtually endless but rarely included.

From 1990 until a few years after the turn of the century, teen pregnancy and birth rates declined by about one-third. However, beginning in 2006, statistically significant increases began to occur in the majority of states. Increases occurred among teens 15–17 and 18–19, and among whites, blacks, and Hispanics. Why such a major change? A likely reason is that funding for abstinence-only sex education tripled during the Bush Administration, while funding for comprehensive sex education languished. Teens were taught that the only acceptable approach to sex was to abstain. Virginity pledges were promoted. Yet several studies found that frequency of sexual activity was no different among participants of these programs than among nonparticipants. A longitudinal study by the Johns Hopkins School of Public Health found that teens who had taken the virginity pledge were not only as likely to have intercourse as other teens, they were also *less* likely to protect themselves when they did. Experts concluded that abstinence-only education provided a negative or faulty view of contraception (Jayson 2009; Thomas, 2009).

With the commencement of the Obama Administration, things changed. President Obama did not promote "abstinence only," and he quietly ended the "gag rule," a Bush Administration policy that prohibited family planning services that received federal funds from mentioning abortion as an option to women with unplanned pregnancies. Under the Obama Administration, from 2012 to 2013 the birth rate for U.S. teens 15-19 years of age fell by 10 percent, to a live birth rate of 26.5 per thousand. That rate remains, however, substantially higher than the teen birth rate of other Western industrialized nations (Teen Pregnancy in the United States," 2015).

Not all teens become pregnant by accident, of course. While statistics often correlate early pregnancy with dropping out of school, evidence sometimes indicates that the relationship may be the other way around. Discouragement at school can lead to pregnancy as a means of escape. What can social workers do to help make schools more hospitable places for their students so that they want to stay and learn? When the question is posed in this way, many creative ideas can be generated—for example, after-school tutorial and recreational programs, family outreach, cultural programs, sex education and self-defense programs, support groups for pregnant teens and young mothers, day care for their children, and the like.

Nutrition and Achievement

Appropriate and sufficient nutrition is very important in helping students do well in school. Research consistently demonstrates that hungry children are more likely to be absent from school, suffer from hyperactivity, and achieve poor grades. They likely experience serious stress at home due the struggle to find enough money to pay for rent and food. Stress and inadequate nutrition lead to further problems for the child, both emotional and physical, such as anxiety, depression, and chronic health problems. Babies and toddlers unfortunate enough to live in food-insecure households are more likely to experience delays in normal development, which can hold them back for their entire lives.

A conservative congress exacerbated the problem of hunger in America in 2013 by cutting the food stamp (SNAP, or Supplemental Nutrition Assistance Program) benefit from $1.70 per meal to $1.40. Because of this, children and families who were already food-insecure became even more so, increasing the risk of poor school performance, developmental delays, and chronic health conditions. Given an average SNAP benefit of only $127 per month, less than three-quarters the minimum cost for a month of healthy meals according to the U.S. Department of Agriculture (USDA), poor families buy the cheapest food they can, which tends to be full of starch and sugar. Many live in areas described by the USDA as "food deserts," places with limited access to fresh produce. A paradox arises: Undernourished children can become obese.

School social workers are in a position to recognize the impact of hunger on their students. They can assist by providing information about possible resources: For example, the WIC (Women, Infant, and Children) program described in Chapter 4 provides supplemental nutrition to pregnant and breast-feeding women and their children up to age 5. Social workers can assist families to apply for reduced-cost school breakfasts and lunches where available. They can inform families about the location and hours of local food banks. But perhaps even more important, social workers can get involved in leadership roles to improve nutrition programs. Imagine members of Congress trying to live on food budgets of $127 per month themselves! The serious harms caused by hunger in this nation are policy-driven and unnecessary. The United States can afford to feed its children adequately. What is required is the will to do so (Picchi, 2015; Ianzito, 2016).

No Child Left Behind and the Every Student Succeeds Act

In an effort designed to help children succeed in school, the No Child Left Behind Law (NCLB) was signed by President George W. Bush in January of 2002. The NCLB involved a sweeping reform of Title I of the Elementary and Secondary Education Act, which was originally passed in 1965. Title I was intended to assist states to provide additional resources for educationally disadvantaged children (Hare et al., 2006).

The NCLB had impressive goals: to set high standards for achievement and to establish strong accountability measures via ongoing standardized testing. Schools whose students did not achieve at the required rate for two years in a row were to lose their federal funding. This soon became a problem: Schools with the greatest majority of poor and minority students, the very schools that needed assistance the most, were the ones most likely to lose funding under the NCLB (Paulson, 2007; Sunderman et al., 2005).

> **Box 8.9 Costs of Child Poverty and Homelessness**
>
> To children whose basic needs are met, *misery* means their parents can't afford to provide the latest designer jeans. To children in poverty, *misery* means not knowing where they will sleep at night because their parents can't afford to provide a home.
>
> In the United States today, hundreds of thousands of children—according to some studies, well over a million—are homeless. They live in cars, or under bridges, or with luck in temporary shelters but with no assurance that they will be able to stay. They are often unable to attend school because they lack an address as proof of residency. If a school with a compassionate policy should allow them to enroll, they have no place to do their homework. They lack decent clothing and shoes that fit. They often go to bed hungry, and hungry children cannot concentrate in a classroom even in the best of schools. If these children should get sick, health care is inadequate or lacking entirely.
>
> Poor and/or homeless children lose out on the education required for economic success in the future. If they have been severely malnourished, their brains may not fully develop. In addition, severe stress triples the blood flow to the muscles of their arms and legs, a "fight or flight" coping strategy intended by Mother Nature to allow people to deal with enemies in the wild by *temporarily* increasing muscle strength. Today the stress response has become chronic for many poor children, depriving their developing brains of essential nutrients because their bodies remain in "fight-or-flight" mode. Thus, their ability to learn in school is impaired. It is sobering to realize that these children represent a large part of America's future.

Not taken into account in the NCLB was what some people have described as "America's dirty little secret": A substantial proportion of American children live in dire poverty. A shamefully large number are homeless. Children whose lives are scarred by poverty and homelessness can rarely concentrate long enough to complete a standardized test, much less achieve a desirable score. Schools and teachers alone simply cannot solve the issue of educational achievement in American schools (see Box 8.9).

The NCLB Act was to be reauthorized by Congress in 2007, but due to its controversial nature, debate was postponed. Finally, in September of 2011, because of Congressional inaction, President Obama issued an executive order permitting states to apply for waivers to the NCLB. Finally, with the introduction of a bipartisan bill crafted by the Obama Administration, Congress replaced the NCLB with a new education law, the Every Student Succeeds Act (ESSA), signed by President Obama on December 10, 2015.

Similar to the NLCB, the ESSA encourages high student achievement, but the tests used to measure achievement are to be state-driven, so as to be more relevant to the particular children they are testing. Federal funding is dedicated to assist the lowest-performing schools. Funds are provided to create new preschool programs, and competitive grants are provided to help replicate high-quality charter schools. Extra supports are recommended for vulnerable communities, with competitive grants provided ("Every Student Succeeds Act," 2016).

Student Achievement: International Rankings

Social work values promote the goal of assisting all students to succeed at school, to help them achieve better opportunities in life, and to maximize their potential. Such goals clearly involve access to good schools so that students are motivated to stay. The good news is that a record 82 percent of teens graduated from high school in the United States in 2013–2014. Moreover, the graduation gap between African-American and white students decreased in 28 states and decreased between Hispanic and white students in 32 states. The gap between students who were economically disadvantaged and all students decreased in 23 states.

Comparing U.S. graduation rates in 2013–2014 with other major countries, however, is sobering. Graduation rates were higher in many other industrialized countries: For example, in Russia, Japan, and Israel, rates were 94 percent, 93 percent, and 87 percent, respectively. Regarding academic achievement, 15-year-old students in the United States fell to 35th on math scores among the 64 nations tested in the 2012 *Program for International Student Assessment*, and 27th on science scores. American students were surpassed in both subject areas by teens living in such surprising countries as Vietnam, Slovenia, and Estonia.

A "Common Core" curriculum was developed in 2009 and 2010 in the United States by a collaboration involving state governors, state officials, working groups of educators, and representatives of higher education. The Common Core is expected to help raise achievement levels of U.S. students. It sets standards for kindergarten through 12th grade in English, language arts, and mathematics. To date, it has been adopted by 42 states, although with much debate (DeSilver, 2015; "Finishing School," 2015; Hinkley, 2015).

Strengthened educational standards alone, however, will not be sufficient to raise U.S. student graduation rates and achievement scores. Hundreds of thousands of students still drop out of school due to poverty and a sense of hopelessness and alienation. Graduation rates would certainly be enhanced if all students could enjoy a decent standard of living, a safe environment, and parents (or parent figures) with the means to participate in their education (e.g., parents not forced by low wages to work multiple jobs so they are rarely available). Social work values thus encourage engagement in policy development to help reduce poverty and its unfortunate effects.

Spiritual Development and Empowerment

Helping empower students to develop the inner strength to remain in school, a challenging environment under the best of circumstances, can involve some unusual and creative strategies. For example, biofeedback techniques dramatically reveal to students the connection between the inner workings of the mind and the mind's effect on the physical body. Students can actually *see* on biofeedback monitors how their angry thoughts lead to increased muscle tension and decreased hand temperature. Students can teach themselves how to calm their own minds and reduce their own physiological stress. A calm mind and reduced physiological stress permit much greater impulse control.

While merely a technique for physiological monitoring if viewed narrowly, biofeedback provides a view into the workings of the inner self. It provides new self-awareness and the ability to modify, intentionally, one's own emotional and physiological stress responses. Many professionals believe that increasing understanding of the mind–body connection, along with the ability to bring about desired emotional and physiological changes, can lead to enhanced personal and spiritual growth (Matuszek & Rycraft, 2003).

Helping assist in the development of students' spiritual growth in the school setting must be commenced with care, as spirituality and religion are often confused. Because

> **Box 8.10 Social–Emotional Learning**
>
> Social–emotional learning involves five key competencies, which can be taught in the classroom. These competencies help students to develop a kind of spiritual resilience without involving any religious instruction. These five key competencies are (1) self awareness, or learning how to recognize one's own thoughts and feelings; (2) self-management, or learning how to respond to others consciously and constructively; (3) social awareness, or learning to better understand why other people think and feel the way they do; (4) relationship skills, or how to better communicate with others, as well as to anticipate the consequences of one's own actions; and (5) responsible decision-making, or learning how to solve problems creatively while remaining true to one's values.
>
> *Source:* Based on Vanessa Vega's *Social and Emotional Learning Research Review* (2015, Dec. 1). Retrieved from http://www.edutopia.org/sel-research-learning-outcomes.

of the legally required and very important separation of church and state, religion must not be taught in the public schools. But there are effective ways to assist in the development of spiritual growth and personal empowerment that are compatible with any religion. One contemporary approach is known as **social–emotional learning** (SEL). SEL involves recognizing emotions and using a variety of methods to regulate responses to stress such as contemplative practice or meditation and breathing exercises (see Box 8.10). An advantage of SEL over biofeedback is the fact that it does not involve any special technology, although more time is required to achieve results.

According to Vega (2015), research has shown that SEL programs reduce misbehavior in the classroom, thus allowing more time for teaching. SEL strengthens student relationships not only with their teachers but also with their families and peers. Students become more self-confident, more self-disciplined, and more motivated; an important result is that they do better academically. Students develop a sense of responsibility and concern for the well-being of others as well as themselves. These skills involve both head and heart. As a result of SEL programs, classrooms run more smoothly.

Current Trends

The rate of child poverty in the United States, more than one child in five, decreased slightly between 2014 and 2015, but will very likely increase in the foreseeable future given the 2016 election of a conservative president and a conservative Congress. That is because conservatives believe that reducing taxes on the wealthy is the way to create more jobs and theoretically reduce poverty, This approach has not worked in the past (remember the economic crash that took place in 2008 as a result of the policies of the conservative G.W. Bush Administration). Meanwhile, the rich get richer: Sixty-two of the world's richest people now possess as much wealth as half the planet (Foroohar, 2016). The super-rich have a great deal of power to control political circumstances because they can make huge campaign contributions (thus making politicians obligated to them); and they don't tend to have much interest in the fate of the poor.

Because schools serve almost all children in this country today, they can provide primary sites for assistance to children living in poverty. But social workers are needed to carry on this important effort. School social work has been a strong and growing field for many decades, but a conservative political climate has led to school budget cuts in recent years. Despite the cuts, the need for these workers continues to grow.

To strengthen their field of practice, school social workers developed the first Specialty Practice Section (SPS) within the NASW in 1994. The School Social Work Association of America was also founded in 1994. These associations are important because they provide forums for development and discussion of important issues in the field and for dissemination of research findings. They also engage in important political action, continuously lobbying government at all levels for increased funding for social work services in the schools.

In 2012, the NASW developed new Standards for School Social Work Services to help guide school social workers in their difficult tasks in modern times. These standards are based on three guiding principles: education and school reform, social justice, and multi-tier intervention ("NASW Standards for School Social Work Services," 2012).

While working at every level of intervention, school social workers today are becoming particularly involved in macro level intervention to stretch scarce resources. Efforts are myriad in scope, including organizing after-school programs, child care programs, weekend recreational programs, parenting classes, substance abuse prevention programs, social–emotional learning programs, and the like. Because of budget cuts, these workers often must become skilled in grant writing in order to finance the programs they struggle to develop.

The trend toward increased numbers of alternative schools and charter schools in the United States has been discussed earlier. The Every Student Succeeds Act (ESSA) will probably enhance their numbers further. Whether alternative and charter schools will improve educational outcomes, especially for poor and minority students, remains a question for further research. The law achieved bipartisan support so it may survive a conservative election, and it promises new funds to help schools with a high percentage of students in poverty. These are the schools that most need social work services.

> **?** Assess your understanding of social work values and their policy implications by taking this brief quiz

AN INTERNATIONAL COMPARISON: SCHOOL SOCIAL WORK IN GHANA

A brief discussion of social work in Ghana, a nation on the west coast of Africa just north of the equator, demonstrates both the similarities and differences in social work services offered in the United States and in this former British colony. With a population of nearly 27 million in 2014, Ghana comprises a very different mix of racial and ethnic groups than the United States. Although only 24.2 percent of Ghanaians were considered in poverty by the World Bank in 2014, the average per capita income that year was only $1,590, compared with an average per capita income in the United States of $55,200 that year ("Ghana Data," 2014; "United States Data," 2014). Ghana, thus, is a poor country by U.S. standards.

Ghana was the first African nation colonized by the British to win independence. It did so in 1957, but, unfortunately, soon fell into a dictatorship. This dictatorship was eventually overthrown, however, and various governments, mostly military, ruled until

1992. A republic headed by an elected president was established at that time and continues today.

Ghana is ethnically diverse, home to more than 100 distinct ethnic groups. More than 50 languages and dialects are spoken. As a result, English, the colonial language introduced by the British, became the lingua franca (the language used for communication between different peoples). The government and the public schools use English as their official language.

Half of Ghana's population is under the age of 20, its median age up slightly from 10 years earlier ("Ghana, Median Age of the Population from 1950 to 2020," 2015). Since 1996, education has been free, compulsory, and universal, although not all children benefit from the law due to poverty, child labor, and **child trafficking**. With so many children to educate, many Ghanaian schools have instituted "shift" systems: One group of children attends school in the morning and another in the afternoon. No special programs are available for children with special needs. Those with minor challenges are integrated into regular classrooms, but children whose needs are severe are simply excluded. Some physically disabled children receive treatment at government rehabilitation centers.

In recent years, a few small schools entirely dedicated to special education have been founded in Ghana's capital and largest city, Accra. Most are too expensive for the average student, however. In 2014, the Reyo Paddock School was launched, operating under the REYO foundation of the United Kingdom, devoted to offering special education services to students of limited means. The foundation plans to expand its offerings beyond Accra in future years because, at this time, rural areas do not have any access to special education services ("Our Special Needs School," 2014).

The British government initiated social work services in Ghana in the 1950s under its Department of Social Welfare, but in 1967 the Ghana Education Service established its own social work service, the School Welfare Service. Truancy and delinquency had increased by that time to alarming proportions. Due to a need for more trained professionals, the Ghana Education Service contracted with the University of Ghana in 1975 to provide professional training for social workers. A two-year graduate program was developed, leading to a diploma in social administration, recognized by the International Council for Social Work Education. In 1990, the University of Ghana initiated a three-year undergraduate program in social work (Dupper, 2000).

School social workers in Ghana serve multiple roles. Families in this nation are matrilineal, which means that children are supported by their mothers' extended families, primarily their mothers' brothers—not their fathers. While Ghana's extended family system was strong prior to colonialism, today the family structure is in disarray due to colonialism's aftereffects. Men are frequently missing, searching for work far away. Poverty is widespread, so many children are mired in child labor or abandoned on the streets. School social workers (known as welfare officers) do their best to assist children who are hungry, homeless, neglected, abandoned, abused, exhausted, and frequently truant. They assist children who are engaged in prostitution; addicted to alcohol, drugs, and gambling; bullied; sold as child laborers, and/or challenged with various physical and other disabilities.

Many poor Ghanaian children become trapped as child laborers, particularly in the chocolate trade. Chocolate is crucial to Ghana's economy, and farms cultivating the trees that grow cocoa beans are widespread in Ghana's central region. Many children work alongside their families on the cocoa farms, making detection of abuse difficult, but a 2014 study by Tulane University found 43 percent of children in cocoa-farming families (two million children) performing work that was dangerous. Many of these children did not attend school (Brown, 2015).

Other unfortunate children are sold by their very poor families to work on cocoa farms. Social workers in Ghana become involved in trying to save these children. One way is by informing and working with anti-trafficking activists. They push chocolate producers such as Nestle and Hershey to increase inspections of chocolate farms to eliminate child trafficking and child labor. There has been significant success in this area, fortunately; in the five years preceding 2015, the number of children missing school in cocoa-growing communities in Ghana fell by 87.5 percent (Brown, 2015). However, over a million children believed to have been trafficked have recently been found working in the Lake Volta region of eastern Ghana ("Ghana," 2015),

To help ameliorate the widespread problems of poverty and hunger, social workers in Ghana organized Ghana's school meal program many years ago, helping provide at least one balanced meal to each student every day. School social workers serve as nutrition officers, making sure that school meals are nutritional and properly prepared. In addition, they serve not only as consultants to teachers regarding the learning needs of particular students, but they directly assist new teachers in finding accommodations for themselves and their children. They arrange school placements for teachers' children, and make sure that teachers' salaries are paid on time. They ensure that each teacher understands his or her duties, obligations, and rights. They organize seminars for teachers on the latest teaching techniques and methods designed to meet the psychological needs of their students.

School social workers in Ghana serve as the primary link between the school and the family. They make home visits to assist families to become more active in their children's education and to help resolve any problems between the school and the home. They assist parents to develop positive parenting techniques and provide family life education programs. They assist parents with children who have minor special needs to keep their children in school. For children who have more serious special needs, school social workers help families find additional resources such as state rehabilitation centers or one of the small private schools devoted to special education described above. They refer parents to appropriate community resources to help resolve other issues such as marital problems and child support disputes.

In addition, Ghanaian school social workers help develop and run parent–teacher associations. The main purpose is to bring parents together to identify common interests and to provide forums for joint parent–teacher discussion and collaboration.

Overall, school social work services offered in Ghana are designed to be preventive—the parent–teacher associations, home and school collaborative activities, nutritional programs, and family life education programs are all designed to help prevent school-related problems or alleviate them before they become serious.

As is common in the United States as well, schools in Ghana could use far more social workers than they actually employ, given the myriad problems that reveal themselves in this setting. It is unfortunate that some trained workers find they need to seek employment elsewhere, even in entirely different

> Assess your understanding of school social work in Ghana by taking this brief quiz.

professions, because of limited school budgets. The School Social Work Association of Ghana (SSWAG) continually advocates for additional employment of social workers in all school settings (Sossou & Daniels, 2002; Dupper, 2003; School Social Work Association of Ghana, 2015).

SUMMARY

- The history of social work in the schools is described. This chapter begins with a case study involving two sisters of Latino ethnic heritage who were referred to the school social worker because of extended truancy. The chapter continues with a brief history of Latinos in the United States. It provides a description of the history social work in the schools, including the reasons for the development of this field of practice.
- Major social work roles in the schools are identified and discussed. As is common to generalist social work practice, school social work roles involve working with individuals, families, groups, organizations, and communities. A difference, however, is that employment in the schools involves working in a secondary setting, one in which social work is not the primary profession represented. Therefore, social workers frequently engage in teamwork with teachers and other professionals in the schools to accomplish their goals. They may also participate in school-linked integrated services such as school-based health centers.
- The impact of different types of diversity in the schools is explained. The impact of one type of diversity in the schools, cultural diversity, is illustrated in the chapter's case study involving sisters of Latino heritage. Language can be a major issue in the education of students of minority ethnic heritage, but also differing cultural norms have a major impact. Diversity is not limited to ethnicity, however. Children with special educational needs comprise another major example. The chapter's second case study entails sexual orientation, another form of diversity.
- Social work values in the school setting and their policy implications are discussed. Social work values guide social workers in helping develop (and hopefully improve) policies in the schools dealing with salient issues such as bullying and other forms of violence; teen sexuality and pregnancy; nutrition and achievement; and emotional, social and spiritual well-being.
- Similarities and differences in school social work as practiced in the United States and Ghana are described. Many services are the similar, including those involving assisting children who are poor, neglected, and abused, along with their families. In both nations, social workers are the primary link between the school and the home. Some services are different. For example, Ghanaian social workers assist teachers to find places to live and serve as school nutrition officers.

Recall what you learned from this chapter by completing the Chapter Review.

9

Social Work with Alcohol and Substance Use Disorders

LEARNING OUTCOMES

- Explain how the profession's history within the substance use disorders field evolved over time.
- Identify the critical components of professional practice.
- Explain the current classification of substances that relate to substance use disorders.
- Compare and contrast the models for prevention and treatment of substance use disorders globally.
- Discuss the social justice and human rights issues in U.S. social welfare policy related to substance use disorders.

CHAPTER OUTLINE

CASE STUDY: Meet Dan Graves 261

The Profession's History in the Substance Use Disorders Field 264
 Early History of Social Work Involvement: Mary Richmond 264
 Social Work Contributions and Leadership Evolve 265

Critical Components of Professional Practice 266
 Values and Ethical Issues in the Alcohol and Drug Use Disorders Field 266
 Problem Solving: Use of Engagement, Assessment, Intervention, Evaluation 267
 Diversity: Gender, Age, Culture and Ethnicity, Lesbian/Gay/Bisexual/Transgender, Disability 275

The Classes of Substances Used 282

CASE STUDY: Meet Dan Graves

Dan was so cold that he knew he might freeze. He looked down at his feet and remembered that he had given his boots to an old man by the train station. Now his broken shoes did little to protect his feet from the snow on the streets. If he could just keep walking, he would not freeze. If he could get a drink, he would feel warm. Dan saw a familiar figure, stooped and hacking with a cough. The man turned into the alley behind the library, his hand in his pocket. Dan followed, and soon both men were sitting in George's cardboard-box shelter, sharing a bottle of brandy. It warmed them as they talked about better times. George had been a preacher in Mississippi until he came north in search of a secure job. That was around 2010, and the secure job had never materialized. Alcohol had eased his disappointment, but it never erased the memories of the family he left behind.

Dan, at 23, was much younger and was not ready to give up hope. True, he had left his wife ... well, not really. Angela had told him to leave because of his drinking. He wouldn't believe that he

> **CHAPTER OUTLINE** *(Continued)*
>
> **Global and Environmental Models of Prevention and Treatment**   286
> > A European Prevention and Treatment Approach: The Harm Reduction Model   286
> > U.S. Model: Alcoholics Anonymous   287
> > Environmental Perspectives   289
>
> **U.S. Social Welfare Policy**   290
> > Shifts in U.S. Social Welfare Policy   290
> > Social Justice and Human Rights vs. Criminalization and Incarceration   291
>
> **Summary**   293

had a drinking problem. He thought it was her imagination. But thinking about Angela hurt too much; he'd better have another drink of that brandy. George had fallen asleep, Dan noticed. Dan looked around for some newspapers to cover George, to keep the cold out, but he saw none. He was feeling sleepy himself, his body exhausted from walking all day on the cold city streets.

When the police found George and Dan, both men were unconscious. For the paramedics who were called, this was the third conveyance of street people to hospitals that evening. The first call had led them to a white woman with a baby, both with frostbite; the baby was listed in serious condition. The second call involved an African-American man, but he had not been drinking, and—although suffering from malnutrition and exposure—he had been admitted in stable condition. George and Dan, also African Americans, were in more serious condition. George had no heartbeat; Dan's was very weak.

St. Francis Hospital was very busy with emergencies that night, but when Dan and George were brought in, the staff rallied. Dan had **hypothermia** (extreme loss of body temperature) and frostbite; one foot appeared to be very damaged. He was admitted to the hospital for further care. After 10 minutes of effort by the emergency room medical staff, George was pronounced dead. It was a bitter cold night in Chicago.

Two weeks later, Dan was talking with the social worker at the Salvation Army Emergency Lodge. Dan had arrived at the shelter the previous afternoon, having been referred there by a social worker at the hospital. Madeleine Johnson, the shelter's social worker, knew about the treatment program he had begun at the hospital, but she questioned him again about his drinking history. Dan instinctively liked this African-American social worker although he was somewhat irritated by the persistence of her questions. He found he could talk fairly easily about his days drinking with high school friends when he was 17. It was much more difficult to talk about what happened later. Admitting that he had lost two good jobs as a computer programmer because of his drinking was definitely not pleasant. But it was true. Having to talk about all this was so hard!

But most difficult and painful to admit was what his drinking had done to his marriage. Angie was so beautiful, and their love had been so deep, so incredible. His pain was unbearable when he thought about Angie. The social worker probed this painful area, too, and she made him talk about Angie and the last time he had spoken with her. For 3 months after Angie had asked Dan to leave and he had begun living on the streets, he would phone her from time to time. He tried to make her believe that he was managing just fine. But he had not telephoned her from the hospital, and he had not given anyone her name, even when he was in critical condition and needed surgery to remove the frostbitten toes of his left foot. Following surgery, he entered the AA program at the hospital. Here he realized and admitted out loud for the first time that he had let alcohol ruin him and that he was an alcoholic. Now, at the Salvation Army Emergency Lodge, he was determined to continue attending AA meetings. The program made sense to him even if it was humbling to have to admit, in front of a group, what alcohol had done to his life.

Madeleine described the AA meetings held every evening at the Emergency Lodge. Dan said that he was serious about ending his drinking. He planned to attend the meetings daily. They also discussed how they would work together to locate employment opportunities for Dan as soon as the doctors said he was well enough to work. When Dan missed an AA meeting on the third day of his stay at the Emergency Lodge, the social worker asked to see him. Dan knew that Madeleine was disappointed that he had missed the meeting; that was a goal he had set for himself. But he was angry, too. He claimed that the meetings were not intended for black men and that he was not—and probably never would be—comfortable with the group. He told her about the comments several of the men made. It was clear they did not want minority members, especially blacks, in their group. Stan, an older man, had been especially outspoken; most of the others, even the two Puerto Ricans, had sided with Stan.

Then Madeleine revealed that she herself was a recovering alcoholic. She too attended meetings and needed the support of others to prevent a return to active drinking. Some AA groups did not meet her needs as an African-American woman and a professional person, so she had searched out and found a group that was right for her. Dan was stunned by her admission and her honesty. After further discussion, Dan resolved to return to AA meetings, but he planned to explore other groups as soon as he was able to walk better on his healing foot.

In the weeks that followed, Dan did attend meetings faithfully. Through meetings and through his interviews with the social worker, Dan grew to better understand himself and his reaction to alcohol. Madeleine was a BSW with 4 years' experience at the Emergency Lodge. She was able to help Dan acknowledge his anger about the misunderstandings and prejudices against African-American people that he encountered in the AA. Dan's trust in Madeleine grew as he discovered that she shared his deep concern about the people like George, even families with children who were living on the streets.

Dan learned from another Emergency Lodge resident that Madeleine and the other social workers had written a grant proposal that just last week had been approved for funding to begin a health care program for homeless people. They would need volunteers, Dan thought. Perhaps there was something he could do to help. He would silently dedicate his volunteer work to his friend George.

After Dan had lived at the shelter for 3 weeks, his doctor said that he could return to work soon. Madeleine and Dan had been talking about Dan's future plans. Now they developed a strategy that involved temporary employment in a service-industry job and evening classes to enable Dan to get back into the computer field. Dan was encouraged to find that the social worker did not want him to settle for a service-industry job for good. But he did need to start somewhere, and he would need income immediately to pay rent for a single room. Dan searched the classified ads in the newspaper for a job that was near public transportation. Within a week, he was hired at a fast-food restaurant. Dan knew that it was only temporary; he had other plans.

Dan registered for classes at the community college immediately. On the day that he began his computer class, he telephoned Angie. He had found a single room that he could afford with his minimum-wage job; he was leaving the shelter the next day. Angie was clearly reluctant to believe that Dan was really no longer drinking. She had heard that story before. Still, she was relieved to hear from him and to know that he was okay. She seemed excited about his computer class. Later, as he was leaving the shelter, Dan thanked Madeleine. She encouraged him to stay in touch with her when he returned for AA meetings and the volunteer work that he would soon begin. Dan sensed her sincerity when she wished him well in the new life he was beginning. In his heart, Dan wished her well, too, for now he understood the special lifelong demands imposed by his battle with alcohol.

The case study of Dan Graves leads us into an exploration of social work in the field of substance disorders. A brief history of social work will reacquaint you with the social work pioneer, Mary Richmond, and with lesser-known persons who also made significant contributions to this field of social work practice. We will then consider some of the ethical issues and value dilemmas that sometimes emerge when working with people with substance use problems. Then we will examine the nature of problem solving and social work practice within this field, giving special attention to the need for social workers to attend to the human diversity of the people we work with, just as the social worker did in the case study with Dan Graves. The substances that are associated with substance use disorders are introduced. The United States tends to treat substance use disorders somewhat differently from other countries, so we will look briefly at these differing approaches. We conclude the chapter by looking at the conflicting directions—*humane* (treatment focused) or *punishment* (imprisonment)—of social policy related to what we think of as substance abuse.

THE PROFESSION'S HISTORY IN THE SUBSTANCE USE DISORDERS FIELD

Early History of Social Work Involvement: Mary Richmond

Mary Richmond's name is already familiar to you. You encountered her pioneering work with the Charity Organization Society in the late 1800s and early 1900s. She proposed the use of the term *inebriety* to replace *drunkenness* and the term *patient* to replace *culprit*. She incorporated the new terminology in an interview guide that she devised for the assessment of clients. Sections of Richmond's interview guide focused on heredity, duration of the drinking behavior, causal factors, drinking habits (when, where, etc.), any current medical treatments needed, and a description of the social conditions in which the person lived. Richmond's insights into the human condition enabled her to elicit information about the client's employment, home and family life, use of drugs in combination with alcohol, and even the potential use of alcohol by women to help them nurse their babies (Richmond, 1917).

As the director of the Russell Sage Foundation's Charity Organization Department in New York City, Mary Richmond was a highly respected and influential social worker. She was also noted for her work as a writer and teacher and is said to have contributed substantially to the acceptance of social work as a profession. Her sensitive discussion of social work practice with "the inebriate" may have helped to move volunteers and, ultimately, social workers away from the extremely rigid, moralistic views of the early 1900s.

Social Work Contributions and Leadership Evolve

The social work literature from 1920 to 1950 contains little reference to intervention with people who had alcohol or substance use disorders. Instead, it appears that social workers tended to work with the spouses or families of such persons. In 1956, Catherine M. Peltenberg wrote in *Social Casework* that the few psychiatrists, psychologists, and social workers who did work in alcoholism treatment programs had to deal with their own as well as societal attitudes that **alcoholism** was a moral weakness and that these persons were morally depraved and lacked character. The year 1956, however, was a turning point. In that year, the American Medical Association proclaimed alcoholism as a disease, making it a treatable illness. Jean Sapir's 1957 *Social Casework* article urging social workers to help change public attitudes toward alcoholism is a classic in the field of social work; it was also one of the first articles to describe an effective working relationship between social work and Alcoholics Anonymous (AA) and an attempt to differentiate those clients who could benefit from referral to AA from those who would not be appropriate candidates for AA. Responding to emerging interest, the Council on Social Work Education commissioned a text, *Alcoholism: Challenge for Social Work Education* (Krimmel, 1971) to assist social work educators.

In 1970, important legislation was passed that was to affect the delivery of services, including social work services, to people with alcoholism. The Comprehensive Alcohol Abuse and Alcoholism Prevention, Treatment, and Rehabilitation Law was the first piece of legislation that recognized alcoholism as an illness in need of treatment. The law established the National Institute on Alcohol Abuse and Alcoholism at the federal level, and it authorized grants to help the states develop alcoholism prevention and treatment programs. With such strong leadership from the federal government, many programs were initiated across the country.

With the 1981 election of President Ronald Reagan, a new era of diminished federal funding for prevention and treatment began. Funding was increasingly shifted to military and police crackdowns on the import and sale of illegal substances and also to imprisoning immense numbers of people whose sentences were drug-related. Insurance companies' decisions to pay only for alcoholism and substance use care delivered in general hospitals led to the closure of many residential treatment centers. Gradually, by the 1990s, new short-term, community-based programs began to be developed. Social workers designed, implemented, and staffed many of these organizations.

Several social work leaders assumed significant leadership positions at the federal level at the beginning of the twenty-first century. Charles Currie, for example, was the first social worker appointed to head up the federal Substance Abuse and Mental Health Services Administration (SAMHSA). Mary Ann Amodeo became the administrator of the Association for Medical Educators and Researchers in Substance Abuse (Steiker & MacMaster, 2008).

Today's social workers encounter people struggling with alcohol and drug problems across all fields of practice. These disorders are often present in relation to other health problems, such as various cardiac diagnoses, or they are contributing to family problems that bring people into counseling, into the child welfare system, or into contact with an employee assistance program (EAP) related to their employment. The prevalence of alcohol and drug use across social work practice was first reported in research

> **? Assess your understanding of the history of the social work profession in the alcohol and substance use field by taking this brief quiz.**

conducted by the National Association of Social Workers, which found that 70 percent of social workers in their study group had worked with these disorders in the previous 12 months (Smith, Whitaker, & Weismiller, 2006). The Dan Graves case study provides one example of a social worker intervening with a person whose alcohol use disorder was clearly a factor in his homelessness.

CRITICAL COMPONENTS OF PROFESSIONAL PRACTICE

The case study at the beginning of this chapter illustrates how many of the critical components or ingredients of practice in this field take place in day-to-day work with people who are experiencing problems related to their use of alcohol or other substances. Social work values are often challenged and ethical dilemmas occur, such as Madeleine Johnson's need to decide whether or not to share her own personal issues with alcohol with Dan Graves. Portions of Madeleine's intervention and her use of the problem-solving process with this client are portrayed, too, in the case study. You will recall that diversity emerged as an important component of her counseling with Dan.

Values and Ethical Issues in the Alcohol and Drug Use Disorders Field

Social workers need to value their clients as unique human beings and to believe in the potential growth and contribution of each client. Madeleine Johnson did this well. She was not burned out by the broken promises of some previous alcoholic clients. Unfortunately, however, social workers and other human service professionals in the past often held very negative attitudes toward this client population. As a result, potential clients and their families sometimes were refused treatment or were shunted to the least experienced staff. One reason for professionals' avoidance of this client population historically was the frustration of working with persons who regularly denied drinking to excess or who denied using other substances. Today these negative attitudes are giving way to a far better understanding of why and how known substances react in the human brain, precipitating behaviors that are commonly associated with alcoholism and other substance use.

The NASW Code of Ethics requires that social workers respect and value the people that they work with and treat them with dignity and respect. The first standard of the code of ethics requires commitment to clients and to their well-being. Respect also extends to avoidance of derogatory language in communication with or about clients. This does not mean that social workers respect or condone all behaviors of the people they work with, but it does support a strengths perspective that compels social workers to find and work with the strengths of people and to affirm and build on their growth potential. Nonetheless, behaviors of clients that threaten either themselves or others take priority over other social work values. The social worker might need to involve police or security personnel or call for emergency responders in the event, for example, of an overdose (NASW, 2015).

Serious problems sometimes emerge from alcohol and drug use. Jobs are lost, indebtedness occurs, and broken promises may lead to severed relationships. Ethical dilemmas occur for the social workers involved when children have to be placed in foster homes, when clients are arrested and jailed, and when suicide or accidental overdose occurs. Not only are issues of confidentiality involved but also the social work value of client self-determination must be set aside in order to take action that will protect clients or others. Social workers across all fields of practice must deal with these challenges since alcohol- and drug-related problems exist prominently in modern society.

Sadly, even professional persons are not immune to problems arising from their own use of alcohol and other drugs. The NASW Code of Ethics, like most other professional ethical codes, addresses **impairment**, a condition in which a professional person's problems including substance use interfere with their ability to practice their profession with competence and integrity. The ethical code requires that social workers who recognize that their own personal problems are threatening their professional performance, thinking, and judgment must take action immediately to address the problem. This could mean taking a leave of absence to obtain treatment, terminating their employment, or taking other appropriate action. The NASW Code of Ethics also addresses the difficult ethical situation that could occur if a professional colleague's substance use is of concern. In this case, the code of ethics recommends that the social worker should discuss her or his concerns with the colleague in an effort to help that person take the necessary action to resolve the problem. If the colleague fails to address the problem, the social worker would have to notify the appropriate authorities such as the social worker's supervisor or administrator within their organization or, if necessary, a social work licensing agency or other appropriate authority. Often ethical issues are very uncomfortable to deal with, but they are an inherent part of one's professional responsibility (NASW, 2015).

> **Ethical and Professional Behavior**
>
> *Dimension of Competency* Values: Social workers understand the value base of the profession and its ethical standards.
>
> **Critical Thinking Question:** How do the profession's values and ethics help social workers to prevent "burning out" when they work within the field of alcohol and drug disorders?

Problem Solving: Use of Engagement, Assessment, Intervention, and Evaluation

The problem-solving or planned change process that has been a part of case studies in many chapters of this book also applies to social work practice in the field of substance use disorders. You may recall that this process includes four phases: engagement, assessment, intervention, and evaluation. Applying those phases to the field of substance use disorders sometimes requires special skills and learned practice behaviors.

Engagement

It would be hard to overestimate the significance of the beginning engagement phase of practice with persons who experience serious problems related to their use of alcohol or drugs. Whether we refer to this as rapport or a therapeutic alliance, the essential ingredient is relationship building. Persons with substance use problems may be frightened, suspicious, angry, or defensive, and they may possibly be in physical pain.

Achieving engagement begins with preparation. As students, social workers learn a set of practice behaviors that starts with thoughtfully reading all available information on the client to prepare cognitively and emotionally to begin work with that person, family, or group. In the initial meeting, even in the greeting, interpersonal skills are used. The social worker invests energy, empathy, and genuine interest in the client. Listening skills are critical to convince the client that the social worker cares and is eager to assist. Interruptions from other staff and telephone calls are avoided so that focus can be given to the client. Engagement does not end with the initial interview. Instead, it continues to thread its way through the work that occurs, whether this is short- or long-term work. Engagement is, in essence, the cornerstone of a constructive, ethical, and professional relationship.

Assessment

Assessment, in this field of practice, is complicated by the variety of substances used. It is further complicated by the need to determine whether there might be underlying depression or another mental disorder, or if the person is responding to a disaster or trauma. Understanding of the causes of alcohol and drug use continues to evolve. Although alcoholism was initially thought to be a sign of weak character development, it is increasingly understood to be a constellation of many types of problems that have genetic, neurobiological, psychological, and environmental contributing mechanisms. A growing body of research points to the potential influence of genetic factors in substance use disorders, especially alcoholism. Currently, it is assumed that genetics are just one of the factors involved. Psychosocial and environmental factors are also known to be powerful contributors, especially in relation to drug availability and motivation for drug use. Additionally, biological and biochemical changes in the brain can now be detected through sophisticated diagnostic tools.

Assessment focuses on gathering information and it is a continuation of the engagement phase. In assessment, the social worker encourages the client to share her or his story. A screening instrument may be used to identify harmful levels of substance use. Multiple screening instruments have been developed, some for use with adolescents and others for adults, older adults, or pregnant women. The World Health Organization's Alcohol Use Disorders Identification Test (AUDIT) is a brief, easily completed assessment instrument. It has been extensively used and researched (see, e.g., King, McNamara, Hasin, & Cao, 2014; Johnson, Lee, Vinson, & Seale, 2013; and Rubinsky, Dawson, Williams, Kiviahan, & Bradley, 2013).

AUDIT is currently the only assessment instrument that has been validated across six countries: the United States, Kenya, Norway, Bulgaria, Mexico, and Australia. It is used internationally with women as well as men, for college students as well as older adults, and it has been translated into many languages. AUDIT provides data that may point to the existence of hazardous, dependent, and harmful alcohol use. These comprise the assessment categories used internationally. Hazardous is the least serious and dependence the most serious of these three levels (Babor, Higgins-Biddle, Saunders, & Monteiro, 2001).

The *DSM-5* (American Psychiatric Association, 2013), the manual used to diagnose mental disorders in the United States, introduced new thinking about substance use disorders in its current edition. Like Mary Richmond's call in the early 1900s to move away from derogatory language describing persons with severe problems with alcohol, the

DSM-5 has replaced the word "addiction" with "substance use disorder" because of its negative connotation and because "addiction" was not well defined. *DSM-5* also discontinued use of the previous edition's concepts of "alcohol dependence" (most serious use pattern) and "alcohol abuse" (use sufficient to cause problems in interpersonal relations but not likely to result in **tolerance**, the continuing need to use larger amounts of alcohol). *DSM-5* introduced an important new understanding: that an actual change occurs in human brain circuits, especially when the substance use disorder is severe and persists past the time when the individual has undergone **detoxification** (the removal of harmful substances from the body).

The National Institute on Drug Abuse (NIDA) provides additional helpful clarification on how the human brain's biochemical system responds to drugs and activates the reward circuit of the brain. Dopamine, one of many chemicals that transport information within the brain, typically regulates pleasure, motivation, and emotion. Many of the illicit drugs work by overstimulating the brain's reward system through flooding it with excessive amounts of dopamine. This drives the compulsive drinking or drug use. The effect is immediate and 2 to 10 times more powerful than other brain rewards such as food or sex. The brain quickly learns to seek more dopamine stimulation, thus physiological craving ensues. At some point, however, the reward circuit of the brain requires more dopamine to achieve pleasure or even just to bring the brain back into normal functioning. This is how tolerance is activated. Instead of pleasure, the person feels lifeless, flat, and depressed; the cycle is poised to begin again (NIDA, 2014).

The 10 substances that *DSM-5* addresses related to substance use disorders are identified and described later in this chapter. For assessment purposes, however, the *DSM-5* breaks down patterns of behavior that relate to the potential course of a substance use disorder. These are shown in Box 9.1. In general all 10 substances addressed by *DSM-5* follow the pattern depicted in Box 9.1. The few exceptions will be identified a bit later in this chapter.

For assessment of severity of substance use disorder across all classes of substances (see Box 9.3), *DSM-5* (2013) suggests the following:

- Mild disorder: 2–3 symptoms
- Moderate disorder: 4–5 symptoms
- Severe disorder: 6 or more symptoms from Box 9.1

For alcohol use, SAMHSA further differentiates levels of drinking. These include **moderate drinking** (one drink a day for women and two for men), **binge drinking** (five or more drinks consumed in a single day within a 30-day period), and **heavy drinking** (five or more drinks on five or more days within 30 days) (SAMHSA, 2015b).

Biological, psychological, and social dimensions must also be assessed. The biological dimension is assessed by reviewing the person's medical history and current health and nutrition. With alcohol use, a drinking history is obtained that incorporates responses to questions about what the person drinks, how much, how frequently, and if other substances are used at the same time. Other questions are asked about when the drinking began, if binge drinking occurs, and if hallucinations or delirium tremors (DTs) have occurred (van Wormer, 1995). The biological assessment provides clues to medical treatment needs.

> **Box 9.1 Criteria/Symptoms for Substance Use Disorder**

Impaired Control:

Criteria 1–4 The person:
1. uses the substance in increasing amounts and/or for a longer span of time than anticipated.
2. expresses a desire to cut back on substance usage; makes unsuccessful attempts to do so.
3. spends considerable time locating, using, and recovering from the substance.
4. experiences craving for the drug (substance).

Social Impairment:

Criteria 5–7 The person:
5. fails to meet obligations related to home, school, or work because of continued substance use.
6. continues use of substance despite interpersonal or social problems that result.
7. decreases or discontinues important activities related to occupation, recreation, or family.

Risky Use:

Criteria 8–9 The person:
8. continues use when it is hazardous to do so.
9. continues use despite awareness that use has caused or worsened a personal problem—psychological or physical.

Pharmacological Criteria (laboratory tests can be used to confirm):

Criteria 10–11 The person:
10. requires increasing quantities of the substance to obtain the desired effect over time (tolerance).
11. experiences unpleasant physiological symptoms (which vary widely by substance) after discontinuing heavy use; may resume use in order to relieve symptoms (withdrawal).

Source: American Psychiatric Association. (2013). *Diagnostic and statistical manual of mental disorders: DSM 5* (5th ed.). Washington, D.C.: American Psychiatric Publishing, pgs. 483–484.

DSM-5 introduced another diagnostic category, the **substance-induced disorders** category. This category is differentiated from the substance use disorders category described in Box 9.1 in that the substance that is ingested creates physiological effects in the central nervous system. These effects can occur with or in the absence of a substance use disorder. Two primary substance-induced diagnoses are intoxication, where symptoms such as exaggerated mood, poor judgment, and belligerence develop quickly after ingestion of alcohol or drugs; and withdrawal, where symptoms of significant distress or impairment occur when heavy use of a substance is discontinued or reduced (2013).

> How does the diagramming offered in this video by Khan Academy further enhance what you've already learned about substance use disorders?
> https://www.youtube.com/watch?v=tPhcRBkVmUM

The psychological dimension of assessment reviews the client's mental health history to determine the possible presence of another underlying mental disorder. Questions are asked about current levels of anxiety, depression, and suicidal thinking as well as unresolved trauma or grief. The connection between substance use and psychological functioning emerges when the social worker explores why the person began using, stopped using, or resumed substance use.

The social dimension of assessment for alcohol or other substance use engages the client in a review of family, friends, co-workers, and other social network relationships. Who has or currently provides friendship and support? Where do stresses and tensions exist? Which relationships have been impacted by the person's drinking or substance use? Are there religious or other organizations or community memberships or involvements that serve to protect against substance use? What about spiritual beliefs and practices? Who and what matter to the client? A careful, thorough multi-dimensional assessment provides insight for the client as well as the professional staff (van Wormer, 1995).

Assessment that explores strengths in addition to the negative, problem-focused facts provides better balance and is respectful. For this reason, engaging people in their own assessment and possibly including close family members or friends can provide an understanding that leads to motivation for change and to an effective and realistic intervention plan. A strengths-based, person-centered assessment process focuses on what people want in their lives. The client's priority may be to salvage the relationship with his girlfriend, not to work on his drinking or drug abuse. This person's motivation to stop or control his substance use may be triggered by the social worker's agreement to work with him to achieve that objective. Questions like "What would you stand to gain if you decide to stop using?" shift away from a blame orientation toward energizing and giving control to the client (Kisthardt, 2009, p. 61).

Once an assessment of the situation has been made and shared with the client, the next step is to develop an intervention plan. Because the problem, the person, and the situation are all unique, the intervention must be creative. An early decision that must be made is where the action should be targeted. Social workers often try to determine what the client wants and what he or she is willing and able to do. Is the person who is actively drinking or using another substance the appropriate client? Perhaps the entire family should be seen as a unit. Perhaps an organization, possibly a worksite, inherently promotes substance use (e.g., a brewery that encourages its employees to drink on the job). If so, quite a different intervention plan would be needed. Are new programs needed in the community? Perhaps vulnerable populations can best be reached through community outreach work. Together, the social worker and client develop an intervention plan.

Intervention

The insights gained from *DSM-5* influence intervention and treatment planning. Planning must now proceed from an understanding of the physiological effect of substance use on human brain circuitry and the significant, sometimes overwhelming craving for the used substance that results. While many different and sometimes overlapping interventions are available, they must be based on understanding and appreciation for the power of the physiological triggers that drive behaviors related to the specific substance that the person used. The social worker and client together seek to select one or more strategies based on compatibility with client needs, culture, and goals. Some possible intervention approaches include the following:

- Inpatient detoxification during withdrawal
- Behavioral approaches
- Family intervention
- Group therapy or self-help groups
- Chemical treatment (prescribed medications)
- Therapeutic communities
- Program development
- Community outreach

Medically monitored intensive inpatient treatment may be needed initially to deal with withdrawal and to identify and treat existing medical problems. For example, Dan

Graves, in this chapter's case study, needed hospitalization. While Dan was still in inpatient treatment, assessment was initiated and he became involved with AA.

Behavioral approaches to intervention seek to change behaviors that are harmful through the use of positive and negative reinforcement. Self-help approaches generally involve groups of persons with similar problems who use what they have learned to help each other. Social workers may initiate and lead such groups, or they may refer people to existing groups. These forms of intervention can be initiated during inpatient care, or they may be implemented with no prior hospitalization.

Interventions that include work with the family often confront patterns of interpersonal relationships and family communications that subtly encourage or excuse excessive alcohol consumption or drug use. Securing the family as an ally in treatment and support for the client can be highly beneficial. Group therapy conducted by social workers, psychologists, or other professionals focuses on the whys of drinking and chemical addiction. Feelings are also explored and worked with in a group environment that is at once supportive and confrontational.

Prescription medications are sometimes used alone or in conjunction with one of the other intervention approaches; they may produce unpleasant effects such as nausea if alcohol is used (Antabuse), or they may block the pleasurable sensation of opiates (Methadone). Therapeutic communities are live-in programs where the resident is intensely involved in individual and group treatment. Always alert to the needs of the community, generalist social workers may reach out to vulnerable persons, such as people living in isolation or on the streets, and offer services that can help them with substance use problems. Sometimes it is necessary to create new services or to put established treatment programs into entirely new areas; suburban communities and rural areas are examples.

Individuals and Families

Work with individuals who have substance use disorders occurs across a wide range of health and social service organizations. It also involves a wide array of interventions. Practitioners across multiple settings have adapted the stages-of-change model of Prochaska, Norcross, and DiClemente to assess, plan, implement, and evaluate interventions with individuals. Their approach helps practitioners to monitor and support the change process:

1. Pre-contemplation: individual is unaware and may not agree that a problem exists
2. Contemplation: individual develops an awareness of the problem and starts to consider whether to begin intervention
3. Preparation: individual intends to make changes soon and may begin making some initial change
4. Action: individual becomes engaged in a change process
5. Maintenance: individual makes continued efforts to sustain the gains previously achieved (Prochaska et al., as cited in O'Hare, 2016, p. 143)

This change process is strengths based; it recognizes that people need to work through a process before they are able to become actively involved in intervention. It does not detract from the knowledge that some regression may occur.

Case management has long been considered a useful approach, too. Rapp (1997) describes his experience using a strengths-based model of case management with persons who use crack cocaine. This approach was so different from and contrary to the medical models previously used with them that clients were initially confused and had difficulty identifying any personal strengths. Nonetheless, Rapp found that they responded well to this approach and subsequent empirical research has demonstrated the effectiveness of brief strengths-based case management in improving linkage with medical and social services that meet clients' needs (Rapp & Lane, 2009).

Much of the family therapy that has been done has kept the person with the substance use problem at the center of the action, while family members learned behaviors to confront, control, and support the person of concern. A newer approach, based on the strengths perspective, gives credit to families that have endured and survived the stress and misery that accompanies substance use by a family member. Instead of viewing the family system as dysfunctional and family members as co-dependents, this approach helps family members identify the strategies they use to survive and manage the chaos that exists when there is active substance use within the family. Reframing is used in discussing behaviors. The simple mechanism of replacing the term *relapse* with *lapse* recharges family energy to assist rather than punish and blame a family member. A lapse, after all, is a setback, quite possibly one that might be predicted when battling a substance use disorder, yet one that is only temporary and can be managed. Family members are encouraged in their caring and support for each other (van Wormer & Davis, 2008, p. 411).

Groups

Although empirical research has not yet demonstrated the superiority of group treatment over other forms of intervention, practical experience has shown that groups offer many advantages. Groups help people to feel less stigmatized by their disorder as they achieve social acceptance from peers. Groups can also be confrontational, making denial of drug use less possible and they can help members achieve a level of self-awareness that is essential to the development of self-control despite difficult struggles with physiological craving.

Social workers use a variety of intervention approaches in their work with groups. Psychoeducational groups, often co-facilitated by a social worker and a physician, frequently use a lecture format to teach members about the body's reaction to alcohol and other chemical substances and the stress reduction and other coping techniques that can be used in recovery. Therapy groups, on the other hand, use member involvement to provide feedback, confrontation, support, and genuine appreciation for progress made in dealing with this difficult disorder. Role-playing is sometimes used to help members learn new behaviors.

Despite the advantages of group intervention, groups are not the best choice for all persons. Clients must be able to function well enough to tolerate the emotional intensity of group encounters. People who have serious, persistent forms of mental disorders, for example, might find some groups devastating. Usually, however, social workers can structure their groups to meet the needs of specific populations or persons.

Self-help groups such as AA and Narcotics Anonymous (NA) typically involve persons who share the same problem and meet together for mutual assistance. Until recently, most self-help groups avoided involvement with professional people. After many years of antipathy between professional groups and organizations such as AA, social workers and other professionals now recognize the value of self-help groups for specific clients, and they frequently refer people to them or combine another form of therapy with self-help group participation. Sometimes, too, social workers will initiate a group for this purpose and then guide the group in developing its own leadership and group processes.

Organizations and Communities

Effective organizational change can potentially benefit a far larger population than one-on-one counseling or group work. Social workers practicing from a generalist perspective often target an organization for change rather than an individual or a group. Social workers on the faculty of universities, for example, sometimes help to initiate support groups for students, faculty, and staff with substance use disorders. Organizational change can result in new or improved prevention or treatment programs. Serving as consultants, social workers help businesses, industrial corporations, and unions to implement EAPs (employee assistance programs) that assist people with substance use issues. Within alcoholism and drug rehabilitation centers, social work staff attempt to effect policies and procedures to ensure that service will be provided in a humane manner.

Another role for social workers is community education. Seminars and workshops are offered by social workers in community centers, churches, or schools. Prevention programs can target specific populations such as youth groups or older adults, religious groups, and ethnic or cultural populations. Educational programs may be offered in the language spoken by the group members or a person from the group may serve as a cultural interpreter, ensuring that the content and communication are truly relevant. This kind of outreach work enables social workers to reach populations that would be less likely to attend seminars at, for example, a hospital or university. The social workers who visit sites where homeless people live or gather can make contact with persons who are using alcohol or chemical substances. Hot food and coffee are a good entrée, especially in cold weather. Community outreach social workers can save lives through early detection and strong emotional support that bring people who are at risk into treatment centers. Recognizing that a considerable portion of health crises are related to (even generated by) substance use, social workers have also begun initiating assessment procedures in hospital emergency rooms in suburbs as well as central city areas. A physician's forceful recommendation for treatment can be a strong motivator.

Evaluation

Throughout the intervention process, social workers monitor their work for effectiveness. Progress notes routinely recorded allow the social worker to critically appraise the impact of intervention. Videotaping groups or sessions can be an asset to evaluation, both for the practitioner and for the clients. Following are some common elements of practice evaluation:

- Assessment of baseline functioning: Strengths as well as problems are targeted for change.
- Progress measurement used systematically throughout the intervention: Measurements are conducted both at specified intervals and at termination.

These may range from informal evaluative discussion to use of outcome measurement instruments.
- Follow-up evaluations: Ideally follow-up contacts are planned from the beginning of service. (Murphy & Dillon, 2011)

Another contribution that research can make to the study of addictions is to provide clear, factual evidence of the impact produced. Social workers in child welfare, family services, the corrections system, schools, and domestic violence centers know so well the tragedy and pain caused by excessive substance use and addictions. A growing body of data now documents the harm that is done. Butcher, Mineka, and Hooley, for example, summarized the work of other researchers who reported on the relationship between heavy alcohol use and likelihood of physical injury, depression existing alongside heavy alcohol use, suicide, and alcohol-involved deaths in automobile accidents (2008). The role of research, though, is to carefully evaluate not only the effectiveness of treatment in terms of the individual receiving care but also the effectiveness of prevention and treatment programs for families, communities, and society.

Diversity: Gender, Age, Culture and Ethnicity, Gay/Lesbian/Transgender, Disability

Generalist practice theory directs social workers to develop intervention plans based on a careful assessment of the individual person within the totality of her or his life situation. Logan, McRoy, and Freeman, as far back as 1987, underscored the need for social workers to take into consideration factors such as the person's gender, age, culture and ethnicity, and the availability of social supports when developing intervention plans.

When people use alcohol or other substances as a response to grief or the overwhelming trauma of disaster or war, this seems understandable to society. Less well understood are the socioeconomic stressors that also exist including the pain and frustration of being poor. Of the various professionals who work in the substance use arena, social workers probably have the best understanding of these stressors.

Women and Children

Among the most vulnerable populations in the United States are women and children. While a smaller percentage of women than men use alcohol heavily, their children are at risk. It is estimated that only a small portion of women with alcohol use disorders receive services. The reasons for this vary, but often women are hesitant to seek treatment due to an outmoded societal attitude that deems it acceptable for men to drink to excess but considers women immoral if they do. Shame prevents women from getting the help they do desperately need.

It is important to recognize that alcohol is a central nervous system depressant. Therefore, it should not be surprising that the result for women who have an alcohol use disorder is that they become increasingly depressed. Women who experience years of abusive relationships may self-medicate with alcohol, which can increase self-disgust. Often suicide ideation and serious marital and family disruption occur before depressed women seek treatment. When depression occurs, too, resumption of substance use is likely. Clearly, there is a need for careful assessment and early treatment of women who would be likely to turn or return to alcohol or other drugs.

Some women need counseling, probably with a female social worker, that focuses on childhood or current experiences with violence and victimization. Family and couple's therapies are helpful to many women, as is parent training, given the guilt that addicted women experience because of their failures in this area. As early as 1994, Rhodes and Johnson reported that teaching women to accept that alcohol has taken power over their lives—which is a tenet of AA and may be more useful with men—is potentially devastating to some women. Instead, they encouraged the use of empowerment approaches, helping women to acquire competence and self-esteem. Empowerment approaches are especially needed for women in shelters, jails, and women and their families served by public health departments. The story of Emilia and Her Baby in Box 9.2 illustrates an empowerment intervention.

Box 9.2   Emilia and Her Baby

When Jasmine Sandoval, MSW, walked into her office at Casa Maria Women's Center, Emilia was already there in the waiting room, her 2-month-old baby asleep in her arms. Emilia looked so much better than she had the night before when Jasmine, doing outreach work, discovered Emilia and her baby in a cardboard box shelter under a railroad viaduct. Emilia's thin body and the dark circles under her eyes still reflected tension and fear, but she smiled slightly when she recognized Jasmine, the social worker who helped her get into a shelter last night.

Jasmine invited Emilia into her office and helped her settle herself and the baby on a comfortable couch. Last night, Emilia told Jasmine about how, at age 17, she had crossed the border into the United States near Laredo, Texas, with several other teens. They hitchhiked to San Antonio, where they hoped to find work. Things didn't work out. Without papers, jobs were not available. When Emilia and another girl agreed to work for a man who offered them employment, he took them to his home and raped both of them, "teaching them," he told them. Soon he brought other men to them for sex and gave them money and the liquor that made this work more tolerable. Emilia lost track of time as drink and drugs mixed with men and sex. When pregnancy made her sick and less desirable, she was forced to leave. One of the men, however, a truck driver, let her travel with him. He dropped her off at a hospital in Houston when she went into labor. That's where she delivered Miriam who, fortunately, was a healthy baby girl.

Her brief hospitalization was a blur in Emilia's memory. Upon discharge, she stayed at a dirty homeless shelter for only two nights. She desperately needed a drink. A woman begging on the street brought her to the viaduct area where 10 people lived in boxes. They shared their food and alcohol and somehow found baby formula for Miriam.

Jasmine began by asking Emilia about the shelter she had spent the night in. Emilia smiled broadly and said that the shelter was clean, with real beds and wonderful food. It seemed like another world to her. Emilia then eagerly asked if they could talk about help from the Casa Maria's Recovery Counseling Program, which Jasmine had offered last night. Looking down at Miriam sleeping on her lap, Emilia said, "My baby is my life now. I will do anything for her. I cannot go on drinking. My baby needs me and she needs a home." Jasmine described the program's individual and group counseling. Emilia interrupted to say that last night she forgot to tell Jasmine that she had stopped using drugs once she knew she was pregnant and she tried to stop drinking but had not succeeded. Jasmine affirmed her for discontinuing drug use when her living situation was so difficult and so saturated with drugs. After further discussion of the Recovery Counseling Program, Emilia asked when she could begin. Emilia attended her first women's group session that afternoon and became one of Jasmine's clients for individual counseling. Their shared Chicana culture was a common bond that enabled Jasmine to gather information and explain the required assessment procedures. Emilia's memory about the forms she had signed at the hospital was almost non-existent but, with Emilia's signed consent, Jasmine began a search for them. At the end of the day, Jasmine and Emilia met with

> **Box 9.2 Continued**
>
> the shelter social worker to begin collaborative planning. It was agreed that Emilia and Miriam could stay for 3 months as long as Emilia complied with the rules, which included no alcohol or drug use.
>
> The first week went well. Emilia was permitted to bring Miriam to daily group meetings, but by the second week she complied with the program's request that Miriam be cared for by a volunteer during group sessions. This proved helpful. Emilia was better focused on group activities and her interaction with the other women improved. They were able to help her learn techniques to deal with cravings for alcohol and learn how to avoid the situations that triggered craving. Emilia began GED classes at the shelter and developed a friendship with a 24-year-old woman who had two children. In her third week, a woman from the viaduct site visited Emilia. The woman brought Emilia a bottle of whisky as a gift. That night, after having several drinks, Emilia voluntarily took the bottle to the shelter receptionist. The next morning, she told Jasmine what she had done.
>
> She had been disciplined and warned by the shelter director but not discharged. Emilia was frightened that what she had done had nearly left herself and Miriam back on the street. Emilia told her story in the women's group. The members were horrified with the danger that Emilia had placed herself in, but they strongly supported her for not giving in to her body's craving for a drink.
>
> This proved to be a turning point for Emilia. In the weeks that followed, she progressed in the group and GED classes. Jasmine helped her to get doctors' appointments for herself and Miriam and to begin to get her legal status resolved. The baby was becoming much more interactive, and Emilia and her baby delighted in their snuggles and play. The shelter social worker began to help Emilia plan for her discharge. Emilia and her friend hoped to find a place they could share so they could care for each other's children when they worked and when Emilia attended ongoing group and individual counseling sessions.

Fetal alcohol syndrome (FAS) is the name given to the abnormalities in children that can result from heavy alcohol consumption during pregnancy. Among the abnormalities that accompany FAS are growth deficiencies, developmental disability, characteristic facial features, cleft palate, small brain, and behavioral problems. There is no cure for FAS. These children often have significant attention deficit, diminished intellectual ability, and problems with judgment. At one time, FAS was thought to affect only the children of very heavy alcohol users, but now physicians urge caution in the use of alcohol in any amount during pregnancy.

The increased media visibility given to the danger of alcohol consumption during pregnancy has had beneficial effects. While decline in consumption is clear, there remain at-risk groups such as young pregnant women in the age range of 15 to 17 whose alcohol consumption places them and their babies at high risk. Brief counseling with women at Women, Infants, and Children community nutrition sites was found to be successful in improving the outlook for newborns in a study reported by O'Connor and Whaley (2007).

Older Adults

A new phenomenon is emerging, not in adolescent drug use, but in the use of illicit drugs by older adults. Baby boomers (generally defined as persons born between 1946 and 1964) have just begun to reach age 65, and they bring with them high lifetime usage of illicit drugs. The most recent data available, the National Survey on Drug Use and

Health, 2013 and 2014, identified the age 50–54-year-old cohort as having the highest lifetime illicit drug use (11 percent) of all age cohorts in 2014. The next highest was the 55–59-year-old group, with 9 percent (SAMHSA, Center for Behavioral Health Statistics and Quality (CBHSQ), 2015, Table 1.11A). Because the 26–29-year-old population historically demonstrated the highest illicit drug use, the older adult data were surprising to many.

Substance use is not usually thought of as a problem for people who are reaching retirement age. There is increasing concern, however, that the physical and social changes that inevitably occur with aging will make these older adults more vulnerable to the effects of current and past drug use. Compounding this is frequent use of over-the-counter medications and some inadvertent misuse of appropriately prescribed pharmaceuticals. Older men statistically demonstrate more substance use problems, but women are actually more likely to begin using alcohol heavily as they age. This may occur when women experience death of their spouse, retirement, or depression, or when psychoactive medication is prescribed, which occurs more frequently for women. This medication, often used to treat depression, may increase the negative effects of alcohol. According to the Hazelden Betty Ford Foundation, the number of older people experiencing substance use problems will double by 2020 (2015). Clearly, a new focus on prevention and care planning is needed for this emerging at-risk population.

Native Americans

The case study at the beginning of this chapter suggests that racism and poverty can be factors in substance use. Native American women clearly belong to several at-risk groups and, perhaps not surprisingly, they have a high rate of children born with FAS. In the United States, there are 562 officially recognized tribes. The rates of FAS vary greatly across the tribes with some tribes having low rates while others, especially the Alaskan tribes, having exceptionally high FAS rates. Native Americans are among the poorest U.S. ethnic populations with approximately 32 percent living below the poverty line. Numerous health disparities exist in addition to FAS. Native Americans also have a history of oppression and trauma, loss of self-determination, displacement, and violence. The Native American death rate from alcohol-related causes is five times greater than that of the white population (SAMSHA, n.d.).

American Indian or Alaska Native peoples also have one of the highest rates of all illicit drug use. The result is exceptionally high rates of suicide, homicide, car accidents, and deaths associated with cirrhosis. The 2014 (most recent available) data across populations show the following facts:

- Native Americans
  Alcohol use: lifetime use 78.4%; past month use: 42.3%
  Illicit drug use: lifetime use 60.8%; past month use: 14.9%
- Persons of two or more races
  Alcohol use: lifetime use 79.6%; past month use: 49.5%
  Illicit drug use: lifetime use 57.9%; past month use: 15.0%
- Native Hawaiian or Other Pacific Islander
  Alcohol use: lifetime use 71.1%; past month use: 37.9%
  Illicit drug use: lifetime use 54.4%; past month use: 15.6%

- Persons classified as white
  Alcohol use: lifetime use 87.0%; past month use: 57.7%
  Illicit drug use: lifetime use 53.8%; past month use: 10.4%
- Asian Americans
  Alcohol use: lifetime use 64.4%; past month use: 38.7%
  Illicit drug use: lifetime use 23.0%; past month use: 4.1% (SAMHSA, CBHSQ, 2015), Tables 1.19B & 2.37B)

The data presented above raise interesting and perplexing questions. What accounts for the surprising differences in alcohol and drug usage among the different ethnic and racial groups? Also, why are usage rates so high for the white population?

SAMHSA has long recognized the need for treatment services for Native Americans. In a study reported in 2012, SAMHSA found that the criminal justice system accounted for nearly half of the Native American referrals made for admission to substance use treatment. This was a considerably higher portion than the referral sources made for all other races. By contrast, referrals made by Native American individuals or through self-referral were significantly lower than other races. This suggests that more outreach and community education work with the tribes may be needed.

Hispanic Americans

In recent years, the Hispanic population in the United States has been increasing more rapidly than most other racial or ethnic populations. The higher birthrate of Hispanics results in a large youth cohort that is an at-risk population, especially among low-income families. The 2014 data for Hispanic substance use follows.

Alcohol use: lifetime use 73.8%; past month use: 44.4%
Illicit drug use: lifetime use 38.9%; post month use: 8.9% (SAMHSA, CBHSQ, 2015, Tables 1.19B & 2.37B)

Compared to previous years, Hispanic people continue to have lower rates of illicit drug use than Native Americans, African Americans, or whites as well as lower rates of lifetime alcohol use than these groups. Past-month alcohol use of Hispanic people, however, has now increased so that it is slightly higher than that of Native Americans and African Americans. However, it remains significantly lower than white Americans. For Hispanics, small rates of increase are emerging in both alcohol and illicit drug use (SMHSA, CBHSQ, 2015).

These increasing rates of substance use are of concern to many Hispanic people as well as the medical and social work professions. Cultural factors are recognized as significant in impacting change. Cultural differences between Hispanic groups, however, are often very great. Family and a close circle of friends are strongly valued among Hispanic people, but within families, cultural norms differ. Mother–son relationships, for example, tend to be central for Cubans and Mexicans. Among Puerto Ricans, mother and sibling relationships are very strong. The strongest familial relationship for Bolivians and Peruvians tends to be to their families of origin rather than spouses or siblings (Comas-Diaz, 1986 & Melus, 1980, as cited in Steiker & MacMaster, 2008).

Research Informed Practice

Dimension of Competency Cognitive Process: Social workers apply critical thinking in their analysis of quantitative data.

Critical Thinking Question: What is the relevance to social work practice with Native American communities of the data presented in this section?

Families can serve as a protective mechanism, thus reducing the need to turn to alcohol or drugs during times of crisis. That powerful sense of family pride, however, can produce overwhelming shame in persons who do engage, especially in illicit drug use. It may isolate people from their families. Because of the traditional sanctions against drinking or drug use by women, this is especially relevant to those women who are minimally acculturated to the majority U.S. culture. Social workers need to be sensitive to cultural differences but also need to help support the cultural facets that sustain identity, integrity, and support that are important to Hispanic people.

African Americans

Significant efforts of African-American churches and schools resulted in a marked decline in the use of alcohol by African Americans. The very steep decline of the lifetime African-American alcohol consumption from nearly 60 percent in 1979 to 47.8 percent in 1997 is historic and unique among the populations studied by SAMHSA. It is evidence of the success that can come from strong commitment and concerted community action. The current data demonstrate that African Americans have sustained a lower rate of lifetime alcohol use (only 75.7 percent) than whites and Native Americans. (The overall rate of consumption for all populations increased considerably from 2000 to the current time.) The current African-American rate is slightly higher than the Hispanic/Latino. The Asian rate, however, was the lowest of the demographic groups tracked by SAMHSA for 2014; this has been a consistent trend for many years (CBHSQ, 2015, Table 2.37B).

In general, there has been a fairly small but consistent increase in illicit drug use over the past 10 years of available data. In 2004, African-American lifetime illicit drug use was 43.3 percent compared with 47.6 percent in 2014. The data for the white population reflect a comparable increase in lifetime use, from 49.1 in 2004 to 53.8 percent in 2014, although the rate of illicit drug use among whites was greater. Both Hispanic and Native American populations showed an increase in illicit drug use from 35.4 to 38.9 percent for Hispanics and 58.4 to 60.9 percent for Native Americans (SAMHSA, 2006 and 2015, CBHSQ, Table 1.19B).

Use of alcohol and drugs and the misuse of prescription medications including opiods have serious consequences regardless of the ethnicity or race of the population in which it occurs. For African-American families, however, drug use has had an especially devastating impact. Drug-related family violence and crime have resulted in the need for shelter care for women and children, imprisonment, and foster care of children. Cocaine use in the past was a gateway to other drugs and also to high rates of HIV/AIDS and other infections and diseases. Recently, opiod prescription drugs have become the gateway to heroin. Families have struggled to remain intact under the pressure of drug use. Grandparents and even elderly great-grandparents have carried heavy burdens when caring for children whose parents were absent from the home.

Persons Who are Lesbian, Gay, Bisexual, or Transgender

People who are lesbian, gay, bisexual, or transgender come from every racial and ethnic group, from all occupations, socioeconomic groups, and from all parts of the United States. This may explain why they do not appear as a separate demographic category within the government statistical reports cited earlier for other groups relative to alcohol or drug use. A 2015 SAMHSA publication, however, refers to research over the past decade that found high rates of drug and alcohol use within the LGBT population (Other Specific Populations). The Centers for Disease Control and Prevention (CDC) also reported that the LGBT population is more likely than the general population to be users of alcohol and drugs, to have high rates of substance abuse, and to be more likely to sustain heavy alcohol use into later adult life (2015). These publications did not provide any data. However, they suggest patterns of drug and alcohol use among persons who are gay, lesbian, bisexual, and transgender.

The CDC report suggests that some gay or bisexual men may have turned to substance use as a response to the homophobic violence they experienced because of their sexual orientation. Heavy use of alcohol and other substances may also have contributed to other social and mental health problems (2015). The likelihood that an LGBT subculture support of alcohol use by gay men and lesbian women grew out of the oppression they experienced has been suggested as long ago as 1995 (Anderson, 1995). Gay bars have served as places to socialize and support each other and, until the recent development of substance-free establishments, this may have impacted the efforts of gays and lesbians who wished to avoid substance use or who were in treatment.

The CDC report also raised concern about use of methamphetamines, which have been found to contribute to increased chances for contracting HIV. Despite much improved understanding of the danger of these practices, some risky sexual behaviors and needle sharing persist and are of special concern (2015).

Among the homosexual community, black males with alcohol use disorders are at special risk of encountering misunderstanding and negative attitudes and stigma that can interfere with treatment. Not only do some treatment programs and professional staff display negativity, but also the African-American community is not always accepting of homosexuality. In addition, some members of the gay community at large are racially biased. Social work intervention can help these clients deal with their substance use problems and also help them locate and link with a positive support system and integrate their sexual identity with their racial identity.

Persons with Disabilities

Persons with disabilities—physical or mental—may use drugs (sometimes their own prescriptions) and alcohol just to make their lives more bearable. If they become dependent on chemical substances, treatment is complicated because it must be adapted to the situation of the specific client. Co-existence of mental disorders and chemical dependence, known as **dual diagnosis**, requires well-coordinated treatment from both mental health and substance disorder treatment programs. When these are not available within the same facility, careful attention must be given to ensure responsible integration of treatment.

Among the more than 600,000 homeless people living on the streets, it is estimated that roughly 10 to 20 percent are persons with dual diagnosis, which is actually a lower percentage than is generally believed. It is unclear whether these people became homeless because of substance abuse or whether homelessness led to substance abuse. People who are homeless are at considerable risk of substance use disorders as well as mental and physical health problems, and violence. Their mortality rate is nearly nine times

> **? Assess your understanding of the critical components of professional practice in the alcohol and substance use field by taking this brief quiz.**

higher than the general population (SAMHSA, 2015a). Not surprisingly, it is extremely difficult for them to comply with treatment regimes or to keep scheduled appointments. Outreach work by social workers is undertaken to try to bring some forms of health care to the streets. Concern about transmission of HIV infection through sharing of dirty needles has prompted needle exchange programs in some communities. Although politically controversial, these programs exist globally.

THE CLASSES OF SUBSTANCES USED

Having reviewed the critical components of social work practice in the field of substance use disorders, we will now review the specific substances that *DSM-5*, SAMHSA, and NIDA generally recognize as those most commonly involved in substance use disorders. Only a few of the prescription drugs currently misused are identified. Some additional substances are recognized by SAMHSA or NIDA but not included in our discussion or Box 9.3. Note that only brief, summary information is provided in Box 9.4.

Alcohol is generally recognized as the most abused substance, not just in the United States but also in many other countries. Alcohol, often mistakenly believed to be an "up" drug is, in reality, a depressant. Repeated use of alcohol, especially in high doses, may be damaging to nearly every human organ. Stomach ulcers, cardiac damage, and cancer of the esophagus may occur. There is risk of suicide during severe intoxication. Attempts to stop drinking often result in nausea and considerable discomfort, which improves with a few drinks, making it very difficult to abstain. Persons with severe alcohol use disorders may require hospitalization for detoxification, as withdrawal from alcohol can result in seizures and death. Treatment requires social support and strong encouragement. It can be compromised when the reminders of alcohol occur and precipitate craving. Despite these challenges, treatment has been successful for many persons.

Caffeine is the only one of the 10 substance classes in Box 9.3 for which there is currently no well-documented substance use disorder, but it has been added to the *DSM-5* list because it does produce both intoxication and withdrawal. Caffeine is present in coffee, tea, chocolate, caffeinated soda, and energy drinks. Low-level caffeine intoxication signs include nervousness, flushed face, and insomnia. More severe caffeine intoxication results in rambling thoughts and speech, muscle twitching, and cardiac arrhythmia. Medical attention may be required for severe caffeine intoxication as it can cause death. Headache is the primary feature of caffeine withdrawal; it may subside in a few days or may last for months. Persons with mental health or substance use disorders, heavy smokers, and prisoners tend to be at high risk if abruptly withdrawn from heavy caffeine use.

Cannabis is the next class of substances in Box 9.3. Marijuana is the most frequently used drug in this category. Marijuana may produce a sense of well-being and relaxation, but it also may result in social withdrawal, anxiety, and even paranoia. It has been found to be useful in the treatment of diseases such as glaucoma and for persons suffering from cancer. It has been approved for medical as well as recreational use in some states in the

Box 9.3 Classes of Substances Related to Substance Use Disorders, Substance Intoxication, or Substance Withdrawal

Substance	Method of Administration	Potential Consequences
Alcohol	Swallowed	Poor judgment, risk of accidents, depression, insomnia, suicide
Caffeine	Swallowed, eaten	Intoxication, dysfunction in work activities, death, withdrawal (headache, fatigue)
Cannabis	Swallowed, smoked	Slowed thinking, impaired memory, risk of accidents
Hallucinogens (Various types of substances used)	Swallowed, absorbed by mouth tissues	Altered perception, hallucinations, nausea, tremors, sleep disturbance, impaired judgment, risk of accidents
Inhalants (Solvents, glues, gases)	Inhaled	Nausea, depression, damage to cardiovascular system, sudden death
Opioids (Includes heroin, analgesics, morphine, codeine, oxycodone, etc.)	Injected, swallowed, snorted	Severe depression/suicide, infections (hepatitis, HIV), violent behavior, death from overdose, withdrawal in infants born to mothers with opiod use disorder
Sedatives (Barbiturates, benzodiazepines), and Hypnotics, Anxiolytics	Swallowed, injected	Reduced pain, sedation, overly aggressive behavior, accidental overdose of sleeping pills (hypnotics), craving and withdrawal of anti-anxiety medication
Stimulants (Cocaine, amphetamine methamphetamine)	Swallowed, snorted, injected	Chest pain, seizures, cardiac arrest; "meth mouth" (tooth decay, mouth sores), infections
Tobacco	Smoked, snorted	Cancer, cardiac and lung disease; environmental cues may precipitate craving and withdrawal
Other Substances Anabolic steroids (Various substances including cortisol, anti-inflamatory drugs, and unknown substances	Injected, swallowed, applied to skin	Blood clotting and cholesterol changes; liver cysts; risky, hostile, or aggressive behavior; symptoms dependent on chemical composition of substance

Source: U.S. Department of Health and Human Services. National Institute on Drug Abuse. (n.d.) Commonly abused drugs. Retrieved from http1://www.drugabuse.gov/DrugPages/DrugsofAbuse.html; and American Psychiatric Association. (2013). *Diagnostic and statistical manual of mental disorders: DSM-5* (5th ed.). (2013). Washington, D.C.: American Psychiatric Publishing.

United States, but it remains an illicit drug in much of the country. Currently, it accounts for over 60 percent of the total illicit drug usage (SAMHSA, CBHSQ, 2015, Table 7.1B).

Hallucinogens are drugs that produce sensory distortions (dreamlike experiences, visual and/or auditory effects). Heavy users of hallucinogens report flashback experiences months after use. LSD, the well-publicized drug of the 1960s, is being used again today. More frequently, however, people are using a variety of other hallucinogenic chemicals including the phencyclidines (PCP and ketamine) that are often synthesized in black-market laboratories. At lower doses, they produce feelings of being separated from mind and body; high doses may result in stupor or coma (*DSM-5*, 2013).

Inhalants have declined in usage, but people do inhale (huff) products such as gasoline, ether, paint thinner, propane, and glue with mixed results. They may hope for a high or improved sexual performance, but they may experience blindness, conjunctivitis (eye infection), or simple disappointment. Youths aged 10 to 17 are especially vulnerable. Most inhalants used today are a mixture of several substances, some unknown; the mixture determines the nature and severity of risk.

Opioids are used medicinally to deaden pain. Vicodin, oxycodone, heroin, morphine, and codeine are among the more commonly used drugs in this category. Because many of these drugs are injected, they present a significant danger for the spread of AIDS and other diseases. This class of drugs can also result in physical craving and addiction. Coma and death from overdose have been occurring with increasing frequency. New production methods have resulted in increased purity and potency of heroin, increasing the possibility of overdose. Opioid use, once primarily associated with low-income populations, is now seen across all ethnic and economic populations. Heroin use, too, has increased in recent years. Physicians and other health care professionals obtain opioids by falsifying prescriptions; their professional credentials and right to practice may be withdrawn by action of state licensing boards or hospitals.

Young woman injects herself with heroin

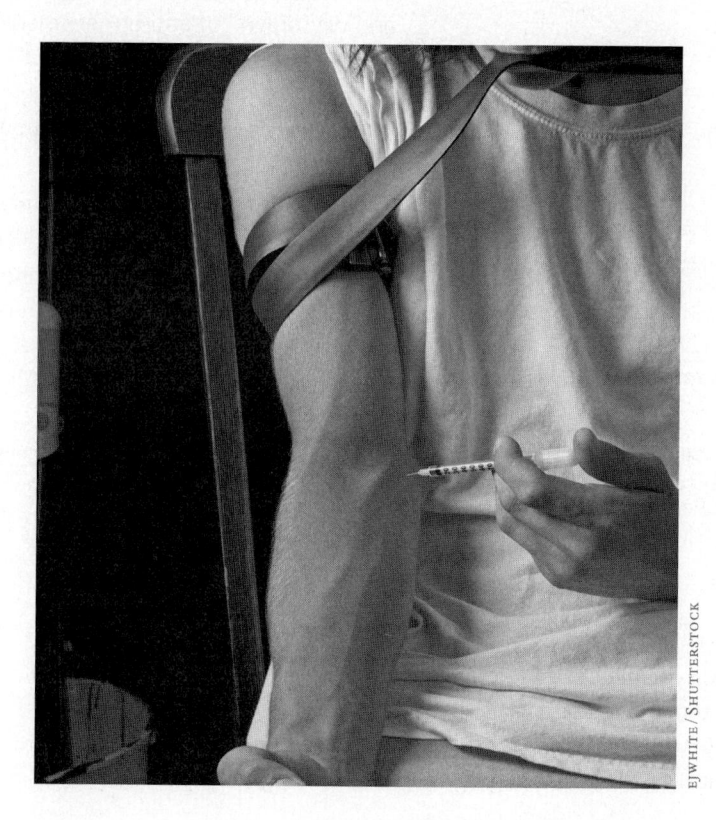

Sedative or hypnotic medication or anxiolytics are a mixed class of substances that are primarily obtained by prescription. Physicians use these drugs to treat various conditions such as insomnia, epilepsy, and anxiety. Tranquilizers and sleeping medications are among the most frequently prescribed substances in the United States. While they can create psychological dependence, they are most hazardous when combined with alcohol or other drugs, causing a condition referred to as **potentiation**, a dramatically increased potential for serious consequences to the health and well-being of the user. Social workers have learned to inquire about prescription drug use when obtaining a drinking history because, when combined with alcohol, they can be truly lethal. Women—perhaps because they see physicians more frequently than men do—are more likely than men to have prescriptions for tranquilizers. They are more likely to become involved in **cross-addiction**, the addiction to two or more substances at the same time. Barbiturates (downers) are included in this class of substances. Their danger is greatest if injected because of the immediate and powerful effect. Withdrawal has the potential for mental disorder, seizures, and even death. Barbiturates are often used in suicides and in mercy killings of animals.

Stimulants are drugs that produce energy, increase alertness, and provide a sense of strength and euphoria. They are prescribed to treat attention-deficit/hyperactivity disorder. This class includes amphetamines and cocaine. Students and truck drivers, among others, use illegally obtained methamphetamines to avoid sleep in order to complete work. The resulting errors in judgment range from a poor exam grade to highway fatalities. "Ice" is a form of methamphetamine that can be injected, swallowed, inhaled, or smoked. An overdose can cause coma and death. Addiction occurs very rapidly, sometimes after only a single use.

Cocaine is now classified as a stimulant. Cocaine is implicated as a cause of child abuse and neglect, family violence, suicide, and unprovoked shootings. Repeated or prolonged use of cocaine can produce withdrawal symptoms, including suicide. Cocaine combined with alcohol results in a dangerous level of toxicity. Crack is a less expensive pellet form of the more expensive and relatively pure powder form of cocaine.

Tobacco, like caffeine, is a commonly used substance that can meet the criteria of a substance use disorder. Although tobacco is used in many forms, the substance use disorder is most likely to occur with heavy daily use of cigarettes or smokeless tobacco, often beginning within 30 minutes of waking. Withdrawal and craving typically begin within 2 days of decreased or discontinued smoking. Clinically significant mood changes of irritability, anger, depression, and anxiety occur as well as difficulty concentrating and insomnia. Tobacco does not result in substance intoxication. Lung cancer, cardiac conditions, pulmonary disease, premature skin aging, and complications of pregnancy such as miscarriage and low birth weight may all result from tobacco use.

Other or unknown **substance-related disorders** comprise the final class of substances capable of producing a diagnosis of substance use disorder. These are substances other than the nine previously described. They may be known substances such as anabolic steroids, antihistamines, nitrous oxide ("laughing gas"), or others that have only limited or quite variable usage. When persons are unable to name the substance they took or they used unidentifiable black market or "designer" drugs, these substances fall into the class of "unknown." A substance use disorder is diagnosed if at least two of the typical symptoms shown in Box 9.1 are present. Substance intoxication can be diagnosed

> **? Assess your understanding of the classes of substances used by taking this brief quiz.**

if the symptoms (e.g., poor motor coordination, euphoria, impaired judgment) develop shortly after the substance is used but then are reversed. Substance withdrawal is often very difficult to diagnose given the considerable variability and range of severity of symptoms (*DSM-5*, 2013).

GLOBAL AND ENVIRONMENTAL MODELS OF PREVENTION AND TREATMENT

Singapore has achieved remarkable success through drug laws that are considered among the strictest in the world. The ironfisted policies of Singapore are unique in the Asian region. Anyone found guilty of trafficking in large amounts of dangerous drugs is subject to the death penalty. Drug users identified through urine tests or medical exams are subjected to mandatory treatment including "cold turkey detoxification" in a drug rehabilitation center for up to 36 months. The community-based portion of the rehabilitation program uses minimal counseling or social work intervention; instead, worship and religious education are emphasized with Islam, Buddhism, and Christianity as the major religions utilized. There is also a well-organized school-based prevention program in which thousands of designated students are responsible for spreading an anti-drug message to friends, schoolmates, and family members (Osman, 2002; Singapore Anti-Narcotics Association, 2008; Teo, 2010).

Germany stands in contrast to Singapore. Germany has a history of alcohol and drug tolerance and has used social workers in drug prevention and treatment programs since the early 1900s. In schools, social workers are a part of the prevention effort. Teams of social work experts assist teachers in preparing educational programs for children. Outpatient treatment programs are said to be dominated by social workers. They also provide case management and individual and group treatment in inpatient facilities. Germany has an extensive network of treatment facilities. Alcohol treatment is handled in a traditional, counseling-focused manner with detoxification, if necessary, completed in a general hospital. Prevention and treatment approaches include distribution of sterile needles, overnight shelters, counseling, case management, and treatment for HIV and other infections (Vogt, 2002).

A European Prevention and Treatment Approach: The Harm Reduction Model

The two models of substance abuse prevention and treatment used most commonly in the United States are the abstinence model and the 12-step recovery program. Both seek a complete and total end to substance use. An alternative but controversial program that is used far more frequently in Europe, Canada, and Australia than in the United States is known as the **harm reduction model**. The intent of harm reduction is to reduce the harm or damage that can occur when people are using chemical substances, including alcohol. The intent is to gradually reduce substance use, but with the recognition that addiction is a powerful force that takes time to change and that people who are using substances can seriously harm themselves and others.

European children grow up in a culture that incorporates alcoholic beverages in everyday life so alcohol use is a norm. Some European countries have a more open attitude toward the rights of people to use various substances, and legal penalties for substance use tends to be quite minimal. Methadone has been used for the treatment of addiction for a long time. Needle exchange programs, in which used needles are exchanged for sterile ones, are much more common in Europe than in the United States. This is the primary treatment for drug addiction in Switzerland, for example. Interestingly, it was the threat of an AIDS epidemic in Europe in the 1980s that generated a groundswell of support for harm reduction programs and policies. Instead of criminalizing drug use, European countries viewed it as a medical or public health issue—not just to protect the health of the users but also to protect the well-being of the public. Programs were set up in the community that provided a safe supply to drug users and to health care professionals for monitoring the use of drugs. Some cities in the United States have created similar programs (van Wormer & Davis, 2008).

From a social work practice perspective, the harm reduction approach is strongly grounded in the strengths perspective. Labeling of persons using drugs or alcohol ("alcoholic," "substance abuser," or other negative terms) is replaced with respect and collaborative relationships. Spiritual as well as social, psychological, and medical needs are met, but clients are in control and afforded the opportunity of making decisions for themselves (van Wormer & Davis, 2008).

Does the harm reduction model work? The World Health Organization (WHO) has found harm reduction strategies to be effective in diverse regions of the world and across multiple public health problems. Because HIV is one of the most serious health problems that WHO addresses, WHO supports programs that exchange clean for dirty needles among drug users. WHO has evidence-based research demonstrating that harm reduction programs prevent the spread of HIV. WHO strongly supports universal access to harm reduction programs for drug injectors (World Health Organization, 2010). Earlier international research showed that countries with liberal harm reduction programs tended to have fewer drug addicts. The Netherlands, for example, had 1.66 drug addicts per 1,000 persons in its population, Belgium had 1.75, Germany had 1.38, compared with the United States' 6.36 (Loebig, 2000). Much more empirical research is needed to evaluate the harm reduction model, but it does pose another alternative to the present prevention and treatment models favored in the United States.

> Watch this video outlining the use of the harm reduction model with substance use disorders. What strengths can you identify in utilizing this approach?
> https://www.youtube.com/watch?v=bnRvzEuP0Yo

U.S. Model: Alcoholics Anonymous

Although it began in the United States, Alcoholics Anonymous (AA) has spread throughout the world, so realistically it can no longer be considered strictly a "U.S. model." In fact, there are 115,326 AA groups in 175 countries (Alcoholics Anonymous, 2015). Also known as the "12-step program," this organization has spawned mutual aid groups for friends and relatives of alcoholics (Al-Anon) and groups for the adolescent children of people with alcoholism (Al-Ateen). In addition, the Adult Children of Alcoholics organization assists people struggling with past childhood experiences that continue to damage their present adult relationships.

Narcotics Anonymous (NA) is structured like AA and uses the same principles and philosophy as AA, including the 12 steps. Cocaine Anonymous functions similarly but is probably not as well known as NA. Alternative self-help groups have borrowed some of the AA philosophy but use other strategies. Rational Recovery, for example, is based on cognitive-behavioral theory that seeks to change self-defeating thinking patterns. Women for Sobriety emphasizes self-respect for women who abuse alcohol. Some groups have emerged that avoid the spirituality of AA and instead focus on personal responsibility. A brief history of AA is provided in Box 9.4.

AA describes itself as a fellowship of people who, in sharing their experiences, seek to help themselves and others in recovering from alcoholism (AA Grapevine, n.d.). AA is generally believed to be very effective, but the nature of AA has made empirical evidence of its effectiveness difficult to document. Part of the difficulty is that there are no records, no therapies, and no paid professional leaders for group sessions. This lack of effectiveness outcome data could lead to concerns by health care professionals as their practice becomes increasingly evidence-based. The Affordable Care Act and other insurance programs will be increasingly scrutinizing effectiveness data in determining payment for treatment programs.

AA, however, does not charge fees and does not depend on payment from health insurance programs. Instead, it relies totally on its own members rather than a paid professional staff to conduct group meetings. Meetings are conducted in community facilities that rarely charge a rental fee. In addition to the 12-step program to recovery from addiction, AA's support system uses experienced members as "sponsors" for new members and for anyone in alcohol use related crisis. The sponsors are all volunteers who are eager to assist without financial compensation.

Box 9.4 The Legacy of "Bill W."

The history of the founding of Alcoholics Anonymous (AA) is an interesting one. Bill Wilson was a stockbroker with a string of failed business ventures and years of alcohol abuse when he met Dr. Robert Holbrock Smith, a physician. Dr. Bob's alcohol abuse was beginning to interfere with his medical practice. Talking together, they discovered, helped Bill deal with his compelling desire for a drink, and it helped Dr. Bob face and begin to deal with his own alcoholism. Bill W.—his "anonymous" name to others in the organization that came to be known as AA—was gregarious, impulsive, and an inspirational speaker. Dr. Bob, a man of few words, avoided public speaking. Dr. Bob's authority, however, molded the new AA organization in many ways. Women were not admitted to AA for years because Dr. Bob opposed their inclusion, preferring to keep AA an exclusively male organization (Robertson, 1988).

AA spread only gradually, yet its appeal touched the lives of many people. By 1939, about 100 persons belonged to AA. They pooled what they had learned from their own experiences and created the book *Alcoholics Anonymous*, a classic that is still known as "The Big Book." It describes the 12 steps, which is the basic process by which members learn to keep themselves sober. After the publication of The Big Book, AA grew rapidly. By 1957, AA had grown to 200,000. Today AA has more than two million members throughout the world.

Environmental Perspectives

In social work, it is important to think about the interactions between persons and their environment. Sometimes environments—neighborhoods and communities—have profoundly negative and harmful impacts on people. Neighborhoods were the focus of a New York City ecological study that linked environmental conditions to deaths resulting from substance abuse. The study found that a low level of homeownership was correlated with exceptionally high rates of drug use. In census tracts with the lowest levels of homeownership, deaths from substance use were exceptionally high. In these areas, whole neighborhoods were left without needed human support and connectivity and invited drug usage. The study demonstrated that the presence of boarded-up, vacant homes was significantly related to the high level of deaths within these census tracts. The study recommended policy initiatives to increase homeownership and build community pride, thus decreasing neighborhood social disorganization. The researchers concluded that instead of focusing exclusively on the rehabilitation of individuals, a very worthwhile approach might be on revitalization of neighborhoods (Hannon & Cuddy, 2006).

> **Evaluate Practice with Individuals, Families, Groups, Organizations, and Communities**
>
> *Dimension of Competency* **Knowledge:** Social workers recognize the importance of evaluating processes and outcomes to advance practice, policy, and service delivery effectiveness.
>
> **Critical Thinking Question:** What factors might social workers need to consider as they think through potential expansion of harm reduction vs. abstinence-based programs designed to benefit communities in the United States?

The recent economic recession in the United States resulted in unprecedented bank foreclosure of millions of homes. As foreclosed homes were abandoned and boarded up, they become an environmental hazard for entire neighborhoods. They were broken into, fires occurred, and they became a location for illicit drug activity. Community action groups, often organized by churches or social service organizations, took initiatives to protect the environment through volunteer neighborhood cleanup efforts, block watches, and community policing. Common Ground, a non-profit organization, challenged the banks that owned these properties to exercise social responsibility in caring for the homes and providing security. When churches, university faculty and students, and neighbors of foreclosed homes united in demanding action, the banks began to respond, thus decreasing the environmental threat to entire neighborhoods.

Some other countries, such as Germany and the Netherlands, utilize an environmental approach to a greater degree than a clinical approach to the treatment of substance use disorders. The Netherlands has historically had one of the most open and liberal substance use environments, with a generous harm reduction program that documented positive outcomes on the health and mortality rates of persons addicted to hard drugs. Their environmental approach is aimed at rehabilitating deteriorating city neighborhoods, reducing poverty, improving safety, and lowering the crime rates. There has been a continued growth of user-friendly places where people can use drugs in a safe environment and obtain outreach and case management services. The city of Rotterdam has a facility designed for elderly drug addicts to receive their drugs in a secure location that meets their special needs. Social workers are involved across the broad range of Dutch substance use programs (de Koning & de Kwant, 2002).

The social welfare policies of countries govern the availability of substance use programs. These policies reflect the values of people within the country. Ireland has been shifting away from a clinical approach toward increased focus on changing the environment. There also appears to be less support for use of law enforcement and prison sentences to treat addiction in a number of countries, including Australia and the United Kingdom.

Dealing with the supply of drugs remains a challenge globally and is understood differently across cultures and nations. Many European countries use prevention and harm reduction programs to decrease demand for drugs. The United States favors incarceration for the use of or dealing in illicit drugs. Singapore uses capital punishment. Today powerful drug suppliers are using small, poor African countries such as Guinea-Bissau as distribution locations to move cocaine and other drugs from dealers in South America into the hands of international traffickers. As early as 2010, a *New York Times* article described the way in which Guinea-Bissau became a point for three-way cocaine trafficking, connecting producers in South America with users in other countries. Sometimes the cargo brought in by planes carried guns as well as cocaine. Extreme poverty and corruption of local officials complicated the efforts of the United Nations, Interpol, the European Union, and the United States to resolve the problem (Traub, 2010).

> Assess your understanding of the different global and environmental models for prevention and treatment of substance use disorders by taking this brief quiz.

U.S. SOCIAL WELFARE POLICY

Shifts in U.S. Social Welfare Policy

A glimpse of history may help us appreciate how the United States arrived at its current, somewhat confused, and definitely still-developing social welfare policy concerning alcohol and drug use. Beginning with the early colonists of the United States, we find that their ship's log shows that it was the Pilgrims' diminished supply of food and beer that resulted in their decision to land at Plymouth in 1620 (Kinney & Leaton, 1995). The Industrial Revolution of the mid-1800s brought enormous social turbulence and strain to family life in the United States. Women in those years were almost totally dependent on their husbands as providers for themselves and their children. Letters and diaries from the 1870s provide ample evidence of wife and child abuse apparently related to husbands' substance use. This was the context that compelled thousands of women into a temperance movement (Lacerte & Harris, 1986).

The Woman's Christian Temperance Union (WCTU) was founded in Cleveland in 1874 to pursue social reform, education, and legislation regarding alcohol use, which came increasingly to be seen as the root of all evil. With another powerful prohibitionist organization, the Anti-Saloon League, the WCTU rallied the vote and was largely responsible in 1919 for the passage of the Eighteenth Amendment (also known as the Volstead Act), which "prohibited" the manufacture and sale of alcoholic beverages in the United States. However, Prohibition of the 1920s proved to be neither enforceable nor fully acceptable to American society. With the repeal of Prohibition in 1933, alcohol use increased steadily until the 1970s, and then leveled off and began to decline by the 1980s.

Opium was widely used in many parts of the world by the 1850s, and U.S. merchants joined in the lucrative opium trade. Drug use in general was so common that, before 1900, narcotics were available from grocery stores and over the counter in pharmacies. Women used them to relieve discomfort related to menstruation and gave their children cough syrup containing opium. In fact, Coca-Cola's original formula contained cocaine! It was not until the Harrison Narcotics Act of 1914 that the use of narcotics for nonmedical purposes was prohibited. The public, which never completely supported the banning of alcohol, did support the suppression of narcotics. Federal laws resulted in increasing control of narcotics, with the 1956 Narcotic Drug Control Act providing the stiffest of penalties, including the death sentence for anyone convicted of selling heroin to a minor.

The 1960s saw a massive increase in the use of drugs. The Comprehensive Drug Abuse Prevention and Control Act of 1970 reclassified the substances, separating alcohol and tobacco from other substances. This left heroin, LSD, and marijuana in a category that brought penalties, including imprisonment, for their sale. (1988 legislation added penalties for possession.) Prevention and treatment funding was appropriated by the 1970 act, although alcoholism treatment centers had actually been developed shortly after the founding of AA in 1935. When the introduction of psychoactive drugs made methadone and antabuse available to treat heroin and alcohol disorders, new treatment programs emerged.

With the advent of the Reagan Administration in the 1980s, the role of the federal government suddenly shifted away from funding treatment and toward use of law enforcement and prison sentences to curtail the use and sale of drugs. Already overcrowded correctional facilities could not accommodate a rush of new offenders, and new facilities soon filled to capacity. In election after election, the public supported prison sentences as an answer to the perceived drug problem. The prison industry became profitable! Despite the perception of the public, use of illicit drugs in the United States actually declined over time. Back in 1979, when the highest illicit drug usage was reported, 14.1 percent of the population of the United States had used illicit drugs in the previous month (SAMHSA, 1998). By 2014 that figure was 10.2 percent (SAMHSA, CBHSQ, 2015, Table 1.19B).

Alcohol and drug concerns remain a potent political issue today Substance use is often linked in the media with crime and has been used to promote lengthy prison sentences. Meanwhile, people who use alcohol pay billions of dollars in federal excise taxes. The government has become dependent itself on income from alcohol. Native American tribes as well as states rely on income from legal, although potentially addictive, gambling. Legalizing the use of marijuana for recreational as well as medicinal purposes is a hotly debated issue (see Box 9.5).

Social Justice and Human Rights vs. Criminalization and Incarceration

In 1971, President Nixon initiated a "war on drugs" to combat the use and trafficking of illegal drugs. With the support of Congress, Nixon increased the criminal penalty for drug dealing. Subsequent presidents and Congresses further stiffened penalties for use and selling drugs and massively funded imprisonment for drug offenses. The criminalization of drugs became so popular with Congress that even the U.S. Sentencing Commission began to question some of the legislation that had been passed. The process of criminalization began with mandatory minimum prison sentences for possession as well as sale of drugs. This focused the country's response to the drug problem on the courts

Box 9.5 Up for Debate

Proposition: Use of marijuana for medical purposes should be legalized across the country.

Yes	No
Legalization would allow doctors to practice medicine more humanely, relieving pain and reducing nausea and vomiting caused by anti-cancer drugs.	There is no empirical evidence that affirms the medicinal value of marijuana to humans.
Hundreds of patients and their doctors have filed applications seeking compassionate use of marijuana.	If the use of marijuana for medical purposes was legalized across the United States, legalization for recreational purposes would immediately be demanded.
Synthetic forms of marijuana such as Marinol are available, but patients have found them to be less effective than marijuana in relieving pain.	Tax dollars should be spent on research to find new alternatives to marijuana.
Marijuana isn't nearly as potentially harmful as numerous other prescription medications in current use.	The Drug Enforcement Administration is firmly opposed to making this illicit, potentially addictive drug available.

> Watch this video produced by Free Spirit Media. How does the information presented align with the text information regarding the U.S. War on Drugs?
> https://www.youtube.com/watch?v=iN31n8Na9VM

and prisons instead of the approach taken by some other countries that focus efforts on prevention and treatment (criminalization vs. medicalization). The United States also spent billions of dollars to intercept drugs in South American countries (von Wormer & Davis, 2008).

Gradually, concern emerged about the lives of people who had been impacted by the criminalization of drug use in the United States. As long ago as 2001, when incarceration for drug offenses had climbed more than 1,000 percent in just two decades (Justice Policy Institute, as cited by McNeece & DiNitto, 2005), people in the United States began to be less supportive of incarceration for minor drug offenses.

The Obama Administration vigorously advocated for change to the Anti-Drug Abuse Act of 1986, which set mandatory minimum sentences for specific drug offenses. When the Fair Sentencing Act of 2010 was passed, it dramatically revised the inequities in crack vs. powder cocaine, as well as other drug-related sentencing. (Crack cocaine is most used by poorer African Americans while the powder form of cocaine is more frequently associated with white, higher-income persons.) The Sentencing Act changed the levels of crack cocaine needed to trigger imprisonment. It impacted sentencing for 3,000 people a year, 80 percent of whom were African Americans (U.S. Sentencing Commission, 2010). The African-American prison population had grown significantly as a result of the war on drugs.

By late 2015, 6,000 additional prisoners' cases had also been reviewed, they were declared no longer of danger to the community, and they were released. Some returned to their home communities, most with planned drug treatment services, but 2,000 were turned over to immigration authorities and deported (Associated Press, 2015). Even before the federal law was passed, some states had begun to change sentencing guidelines related to drug offenses. The continuation of this reform effort remains an important social justice concern, since 86 percent of all U.S. prisoners are in state (not federal) prisons. When the 2016 election reflected growth of conservative political sentiment favoring "lock them up" policies, there was less pressure on state governments to release drug offenders.

The marijuana legalization effort (see Box 9.5) has gained momentum, too, in recent years. Even though marijuana is still illegal under federal law, by 2015, states had rapidly begun to legalize it for medical or recreational use, or both. Some states discontinued incarceration for possession of small quantities of marijuana. The federal government advised Native American tribes that they could grow and sell marijuana (Wozniak, 2014). In Canada, Prime Minister Trudeau appointed an advisory committee to study potential legalization models (Angell, 2015). Federal decriminalization of marijuana, if and when it occurs, could further reduce the prison population, but concerns remain about marijuana as a source of substance use disorder that poses a risk to individuals and communities.

DSM-5's work to decrease the stigma of substance disorders through improved understanding of addiction as a disease of the brain is a significant step toward advancing a healthier society. In the past several years, we have also seen growth toward decriminalization of minor substance use offenses. Other human rights and social justice issues related to substance use remain to be tackled. This includes the limited time juvenile courts sometimes give parents to demonstrate recovery in order to avoid permanent termination of their parental rights. The future for human rights and social justice promise to be much brighter as change continues to evolve in the field of alcohol and substance use disorders.

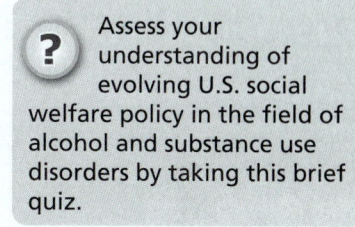

> **?** Assess your understanding of evolving U.S. social welfare policy in the field of alcohol and substance use disorders by taking this brief quiz.

SUMMARY

- The social work profession's history within the substance use disorders field and its evolution over time are explained.
- The components of social work practice in the alcohol and substance use disorder field of social work practice are identified: ethical issues, the use of problem solving process, and human diversity.
- The current classification of substances that relate to substance use disorders are explained.
- The models for prevention and treatment of substance use disorders globally are compared and contrasted.
- The social justice and human rights issues in U.S. social welfare policy related to substance use disorders are discussed. Evolving U.S. social welfare policy related to decriminalization and criminal justice reform held promise for the future of human rights and social justice for people with substance use disorders. Now, however, the more pro-incarceration, conservative public sentiment threatens this social justice reform.

> **✓** Recall what you learned from this chapter by completing the Chapter Review.

10
Social Work with Older Adults

LEARNING OUTCOMES

- Describe the history of social work with older adults.
- Identify and discuss major characteristics of older adults today.
- Discuss major issues concerning older adults and their families.
- Describe social policies relating to older adults, past and present.
- Identify major end-of-life issues for older adults.

CHAPTER OUTLINE

CASE STUDY: Caring for Abbie Heinrich 294

Social Work with Older Adults: A Brief History 299
    The Importance of Generalist Social Work 300
    Gerontological or Geriatric Social Work 302
    Empowerment Practice 303

Who Are Our Older Adults? 303
    Geographical Distribution 303
    Marital Status 304
    Education 304
    Employment 304
    Economic Status 305
    Housing 306
    Health: Physical and Mental 307
    Alzheimer's Disease and Related Dementias 308
    Ethnicity 309
    The Environment and Older Adults 310

Older Adults and Their Families 311
    Daily Life in Later Years 311
    Research on Family Strengths 311
    Ethnic and Cultural Minorities 312

CASE STUDY: Caring for Abbie Heinrich

A loud voice wailed persistently. Pat Smythe, BSW, who was toiling over some complicated paperwork at Oak Haven Nursing Home, tried to ignore it at first. He suspected the voice belonged to Abbie Heinrich. Abbie frequently turned on her call light and then yelled if help didn't come quickly. The care staff, occupied with other patients, took time to respond. To make matters worse, Abbie sometimes hit her call light button by accident. Rheumatoid arthritis had left her arms and legs severely contracted so that her movements were clumsy. Aides who responded to Abbie's light sometimes found they weren't needed. So they might ignore the light, muttering, "There she goes again."

Abbie's voice began to take on a hoarse, desperate tone. Pat decided to check on her himself. He put his paperwork aside and headed down the long hallway. He found a frail old woman lying flat on her back with her eyes closed but mouth wide open, emitting insistent cries.

"Abbie!" Pat called loudly, as she was hard of hearing. "What's going on?"

Abbie's eyes flew open, a startlingly clear blue beneath her crown of silver hair, direct and challenging. "Nobody comes when I turn on my call light," she accused, as articulate as any member of the staff. "I turned my light on over half an hour ago."

"I'm really sorry, Abbie," Pat said sincerely. "The aides must be very busy today. What do you need?"

"A pain pill," Abbie responded. "My back is hurting something terrible today."

"I'll stop at the nursing station and let them know, Abbie," Pat said soothingly. After a few gentle assurances, he left to find assistance.

Pat found the charge nurse for Abbie's floor, Cindy Murphy, RN, down the hall, and told her about the request for a pain pill. Cindy said thoughtfully, "You know, Pat, Abbie has been asking for a lot more pain medication lately. Maybe we should reevaluate her level of need."

"She is due for a staffing soon," Pat replied. "Let's talk about her pain medication at the next meeting."

Pat was responsible for organizing quarterly meetings for all 80 of his clients, so he sent notices to Abbie's county social worker, Helen Haines, and to Abbie's only "family," a community volunteer named Harriet Locke who served as her **power of attorney** for health care. He checked back with Cindy, the nurse, and was able to schedule a meeting time that would work for everyone.

Organizing meetings took a lot of Pat's time, but his work responsibilities comprised a great deal more. He held conferences with families to help them understand issues such as living wills and powers of attorney. He mediated roommate disputes; counseled patients with personal problems; made referrals to other departments of the nursing home and to external resources, such as clinical social workers or psychiatrists; filled out numerous forms required by private **insurance** plans, Medicaid, and Medicare; and even, on occasion, used his handyman skills. For example, Pat had become proficient at cleaning filters in hearing aids and changing batteries, tasks too small to refer to the maintenance department. Needless to say, there was no such thing as a typical day for Pat Smythe at the nursing home.

Helen Haines, BSW, worked for the Department of Human Services in the rural county where Abbie Heinrich was born and raised. Helen was assigned to the unit serving people with developmental disabilities. Many of her 60 clients lived in family care homes out in the community. Helen was responsible for monitoring the care they received. Besides consulting with her individual clients, Helen needed to cultivate professional relationships with biological families, family care home staff, group home managers and staff, sheltered workshop managers and staff, state Developmental Disability Services Office personnel, social workers in nursing homes such as Oak Haven, and the like. Her work was complex

CHAPTER OUTLINE (Continued)

Gay and Lesbian Older Adults 313
Older Adults as Caregivers;
   Grandparent-Headed Families 313
Caregiver Stress and the "Sandwich
   Generation" 314
Elder Abuse and Self Neglect 315

Social Policy and Older Adults: Past to Present 316

Family Care 316
Early Pension Plans 316
Trends in American Private
   Pensions 317
Social Security Today 317
Supplemental Security Income 319
Housing Assistance 319
Medicare and Medicaid 320
Food Stamps, or the Supplemental
   Nutrition Assistance
   Program 321
The Older Americans Act 322
The Social Services Block
   Grant 322
Values and Public Policy 323
The "Continuum of Care":
   Prolonging Independence 324
Emerging Lifestyle Trends and
   Innovative Programs 328
An International Perspective:
   The Netherlands 329

End of Life Issues: Care Needs, Religion, and Spirituality 331

Coming to Terms with Long-Term
   Care 331
Death and Dying 331
Spirituality and Religion 331
Hospice Services, Palliative
   Care, and Complementary
   Therapies 333
Social Work with Older Adults:
   A Growing Future 333

Summary 334

and required facilitating cooperation among many different community agencies and staff to secure the best possible care for her clients. Helen's job title was **case manager**, but in addition to "managing cases," she frequently was involved in community organization work. For example, she often testified at county and state budgetary hearings, describing the need for additional services. She sometimes took clients with her to tell their stories. It distressed her that so many local residents attending the hearings opposed additional services for their vulnerable fellow citizens because of the fear of higher taxes.

> ### Ethics and Professional Behavior
>
> *Dimension of Competency* Skills: Social workers use reflection and self-regulation to maintain professionalism in practice situations.
>
> **Critical Thinking Question:** Given the NASW Code of Ethics' concern about keeping professional "boundaries," do you think Helen's visits to Abbie on her own time indicated a lack of skill in maintaining appropriate professionalism?

A growing proportion of Helen's clients with disabilities were older adults. She found it necessary to consult regularly with social workers in nursing homes where many of her older clients resided. Once every year, for example, all nursing home clients had to be re-assessed according to Medicaid regulations to make sure their placements and levels of care were appropriate. Helen met with Pat Smythe at Oak Haven Nursing Home more frequently than she met with most nursing home workers. That was because Helen served as Abbie's power of attorney for financial matters and also because Abbie Heinrich was an unusual case. She had absolutely no family left, and, while totally bedridden, she was mentally sharp and needed to socialize. Only social workers were available to check that Abbie had sufficient clothing, to purchase personal toiletries, or to buy the occasional box of chocolates Abbie loved. Helen took more time helping Abbie than she actually had, meaning that she sometimes visited the old woman on her own time. The county discouraged case managers from visiting "unfunded clients" by assigning large case loads. Abbie was classified as an "unfunded client" because the county could not receive partial reimbursement from the state for the cost of supervisory visits by one of its case managers. Only clients participating in special programs providing "community care" were eligible for state funding (this will be explained in more detail later). Helen knew that she was going beyond the requirements of her job description by visiting Abbie regularly. She also knew that in some ways she had a dual relationship with the elderly woman, a genuine closeness as well as a worker–client relationship, and that the social work code of ethics counseled caution with respect to dual relationships. But Helen had learned from experience that Abbie was much less depressed about her dependent condition when she received regular visits, and, practically speaking, Abbie needed someone to buy clothing and other personal items for her. The NASW Code of Ethics states that the social worker's primary ethical responsibility is to promote the well-being of clients. Helen was doing just that.

Helen knew her attention and **advocacy** were crucial for Abbie. In the recent past, she had advocated on Abbie's behalf with a psychiatrist, as the psychiatrist had prescribed medication for anxiety that gave Abbie terrible nightmares. Abbie had asked the psychiatrist to stop prescribing this medication, but instead he had prescribed an additional medication that was supposed to quell the nightmares. It didn't, and Helen feared from her extensive experience with older clients that two strong medications would be too much for Abbie's frail body. She discussed this problem with the psychiatrist, but he was unwilling to heed either her or Abbie's concerns. Finally, Helen persuaded Abbie's regular physician to take over all medication; this physician listened to Helen's suggestions and, at last, Abbie could sleep again.

Helen knew Abbie needed her services, but still, given her ever-increasing work load, she had recently told the frail old woman that she might have to cut back on visits in the future. Abbie had been a client of Helen's county's Department of Human Services for nearly 25 years. An only child, she had been crippled with polio when she was three years old. Her parents had cared for her at home for nearly 50 years, but then her mother had died and her father became too frail to carry on alone. County social workers placed Abbie in a **group home** where she had thrived. Abbie even participated in a **sheltered workshop** for a time and became a favorite because of her active mind and strong sense of humor. But, cruelly, disease struck again, this time in the form of rheumatoid arthritis. The group home could no longer meet Abbie's physical needs. At that time, Helen had hoped to place Abbie in a skilled **family care home**, but Abbie now required 24-hour care. She needed to be turned regularly throughout the night to prevent bed sores, as she could no longer turn herself. If Abbie were to be placed in a skilled family care home and participate in a community day care program, the state would pay 60 percent of the cost, but the county would have to fund 40 percent. The county's portion would run more than $60,000 annually. The county, unfortunately, was having budgetary problems because more and more **frail elderly** and disabled people were requiring assistance. So Helen was told to place Abbie in a nursing home where Medicaid, funded by the federal government and the state, would pay the whole bill.

Helen had recently asked Pat Smythe if he could help her find a volunteer for Abbie, as Abbie's former power of attorney for health care, a retired social worker, was moving away. A new power of attorney was needed. Although Helen served as Abbie's power of attorney for financial matters, county policy would not allow her to take on both roles due to potential conflict of interest. Pat turned to the Volunteer Department, but there was no one available. He then tried the Department of Pastoral Care and found Harriet Locke.

When the date for Abbie's staffing meeting arrived, Pat Smythe, Cindy Murphy, Helen Haines, and Harriet Locke all met at the old woman's bedside. Because Abbie was alert and capable, she was an integral part of her own staffing meeting. Pat initiated the discussion.

"Hello, Abbie," he began conversationally. "How are you today?"

"Not so good," Abbie replied. "The pain is bad again today."

"Where does it hurt, Abbie?" Pat asked.

"My back, mostly," she replied.

"On a level of 1 to 10, where '1' means no pain and '10' means such strong pain you can't bear it, where would you say your pain is today?" Pat inquired.

"It's about a 7," Abbie replied. At this point, Cindy, the nurse, joined the conversation. "Is your pain worse today than it was yesterday, Abbie?" she asked. "It was about the same yesterday," Abbie replied. "My back hurts bad all the time."

The high pain level concerned everyone present, and it was decided that Cindy would consult with Abbie's doctor. Perhaps the pain medication needed to be changed or provided on a regular, scheduled basis. Pat then asked Abbie if she had any other issues she wanted to discuss. Abbie complained that the nursing home staff members were slow in responding to her call light. Cindy apologized, explaining that staff members were busy, but promised to ask the aides to respond to the light more quickly. Next, Abbie requested a different roommate, one that she could talk to, because her current roommate was deaf.

Abbie then remarked that her own hearing aid wasn't working properly and that she was almost out of her favorite hand lotion. Two of her best blouses hadn't returned from the laundry, and she was afraid they were lost. Pat promised to investigate the whereabouts of the blouses and to check the hearing aid himself. He promised to have the hearing aid representative who came to Oak Haven every week take a look at the device if he himself couldn't fix it. Pat explained to Abbie that he couldn't provide a different roommate, however—there was no one else available. Softly, as an aside that Abbie couldn't hear, Pat explained to the others that Abbie needed a deaf roommate as she yelled so often that her two former roommates had requested different rooms.

Helen promised to purchase hand lotion and new hearing aid batteries using Abbie's tiny Medicaid allotment, which she managed as financial power of attorney. Cindy offered another idea—she said she would ask the nurses' aides to greet Abbie and make a little fuss over her even when they were coming in to assist the roommate. That might help Abbie feel less lonely.

Helen had a sudden thought. "It's such a shame," she remarked, "that Abbie can't occupy her mind with reading. She used to love to read, but now she can't even hold a book."

"What about getting her recorded books?" Harriet, the new volunteer, suggested.

"That's not a bad idea," Pat replied. "The local library brings recorded books to the nursing home every two weeks, mostly CDs. But we have a very limited supply of CD players to loan out here." He turned to Helen. "Does Abbie have enough money in her account to purchase a CD player of her own?

"I wish it were so," Helen replied. "I think Abbie would enjoy listening to books very much—but, unfortunately, there is nowhere near enough money in her account."

Everyone looked sad as they remembered that Abbie was completely dependent on Medicaid and that Medicaid's personal allowance barely covered the cost of a haircut every couple of months.

"Tell you what," said Harriet. "if Abbie says she is interested in listening to recorded books, I'll ask her if she would accept a CD player as an early birthday present. I'd be glad to buy one for her."

"That's good news," Helen said quickly. "Listening to stories might help distract Abbie from her pain as well as provide her with something she could enjoy."

"I agree. I think listening to recorded books would be very good for Abbie," said Cindy, the nurse.

"If Abbie is interested," Pat said, "I can have the Activities Department put her name on their list for the library's outreach program right away. We could probably get some books for her next week."

"Abbie," Pat continued more loudly, turning to the older woman who was straining to hear, "I know it looks like we are plotting in whispers. I apologize. We're talking about books—do you think you might enjoy listening to recorded books, books you could listen to where you wouldn't need to use your hands to turn any pages?"

Abbie's blue eyes gleamed. Her mouth opened in a wide smile, showing every one of her false teeth. "Oh, yes!" she said. "I used to love to read, especially mystery stories. Can you bring me mystery books? Lots of them?"

Then she paused and her face fell. "But how could I listen to them?"

Pat explained about the CD player.

And so it was decided. In Pat's next quarterly report, he recorded that Cindy would have Abbie's pain medication reevaluated, that Helen would bring needed personal supplies, and that Harriet would provide a CD player. Pat would search for the missing clothes, check Abbie's hearing aid, and make a referral to the Activities Department so that she could receive recorded books from the library. Now, he reflected, all he had to do was meet the needs of his other 79 clients.

SOCIAL WORK WITH OLDER ADULTS: A BRIEF HISTORY

Older adults have served as role models and mentors to younger generations throughout human history, providing care and guidance instrumental to survival of the human species. In the United States, the contributions of older adults were recognized and older people were viewed in a positive light as survivors who had mastered the secrets of long life well into the nineteenth century. But by the turn of the twentieth century, this perception had changed. The focus turned to the problems of older persons, rather than their wisdom and strengths.

In the early years of the profession, social workers worked with older adults in institutions and in their own homes where possible, but such work was not emphasized as a special field until the number of older people began to increase significantly. Nathanson and Tirrito (1998) note that social work with older adults shifted its focus over time. In the early 1900s, the profession focused on alleviation of social ills through pursuit of social programs. Then, during the 1920s, the focus shifted to developing practice methods for work with individuals. One school, using Sigmund Freud's psychoanalytic theories, concentrated on treating individual psychopathology among older adults. A second school, the functional school, emphasized the use of health, growth, and self-determination along with social programs to help alleviate problems of older persons. Then, after the onset of the Great Depression in the 1930s, the emphasis shifted to alleviation of poverty.

Social workers have been instrumental in improving conditions for older adults. For example, Harry Hopkins, a social worker, led the nation's relief efforts during the great depression. Hopkins worked hard to achieve passage of the Social Security Act, crucial for the survival of many older Americans ("Hopkins Led Nation's Relief Effort," 1998). Another social worker, Bernard E. Nash, organized the first White House Conference on Aging in 1961. This significant conference, which reconvenes every 10 years (most recently in 2015), has led to such important legislation as Medicare and the Older Americans Act. Nash later became Executive Director of the American Association of Retired Persons (AARP) ("About Bernard Nash," 2007). Rose Dobroff, also a social worker, founded Hunter College's Brookdale Center on Aging in 1975 and served as its director until 1994. In 1995, President Clinton appointed Dobroff to the policy committee of the White House Conference on Aging and to membership on the Federal Council on Aging. She co-chaired the U.S. Committee for the Celebration of the United Nations Year of Older Persons in 1999 ("Rose Dobroff, DSW," 2001). Soon after the Great Depression, social work practice tended to focus once more on addressing the problems of individual older adults. In the 1960s, however, the War on Poverty inspired a shift back toward developing programs to alleviate the widespread social disadvantages they experienced. Legislation such as Medicare and the Older Americans Act (to be discussed later in this chapter) improved the lot of the elderly as a whole. Today the profession recognizes the need for multi-faceted approaches: addressing social ills *and* developing improved practice methods with individuals and families.

The National Association of Social Workers has developed several continuing education courses to help social workers understand the most important issues surrounding working with older adults as well as an aging credential for social workers (Nadelhaft, 2006). The most recent credentials are as follows (NASW, 2016):

- Certified Social Worker in Gerontology (CSW-G) at the BSW level
- Certified Advanced Social Worker in Gerontology (CASW-G) at the MSW level
- Certified Advanced Clinical Social Worker in Gerontology (CACSW-G) at the advanced clinical level

The Council on Social Work Education, recognizing a need for more social workers prepared to work with older adults, has developed the National Center for Gerontological Social Work, also known as the CSWE Gero-Ed Center. The center provides many resources for social work programs across the nation to encourage and assist in the development of curriculum dealing with issues of later life.

The Importance of Generalist Social Work

Work with older adults requires practitioners who can operate from a generalist framework; every level of intervention is required, from individual to community. The generalist approach is illustrated well by the work of both of the social workers in this chapter's case study, Pat Smythe and Helen Haines.

Pat Smythe, for example, worked with all 80 of his clients on an individual basis. He frequently met with Abbie individually because she was so alert and yet so frustrated due to her pain and physical limitations. Pat met regularly with family members of most of his clients, answering questions and including them in care conferences. Abbie didn't have any family members left, so Pat took care to consult with Abbie's county social worker, Helen, and the new volunteer, Harriet. Pat used his group work skills effectively in leading quarterly staffing meetings and his organizational skills in arranging and coordinating those meetings. He also helped organize and coordinate a residents' council within the nursing home. In the wider community he, like Helen, lobbied at county and state levels for better funding for services for his indigent clients.

Helen Haines also took care to utilize every level of social work intervention. She met regularly on an individual basis with her clients with disabilities, their biological families, their foster families, their group home care staff, and the like. She organized or participated in care conferences for her clients on a regular basis, wherever they happened to live. She frequently intervened in various organizational settings where her clients were placed to improve the quality of their care. For example, when Abbie complained about the quality of the food she was provided at Oakwood Manor, Helen consulted with Pat Smythe, who called in the home's dietitian. At the community level, Helen frequently lobbied to increase funding to improve services for her clients. Where funding was not available, Helen was creative, sometimes calling on volunteers (see Box 10.1).

Box 10.1 Abbie and the Volunteer

"Abbie," murmurs the volunteer, Harriet, peering down into the old woman's face, noting the closed eyes and moving lips, "today I've brought your DVD player." The CD player Harriet had brought previously had been a big success.

The blue eyes fly open, clear and bright as the Utah desert sky. Recognition dawns, and the eyes smile as wide as the mouth full of false teeth. "Oh, they're beautiful," Abbie says. She means the flowers the volunteer holds in her hands.

"For you, Abbie," Harriet says, lowering the flowers so the old woman can see them, her head still upon the pillow. "A bit of spring. Shall I put them in a vase for you?"

"Yes, yes," Abbie says.

When the flowers are in their vase and the conversation resumes, the volunteer says, again, "And today I've brought you your new DVD player, Abbie."

The blue eyes narrow. "I'm not so sure about that machine," she says. "I have my Bible channel on the TV, and I get the news, and the Gospel, and that's what I want to hear."

"But, Abbie," says Harriet, who has spent a weekend finding just the right DVD and a table stand for it small enough to fit in her half of the little nursing home room, "wouldn't you like to see movies? They'd show right on your TV screen. Like the movie *The Sound of Music*. Wouldn't you like to see that?"

"Saw it when I was younger," says Abbie. "Didn't like it. I like my Channel 30, where they teach every chapter of the Gospel. I think you should watch Channel 30. You know, only those who are saved are going to go to heaven. I've been praying for you, but it would help if you would watch Channel 30."

"But, Abbie," says the volunteer, "we could get Gospel movies—maybe like *The Ten Commandments*. You'd have more choice of things you'd be able to watch."

"Saw it," she said. The blue eyes closed.

"But, Abbie, remember your care conference last week, when the nurse and the social worker asked you about a DVD player and you said you might like one?"

"Well, I wasn't sure that day, and there was a lot else we were talking about, like fixing my hearing aid again."

"Wouldn't you give the DVD a try, just once? Try something new?"

"Well, I suppose I might—but you know, I couldn't see it anyway."

"But Abbie, you watch TV all day!"

And then the volunteer stops. Stares down at the ancient figure, tiny in the bed below her. Legs contracted into a froglike heap beneath the blankets. Arthritic hands contracted into flannel-covered braces. Head propped carefully on a pillow on a hospital bed that has cranked lower year by year, year by year, easing pressure on a painful back.

Harriet suddenly sees Abbie's eyes in her own mind's eye—closed—always—when she comes to visit—the TV always on. She lowers herself by the bed, tips her head back where Abbie's is tipped and sees—only the ceiling, only the ceiling.

"Oh, Abbie," Harriet sighs. "You don't watch TV at all, do you?"

"Not anymore," Abbie replies. "But I hear it. I hear my Gospel every day. And last week I saw an angel. Right in my room. She had the most beautiful smile."

"Tell you what, Abbie," says the volunteer. "I'll return the DVD."

Gerontological or Geriatric Social Work

Pat Smythe and Helen Haines can be described as gerontological or geriatric social workers. In this context, the terms *gerontological* and *geriatric* are virtually interchangeable, although *geriatric social worker* is the term usually used in settings involving health care. The work requires creativity, flexibility, and dedication of purpose. In return, it is rewarding and often exciting. Results may be tangible and immediate or take considerable time, but older adults can be stimulating and appreciative clients.

Many social workers who work in gerontological or geriatric settings have MSWs. A good deal of education for work with older persons takes place at the master's level, but increasing numbers of BSWs are being hired today in a variety of settings serving this population. As the number of older adults grows, so does the need for professionals to serve them. Hence, the necessity has grown for educational resources for undergraduate social work programs to better prepare BSW's to work in this field. The NASW's new CSW-G credential helps encourage increased preparation, and the CSWE's Gero-Ed center was developed to promote social work education at the BSW as well as the MSW level (see Box 10.2).

Case management, or coordination of care, is a major task for social workers who work with frail or ill older adults. Major goals of this kind of case management include the following:

1. Helping older adults remain in their own homes and communities as long as possible
2. Helping older adults and their families cope with increasing dependency needs (e.g., living with a family member, assistance with finances, nutrition)
3. Helping older adults and their families assess the need to move to a more protected environment (such as an assisted living setting or nursing home)

Case managers need to monitor client services to make sure they truly meet the needs of each particular client, and that they assist clients and their families to navigate the complex systems of services, programs, and agencies that serve older adults (Rosengarten, 2000).

Box 10.2 Gerontological Social Work

Gerontological social work is practiced in a wide range of settings. Some settings are community-based, such as senior centers, which serve active older adults. Others are institutional, such as nursing homes, which provide care for the frail elderly dealing with chronic illness and disability. New roles for gerontological social workers have been emerging in recent years, such as leadership in the creation of elder-friendly communities and new models of "aging in place." Family work is extremely important as well because of the central role of informal caregivers to the care of older adults.

Based on information from the National Center for Gerontological Social Work Education (CSWE Gero-Ed Center).

Empowerment Practice

Social workers are encouraged to use an **empowerment** model when working with older adults to help them enhance coping skills through consciousness raising, education, and support. Healey (2003) suggests that empowerment with older adults should include three basic strategies: assisting older adults, individually and collectively, to define their own needs; promoting conscious awareness of social and economic injustice; and encouraging political action.

Senior centers can be effective settings to help empower older adults, providing supportive environments to engage in consciousness-raising and promoting political action about issues of importance to them. Encouraging older persons to join advocacy groups such as the AARP or the Gray Panthers can also aid in the process of empowerment, as can working with organizations such as Generations United. Generations United encourages members of different generations to work together to develop policies that stimulate cooperation with attention to the long-term future; it has developed an Intergenerational Legislation Impact Assessment tool to help evaluate proposed legislation as well as current public policy to determine probable affects on people's lives across the generations ("Generations United," n.d.).

> **?** Assess your understanding of the history of social work with older adults by taking this brief quiz.

WHO ARE OUR OLDER ADULTS?

In terms of both total number and percentage of the population, more and more Americans are reaching the age of 65. In 1900, approximately 3.1 million Americans were over 65, or about 4.1 percent of the population. By 2014, however, the percentage of Americans over 65 had more than tripled, comprising 14.5 percent of the population, about one person in seven, fully 46.2 million people. This population is expected to more than double to 98 million by 2060 ("A Profile of Older Americans," 2015).

Should a person over 65 be considered "old"? Traditionally, 65 has been considered old indeed—time to retire. That is because life expectancy as recently as 1900, the turn of the last century, was only 47 years. Today, however, life expectancy in the United States is more than 78 years, and there are 6.2 million people alive today who are over 85, a number expected to triple by 2040. There are more than 72,000 people over 100 living in the United States as well, more than double the 1980 figure. Thus, 65 doesn't seem as old as it once did! ("A Profile of Older Americans," 2015).

Perhaps surprising to some, the average lifespan of Americans is not the highest in the world. We do not even fall among the top 10 nations for longevity. These are Monaco, Japan, Singapore, Macau, San Marino, Iceland, Hong Kong, Andorra, Switzerland, and Guersey. The United States falls an unimpressive forty-third ("Life Expectancy at Birth," 2015).

Geographical Distribution

Contrary to popular belief, most older adults do not move to warmer climates immediately upon retirement. In fact, older people are far less likely to move than adults of other age groups. For example, between 2014 and 2015, only 4 percent of older adults moved, as compared with 13 percent of younger people. Of those who moved, 60 percent stayed within the same county. Only about a fifth of older adults who moved went out of state. Over 60 percent of adults over 65 live in only fourteen states: California, Florida, Texas, New York, Pennsylvania, Ohio, Illinois, Michigan, North Carolina, New Jersey, Georgia, Virginia, Arizona, and Massachusetts. In three states, Florida, Maine, and West Virginia, persons over 65 comprised 18 percent or more of the population. More than 80 percent of persons over 65 live in metropolitan areas ("A Profile of Older Americans," 2015).

Marital Status

Marital status is an important factor for older adults because at this stage of life a spouse is a significant resource for independent living. Older men are far more likely to be married than older women. In 2015, 70 percent of men but only 45 percent of women were married. Thirty-four percent of older women were widows, and almost half of women over 75 lived alone (A Profile of Older Adults, 2015). An older widow's chance of remarriage is low because there are more than three times as many widows as widowers. Women generally take care of their husbands until they die, and then the women have to cope on their own.

Education

The educational level of older adults is increasing significantly. In 1970, only 28 percent of older adults had high school diplomas. By 2015, 84 percent had, and 27 percent held bachelor's degrees or higher. The percentage of persons who had completed high school varied considerably by race: 89 percent of whites, 74 percent of Asians, 75 percent of African Americans, 64 percent of Native Americans, and 54 percent of Hispanics ("A Profile of Older Americans," 2015).

Employment

Many older Americans seek work, primarily for economic reasons. In 2015, 8.8 million (18.9 percent) of Americans age 65 and over were working or seeking work, including 4.8 million men (24 percent) and 4 million women (15.3 percent). They comprised approximately 5.6 percent of the paid labor force.

Patterns of participation in the paid labor force in the United States have changed over time, of course. Labor force participation of men over 65 decreased steadily from 66.6 percent in 1900 to 15.8 percent in 1985; it stayed between 16 and 18 percent until 2002 but has been increasing since then to over 20 percent today. The participation rate for women over 65 rose slightly from 8.3 percent in 1900 to 10.8 percent in 1956. It fell to 7.3 percent in 1985, and was between 7 and 9 percent from 1986 to 2002. Beginning in 2000, however, labor force participation of older women has been steadily rising to over 15 percent today. This increase is especially noticeable among those between 65 and 69 ("A Profile of Older Americans," 2015).

Because the huge baby boom generation reached the age of 65 in 2010, it is likely that more and more older adults will need to remain in the paid workforce, at least part-time.

Traditional pension plans providing adequate income for retirement are becoming increasingly rare. Most private pension plans have been replaced by 401(k) plans, which leave all risks to individual employees. Such plans require employees to invest their own money in their own special accounts for retirement purposes. The money they put in is tax free, but taxes must be paid when the money is later withdrawn in retirement.

The recession that struck in 2008 hit older adults hard, decimating their regular savings and their 401(k) plans. The value of their homes fell significantly. Moreover, public pension and health insurance funds for employees, funds that had been considered secure, were found to be underfunded by over $1 trillion in 2008, according to the Pew Center on the States (*before* the collapse of Wall Street and the real estate market) (Toedtman, 2010).

Economic Status

While economic conditions among older persons are a concern today, circumstances are better than they were in the mid-twentieth century. In 1960, fully a third of older Americans were poor. Their economic situation improved in large part due to federal government initiatives such as indexing Social Security benefits to inflation, health insurance from Medicare, and Supplementary Security Income (see Chapters 4 and 7). The greater financial stability of older adults today has been widely publicized and, unfortunately, tends to pit elders against other groups competing for resources. However, many retired people experience great difficulty making ends meet and have to seek paying work. This is especially true since the recession beginning in 2008.

In 2014, more than 4.5 million older Americans (over 10 percent) had incomes below the official U.S. poverty line. Another 2.4 million (5.3 percent) of older adults were "near-poor" (had income less than 125 percent of the poverty level). Moreover, the official U.S. poverty line formula assumes that people over 65 eat less than younger people. This may or may not be true for any given older adult. Furthermore, the poverty line is determined simply by multiplying the cost of the U.S. Department of Agriculture's *emergency* food basket times three. It was formulated according to 1955 consumption patterns, when food comprised about a third of the average household budget.

But housing and health care costs have risen much faster than food prices since 1955. Yeoman (2010) points out that the poverty line determination method is obsolete; it doesn't even take into account the geographical area in which a person lives. The cost of living is much higher in northern metropolitan areas, for example, than in southern rural areas.

The U.S. Census Bureau developed a new poverty measure, the Supplemental Poverty Measure (SPM), in 2011. It does not replace the official poverty measure, but its findings are revealing. It takes into account regional variations in the cost of housing and the impact of non-cash benefits such as food stamps and low-income tax credits, along with the effects of non-discretionary expenditures such as medical out-of-pocket costs (MOOPS). According to the SPM, fully 14.4 percent of older Americans were poor in 2014, largely due to MOOPS ("A Profile of Older Americans," 2015).

Members of ethnic minority groups and women are especially likely to be poor among older adults. The percentage of people of African-American or Hispanic heritage with incomes below the official poverty level in 2014 (19.2 and 18.1 percent, respectively) was over twice as high as that of older whites (7.8 percent). Poverty increases with age and is higher among women than men (12.1 percent vs. 7.4 percent in 2014). The highest poverty rate in 2014 was experienced by older Hispanic women living alone, 35.6 percent ("A Profile of older Americans," 2015).

Social Security is a major source of income for more than 90 percent of older Americans today, lifting many out of poverty. Without Social Security benefits, in 2014 more than 41.5 percent of older adults would have had incomes below the official poverty line. In 2015, Social Security benefits accounted for 39 percent of the income of all older Americans; 53 percent of married couples and 74 percent of unmarried people received 50 percent or more of their income from the program. Social Security provided benefits to more than 59 million Americans in 2015, with an average monthly benefit for a retired worker of $1,350 (Van de Water, Sherman, & Ruffing, 2013, "Social Security Basic Facts," 2015; "Policy Basics, Top Ten Facts," 2016).

When the Social Security Act of 1935 was passed, the program was not intended to be a sole source of income but rather to supplement people's pensions and savings. However, for many older adults, pensions and savings are non-existent. The poorest elderly can receive Supplemental Security Income (SSI, see Chapter 4) in addition to any Social Security income for which they may be entitled, but SSI even in combination with Social Security does not usually raise its recipients' total income above the poverty line.

Economic Status and Life Span

A person's economic status has a strong effect upon his or her life span. A research team at MIT studied this issue over a period of years, 2001–2014. They found that among men, the richest 1 percent lived an average of 14.6 years longer than the poorest 1 percent, and that among women, the richest 1 percent lived an average of 10.1 years longer than the poorest 1 percent. Differences in life span across income groups increased over the time of the study (Chetty et al., 2016).

Housing

Despite the popular belief that most older adults live in nursing homes, in fact, only about 4.2 percent resided in one of these institutions at any one time in 2015 (5 percent over the course of the year). The percentage increases to more than 24 percent for people over 85, however, and more than 50 percent for those over 95. The average person of 65 has a one in four chance of requiring nursing home care at some point (Demko, 2016). The cost is high: Over $81,000 per year for a semi-private room and over $90,500 for a private room with an average stay of about two years (Mullin, 2013; Genworth, 2016). Nursing home costs increase significantly every year.

Older heads of household usually own their own homes (81 percent) rather than renting (19 percent); about 65 percent of these homeowners own their homes free and clear. Not surprisingly, their houses are older on average than those of younger people (median year of construction is 1972 compared with 1976 for all homeowners); 2.7 percent of the houses have physical problems such as rotting window frames or leaky roofs, or problems with plumbing, wiring, heating, etc. About 45 percent of older homeowners spend more than a quarter of their income on housing; 39 percent for owners and 69 percent for renters ("A Profile of Older Americans," 2015). Although many of the poorest older Americans need safe, low-cost housing, the federal government has not invested in constructing additional units of public housing for many decades.

Health: Physical and Mental

The physical health of older adults is better than younger people may believe. In 2012–2014, for example, 44 percent of noninstitutionalized older adults rated their health as excellent or very good (compared with 55 percent of adults aged 45–64). But ethnic minorities were less likely than whites to report their health as excellent or very good: only 27 percent of older African Americans, 31 percent of older Hispanics, 34 percent of Asians, and 28 percent of Native Americans, as compared with 48 percent of whites ("A Profile of Older Americans," 2015).

Most older people experience at least one chronic health condition. Of these, the most frequently reported are hypertension, arthritis, heart disease, cancer, diabetes, and sinusitis. Approximately 30 percent of older adults who reside in the community have difficulty performing some of their **activities of daily living** (**ADLs**) such as cooking, eating, dressing, bathing, toileting, moving around the house, and cleaning house; the percentage increases dramatically as these adults grow older. Approximately 36 percent of older adults reported some type of disability in 2014 (difficulty in hearing, seeing, thinking, walking, or self-care). Almost one-quarter had an ambulatory disability; 15 percent a hearing disability and 7 percent a vision disability. Nearly 15 percent needed some kind of personal assistance as a result.

Disability increases with age and can lead to nursing home care. Of older people receiving Medicare who reside in nursing homes, 96 percent have difficulty with one or more ADL, and 83 percent have difficulty with three or more. Many have severe cognitive impairments. Approximately 1.5 million older adults live in nursing homes today; almost half are over 85 years old. ("A Profile of Older Americans," 2015; "HHS Proposes to Improve Care," 2015).

> **Research Informed Practice**
>
> ***Dimension of Competency*** **Skills:** Social workers understand the processes for translating research findings into effective practice.
>
> **Critical Thinking Question:** The statistics presented in this section took considerable research to assemble. How can social workers use these findings to increase their practice skills with older adults?

In 2015, the U.S. Department of Health and Human Services (HHS) issued a proposal designed to improve the care and safety of older adults residing in nursing homes. It included upgrading the training of staff regarding dementia and abuse prevention, making sure the personal goals and preferences of residents were included in their care plans, strengthening residents' rights, and requiring a greater provision of food choices. The recommendations of this proposal became HHS regulations in November, 2016 ("HHS Proposes to Improve Care," 2015; "Medicare and Medicaid Programs," 2016).

Health Insurance

Despite the great improvement in availability of medical care for older adults through the Medicare and Medicaid insurance programs, which cover virtually all older people, elders today face substantial health costs that are not covered. Medicare covers mostly acute care and requires beneficiaries to pay part of the cost; **premiums** and **co-insurance** make appropriate medical care out of reach for many. Approximately half of health spending must therefore come from other sources. Some older adults (approximately 53 percent) purchase additional private health insurance, and 8 percent have military-based health insurance. The most impoverished people living out in the community usually receive assistance from Medicaid (7 percent). More than 63 percent of Medicare beneficiaries living in nursing homes receive assistance from Medicaid, but first they must have exhausted their own private assets. As noted above, the cost of nursing home care is prohibitive for most people. Medicare pays for certain qualified short-term stays only ("Overview of Nursing Facility Capacity, Financing and Ownership," 2013; "A Profile of Older Americans," 2015).

Another problem for older people dependent on Medicare is the issue of prescription drugs. Until 2006, persons enrolled in Medicare received no assistance in purchasing prescribed medications. Finally, 40 years after Medicare was first enacted, a bill authorizing a drug benefit (known as Medicare Part D) was passed in 2005 under the Bush Administration, taking effect in 2006.

Medicare Part D as originally designed was very confusing. It contained a provision whereby after a small amount of money was spent by the older person on prescription drugs, a "donut hole" was encountered where the person had to pay full cost again. Congress invented the "donut hole" in large part because drug companies hired more than 800 lobbyists (spending more than $100 million) to pressure Congress to forbid the government to negotiate prices or price controls. This made drug coverage so expensive for the government that the "donut hole" was required to make the new program financially feasible ("The New Medicare 'Part D' Drug 'Benefit,'" 2006).

President Obama's Affordable Health Care Act includes provisions to fill the donut hole by 2020. However, the ACA's future is uncertain as this chapter is being revised because of the election in 2016 of Donald Trump as president along with a conservative Congress.

Mental Health Challenges

Mental health challenges tend to increase with age. That is because the aging process is inevitably accompanied by personal losses. One's bodily strength inevitably declines, for example, and a person tends to suffer more chronic illness. Spouses, family members, and friends may die. Retirement brings loss of income and loss of the worker role; age discrimination limits a person's ability to secure paying employment. The older adult can gradually lose the necessary resources to remain independent, leading to depression.

Nevertheless, many older persons cope remarkably well with the losses they encounter and maintain their optimism and resilience. Community resources and supports such as senior centers and Meals on Wheels can make a crucial difference in sustaining both the physical and mental health of older adults.

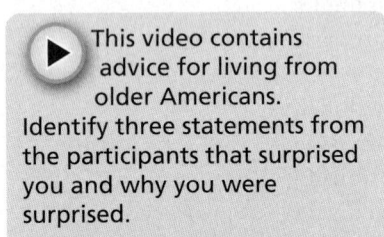

> This video contains advice for living from older Americans. Identify three statements from the participants that surprised you and why you were surprised.
> https://www.youtube.com/watch?v=j9WhqZ0BNas

Alzheimer's Disease and Related Dementias

Alzheimer's disease is one of the most serious chronic conditions afflicting older adults today. Nearly half of nursing home residents today have Alzheimer's disease or related **dementias**. Dementias warrant a special section in this chapter because they affect *both* physical and mental health. Alzheimer's disease often presents first as memory impairment, but it can be difficult to distinguish from related dementias. Other dementias can initially present as memory impairment, but while the usual early symptom of Alzheimer's is memory impairment, the usual first symptoms of related dementias include visual and motor impairment, behavioral changes, and sleep disruptions. Dementias progress over time so that the afflicted person may no longer recognize family and friends, experiencing confusion, distress, and eventually early death.

Alzheimer's disease was first described by Alois Alzheimer in 1906. It produces tiny lesions in the brain. Affecting more than five million older Americans today, it causes irreversible damage to one's brain, including memory loss, behavioral and psychological disorders, and the inability to carry on self-care functions (ADLs). Symptoms of Alzheimer's disease are progressive; eventually, the afflicted person loses use of both body and mind. People with this condition generally live four to six years after diagnosis but some live as long as 20.

Societal costs of Alzheimer's disease are enormous. It is the seventh leading cause of death, and incurs approximately $215 billion in annual costs. It takes the time and energy of more than 10.9 million unpaid caregivers who may themselves develop severe depression due to stress ("Alzheimer's Facts and Figures," 2010; "Alzheimer's Disease and Related Dementias," 2015).

Despite the dismal long-term prognosis for Alzheimer's patients, new treatments are being developed that can help slow the progression of symptoms. These include medications for depression, psychosis, and agitation. Preventive measures are also being investigated, including modifications in diet and exercise. Vaccines have been tested, but to date have not been found safe or effective (Park, 2015).

While Medicare, Medicaid, and private insurance pay for much necessary medical care, families assume most of the cost and provide most of the personal care. Families of these patients need attention: At least half of primary caregivers develop significant psychological distress. Prolonged stress is likely to develop into physical illness (Small et al., 1997; "Alzheimer's Disease and Related Dementias," 2015).

Providing supportive care to families of Alzheimer's patients can be an important role for social workers; social workers can also help maximize the functioning of afflicted elderly people by helping them exercise whatever faculties they have left. Structured small-group activities are excellent for this purpose and are comparatively easy to organize in nursing home settings (Naleppa & Reid, 2003).

In 2015, the U.S. Department of Health and Human Services announced a plan to address the challenges presented by a growing population of older adults, some of whom will contract Alzheimer's or related dementias. The plan proposed providing supports to communities offering special services for people with Alzheimers and their families ("Combating Alzheimer's and Other Dementias," 2015).

Ethnicity

The population of older Americans is becoming increasingly diverse. In 2008, for example, 19.6 percent of persons over 65 were of ethnic minority heritage. But by 2014, older adults of minority heritage comprised 22 percent of this population. African Americans constituted 9 percent of older persons in 2014; Hispanics (of any race) constituted

8 percent; Asian or Pacific Islanders, 4 percent; and Native Americans, 0.5 percent. Persons who identified themselves as belonging to more than one race constituted about 0.7 percent.

Life-span expectations differ among various ethnic groups. For example, only 8 percent of all persons of racial and ethnic minority heritage had attained the age of 65 or older by 2014, whereas nearly 18 percent of non-Hispanic whites had ("A Profile of Older Americans," 2015).

The Environment and Older Adults

Older adults are particularly susceptible to environmental hazards because they have accumulated a lifetime of exposure. In terms of national policy, this is a major problem because the cost of health care will increase as the population of older adults increases in number and percent. These environmental hazards are significant (see Box 10.3).

Environmental pollutants can exacerbate health problems such as asthma, Chronic Obstructive Pulmonary Disease (COPD), cancer, and heart disease—conditions particularly devastating to older adults. The Environmental Protection Agency (EPA) has developed an Aging Initiative to educate the public on environmental hazards for this population. Hopefully, the nation will continue the policy changes to reduce pollution initiated by the Obama Administration. However, these have been vehemently opposed by a conservative Congress. Older adults themselves are becoming increasingly involved in confronting environmental hazards. For example, the Environmental Alliance of Senior Involvement (EASI) was initiated in 1991 as a partnership between the U.S. Environmental Protection Agency and the American Association for Retired Persons. Today it includes more than 300 national partners such as the National Wildlife Federation, the National Association of Physicians for the Environment, and the National Park Foundation. In 1997, the first statewide Senior Environment Corps was created through a partnership between EASI and the state of Pennsylvania. In addition, voluntary organizations such as the Raging Grannies Action League conduct demonstrations to protest environmentally unsafe practices such as fracking (a means of extracting oil which results in major air and water pollution, and possibly earthquakes) and mile-long oil trains, which travel through densely populated areas on old unsafe tracks ("About Us," n.d.; "EASI Does It," n.d.).

> **?** Assess your understanding of the major characteristics of older adults today by taking this brief quiz.

Box 10.3 Environmental Hazards Affecting the Health of Older Americans

- **Indoor air pollutants:** radon, second-hand smoke, and carbon monoxide
- **Outdoor pollutants:** ozone, lead, and particulate matter
- **Drinking water contaminants:** microbes, disinfectants, and byproducts
- **Pesticides:** the health effects depend on the type of pesticide
- **Heavy metals:** lead and mercury (primarily from coal-fired plants)
- **Temperature extremes:** resulting from climate change

Source: Based on "What Is the EPA Aging Initiative," U.S. Environmental Protection Agency, www.epa.gov/aging.

OLDER ADULTS AND THEIR FAMILIES

Daily Life in Later Years

Young people often believe that older adults have plenty of time to do whatever they want because they are no longer required to earn a living and their children have left home. These young adults may fantasize that older persons spend most of their time resting (perhaps since young people themselves often need more rest!). Perhaps surprisingly, however, the daily life of most older adults is filled with activity, even those "empty nesters" who have fully retired from paid employment. Their lives are full, and they have as many (or more) interests, goals, and aspirations as younger people (Hodge, 2008).

Given freedom to spend their time more as they like, older people soon fill it with activities such volunteer work, hobbies, travel, visiting friends and relatives, attending classes, engaging in exercise programs—so that a common wail among the newly retired is "I can't believe it—I don't have any more time now than I ever did!" Older adults are valuable and productive members of society. They have taken over a good deal of the volunteer work that formerly was done by married women in the days when married women were unlikely to have paid employment.

Research on Family Strengths

There is a myth in our times that Americans abandon their elders, callously storing them away in nursing homes, never to see them again except perhaps at funerals. Although such tragedies undoubtedly do occur, research consistently refutes this myth for most families. For one thing, older adults in need of long-term care have been

Senior center activities promote social interaction among older adults

relatively rare until recent times. Stories about families caring for parents until death in the early days of this country may have been true, but that death would probably have occurred rather quickly. The average life expectancy in 1900 was more than 30 years less than it is today.

The truth is that more families are caring for elderly members today than ever before, and for many more years. In 2013, 40 million family caregivers provided approximately 37 billion hours of care with an estimated economic value of $470 billion. About two-thirds of caregiving is provided by women. Although many men provide caregiving as well, women spend about 50 percent more time at this task than men. Most family caregivers are also in the paid work force; nearly two out of three workers between the ages of 45 and 74 provide care for an aging parent, a spouse or partner, a relative, or a friend. Stress can lead to illness on the part of the caregiver, and loss of paid working hours due to illness can result in loss of future retirement income and social security benefits. For this reason, a few states (for example, California, Rhode Island, and New Jersey) have developed policies requiring paid family and medical leave allowing working caregivers to better manage their multiple responsibilities (Feinberg, 2014; Reinhard et al., 2015; "Women and Caregiving, Facts and Figures," 2015). Most states have no such laws, however, and there is no national requirement.

Greene (2000) points out that family developmental tasks have traditionally centered on the nuclear family and childrearing. Families today, however, increasingly encounter developmental tasks in later life, especially dealing with issues of dependency in older adults. This involves both a realistic acceptance by the older adult of strengths and limitations, and the ability of the adult child to accept a caregiving role.

Ethnic and Cultural Minorities

The number of older adults who are members of ethnic minority groups is growing faster than average. Because of discrimination and other factors, minority elders are especially vulnerable to poverty and are likely to have an increased need for social services. Such services should be carefully designed to meet the needs of particular clients in light of their cultural backgrounds.

Cox (2005) points out that work with ethnic and cultural minorities requires the recognition that social workers must be knowledgeable about the values, beliefs, and traditions of their clients. Such knowledge requires ongoing, sensitive communication, necessitating some fluency in the language and dialects of the persons being served. In addition, sensitivity to nonverbal cues is important, including gestures, posture, and eye contact. These can have very different meanings to members of diverse groups.

Recognizing one's own biases is essential for the social worker who serves older adults of diverse cultural backgrounds. Older persons may cling to traditional values to an extent not experienced with younger clients so that acceptance of difference is especially important in working with this population.

Services should reflect appropriate roles for the life cycles of diverse individuals, and they must be accessible to elders who may cope with mobility and other disabilities. Family circumstances should be assessed and presenting problems defined in terms of family and community mores.

Gay and Lesbian Older Adults

Another numerical minority that has had to learn to live in at least two different cultural worlds simultaneously comprises gay and lesbian older adults. If they are female, persons of color, or poor, they have had to survive multiple barriers. Many older adults have chosen not to reveal their sexual orientation for fear of rejection by family and friends. Yet many serve as caregivers for parents, spouses, or partners.

Gay and lesbian older adults have the same concerns as all older adults: health care, housing, employment, transportation, and so forth. They need support, both formal and informal, to help cope with the ongoing concerns of old age. This represents a challenge for social workers because many gays and lesbians still choose to remain invisible due to fear of social stigma and prejudice. Despite the improving social climate for this population, many people remain isolated and alone.

The Supreme Court ruling in 2015 legalizing gay marriage should help stabilize family life among older gays and lesbians. Unfortunately, however, most states still lack laws that would protect them from job discrimination, housing discrimination, etc.

Older Adults as Caregivers; Grandparent-Headed Families

Family members do not just assist their older adult relatives. Older adults are often the primary caregivers themselves. First of all, many care for each other. Married elderly, for example, particularly women, frequently take care of a spouse through long-term illness, including dementia, right up until death brings release. Many other older adults care for relatives and friends.

Older people also frequently care for children. Sometimes they provide child care for grandchildren while the children's parents work. But more than that, today many families are headed by older adults who are assuming increasing responsibility for raising grandchildren. In 2014, 554,000 grandparents over 65 had primary responsibility for the care of grandchildren who lived with them. More than 2.2 million grandparents over 65 lived in a household with a grandchild present ("A Profile of Older Americans," 2015).

Primary reasons compelling many children to be cared for by their grandparents are substance abuse, incarceration of the parents, and child maltreatment. Custodial grandparents often suffer increased health problems because of their additional responsibilities. Others experience increased psychological distress and social isolation. Innovative programs have been developed in a few places to help support their caretaking efforts, such as case management, support groups, parenting skills groups, respite care, assistance with legal concerns such as adoption, and welfare benefits; informational audiotapes regarding health, caregiving, and well-being have been developed to assist (Kropf & Wilks, 2003; "A Profile of Older Americans," 2015).

Many older adults adopt children. For example, elders who were serving as foster parents in 1997, the year of the Adoption and Safe Families Act, frequently decided to adopt their wards. This act encouraged states to speed up adoptions of children unlikely to have the opportunity to return to their biological families. Rather than risk losing the children in their care, many foster parents over the age of 60 decided to adopt. Because children older than five are considered hard to place, many of the older adults who applied were allowed to do so. Even an 80-year-old received permission to adopt (Stevens, 2001).

Box 10.4 Senator Barbara Mikulski

From a young age, Barbara Mikulski wanted to make a positive difference in her community. She grew up in East Baltimore and worked at her family's grocery store, often delivering groceries to homebound neighbors including many older adults.

Barbara decided to become a social worker. She earned her MSW at the University of Maryland School of Social Work, and then worked for Catholic Charities and the Baltimore Department of Social Services. When she learned there were plans to run a 16 lane highway right through Baltimore's Fells Point neighborhood, she became active in community efforts to stop it. Her efforts helped to prevent the road from being built.

Spurred on by her experience with social activism, Barbara Mikulski decided to run for political office and was elected to the Baltimore City Council in 1971. In 1976 she was elected to the U.S. House of Representatives. She served in the House for 10 years until elected to the U.S. Senate in 1986. At that time, she was 50 years old. She served continually in the Senate from 1986 until January 3, 1917. She has been an inspiration for many social workers, and hopefully will serve as a model for social work students today.

As senator, Barbara Mikulski put her values into action—she worked tirelessly to make quality education accessible to all students; worked to improve programs for seniors, including Medicare; supported Alzheimer's and stem cell research; pursued women's health issues; worked toward competent health care for veterans; and supported volunteerism and national service programs such as AmeriCorps.

Source: Adapted from Senator Barbara Mikulkski's website: http://mikulski.senate.gov/About/Biography/index.cfm.

Beyond caring for members of their immediate families, many older adults today are caregivers for their communities, their states, and even the nation. An inspiring example is Senator Barbara Mikulski (see Box 10.4).

Caregiver Stress and the "Sandwich Generation"

> In what specific ways does this video highlight the challenges for the Fischer family, especially parents Celeste and Scott, as "sandwich generation" caregivers?
>
> https://www.youtube.com/watch?v=LO4OkoRiigc

While millions of families provide care to their older members with good will and grace, providing help to older adults can be stressful. Activities of daily living such as shopping, cooking, cleaning, helping with laundry, and bathing all take time and money. Even more time is required when caring for an older person who is ill. Since most caregivers work outside the home as well, it is clear caregiving takes a toll on the giver.

In addition, many caregivers have children as well as older family members for whom to care: Caregivers with responsibilities to the generation both above and below are sometimes known as the **sandwich generation.** Their conflicting duties create additional stress.

According to the American Psychological Association, mothers in the "sandwich generation," women aged approximately 35–54, feel more stress than any other age group as they struggle with caring both for growing children and aging parents. Nearly 40 percent of both women and men in this age group feel overextended, but more women than men report experiencing extreme stress because they provide the most care. Financial worries increase at this time as well because of concerns about saving for children's college education as well as saving for retirement ("Sandwich Generation Moms Feeling the Squeeze," 2016; see Box 10.5).

> **Box 10.5 The Sandwich Generation**
>
> Dora was married with two young sons when her mother, a widow, had a stroke and needed help with dressing, bathing, shopping, and housecleaning. Both Dora and her husband worked full-time, Dora as a hospital receptionist and her husband as a mechanic. Dora could not go to live with her mother, who had her own apartment a few miles away, because of responsibilities to her husband and children. In addition, there was not enough room in Dora's home for her mother to move in. So with great difficulty, Dora arranged for part-time help for her mother to assist with daily needs such as bathing and eating lunch, but the ongoing chores of shopping and housecleaning fell to Dora. She drove to her mother's apartment every morning after getting her sons ready for school to help her dress and eat breakfast. Dora stopped by her mother's apartment every evening to make sure she was safe and to make dinner before going home to make dinner for the rest of her family. The work was exhausting, and Dora felt guilty about the time taken away from her husband and children. Finally, thankfully, Dora's mother recovered enough to manage her own affairs.

Elder Abuse and Self Neglect

According to the National Center on Elder Abuse, we do not know with certainty how many people are suffering from elder abuse and neglect although studies indicate that women are abused at a higher rate than men and that abuse increases with age. Reasons for lack of reliable data include the fact that an older person may be unable to report abuse due to cognitive deficit or physical limitations, may be unwilling to report due to fear of retaliation, or may be unwilling to report because of not wanting to get a family caregiver in trouble. Thus, a great deal of elder abuse goes unreported (Statistics/data, n.d.).

Most families do their best to provide for their older members. But given the pressures of caregiving, it may not be surprising that reports of elder abuse are rising nationwide. One large study found that between 7.6 and 10 percent of study participants had been abused or neglected in the recent year. In another study, 44 percent of nursing home residents reported that they had been abused during the previous year, and a sobering 95 percent of residents reported neglect of themselves or other residents (Statistics/Data, n.d.). Increased social services to older adults and their families, including day care for frail elderly and **respite care**, or temporary relief for caregivers, could help prevent a large proportion of the elder abuse and neglect occurring today.

Abuse and/or neglect may occur in several ways (Kosberg & Nahmiash, 1996; Naleppa & Reid, 2003; Statistics/Data, n.d.):

- Physical maltreatment in which pain or injury is inflicted
- Sexual abuse
- Verbal or emotional abuse in which a person is insulted, humiliated, or threatened
- Material or financial abuse in which money or property is misused
- Passive or active neglect, or not providing adequate food, shelter, and other necessities for daily living
- Violation of civil rights or forcing someone to do something against his or her wishes

- Resident-to-resident abuse in long-term care facilities
- Self-neglect in which a person retains responsibility for his or her own care but manages poorly in areas such as nutrition and hygiene

Self-Neglect

Self-neglect is especially common among older adults and can raise serious ethical dilemmas for social workers who serve this population. Many elderly people choose, for example, to live in their own homes, but they may grow too frail to cope well alone. Housekeeping suffers or is non-existent and meals become minimal, lacking in nutrition.

Some older homes are in such need of repair that they provide unsafe living environments. Some older adults suffer injuries that temporarily prevent them from being able to carry out necessary activities of daily living such as feeding and dressing, yet they still do not want to leave their homes. In spite of urging from their families, older adults often refuse to move to safer living situations such as assisted living facilities or nursing homes. Thus, social workers who work with this population face ongoing ethical dilemmas concerning client self-determination versus physical safety.

> **?** Assess your understanding of major issues concerning older adults and their families by taking this brief quiz.

SOCIAL POLICY AND OLDER ADULTS: PAST TO PRESENT

Family Care

Historically, before governmental social policies dealing with older adults were developed, services to the elderly were provided almost entirely by their families. This was workable because of the short life span that was the norm at that time and because there were many tasks an elderly parent or relative could perform as a way of reciprocating.

By the late 1800s, however, industrialization had changed family patterns. Grown children tended to move to the cities. Individual achievement as a value took precedence over loyalty to one's extended family. The nuclear family supplanted the extended family as the primary locus of responsibility. Changes such as these undermined family support systems for older adults. The need for new forms of support began to appear. In early times, the only alternatives were the church or almshouse. Later, **pension plans** were established in some countries.

Early Pension Plans

Germany initiated a compulsory **pension** program in 1889 that provided a regular source of income for older, retired workers. Employers, workers, and the state each contributed equal amounts to the financing. Britain introduced a pension program in 1908, which permitted general tax revenue to be transferred to elderly poor persons (Huttman, 1985). By comparison, the United States has been slow in developing universal pension plans for the elderly. Some states had pension plans by the 1920s, but they all required a means test (only people with very low incomes could qualify).

Not until the Great Depression did this country enact a nearly universal pension plan for the elderly, via the Social Security Act of 1935. The intent of Title II of this act was to stabilize income for older Americans without the appearance of the "dole," or a government handout. People were required to contribute to Social Security through a special tax during their working life. Thus, they could perceive the program as a contributory "insurance" plan, not charity. Workers who were required to pay Social Security taxes were eligible to receive benefits after retirement, whether rich or poor. In 1939, coverage expanded to include widows and children. Eventually, many other categories such as self-employed people, farm and domestic workers, government workers, the military, and religious personnel were included (Huttman, 1985).

Trends in American Private Pensions

In recent generations, American workers grew accustomed to receiving not only government Social Security benefits but also substantial retirement benefits from the companies for which they worked most of their lives. This situation has changed, however. Not only do workers tend to change jobs frequently today, due to both personal choice and involuntary layoffs, but companies have seriously underfunded the private pensions they promised. The federal government guarantees benefits through the Pension Benefit Guarantee Corporation (PBGC), but this entity faces a gap of billions of dollars between obligations and income ("Smoothing the Way to Retirement Pay," 2006).

In late 2006, the federal government passed the Pension Protection Act, requiring employers to fund pension plans fully (up from 90 percent). While this legislation helps protect American taxpayers from having to subsidize underfunded company pension plans, an expected side effect was that fewer companies would offer such plans (Trumbull, 2006).

Today only about half of employees have access to any kind of retirement plan through their workplace, and the number is steadily decreasing. In recent years, most employers have transferred the entire risk of financing retirement to their employees. They have replaced what once were defined benefit plans (plans promising specified income at retirement) with what are known as 401(k) plans. Employees can contribute to a 401(k) plan tax-free, with taxes deferred until money is withdrawn in retirement. Unfortunately, few employees have any training in investing or managing investment risk, however, and fees charged by financial firms to run the plans can reduce a retirement nest egg by as much as 30 percent (Sherter, 2014). Americans today are largely on their own to finance retirement.

Social Security Today

Social Security is a federal **entitlement program**, a program in which a legal right to receive benefits has been bestowed by law on people who meet certain eligibility criteria. It is financed through taxes: Both employers and employees pay 6.2 percent of an employee's salary in Social Security taxes for a combined total of 12.4 percent. The tax applied to salaries up to $118,500 in 2016; the amount of income taxed for Social Security purposes rises according to the Consumer Price Index. Social Security assists more than retired workers: Retired workers received 72 percent of all Social Security benefits in 2016, but disabled workers and their dependents received 15 percent, and survivors of deceased workers received 10 percent.

Because of the increasing financial insecurity many people are experiencing due to loss of traditional pension plans, Social Security benefits are more important today than ever before. Benefit levels are indexed to inflation, which can help keep poverty at bay. Indexing, however, has become a political football in recent years as conservative politicians attempt to chip away at the program.

Ninety percent of persons over 65, more than 48 million, receive Social Security benefits; in 2016, the average monthly payment to this category of beneficiaries was $1,350. Social Security benefits were never designed to supply a worker's total retirement income, but rather to supplement private pension plans and personal savings. However, as previously discussed, private pensions have largely disappeared. Most employees today must finance their own retirement "pension," usually through investing in **tax-sheltered annuities** such as 401(k) plans. Employers sometimes offer to match employee contributions to such plans ("Policy Basics, Top Ten Facts" 2016).

Savings by Americans which could supplement their Social Security retirement incomes are very small: one third have no retirement savings at all, and an additional 23 percent have less than $10,000. Women are worse off than men: two-thirds of women have nothing, or less than $10,000, compared with just over half of men with savings that low. An important reason for the difference is the gender pay gap, along with the fact that more women take time away from the paid job market to raise their children (Kirkham, 2016).

Because of the great number of workers initially paying into the Social Security program per beneficiary, the fund developed a huge surplus; today it has a combined trust fund of $2.8 trillion. The surplus is invested in interest-bearing Treasury securities and generates substantial interest. According to projections in 2016, interest income plus redemption of the government securities should allow full payment of benefits until 2034. At that time, income generated by Social Security taxes alone will provide about three-fourths of the scheduled benefits through 2089 ("Social Security Basic Facts," 2016).

Conservatives foment fear that the Social Security program is nearly bankrupt and will not be available for today's young workers when they retire. They point out that the government securities will need to be redeemed to permit payment of full benefits in the near future. However, these government securities are as sound as those purchased by individuals as investments, and such investment are considered very safe. It is true, however, that some government moneys now allocated to other purposes may need to be re-allocated to the Social Security program to redeem the securities.

The Social Security program could be made sound for the foreseeable future with a few minor adjustments, for example, by allowing an individual's full income to be taxed for Social Security purposes (e.g., raising Social Security taxes on wealthy persons), by raising the tax rate slightly for everyone, and/or by modifying benefit levels slightly ("Policy Basics, Top Ten Facts," 2016). The program has already been modified by raising the age at which a person can retire with full benefits. Originally, the full benefit could be obtained when a worker turned 65. Today that age is 66 for people born between 1943 and 1954. It will gradually rise to 67 for those born in 1960 or later. Another modification that has been made is the requirement for retirees to pay income taxes on 85 percent of Social Security income, even though they already paid taxes on the 50 percent they contributed themselves while working. This change occurred under President George H. W. Bush, a conservative who said "Read my lips, no new taxes." Apparently he meant except for the elderly.

Conservatives argue that the program should be privatized to allow maximum returns to investors (i.e., those who happen to be lucky). However, Jeanne Marsh, in an editorial in *Social Work* (2005) pointed out the dangers of such a plan. Because retiree benefits would continue to be paid in full for a time while a percentage of worker payments would be diverted to private accounts, the cost to taxpayers to fill the gap would be massive. At the same time, retirement security for the average worker would be greatly reduced due to the substantial and ongoing risks of the stock market.

Social Security is an extremely important program assisting nearly 60 million Americans today.. The program is especially helpful to workers who tend to earn less, such as minorities and women, because the system returns a greater percentage of pre-retirement earnings to lower-wage workers than higher-wage workers ("Social Security Basic Facts," 2016; "Status of the Social Security and Medicare Programs," 2015). A realistic worry is that the new conservative president and Congress will try to privatize it.

Human Rights

Dimension of Competency **Values:** Social workers understand that every person has fundamental human rights such as an adequate standard of living and adequate health care.

Critical Thinking Question: Use your critical thinking skills to decide whether social work values would support the Social Security system's policy of returning a greater percentage of pre-retirement earnings to lower-wage workers than higher-wage workers.

Supplemental Security Income

Supplemental Security Income (SSI), another federal entitlement program, was initiated in 1972 as an amendment to the Social Security Act of 1935. As explained in Chapter 3, this program was developed to reduce the stigma of public assistance for three categories of poor people: older adults, persons who are blind, and persons who have other disabilities. SSI established uniform national eligibility requirements and benefits, and people can apply for benefits through federal Social Security offices rather than local "welfare" offices. Benefits, however, remain very low. A few states offer SSPs, or State Supplementary Programs, for the poorest elderly to augment income from SSI.

Housing Assistance

As noted earlier in this chapter, the majority of older adults own their own homes, but many struggle to make ends meet and cannot afford such a luxury. To assist with this problem, the Federal Housing Assistance Program, through the U.S. Department of Housing and Urban Development (HUD), subsidized nearly two million apartments for poor people, about half of them for the elderly, for many years (Salamon, 1986). However, the Reagan Administration slashed HUD funding after his election in 1980.

As a result, affordable housing has been increasingly out of reach for all of the nation's poor, including older adults. A Republican Congress tried to cut HUD funding entirely during Clinton's tenure as president. To save the department, the Democratic Clinton Administration converted HUD programs into a system of block grants to the states in 1996 (Popple & Leighninger, 1999). Then, in 1998, Clinton signed the Quality Housing and Work Responsibility Act, which transferred primary responsibility for publicly assisted housing to local Public Housing Authorities (PHAs). Under this act, PHAs can consider applicants' employment histories in admissions decisions; tenants in TANF programs who do not meet work requirements can be evicted (Karger & Stoesz, 2010).

The Republican G.W. Bush Administration continued to reduce funding for low-income housing, but fortunately HUD survived. Today it provides three major programs to assist low-income families with housing needs: public housing, Section 8 Project-Based Rental Assistance (PBRA), and the Section 8 Housing Choice Voucher Program.

The public housing program, while overseen by HUD, is administered by some 3,000 local public housing agencies. About 20 percent are located in rural areas. Most local agencies own and manage their own housing developments that assist 2.2 million low-income Americans today. About 30 percent are elderly. While approximately 85 percent of public housing units meet HUD safety standards, nearly all were built before 1985, and many require serious renovations for which Congress has not allocated sufficient funds.

The Section 8 Project-Based Rental Assistance (PBRA) programs assist two million Americans today, of whom 46 percent are older adults. PBRA programs contract with private owners to rent units in their housing developments to low-income families. Most owners are for-profit entities, but non-profits comprise a significant share. About 13 percent of Section 8-PBRA assisted units are located outside of metropolitan areas.

The Section 8 Housing Choice Voucher Program has become the largest federally assisted housing program of all, assisting more than five million people today. About 21 percent are elderly. Low-income persons and families can use vouchers to pay for housing they find themselves on the private market. Participants in all of these programs must be very low-income ("Policy Basics, Section 8," 2015). Most programs have long waiting lists.

Medicare and Medicaid

Before 1965, most health care costs for older adults were paid by the elderly themselves, with the result that many lacked any care at all. This situation greatly improved after the 1965 passage of Medicare, Title XVIII of the Social Security Act. All persons over 65 qualify for Medicare benefits. Part A covers hospital expenses; part B deals with outpatient costs. Because of out-of-pocket costs such as premiums and co-pays, Medicare Advantage plans, less expensive for the older adult, have been introduced by private companies, but participants must go to in-plan health providers for their care.

Medicare Part D (coverage for prescription drugs) was enacted in 2005. Beginning in 2016, Medicare will pay doctors for end of life counseling, or discussions with patients providing information about care options at different stages of their lives. (See Chapter 7 for an extensive discussion of Medicare.)

Medicaid also came into being in 1965 through an amendment to the Social Security Act, Title XIX. Medicaid was designed to aid older adults with very low incomes. This is the program that paid for nursing home care for Abbie Heinrich of our chapter's case study. Medicaid is administered under each state's public welfare system, and benefits differ from state to state. Costs are shared between state and federal governments.

Since 1993, a federal law has required that states recover the money spent on medical care for a Medicaid beneficiary after the beneficiary dies. In many cases, the only asset to seize is the deceased recipient's former home. This requirement is exempted if a surviving spouse or child under 21 lives in the home, but often the person living there is an adult child who cared for the deceased for many years. This dedicated caretaker is evicted if unable to buy the home. Often the families involved are pitifully poor (Green, 2006).

Food Stamps, or the Supplemental Nutrition Assistance Program

The food stamp program, also discussed in Chapter 4, is a federal entitlement available to poor older adults. The program is also known today as SNAP, or the Supplemental Nutrition Assistance Program. Eligibility requirements involve both income and the number of persons in a given household who presumably share income.

Older Americans who are eligible for SNAP/food Stamps are significantly less likely to participate in the program than younger people. In 2011, three out of five eligible older adults failed to apply for SNAP benefits. Reasons include lack of information, the stigma of **charity**, mobility barriers, complexity of application processes (including technology), and low benefits. In 2012, four million older adults participated in SNAP in an average month, nine percent of all participants. The average benefit for a single older adult over 60 in 2012 was only $119 per month ($176 for a household with two older adults). Despite low benefits, the SNAP program lifted 4.9 million people out of poverty, 346,300 of whom were seniors over 65 ("Combating Food Insecurity," 2015; see Box 10.6).

Box 10.6   Bertha Talbot

Bertha Talbot had just turned 56 when her husband, George, a retired school teacher, died unexpectedly of a heart attack. The two had had a traditional marriage: George brought in the family income while Bertha served at home as full-time wife and mother of six children.

At the time of George's death, the children had all left home and moved to other states in pursuit of work. They returned home for George's funeral, but soon left again.

Fortunately, George Talbot's former employer had provided him with a pension when he retired, and Bertha now received a percentage of that pension as his widow. But she was too young to receive a widow's benefit from Social Security—this would not be available until she turned 60. Moreover, because housekeeping and raising one's own children are not considered "work" under this act, Bertha would never receive Social Security benefits of her own achieved by her own labor. Bertha soon found herself struggling to make ends meet. One day, after church, her minister asked how she was doing since George died. She broke down in tears. She said she was thinking of trying to find a paying job but didn't know where to begin. She had no experience with paid work, but she was running out of money to meet living expenses. The minister suggested she might consult with the County Aging and Disability Center. A few days later, he took Bertha himself.

The County Aging and Disability Center was a lifesaver for Bertha. The social worker there told her about the Homestead Tax Credit, which allows low-income persons to pay reduced property taxes. The social worker encouraged her to apply for food stamps and helped her fill out the long application form. The worker also encouraged Bertha to attend a senior center in the neighboring county.

With great hesitation, Bertha visited the senior center. She was received with such welcome that she decided to return to try one of the congregate meals. That way, she met a man named Curtis, and a year later they were married.

There was an interesting twist to Bertha and Curtis' marriage, however—one becoming more common among older adults today for similar reasons. Bertha knew she would lose the pension George had left her if she formally remarried. She would also lose her widow's benefits under Social Security when she turned 60. So, with the knowledge and understanding of her minister, who conducted the marriage ceremony with full blessings, Bertha and Curtis did not record their marriage at the courthouse. Bertha knew she had earned this small amount of financial security—her unpaid work at home had enabled George to carry out the paid job that had left *him* a pension, plus Social Security benefits.

The Older Americans Act

The mid-1960s were important years for the elderly. The Older Americans Act of 1965 focused on coordinating comprehensive services for all people over 60, not just the poor. It established the Administration on Aging at the federal level and authorized state units and local area agencies on aging. These agencies assess the needs of the older adults and try to develop programs to meet them. State and local autonomy is permitted within federal guidelines. In 1993, President Clinton raised the position of commissioner of the Administration on Aging to an assistant secretary level (Torres-Gil & Puccinelli, 1995).

Funding under the Older Americans Act has always been low. Still, it supports nutrition programs, senior centers (which often house the nutrition programs, low-cost congregate meals for all persons over 60), and information and referral services. In 1999, the National Family Caregiver Support Program was authorized under the act, calling for coordination between state and other community service programs to provide support services for caregivers. When the act was reauthorized in 2006, it included a provision allowing the Assistant Secretary for Aging to establish Aging and Disability Resource Centers in every state ("Older Americans Act," n.d.; "Administration on Aging," 2010).

Aging and Disability Resource Centers serve as resources where senior citizens, adults with disabilities, and their families are connected with information about needed services including home health and hospice agencies, homemaker service providers, legal services, senior centers/senior dining, support groups, transportation services, nursing home ombudsmen, assistance with Alzheimer's disease, substance use disorders, and abuse and neglect. These agencies are especially important in rural areas, where services are scarce.

In these times of social service cutbacks, many argue that services should be provided only for older adults who are also poor or have a disability. However, others point out that two-tiered services separate people according to economic status, placing a stigma on services.

National organizations such as the AARP and the Gray Panthers support offering services to all elderly people. (See Box 10.7.)

Participants in the White House Conference on Aging in 2015 strongly advocated reauthorization of the Older Americans Act. One in five older adults—11 million people—benefitted from its services. It had last been reauthorized in 2006 and funding was at serious risk. Finally, in a rare bi-partisan action, Congress reauthorized the act in April, 2016 (Blancato, 2015; "Aging in 2015," 2015; "Congress Renews Law," 2016).

The Social Services Block Grant

Before the 1970s, people who applied for financial assistance received services from social workers in public welfare departments, who assessed social service needs while determining eligibility for financial aid. Beginning in the early 1970s, eligibility for financial aid was determined by clerical staff who made no further needs assessment (Cox & Parsons, 1994).

Social services for older adults began to be funded by the Social Services Block Grant in the mid-1970s. It is a limited source of financing for services such as case management, adult day care, protective services, homemaker services, health-related services,

Box 10.7 Up for Debate

Proposition: Services under the Older Americans Act should be means-tested.

Yes	No
Funding under this act is low so that services should be limited to the most needy.	All older Americans benefit from balanced meals and an opportunity for social interaction.
Taxpayers are unwilling to subsidize services for all elderly.	All taxpayers will one day be elderly. Services for all can help make old age a rewarding experience for everyone.
Poor elderly need help the most.	Services limited only to the poor separate people according to economic status and place a stigma on services.
Because money is scarce, it should be targeted to poor people.	Limiting services to the poorest people pits the non-poor against the poor, rather than encouraging all older adults to develop cooperative self-help efforts.
Taxpayers may resist using tax dollars to provide universal services for all older adults.	If most taxpayers know they will be denied services when they get old because they are not poor, no wonder they protest using tax money to provide these services for others.

and transportation. Originally known as Title XX of the Social Security Act implemented in 1975, this program was renamed and modified under the Omnibus Budget Reconciliation Act of 1981 (Eustis, Greenberg, & Patton, 1984). Today the Social Services Block Grant continues to help fund community-based services for older adults and those with disabilities. Funding is very limited and states are allowed freedom in determining how to use it (Karger & Stoesz, 1998; "Social Service Block Grants," 2016).

Values and Public Policy

Funding for programs for older adults involves national policy choices; such policy choices translate into dollar terms the values of those who determine the policy. Should all older American adults be offered tax-supported services such as congregate meals, for example, or only the poorest, frailest elderly?

The debate around privatizing Social Security and social welfare programs in general relates far more to economic and political values than to values concerning the well-being of others. Conservatives trying to privatize social welfare programs appear interested primarily in promoting the free enterprise system so private businesses can generate profits and taxes remain low, rather than making sure people in need of services receive them.

Policy Practice

Dimension of Competency Values: Social workers assess how social welfare and economic policies impact access to social services.

Critical Thinking Question: In what ways do you think values can affect economic policies, which in turn impact access to social services?

The "Continuum of Care": Prolonging Independence

Most older adults want to maintain independence as long as possible. Recognition of this preference has led to the concept of the **continuum of care.** Highly relevant is the principle of "least restriction," that an intervention designed to meet a special need should present the least amount of interference with normal life patterns while meeting the need in the most beneficial way possible. Generally, whatever can be done to enable the older person to remain in his or her own home setting (the **least restrictive environment**) is appropriate.

Figure 10.1 illustrates the major components of a long-term continuum of care for older adults. The diagram illustrates how many services for the elderly can fit into more than one category; for example, nutrition programs can be offered either in the home or in the community, perhaps at a senior center. The following sections briefly describe each major category of care (see Figure 10.1).

Least Restrictive

In-Home and Community:
- Monitoring services
- Homemaker and home health services
- Nutrition programs

(In-Home: Monitoring services, Homemaker and home health services)

- Legal/protective services
- Senior centers
- Community medical and mental health services
- Dental care
- Adult day care programs

(Community: Nutrition programs through Adult day care programs)

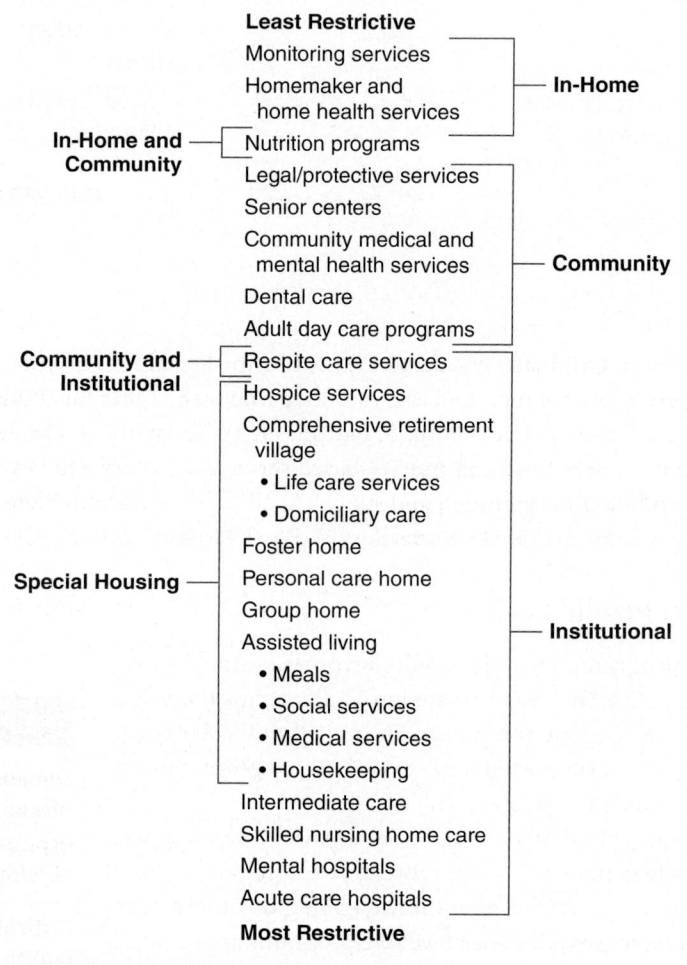

Community and Institutional:
- Respite care services
- Hospice services

Special Housing:
- Comprehensive retirement village
  - Life care services
  - Domiciliary care
- Foster home
- Personal care home
- Group home
- Assisted living
  - Meals
  - Social services
  - Medical services
  - Housekeeping
- Intermediate care
- Skilled nursing home care
- Mental hospitals
- Acute care hospitals

(Institutional: Respite care services through Acute care hospitals)

Most Restrictive

Figure 10.1 Components of Long-Term Care for the Elderly

Source: Adapted from R.R. Greene (1986). *Social Work with the Aged and Their Families.* (p. 177). New York: Aldine de Gruyter.

In-Home Services

Monitoring services usually involve telephone calls to make sure that an older person is alive and well and to provide support and reassurance. Today, electronic devices are available where the push of a button alerts special services to investigate potential emergencies.

Homemaker services involve housecleaning, laundry, shopping, minor home repairs, yard work, and other routine chores. A more intensive kind of homemaker service may involve personal care, such as help with bathing and dressing. Home health aides provide medically oriented care, under the supervision of a skilled nurse. Home health aides may change bandages, give injections, and take a client's blood pressure.

Medicare and Medicaid pay for some of these services, but eligibility requirements are complicated and restrictive. Sometimes older adults can receive homemaker services at low cost by applying to an agency partly funded by the Older Americans Act or the Social Services Block Grant. Most people need to purchase these services privately, however.

Community Services

Nutrition programs can help older adults remain in their own homes. Meals on Wheels is a well-known example. In some communities, programs funded under the Older Americans Act provide congregate meals daily at senior centers or other sites.

Occasionally, family or other caretakers abuse or neglect older people. Protective services for the elderly are a fairly new phenomenon; in 1968, fewer than 20 communities had such programs (Dunkel, 1987). Today, however, almost every state requires helping professionals to report suspected abuse or neglect of older adults.

Senior centers are important means for older adults to maintain social interaction. Many are privately funded and administered by organizations such as churches or by local cities or counties. Some centers receive funding through the Older Americans Act or Social Service Block Grants.

Community medical and dental services include private-pay arrangements that older adults finance themselves as well as public services financed partly by Medicaid and Medicare. An important public policy issue involves how much of their own medical costs older adults should have to finance themselves.

Community mental health services can help older adults cope with various stresses of living, including the stress of caring for a spouse who is ill. Mental health services also can assist other family caregivers. For example, a daughter or a daughter-in-law may have to give up a paying job and most personal freedom to provide round-the-clock care for an elderly relative. Mental health services may assist the caretaker.

Adult day care services provide regular programming outside the home to supervise and maintain older persons who cannot get through the day alone. Many older adults who spend their days in adult day care programs live with relatives who regularly assist them but must work outside the home during the day.

Institutional Services

Some institutions, including nursing homes, offer a service called respite care, whereby an older person resides in the institution for a few days, a week, or even a month. This temporary arrangement allows family caretakers to take a break, go on vacation,

Pet therapy enriches nursing home living

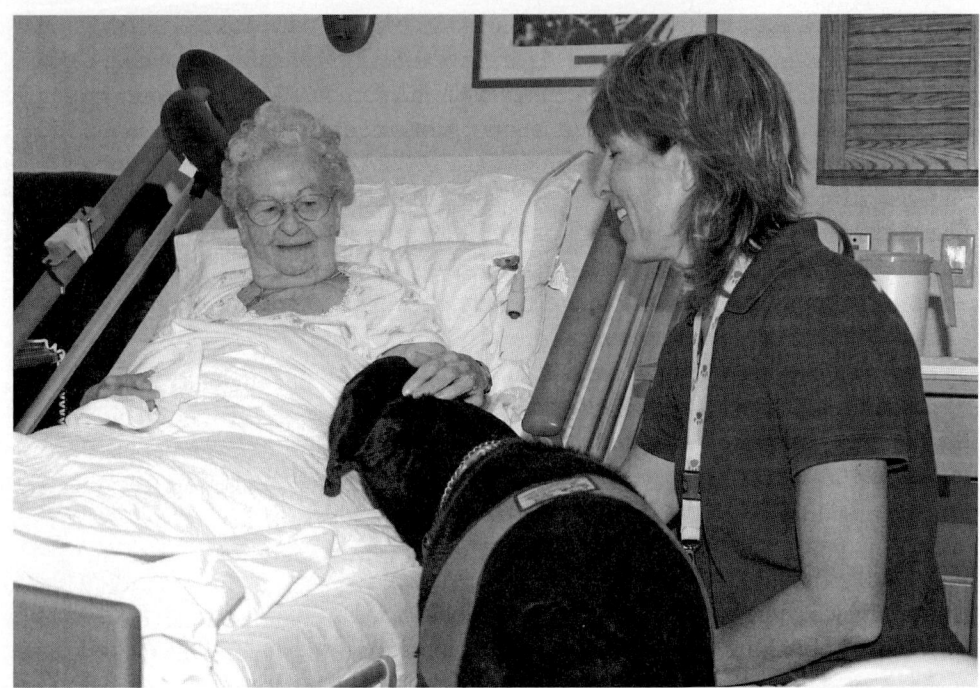

or otherwise "recharge their batteries" physically and emotionally. After the respite, the elder returns home to their care. Many institutions also offer day care services as described above.

The next several categories in Greene's continuum of care (Figure 10.1) are institutional in that they involve long-term care outside the older person's home in an institution such as a hospital or nursing home. Greene also places them in the subcategory of special housing, however, because the service is sometimes offered in a person's home or in a small homelike setting. The first of these services is hospice care, or care for the dying. The purpose of hospice care is to help the patient die with dignity and with as little pain as possible. Medicare will pay for hospice care for persons whose prognosis indicates that they have six months or less to live. (Medicare pays the medical charges, but not room and board.)

The next item with both institutional and special housing aspects is the retirement village. Many retirement villages offer lifetime care with a continuum of services; many are private, non-profit arrangements established by religious denominations. Older adults who are economically advantaged may purchase lifetime rights to an apartment or other housing unit. Some such programs offer the option of purchasing congregate meals. Many include a domiciliary option, or a large housing unit where a number of elderly people live and are offered personal assistance and meal services. The most advanced retirement villages include skilled nursing home care as needed.

Some older adults reside in foster homes or in small group homes, where they can receive individual attention and protection if needed as long as ongoing medical attention is not required. Others live in larger **personal care homes**, which usually provide meals and are sometimes called nursing homes because the services of nurse's aides are available to help with bathing, eating, dressing, and the like. Technically speaking, however, a personal care home is not a nursing home because very limited nursing care is available.

An increasing demand for community living options for older people who need some level of assistance, but do not need an environment dominated by nursing requirements has led to the development of an option known as **assisted living**. Assisted living is a step between independent living and living in a nursing home. The term became recognized nationally after the Assisted Living Federation of America was incorporated in 1992 ("About ALFA," 2007). Older adults who reside in assisted living settings have their own small apartments including kitchens, bedrooms, and bathrooms. The environment is much more attractive than a room (usually shared) in a personal care home. Yet the same services are available: assistance with cooking, shared meals when desired, assistance with activities of daily living (dressing, bathing, laundry, housekeeping, etc.), and occasional nursing care as needed. Unfortunately, assisted living is usually available today only to people with significant financial means.

The institutional settings that provide the most restrictive environments for care of older adults are nursing homes and hospitals. Most elderly people do whatever they can to avoid them. However, because living into one's 80s and 90s is becoming common, an increasing number of older adults face an eventual move to a nursing home. These facilities provide the only reasonable alternative to 24-hour family or hospital care when an older person is very ill or very frail. This is the setting that provided life-giving care to Abbie Heinrich of our chapter's case study.

Fortunately, nursing homes now are professionally organized and staffed. Many, especially the non-profits, provide responsible services along with opportunities for older adults to enjoy the companionship of peers. "Intermediate care" and "skilled nursing care" are categories that reflect the level of nursing care provided. The former is less intensive than the latter, and monthly fees are lower. Abbie Heinrich, with her extensive physical challenges, required the highest level of skilled nursing care (see Box 10.8).

Box 10.8 Making Nursing Homes Livable

For many older persons, having to move to a nursing home is experienced as the "kiss of death." The belief is that they are going there to die, and quite naturally they become despondent, depressed, and lonely. Sadly, two frail older persons can live in adjoining rooms, sometimes even in the same room, yet crave company and never think it worthwhile to get to know each other as they are "only going to die." To alleviate this unfortunate state of affairs, progressive nursing homes encourage their residents to engage in activities ranging from reminiscence groups to exercise groups to music and arts and crafts. Many homes bring in volunteers as "friendly visitors," including young children. Children can be especially effective as visitors to frail older adults; their very presence seems to transfer a sort of vibrant energy.

In the best nursing homes today, it is not uncommon to see bird cages full of active parakeets chattering away in day rooms, surrounded by smiling residents enjoying the sounds and the vibrant colors. Therapy programs bring in dogs and cats; the response of older residents to these feline and canine visitors is overwhelmingly positive. Plants are brought in to add color and a sense of purpose to the lives of residents who often "adopt" them and lavish time and attention upon them. Such stimulating sights, sounds, and activities can dramatically decrease depression and loneliness among older adults residing in nursing homes.

Unfortunately, because many nursing homes are administered by for-profit private organizations today, staffing levels are low to maximize profits. Non-profit homes provide nearly an hour more care per resident per day and nearly twice as much care from registered nurses. Federal rules require only eight hours of registered nursing and 24 hours of licensed nursing care per day in any given facility, so large homes can have the same size staff as small ones. Many states have their own regulations, but state inspectors underreport deficiencies due to staff shortages of their own. Cuts in Medicaid reimbursements have also contributed to nursing home understaffing. These institutions should be utilized only when less restrictive alternatives have been exhausted ("Nursing Homes, Business as Usual," 2006).

The Affordable Care Act passed by Congress in 2010, promoted and signed by former President Obama, includes a provision titled the Elder Justice Act, designed to help improve nursing home quality (Sebelius, 2010). In 2015, as discussed earlier in this chapter, the Centers for Medicare and Medicaid Services proposed new regulations that would update quality and safety requirements of more than 15,000 nursing homes for the first time in 25 years. These regulations to help improve the care of older adults were adopted in 2016, but were immediately endangered by the election of a conservative president, Donald Trump, and a conservative Congress.

Rural versus Urban Issues

Services to assist older adults to live independently in the community are scarce almost everywhere, but gaps in the continuum of care are far more likely to occur in rural areas. Even where important programs such as congregate meals and adult day care exist within a given rural county, transportation over long distances may be required to obtain them; thus, many seniors and their families are effectively blocked from participating in their benefits. Many rural areas are completely lacking in crucial services such as senior centers with congregate meals, Meals on Wheels, affordable housekeeping help, medical screening services, adult day care programs, and the like. The result is that too many seniors in rural areas who become frail and ill find that their only option is to enter a nursing home.

Emerging Lifestyle Trends and Innovative Programs

Many factors complicate the lives of older adults. Perhaps most important is the great recession that began in 2007. It decimated savings and stock holdings and undermined the value of homes. The risk of poverty for older adults greatly increased, especially for women, who are more than twice as likely to be poor as older men.

Another major issue confronting retirees is the high cost of health care. Even with Medicare, a recent study estimates that a 65-year-old couple retiring in 2013 would need $220,000 to cover future medical expenses. Moreover, the cost of long-term nursing home care is prohibitive for middle class people, who have too many assets to qualify for Medicaid but nowhere near enough money to finance living in a nursing home.

Additionally, due to the falling birth rate, fewer informal family caregivers are available to assist older adults today. Nearly a quarter of baby boomers have never had children, and a third of adults 45–65 have never married, so there is no spouse to rely on.

Baby boomers have a history of creating social change to address social problems, however, and they continue to do so. Starting about 15 years ago, groups of friends and neighbors began getting together to discuss new challenges they were facing, such as caring for elderly parents and meeting increasing care needs of their own. Informal support groups gradually developed into organized self-help networks in which neighbor helped neighbor, and neighbor even began living with neighbor. The Golden Girls Homes in Minneapolis is an example. This organization coordinates house sharing and holds regular meetings to help with logistics. Another example is the Village to Village network, which has been the catalyst for 110 self-help villages around the country with another 120 in development. The first was Beacon Hill Village in Boston, established in 2002.

> Watch this news clip about the Golden Girls Network. What are the primary benefits of this network identified by users?
> https://www.youtube.com/watch?v=uCP-r5iMfB4

While most older adults hope to "age in place," this desire may not be possible because their homes are ill-equipped to meet special needs. Older homes may have steep stairways, narrow doorways that do not allow wheelchairs, bathrooms that are not equipped for people with disabilities, etc. Most older adults do not have the means to finance necessary modifications. Cooperative self-help organizations, however, provide volunteers with multiple skills who not only enable older people to remain in their own homes but also to do so in a community context, which helps prevent loneliness.

Many projects known as "co-housing" are developing independently around the nation: Housing units intentionally designed by groups of people that provide private bedrooms with baths but shared kitchen and living room facilities. These ventures are financed through contributions from each member. Shared living arrangements such as these represent a growing movement to create new ways for people to grow old while supporting one another. Unlike most social movements, which tend to be started by young people, members of these groups began working together in their 60s and 70s. About two-thirds are women (Hager, 2015; Blanchard, 2014; "The National Movement," 2009).

An International Perspective: The Netherlands

Provisions for older adults in the United States today could clearly be improved, and research regarding services provided by other nations may provide new ideas. The AARP surveyed 16 industrialized nations (including the United States), weighing 17 criteria; that survey concluded that the country providing the best care for its older citizens in the early years of the twenty-first century was The Netherlands (Edwards, 2004).

International rankings have changed, however, according to The Global Age Watch Index 2015, which assessed 96 countries based on four domains: income security, health, capability (including employment and educational status), and an enabling environment (one promoting civic freedoms and access to public transportation). By this report, Norway came in first in terms of being the best country for older adults to live in; the Netherlands fell to sixth, and the US came in 9th (Miller, 2015).

The change in ranking for the Netherlands reflects the fact that since the 1980s, the country has been transitioning from a welfare state to one based more on individual responsibility and achievement primarily to cut costs for the government. In 2007, the Social Support Act called for increased local autonomy and responsibility by nongovernmental bodies (Smits et al., 2013).

Still, Dutch citizens remain largely protected from poverty, and social policy in The Netherlands is designed specifically to prevent social exclusion of older persons. The central government provides a policy framework that specifies the various responsibilities of finance agencies and service providers. Older people are encouraged to make their own decisions regarding the services they need. "Custom-made care," or care designed to meet the needs of each unique individual, is a central concept in The Netherlands' social policy (Ex, Gorter, & Janssen, 2004; Smits et al., 2013).

All older adults in The Netherlands receive a full old-age pension at age 65 whether or not they have worked outside the home (approximately $1,069 for a single person in 2013, $741 per person for couples, married or not), but they must have lived in the country for at least 50 years between the ages of 15 and 64. Every older adult also receives a "holiday allowance" in May, in time for a spring celebration. Seven days' free travel are provided on the nation's efficient railway system, and museums, movies, concerts, and holiday motels offer discounts. Government health insurance covers not only medical care, including prescription drugs with tiny co-payments, but also hospital care and coverage for nursing home care if needed, both short and long term (Smits et al., 2013; "State of Affairs of Social Security," 2014).

The Dutch pension system is built upon three pillars: the universal flat-rate state pension (described above), supplementary occupational pensions covering 95 percent of all employees (under pressure since the great recession), and voluntary private pensions purchased through insurance policies with a tax incentive from the government. Thus, almost all native-born older citizens of the Netherlands are financially secure; most own their own homes mortgage-free. The poverty rate of older adults in the Netherlands is the lowest in the world according to a recent study, only 1.7 percent. Other studies have indicated higher percentages, but there is no doubt that most Dutch elderly enjoy a secure living. Many of the elderly who *are* poor are non-Western immigrants, people who have not lived in the Netherlands long enough to qualify for benefits (Smits et al., 2013; "Elderly Poverty," 2016).

Comprehensive services can be provided to most older adults in The Netherlands because the government controls almost all health care costs (drugs, physicians' services, hospital care, etc.). Taxes are higher than in the United States, but public attitudes support this trade-off. In general, younger people support generous treatment of older adults because older people are viewed as having earned assistance; they also recognize that the time will come when they themselves will need help (Edwards, 2004).

Interestingly enough, The Netherlands, like the U.S. state of Oregon (and five other states), allows older people who are in extreme pain to request medication from their physicians to enable a peaceful death by choice. The Netherlands' law is broader than Oregon's in that the excruciating pain justifying such a request may be psychological, not just physical. Two independent physicians, one a psychiatrist, must review and accept the request in order for it to be carried out. Assisted death or euthanasia has been the subject of ongoing debate in The Netherlands for the past 30 years and may only take place in the condition of voluntary request (Mackelprang & Mackelprang, 2005; Smits et al., 2013).

? Assess your understanding of social policy relating to older adults, past to present, by taking this brief quiz.

END OF LIFE ISSUES: CARE NEEDS, RELIGION, AND SPIRITUALITY

Coming to Terms with Long-Term Care

We usually do whatever we can, both personally and collectively as a society, to live longer lives—and we are succeeding. That is the good news. Ironically, however, it is also bad news in some ways. Longer lives present new problems. Long-term care is a major one. It requires considerable financial outlay for which most of us are unprepared and raises important issues regarding quality of life.

A few older adults have purchased private long-term care insurance to assist with nursing home care should they require it. Medicare is not a serious resource because it covers only short periods of skilled nursing home care after a hospital stay. Most elderly people cannot afford to pay, so a majority receive help from Medicaid—but to qualify for Medicaid, they must spend virtually all of their savings first; it is not uncommon for an older couple to have to divorce in order for the ill spouse to qualify for Medicaid so that the healthy spouse is not impoverished (Fischer, 2010).

Medicaid payments to nursing homes are lower than the fees charged to private clients, and they do not usually cover the full cost of care. Most nursing homes, therefore, accept private-paying clients first. When private-paying clients' money runs out, they turn to Medicaid. Most nursing homes will allow these people to stay, but had they originally applied as Medicaid clients, their chances of admission would have been minimal. Frail older adults who have experienced lifelong poverty find nursing home care very difficult to obtain. Abbie Heinrich of our chapter's case study was lucky in a way—she was admitted to Oak Haven many years ago when Medicaid payments still met the true cost of care.

When an older adult needs round-the-clock care, care at home can be more costly than nursing home living. Hence, many seniors who desperately want to avoid the nursing home end up there anyway.

Death and Dying

Older adulthood involves many life changes, as noted previously. The possibility of death begins to feel very real. By this time, the older person has lost members of his or her family, and probably friends. Coping with such loss often awakens spiritual concerns—not only for the older adult but for the social worker. Questions may arise such as "Does life have meaning?" "Does *my* life have meaning?" "Will death be the end?" "What, if anything, comes next?" Even if clients do not ask these questions aloud, both they and their social workers may wonder.

Spirituality and Religion

Spirituality and religion are important to older adults since they address questions such as those posed above. Until recently, social workers have tended to avoid discussions of these issues, referring them instead to the clergy. It is, of course, important to involve clergy where available. Still, many clients do not belong to a church and feel embarrassed about asking to see a clergyperson who is unknown. The social worker, on the other hand, may be a person with whom they already feel comfortable, so workers are encouraged to discuss spiritual issues if requested.

Of concern, of course, is that social workers and clients may have very different religious orientations. **Religion** involves a formal belief system as taught by a particular church or theological tradition, whereas **spirituality** refers to a process involving a universal search for meaning. It is important for social workers not to impose religious beliefs on clients, but regardless of a social worker's personal religious orientation, it is entirely possible to assist clients—even of very different traditions—to cope with spiritual issues. Encouraging clients to reminisce about their lives can help them work through meaning-related questions. Allowing clients to talk about their beliefs, whatever they may be, can help them clarify these beliefs in ways that may comfort them. Social workers themselves may find it helpful to clarify their own religious and/or spiritual beliefs. A spiritual grounding can help a worker cope with the fact that clients do die.

Near Death Experiences

There is an interesting literature on near-death experiences (NDEs), which seem to help reduce the fear of dying for both social worker and client. The near-death experience, in which all vital signs have ceased but the person is later revived, was first studied by sociologist Raymond Moody (1976). The phenomenon has been investigated since by many others. According to Dr. Dean Radin (2006), author and lead scientist at the Institute of Noetic Sciences in California, NDE's have been found to involve several distinctive experiences. These include (a) floating above one's body, (b) entering and moving along a tunnel, (c) experiencing an intense and beautiful light, (d) encountering deceased loved ones, and (e) sometimes having to decide whether to return to one's body. People who return to the body often feel regret because the out-of-body state felt exceedingly blissful (pp. 40–41).

Radin reports that in three studies of 496 patients with cardiac arrest (Dutch, British, and American), between 11 and 18 percent of patients had an NDE. Profound, positive personality changes were present in these people at follow-up studies two and eight years later.

Stephan Schwartz makes the intriguing observation that consciousness as an entity in itself is being studied today in many laboratories around the world; results indicate that consciousness may be "nonlocal," or not confined to the brain. Schwartz reports that ongoing double-blind and triple-blind research is producing evidence that consciousness is "nonlocal" with statistical odds against chance of one in a billion. If consciousness is not confined to the brain during life, Schwarts asks, what could this mean regarding its possible survival beyond physical death of the body (Schwartz, 2016)?

Patients who have registered clinically brain dead on electronic monitors have reported extensive, detailed, coherent near-death experiences. How can a dead brain experience anything at all? It seems as if consciousness may involve more than the brain. Arguments to this effect are ongoing and the studies that they instigate are intriguing; they suggest that the current materialistic paradigm of western science may be too limited and that life on this earth may not be all there is.

End of Life Decisions

End of life decisions can be particularly challenging. Some clients, usually when suffering extreme pain, ask for assistance in ending their lives (euthanasia, or physician-assisted suicide). How is a social worker to respond? Religion is particularly important here because many religions, at least as practiced today, prohibit euthanasia even under circumstances of extreme pain. However, six American states permit it. The first was Oregon in 1994. Oregon permits people who have a life expectancy of six months or less and who are suffering extreme physical pain to ask their doctors for medication to end their lives. Oregon's Death with Dignity Act was upheld by the U.S. Supreme Court in the *Gonzales v. Oregon* case (Stoesen, 2006). In 2008 the state of Washington passed a law similar to Oregon's. Euthanasia was accepted by the Montana Supreme Court in the *Baxter v. Montana* case in 2009; the court's 5-4 decision indicates how contentious this issue was (and still is). In 2013, Vermont passed a law similar to Oregon's, followed by California in 2015 and Colorado in 2016. All of these laws require residency in the respective state, two oral requests for assistance, and one written request.

The NASW does not take a formal position with respect to euthanasia, but affirms the principle that patients have the right to make their own health care decisions.

Hospice Services, Palliative Care, and Complementary Therapies

Hospice services are designed to assist people to cope with the dying process in a more humane and personal way than can be provided in traditional hospitals. While it is important for social workers to help their clients identify all options available to them, advocacy regarding pain management is especially important. People in terminal situations who are not in pain are much more likely to choose to live as long as possible.

The catalyst for the hospice movement in the United States was Dr. Elizabeth Kubler-Ross, who published her famous book, *On Death and Dying*, in 1969. In it she lamented the mechanized treatments provided by traditional hospitals and advocated for care of the whole person, including psychological and spiritual needs. The first hospice in the United States was opened in 1974 (Seeber, 1995). Today hospices exist in all 50 states.

Hospice services include medical care and psychological and spiritual counseling for patient and family, and bereavement services for the family after the patient has died. Pain management is a primary concern. Patients can be accepted by hospice programs when life expectancy is six months or less, and comfort rather than cure is the goal. Hospice care may be offered in one's own home or in homelike residential facilities; many services are covered under Medicare.

Palliative care is another choice for older adults. Its focus is on pain management and symptom control. While hospice programs are designed specifically for persons who are terminally ill, palliative care is designed to help anyone with a serious illness. Palliative care programs may be offered in hospitals, outpatient clinics, long-term care facilities, hospices, or at home. Curative treatments may continue under palliative care, and some treatments may be covered by insurance ("Get Palliative Care," 2012).

Social Work with Older Adults: A Growing Future

Older adults in this country and around the world are growing in number and proportion every day. Even with the predictable waxing and waning of public financing for social services for older persons, reflecting shifts in the values of the politicians in power and the people who elect them, older adults are developing growing political sophistication.

> **Box 10.9 Employment of Social Workers with Older Adults**
>
> Employment of social workers is expected to increase by 12 percent during the 2014–2024 decade, faster than the average for all occupations, and the employment of social workers in health care is projected to grow 19 percent, much faster than the average for all occupations. The reason is that the growing population of older adults will need assistance adjusting to new lifestyles, medical treatments, and medications.
>
> Based on the Bureau of Labor Statistics, U.S. Department of Labor, *Occupational Outlook Handbook, 2016–17 Edition*. Retrieved from http://www.bls.gov/ooh/community-and-social-service/social-workers.htm.

As a group, they are making themselves heard at all levels of government. Their needs are many. Thus, employment for social workers in the field of aging, despite the election of a conservative president and Congress in 2016, will probably continue to grow into the foreseeable future (see Box 10.9).

Social workers who work with older adults encounter a varied and challenging client population. These are people who have led full lives and have developed the wisdom and perspective that come with many years on this planet. Older people are fascinating, enriching clients who can enlighten social workers as well as command their skills.

On the other hand, probably no other field of social work requires so much soul-searching on the part of the practitioner. Older adults are manifestly nearing the end of their journey on earth, and this certainty makes many thoughtful workers ponder the "meaning of it all."

Assess your understanding of end-of-life issues for older adults by taking this brief quiz.

SUMMARY

- The brief history of social work with older adults is described, along with a discussion of the importance of generalist practice utilizing an empowerment approaches.
- Major characteristics of older adults today are identified and described: geographical distribution, marital status, education, employment, economic status, housing, mental and physical health, Alzheimer's and related dementias, environmental hazards, and ethnicity. The risk of poverty increases with age and is especially serious for members of ethnic minority groups and women. Those with lower incomes suffer the greatest problems in terms of health and adequate housing.
- Major issues concerning older adults and their families are discussed. Most families are active in helping their older members cope with special needs. Because people are living longer today, more families are contributing to the care of older relatives than ever before, and for many more years. Middle-aged children, especially middle-aged women, may find themselves part of the "sandwich generation," people who have children to care for in addition to elderly relatives.

Older adults themselves often serve as caregivers for grandchildren whose parents can no longer cope and for spouses, friends, and neighbors. Social workers can help families deal with the many stresses involved in intergenerational care.
- Social policies relating to older adults, past and present, are described, beginning with the first pension plan, developed in Germany. In the United States, pension plans and federal entitlement programs such as Social Security, Supplemental Security Income, housing assistance, health insurance, and food stamps help older adults meet their financial and material needs. Other limited services such as information and referral, congregate meal programs, low-cost homemaker aids, and protective services are provided under the Older Americans Act and the Social Services Block Grant. However, need for services outstrips supply, and a large burden of care today falls upon families, creating intergenerational stress. A continuum of care helps older adults maintain independence for as long as possible. Social policies assisting older adults in the Netherlands are offered in comparison to those in the United States.
- Major end-of-life issues for older adults are identified. Given increasing longevity, the need for attention to long-term care has heightened in importance, not only for older adults but for their families and society as a whole. Long-term care in nursing homes is prohibitively expensive. Hospice and palliative care programs have grown due to growing need for pain and symptom relief. Spiritual needs of older adults present a growing challenge, a responsibility no longer assigned to clergy alone. Social workers themselves may find themselves spiritually challenged as they work closely with clients who are facing a final transition.

> Recall what you learned from this chapter by completing the Chapter Review.

11

Social Work in the Criminal Justice System

LEARNING OUTCOMES

- Trace the history of the criminal justice system in the United States.
- Describe the components that comprise the criminal justice system.
- Explain how the profession of social work is practiced within the criminal justice field of practice.
- Discuss the social, economic, and environmental justice issues that exist in the criminal justice system in the United States.

CHAPTER OUTLINE

CASE STUDY: Alan Martin's Social Work Identity Crisis 336

History of the Criminal Justice System 339
- European Historical Roots of Criminal Justice Systems 339
- History of Criminal Justice Systems in the United States 340
- Social Work Emerges: Progressive Contributions of Jane Addams and Hull House Staff 340

Components of the Criminal Justice System 341
- Enforcement 342
- Courts 344
- Correctional System 345
- Juvenile Justice System 351

Social Work Practice in the Criminal Justice System

CASE STUDY: Alan Martin's Social Work Identity Crisis

Alan Martin slumped in his chair and sighed. Then he picked up the file again. Another new case had just been added to his already overloaded caseload. You're letting yourself burn out, he thought. Then, reminding himself that he was just tired but he could go home soon, he picked up the telephone and dialed the number he had found in Brian Cook's folder. He talked briefly with Brian's mother, Laura Cook, scheduling an office appointment with Brian for Friday. The file showed that Brian had been released on parole from the state juvenile corrections center just 5 days ago. He had served 2 years of a 5-year sentence for selling illicit drugs. He had apparently been a model prisoner.

The telephone rang, and Alan reached for his notepad—an emergency; the police had just arrested another of his clients, a 13-year-old, for selling cocaine at the bus stop across the street from a school. There had been a scuffle; weapons were involved. One officer and the 13-year-old were badly injured and being transported to the hospital by ambulance. A picture of 13-year-old Ramon flashed through his mind: a bright, defiant, angry kid whose father died 6 months ago. Without hesitation, Alan replied to the voice on the phone: "I'll be at the hospital in 10 minutes." It was very late when Alan finally got home that night.

Alan Martin was an experienced BSW social worker who had worked in the criminal justice field for 6 years now, initially in adult probation and parole and, for the past 6 months, in Youth Correctional Services. Alan was respected by his colleagues, police, and judges. Among his clients, he was viewed as tough, demanding, and fair. Once actively involved with the National Association of Social Workers (NASW) and careful to sustain continued professional learning activities, Alan had gradually drifted away from identification with his profession and, in fact, had forgotten to renew his NASW professional membership. Alan felt vaguely unsettled with his life and his work.

On Friday, minutes before Brian Cook's scheduled appointment, Alan pulled out his file. Brian's 14-year-old face stared back from the photo taken at the time of his arrest 2 years ago. This image was quite a contrast to the older-looking, broad-shouldered, passive but mistrustful person he had met at the correctional facility 2 weeks ago. Kids who weren't criminals before they arrived at that place were quite likely to be so by the time they were released, Alan thought as he snapped the file closed and went out to get Brian from the drab, vaguely filthy waiting room.

CHAPTER OUTLINE *(Continued)*

Social, Economic, and Environmental Justice   358
   Environmental Perspective: Communities at Risk   359
   Environmental Perspective: Community Strength, Restoration, Spirituality, and Resilience   359
   Global Context   360
   Promoting Human Rights and Social Justice   362
   The Death Penalty   365
   Reforming Juvenile and Adult Criminal Justice Systems   367

Summary   372

Their first session in Alan's office included a review of the parole contract. Brian's cool, almost sullen expression was annoying. Alan found himself talking loudly, lecturing Brian about the consequences of failure to abide by the terms of the contract. He told Brian about the procedure for providing a urinalysis to check for drugs each time he came in. He was angered by Brian's comment: "So, you don't trust me. I told you I don't do drugs."

"No, I don't trust you," he responded, using the very words he didn't like but often heard other parole officers use. Further annoyed with himself for having said this, Alan changed the subject to school. Brian said that he had enrolled in and started attending classes this week but hated the school. Alan ignored this, instead warning Brian about associating with anyone related to his conviction, especially Shari, the girl for whom he had purchased drugs.

After Brian left the office, Alan returned the telephone call that had come in from Ramon's mother. She was at the hospital; Ramon was not doing well, but she couldn't understand the doctor's explanation about what was happening to him. Alan decided to stop by the hospital during his lunch break. The expression of the policeman guarding the room told Alan that all was not well. One look at Ramon's face, contorted with pain and discolored by jaundice, confirmed that Ramon was in serious condition. Alan beckoned Ramon's mother to follow him. Tearfully, she told him that in her heart she did not think that Ramon was going to live. She didn't know what was wrong; she was terrified. Alan searched frantically for a nurse, finally finding one who would talk with them. The nurse was dignified but cold. Ramon had developed an infection related to the gunshot wound in his abdomen. He was not responding to antibiotics. His lab reports this morning were very bad. She certainly didn't know why these teenage criminals thought they could get away with fooling around with guns. As she turned to leave, Alan heard her say, "Sometimes they have to pay the price." Struck to the core by her remark and instantly, painfully aware of the negative attitudes he had been developing, he turned to Ramon's mother, hugging her to defend her from the added pain of the nurse's remark. He took her to a quiet corner, explained what the nurse had said about the seriousness of the infection, and sat with her for a time while she cried. Alan left when Mrs. Perez's sister arrived. That night Ramon died.

Thoughts about Ramon's tragic death and the judgmental attitude of the nurse troubled Alan for weeks. Attending Ramon's funeral service was very difficult, but it refreshed him spiritually and strengthened his determination to fight for real justice, a justice built on dignity and respect for people, not on retribution and various prejudices. Alan began to make time at night to do a bit of reading—some light short stories that were delightful and refreshing and some professional articles from social work journals. Re-reading the NASW Code of Ethics renewed Alan's awareness that as a professional person he was responsible for the quality of his own practice. In his work with his clients, Alan now consciously struggled to become more self-aware and more attuned to the reality of their lives.

On the day that Brian Cook was scheduled to see him again, Alan received a report from the school indicating that Brian was not attending classes. This was a violation of his parole contract, and it also raised questions about what he was doing with his time. Was he back into the drug scene again? Alan confronted Brian with all of this. To his annoyance, Brian insisted that he was attending school. Brian added: "I know you won't believe me about this. You don't believe anything I say." Alan showed him the report, but Brian insisted that he was attending school even though he hated it. Then, despite the report, Alan decided to suspend his disbelief until he and Brian could check out the report together. Brian was quite surprised when Alan proposed this. Together they drove to the school in Alan's car.

On the drive, Alan encouraged Brian to talk about his classes. By the time they reached the school, it seemed more and more likely that Brian really had attended at least some of his classes. They were fortunate in being able to meet briefly with two of Brian's teachers, who affirmed that Brian had indeed been in class. Both gave Brian suggestions about how to improve his work. When Alan presented their case to the school attendance clerk, she reviewed her records and found that a mistake had been made.

Back in the car, Brian smiled for the first time. He said, "This time truth was on my side." Alan agreed. Suddenly Brian's expression changed. He said, "I can understand better now about truth. … I was lied to and I actually did lie to you, too." He explained that Shari had promised him when he was convicted that she would be true to him while he was away. He counted on that. Since getting out he had been trying to contact her, but she wasn't returning his phone calls. Today he found out that she was pregnant and due to have a baby shortly. So he had been lied to. And he had lied to Alan, too, when he agreed not to contact Shari. When Brian looked up at Alan, there was pain in his eyes. It was quiet in the car for several minutes; Alan let the silence hang in the air unbroken, feeling Brian's pain. Then he said, "OK, Brian let's start over now … and we'll begin by trusting each other."

Engagement

Dimension of Competency: *Cognitive and Affective Reactions* Social workers understand how their personal experiences and affective reactions may impact their ability to effectively engage with clients.

Critical Thinking Question: How was Alan Martin able to use painful, difficult circumstances in his clients' lives to reconnect with his social work professional values and skills and to effectively engage with Brian?

In this chapter's case study, Alan Martin could be said to be "burning out" in his job. His identity with the social work profession and its values and ethics were slipping away. His ability to engage with Brian was compromised; he did not initially trust Brian. Yet the case study concluded with the social worker and his client totally and constructively redefining their working relationship. And Alan Martin reestablished his identity with the social work profession.

Following the case study, this chapter introduces the history of criminal justice to help us understand how the criminal justice system evolved into such a challenging yet rewarding system for social workers to work in. We will then consider the multiple components that comprise the criminal justice system, all of which provide opportunities for social work employment. Next, social work practice in several different components of the system will be described. We will conclude the chapter by looking at the potentially exciting and very controversial social and environmental justice challenges emerging in social welfare policy related to criminal justice.

HISTORY OF THE CRIMINAL JUSTICE SYSTEM

European Historical Roots of Criminal Justice Systems

The history of criminal justice is one that has slowly evolved out of a distant past when punishment for misdeeds was instantaneous and severe. Archaeological findings have provided evidence of the use of beatings and slavery for those who violated societal norms in ancient times. In the enlightened period of Greek civilization, around 400 B.C., new ways of looking at criminal behavior emerged. Hippocrates insisted that natural causes, rooted in the environment and in the family, shaped behavior more significantly than did evil spirits.

Evidently such enlightenment failed to continue, for by the Middle Ages in Europe severe punishments were being used: branding, cutting out an offender's tongue, public hanging, beheading, and burning at the stake. In the 1600s, the colonists brought many of these punishments to America. Following the Revolutionary War in America, the Pennsylvania Quakers became alarmed about the harshness of punishments being used. They believed that offenders could be reformed if their environment was separated from that of persons who were influencing them and exposing them to criminal practices. They thought that this separation would encourage them to become penitent and change their behaviors; this was the origin of the term *penitentiary* and it was this thinking that led to the birth of the present prison system.

In France, the Napoleonic Code of 1807 created a new and more humane approach to Western society's thinking about criminal justice for children. The Napoleonic Code established a minimum age at which children could be charged and punished for offenses. Thus was born the principle of differentiating juvenile from adult crime. Separate correctional facilities for children—facilities then known as refuges—began to be provided in the United States in the early 1820s. These privately funded, supposedly charitable organizations unfortunately grew into large institutions characterized by severe discipline.

During the 1800s, England began the practice of transporting excessive numbers of convicts to other lands. It served the purpose of excluding the lawbreakers from the law-abiding community. Prisoners were taken by boat to Australia, for example, and left there. They were no longer a significant financial burden and the prisoners no longer posed a threat to the home country. Interestingly, these were some of the first immigrants to Australia and they ultimately formed well-functioning civil governments in their new land. In the mid-1800s, Captain Alexander Maconochie, who was responsible for the British penal colony on Norfolk Island in the South Pacific, devised and promoted a concept of conditional release for prisoners, which was the first known parole system.

History of Criminal Justice Systems in the United States

Although the United States did not follow England's practice of transporting convicts to other locations, the early colonists brought European systems of harsh punishment and imprisonment to this country. John Augustus, a Boston shoemaker, is credited with the establishment of probation. In 1841, Augustus requested permission of the courts to serve as surety—to accept personal responsibility and provide supervision—for a man charged with drunkenness. That first successful experience led Augustus to continue his work with other offenders. In 1869, the Commonwealth of Massachusetts created the first formal position for probation work; the agent was required to appear at criminal trials of juveniles, to locate suitable homes for them, and to supervise them. In 1878, Boston began to provide probationary supervision for adult offenders.

At about the same time, the system of parole evolved. The first correctional system in the United States to experiment with the concept was the Elmira Reformatory in New York State in 1877. The use of parole soon became an accepted principle in corrections in the United States.

By the early 1900s, juvenile courts began to be established across the United States. A special concern of juvenile courts was provision of competent, professional service for children. These courts looked to the new profession of social work for staff to assist juvenile court judges. In contrast, the adult probation and parole agents of the time represented a variety of disciplines but tended to use sheriffs and people with police experience. Gradually, this area too was professionalized, but even today probation and parole agents come from a variety of disciplines with quite different philosophical approaches to criminal justice.

Social Work Emerges: Progressive Contributions of Jane Addams and Hull House Staff

Jane Addams of Hull House and Edith Abbott, dean of the School of Social Service Administration at the University of Chicago, provided much of the leadership, teaching, and research in correctional social work in its early days. Abbott, for example, studied crime and incarceration of women during the Civil War and World War I. Florence Kelley, another of the Hull House residents, was an attorney who advanced the social work profession through the creation of the U.S. Children's Bureau and by developing training programs for the Children's Bureau staff. She also worked to develop child labor laws (Edwards, 1991, as cited in Barker & Branson, 2000). The social work profession, in its infancy, was also assisted by another attorney, Sophonisba Breckinridge, who helped bring training of social workers into universities and, in fact, became the dean of one of the earliest schools of social work, the University of Chicago's School of Social Service Administration (Quam, 1995, as cited in Barker & Branson, 2000). The early schools of social work taught courses on law and social work, and, indeed, much of early social work practice was within courts, child welfare agencies that involved court investigations, and probation and parole systems.

Social casework was introduced within the U.S. Bureau of Prisons in the 1930s. By that time, society had begun to accept Freudian concepts of causation of behavior. Increasingly, counseling for prisoners incorporated some of this theory. The federal prisons were fraught with riots resulting from overcrowding, understaffing, and overall poor prison conditions. Reform efforts introduced social casework as part of a rehabilitation effort. Kenneth Pray (1945), a community organizer and educator, helped to clarify the role of social casework in the prisons with his writings in the 1940s.

Police social work programs grew out of demonstration projects initially funded by the federal government's Law Enforcement Assistance Administration in the 1970s. Harvey Treger, of the Jane Addams School of Social Work at the University of Illinois, was probably the most significant figure in the development of this field. Victim/witness programs were also initially created through governmental funding.

Innovations that occurred in probation and parole in more recent years include the use of home confinement, electronic monitoring, intensive supervision as a substitute for incarceration, and restitution. Victim/witness programs, police social work, alternatives to incarceration, and forensic social work have also continued to evolve. All of these programs brought social workers in the corrections field opportunities for new approaches to practice. The expansion of prison privatization resulted in custodial care with minimal attention to prisoner rehabilitation. Many of the private prison facilities were located in southern states but were frequently used to house prisoners from northern states. The already frail linkages between prisoners and their families became even more tenuous.

Today social workers and social work students are renewing their interest in police social work, probation and parole, victim/witness assistance programs, domestic violence services within district attorney's offices, and alternative-to-incarceration and prevention programs. Within this context, **forensic social work** is developing and evolving. Forensic social work is viewed by many as a highly specialized area of practice related to the law, while for others forensic social work encompasses practice across broad areas including all of criminal justice as well as areas of child welfare and mental health (Ashford, 2009). The broader definition acknowledges BSWs as well as MSWs as engaged in forensic practice (van Wormer, Roberts, Springer, & Brownell, 2008). Forensic social workers utilize expertise in legal matters related to child welfare, juvenile offenses, divorce issues such as custody determination, and various areas of dispute negotiation. Forensic social work will be further described later in this chapter.

> Assess your understanding of the history of the criminal justice system in the United States by taking this brief quiz.

COMPONENTS OF THE CRIMINAL JUSTICE SYSTEM

Alan Martin, the social worker in this chapter's case study, was experienced in the adult as well as juvenile corrections systems. In his practice, Alan worked with all of the subsystems of the criminal justice system. Sometimes referred to as the three Cs (cops, courts, and corrections), the criminal justice system in the United States grew out of the system brought to this country by colonists from England. Over time, it developed into a complex and somewhat fragmented system, with separate subunits that did not always interact effectively. It acquired a strange and somewhat inconsistent combination of goals: to punish, to deter crime, to rehabilitate, and to remove criminals from society.

Specific laws and regulations pertain to each of the three criminal justice system areas. Social workers will need to learn the laws and regulations that guide the area of the criminal justice system in which they work. A police social worker, for example, will develop an understanding of arrest procedures, statutory rape laws, and laws pertaining to child and spouse abuse. A social worker serving as a parole agent, such as Alan Martin in the case study, will become familiar with the administrative law that defines the responsibilities of probation and parole agents, with parole contracts and with revocation procedures.

Two terms that will be used in the remainder of this chapter and that should be understood by all informed citizens, need further definition: *misdemeanor* and *felony*. A **misdemeanor** is a relatively minor offense but certainly more serious than a misdeed; it is punishable by fines, probation, or a relatively brief jail or prison sentence unless taken to extreme or done repeatedly. A **felony** is a serious crime. Murder, rape, and armed burglary are felonies, while defacing public property is a misdemeanor. Assault could be a misdemeanor, while aggravated assault (involving deadly force or intent to rob, kill, or rape) would be considered a felony. Under federal law and also in many states, the consequence of a felony is a prison sentence of one or more years; the most extreme penalty for a felony is the death penalty. Professional people, such as social workers, may be prohibited from being licensed or certified to practice in their state if they have a criminal record.

Two additional terms, *probation* and *parole,* were encountered in the Alan Martin case study, and these terms will be used frequently in this chapter. It is important to understand the differences between the two. **Probation** is a sentence, following conviction for a crime, in which the offender is ordered to undergo supervision for a prescribed period of time instead of serving that time in prison. Brief sentencing to jail may precede release under probation, but the majority of the sentence may be served in the community if the terms of the probation contract are met. A court-designated probation officer, who may be a social worker, provides the community supervision. In **parole**, a person has served a portion of his or her sentence in prison and then receives an early release to complete the sentence in the community under supervision. In probation, the prison sentence is said to be suspended in that the person does not normally go to prison unless revoked (sent to prison) because of behavior that violates the probation contract. Persons on parole, too, can be returned to prison for the remainder of the sentence.

Let us now examine the three major components of the criminal justice system in the United States and the interesting ways in which social work as a profession has found a niche in each of these areas.

Law Enforcement

When we speak of **law enforcement**, we are essentially referring to the police. The police, as law enforcement officers, comprise the first of the three areas of the criminal justice system. What exactly is the role of the police? It is much broader than most citizens realize.

Police are responsible for responding to citizens' complaints and for questioning and apprehending persons. Before charging a person with a crime, however, police have considerable decision-making responsibility. Police decide whether a charge is warranted or another alternative might be considered. Current law determines the officer's decision. Prevailing public sentiment or the political climate might also be influential and might, in part, account for the tougher sentencing of youths in recent years. Often it is a matter of chance, visibility (as in a high-crime neighborhood that is under greater scrutiny than other areas), or past behavior that determines whether a violation of the law even results in contact with the police. Shopkeepers, school authorities, and neighbors may be more prone to call the police in some parts of the city or community than in others.

In addition to responding to criminal complaints, police are also responsible for keeping the peace. In this role, they encounter families in crisis, domestic violence, suicidal behavior, and substance abuse. One of the frustrations of police officers is that they receive little recognition by the community or even by the police system itself for the human services they routinely provide.

Police social work is the practice of social work within police departments, within courthouses, or in jails. Police social work is still a relatively underdeveloped area of social work practice, but it appears to be an expanding area of the profession. Police and social workers share a common concern about personal and family crisis situations. A considerable portion of police calls are of a social service nature because people are most likely to call the police when they don't know where else to turn for help. In communities where police social workers are available, dispositions of cases frequently result in redirection from the criminal justice to the social service system.

When police departments first employed social workers, they were assigned to youth services. Their tasks included resolution of parent–child conflicts; referral of children to child guidance or child psychiatric clinics; assessment of child abuse, neglect, and abandonment situations; and a variety of crisis roles. Police social workers have proven their value in domestic dispute situations. Because these are some of the most dangerous cases for police, police social workers' ability to ease the tension in such situations, as well as to assess and intervene, has impressed police departments.

Cases handled by police social workers may include traffic accidents and fatalities, child abuse, suicide, alcohol and substance abuse, mental health emergencies, and family disputes. Social workers provide crisis intervention, brief individual or family counseling, referrals, victim assistance and sexual assault intervention, as well as community crime prevention efforts. The same problem-solving process used in other areas of generalist social work practice applies to police social work. Skill in engaging clients and quickly forming effective, empathic, respectful working relationships is an essential asset in volatile situations. Psychosocial assessment requires collecting and organizing information, but in police work, risk factors must be especially carefully determined. This is true in domestic disputes and child abuse, and even lethality potential must be considered in cases involving potential suicide or homicide. Intervention often involves negotiation, mediation, and advocacy, and it is generally handled collaboratively with police officers. As an intervention concludes, police social workers often engage the clients, police personnel, or other community representatives in evaluating the results of the intervention effort. Follow-up contacts may be considered at this time, too (Knox & Roberts, 2009).

Police social workers are obviously not confined to desks in police departments. In addition to home visits and crime scene crisis work, they are increasingly involved in crime prevention work in the community. Often, a team consisting of a social worker and a police officer seeks to prevent crime through educational programs provided to youth groups, in the schools, or to civic associations. Today, suburban police systems are in the forefront of community organization work with police personnel participating in and often leading community action efforts related to crime prevention, the development of youth services, drug courts, and even the reform of mental commitment laws. Their professional education makes police social workers especially well suited for such responsibilities.

The Courts

Courts exist at the federal, state, and local levels, and they range from municipal courts to the highest court in the land, the U.S. Supreme Court. Courts have two primary functions: civil and criminal. Civil functions deal with the rights of private citizens and may result in fines or monetary damages. Criminal functions involve determination of guilt or innocence; punishment such as a prison sentence may result. In the criminal court system, a case begins with an arrest.

Some persons may have charges against them dropped and, therefore, they discontinue their involvement in the criminal justice system. In fact, at each step along the way—from the point of police questioning through arrest, charging, and sentencing—a certain percentage of persons exit the system. Only a fraction of those initially detained for questioning are actually found guilty and incarcerated. In this "criminal justice funnel," the top of the funnel represents all the crimes that have been committed. The people who exit the system along the way are found in the slanting sides of the funnel. At the bottom of the funnel are those persons actually prosecuted and sent to prison—approximately three percent. As research studies described later in this chapter suggest, racial biases may be among the factors that influence decisions at each step from questioning through incarceration.

Social workers are increasingly found in the courts of the United States, where they serve in several interesting ways. One role for social workers is work with and on behalf of victims of crime. Social workers were among the pioneers of victim/witness programs. These programs, often housed in the local district attorney's office, assist people who are intimidated by the legal process. Programs to help battered women through the court system were among the first to emerge. Today social workers assist victims of domestic abuse to obtain restraining or harassment no-contact orders, and they serve as client advocates in the courts. Persons who are injured in crimes are also provided services that emphasize compassion, affirmation, and emotional support.

Testifying in court is a responsibility for social workers in child and family services; across all areas of criminal justice and forensic social work, this is a primary area of expertise. NASW has a variety of resources that help to prepare social workers, beginning with how to deal with receipt of a **subpoena** (an order to appear in court on a specified date). Another role for social workers in the court system is that of work on behalf of the court in conducting a **presentence investigation**. If a case goes to court and the person is convicted, a presentence investigation may be requested by the judge. Probation officers, many of whom are social workers, conduct presentence investigations; the investigations typically involve both office and home visits with family members, the client, and other collaborative sources. The report is likely to be very detailed and comprehensive, including a social history and descriptions of the home and work environment, education and employment, and physical or mental health problems, as well as an identification of the existing social supports of the person who was convicted. The concluding recommendation often evaluates the potential risk if the person convicted remains in the community. If sexual assault or physical injury has been inflicted on a child, the need for protection of the victim becomes a primary concern in the presentence investigation. The social worker's recommendation tends to be highly valued by the courts.

A decision to sentence will involve a jail term, probation, or imprisonment. Note that there are significant differences between jail and prison. A **jail** is a correctional facility used for short sentences or for detaining persons while they await a court hearing. A **prison** is used for lengthier sentences, generally for a number of years. In passing sentence, judges are required to abide by the legal code, which provides parameters for the length of imprisonment; therefore, judges' options are somewhat limited.

Alternatives to prison are less costly than prison, and they are a good deal more humane than a prison sentence. Any alternative program mandated by the court is usually attached to a sentence of probation. **Community-service sentencing** usually requires work without pay in a private or governmental human service organization for a specified period of time. **Restitution** programs require compensation to the victims (usually monetarily) for losses suffered as a result of the criminal offense. Restitution sentences are used by juveniles as well as adult courts. Restitution is most frequently used in conjunction with property crimes, which are the most prevalent of all crimes committed. Social workers who work with restitution often find that a monetary payment has less long-range meaning than the experience of facing the victim, explaining the offense, and seeking to restore the loss.

The Correctional System

The correctional system is that part of the criminal justice system that uses imprisonment, probation, parole, and various alternatives to change the behaviors of persons convicted of crime. The two major components of the correctional system in the United States are prisons and community-based programs. Each of the 50 states has its own correctional system with varying structures, sanctions, and administrative laws. At the local level, some counties and cities also operate correctional facilities and probation departments. The federal government has the Bureau of Prisons, which operates the federal prison system and is a component of the U.S. Department of Justice, and a federal probation system operated by the courts. In addition, the Department of Defense maintains military prisons. There is considerable variety of organizational structures as well as weak linkages among these many systems.

Prisons

Across jurisdictional systems, prisons are classified as minimum-, medium-, and maximum-security facilities. Until recently, all prisons were owned and administered by governmental bodies, but private enterprise has created a very profitable prison industry in some parts of the country. There has been considerable construction of new prisons, yet they tend to be extremely overcrowded, housing populations in excess of their capacity day in and day out. Juvenile facilities are separate from prisons for adults. They too tend to be seriously overcrowded, presenting the same health, safety, and security problems found in adult facilities. Smaller, community-based correctional programs serve as prerelease centers, halfway houses, and group homes.

The various jurisdictions have different procedures for assigning persons to correctional facilities. Often newly sentenced persons are observed in specially designated reception facilities for several weeks while vocational and psychological testing is done to help select the most appropriate prison facility. Social workers participate in the evaluation procedure, gathering social history data or supplementing information already available if a presentence investigation was done.

The prison population in the United States grew at an astounding rate beginning in 1990 until 2011, when small decreases began to appear in the data published annually by the U.S. Department of Justice, Bureau of Justice Statistics. Historically, males have been incarcerated at a much higher rate than women, which is demonstrated by the data in Box 11.1. The *Sourcebook of Criminal Justice Statistics Online* is the primary publication source, but unfortunately there is a rather considerable delay in availability of their data. As of this writing it appears that the incarceration rate in the United States has continued to decline slightly since 2012, most recent year of published data. This decline is represented among female as well as male incarceration rates. Nonetheless, imprisonment today in the United States still remains at very high rates.

Box 11.1 Sentenced Male and Female Prisoners under Jurisdiction of State and Federal Correctional Authorities 1930–2012 (by rate per 100,000 residents)

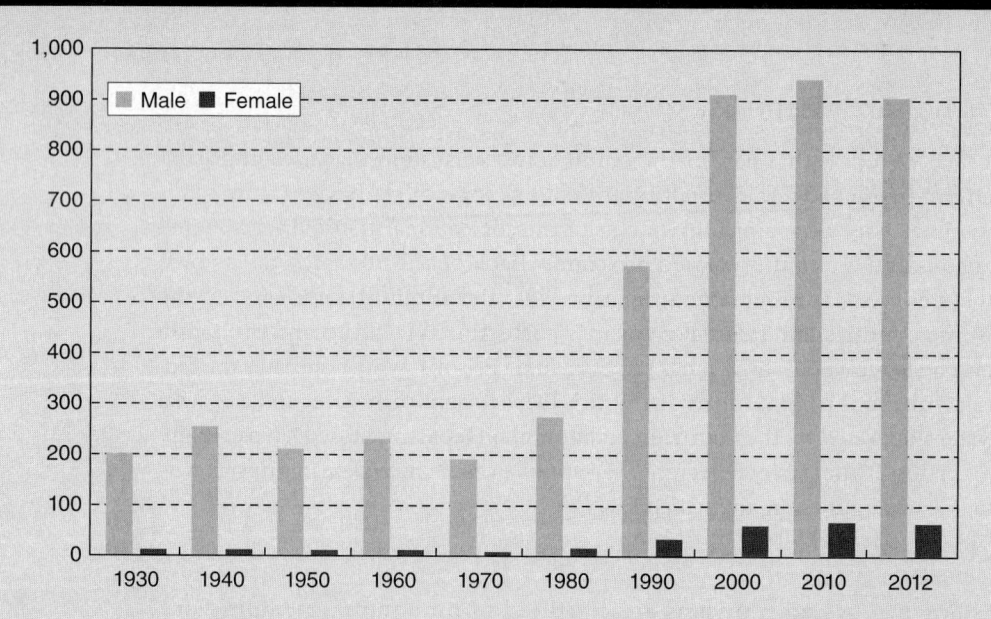

Source: U.S. Department of Justice, Bureau of Justice Statistics; Table 6.28.2012, Number and rate (per 100,000 U.S. residents population in each group) of sentenced prisoners under jurisdiction of state and federal correctional authorities on Dec. 31, *Sourcebook of Criminal Justice Statistics Online* (2013). Retrieved from http://www.albany.edu/sourcebook.

There has been increasing public interest in criminal justice in recent years. It has become a politically charged topic, with politically conservative groups calling for increased use of prison sentencing, with longer sentences and less availability of parole, while liberal groups have called for less reliance on incarceration to deal with societal problems, especially substance abuse. There is growing awareness of the disproportionate level of drug offenses resulting in imprisonment relative to sentencing for other offenses, including far more violent offenses. While the U.S. Department of Justice had no updated data on drug-related imprisonments for correctional facilities under the jurisdiction of state and federal authorities, more current data from the Federal Bureau of Prisons is shown in Box 11.2. These data reflect the enormous number of persons who remain incarcerated in federal prisons (and very likely in state prisons as well) for drug offenses. These data have not changed significantly despite action taken by the courts and the Obama Administration in 2014–2015 to change drug-sentencing policy for new offenses and to release large number of persons previously convicted for low-level drug offenses.

> Watch this news clip from Voices of America (VOA). What are the benefits of reduced sentences for nonviolent drug offenses?
> https://www.youtube.com/watch?v=4bsfiUmLX9M

In recent years, there has also been increasing concern about the increase in the rate of imprisonment of women and the unique but unmet needs of women prisoners. As van Wormer points out, women "are receiving treatment in a system run by and designed for men" (2010, p. 3). The same classification system tends to be used for both male and female prisoners, yet research demonstrates that women prisoners are significantly less of a threat to other inmates or to the outside community should they escape.

Box 11.2 Offenses of Inmates within the Federal Bureau of Prisons, December 26, 2015

Offense	# of Inmates	% of Inmates
Banking and Insurance, Counterfeit, Embezzlement	649	0.4
Burglary, Larceny, Property Offenses	7,945	4.3
Continuing Criminal Enterprise	429	0.2
Courts or Corrections	780	0.4
Drug Offenses	86,080	46.5
Extortion, Fraud, Bribery	12,024	6.5
Homicide, Aggravated Assault, and Kidnapping Offenses	5,545	3.0
Immigration	17,354	9.4
Miscellaneous	1,521	0.8
National Security	83	0.0
Robbery	7,055	3.8
Sex Offenses	14,266	7.7
Weapons, Explosives, Arson	31,292	16.9

Source: Federal Bureau of Prisons, *BOP Statistics: Inmate Offenses*; Dec. 26, 2015. Retrieved from https://www.bop.gov/about/statistics_inmate_offenses.jsp.

Instead of basing the system on risk, Farr (2000) calls for a prison classification system for women based on need in treatment areas such as substance abuse counseling; obstetric and gynecological health care; improving the connections between women and their children; instituting parenting skills training; and treatment for the mental disorders, such as depression, that appear to be more prevalent among women prisoners. Strengths-based approaches are gradually emerging, too, in group work with women inmates and in preparation programs as women, especially older women with lengthy sentences, plan their return to the "free world" (van Wormer, 2010).

Prison social workers are prisoners' links to their home community. In women's prisons, for example, it is often the prison social worker who communicates with the foster care agency when children have been placed in care pending the mother's release from prison. Family members often have great difficulty accepting the imprisonment. Feelings of anger, abandonment, fear, and denial have to be worked with. Just as families need to make very difficult adjustments when a member is imprisoned, other social, emotional, and economic adjustments are required when release from prison is anticipated. It would be wonderful if all prisons had social workers with sufficient time to provide these services. The reality is that some prisons have no social work staff at all, and other prisons have so few social workers that staff must carefully prioritize their tasks.

Although social workers are members of the prison staff, they do serve as communication facilitators between inmates and other prison staff. As advocates for prisoners, social workers attempt to secure resources, such as access to scarce educational, social service, or vocational programs. Social workers advocate with prison administrators for changes in policies or procedures affecting the inmate population. They also promote an exchange of information between families of inmates (especially children in foster care) and the prisoners. During medical emergencies, prison social workers provide updated medical information between family members and prisoners and, if appropriate, with other segments of the prison community.

Prison riots have demonstrated the role of social workers in negotiation. Social workers have been selected by prisoners to present their issues to administrators and to the outside world. Given the serious overcrowding of prisons today, most prison facilities experience tension and violence almost daily. Fighting between prisoners is a common occurrence. Violence in prisons is not limited to inmate-inflicted abuse, nor is it only a function of modern times. Inmates of some of the early prison facilities were forced to work as servants in the homes of wardens, where many abuses were suffered, including beatings and death for disobedience. Female prisoners have always been subject to sexual abuse. Lawsuits filed on their behalf and public investigations into such abuses have resulted in the implementation of procedures that require a formal hearing and response to the complaints of inmates in correctional facilities, but this has not eliminated exploitation or violence.

The absence of heterosexual outlets encourages same-sex relationships in prisons and jails. These relationships may provide some level of comfort and closeness, but they may also produce jealousies, heated altercations, and acts of reprisal for unfaithfulness. Especially in prisons that are overcrowded, rape also occurs, sometimes with extensive physical injuries.

In prison and jail facilities, social workers seek to reduce violence by building bridges between inmates and staff, by helping prisoners develop or enhance their sense of self-worth, and by reducing the inmates' sense of powerlessness. Behavior rehearsal and role-playing are used to teach new behaviors or to modify existing actions. Educational and skill-building programs are implemented. Techniques including reality therapy, behavior modification, transactional analysis, and educational programs are used, depending on the social worker's level of skill and on inmates' needs.

Community-Based Corrections

Community-based corrections are programs that provide an alternative to incarceration. Probation and parole, the major community-based programs, require ongoing supervision until the original sentence is concluded. The person providing that supervision is generally referred to as a parole (or probation) agent or officer. Preferences regarding the use of *agent* or *officer* vary among the many federal, state, county, and city jurisdictions; we will use *agent*. Most state probation and parole positions require a bachelor's degree in social work or criminal justice. Federal positions require 1 year of graduate courses in addition to a bachelor's degree. Sometimes a related degree is acceptable.

While parole provides for the early release of a prisoner from a penal institution, probation permits the offender to avoid imprisonment, remaining in the community to serve her or his sentence. Both parole and probation are conditional; that is, if the terms of the probation or parole agreement are violated, the offender may be subject to **revocation** (may be returned to prison for the remainder of the sentence). The terms of the agreement are identified in a contract signed by the client and the agent. The contract clearly identifies the terms of each person's conduct and may include the following:

- All arrests or police contact must be reported to the agent immediately.
- Make yourself available for searches or tests.
- No change of employment or residence may be made without permission.
- Leaving the state without permission is not permitted.
- Purchase of or selling, trading, or operating a motor vehicle requires advanced approval.
- Money may not be borrowed or items purchased on credit without advanced approval.
- Purchase or possession of firearms or other weapon is not permitted without advanced approval.
- Voting in any local, state, or federal election is prohibited.
- Reporting to the assigned agent as requested is required.
- Payment may be required for monthly supervision by the agent or for polygraph testing, if requested.

The items listed above are routinely included in the Community Supervision Rules of the State of Wisconsin, Department of Corrections. Additional space is usually provided for specific terms related to the individual client.

Helping people to meet the terms of the probation or parole agreement is a key function of the social worker. In truth, the client's life is subject to almost continuous scrutiny by the social worker. Developing a relationship of trust with a corrections client is not always easy. It requires skill and commitment from the social worker.

Alan Martin, the social worker in the case study, carried many of the responsibilities of both parole agent and probation agent. As a professional social worker in the role of parole agent, Alan Martin sought to apply the knowledge, values, and skills of generalist practice that he had learned while in college. He used the same problem-solving steps cited in Chapter 1, a process that underpins all generalist social work practice. If Brian Cook had been sentenced by the judge to probation instead of prison, Alan might have been assigned as his probation agent. The role of the probation agent is very similar to that of the parole agent, so Alan would have engaged Brian in the same problem-solving work that was done during Brian's parole.

The correctional system requires the agent, in this case Alan Martin, to assist the client in meeting the terms of the probation agreement. The same contract form, citing the very same terms, may be used for both probation and parole. The probation client generally has not left his or her home community as a result of the conviction and sentence; therefore, the agent has the advantage of working with a person who is still connected to family, neighborhood, and job or school. The pressing need to find housing or employment—so often the case with parole clients—is not usually present, nor is re-integration into the community an issue to be worked through.

Probation and parole agents often have extremely large caseloads. They range widely, from 20 to 100 clients. This makes it difficult for some agents to know their clients well. Often they use much of their time managing crises and barely spend more than 15 minutes with the client who reports for scheduled monthly meetings. Technology—computers, cell phones, fax machines—helps probation and parole agents handle heavy workloads. Some agents may use technology to work, in part, from their homes.

Probation and parole departments have analyzed the workload and have found that there are identifiable corrections populations that need more time and greater expertise than others. Accordingly, some jurisdictions have created separate units to work with persons who are mentally ill, for example, or those whose crime involves use of illegal drugs or sex offenses. Social workers in specialized units usually have a smaller caseload; frequently they have MSW degrees plus experience.

One approach to minimizing **recidivism** (the repetition of criminal behavior resulting in return to prison or reinstatement of a prison sentence) is **risk rating** in which clients with higher risks of recidivism are placed under closer and more frequent supervision. A risk-rating assessment is now used in most state and county probation and parole departments as well as in Canada and Australia. The National Center for Crime and Delinquency and other corrections agencies have done considerable work to validate the risk assessment instruments that are used. A high score on the risk rating assessment would suggest the need for a maximum level of supervision; a low score normally results in a minimal level of probation or parole supervision. Generally, a minimum level of supervision or monitoring would involve contacts only once every 3 months, although more frequent telephone or mail-in reports might be required. By contrast, a maximum level of supervision could involve office visits every 2 weeks and possibly a home visit every month.

Interestingly, data from the Bureau of Justice Statistics demonstrate that the number of persons in state and federal probation and parole programs has begun to increase. Over 30 years, from 1980 to 2010, the number of persons on probation and parole increased from 1,338,535 to 4,275,952 and by the end of 2014 (most recent available data), the total reached 4,708,100. Interestingly, the population on probation declined while the parole population increased (Bonczar, Kaeble, & Maruschak, 2015). If support for criminal justice reform continues, the result could be an ongoing expansion of community corrections.

Intensive probation is a specialized category of probation for persons who have committed violent crimes or who have displayed violence or hostility and are considered to be of high risk. This form of probation utilizes frequent client contacts—daily or at least several contacts per week. Electronic monitoring using wrist or ankle bracelets (increasingly with GPS) also provides a means of controlling clients' movements. Intensive probation is more cost-efficient than imprisonment and provides a relatively high level of community protection. It is also useful with special client populations such as those who chronically abuse alcohol or drugs.

No other area of social work practice gives the social worker as much police authority as probation and parole. This includes authority to seize property, search clients' premises, and even to handcuff and arrest. The agent also has the right to recommend a client's return to prison if terms of parole are not met. Agents may require clients to participate in treatment such as substance abuse counseling or batterers' group therapy. With house arrest, people are confined to their homes with electronic or computer surveillance ensuring that they do not leave. This power cannot be taken lightly.

Several other forms of community-based corrections programs exist. Some, such as victim–offender mediation and restitution, have already been described. Informal diversion and community service requirements are consistent with the principles of restorative justice, which values healing over punishment and retribution. Informal diversion is used with first offenders or for minor offenses and is most common in juvenile justice systems. With informal diversion, an authorized intake worker (sometimes a social worker) or officer obtains agreement from the offender to abide by the law and, possibly, to make restitution, in lieu of being prosecuted for the offense. This is both humane and cost-effective. Community service may be a component of diversion, or it may be the sentence following conviction. It requires unpaid labor that is useful to the community and that, when possible, utilizes the client's knowledge or skills.

The Juvenile Justice System

The juvenile court system evolved from quite a different philosophy than the adult court system and came out of the pioneering and social reform work of Jane Addams and Hull House workers, among others. Established in 1899 in Chicago, it was born of the belief that children were not fully developed human beings capable of making judgments about their behavior or controlling their lives in the same way adults were expected to do. Juvenile courts were designed to intervene when children misbehaved or were in need of protection. There was a strong belief that children could be rehabilitated. Treatment was stressed, as well as separation of the child from adult court systems. Juvenile court proceedings were conducted informally, often without legal representation.

While Addams and her Hull House colleagues in Chicago spearheaded social reform including the founding of the first juvenile court in 1899, Margaret Murray Washington (wife of Booker T. Washington) was actively pursuing similar goals in the South. The pioneers of this movement were later referred to as the "child savers" because their efforts led to the establishment of child labor laws, kindergartens, compulsory school attendance, and, perhaps their most ambitious project, the development of a juvenile justice system (Moon, Sundt, Cullen, & Wright, 2000). Removing children from the adult court and prison system was a major breakthrough. It required the skills of noted civic leaders like Washington, whose personal involvement led to the development of Mt. Meigs Reformatory for Juvenile Law-Breakers in Alabama and the Mt. Meigs Rescue Home for Girls (Dickerson, 2001).

From the beginning, social workers were a major presence in the day-to-day operation of the children's courts and juvenile justice programs. By the 1960s, a major philosophical shift occurred. After two landmark Supreme Court decisions, primarily the 1967 case, *In re: Gault,* formal legal processes were instituted within juvenile courts, affording children increased legal protections. No longer could the courts imprison or detain children without due process. An **adversarial court** evolved in which attorneys representing the prosecution and attorneys representing the defense were permitted to engage in cross-examination. Children's courts quickly lost their former informal environment in which parents, children, judges, and social workers talked across a table. Constitutional rights and legal processes increasingly became paramount. Legal issues emerged relating to detention, search and seizure, and questions about transfer of children to adult courts.

Today, youth encounters with the juvenile justice system proceed through several phases: arrest, intake, detention, adjudication, and disposition. Behaviors in violation of the law bring youths into contact with the police. The officer determines whether to file charges. While there is considerable variability across states in the United States, most youths who come in contact with police are not arrested but are instead given a warning, or the problem is resolved in some other way. The Juvenile Justice and Delinquency Prevention Act of 1974 discontinued the earlier practice of jailing youths for offenses such as curfew violations and truancy and required that arrested youths be separated from adults in jails or prisons. As a result, juvenile detention centers were constructed. They are now the locations that receive arrested youths. In rural areas, where juvenile facilities do not exist, youths may be held in jails, but they are kept in cells separate from adults.

Following arrest, an intake process is begun. The intake process will conclude with a decision to detain, dismiss, or make some other disposition of the case. The risk-and-needs assessments that are increasingly part of the intake process may affect the disposition decision. Juvenile court or probation officers (often social workers) generally conduct the intake-and-assessment process. The data collected include any history of past offenses, violent or aggressive behavior, mental health or substance abuse needs, family or peer problems, educational deficits, medical problems, and sexual abuse history. In addition, information is gathered from parents, police, schools, and other health and social service organizations.

Youths' entry into the juvenile justice system is influenced by a pattern of social and medical needs and by poverty, race, and ethnicity factors that place some youth at increased risk. Researchers Maschi, Hatcher, Schwalbe, and Rosato (2008) suggest that schools, among other human service agencies, accept increased responsibility for identifying needs and for referrals to appropriate services in order to prevent vulnerable children from becoming involved with the juvenile court system. They also suggest increased diversity training for police, judges, and the professionals involved in the juvenile justice system.

Social workers in juvenile detention centers regularly provide individual and group counseling, often with a behavior change focus. Juvenile court work ideally includes service to families as well, but significant staff shortages often preclude the provision of significant family service.

Social work parole agent reviews parole contract with youth prior to release from a juvenile correctional facility

Adjudication, the next phase, refers to the decisions made by the juvenile court judge when the charge against the youth is reviewed. The court may decide to drop all charges, but if instead the youth is found guilty, sentencing follows. The **disposition** of a case entails the carrying out of the court order. Probation is the most common sentence in juvenile courts. It is similar to adult probation and may require regular monthly contacts or more intensive and frequent meetings with a probation agent, who is often a BSW social worker. Restitution and/or community service may be a component of probation or may be court ordered as an alternative to probation. If the assessment done at intake identified the need for mental health or substance abuse treatment, placement in a community-based residential treatment program or group home may be court ordered. Serious crimes or frequent offenses may result in sentencing to a juvenile prison. Sentencing is for a specified number of years. Juvenile prisons are typically designed as a series of cottages, a school, and administrative facilities, all enclosed by walls topped with razor wire. Parole, which resembles probation, typically follows incarceration.

Another possible disposition of a juvenile justice case is waiver to adult court for sentencing. This action, which is used with increasing frequency, is generally reserved for serious or violent criminal behavior. Serious and violent crimes, however, have actually declined. Currently there are approximately 10,000 children in adult jails and prisons, 3,000 of whom have been sentenced to life without parole. Children in adult prisons are at substantial risk of being sexually assaulted or to commit suicide. The Equal Justice Initiative is one of a growing number of organizations and individuals challenging the sentencing of children to adult prisons ("Children in Prison," 2016).

> ▶ This video explores problems within our juvenile justice system. What information was most surprising to you, and why? Which statistics confirmed information you already knew?
> https://www.youtube.com/watch?v=9yuol0tjMzc

> Assess your understanding of the components of the criminal justice system by taking this brief quiz.

As a part of his justice reform initiative, President Obama used his executive authority in 2016 to ban solitary confinement for child prisoners in federal prisons ("President Obama Bans Solitary Confinement for Juveniles in Federal Prisons," 2016). Bernstein, in her 2014 book, *Burning Down the House: The End of Juvenile Prison*, called for an end to *all* imprisonment of children.

SOCIAL WORK PRACTICE IN THE CRIMINAL JUSTICE SYSTEM

Opportunities abound for social workers in the field of criminal justice. There are also employment opportunities at all levels of federal, state, and local government as well as with private organizations. Salaries tend to be good, and there are additional opportunities for advancement to administrative positions. While only a small percentage of social workers enter this field, a larger percentage of BSWs than MSWs do so. Increasingly, too, student social workers are becoming excited about the prospect of working to humanize the criminal justice system. They will need to be armed with an understanding of the value dilemmas that confront practitioners in this field of practice.

Value Dilemmas for Social Workers

The use and abuse of authority represent one of the most consistent value dilemmas for social workers in criminal justice settings. For one thing, the legal system gives the probation or parole agent substantial policing authority and responsibilities, and this may well conflict with—or at least appear to conflict with—the professional obligations to a client that are defined in the NASW Code of Ethics.

The code of ethics's strong emphasis on confidentiality presents a dilemma since social workers in criminal justice settings are required to testify, as requested by the courts, regarding their conversations with clients and to report any new or suspected offenses. This requirement may place special strain on the relationship between social workers and the people they work with. Hard decisions sometimes have to be made by the social worker. If a teenaged girl, on probation for running away, admitted to a probation officer that she had been running away because of her father's sexual abuse, the social worker would feel sorry about having to violate the confidence so painfully shared by the teenaged girl, but there would be no doubt that this situation would have to be reported and assessed further.

Another dilemma relates to the profession's long struggle with the issues of coercion. No other field of practice presents social workers with the dilemma of having 100 percent of their clients as mandated—forced to see them by the law. This potentially sets up a negative working relationship from the start and promotes conning, where clients tell social workers just what they think social workers want to hear and nothing more. The criminal justice system, which has a history of negative attitudes and disrespectful treatment of clients (who are referred to as "offenders" and "inmates"), sometimes creates an environment of distrust and hostility. Social workers actually do sometimes become agents of social control, enforcing specified behaviors from unwilling clients. Social work students often ask: "Is this a professional, even an ethical role?" One response is that social workers often work in environments in which some level of persuasion or coercion occurs in order to protect the best interests of individuals or to sustain societal stability. In fact, there are always limits to individual self-determination since human beings live in societal systems that are defined by their attempt to meet the greater good of the entire community. But sometimes societal systems are repressive, abusive, and unjust. Social workers do not wish to become agents of repression. Provided this is not the case, the social control role can be a legitimate professional role if it is practiced with care and critically analyzed, and if the social worker also seeks changes within the organization needed to humanize it and make it responsive to the needs of its clients as well as the larger society.

Forensic Social Work

Forensic social work is a relatively new and evolving field of social work practice. While forensic social work can be broadly defined to include almost all areas of social work practice in criminal justice, the more narrow definition views it as a specialized area of practice built on in-depth knowledge of the law and litigation in civil and criminal justice. Courts, for example, may request an evaluation and recommendation for the purpose of determining child custody in a divorce situation or following the death of a sole parent. After a careful psychosocial study including interviewing the child, the social worker will provide testimony as an unbiased expert to assist the judge in determining what is in the best interests of a child or children. Similarly, social workers may assist in mental competency hearings when defendants' criminal behaviors appear to be related to mental illness or developmental disability (Ritter et al., 2009).

Forensic social workers may also be requested by the court to conduct a presentence investigation, or they may be asked to obtain information from the family of, for example, a child who has been physically or sexually abused. The forensic social worker may be asked by the court to recommend "ways to resolve, punish, or rehabilitate those found guilty of crimes or negligence in civil actions" (Barker & Branson, 2000, p. 16). If the forensic social worker recommends community service, for example, the court may further ask that social worker to facilitate and monitor the sentence.

In recent years, some medical examiners' offices have begun employing forensic social workers to assist in their investigations and to help them with the sensitive communication of painful information to victims, families, or friends related to criminal events. Following autopsies, for example, the medical examiner or coroner often must share complex but horrific information not only with the police but also with the victim's family members. Social workers can partner with the medical examiner to ensure that people understand fully the information that is provided. Social workers' expertise in dealing with the often overwhelming emotions of that traumatic event is exceptionally helpful. An example of this kind of forensic social work appears in the Box 11.3 Forensic Social Work Case Study.

Forensic social workers may be employed by court systems or other organizations on a full- or part-time basis, or they may function as private practitioners. They are highly specialized and function only within their areas of expertise. The National Organization of Forensic Social Work has been in existence for approximately 30 years. In 2011, it initiated the *Journal of Forensic Social Work*; it also offers annual conferences. Readers might wish to visit this organization's website for additional information.

Box 11.3 Forensic Social Work Case Study

The local TV website for additional information on the body that had been found frozen in ice and snow early that morning on N. Oak Street. The body was that of a young woman clad in a light jacket and clothing not fit for the sub-zero weather. Police questioned people living in nearby homes, but no one seemed to have heard or seen anything unusual during the night. No one could identify the body, which was then transported to the medical examiner's office.

The team that was on duty that morning consisted of the chief medical examiner and his two assistant medical examiners—all physicians with specialties in forensic pathology—and an MSW social worker, Colleen Jackson and her student, Marsha Holton. Together the team reviewed the few facts that were available from the police report. They checked to see if any phone calls or emails had been received from someone searching for a missing person, but none had. After the body was photographed and carefully examined by one of the medical examiners, the team reconvened. The photograph showed the body to be that of a slender, young white woman, probably in her early twenties, with bright red hair and heavy makeup. The examination revealed no visible trauma to the body or any clear cause of death beyond freezing. The first problem to be solved was to determine the identity of this young person, if possible. Colleen suggested that she and Marsha might attempt to obtain additional information by interviewing people in the neighborhood where the body was found. The team agreed to this plan. Dr. Jim Marcoli would also start a preliminary autopsy immediately.

Armed with photos of the body, Colleen and Marsha set out. They learned that students from one of the two universities in the city occupied many of the apartments in the area. Dr. Marcoli telephoned to say that while no chemical substances were found in his autopsy, body fluids had revealed ample evidence of alcohol sufficient to cause loss of consciousness. There was no indication of any physical violence. Colleen and Marsha used this information to begin asking people in the area about any parties that might have taken place in the previous 24 hours. Three blocks from the site where the body was discovered, an older woman in a fourth-floor apartment complained vigorously about a very loud party the previous night in the apartment above hers. She had not mentioned this to the police because she had complained many times about the parties in that apartment, to no avail.

As Colleen and Marsha set out to interview the people who had begun returning to the apartment building in the evening, a telephone call came in from the office. A woman from a rural area 50 miles north of the city had called asking about the body that had been found. She was frantic because she was unable to reach her daughter, a student at the university. Colleen decided to talk with this woman. Meanwhile, Marsha would try to interview residents of the building.

Marsha was lucky to find three young people just returning to the fifth-floor apartment above the older resident. They reluctantly let Marsha into their apartment. It was a mess with discarded cans and bottles of alcoholic beverages everywhere, remnants of snack food, and the TV still blaring. Despite their shock and initial distrust when they found that Marsha was from the medical examiner's office, they did respond to Marsha's calm approach and her gentle manner. She informed them that she was also a student and that her primary concern was in trying to identify the young woman who had died in their neighborhood the previous night. Marsha did not show them the picture of the body, but when she described the bright red hair of the young woman, the three students exchanged glances and then acknowledged that someone of that description had been at their party the previous night. She seemed to have been drinking before she arrived. She was loud, and, late in the evening, she and another girl got into a huge argument over one of the guys, who tried to break it up. They only knew her only as Amanda. Amanda had been drinking heavily, and she stomped out of the apartment in a rage probably around midnight. The students agreed to be available if Marsha had further questions. Back at the car, Marsha shared her information with Colleen. Colleen quickly told Marsha that the woman she had talked with was on her way to the city. Her daughter's name was Amanda; she had bright red hair. The woman's husband was in the military, stationed at

(continued)

> **Box 11.3 (continued)**
>
> a base on Guam, a U.S. island in the West Pacific; she had already contacted him. She was desperate to know if the body was that of her daughter.
>
> Two hours later, Colleen, Marsha, and Dr. Marcoli met with Simone Anderson. Her likeness to that of the dead girl was immediately apparent. After taking some time to prepare her for what she was about to experience, Colleen and Dr. Marcoli accompanied her to the autopsy area, where with desperate grief Simone identified the body as that of her 20-year-old daughter. Back in her office, Colleen and Marsha helped Simone to vent her grief and tell her story about how she had tried so hard to help Amanda with her drinking problem but now, away at college, Amanda had apparently started binge drinking again. Colleen encouraged Simone to call her husband again and offered to place the call when Simone's hands trembled uncontrollably with the phone. After Simone reached her husband and they shared their horror and grief, Amanda's father asked to speak with Colleen. Colleen instructed him in the procedure he could follow with his commanding officer to obtain the military's help in getting him back home immediately. Colleen and Marsha stayed with Simone, consoling her, helping her to call her sister, and eventually helping her to understand what she would need to do next in completing the paperwork required by the police department. Simone clung to Colleen and tearfully whispered her gratitude as her sister arrived and prepared to take Simone back home.
>
> Marsha and Colleen talked together for a long time after Simone left, processing this emotional experience. Dr. Marcoli stopped by the office and thanked Marsha for her fine work in enabling the three university students to share their knowledge, which helped the medical examiner's office in their task of determining the cause of Amanda's death. Dr. Marcoli also commented on how much more sensitively and humanely this situation had been handled than in the time before social workers were part of the medical examiner's office team.

Social Work with Groups and Organizations

Although most of the discussion up to this point has focused on criminal justice social work practice with individuals and families, there is a growing trend toward work with groups and entire organizations. Persons who have been sexually abused, domestic violence victims, and perpetrators are often most effectively helped with groups. Mothers of sexually abused children, for example, can be helped through the use of mutual aid groups where the strong support and empathy of group members enable many to heal. Similarly, groups enable women who experienced sexual abuse to share intimate, painful experiences of devastation they had never revealed before. They, too, learn to deal with their anger and grief as they acquire self-forgiveness and the ability to empathize deeply with others (Schiller & Zimmer, 2005). As they regain self-respect, they are significantly better able to nurture their children.

Group work with men who have abused others in intimate relationships, interestingly, works with some similar themes. Trimble (2005) described such groups, noting that although the men were typically court-mandated, their fear of intimacy, angry feelings, and lack of self-respect emerged in group sessions. The detailed and painful sharing of ugly past experiences of their abuse of others was made possible by the emotional environment of the group. The men were able to regain self-respect as they learned to control their behaviors. The social worker's use of strengths perspective helped them learn about and use the gentle, nurturing part of themselves whether or not they were ever able to return to the relationships that they had abused.

Group work has been shown to be especially useful in prisons. In women's prisons, groups can provide much needed educational experiences related to high-risk behaviors ranging from unprotected sex to sharing of dirty needles. Well-designed groups can be educational, emotionally supportive, empowering, and nurturing, as well as fun-loving and entertaining. Confronted with the daily disrespect, control, and authority of the prison system, social work groups can be especially meaningful and effective (van Wormer, 2010). Problems with anger management may also be a complication of daily life in prison. In prison, for example, it is not uncommon for guards to demand that a work task, such as scrubbing a floor, be repeated several times even though it was satisfactorily completed initially. An inmate may have to share a small cell with a person who is verbally or physically abusive. Anger, frustration, depression, and mental deterioration are common in prisoners. Groups can help prisoners verbalize their upset and dissatisfaction.

Evaluation

Dimension of Competency: *Knowledge*
Social workers understand that evaluation is an ongoing component of practice with individuals, families, groups, organization, and communities.

Critical Thinking Question: How could social workers use evaluation procedures to continually improve their group work within prisons?

Group work can also be the primary problem-solving approach used in community-based homes for adolescents just released from correctional institutions. Because peer influence is so significant during adolescence, group work can sometimes be more beneficial than individual work with this age cohort. Establishing communication and relationships with withdrawn, socially immature teenagers is often an important goal for social workers in group homes.

Group home placement can be a desirable intervention plan, but a limitation is the high rate of staff turnover. To keep the group home or community-based correctional facility functioning, the social worker must tackle organizational tasks such as training the youth care staff, helping them understand and work more effectively with the residents. Youthful residents of group homes are often violent, impulsive, and very difficult for staff to work with; therefore, group sessions, in which problems of the home or the unit are discussed by staff and residents, are beneficial. The ability of the staff and the group home as an organization to meet the needs of this complex resident population depends heavily on the effectiveness of the social worker.

When social workers are the administrators of community-based correctional facilities and group homes, they are responsible for the budget, for recruitment and supervision of staff, and for the quality of care provided. A BSW holding the middle-management position of house manager is responsible for the day-to-day operation of the home, for direct supervision of staff, and for program planning for the residents. Whether serving as a house manager, an administrator, or a parole agent, social workers have a professional responsibility to help make their organization as humane, just, and responsive to clients as possible.

Assess your understanding of how the profession of social work is practiced in the criminal justice system by taking this brief quiz.

SOCIAL, ECONOMIC, AND ENVIRONMENTAL JUSTICE

Criminal justice is a field of social work practice that brings police, police social workers, and probation and parole agents into communities that are known to people of those communities as high-crime areas. Prison staff, including social workers, psychologists, and nurses also work in institutional environments where there is risk of violence and where imprisoned people are often housed in degrading, even unclean conditions. The social work person-in-environment perspective implies that we need to consider the impact on our clients of the physical space in which they live and work.

Environmental Perspective: Communities at Risk

Too often in social work, we tend to ignore the immediate environments where people live, spend their daily lives: their homes, apartments, offices and job sites, schools, even their cars, bars, faith communities, gardens, and neighborhood stores. We could argue about whether crime causes deterioration in neighborhoods or whether neglected neighborhoods cause crime, but it is pretty clear that dilapidated, poorly cared-for properties and crime generally coexist.

In probation or parole work, social workers' responsibility to their employing organization (usually the county, state, or federal government) is to try to prevent additional criminal activity in the persons they are supervising. When the social worker visits the client, however, many problems emerge in addition to the crime that resulted in a sentence of probation. Often the client's environment is filled with guns, drugs, and violence. Family, school, and even employment (if the client is lucky enough to still have employment) may actually promote rather than deter criminal activity.

Increasingly we are asking why these communities and the families that live within them are at risk. We can see what is present in the community, but we also need to ask what is missing. Data presented earlier in this chapter reflected the disproportionate imprisonment of youth and young adults as a result of drug-related arrests. The longstanding, serious consequences of these arrests for the fabric of community health and well-being emerged from Travis's research as early as 2004. Travis's research demonstrated that specific blocks in urban neighborhoods predictably incarcerate much larger numbers of individuals, and they tend to be imprisoned in facilities located at considerable distance from their home neighborhoods. In Brooklyn, New York, for example, one out of every eight parenting-age man was sentenced to jail or prison every year.

The impact on families and neighborhood environments is dramatic. Older adults, for example, can anticipate raising grandchildren and even great-grandchildren. Children grow up not knowing their fathers and, increasingly, their mothers. The economy of many already impoverished communities suffers. Pinard's 2010 study of the collateral consequences of incarceration also identified several ways in which possession of a criminal record threatened the likelihood of successful re-integration into society. He found that access to public housing was restricted for individuals with certain offenses. Employment restrictions existed for persons with felony convictions. Criminal background checks, which quickly identify misdemeanors and felonies, are required by large numbers of employers who might otherwise be likely to hire persons following release from prison. Pinard noted that cash assistance and even food stamps have been denied to persons convicted of felony offenses, and the majority of states also ban voting by persons serving time on probation or parole for felony offenses.

Environmental Perspective: Community Strength, Restoration, Spirituality, and Resilience

Dennis Saleebey, whose strengths perspective enriches social work practice today, was a firm believer that small changes in environment could bring big changes in the behavior of people. Citing what he refers to as the "Broken Windows" theory, he suggests that creating small changes, such as repairing or replacing broken windows, in areas where crimes occur reap dividends in crime reduction. "If a neighborhood or space looks like no one cares for or about it, then criminals are less likely to be restrained in their activities there" (2006, p. 242).

The strengths perspective tells social workers that all social systems (individuals, families, groups, organizations, and communities) have strengths. We sometimes have to look hard to find them. Supposedly bad or high-crime neighborhoods have strengths, too. They have vibrant faith communities, schools, hardworking people, and children full of energy and spirit. Often they contain large, old, ornamented, beautifully designed housing stock. Sometimes small changes, such as fixing a sagging porch or painting a picket fence, can mobilize other improvements in a community and contribute to an overall change in the neighborhood environment. Green space can be created out of abandoned parking lots. Flower or vegetable gardens add color and beauty. They present an alternative to bars as places for people, old and young alike, to congregate, coming out of the fearful isolation of their homes to chat, share stories, and nurture neighborly networks.

Some of these exciting changes are already underway. Churches and faith communities have been a wellspring of energy and creativity in promoting community health and healing in many areas. While many American religious denominations support restorative justice, the American Baptist Church provides resources to enable churches to mediate community conflicts, especially those involving cultural differences. To sustain or rebuild family relationships, some churches have developed programs that enable children to visit parents in prison. Others offer social services and mentoring programs and provide church space for free health clinics, child care centers, and food pantries and as meeting places for women's alcohol and drug support groups, youth groups, and even for probation and parole agents to meet with their clients. Volunteers from many faith groups are increasingly working with local residents to build the capacities of neighborhoods and to organize political action to improve American social welfare policies that impact poverty.

The resurgence of faith community resources could not have come at a better time. The extraordinarily high rates of incarceration over the past several decades are just now beginning to pose new challenges. Some prisoners are reaching the end of their sentences and are being released to the community, some on parole but many with no mandated ongoing supervision because their sentences have been served in full. In addition, whole new cohorts of prisoners are being given early release as the disparity of drug sentences is being successfully challenged.

Global Context

The world we live in has become increasingly small. Events that take place in one country are now communicated instantly around the globe. The United States has gained a very negative reputation in other parts of the world for its prisons, its sentencing, and its entire criminal justice system. The United Nations considered the United States to be in violation of the International Covenant on Civil and Political Rights, which bans the execution of juveniles, until 2005 when the U.S. Supreme Court finally banned execution of children. Today the international community remains concerned about treatment of people in U.S. prisons, overcrowding, shackling of women prisoners during labor and childbirth, over-utilization of incarceration, and the death penalty. The international community has also expressed alarm with the U.S. detention of non-citizen immigrants suspected of terrorist acts and the use of military commissions to try cases of noncitizens.

For many years, the United States had the highest rate of imprisonment of all countries in the world. That was true in 2001 when the world average rate was 140 out of every 100,000 persons in the population. At that time, the U.S. rate of imprisonment was 702, compared with Russia's 635 and South Africa's rate of 406, the three top worldwide rates (International Centre for Prison Studies, 2001). For many years prior to that, Russia's rate was consistently the highest and, before apartheid ended in South Africa, that country had the highest incarceration rate in the world (Mauer, 1994). By 2016 (most current available data), the average world population imprisonment rate was 144 and over half of all 221 countries had a rate of 150 or less. The U.S. rate remained the highest in the world, except for the tiny island country of Seychelles off the coast of East Africa (Walmsley, n.d.). Box 11.4 provides a sampling of incarceration rates worldwide. As you read through it, pay special attention to the enormous variation in countries' sentencing practices. What these data do not show is the length of imprisonment for specific crimes. In general, however, the United States tends to sentence people to much longer prison terms than other countries.

An observation that was articulated by Walmsley, an international authority on criminal studies research, to the United Nations in 2001 remains valid today: Increasing crime rates are not the cause of overutilization of incarceration, but increased fear of crime and strong desire for retribution, especially among policy makers, drive the massive incarcerations in some countries. Data on incarceration and rate of imprisonment internationally also suggest that human rights are globally impacted by over-utilization of imprisonment.

Box 11.4 Incarceration Rate for Selected Nations, 2016 (per 100,000 Population)

Seychelles (East Africa)	799	Canada	106
United States of America	698	France	100
St. Kitts & Navis (Caribbean Islands)	607	Italy	87
Russian Federation	446	Switzerland	84
South Africa	293	Denmark	61
Mexico	212	Finland	57
United Kingdom	148	Sweden	55
Spain	133	Japan	48
China	119	India	33
Kenya	118	Central African Republic	16

Source: Institute for Criminal Policy Research, (2016). *World prison brief: Highest to lowest prison population rate*. Retrieved from http://prisonstudies.org/highest-to-lowest/prison_population_rate?field_region_taxonomy_tid=All.

Promoting Human Rights and Social Justice

The United Nations' Universal Declaration of Human Rights of 1948 and its more recently developed sections provide a basis for agreed-upon international guidelines to human rights. While the United Nations does not have strict enforcement powers, it does set goals for nations and requests progress reports on identified needs. Member states of the United Nations also seek to hold other nations to the principles affirmed in this document. The United States signed the Universal Declaration of Human Rights; however, the U.S. Senate has never ratified it. The Universal Declaration of Human Rights, however, remains a respected legal instrument that is used to effect change globally.

In many respects, the NASW Code of Ethics parallels the Universal Declaration of Human Rights as it asserts the rights and dignity of all persons and calls social workers to culturally competent practice. The entire final section of the NASW Code of Ethics, which deals with social workers' ethical responsibilities to the broader society, appears to have been written from a global social justice perspective. The social justice issues that this chapter has identified within the criminal justice area are clearly addressed, whether from a national or an international perspective. The code requires that social workers work toward improving access to basic human needs, promote social justice safeguards for all people, and seek an end to discrimination (NASW, 2008). The human rights perspective of the NASW Code of Ethics invites social workers to think globally and to appreciate the interdependence of all people and all nations.

Amnesty International (AI) is one of several international organizations seeking to ensure human rights for persons who are members of the lesbian, gay, bisexual, and transgender (LGBT) community and to achieve the decriminalization of homosexuality. Globally, gender identity and sexual orientation are often punished by local criminal justice systems through torture, imprisonment, and even execution. AI has identified threats of violence, arrests, and torture of LGBT human rights activists in Uganda, Latvia, and Malawa (Amnesty International USA, 2010). It should be noted that the NASW Code of Ethics calls upon social workers to work to achieve social policies that ensure justice and human rights for all people including persons who are LGBT or who are distinguished by gender identity or expression. War, too, adds vast numbers of political prisoners and even migrants fleeing war increase the numbers of persons arrested, incarcerated, and denied their human rights.

The environment of prisons in the United States and in many other countries as well makes them breeding grounds for abuses of many kinds. AI is the primary organization that works on these issues internationally. In 2000, AI filed a briefing with the United Nations, alleging that the treatment of prisoners in the United States was in violation of the United Nations Convention against Torture and Other Cruel, Inhumane or Degrading Treatment or Punishment. When the United States ratified this UN convention in 1994, it agreed to abide by the principles of the convention.

AI's listing of concerns included some of the following:

- Beatings, excessive force, and unjustified shootings by police officers
- Physical and mental abuse of prisoners by prison guards, including use of electroshock equipment to inflict torture or ill treatment
- Sexual abuse of female prisoners by male guards
- Prisoners held in cruel conditions in isolation units

- Failure to protect prisoners from abuses by staff or other inmates
- Inadequate medical or mental health care
- Overcrowded and dangerous conditions in some facilities
- Racist ill treatment of ethnic or racial minorities by police or prison guards
- Cruel conditions on death row and violations of human rights standards in the application of the death penalty (Amnesty International, 2000)

Progress has occurred in some areas. All 50 states now have legislation intended to protect women from sexual abuse by guards and corrections staff. The Federal Bureau of Prisons barred shackling of pregnant prisoners in 2008. The majority of state and local prisons, however, have no legislation banning such practices as the use of shackles or restraints during labor and delivery. AI has also consistently recommended that children be incarcerated or placed in solitary confinement only as a last resort, and that the death penalty be discontinued for children and for people with cognitive disabilities.

Social workers can promote social justice for prisoners by supporting the efforts of AI and other organizations advocating reform. Indeed, social work students on some college campuses are actively working with AI campus chapters to secure humane treatment of prisoners in the United States and internationally. Action is often targeted at specific areas of injustice.

One of the most dramatic examples of social work activism on behalf of women prisoners occurred a number of years ago in Michigan. A group of Michigan social workers and students engaged a Detroit city council member, a coalition of community leaders, and the state Department of Corrections in the development of the Women and Infants at Risk (WIAR) program. Students initiated action when they learned that "belly chains" were used to secure women in labor when they were transported from the prison to the hospital for delivery, guards (male or female) remained with the women throughout

Social work student lobbies state congressman on proposed reform legislation

delivery and their brief hospitalization, and the babies were separated from their mothers when the women were returned to prison. The WIAR program that was created moved pregnant women from the prison to the WIAR community residence months prior to delivery, provided them with maternity clothes (not normally available to prisoners), prenatal classes, and nutritional supplements. When the women went into labor, they were admitted to the local hospital where they delivered their babies. They were not chained or shackled during transport, during labor, or following delivery. They returned to the WIAR home and were able to care for their babies for a full month before returning to a reduced level of work responsibilities at the prison (Siefert & Pimlott, 2001).

Human Rights and Justice

Dimension of Competency: *Skills* Social workers utilize strategies to promote social and economic justice and human rights.

Critical Thinking Question: What strategies and actions might social workers use to creatively address today's compelling social justice issues in the criminal justice system?

The students and social workers who created the WIAR program clearly understood the forms of injustice within the prison system. They used their knowledge and skills to advance social justice for mothers and their infants. But this is barely a beginning. In the criminal justice system, numerous social justice issues remain to be addressed by social workers in collaboration with other human rights advocates.

It is important to remember that the way we vote and how we interact with our elected representatives determine the nature of our criminal justice system. The liberal and conservative political ideologies that were discussed in Chapter 2 typically drive voting behaviors and lead to social policy decisions that have enormous impact on our criminal justice system. The strength of political conservatives in past years resulted in increasing use of imprisonment, longer sentences, and less concern about rehabilitation. This approach, however, ignored the simple fact that after a severe prison sentence and with minimal rehabilitation or preparation, most prisoners will someday be released back into the community.

The disproportionate sentencing of black Americans has emerged as one of the most significant social justice issues confronting the U.S. criminal justice system. Media coverage of young black males being killed by police has focused public attention on all aspects of the criminal justice system's treatment of race in apprehension, charging, and sentencing. The data on sentenced prisoners illustrate this disparity:

- Blacks comprise 35.8% of the prison population
  Blacks comprise 13.2% of the U.S. population
- Hispanics comprise 21.6% of the prison population
  Hispanics comprise 17.4% of the U.S. population
- Whites comprise 33.6% of the prison population
  Whites comprise 77.4% of the U.S. population (Carson, 2015; U.S. Census Bureau, 2015)

The largest age cohort of the prison population is the age 30–39-year-old group. The Bureau of Justice Statistics data analysis found that of all black males of that age range in the U.S. population, 6 percent were in prison. Again, disparity in incarceration emerges when the black male incarceration rate is compared with only 1 percent of the white 30–39-year-old male population and 2 percent of the Hispanic male population in the same age range. Incarceration is only one piece of the criminal justice system, but it has a profound impact on the lives of people.

The Death Penalty

Another social policy issue relates to **capital punishment**, the death penalty. Since its founding, the ultimate penalty for criminal conduct in the United States has been death. It remains a hotly debated issue. Some people believe that since "justice should fit the crime," it is logical that a person who commits murder should be punished with death. When the former U.S. president George W. Bush was governor of Texas, he favored a continuation of capital punishment in his state because he liked legal practice the way it was and saw no reason to change it. The U.S. Conference of Catholic Bishops expressed an opposing view in 1999; its statement opposed capital punishment "not just for what it does to those guilty of horrible crimes, but for what it does to all of us as a society" (p. 2).

Canadians find the death penalty unacceptable and Canada does not have capital punishment. Nor do most of the other industrialized nations of the world. The European Union bans the use of executions by member nations. Some nations refuse to extradite prisoners to the United States because of the U.S. death penalty. Many U.S. organizations—including the NASW, the American Bar Association, the American Civil Liberties Union (ACLU), and various religious organizations—are calling for the suspension or discontinuation of the death penalty. Inadequate legal representation for poor persons, racial bias, execution of children and mentally impaired persons, and execution of innocent persons are among the concerns of opponents of the death penalty. In recent years, DNA testing has confirmed the innocence of a number of persons sentenced to death. The ACLU has called for a moratorium on capital punishment in the United States.

In 2016, 3,261 persons were under sentence of death in federal or state prisons (Death Penalty Statistics). Detailed information from the Bureau of Justice Statistics provided a racial breakdown for sentenced persons in 2013 (most recent data available); 41.9 percent were black, 14 percent were Hispanic, and 55.8 percent were white. Women represented only 2 percent of the persons on death row. In 2013, 39 persons were executed, one-third of whom were black. Until one recalls that blacks comprise 13.2 percent of the U.S. population, the data may not suggest racial disparity in capital punishment sentencing. Comparing the 13.2 percent of black people in the population with the data showing that nearly 42 percent of the prison population sentenced to death was black persons and that black persons were 33 percent of prisoners executed does reveal disparity (Snell, 2014).

Racial disparity can influence sentencing decisions in ways that most people are not aware of. Cohen and Smith (2010), for example, observed that federal prosecutors can sometimes avoid the harshest of punishments by trying to take potential death penalty cases to federal court rather than state district courts, where death penalties are handed down much more frequently. Federal districts are geographically much larger than state jurisdictions and the federal court jury pools tend to be predominately white and represent largely white populations. Death sentences rarely occur in these courts. A 2011 article examined quite a different phenomenon. It strongly suggested that bias in favor of the death penalty may arise in southern states when the Confederate flag is flown at death penalty trials. This article specifically identified the Caddo Courthouse in Louisiana where, since 1972, 16 men and one woman have been sentenced to death; all but four were black, thus strongly suggesting racial bias. The flag is said to carry a stark reminder of the lynchings that took place in that area, as well as a not-so-subtle racially biased message that is "not to be underestimated" (Trenticosta & Collins).

Currently, 32 states still have capital punishment laws, but in 2014 only seven states executed a total of 35 prisoners. From a human rights perspective, some progress is being made in the United States. Maryland, repealed its death penalty law in 2013; Connecticut, repealed the law in 2012; and New Mexico in 2009. Prior to that, New Jersey ended capital punishment in 2007 and New York in 2004 (Snell, 2014). In 2016 California, Nebraska, and Oklahoma, however, voted to protect capital punishment. California moved to speed up executions of death row inmates (Schuppe, 2016).

In 2005, the U.S. Supreme Court struck down the juvenile death penalty by a narrow 5–4 decision, citing the state laws authorizing capital punishment for 16- and 17-year-old offenders as unconstitutional. At that time, the United States had the dubious distinction of being one of only six nations worldwide that had a juvenile death penalty law. Sadly, Human Rights Watch observed that two-thirds of all child death penalty executions in the world since 2002 have been carried out by the United States.

Arguments for and against capital punishment are shown in Box 11.5.

Capital punishment for mentally ill persons has become a social policy issue. This is clearly a thorny issue; mental illness ranges widely, from forms of illness that can be well managed to circumstances of truly severe impairment. Decisions would have to be made, too, about those persons who became mentally ill while in prison vs. those who, like Kelsey Patterson, clearly demonstrated profound mental illness at the time of the offense.

Box 11.5 Up for Debate

Proposal: The death penalty should be abolished in the United States.

Yes	No
The death penalty is cruel and inhumane, a fact that is acknowledged by almost all other industrialized countries in the world.	The death penalty is "just rewards" for the crime of murder.
Governments have no more right to take a life than does a person.	Each government has a right and an obligation to determine appropriate sentences. In the United States, the Supreme Court has ultimate authority to determine the constitutionality of laws enacted by state courts.
Capital punishment is not a deterrent, and it does nothing to protect citizens against crime.	As a result of capital punishment, thousands of people have been executed over the years, all of whom represented a threat to society.
As recent DNA evidence has demonstrated, there is always the potential for execution of an innocent man or woman.	With technology such as DNA laboratory findings, there will be very little future likelihood of state execution of innocent persons.
There is clear racial, socioeconomic, and even geographic discrimination in the way in which offenders reach death row and are subject to execution.	The majority of persons subject to the death penalty and executed by the United States are white males.
Capital punishment is a failed, morally wrong social policy.	The death penalty should be expanded to include accomplices and others indirectly involved in committing a murder.

Kelsey Patterson, a 50-year-old man diagnosed with paranoid schizophrenia, was apprehended as he walked naked down a street near his home on a warm fall afternoon, mumbling incoherently. He was found to have committed a double murder for which no clear motive was established. Kelsey Patterson was executed by the state of Texas in 2004. Further complicating the death penalty issue related to mental illness is an awareness that persons with mental illness might never have found their way into the criminal justice system if they had received mental health treatment in the first place.

Reforming Juvenile and Adult Criminal Justice Systems

Since 1996, juvenile crime has declined steadily and has now fallen to a level last seen in the 1970s. The juvenile crime rate, in fact, has declined even more substantially than adult crime. Violent crime for juveniles (under age 18) decreased markedly, according to the U.S. Department of Justice (2015). In 1 year alone (2013 to 2014), the total number of arrests for crimes committed by juveniles fell from 875,262 in 2013 to 804,104 in 2014. Murder rates over those 2 years dropped from 614 to 590, and robberies fell from 15,932 to 15,312. The total number of arrests for violent crimes among juveniles dropped by 1,528, from 43,651 in 2013 to 42,123 in 2014 (FBI, 2014; FBI, 2015). This continuing decline in juvenile crime, however, does not match the perception of communities. Public attitudes still support punitive policy for youths, but slowly there is increasing recognition that the current juvenile justice system is not working. Many professional persons involved with juvenile justice have sought change for several years.

As early as 1998, Jensen and Howard (both social workers) proposed looking at the social context that places youths at risk for delinquency, including factors such as poverty, family instability, and substance abuse. They suggested developing prevention programs targeted at youths known to be at high risk for anti-social behavior and investing in community economic development aimed at providing opportunities for young people. At the same time, Scott and Grisso, an attorney and a psychiatrist, urged the incorporation of understandings from developmental psychology in social policymaking. They pointed to continuing statistics showing that delinquent behavior is both fairly common in adolescence and likely to conclude as youths become young adults. Adolescents' knowledge base and decision-making abilities are sufficiently immature, they stated, that it impairs their ability to make sound judgments when they are read their rights, at arrest, and in their ability to stand trial. Immature judgment is often involved in the behavior that leads to arrest. They concluded that severe sanctions (transfer to adult courts, imprisonment in adult jails, severe sentences) on youths for first offenses, even for serious crimes, are not in the best interests of the youths or of society (1998). That, of course, was the belief of Jane Addams when she and her Hull House colleagues founded the first the first juvenile court in the United States in 1899.

The focus on rehabilitation and acknowledgement that "juvenile" brains did not have the same capacity of adult brains in decision-making began to slip away in the 1970s and 1980s. Increases in juvenile crime led to the perception that the criminal justice system had become too lenient with youths. During the 1980s and 1990s, state legislatures passed legislation that shifted juvenile courts away from a rehabilitation focus toward increasingly treating juvenile offenders as adult criminals. Forty-five states in the

> Watch this TEDx talk by social worker Bobby Lefebre. What is his message about the correlation between environmental justice and working with juveniles in the corrections system?
>
> https://www.youtube.com/watch?v=Uw5qLiQERBg

1990s defined procedures that permitted juvenile offenders to be transferred from the juvenile court to the adult criminal justice system, thereby enabling adult courts to try, sentence, and imprison juveniles as if they were adults. Gradually in some states, youths aged 16 or older, or children charged with certain heinous crimes, were automatically transferred to adult court. They then automatically entered the adult criminal justice system. Other state legislation expanded the sentencing options of juvenile courts resulting in adult court sentences, in some cases as long as life-without-parole or death sentences.

By 2011, some states developed discretion provisions. These provisions gave prosecutors the right to decide whether to file charges in adult (or juvenile) court, depending on the nature of the crime. Today many states have laws that exclude certain crimes such as murder from being prosecuted in juvenile courts. Additionally, states have set upper age limits for juvenile court cases; in 2010, 13 states defined 15 or 16 as the line between juvenile and criminal court. Pennsylvania has no minimal age for prosecution of murder; the age designation for some other youth crime in Pennsylvania is 14 or 15 (Sickmund & Puzzanchera, 2014).

Slowly, ever so slowly, some reform is coming to juvenile justice systems. Blended sentencing laws were approved by 14 states in 2011. These laws built in some flexibility, enabling juvenile courts to order adult criminal court sentences and/or adult criminal courts to impose a juvenile court sentence (usually much less harsh). The result has been that some judges will give both an adult sentence and a juvenile sentence, with the adult sentence suspended if the youth successfully completes the requirements of the juvenile sentence. The U.S. Supreme Court, in the 2012 *Miller v. Alabama* case, made history by striking down existing mandatory life-without-parole sentences for juvenile offenders. This did not eliminate the possibility of a juvenile life-without-parole sentence; this remains an option available to the courts, but states may no longer mandate a life-without-parole sentence for murder, as had been the case. The Supreme Court terminated the death penalty for juveniles in 2005 (Sickmund & Puzzanchera, 2014).

In both landmark decisions, the court reaffirmed the need to distinguish between children and adults in sentencing. After *Miller v. Alabama*, states began changing their laws. California's revised 2012 law permitted persons serving a life-without-parole sentence stemming from a juvenile conviction to petition for a new sentence. North Dakota's 2013 law required a presentence investigation to identify any mitigating circumstances before the court could sentence a juvenile to life imprisonment. In 2013, Wyoming's legislation stated that persons sentenced to life in prison would become eligible for parole consideration after serving 25 years. Iowa's governor used his authority to commute 38 prisoners' life-without-parole sentences ... to 60-year prison terms (Sickmund & Puzzanchera, 2014). In 2016, the day after the U.S. Supreme court required states to retroactively apply the *Miller v. Alabama* ban on mandatory life-without-parole sentences for juveniles, President Obama used his executive privilege to ban solitary confinement for youths held in federal prisons. Justice Kennedy, in handing down the Supreme Court's decision, affirmed the belief of the court that even children who commit heinous crimes have capacity for change. President Obama, following his announcement banning solitary confinement for juveniles, expressed his belief that solitary confinement has devastating effects on people, makes it difficult for them to re-enter society as productive citizens, and can result in suicide. As a result, it should be used sparingly even with adult prison populations (EJI, 2016).

Reform of the juvenile justice system, if it is to return to the spirit and intent of Jane Addams and acknowledge the special needs of children, has many challenges ahead. With approximately 10,000 children still incarcerated in adult prisons and jails every day, attention needs to be paid to the dangers lurking in these environments. Inmates in adult prisons tend to be much older, while juvenile offenders are usually between 15 and 17 years old. The adults in these facilities tend to be physically bigger and stronger and have more violent criminal histories. The sheer size of adult facilities, often holding upward of 1,000 prisoners, further complicated by overcrowding, creates an environment that, at best, fails to nurture rehabilitation and, at worst, puts youths at risk of theft, battery, and sexual assault by older prisoners and sometimes by guards. Soon the question may arise: if it is really in the best interests of society or of juvenile offenders to incarcerate them in adult facilities.

Perhaps it is time, too, to think about how children enter the criminal justice system. Zero-tolerance policies of schools, policies that punish behavior problems with police referral, sweep large numbers of children into the juvenile justice system. This is sometimes referred to as the "school-to-prison pipeline." In recent years, metropolitan city schools have significantly increased police presence within public schools. Inner-city students of color and students from families struggling with poverty are disproportionately affected by zero-tolerance policies (Friends Committee on National Legislation, 2015). An option to be considered might be one of replacing the police presence with that of services to help the children, teachers, and families. This would mean providing schools with more than just one school social worker, psychologist, nurse, and counselor. In fact, most schools today share one social worker, psychologist, etc., among several schools so their presence is far from equal in number to that of police. The school-to-prison effect of zero-tolerance policies demands reconsideration.

Criminal justice reform was emerging more fully in the adult criminal justice arena than in juvenile justice systems. In 2015 and early 2016 there appeared to be a new willingness to talk and to work on systemic reform for the adult criminal justice system in the U.S. Congress. Both political parties agreed that the system needed reform, that too many Americans were locked up in prison. The cost to taxpayers for massive incarceration was a major concern for political conservatives. Injustice to individuals, families, and communities, especially for people of color, was the primary concern advanced by liberals. Sentencing reform, the state of prison environments, re-entry programs for persons returning to the community, and police-community relations were major reform issues.

A number of bills were initiated by Congress in 2015, most building on the 2010 **Fair Sentencing Act**, landmark legislation that reduced the racially discriminatory sentencing disparity between crack and powder cocaine possession, stemming from laws passed in the 1980s. The Sentencing Reform and Corrections Act, introduced in 2015, was expected to be acted upon by both the U.S. Senate and the House of Representatives before the end of the legislative year in 2016. This bill would decrease the sentencing guidelines for some drug-related crimes. The Senate version would also create several new mandatory minimum sentences (including a mandatory 5-year minimum sentence for providing controlled goods to terrorists or to anyone involved with the development of weapons of mass destruction). It also provided programs for the compassionate release of prisoners who were elderly and considered non-violent and for a pre-release program aimed at decreasing recidivism (GovTrack.us, 2015). Advocates for sentencing reform especially favored the portion of the bill that permitted the reduction of sentences for some prisoners currently held on drug charges.

The Sentencing Reform and Corrections Act was considered to be an update and it incorporated much of the content of the Smarter Sentencing Act, which had also been introduced with bipartisan sponsorship in 2015. The Smarter Sentencing Act focused on non-violent drug offenses and reduced the current sentences of persons convicted for low-level drug offenses from 5-, 10-, and 20-year mandatory minimum to 2-, 5-, and 10-year sentences for specified drug offenses. It also reduced mandatory life-without-parole sentences of persons convicted for their third drug-related crime to a minimum term of 25 years. This bill would not be retroactive; therefore, it would only affect persons coming up for sentencing, not persons already imprisoned, except that it did provide an opportunity for persons imprisoned for crack cocaine offenses to petition the court for fairer sentences. The bill did not change sentencing for gun, violent, or sex-related offenses.

Criminal reform advocacy groups strongly supported these two bills. The Friends Committee on National Legislation, a Quaker lobby organization, worked toward passage of the Smarter Sentencing Act, favoring restoration of judges' discretion in sentencing and the retroactivity of the old Fair Sentencing Act of 2010 (Friends Committee on National Legislation, 2015). A non-profit organization, the Families against Mandatory Minimums, saw the bill as helpful in cutting back on the federal criminal justice system's sentencing of "innocent and well-meaning people" who had unintentionally, sometimes unknowingly, violated laws (FAMM, 2015, p. 3). This was one of several criminal justice reform efforts that sought to shift away from mandatory sentencing entirely in the belief that sentencing flexibility permits courts to recognize the uniqueness of each person and the nature of the crime. Following the 2016 election, hopes faded that this reform bill would sustain sufficient support to pass either House of Congress.

At the end of 2015 (prior to the 2016 election), 6,000 prisoners were granted early release from federal prisons due to earlier changes in the drug sentencing law. Although approximately 2,000 were foreign nationals who were immediately deported, the remainder were moved into halfway houses or placed on probation, some under electronic home confinement. Some states developed re-entry programs for their returning prisoners (Associated Press, 2015). Additionally, President Obama commuted the sentences of 95 federal prisoners, five of whom were serving life-without-parole sentences and had been convicted of nonviolent crimes (ACLU, 2015).

The emergence of the Black Lives Matter movement riveted the country's attention to police–community relations following police shootings and police abuse of black people. Black Lives Matter is a national organization that was formed following the shooting of Trayvon Martin in 2012, but it has grown to become an organization that is working both to affirm all black people and to fight for the lives as well as the human rights of all black people (Black Lives Matter Network, n.d.). Tragically, police shootings have continued in the years since Trayvon Martin's death, leading to deteriorating relationships between police and communities. In an effort to improve policing practices, reduce the lethal use of force, and improve police–community relations, the U.S. Conference of Mayors published a set of recommendations. Police departments were strongly advised to develop hiring practices that would ensure that the police force was reflective of the community it served. Officer training was to concentrate on alternatives to lethal force, when possible, and methods to defuse escalating incidents as well as approaches to identify and safely handle persons exhibiting symptoms of mental illness (2015).

Racial profiling and disparity in the arrests of people of color have been longstanding human rights problems in the United States, which, especially in conjunction with police shootings in recent years, has fueled poor police–community relations. Historically, racial profiling was targeted primarily at people who were black, but the terrorist attacks on the United States in 2001 quickly expanded profiling to members of Arab, Muslim, and other South Asian communities. Immigrants and entire Latino communities have also experienced profiling. The Black Lives Matters movement, along with the ACLU and other organizations, are working to stop racial profiling, which includes interrogations, arrests, searches, detention, and even social media monitoring. In 2015, the executive director of the ACLU of Oregon reported that persons using the Black Lives Matter hash tag were experiencing secret, illegal surveillance by the Oregon Department of Justice. The executive director of the ACLU of Oregon called for the state attorney general to initiate reforms (Rogers, 2015).

Reform of the criminal justice system does not end with issues related to policing. The entire corrections area—prisons, re-entry programs, probation, and parole—and the courts are all interconnected and need attention. Many prisons are now very old, with crumbling, stone wall interiors as well as exteriors. They are difficult to keep clean and properly ventilated. They present health concerns for prisoners and staff alike. Perhaps most at risk are older adult prisoners with lengthy sentences whose health care problems include incontinence, high blood pressure, hearing and vision loss, diabetes, cardiac disease, cancer, dementia, and the need of wheelchairs and walkers. Most prisons are not adequately staffed to deal with the advancing age and disabilities of prisoners, although some prisons now have hospice units ("Aging Inmates Prompt Creation of Assisted Living Center at Washington Prison," 2010).

Surely reform of the prison system needs to begin with the question of why these people are still being held in prisons. Are they of danger to the community? Obviously, there are numerous other concerns about prisons and prison environments, the growing need for re-entry programs for persons coming out of prisons, and community practices that include discrimination against persons with felonies in hiring, housing, and access to health care. Reforming the juvenile and adult criminal justice system is a complex process and it faces many challenges.

Some of the enthusiasm for reform, however, was lost when the 2016 election brought "law and order" candidates into office across the country. Much of the country's attention was riveted to the startling volatility of the presidential campaign which was marked by verbal assaults on women, people with disabilities, Muslims, and racially diverse populations. The FBI reported a seven percent increase in hate crime in 2015 including a 67 percent increase in offenses targeting Muslims. Jewish people, African Americans, women, and gays and lesbians were also targeted. Following the election, hate crime incidents spread to college campuses, houses of worship, and other public places (Johnson, 2016). The new president pledged to bring back order to the streets and public places of America. He stated that he would use his authority to roll back the Obama reform initiatives that were soft on crime, such as the early release of persons convicted of nonviolent drug offenses (Schuppe, 2016).

The future of criminal justice reform may await renewed action by Congress and at the state level, where interest in pursuit of human rights change is led by organizations and individuals, among them local faith communities, social workers, attorneys, and prosecutors among others, who seek to heal and repair what they see as a broken justice system. It is speculated that Trump's business sense and Congressional intent to reduce government spending may, in time, coalesce and sustain some of Obama's executive orders related to reduced sentencing for non-violent offenses and other criminal justice initiatives (Schuppe, 2016). Of course there is also the possibility that state and federal legislative bodies may instead increase the use of incarceration and expand the private prison industry. In that case, social justice advocates will need to be ready to respond quickly and creatively.

Then conclude this section with the existing final sentence of the section. The energy and passion of people awakened by the 2016 election (especially people who did not vote) and the evolving political environment have potential for creative social justice reform, including humanitarian reform of the U.S. criminal justice system.

> Assess your understanding of the social, economic, and environmental justice issues that relate to criminal justice in the United States by taking this brief quiz.

SUMMARY

- The history of the criminal justice system in the United States is traced. The chapter begins with a case study that depicts a probation/parole social worker, Alan Martin, experiencing his own identity crisis while working with the mother of a youth who dies following an exchange of gunfire with police, and with a youth who Alan helps to re-enter the community following imprisonment. Alan's renewal of his social work values and commitment to his profession forms the background for an examination of the historical development of social work in the field of criminal justice.
- The components that comprise the criminal justice system are described: law enforcement, the courts, the correctional system, and the juvenile justice system.
- The profession of social work and how it is practiced within the criminal justice field are explained, with special attention given to the value dilemmas social workers experience in this field of practice. Forensic social work, a new area of practice, is explored with a case study provided to illustrate practice in a medical examiner's office. Group and organizational system practice is also described.
- Social, economic, and environmental justice issues that exist in the criminal justice system in the United States are discussed. The new, evolving political environment that poses both opportunities and challenges for those who are committed to humanitarian reform of the American criminal justice system are acknowledged.

> Recall what you learned from this chapter by completing the Chapter Review.

12

Developmental Disabilities and Social Work

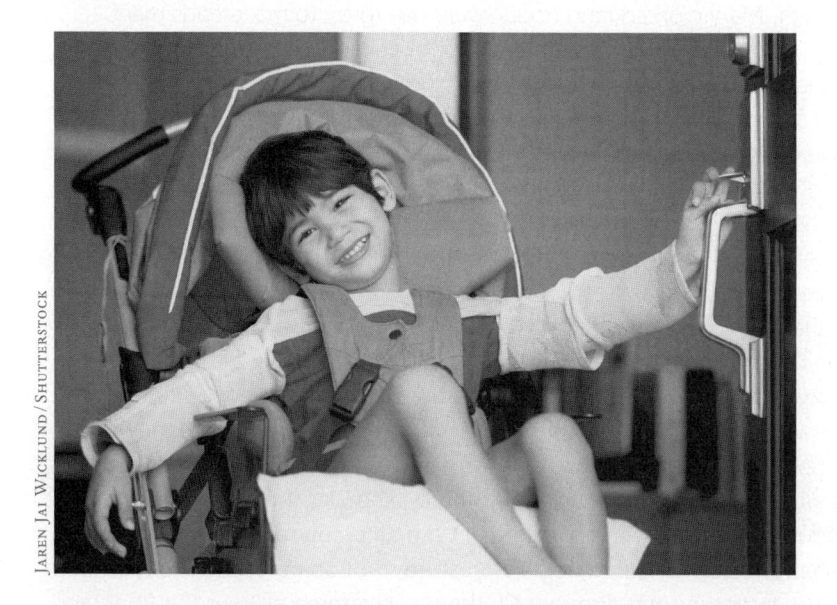

CASE STUDY: Mary and Lea Perkins

Mary Perkins called the Department of Social Services (DSS) early one morning. Her teenage daughter, Lea, had been sexually assaulted by an unknown person during the night. The attack had taken place on the front steps of the family apartment. Mary had already called the police, but then she decided to call the DSS as well because she believed that Lea was out of control and needed help. The girl had disobeyed Mary's curfew rules again, contributing to her traumatic experience. Moreover, she had skipped school almost daily for months. Mary asked the DSS for help in supervision. She knew the department offered these services because her older daughter, Lorraine, already received them. Lorraine had been arrested for drug possession the year before, and the court, under a CHIPS (child in need of protection) petition, had ordered DSS supervision.

LEARNING OUTCOMES

- Describe the history of services to people with disabilities.
- Identify and discuss major types of developmental disabilities.
- Describe contemporary social work practice with people who have disabilities.
- Explain social justice issues that pertain to human diversity involving disabilities.
- Discuss the disability rights movement and its causes.

CHAPTER OUTLINE

CASE STUDY: Mary and Lea Perkins 373

Services for People with Disabilities: A Brief History 378
- Pioneering Efforts 378
- Training Schools 379
- Protective Asylums 379
- The Eugenics Movement 380
- New Research, New Attitudes 381
- Normalization and the Deinstitutionalization Movement 382
- Deinstitutionalization as a Goal 382

Types of Developmental Disabilities 384
- Developmental Disabilities: What Are They? 384
- Difference between *Disability* and *Developmental Disability* 384
- Categorical vs. Functional Definitions of Developmental Disability 384
- Intellectual Disability 384
- Cerebral Palsy 386

373

CHAPTER OUTLINE (Continued)

    Autism Spectrum Disorders   386
    Orthopedic Problems   388
    Hearing Problems   389
    Epilepsy   390
    Traumatic Brain Injury   390
    Learning Disabilities   391
    Emotional Disturbance   392
    Fetal Alcohol Spectrum Disorders;
        Cocaine-Exposed and Other
        Drug-Exposed Babies   392
    Overall Prevalence and
        Co-Occurrence of
        Disabilities   393
    The Continuum of Care   394

Social Work Practice with People Who Have Disabilities   395
    Education for Work with People
        Who Have Disabilities: CSWE
        Educational Policy   395
    NASW Code of Ethics   395
    Institutional Settings   396
    Community Settings   396
    Genetic Counseling   397
    Spirituality Dimensions   397

Human Diversity and Social Justice   398
    Providing Supportive Services to
        Diverse Families: A Chinese
        Illustration   399
    Asian Americans: A Brief
        History   400
    Social Justice Issues and
        Disability   401
    Mismatch between Person and
        Environment   401
    Discrimination   401
    Empowerment, Self-Determination,
        and Self-Advocacy   402

The Disability Rights Movement, Social Policy, and Appropriate Terminology   403

Shortly after Mary's call for help, a neighbor called to report Mary herself for neglect, complaining that the mother was rarely home and allowed her children to "run wild all day." The case was scheduled for investigation. The social worker making the initial contact regarding Lea found a mother who was overwhelmed by the demands of parenting three children: Lorraine, 16; Lea, 14; and Jeff, 11. Mary was openly seeking assistance. The children's father was not a resource for her. Alcoholic and unemployed, he had abused the mother physically and emotionally for years. Mary had recently secured a divorce; social workers at a local women's shelter had assisted her. With three children to support on her own, Mary worked long hours every day to try to make ends meet.

Because of Mary's admitted lack of control, Lea was at risk for foster placement. The case was contracted out to a private agency according to a service agreement reflecting a trend toward privatization. The agency assigned the case to its Home Base program, which provided intensive in-home intervention designed to prevent foster placement. According to the agency's contract with DSS, services could be provided in the home setting for up to three months, for four hours per week. If in-home intervention failed, foster care would follow. The Home Base program assigned the case to one of its social work student interns, Jenny Chambers.

New to her internship, Jenny felt understandably anxious when she read the referral information. She tried to make an appointment right away, but the Perkins' telephone had been disconnected. Jenny sent a note to schedule a late-afternoon appointment, when she hoped Mary would be home from work. Thankfully, she was. Mary met Jenny at the door and invited her in graciously. With an embarrassed smile, she raised her arms upward in a helpless gesture, motioning at the room around her. It was in total disarray. Clothes lay scattered all over the floor, and dishes overflowed the sink. "I'm so sorry," Mary said softly. "I tried to clean up last night for your visit, but the children wouldn't help, and they messed everything up again today. I might as well not have bothered."

Jenny took a deep breath and smiled at the mother warmly, complimenting her on the one item she could see giving her an opportunity to do so, an appealing family picture hanging on the wall.

Mary began to talk about her troubles. Jenny soon learned that the family not only lacked a telephone but heat as well. In addition, the rent was three months overdue, and the landlord was threatening eviction. Mary cried as she told Jenny that as her bills piled up, she simply did not know what to do, so she threw them in a grocery bag and tossed the bag in her bedroom closet. That way she could pretend they were gone. But the children made her so nervous she withdrew into the bedroom early in the evening and shut the door. Part of this problem was that two teenage boys, Lorraine's boyfriend and one of his buddies, stayed in the apartment most of the time. They had been rejected by their families, and Mary felt sorry for them. To add to the confusion, Lea had recently thrown a frying pan at a friend's mother during an argument and had been arrested for assault. The neighbor had taken out a restraining order, and there would be a court appearance for Lea soon.

Jenny's social work courses at school had prepared her to look for strengths and resilience. She was grateful, as otherwise she suspected she would feel overwhelmed listening to Mary's situation. She began consciously searching for strengths. She already knew of one: Mary had read Jenny's note and kept her appointment. There were several others. Mary had tried to clean her apartment for Jenny's visit. Two of her three children were attending school. She wanted to hold her family together. Prior to the neglect charge, Mary had had the strength to request assistance for Lea. Now that the DSS was considering foster placement, Mary was willing to do whatever she could to prevent that from happening. She worked long hours due to economic necessity, not because she wanted to neglect her children. She was managing a full-time job responsibly. Like many poor people, she was generous, sharing her meager resources with two needy teens who were not even related to her.

> **CHAPTER OUTLINE** (Continued)
>
> The Americans with Disabilities Act of 1990 and the Civil Rights Act of 1991   404
> Global Efforts on Behalf of People with Disabilities   406
> Value Dilemmas and Ethical Implications   406
> Current Trends   407
>
> **Summary   409**

Jenny next talked with Mary about Lea. Mary felt sorry for her daughter about the sexual assault but was also angry with her, as Lea had disobeyed Mary's curfew rules. Jenny asked how Lea usually behaved. Mary described Lea as "out of control, disrespectful, and nasty." Mary frankly stated that she felt exhausted from trying to function as a parent. But she did not want to lose her daughter, as so many of her neighbors had lost their children. Lea could be killed or injured on the street, for example. She could end up in foster care due to the neglect charge or to repeated truancy. Mary said that Lea probably refused to go to school because she was a very poor student and had been left back the year before.

On a hunch, Jenny asked Mary about her own experience as a student. To her surprise, she learned that this mother had an intellectual disability. School had been a desperate struggle for her, but a special education program had been opened when she was in her early teens. A teacher had referred her for evaluation, and she was placed in a class for children with mental retardation. While ashamed at first, Mary began to blossom with the new attention she was receiving. During her senior year, she participated in a school-to-work program, where she learned to assist in a physician's office. That education had served her well: Mary worked in a physician's office still.

"Was it possible that Lea, too, had an intellectual disability?" Jenny wondered. Could a special education placement make a positive difference for her? Certainly a referral for assessment was in order. And what about Mary's unusual coping style? Could her disability help explain the bag of unopened bills? Jenny also learned that Mary was taking prescribed medication for anxiety. Anxiety, too, could affect Mary's coping skills.

Before Jenny left her appointment with Mary, she made another to talk with Lea. When she returned two days later, Lea was waiting for her. A slim, attractive young girl with auburn hair and expressive blue eyes, she was dressed in baggy jeans, an old sweatshirt, and torn sneakers. Lea told Jenny straight away that she was tired of being poor and wanted to move out of the "ghetto," as she described her neighborhood. People who lived there were looked down upon as "criminals or bums." Lea admitted that she used alcohol to feel better and had been drunk the night of the sexual assault. She was having difficulty sleeping now because of flashbacks and nightmares.

She admitted that she was fighting a lot at home and had recently been arrested for attacking a friend's mother who had been yelling at her.

Jenny recognized the emotional turmoil Lea was experiencing and the associated behavioral problems. However, she also recognized many strengths. Lea had kept her appointment with Jenny and talked to her with surprising candor for a first interview. She could express her feelings verbally. She was aware that some of her behavior was inappropriate. She was aware of her external environment and its dangers, even though she was careless about protecting herself. Lea also expressed a strong interest in sports. Jenny thought this might help lure the young girl back to school.

Jenny met next with Mary and Lea jointly. Together an intervention plan was developed, including a contract that was signed by all parties. The contract called for (1) school attendance and educational testing for Lea; (2) house rules for Lea; (3) consequences for Lea if she did not follow the rules, which Mary must enforce; (4) therapy for both mother and daughter; and (5) convincing DSS not to place Lea in foster care. (This was the component that motivated Lea to agree to the other conditions.)

Intervention

Dimension of Competency: *Cognitive and Affective Reactions* Social workers understand that intervention is an ongoing component of practice on behalf of diverse individuals.

Critical Thinking Question: How did Jenny use her understanding of Lea's cognitive and affective reactions to the environment in which she was living to develop appropriate intervention plans?

To make the contract feasible, Jenny assisted the family in dealing with some very practical matters: the rent, the telephone, and the heat. She reviewed with Mary every bill in the grocery bag. She role-played talking with the landlord and encouraged Mary to approach the man in person. A payment plan for the back rent was successfully negotiated. Next, Jenny encouraged Mary to talk with the telephone company. A payment plan was worked out, and service was restored. Jenny found a state energy assistance program and encouraged Mary to call for more information. Mary did so, and her heating bill was substantially reduced with funds from the energy assistance program. Another payment plan was worked out. Heat was restored.

But if Mary were to meet the conditions of the payment plans for rent, telephone, and heat, something would have to be done to balance her income and expenses. So Jenny helped Mary develop a budget. That involved a great deal of effort. While many single mothers are unable to make ends meet due to inadequate wages, Jenny suspected that Mary might have an especially difficult time due to her intellectual disability, so she showed Mary how to write her income and expenses on paper and how to record her payments. When she realized there was no way Mary's income could meet expenses, she helped the hardworking mother apply for food stamps. She shopped with her for groceries and showed Mary how to compare prices and use product coupons and the debit-like card she received from the food stamp program. Jenny even helped Mary plan simple meals, demonstrating how she could save money by avoiding fast-food takeout.

Through these efforts, Jenny and Mary together realized that feeding two extra teenagers was impossible on Mary's income. Moreover, Mary recognized that their presence had a lot to do with her withdrawing to her bedroom every evening. With Jenny's coaching, she found the courage to tell the boys that they would have to find another place to stay. Jenny offered to help them approach their parents or to refer them for foster care. The boys opted for help in talking to their parents and soon went home.

Now Jenny decided it was time to clean up the Perkins' apartment, if Mary was interested. She was. Jenny moderated a family meeting, where Mary assigned regular chores to herself and the children. Together, they drew up a chart to record their accomplishments, displayed conspicuously on the refrigerator. While Jenny did much of the initial cleanup work with the family, gradually they took over.

Getting Lea to go to school or to attend therapy was not easy. The girl finally agreed to attend school only after her probation officer threatened to put her in juvenile detention if she didn't. (Lea had been put on probation for the frying pan incident shortly after Jenny began working with the family.) She then agreed to attend if Jenny would accompany her. Jenny agreed and then referred Lea for a special education evaluation. Only after several meetings with Jenny, the special education staff, and Lea would Lea attend school on her own. Jenny also found she had to accompany Lea to her first few therapy sessions to get her to go.

Assessment by the special education program determined that Lea did not have an intellectual disability. Her intelligence tested above average, in fact. However, she did have another disability, emotional disturbance (ED). Lea demonstrated disturbance in three environments: school (truancy), home (disobedience), and community (fighting behavior). Moreover, Lea's therapist submitted a diagnosis of posttraumatic stress disorder (PTSD). The PTSD related not only to the recent sexual assault but to prior physical and sexual abuse by her father, which the therapist reported to DSS for further investigation. Lea soon began receiving special services at the school and became a much happier person. She joined the girls' basketball team, making new friends. Her grades improved dramatically. Lea's lively blue eyes flashed with pride as she told Jenny about her new accomplishments.

To Jenny's dismay, however, Mary Perkins initially did not follow through with parts of her contract. She did not attend therapy, nor did she often enforce consequences when Lea broke house rules. Lea continued to roam the streets at night and, because the rapist remained at large, danger was real. Jenny sometimes wondered if foster placement might not be appropriate after all. Mary seemed to say one thing and do another. However, after much deliberation, Jenny decided to trust in the underlying love between mother and daughter.

Believing in the power of a strengths-based approach, Jenny continued to meet and talk with Mary regularly. She learned that Mary had suffered physical and sexual abuse from her own father. Jenny was then able to help the mother understand Lea's trauma (and need for firm parental protection) in terms of her own. Jenny helped Mary understand that she needed to serve as a role model for her daughter and to maintain consistent discipline to help Lea gain a sense of security and importance. Finally, Mary began to attend therapy, which helped her deal with long-term anxiety and develop the strength to enforce her own house rules.

As the initial three-month contract with DSS came to a close, Jenny did not believe that either Mary or Lea was ready to carry on without assistance. She applied for, and received, a six-week extension. By the end of that time, the situation had stabilized. Lea was attending school every day on time, participating in the ED program, and actually earning As. Mother and daughter were attending therapy regularly, reporting that it was useful. Mary was writing down on paper her behavioral expectations and consequences for Lea and enforcing them. She was discussing possible alternative living situations for Lea if her expectations were not met. Lea was following the house rules.

> **Evaluation**
>
> **Dimension of Competency:** *Skills* Social workers understand that evaluation is an ongoing component of social work practice with, and on behalf of, diverse clients.
>
> **Critical Thinking Question:** How do you think the agency supervisor evaluated Jenny's practice skills (from low to high) as a result of the information she received from Mary?

Termination wasn't easy for anyone. Lea, in fact, said she felt "sad and out of control" when Jenny reminded her that their time was coming to a close. Jenny helped Lea recognize that she had many other caring people in her life now, such as her therapist and the special education staff. She reminded Mary and Lea that they could call the agency for services again if needed, but that she herself would no longer be an intern there. Jenny was sad at the end of her allotted time with the family, as she had grown fond of every member.

A few weeks later, Jenny's supervisor visited the family to evaluate Jenny's work. In response to her questions, Mary replied, with tears in her eyes, that Jenny had been "an awful nag, but we miss her terribly."

SERVICES FOR PEOPLE WITH DISABILITIES: A BRIEF HISTORY

Pioneering Efforts

Throughout most of history, very little has been done for persons with disabilities. At one extreme (ancient Sparta), individuals unfortunate enough to have an obvious disability were left outside to die of exposure. Native Americans, on the other hand, allowed people with disabilities to live unharmed as children of the Great Spirit.

There are a few early recorded efforts to make special provisions for persons with disabilities. In the 1300s, a colony of persons with mental retardation (persons with intellectual disabilities, to use today's terminology) was established in Belgium, and, in 1325, King Edward II of England issued a statute distinguishing between people with intellectual disabilities and those afflicted with temporary mental illness. He established guidelines to protect the rights of "idiots" and to provide for their daily care (Dickerson, 1981). Later on, the Elizabethan Poor Law of 1601 provided limited food and shelter for people with disabilities (along with the elderly, people with mental illness, and the sick). Apparently, no thought was given to providing services or education to improve the lives and opportunities of such individuals.

France provided the pioneers who first educated persons with disabilities. Jacob Rodriguez Pereira demonstrated that people with speech and hearing problems could be taught to read words and to add simple numbers. By the late 1700s, Pereira had become so famous for his work that he was honored at the court of King Louis XV. Later, in the early 1800s, Jean Marc Gaspard Itard took on the education of a young boy, about 12 years old, whom he named Victor. The boy had been discovered living in a forest in France in 1799, and Itard hoped to help him learn how to function as a normal human person. Itard worked intensively on this goal for about five years. The extent of Victor's intellectual disability was too great, however, and Itard initially considered the project a failure. However, he was able to teach Victor basic self-care skills such as feeding and dressing. The boy remained mute but learned to read and write a few words. The French Academy of Science, impressed by Itard's accomplishments, recognized him and asked him to write a report. The result became a classic, *The Wild Boy of Aveyron* (Patton, Blackbourn, & Fad, 1996).

Another Frenchman, Itard's student Edouard Seguin (who was also influenced by Pereira), worked with small groups of children with intellectual disabilities in a hospital in Paris in the mid-1800s. Seguin demonstrated that these children could be taught to speak, read, obey instructions, and accomplish simple tasks.

Training Schools

At the same time Seguin was working with children with intellectual disabilities in Paris, a Swiss physician named Johann Guggenbuhl started a residential facility for people afflicted with cretinism. Cretinism is common in mountainous regions of Europe. Caused by a thyroid deficiency, it results in severe intellectual disability and physical crippling. Guggenbuhl was inspired by a religious vision; he was determined to prove that these people could be taught. Guggenbuhl succeeded in his long-term goal, stimulating further work with people with disabilities all over the world, including the development of training schools in the United States. In the short run, he ran into trouble, however, partly because he misunderstood the causes of cretinism. Like others of his time, Guggenbuhl thought the condition was caused by poor diet, unclean air and water, and lack of sunlight. He corrected these problems in his training school but promised too much in too short a time. His facility was closed in 1858.

In 1848, Dr. Samuel Gridley Howe, an American reformer, traveled to Europe and visited Guggenbuhl's training school and Seguin's hospital program. Back in the United States, he lobbied for funds to begin similar work. He established training schools for children with disabilities in Massachusetts, New York, and Pennsylvania during the late 1840s and early 1850s. These schools were small and usually served fewer than 20 children each; their goal was to prepare children with disabilities (such as vision impairment or mild intellectual disability) for productive adult lives in the community. Admission was limited to those children who were considered to have the most potential for **rehabilitation** and eventual discharge.

Seguin immigrated to the United States in 1848 after the rise of Napoleon III, a dictator with whom he had political and religious differences. As Seguin became active in the early movement establishing training schools for children with disabilities in America, he advocated for small facilities, each ideally serving no more than 20 children, so that each child could receive individual attention and planning. He suggested that these institutions be built near cities and towns so that younger children could receive instruction by parents, who, in turn, could be coached by the training staff of the school. Seguin's intent was that children should be returned to the community when they gained sufficient skills (Switzky, Dudzinski, Van Acker, & Gambro, 1988).

Protective Asylums

Because of the lack of other resources for people with developmental disabilities in the community, the vision of the training school as a small institution to educate a few children with disabilities for community living was soon overwhelmed by the demand for protective shelter for people with disabilities of all kinds. By the 1870s, parents and relatives were begging the schools to take on the daily care of their family members with disabilities. The training schools quickly turned into huge impersonal institutions. They tended to be built in rural areas, which isolated the residents from the rest of society. To reduce costs, higher-functioning residents were set to work the land, so their education was abandoned in favor of using their abilities as a means of producing income for the asylums. Other talented residents were required to cook, clean, and provide personal care for the less able. Thus, tax input to support the institutions could be kept low, reducing taxpayers' complaints.

Custodial care, rather than education or rehabilitation, became the purpose of these large asylums. By the late 1860s, Samuel Gridley Howe was advocating that the institutions be closed. He urged that their residents be reintegrated into society rather than being segregated into the cheaply built, warehouse-style, oppressive facilities designed to provide mass management rather than individualized care.

The Eugenics Movement

The institutions were not closed, however. The next period of history was one that demeaned people with developmental disabilities and tended to keep them not only socially isolated but also despised. By the 1880s, social Darwinism was in full swing. Its advocates took Charles Darwin's fascinating discoveries regarding evolutionary trends in whole physical species and inappropriately applied them to single individuals within the species called *Homo sapiens* in a way Darwin never intended. Social Darwinists preached that because persons with disabilities were "inferior," they were second-class citizens and taxpayers should not be required to assist them. In fact, it was better that they be allowed to die off according to "natural law."

Members of the eugenics movement whipped up a hysteria of fear regarding people with disabilities. A book in 1883 by the English scientist Francis Galton, a cousin of Darwin, asserted that people with intellectual disabilities committed terrible crimes and that "morons" were multiplying like rabbits compared with the rest of the population. Galton insisted that people with intellectual disabilities were spreading venereal diseases and sexual immorality. Frightened by such assertions, eugenicists (people who believed that human perfection could be achieved if those they regarded as defective were eliminated) clamored successfully for massive sterilization of people with intellectual disabilities (Patton et al., 1996). They called for confinement of people with all types of disabilities in segregated, jail-like institutions from which there could be no escape without sterilization. Social Darwinists and eugenicists were natural allies.

The eugenics movement took strong hold in both the United States and Europe in the late nineteenth and early twentieth centuries, and many people today are still in the sway of its viewpoint. Perhaps its most horrific manifestation was Hitler's "final solution" in the 1930s and 1940s. It is estimated that Hitler slaughtered 250,000 people with disabilities in pursuit of his idea of perfection (Rothman, 2003).

A third social influence tending to demean people with disabilities was the development of the standardized intelligence test. The most famous IQ test of the time was devised by the French psychologists Alfred Binet and Théodore Simon. It was in widespread use by the early 1900s. The intelligence test placed powerful labels such as "moron" on individuals with intellectual disabilities and tended to set in stone other people's ideas of the potential of a person with disabilities. "Once feebleminded, always feebleminded" became a belief of the times. With such an outlook, why establish educational programs for people with disabilities?

Between 1880 and 1925, institutions for people with disabilities grew into huge facilities designed for subhuman "animals"; the model was that of the hospital, where everyone residing therein was viewed as "sick"; where living units were called "wards"; and where the residents were prevented from "hurting themselves" by being confined to locked wards with barred windows, little or no furniture, and nothing in the way of comfort or hope. Dehumanizing routines removed almost all opportunity for persons with disabilities to learn to live like people without disabilities; the "inmates" or "patients" truly seemed subhuman by the time the institution was through with them (Switzky et al., 1988).

New Research, New Attitudes

In 1919, W. E. Fernald published a study of what happened to 1,537 residents with disabilities who were released from institutions between 1890 and 1914. He delayed publication of his results because they astonished him; he had previously supported the "social menace" theory. Fernald found that most of the men and women released exhibited socially acceptable behavior. Few married or bore children; many became self-supporting. Fernald conducted another study in 1924 of 5,000 children with intellectual disabilities in Massachusetts schools and found that fewer than eight percent exhibited any kind of antisocial behavior (Switzky et al., 1988).

Other studies of the time demonstrated similar results. For example, Z. P. Hoakley investigated people discharged from public institutions in 1922 to determine how many had to be readmitted within one year; his results demonstrated that only six percent of males and 13 percent of females had to be readmitted. H. C. Storrs investigated 616 adults discharged from an institution in New York State in 1929 and found only four percent were readmitted (Willer & Intagliata, 1984).

Attitudes toward people with disabilities began to improve in the 1920s, partly as a result of research but mostly because of the passage of time and the gradual dying down of the eugenics hysteria. Institutions made attempts to "parole" their highest-functioning residents into the community, at first to relatives' homes and later, by the 1930s, to family care homes. Some institutions developed "colony" plans that relocated residents to smaller institutions intended to provide more normal, but still supervised, living arrangements. Some of the colonies were farms, where residents could be nearly self-supporting; some were located in towns, where residents could work in factories.

Economic factors interfered with the process of **deinstitutionalization**. The Great Depression of the 1930s made it impossible to find community-based jobs for all who could perform them. World War II improved public attitudes toward people with disabilities because so many war veterans came home with serious disabling conditions, but the war effort itself drained money away from other pressing social needs. Although the rate of institutional growth slowed during the 1940s, admissions to institutions continued to exceed discharges during this entire period, despite attempts at community placement (Willer & Intagliata, 1984).

Normalization and the Deinstitutionalization Movement

Normalization is a concept that was first developed in the Scandinavian countries in the 1950s. The principle can be summarized as "making available to persons with mental retardation, as well as to persons with other handicapping conditions, patterns and conditions of everyday life that are as close as possible to the norms and patterns of mainstream society" (Switzky et al., 1988, p. 32). The idea took shape in the 1950s and continues to evolve today.

Normalization involves the recognition that people with disabilities are people first, people who simply happen to have physical or mental disabilities with which they must cope. They deserve caring, humane assistance. Parent groups such as the National Association for Retarded Citizens, organized in 1950, known today as the American Association on Intellectual and Developmental Disabilities, (AAIDD), as well as professional organizations such as the National Association of Social Workers (NASW), have provided leadership in this direction. The goal has not yet been achieved, but steps are being taken in the right direction, as illustrated in the case of Sandra McLean in Chapter 2 and Mary and Lea Perkins in this chapter's case study.

Normalization for a person with disabilities requires a plan of care providing for education, training in daily living skills, community-based rather than institutional care, and an opportunity for employment or some other occupation designed to maximize one's potential for independent living. Deinstitutionalization of persons with disabilities came to be perceived as part of the overall thrust of the 1960s toward upholding the rights of minority groups. Funding has been a continual problem in achieving this goal, however, as also is illustrated in the McLean case in Chapter 2. Zoning is another barrier keeping group homes for people with disabilities out of residential neighborhoods. Both problems illustrate that people without disabilities still discriminate against those who are less fortunate.

Deinstitutionalization as a Goal

An important piece of legislation, the Developmental Disabilities Act of 1969, called for establishing planning councils and advocacy agencies in every state. The act created a service structure that could help make deinstitutionalization a realistic goal (Parkinson & Howard, 1996). Also very important was the Rehabilitation Act of 1973, which established the first community-based Centers for Independent Living (CILs). Where available, CILs today provide information and referral services, peer support, and independent living and self-advocacy training for people with disabilities (Putnam, 2007).

The deinstitutionalization movement accelerated during the 1970s and 1980s. This acceleration was spurred in part by court decisions. For example, in 1971, a class action lawsuit was initiated on behalf of patients with mental illness at Bryce State Hospital and residents with cognitive disabilities at the Partlow State School, both in Alabama. The 1972 decision of the U.S. Supreme Court in *Wyatt v. Stickney* (cited in Willer & Intagliata, 1984) affirmed not only that institutionalized people have a constitutional right to **habilitation** services (services designed to help one achieve and maintain one's maximum level of functioning) but also that mildly or moderately intellectually disabled persons should be admitted to institutions only if this is the least restrictive environment available (Willer & Intagliata, 1984).

Teen boy with a disability enjoys playing basketball

The economic climate of the early 1970s also helped the deinstitutionalization movement. The economy was strong, helping provide funding for staff to organize community placement and permitting employment for the more independent of those discharged. That deinstitutionalization occurred at a dramatic rate has been well documented by research. Between 1967 and 1988, for example, the percentage of people with developmental disabilities residing in institutions dropped from 85 to 34 percent (Wolfe, 1992).

Figures such as these probably overstate the reality experienced by people with disabilities, however. As inflation became a severe problem in the late 1970s, the coalition fueling community placement (political conservatives who desired reduced government spending and liberals who wanted more humane care) fell apart (Segal, 1995). Many people simply were shifted from large state institutions to private custodial settings such as nursing homes because they were cheaper. Many of the new settings provided inadequate services for the population they absorbed. It has been suggested that, sadly, *reinstitutionalization* better describes what actually happened to many people (Johnson & Surles, 1994).

Fortunately, today most parents bring up their children with developmental disabilities at home. Special education services in the schools (discussed in Chapter 8) make this challenge more feasible. In addition, many larger communities and urban areas provide special services for persons with disabilities including recreational and job training programs. However, when parents become elderly or die, special housing may be required. Such housing is in short supply, so many people with disabilities still end up in nursing homes.

> **?** Assess your understanding of the history of services for people with disabilities by taking this brief quiz.

TYPES OF DEVELOPMENTAL DISABILITIES

Developmental Disabilities: What Are They?

Some developmental disabilities are so obvious that everyone agrees the person so affected is, indeed, "disabled." A clear example of such a disability might be a bone deformity such as a club foot that makes it difficult for the afflicted individual to walk. On the other hand, some disabilities, while just as real, are much less visible. This was the case with Mary and Lea Perkins, both of whom coped with developmental disabilities that could not be seen. In addition, many children today are diagnosed with "learning disabilities," which require painstaking assessment of problems in reading, spelling, and writing to be detected.

Difference between *Disability* and *Developmental Disability*

Many disabilities are truly disabling but are not "developmental." For example, President Franklin D. Roosevelt became confined to a wheelchair in midlife because of polio; he was disabled, but not developmentally disabled. According to the federal definition of **developmental disability**, the condition must occur before the affected individual has reached the age of 22.

How developmental disability is defined is not just an academic exercise. The definition affects real people in very real ways. For example, funds reserved for special education services for people with developmental disabilities may be spent only for those who qualify for that funding under the legal definition. A person who may need reeducation in midlife due a disease like polio or some kind of serious accident will not qualify for the services that assisted Mary and Lea Perkins in the public schools.

Categorical vs. Functional Definitions of Developmental Disability

Some states define developmental disabilities according to category—for example, intellectual disability or cerebral palsy. Persons who fall into these categories are eligible for whatever financial aid is provided by state law for such classifications.

The federal definition of disability, on the other hand, is functional. For a given person to qualify for federal funds, his or her disability must be severe in function and the functional impairment must be chronic (of extended duration). The disability must significantly limit the person's ability to live independently and be self-supporting. Therefore, a person who might qualify categorically for state aid because of a mild disability might not qualify for federal aid.

Developmental disabilities appear in many forms. Let us describe 10 major diagnostic categories (see Box 12.1). In addition, we will discuss fetal alcohol syndrome (FAS) and cocaine- and other drug-affected babies.

Intellectual Disability

Intellectual disability has previously been known as mental retardation, but President Obama signed "Rosa's Law" in 2010, requiring that references to mental retardation in

> **Box 12.1 Major Categories of Developmental Disabilities**
>
> | | |
> |---|---|
> | Intellectual disability | Epilepsy |
> | Cerebral palsy | Traumatic brain injury |
> | Autism | Learning disabilities |
> | Orthopedic problems | Emotional disturbance |
> | Hearing problems | Co-occurrence of disabilities |

federal law be changed to "intellectual disability." Intellectual disability is caused by a wide variety of factors. Sometimes it results from injury at birth, as in the case of Sandra McLean in the Chapter 2 case study. Sometimes the mother has had a serious illness during pregnancy (measles is a well-known example). In recent times, the Zika infection carried by a mosquito has been linked to microcephaly ("small head") in newborns, resulting in cognitive disabilities. If a woman with Zika becomes pregnant, the infection can spread to her fetus. In early 2016, the Zika virus was identified in the United States, along with nine Zika pregnancies. Two of the pregnant women chose to have abortions. Two pregnancies ended in miscarriages. But one resulted in a baby with severe microcephaly (Dennis & Cha, 2016; What We Know, 2016). Sometimes, as with Down syndrome, the cause of cognitive disability is genetic and involves chromosomal abnormalities. Sometimes the problem involves inadequate nutrition for the pregnant mother, a terrible potential side effect of poverty. Early infant nutrition has an effect as well, as does early sensory stimulation. A mother's drinking, smoking, or drug use may result in the intellectual disability of her child. Some conditions may be reversible with early intervention.

A child who has an intellectual disability is unable to learn at the rate most children do or cannot apply what is learned in the normal way to requirements of daily living. Preschoolers with this diagnosis tend to learn more slowly than other children to crawl, sit, walk, and talk. Such school-aged children have difficulty developing academic skills and often social skills as well. Such adults have trouble living and working independently in the community, although they may do well with supervision and other assistance.

The American Association on Intellectual Disabilities (AAIDD, previously the American Association for the Mentally Retarded, or AAMR), provides a definition of intellectual disability. This definition includes the following factors:

- The person has severe limitations in intellectual functioning—a person's ability to learn, reason, and solve problems.
- The person has severe limitations in adaptive behavior—a person's social, practical, and conceptual skills.
- These limitations begin before age 18.

While the criteria for diagnosing intellectual disability is generally a score of 70 or less on an IQ test, the AAIDD cautions that the IQ score is only one aspect of determining the presence or absence of an intellectual disability. Other tests determine the extent of any limitations in adaptive behavior: conceptual skills, social skills, and practical skills such as feeding and dressing.

Both Sandra McLean of the Chapter 2 case study and Mary Perkins of this chapter's case study suffered from intellectual disabilities. Sandra's disability was profound, but Mary's was mild and, with appropriate support, she could live a normal life.

Cerebral Palsy

Cerebral palsy results from damage to the brain, usually before or during birth. It takes three major forms: spastic, athetoid or dyskinetic, and ataxic. Some children manifest elements of all three types. Cerebral palsy may affect the entire body or only parts, such as various limbs. Spastic cerebral palsy is the most common form; approximately 80 percent of affected individuals have this type. Movement is difficult, slow, stiff, and sometimes jerky. Intellectual disability frequently, but not always, accompanies this condition. Children with spasticity in both arms and legs (spastic quadriplegia) usually cannot walk.

The athetoid or dyskinetic type is manifested in 10 to 20 percent of individuals with cerebral palsy. Movement may be continuous but random and uncontrolled, especially under stress. Facial features may also move in an uncontrolled manner. The walking gait is lurching.

Ataxic cerebral palsy is the least common form, manifested by 5 to 10 percent of affected individuals. It is primarily a balance disorder; children with this disability may walk with feet spread wide apart for stability. Movements that require precise coordination (such as writing) present special difficulties for these children.

According to the Centers for Disease Control and Prevention (CDC), about 1 in 323 children have cerebral palsy, and the condition is more prevalent in boys than in girls. Causes include infections to the mother during pregnancy, insufficient oxygen reaching the fetus, premature birth, lack of oxygen to the baby during birth, blood diseases, and other birth defects. Many children with cerebral palsy have co-occurring disabilities—41 percent also have epilepsy and 7 percentalso have some type of autism spectrum disorder. ("Facts about Cerebral Palsy," 2015; "What You Need to Know," 2014).

> ▶ Matthew Simpson has spastic cerebral palsy. What symptoms of his condition are directly visible in this video? How has he overcome the physical limitations of his disability?
> https://www.youtube.com/watch?v=VUtJ9VTTK_g

Autism Spectrum Disorders

Autism spectrum disorders (ASD) comprise several conditions that at one time were considered separate. Today, three conditions commonly included in ASD are autistic disorder, pervasive developmental disorder not otherwise specified (PDD-NOS), and Asperger syndrome (Facts about ASD, 2015).

The prevalence of ASD has increased dramatically over the past few decades. Today, it affects approximately 1 in 68 children (1 in 42 boys, 1 in 189 girls). The disorder affects members of all races and socioeconomic groups ("Data and Statistics," 2015). Symptoms of ASD include the following:

- Having trouble relating to others
- Not being at all interested in others
- Not liking to be held or cuddled
- Avoiding eye contact; wanting to be alone
- Appearing unaware when other people speak to them

- Echoing words or phrases repeatedly instead of conversing normally
- Having trouble expressing personal needs

Symptoms of a disorder begin to appear when the child is around 18 months old. As infants, they seem normal. Most children with ASD can be helped with early intervention, but symptoms are usually lifelong. Children with Asperger syndrome have the best chance of living a normal life because their symptoms are milder, they learn to speak at the expected age, and they have normal intelligence.

The causes of autism are not understood. At one time, parents were blamed for being aloof and unresponsive, but this theory has thankfully been proved false. Other theories today are held with great passion, including that mercury-based preservatives in vaccines might set off the syndrome, or multiple vaccines given at once might do so. Research has not substantiated these theories, but it has found some possible genetic factors (e.g., if one identical twin has ASD, the other is affected 36–95 percent of the time; ASD seems to occur more often in people with certain chromosomal abnormalities) ("Data and Statistics," 2015).

A great difficulty for parents with children who are diagnosed with ASD is that they appear perfectly normal at birth and during early infancy; the parents are thus not prepared for the challenges they will later encounter (see Box 12.2).

Box 12.2 Danny Hensley

When Danny came into this world, his parents were overjoyed. He was a beautiful baby, born with all ten fingers and toes and an adorable little face with fine regular features. He seemed to be in perfect health. He developed normally—he stood up at about a year of age, took his first wobbly steps a couple months later, and said his first words soon after that. Danny's proud parents loved to show the little boy off to aunts, uncles, grandparents, and friends. He seemed to grow cuter by the day.

Then something went wrong. When Danny was a little over 18 months old, he began to rock back and forth repetitively. He stopped smiling at his parents. He stopped speaking the words he had previously learned. Even worse, by age two, he had stopped responding to his parents' words. Danny's parents wondered if the little boy had developed some kind of hearing loss, so they took him to an audiologist who specialized in testing children. They learned from the audiologist that Danny could hear perfectly well, but he apparently couldn't make sense of the sounds he heard. To the parent's dismay, the audiologist suggested Danny be evaluated for possible autism.

Diagnostic tests indicated that Danny had indeed developed autistic disorder. His parents were devastated. Fortunately, the professionals who tested Danny assured them Danny's condition was not their fault. They explained that the cause for autism was unknown and referred the parents to an early learning center established by a private organization to assist infants suspected to have developmental disabilities. There, special services could help Danny begin to develop necessary life skills as nearly normal as possible. His parents could receive counseling for how to cope with Danny's behavior at home, which was becoming increasingly challenging.

When Danny turned three, he was enrolled in the special education program of a public school. An Individualized Education Plan (IEP) was developed to address his special needs. Special services continued for Danny right through high school. His parents continued to seek supportive counseling from time to time, especially after twin daughters were born.

(continued)

> **Box 12.2 (continued)**
>
> The twins required considerable time and attention themselves and Danny's special challenges did not diminish as he grew older. The boy seemed to live in a world of his own, unaware of the needs of others.
>
> Danny demonstrated little interest in relating to his sisters or even to his parents. The parents began to wonder if Danny could ever learn to relate normally to another living being. When Danny was in his early teens, however, a family friend referred them to a therapeutic riding program where children with disabilities could learn to ride and work with horses. The parents decided to give it a try. To their amazement, Danny hugged his therapy horse the very first day. He actually whispered to the animal. The animal nickered back softly. A partnership was born.
>
> When Danny graduated from high school, he did not want to go to college. However, like many other boys his age, he hoped to begin living independently of his parents. The social worker for the special education program at Danny's school, aware of Danny's love for horses, suggested he might be able to find work on a farm. She referred Danny to a job placement program for people with disabilities. Due to Danny's experience with horses, the placement counselor there, another social worker, had an idea. Farm owners had recently contacted the counselor because they were having difficulty keeping long-term help. The work they offered required long hours and extensive physical labor. They raised horses and cattle and kept milk cows that needed to be milked twice every single day without fail.
>
> Danny was young and strong and enjoyed spending time with animals. Despite his autism, his intelligence was normal. He realized this farm could provide a means of gaining independence. Still, he worried about what it would be like to have to talk with the owners. He realized people had to interview for jobs, and he was afraid he would be unable to survive an interview successfully.
>
> The social worker at the placement agency reassured Danny, however, by explaining to him that hardly any young man right out of high school would know how to interview very well. The worker asked Danny if he would be willing to role play an interview. Danny agreed to try. The first trial didn't go very well at all, but the worker assured Danny that he could learn to do better. He gave Danny some interviewing tips and then conducted another interview—and then another and another.
>
> When the social worker believed Danny was ready, he arranged an interview with the farm owners. Danny not only got the job but also found a new home as well because the farm came with a caretaker's cottage. The placement agency provided Danny with a **job coach** to assist him for the first couple of months until it was clear the boy could handle his responsibilities. Danny was now on track toward living a life as satisfying as that of any person without a disability.

Orthopedic Problems

Orthopedic problems include a wide variety of physical disabilities, such as problems with physical functioning of bones, joints, and muscles. Spina bifida is a well-known example. A child with this condition is born with an incomplete spinal column so that nerve impulses cannot reach the legs and the child cannot walk. Other examples of orthopedic problems include bone deformities, missing limbs, club feet, or extra fingers and toes. Some such problems can be corrected at birth by surgery or more gradually by corrective appliances such as braces.

Children with minor orthopedic problems may not be classified as developmentally disabled because functional impairment is not severe enough to meet the definition. Other children with severe orthopedic problems may receive services under a different classification (e.g., cerebral palsy). For this reason, the exact prevalence of orthopedic problems in the United States is difficult to determine.

Young man in wheelchair with pensive expression

Children with physical impairments may experience rejection, embarrassment, feelings of insecurity, stigma, and so forth. Today such challenges may be compounded with insensitive messages transmitted by thoughtless peers via computer or cell phone text messaging. Social workers need to be sensitive to the emotional challenges that these children face in addition to the physical ones.

Hearing Problems

Hearing problems can cause massive developmental disabilities, and they are one of the most common birth defects. Nearly 3 in 1,000 babies in the United States are born with some degree of hearing impairment, or about 12,000 each year. Children who are hearing impaired are often diagnosed incorrectly as having a cognitive disability because their language development is so grossly delayed that they cannot be tested accurately. Without language development, the thinking process may be hampered, and social development is drastically impacted.

Hearing loss may range from mild to profound. Conductive hearing loss occurs when something interferes with sound passing through the outer or middle ear so that sound does not reach the inner ear. Such conditions may include wax, infections, or ruptures of the eardrum, and they are usually treatable. Sensorineural hearing loss usually occurs when the hair cells in the inner ear cannot detect incoming vibrations or when neural impulses are not transmitted to the brain. Some children suffer from both conditions, which is called mixed hearing loss.

Hearing loss may be present at birth (congenital hearing loss) or developed later in life. About half the cases present at birth are caused by genetic factors. About a quarter of cases are linked to a mother's illness during pregnancy (e.g., German measles, herpes, syphilis, or exposure to some other infection) or to complications after birth, including head injuries, childhood infections, medications, and ear infections. About a third of babies with hearing loss have other disabling conditions as well, such as Down syndrome ("Hearing Loss in Children," 2015; "Hearing Loss," 2014).

Epilepsy

Epilepsy is a disorder of the brain that causes **seizures**. This disorder involves changes in the electrical activity of the brain. Only when a person has suffered two or more seizures is a diagnosis of epilepsy made, however, because seizures can occur due to other medical problems such as low blood sugar, alcohol or other drug withdrawal, or high fever.

Not all seizures are noticeable to a bystander—sometimes the affected person simply seems to be staring off into space. Other seizures, however, cause an affected person to fall to the ground, to shake violently, and to lose consciousness. Epilepsy affects different people in different ways because the condition has many causes and there are many different types of seizures. Seizures are classified into two groups: generalized seizures affecting both sides of the brain and focal or partial seizures, affecting only a part of the brain.

According to recent estimates, about 1 percent of children have been diagnosed with epilepsy, or about 750,000 children aged 0–17. About 1.8 percent of adults have been diagnosed with the condition, approximately 4.3 million. About 0.6 percent of children (460,000) have active epilepsy (are taking medication to control the condition or else have had a seizure in the past year), and 1 percent of adults (2.4 million) have active epilepsy. All together, about 2.9 million people in the United States have active epilepsy.

For two out of three people, the cause of epilepsy is unknown, but there are identified causes for some cases: stroke, brain tumor or infection, traumatic brain injury, loss of oxygen to the brain during birth, genetic disorders such as Down syndrome, and neurologic disorders such as Alzheimer's Disease ("About Epilepsy," 2016; "Epilepsy Basics" 2015).

Traumatic Brain Injury

Traumatic brain injury includes any trauma to the head that causes brain damage. Brain injuries generally occur in three ways: through blunt injuries, as when the head is hit by a fixed or moving object (such as a windshield or a baseball bat); penetrating injuries, as when the head is penetrated by an object such as a bullet; and compression injuries, as when the head is crushed.

Head injuries may result in fractures or broken or dented skull bones. Loose bone fragments may place pressure on the brain. Concussion, or temporary loss of consciousness, may occur. Severe blows may cause contusions, or bruising of the brain tissue. Lacerations of the head may tear brain tissue.

Symptoms of mild traumatic brain injury include headache, confusion, dizziness, blurred vision, ringing in the ears, memory loss, agitation, lack of inhibition, and loss of concentration. Persons with moderate to severe traumatic brain injury may experience a serious headache that continues to worsen, repeated vomiting, convulsions or seizures, dilation of one or both pupils of the eyes, slurred speech, loss of coordination, and increased confusion.

Approximately half of severely head-injured patients will require surgery to remove ruptured blood vessels or contusions. The severity of any long-term disabilities resulting from traumatic brain injury depends on the severity and location of the injury in the brain, the age of the person who received the injury, and his or her general health ("NINDS Traumatic Brain Injury Information Page," 2010; "What Is Traumatic Brain Injury," 2016).

Learning Disabilities

Some children have disabilities that interfere with their ability to read, write, or do mathematical calculations. They may also have trouble listening, speaking, or thinking. Often these children appear perfectly normal until they go to school, where they encounter a whole new set of demands. They score normally on IQ tests, but somehow they do not seem to perceive written language in the same way that other children do. While they may be able to read written words, many cannot translate their meaning. No matter how hard they try, these children seem unable to learn in the usual way. Although there is much about learning disabilities that we do not understand, a number of techniques have been devised to help children so afflicted.

The Individuals with Disability Education Act (IDEA) defines "learning disability" as:

> a disorder in one or more of the basic psychological processes involved in understanding or in using language, spoken or written, that may manifest itself in an imperfect ability to listen, think, speak, read, write, spell, or do mathematical calculations, including conditions such as perceptual disabilities, brain injury, minimal brain dysfunction, dyslexia, and developmental aphasia.

In general, for regulatory purposes, the inability to learn cannot be the result of low intelligence, socioeconomic circumstances, or poor sensory skills. The most frequent method of identifying learning disabilities involves measuring and comparing ability and achievement in the school setting. Thus, the disabilities are rarely identified before a child goes to school.

Learning disability is an umbrella term encompassing a number of more specific disabilities such as dyslexia, a language and reading disability; dyscalculia, a disability involving math skills; and dysgraphia, a disorder resulting in illegible handwriting. This disability varies widely from person to person ("Learning Disabilities," 2010; "What Are Learning Disabilities?" 2015).

Technology today can be of tremendous help to children with learning disabilities. For example, children with dyslexia can use speech recognition software to read written text aloud, and children with dysgraphia can have words typed out as they speak. Access to such software is an important social justice issue today because the technology is financially out of reach for many children (Casey, 2015).

Emotional Disturbance

Many terms have been used to describe emotional or behavioral disorders, but the term currently used in the Individuals with Disabilities Education Act (IDEA) is *emotional disturbance*. IDEA defines this disability as follows:

> a condition exhibiting one or more of the following characteristics over a long period of time and to a marked degree that adversely affects a child's educational performance—
>
> 1. An inability to learn that cannot be explained by intellectual, sensory, or other health factors.
> 2. An inability to build or maintain satisfactory interpersonal relationships with peers and teachers.
> 3. Inappropriate types of behavior or feelings under normal circumstances.
> 4. A general pervasive mood of unhappiness or depression.
> 5. A tendency to develop physical symptoms or fears associated with personal or school problems.

Emotional disturbance is an umbrella term including (but not limited to) anxiety disorders, bipolar disorder (sometimes called manic depression), conduct disorders, eating disorders, obsessive-compulsive disorder (OCD), and psychotic disorders.

Families who have children with emotional disturbance often need help in understanding their children's condition and in learning how to cope effectively. In this chapter's case study, Lea Perkins demonstrates emotional disturbance.

According to CDC data, approximately 8.3 million children (14.5 percent) aged 4 to 17 years of age have parents who have sought help from a health care provider or a school staff member about their child's emotional or behavioral difficulties. Nearly 2.9 million children have been prescribed medication for these difficulties ("Emotional Disturbance," 2015).

Behaviors observed in children who have emotional disturbance include hyperactivity (short attention span, impulsiveness); aggression (acting out, fighting); withdrawal (avoiding others); immaturity (inappropriate crying, tantrums); and learning disabilities (performing academically below grade level). Children with the most serious disturbances may demonstrate severe anxiety, major mood swings, distorted thinking, and disturbed behavior.

Fetal Alcohol Spectrum Disorders; Cocaine-Exposed and Other Drug-Exposed Babies

Fetal alcohol spectrum disorders (FASD) result from women drinking alcohol during pregnancy. The alcohol a pregnant woman drinks passes to her fetus through the umbilical cord. There is no safe amount of alcohol a pregnant woman can drink, and all types of alcohol are dangerous, including wine and beer. A major problem is that about half of the pregnancies in the United States are unplanned. As a result, even a woman who knows she should stop drinking when pregnant does not do so because she is unaware she has conceived a child. Once a mother knows she is pregnant, she should stop drinking immediately to prevent any additional alcohol-related damage to the fetus ("Prevalence of FASDs," 2015).

Fetal alcohol syndrome (FAS) lies at the most severe end of the FASD spectrum. FAS may result in fetal death. Babies born with FAS have low birth weight and abnormal facial features. Children with FAS have growth problems and other developmental issues such as intellectual disabilities, short attention spans, poor memories, learning problems, communication problems, and vision and hearing problems. While estimates vary, a recent study by the Centers for Disease Control and Prevention (CDC) finds that 0.2 to 1.5 infants out of every 1,000 are born with FAS in the United States. However, an assessment of school-aged children determined that 6 to 9 of 1,000 of school children were believed to have FAS ("Prevalence of FASDs," 2015).

Alcohol-related neurodevelopmental disorder (ARND) is the next most serious level of FASD. Children with ARND are likely to have intellectual disabilities, short attention spans, and difficulties with impulse control. They are likely to have poor judgment and do poorly in school.

Alcohol-related birth defects (ARDB) are the mildest form of FASD, but people born with ARBD may experience ongoing problems with the heart, kidneys, bones, hearing, or a combination of difficulties such as these.

Many women are aware that heavy drinking can cause harm, but far fewer realize that light to moderate drinking can also be harmful depending on the developmental stage of the fetus. In addition, many thousands of women use cocaine and/or other drugs such as marijuana, heroin, or Ecstasy during pregnancy, also placing their unborn children at serious risk of birth defects. Unfortunately, like alcohol, cocaine and other drugs pass through the mother's placenta and umbilical cord into the fetus.

Drugs can trigger labor so that many cocaine-exposed or other drug-exposed babies are born prematurely. Those who survive are likely to have intellectual disabilities and visual and hearing impairments. Cocaine babies tend to have small heads, which possibly indicate small brains. Many appear to experience drug withdrawal; the babies are irritable and jittery, making it difficult to bond with caretakers. However, other factors may impact these children making it difficult to understand how many of their limitations are actually drug related—maternal nutrition, extent of prenatal care, and socioeconomic and environmental conditions are also important factors ("Cocaine," 2010).

Many people are aware that alcohol and drugs such as cocaine can harm a fetus, but fewer are aware of the dangers of nicotine. Nicotine, like other addictive drugs, results in long-term changes to the fetal brain such as increased levels of the neurotransmitter dopamine, which controls sensations of reward and pleasure. Pregnant smokers have a higher risk of miscarriage, stillborn babies, premature births, and low birth weight babies. If a woman smokes a pack of cigarettes a day while pregnant, her child has nearly twice the risk of becoming addicted to tobacco. The child is also more likely to suffer learning and behavioral problems ("Drug Facts, Cigarettes and Other Tobacco Products," 2015).

Overall Prevalence and Co-Occurrence of Disabilities

According to ongoing research conducted by the Centers for Disease Control and Prevention (CDC), approximately 15 percent, or one in six children aged 3 through 17 have one or more developmental disabilities today. Some of these disabilities originate during the pregnancy of the mother; others occur during birth or during the child's developmental period. Disabilities often impact a child's daily functioning and may be lifelong, although early intervention can help some children achieve a more normal life ("About Us," 2015).

People who suffer from more than one disability at a time have a condition known as co-occurrence of disability. Sandra McLean, introduced in Chapter 2, suffered from both epilepsy and intellectual disability. Persons with cerebral palsy and autism frequently also have intellectual disabilities. Children with FAS and those who are exposed to cocaine characteristically suffer multiple disabilities. It is important to remember that all disabilities involve psychological and social dimensions, which must be assessed and addressed.

The Continuum of Care

Many people with developmental disabilities, especially children, require special care. A **continuum of care** helps meet the need. Ideally, this care is provided in the **least restrictive environment**, the most normal environment in which a person's special needs can be met.

The continuum of care begins at home because that is the least restrictive, most normal environment in which children can be raised. Children with special needs present special challenges, however, so **respite care** to help prevent burnout of family caregivers can be crucial to the success of care in the home. Later on, grown children with developmental disabilities, especially those who have received early intervention services, may be able to live independently in homes or apartments of their own, with appropriate assistance. In this chapter's case study, Mary Perkins was able not only to live independently but also to raise a family. However, she needed assistance from social workers.

Adults with disabilities may do well in boardinghouse-type arrangements with room, board, and a minimum of supervision. Days may be spent in **activity centers** or **sheltered workshops** (places of employment that provide special training and services for people with disabilities). Some adults with developmental disabilities are able to hold jobs in regular work settings, especially with the assistance of **job coaches**.

Foster homes, or **family care homes**, are the next step along the continuum of care. They provide family-like settings with foster parents. Lea Perkins would have been placed in one had her mother, Mary Perkins, not been able to improve her parenting skills. Next, somewhere near the middle of the continuum of care, are small group homes. These facilities are staffed by aides and skilled professionals who provide care, supervision, and training for up to eight people.

L'Arche USA, a pioneering organization, provides family-like group homes in small communities where people both with and without disabilities can share their lives. L'Arche communities began in France in 1964; the first L'Arche community in the United States began in Erie, Pennsylvania, in 1972. Today there are 18 L'Arche communities across the United States and five more under development ("Communities of L'Arche, USA," 2016).

Nearing the institutional end of the continuum of care are nursing homes. Nursing homes range from those providing only room, board, and minor personal assistance to those offering skilled nursing care for persons with extensive physical needs. When large numbers of people with disabilities were moved to nursing homes in the 1970s, many of these facilities developed special programs for them. Unfortunately, however, many did not, and almost 20 years passed before federal Medicaid regulations required special certification and appropriate programming.

At the far end of the continuum of care are the large state institutions, where people with disabilities reside in highly restrictive, regulated environments. Today, people who live in these facilities have severe and multiple disabilities.

> **?** Assess your understanding of types of developmental disabilities by taking this brief quiz.

SOCIAL WORK PRACTICE WITH PEOPLE WHO HAVE DISABILITIES

Social workers have assisted people with disabilities for well over a century. Early in the history of the profession, Charity Organization Society (COS) workers investigated the needs of people with disabilities. Their work was described by Mary Richmond in her classic text *Social Diagnosis* (1917). Richmond, a leader in the COS, devoted an entire chapter to "The Insane—The Feebleminded." Her work helped promote the work of practitioners in this field.

Education for Work with People Who Have Disabilities: CSWE Educational Policy

Today, social work education can offer an excellent background for working with people with disabilities because of its person-in-environment perspective. For many years, however, the Council on Social Work Education (CSWE) seemed to overlook the opportunities and need for work in this area. It was not until 2001 that the *CSWE Educational Policy and Accreditation Standards* included disability as a category for which programs are required to provide learning contexts to promote understanding and non-discrimination (Council on Social Work Education, 2001; May & Raske, 2005).

Fortunately, the *Final 2015 Educational Policy*, developed and approved by the CSWE Commission on Educational Policy (COEP), states clearly under Competency 2, "Engage Diversity and Difference in Practice," that "disability and ability" are aspects of diversity that every social work education program must address (Council on Social Work Education, 2015).

NASW Code of Ethics

The National Association of Social Workers (NASW) has developed a comprehensive code of ethics that includes important provisions relevant to service to people with disabilities (NASW, 1999). Following are the most pertinent provisions:

- The social worker must guard the rights and interests of clients who may be unable to make prudent decisions due to cognitive or other disabilities.
- The social worker must not discriminate against, or condone **discrimination** against, persons who have disabilities.
- The social worker should try both to prevent and to eliminate any exploitation of persons with disabilities.

Together, the CSWE and the NASW provide important guidelines for social work practice with people who have disabilities. Institutional and community practice settings are described below, as are additional helpful services for this population.

Institutional Settings

Traditionally, social workers have tended to work with people with disabilities in institutional settings such as hospitals and nursing homes. That is because persons with disabilities have routinely been institutionalized in the past, given the attitudes of the wider society. People with severe disabilities tend to reside in institutions even today, and social workers are employed in these settings. Their roles are multi-faceted, including providing direct services to clients, program development, administration, and evaluation. As direct service providers, social workers usually function as members of rehabilitation teams, engaging in assessment and referral, education, and advocacy. They often serve as primary liaisons with residents' families.

Community Settings

Today, more and more social workers are working with people with disabilities who are living out in the community, as illustrated in this chapter's case study. As the service system continues to shift from an institution-based model toward a community-based one, social work roles have evolved to encompass increasing amounts of "boundary work," or intervention between and among social systems. Such work includes educating people with disabilities and their families about their civil rights and appropriate programs and services in the community that may be of assistance. Important social work roles involve information and referral services, social brokerage between families and larger systems, and advocacy. Assisting in the development of new or additional services and programs that are widely needed is another important role.

Beaulaurier and Taylor (2001) offer a useful framework for services intended to assist people with disabilities:

1. Assist people with disabilities to expand their range of options and choices.
2. Prepare them to be more effective in dealing with professionals, bureaucrats, and agencies that often do not understand or appreciate their need for self-determination.
3. Mobilize and help groups of people with disabilities to consider and advocate for policy and program alternatives that can improve their situation.

Within the community, then, social workers need to assist clients with disabilities to advocate for programs and services that will allow them to maintain their sense of personal dignity and maximize their independence. Within the family, social workers can be helpful in assisting parents to develop positive expectations for their children with disabilities and to cope with the stresses of daily living. Individual, group, and family counseling may be helpful, as can parent training groups and parent-to-parent programs. Respite care and other supportive services such as day care may be crucial in ensuring the success of family care. A systems-based, empowerment approach recognizing and building on family strengths is important.

Another role for the social worker in the area of disabilities is that of job coach, or employment specialist, in a supported employment setting. **Supported employment** is a vocational option that provides individualized supports to people with disabilities, so they can achieve their goals in the workplace, especially in integrated settings where people with disabilities work alongside those without disabilities. The role of job coach helps ensure the success of supported employment. This specialist provides direct services to the consumer such as assessing skills, locating jobs, contacting employers, making job placement arrangements, providing onsite training, assisting with work-related issues, and providing other types of support as needed (Wehman, Inge, Revell, & Brooke, 2007).

Genetic Counseling

Genetic counseling is another important role for social workers in this field. Scientific knowledge of genetics and its impact on birth defects is expanding exponentially. Genetic counseling translates scientific knowledge into practical information. Genetic counselors work with people who may be at high risk for inherited disease or abnormal pregnancy, assessing their chances of having children who are affected and helping them decide what to do ("Genetic Counseling," 2007; "Definition of Genetic Counseling," 2016). (See Box 12.3.)

Spirituality Dimensions

People with disabilities confront special challenges and spiritual sustenance can help them meet these challenges. Morrison-Orton (2005) conducted an important study to find out what, if any, strategies involving spirituality and/or religion were utilized by social work practitioners in assisting clients with disabilities. She conducted in-depth interviews with 15 rehabilitation specialists. Sadly, she found that not a single one was aware of the many empirical studies showing a positive relationship among spirituality, religion, belief, and healing (Dossey, 2003; Schlitz & Amorok, 2005).

However, Morrison-Orton did find that 11 of the 15 participants believed that the helping relationship itself was spiritual and that the relationship was the catalyst for positive change. She writes:

Box 12.3 Up for Debate

Proposition: Genetic testing should be encouraged for people planning to have children.

Yes	No
Genetic testing can help reduce the overall incidence of developmental disabilities.	Any life is worthwhile, even one with a disability.
A life with a disability may bring much struggle and little satisfaction.	Many people with disabilities express strong satisfaction with their lives.
Family members, especially caregivers of people with disabilities, experience heavy burdens.	Many families find special rewards in providing care to members with disabilities.
Society as a whole is burdened by the special needs of people with disabilities.	People with disabilities are citizens who have the right to full participation in society like all other citizens.

Overall it can be said that the participants went through three stages during the interview. In sequence all but one person went through the same process. The first step in the sequence was the initial denial of any and all use of spiritual or religious strategies. Second was awareness that they could not separate themselves from their spiritual or religious beliefs. Therefore, they did engage in spiritual or religious ways of behaving that enhanced their skills as rehabilitation professionals and were used in their own personal coping with this sometimes-difficult work. Third was the insight that they directly used the strategies in practice with clients. Related to this was the dawning belief that there should be more training (in these areas) while they were in school and on-going professional education once they left school (2005, p. 32).

> Assess your understanding of social work practice with people with disabilities by taking this brief quiz.

Larche communities, described earlier in this chapter, are grounded spiritual values. They affirm that every person is sacred and unique, and that persons with disabilities have special gifts for touching the hearts of others. L'Arche communities are created so that people with and without developmental disabilities can enjoy mutual friendships rooted in faith and love ("Who We Are," 2016).

HUMAN DIVERSITY AND SOCIAL JUSTICE

Persons with disabilities can be viewed as members of diverse populations, in particular as members of diverse populations that are vulnerable to discrimination by the wider society. As discussed previously, discrimination in the past led to people with disabilities being warehoused for years in prison-like facilities. People with severe disabilities are frequently still institutionalized today, often in private nursing homes that have few facilities for this population. Social workers are urged to advocate for all persons with disabilities and to prevent institutionalization wherever possible. Today many people with disabilities are actively advocating for themselves and others like them, working toward achieving the most normal lives possible and maximizing their potential (see Box 12.4).

Box 12.4 Strengths of People with Autism

People with autism demonstrate diverse strengths and abilities, not only disabilities. For example, Temple Grandin, PhD, a woman with autism, has become prominent in two professional fields. First, she is the author of at least seven books and a DVD dealing with various aspects of autism. She has labored tirelessly to teach parents and professionals how to help children who have the disorder to build on their special talents and achieve their highest possible functioning. Dr. Grandin has become famous for her insightful writings about what it is like to grow up with autism. She hosts frequent conferences on autism around the nation.

In addition, Dr. Grandin is famous for her work helping people to understand how animals think and feel. For her, the experience of autism has provided important insights into this usually hidden realm. To date, Dr. Grandin has written two influential books on the topic. One well-known result is more humane treatment of cattle on their way to the market.

Dr. Grandin maintains a website where people can send questions and request advice. She responds openly over the Internet so that all interested parents and professionals can be assisted.

Source: Temple Grandin Books. Retrieved from http://www.templegrandin.com/templegrandinbooks.html.

Preventing warehouse-like institutionalization of persons with disabilities requires a continuum of care available in the community. Fortunately, the service system in the United States moved from a primarily institution-based model prior to the late 1960s to a community-based model in the 1970s and 1980s (Freedman, 1995). This positive change was advanced by the Developmental Disabilities Act of 1969 and the Americans with Disabilities Act (ADA) of 1990, which will be discussed later in this chapter. It was further advanced in 1999 by the Supreme Court's Olmstead decision. This decision, *Olmstead v. L.C.*, interpreted Title II of the ADA to require states to provide services in the "most integrated setting" appropriate for a given person (Rothman, 2003).

What makes even the most integrated setting appropriate for a given client may differ according to that client's cultural heritage. Following is a description of supportive services offered to a Chinese family.

Providing Supportive Services to Diverse Families: A Chinese Illustration

Barnwell and Day (1996) note that different ethnic and cultural groups utilize professional services at different rates and provide professionals with different amounts and types of information. Cultural perspectives differ as to the meaning of disability, the causes of disability, and the appropriate roles of families with respect to disability. What may be experienced as a terrible tragedy in one culture may in another be experienced as God's will and an opportunity to serve. Professional intervention must take account of these cultural differences.

Liu (2005) offers an interesting example of differing cultural perceptions of disability from a Chinese point of view. In many areas of China, Liu writes, disability is viewed as a punishment for sins committed in past lives—sins committed either by the person with a disability or by that person's parents. Thus, a stigma is attached to disability and families experience a sense of shame, guilt, and fear of social disgrace. A Taoist priest may be sought to perform rituals to try to seek a cause or a solution.

Because the family is the most fundamental unit of society among the Chinese—three generations living in one household is still common—it is important for social workers to do whatever possible to establish strong working relationships with extended family members. Liu points out, however, that the family in China today is more diverse than in the past because of the 10-year Cultural Revolution, which separated many families and undermined respect for the elderly.

The one-child-per-family policy in China, established after World War II and only very recently modified to allow certain married couples to have two children, has also undermined the traditional family system (Walsh, 2015). As an important example, there may no longer be a son's wife to care for his parents, as was the traditional custom. Hence, the social worker must carefully assess family structure as part of the intervention process. Competence in the Chinese language is also helpful to achieve best outcomes. In addition, social workers need, with great sensitivity, to help the family understand the cause of disability from a more neutral (less blaming) point of view and to discuss possible treatment options (see Box 12.5).

> **Box 12.5   The Importance of Cross-Cultural Competence: The Case of Sun**
>
> Sun, a Chinese American woman of 25, had a moderate cognitive disability. She was blind and nonverbal as well. Sun could understand Cantonese, the language spoken by her parents with whom she lived, plus a few English words, but she could not respond to any questions except by making little noises and nodding or shaking her head. Sun's original case manager placed her in a day treatment program for persons with cognitive disabilities. She seemed comfortable enough there, but she did not seem to grow in skills or understanding. When Sun's case manager asked her parents if they were satisfied with her placement, the parents just nodded and smiled.
>
> Then a new social worker was assigned to Sun's case. This worker spoke fluent Cantonese. The worker soon learned that Sun's parents really wanted their daughter to be placed in a special school for the blind, not a program for the cognitively disabled, but they had not been able to communicate their wish to the former case manager due to the language barrier. The former worker spoke only English, whereas the parents spoke only Cantonese.
>
> The new social worker searched for and located an excellent program for persons with visual impairment near enough to Sun's home for her to attend. Sun was enrolled in this program. She soon was thriving there. She took part in many activities designed for persons who were blind; she became much more active and appeared significantly happier than before. Sun's parents were sincerely pleased with the change, and the young woman blossomed.
>
> Source: Stone, J.H. (2005). *Culture and disability: Providing culturally competent services*. Thousand Oaks, CA: Sage Publications, Inc.

Asian Americans: A Brief History

People of Chinese descent comprise the largest subgroup of Asian Americans in the United States today. Asian Americans as a whole comprised approximately 19.4 million persons in 2013, of whom 4.3 million were Chinese ("Facts for Features: Asian/Pacific Heritage Month: May 2015," 2015). Other Asian Americans originate from Japan, India, and the Pacific Islands.

Diversity and Difference

Dimension of Competency: *Skills* Social workers understand how diversity and difference shape the human experience; social workers present themselves as learners to members of diverse constituencies.

Critical Thinking Question: What professional skills did Sun's new case manager possess (which her predecessors apparently did not) that allowed her to improve services for Sun and Sun's family? (See Box 12.4).

The Chinese were the first Asian people to come to America in large numbers. They arrived in relatively recent times, toward the middle of the nineteenth century, attracted by economic opportunity. In Hawaii, the Chinese worked as sugar plantation laborers, and in California they took part in the Gold Rush of 1849. Many became construction workers for the Southern Pacific Railroad. Their success led to fear of competition, which culminated in the Chinese Exclusion Act of 1882, barring further immigration. People of Chinese descent were denied citizenship and the right to intermarry (Lum, 1992).

Large numbers of Japanese emigrated during the early twentieth century in response to the need for farm workers in California. The Immigration Act of 1924 closed the door to immigration of Asians after that time, however. This law set low immigration quotas for dark-skinned people of all nationalities and excluded Asians entirely. Then, after the bombing of Pearl Harbor in 1941, Japanese Americans were forcibly interned in camps for the duration of World War II. Their property was liquidated and never returned. Although the U.S. Supreme Court in 1944 declared this treatment unconstitutional, it wasn't until 1988 that Congress accepted petitions for redress of grievance. The settlement even then was token—$20,000 for each living survivor.

The 1965 Immigration Act changed U.S. policy to make it more equitable to people of diverse racial and ethnic heritages. Political refugees from the Philippines and Korea included many educated Asian professionals at that time. Then the Vietnamese War brought waves of refugees from Vietnam, Laos, and Cambodia, particularly after the fall of Saigon in 1975. The early refugees were highly educated people who had been allies of the Americans, but later refugees included less privileged people who experienced much more difficulty adjusting to life in the United States.

Traditional values still strongly affect Asian family life today. These values include deference to parental authority and the expectation that children will sacrifice personal ambition to meet family needs. Families may experience stress when children encounter other values and begin to question differences. This type of stress, of course, is experienced across generations by all immigrant groups.

Social Justice Issues and Disability

In an **accommodating** environment, a person with a disability can often function independently and at a high level of performance. Such a situation is ideal, but sadly too uncommon. Barriers to independent functioning include a serious mismatch between person and environment and enduring discrimination. Conversely, **empowerment** practice, self-determination, and self-advocacy can assist people with disabilities to have more control over their own lives.

Mismatch between Person and Environment

Putnam (2007) points out that disability may be viewed as a "mismatch" between a person's abilities and his or her environment. In other words, where there is a problem related to disability, that problem is a result of the interaction between person and environment and not the individual's issue alone. For a person with a disability to function at a high level, the environment must be modified to accommodate the person's needs. Along these same lines, May (2005) asserts that *disability* and *impairment* are not inherently linked. These observations are important. For example, Mary Perkins, with her intellectual disability, could have functioned without assistance in a less hazardous environment and would not have been viewed as impaired. Lea Perkins would not have developed her disability of emotional disturbance at all had she been fortunate enough to live in a safe environment. Once Lea received supportive services, she could function as well as any other teenager with no sign of impairment.

Discrimination

Instead of understanding and accommodation, however, persons with disabilities frequently experience discrimination. It is important, therefore, for social workers to recognize that social justice issues are inherently involved in working with this vulnerable minority population. Advocacy is a very important role for the social work professional, and it is important for the worker to assess the client's own strengths, resources, and limitations as well as the strengths, resources, and limitations of the environment in which the client lives.

Smart (2001) reminds us that there are four important resources professionals can bring to their work with clients who have disabilities: hope, ideas, understanding of the prejudices and discrimination they face, and a willingness to stand by them. Jenny Chambers, in our chapter's case study, brought these very resources to Mary and Lea Perkins, and the result was that their quality of life was very much improved.

Empowerment, Self-Determination, and Self-Advocacy

In addition to advocating for their clients, standing by them and offering hope, ideas, and understanding, the effective social worker will assist people with disabilities in strengthening important personal qualities and skills. Assistance should include education in empowerment, self-determination, and self-advocacy.

Empowerment is an attitude, a process, and a set of skills involving the ability to gain some control over valued events, outcomes, and resources. Empowerment requires genuine choices and the power to make one's own decisions and is strongly in accord with social work's professional value of self-determination (Gilson, 1998).

People with disabilities, like other people, want to have as much control over their own lives as possible. Even people with severe disabilities can make decisions for themselves if they have access to support services, barrier-free environments, and appropriate information and skills. The desired outcome is independent living wherever possible.

The empowerment model strongly encourages self-determination and self-advocacy among people with disabilities, both as individuals and in groups. A national movement modeled after the civil rights movement has been active over the past few decades: The AAIDD describes some of its premises in a 2015 "Issue brief." These include the following:

> In this video, the founder of Self Advocates Becoming Empowered (SABE), Nancy Ward, is asked for her input regarding the Elementary and Secondary Education Act and its impact on higher education for individuals with disabilities. How has large-scale advocacy (such as what SABE has been involved in) led to greater college/university community inclusion for students with disabilities?
>
> https://www.youtube.com/watch?v=vaXFlsawk00

- People with disabilities are able make their own choices, set their own goals, make decisions, solve problems, attain self-awareness, and advocate for themselves.
- Self-determination increases across a person's lifespan and should be endorsed in public policies involving education, employment, health, and community living.
- Additional research should be undertaken to make sure that societal practices support the best possible skill development and self-determination among persons with disabilities.

The concepts of empowerment, self-determination, and self-advocacy do not mean that society (or social workers) should abandon people with disabilities to struggle alone. It means, instead, that society must recognize that the individual with a disability is not the problem; the problem is an environment that discriminates, does not provide viable choices, and does not meet the special needs of all its citizens.

Self-advocacy goes beyond individuals advocating for themselves alone. It also involves groups of people with disabilities working together to fight discrimination, gain more control over their lives, and work together toward greater justice in society. Toward this end, a national organization called Self Advocates Becoming Empowered (SABE) was founded in 1990. SABE is a major self-advocacy organization in the United States. It has been working toward the full inclusion of people with developmental disabilities in the community throughout all 50 states for many years. It is a non-profit advocacy organization run by a board of self-advocates representing nine regions of the country. Collective efforts such as SABE's hopefully can lead to new legislation bringing important advances in social policy affecting people with disabilities.

> **?** Assess your understanding of human diversity and social justice taking this brief quiz.

THE DISABILITY RIGHTS MOVEMENT, SOCIAL POLICY, AND APPROPRIATE TERMINOLOGY

Disabilities have been viewed historically as medical problems or personal tragedies. This prevailing view began to be challenged in the 1960s, when, along with other minority groups, people with disabilities sought to redefine their identities and to change popular perceptions of the sources of their problems (Christensen, 1996). By the late 1960s, first in Scandinavia and then in the United States, a disability rights movement developed, advocating that people with disabilities should be seen as "subjects in their own lives rather than simply as objects of medical and social regimes of control" (Meekosha & Jakubowicz, 1996, p. 80). Community prejudice and discrimination were overtly identified as major barriers preventing people with disabilities from taking control of their own lives. As a salient example, until the late twentieth century, some American cities, including Chicago and Omaha, actually had "ugly laws" that banned people with disabilities from appearing in public (Rothman, 2015).

The crux of the new thinking, as noted by Beaulaurier and Taylor (2001), was that an individual's disability in itself was not so much the problem as the lack of accommodation provided by the wider society. Lack of accommodation was usually not so much a result of hostility as from failure to consider everyone's needs. Those who became involved in the disability rights movement determined to get the requirements of people with disabilities onto the national agenda (see Box 12.6).

In the United States, the disability rights movement promoted deinstitutionalization and independent living and helped secure the passage of the Developmental Disabilities Act of 1969. The movement was strengthened in the 1960s by the civil rights movement. Then, in the late 1960s and early 1970s, thousands of veterans returned from the Vietnam War with extensive disabling conditions, both physical and emotional. Their added influence helped achieve passage of the federal Rehabilitation Act of 1973. Title V of this act prohibits recipients of federal funds from discriminating against people with disabilities in employment, education, or services.

The Rehabilitation Act of 1973 was followed in 1975 by the Developmentally Disabled Assistance and Bill of Rights Act and the Education for All Handicapped Children Act, which later became IDEA, the Individuals with Disabilities Education Act (Meekosha & Jakubowicz, 1996; Asch & Mudrick, 1995; Pardeck, 1998; Rothman, 2003).

> **Box 12.6 The Disability Paradigm**
>
> The disability paradigm asserts that any study of the experience of people with disabilities should include multiple variables including the following:
>
> - Processes in which performing social roles and tasks produces discrimination
> - Discriminatory treatment of people with disabilities produced by societal organization
> - Recognition that impairment does not imply tragedy or low life satisfaction
> - The reality that people with disabilities are an oppressed minority
> - The need of everyone, not just those with disabilities, for services that help them live independently
> - The knowledge that everyone, due to passing time, will eventually experience disability
> - The rejection of the idea that there is "normal" human behavior on which social policy should be based
> - The reality of pervasive discrimination against people with disabilities
>
> Source: May, G.E., & Raske, M. (Eds.). (2005). *Ending Disability Discrimination: Strategies for Social Workers*, Boston, MA: Allyn & Bacon, pp. 82–83.

As publicly signaled by appropriate terminology in IDEA, sensitivity is needed with respect to terminology. Certain commonly used phrases and adjectives can be experienced as demeaning and inappropriate. For example, in IDEA, the term *handicap* is replaced by the more neutral term *disability*. And, as noted previously, the more recent Rosa's Law replaces the term *mental retardation* in federal law with *intellectual disability* ("Self Advocates Becoming Empowered," 2015).

Another major piece of legislation promoting disability rights, the Americans with Disabilities Act (ADA), was passed in 1990; it was greatly strengthened by the Civil Rights Act of 1991. These acts are described next.

The Americans with Disabilities Act of 1990 and the Civil Rights Act of 1991

The Americans with Disabilities Act (ADA) was designed to assist all people with disabilities, not just those with developmental disabilities. Its purposes are identified in its Section 2 as providing a mandate for ending discrimination, providing standards of treatment for people with disabilities, and creating a central role for the federal government in enforcing these standards. Title I of the act makes special requirements of employers. One is that employers with 15 or more employees may not discriminate against people with disabilities who are otherwise qualified. Another is that employers must make accommodations for people with disabilities. The law intends that the accommodations should be "reasonable." Existing physical barriers, for example, need to be remedied only if this can be done without much difficulty or expense.

Other titles of the ADA call for reasonable access to public services (e.g., special accommodations as needed to allow usage of buildings, buses, and trains) and accessibility to public accommodations such as restaurants, hotels, theaters, schools, day care centers, colleges, and universities. Telephone companies must provide telecommunications services for hearing-impaired and speech-impaired persons (see Box 12.7).

> **Box 12.7 The Americans with Disabilities Act Recognizes Discrimination**
>
> Section 2 of the Americans with Disabilities Act states, among other things, that historically, society has tended to isolate and segregate individuals with disabilities, and, despite some improvements, such forms of discrimination against individuals with disabilities continue to be a serious and pervasive social problem; discrimination against individuals with disabilities persists in such critical areas as employment, housing, public accommodations, education, transportation, communication, recreation, institutionalization, health services, voting, and access to public services.
>
> Unlike individuals who have experienced discrimination on the basis of race, color, sex, national origin, religion, or age, individuals who have experienced discrimination on the basis of disability have often had no legal recourse to redress such discrimination. . . .
>
> Source: Quoted from Section 2, "Findings and Purposes," Public Law 101–336, Americans with Disabilities Act of 1990.

The Civil Rights Act of 1991 strengthened the ADA by allowing jury trials and compensatory and punitive damages in accord with those available to minorities under the Civil Rights Act of 1964. Complaints are handled by the Equal Employment Opportunity Commission (EEOC). It is interesting that a large number of job discrimination suits were filed with the EEOC by people with disabilities that no one anticipated because they were invisible. The first plaintiff to win a monetary award, for example, experienced job discrimination related to a diagnosis of cancer (Pardeck, 1998).

Pardeck (2005) notes that over the years, the Supreme Court has had a profound effect on the ADA. Some rulings have limited the scope of the law. For example, in 2002, a plaintiff with carpal tunnel syndrome lost her case as the court did not consider the condition serious enough to be covered under the ADA. In 2004, however, the law was strengthened when the court upheld the right of disabled individuals to sue the states for equal access to public services and facilities in *Tennessee v. Lane* (Richey, 2004). Interpretations of the ADA continue to change regarding what is considered a disability and what must be done to accommodate the disability. Supreme Court decisions have fluctuated over time, with only some meeting the needs of the plaintiff with a disability (Bagenstos, 2009).

The Supreme Court has not made another major decision pertaining to disability in recent years, but serious challenges for this population continue. Poverty and unemployment rates remain high, for example. In 2012, the poverty rate for people with disabilities aged 18–64 was 28.4 percent (4.3 million persons) as compared to a rate of 12.5 percent for the same age group of people without disabilities ("Poverty in the United States," 2013). In 2016, labor force participation by people with disabilities was only 19.5 percent as compared to 67.9 percent for people without disabilities, and the unemployment rate for people with disabilities was twice that of people without disabilities ("Disability Statistics," 2016). Thirty percent of cases of workforce discrimination accepted by the U.S. Equal Employment Opportunity Commission in 2015 involved disability ("EEOC releases," 2016).

In 2014, President Obama signed the Workforce Innovation and Opportunity Act to help all job seekers, including persons with disabilities, access services that might assist them in their search. To help achieve the purposes of the act, the Advisory Committee on Increasing Competitive Integrated Employment for Individuals with Disabilities was created. Hopefully, this act and the committee

> ▶ How do Pat Puckett's statements align with the chapter with regards to discrimination, empowerment, and self-advocacy?
>
> https://www.youtube.com/watch?v=QYZ4mTJaO8c

it has created will be of genuine assistance to people with disabilities ("Advisory Committee on Increasing Competitive Integrated Employment for Individuals with Disabilities," 2015). However, the election of a conservative president, Donald Trump, who insulted various minority populations during his campaign, as well as a conservative Congress in 2016, placed in jeopardy any additional assistance to people with disabilities. Increased aid would require tax-generated allocations of funds from the government, whereas, by contrast, the primary goal of the conservative agenda was cutting taxes for people with wealth.

Global Efforts on Behalf of People with Disabilities

Discrimination against people with disabilities is not confined to the United States. Rather, it is a worldwide phenomenon. For this reason, the United Nations, an international organization often more visionary than its individual member states, determined to address the matter in 2006. The outcome was the Convention on the Rights of Persons with Disabilities in 2007. The convention achieved the highest number of signatories in UN history on an opening day ("Convention on the Rights of Persons with Disabilities," 2007).

The convention adopts a broad categorization of persons with disabilities and reaffirms that all persons with all types of disabilities must enjoy human rights and fundamental freedoms. It clarifies and qualifies how all categories of rights apply to persons with disabilities. Through the convention, the United Nations has initiated international acknowledgment of issues pertaining to, and the rights of, persons with disabilities.

By 2016, the convention had 160 signatories ("United Nations Treaty Collection," 2016). As with the UN Convention on Human Rights, however, not all nations that have signed the treaty have also *ratified* it. Ratifying would make them legally obligated to meet its provisions. The United States is one of those nations which has signed but not ratified the treaty. A two-thirds majority vote would be required in the US Senate, unlikely in the foreseeable future due to the conservative majority.

Value Dilemmas and Ethical Implications

Both personal and professional values come into focus in social work with people with developmental disabilities. Today, because of new knowledge of genetics and new medical procedures, value issues in this field are more complex than ever. Some of these issues are identified next.

Complex Issues

Today genetic counseling is available to all those who request it. This type of counseling makes it possible for a couple to know beforehand if they run a substantial risk of abnormality in a pregnancy. Should a concerned couple seek this type of information? What should they do if a substantial risk is identified?

A procedure called amniocentesis can identify many types of fetal abnormalities during a pregnancy. Corrective measures sometimes can be taken in utero, but sometimes nothing can be done. Should such a pregnancy be continued? Does this question involve absolute principles? Or can it involve consideration of probable quality of life for the fetus? For the family?

Social workers advocate self-determination. But who is the client in cases such as these? The fetus? The family members who will need to provide ongoing special care? Individual and family systems are both legitimate focuses for intervention, and the different systems might make different choices. Whose choices should be honored? But how can one even know what choice a fetus might make? Would it depend on the severity of the disability?

Perhaps if society provided sufficient supports to family caregivers, sufficient options such as universal access to respite care and day care services, choices could be made that would satisfy every member of a family. But increasing available family supports requires advocacy and political action in a larger arena. The NASW Code of Ethics provides a guide to expanding choice (see Box 12.8).

The Americans with Disabilities Act of 1990 and the Civil Rights Act of 1991 discussed earlier are important examples of legislation aimed at improving social conditions and promoting social justice for people with developmental disabilities. People with disabilities themselves, their families, social workers, and many, many others participated in the effort that resulted in these new laws.

Social workers may be able to affect social policy directly through their work if they should have an administrative position. Even with direct-service positions, however, social workers may help create change by writing informed letters to their agency administrators or to influential legislators. They may serve as expert witnesses at legislative hearings. Social workers may be even more active in creating policy by running for and holding public office. There is a great deal of work that still needs to be done with, and on behalf of, people with disabilities.

Current Trends

Because community care today so often means ongoing care by the family, a continuing trend is collaboration between families and professionals such as social workers. The strengths, or empowerment, model has helped encourage a paradigm in which families are viewed as competent, full partners in professional service, as illustrated in this chapter's case study with Mary and Lea Perkins. The role of social workers is primarily to assist families and consumers of services to meet their own goals. Mutual respect, trust,

Box 12.8 Social and Political Action

The NASW Code of Ethics provides guidance for social workers in the area of social and political action. According to the NASW, desirable ethical actions include the following:

- Becoming involved in political action in order to expand opportunities for self-determination for all client systems
- Becoming involved in political action to help ensure that all people have equal access to the resources they need, including employment
- Becoming aware of the impact of social policy on practice options
- Advocating for policy changes that can improve societal conditions
- Working to expand choice for all people, especially for populations that are vulnerable to exploitation and oppression

and open communication are imperative, as well as an atmosphere in which cultural traditions, values, and diversity are acknowledged and honored (Liu, 2005; Rothman, 2003).

Although community care, especially care by one's own family, may be the option of choice for the individual with disabilities, caregiver stress among family members is an ongoing concern. For example, one study of parents of children with autism found that while their divorce rate is about the same as the divorce rate for parents of children without disabilities until the child reaches the age of 8, their divorce rate remains high after that age is reached, while it goes down significantly for parents of children without disabilities (Devitt, 2010). Such a study indicates the toll a disability can wreak on families.

Family supports known as "wraparound services" are available in many communities today. Wraparound services usually assist families with children who have behavioral disabilities so severe they are at risk of placement in residential care. Services include diagnosis and treatment, family support services, and any other community supports recommended to make it possible for a child to remain at (or return to) home. A special service plan is often developed by a Family Assessment and Treatment Team (FAPT). The team may include members of the local Department of Social Services, the juvenile court, the school, and other agencies such as the local Community Services Board ("Wraparound Services," 2015).

As children with disabilities grow up and see their age-mates leaving home, they also frequently desire to live independently of their families. Independent living benefits not only the children but also their families, as it provides relief from caregiver stress. Special housing is often required, however. Today there is nowhere near enough special housing to meet the need. Part of the issue is that people with different disabilities require different supports. For example, people with impaired mobility have very different housing requirements than people with intellectual disabilities. Another part of the issue is budget cuts—special housing is usually put on the chopping block during hard economic times. Group homes and rent-assisted public housing for people with disabilities have long waiting lists today—years long in many communities.

The increasing lifespan of people with disabilities is another major trend, made possible by advances in medicine. While increasing lifespans should be something to celebrate, the problem is that there is not enough special housing to meet the needs of the older population with disabilities. In many cases, assistance from parents is no longer available; parents have died or become disabled themselves. A horrifying result is that huge numbers of people with disabilities become homeless.

New hope was offered in 2010 to all homeless people—an Obama Administration program named *Opening Doors* designed to end veteran and chronic homelessness by 2015 and to end homelessness among children, families, and youth by 2020. The federal Department of Housing and Urban Development (HUD) prepares annual reports measuring progress toward these goals. HUD's 2015 *Annual Homeless Assessment Report to Congress* found that significant progress was indeed being made in reducing homelessness in America between 2010 and 2015, but the problem was far from solved. There was a decrease of 11 percent in overall homelessness and a 26 percent drop in "unsheltered" homelessness. Veteran homelessness declined by 36 percent and chronic homelessness by 22 percent.

Many people with disabilities have undoubtedly been assisted through *Opening Doors*, although the 2015 HUD report did not factor out this population. The report found that while some communities were continuing to make progress toward ending homelessness, others were stymied because of lack of affordable housing and budget shortages.

Adults with disabilities comprise about 17 percent of those helped by Section 8 public housing today, a program overseen by HUD. Section 8 tenants, as discussed in Chapter 10, must be very low income. They pay approximately 30 percent of their income, whatever it might be, toward rent. Many adults with disabilities who could not otherwise afford independent accommodations have been enabled to do so by this program. However, no new rental units have been built for decades. The Consortium for Citizens with Disabilities (CCD), while praising many provisions in President Obama's proposed 2017 budget, lamented that proposed funding for public housing was sufficient only to maintain current units, while additional funds for new units were urgently needed ("CCD Response," 2016).

Social workers should have many opportunities to work with people with disabilities in coming years because the number of people with disabilities is increasing and more efforts are being made toward providing community-based supports for this population. More and better community services are clearly needed, not only for young people with disabilities but for the ever-increasing numbers who survive into old age.

> **?** Assess your understanding of the disability rights movement, social policy, and appropriate terminology by taking this brief quiz.

SUMMARY

- The history of services to people with disabilities is described. The chapter begins with a case study illustrating contemporary, community-based social work with people with disabilities. It presents a brief history of services to this population. For centuries, people with disabilities were overlooked or incarcerated. Reformers such as Frenchmen Pereira, Itard, and Seguin demonstrated that people with disabilities could be taught in training schools. Huge institutions soon replaced training schools, however. Then, in the 1920s, research proved that people with disabilities released into the community could lead productive lives. The concept of normalization spurred efforts toward removing people from large institutions and placing them back in the community. While social workers traditionally have worked primarily with people with disabilities in institutional settings, today community-based settings are preferred.
- Major types of developmental disabilities are identified and discussed. The differences between categorical and functional definitions of disability are important because of effects on funding resources and eligibility for service. Ten major categories of developmental disability are discussed: intellectual disability, cerebral palsy, autism, orthopedic problems, hearing problems, epilepsy, traumatic brain injury, learning disabilities, emotional disturbance, and co-occurrence of disability. Disabling effects of alcohol, cocaine and other drugs are also described.
- Contemporary social work practice with people who have disabilities is described. Both the Council on Social Work Education and the National Association of Social Workers address social work practice with people with disabilities. Social workers assist people with disabilities and their families in diverse settings

- ranging from institutions to the wider community, and provide diverse services including genetic counseling and spiritual nourishment.
- Social justice issues that pertain to human diversity involving disabilities are described. Clients with developmental disabilities are diverse, not only with respect to their special needs but also their membership in diverse cultural groups. Thus, cultural competence is important for social workers. A case example involving a Chinese family including a daughter with physical and intellectual disabilities is provided. Social justice issues pertaining to people with disabilities include the mismatch between person and environment, and discrimination. Social workers engage in empowerment practice assisting clients with disabilities to exercise self-determination and self-advocacy.
- The disability rights movement and its causes are discussed. The disability rights movement, which works toward empowerment of people with disabilities, helped lead to the passage of The Education for All Handicapped Children Act of 1975 (currently known as the Individuals with Disabilities Education Act), the Americans with Disabilities Act of 1990, and the Civil Rights Act of 1991, among others. However, competition for scarce resources makes implementing these laws difficult. Resources assisting people to live in the community are limited, particularly special housing for those who wish to live independently. The Convention on the Rights of Persons with Disabilities, adopted by the United Nations in 2007, lends hope that this population will receive increasing social justice efforts in the United States and around the world in the coming years.

> ✓ Recall what you learned from this chapter by completing the Chapter Review.

13

The Social Work Profession Looks to the Future

LEARNING OUTCOMES

- Explain how globalization affects social workers and social work practice.
- Identify the major social forces that are transforming the world.
- Describe what the future of the social work profession holds in terms of employment opportunities and future challenges.

CHAPTER OUTLINE

CASE STUDY: Rachel Fox: Student Social Worker in an International Field Placement 411

Social Work: A Profession at the Edge of Change 415
- National and International Strategic Planning 417
- Globalization: Relevance to Social Work 418

The Major Forces Driving Transformation of the World 420
- Demographic Trends 421
- The Changing Immigrant and Refugee Population 425
- Political Forces 428
- Economic Trends 433
- Technological Trends and Biomedical Advances 435
- Environmental Sustainability 440

The Future of the Social Work Profession 442
- The Social Work Workforce: Employment Projections, Social Worker Shortages 442
- The Grand Challenges and Contributions of Social Work 443

Summary 445

CASE STUDY: Rachel Fox: Student Social Worker in an International Field Placement[1]

At first, time had moved slowly, but near the end of the internship the time to leave had come quickly. Rachel reflected on her internship in South Africa during the 21-hour flight back to the States,

[1] The Rachel Fox case study was contributed by Nicholas P. Smiar, PhD, ACSW, Professor Emeritus, University of Wisconsin-Eau Claire, with input from his student, Rachel Fox. Nick Smiar has extensive experience with international field placement of social work students.

remembering that day two years ago, when a South African social worker spoke to her policy class on campus. It was then that she decided to apply for the internship in South Africa. A year later, she was required to interview with social work internship faculty and a South African supervisor. She described to them her experiences in other countries, including summers spent in France with family, and her interest in South Africa. She was very pleased to learn that she had been accepted for an internship in a child welfare agency in the Western Cape of South Africa for that fall. Her friend Emma, another intern, would accompany her.

The next six months were spent finishing her social work classes and preparing for the internship. She met with the three other interns and a coordinator and spent many hours reading about the history of South Africa, about social work and social services, about South African social welfare policy (especially the new Children's Bill), and about cultures, customs, and languages. She even began to learn the basics of Xhosa, the local native language. She applied for her passport, a student visa, and registration as a student social worker.

The actual trip to South Africa seemed to take forever, but finally Rachel was at King William's Town Child and Youth Care Center in a small city in the Eastern Cape Province. It took a few days for both interns to overcome their jet lag and to go through the agency orientation. At first, it was difficult to come to know the staff, especially the black staff members, who were primarily Xhosa speakers. As Rachel entered into her work, she discovered that there was a divide between the white staff and the black staff, which was partly cultural and partly a result of the past apartheid policies, so she made a concerted effort to work with the black staff. She also had to deal with the language divide as she struggled to learn Xhosa, with its clicks and other unusual sounds. She did learn enough to be polite and to know what was being said, but not enough to be fluent with her clients and their families. She had to rely on interpretation for part of her work.

Rachel and her student friend, Emma, entered the work gradually, first learning all of the services of the agency and then developing a working knowledge of the social work processes of the agency and of the provincial department of social welfare. They had had to reframe their understanding of social welfare policy and of social work itself because they were in a different policy environment, in a country with a unique recent history and a parliamentary polity. Rachel learned that the basic policy principle is *Ubuntu*, from the Xhosa saying: "A person becomes a person through other persons."

Rachel and Emma had already become familiar with the Children's Bill, the first major revision of child welfare policy since 1983. Both interns quickly discovered that they actually knew more about the policy than most of the social workers with whom they were working because although the law had been passed two years previously, the implementation was slow; the regulations were still being drawn up. That was definitely a challenge in the child welfare environment. However, the agency social workers would gather for case discussions and to learn more about the Children's Bill and its implementation. Rachel also observed what seemed to her to be ethical lapses when case files were not secured or confidential information was discussed openly, without safeguards; but she learned that a code of ethics had just been drawn up by the South African Council for Social Service Professions (SACSSP) and had not yet been integrated into social work education. Another major challenge was working with the social workers in the public department of social welfare. These social workers had very large caseloads and were generally non-responsive when it came to permission to return a child to his or her family.

The saddest part of Rachel's experience was working with very young children who were HIV-positive or had AIDS. The agency had a residential unit for infants, many of whom were infected or were orphans of AIDS. Many of the parents had died of the disease. HIV and AIDS, Rachel learned, are everyday realities in South Africa, which has the highest HIV–AIDS rate per capita in the world, and the country has only recently begun to address the problem with clinical treatment and prevention. This was not Rachel's only experience with the health care system. One day, while driving to an appointment, Rachel was injured in an auto accident. She learned firsthand about the two health care systems, one for the poor and one for those who had private insurance. In her work at the agency, she had already seen the system for the poor when the young children with HIV or AIDS were sent to the local public clinic, where care was not the finest. When a white boy became sick, he was taken to the private clinic and received good quality care; when a black girl became sick, she was taken to one of the inadequate public clinics. Now Rachel saw for herself a very different system from the public clinics where she had to take children for care. She experienced the other private system, where she received far better care. Unfortunately, however, for some time following the accident she could no longer pick up the infants, who wanted so much to be held.

As a primary part of her fieldwork, Rachel helped three families to reunite. This involved navigating the social welfare system, advocating for her clients, squeezing permissions out of public social workers, and helping to make placement arrangements in very poor communities with few resources. She saw people with very few material possessions who struggled every day to survive but would help neighbors in need. She saw *ubuntu* in action and came to understand the strong communal ties and traditional values among the Xhosa people. She experienced the bedrock faith of the people when she attended a local Baptist church, when she heard a prayer before every social work or community meeting, and when she heard the workers sing hymns whenever the start of a meeting was delayed.

One of the first children Rachel heard about when she arrived at the children's center was James. James had spent most of his life in residential care. When she arrived at the Child and Youth Care Center, everybody talked about James because he was the most challenging case that the center was dealing with at the time. Although there was uncertainty about how to proceed with James, it was decided that Rachel could work with him. James was 11 years old; he had been removed from his home when he was 5 years old. He lived in a single-parent household and had experienced a difficult childhood. His mother tried to kill him twice, and it was suspected that she had also prostituted him out for extra income. James had lived at several different child care centers before he ended up at Rachel's field placement agency. By the time Rachel arrived, he had been there six months and he was not attending school. He had initially attended school but was removed when he stabbed a classmate with a pencil and threatened a teacher. There were no public schools in the area that would accept him as a student.

Once Rachel became familiar with the case, she set up a team that would meet on a weekly basis and focus on James. This team consisted of the director of the facility, who had worked closely with James, the social work supervisor, and the child care workers from James's unit. This team worked together so that everybody had the same information and provided consistency in James's life. James was given incentives for good behavior. When the team discovered that money was an important motivator for James, they set up an allowance that James could earn by doing his chores and following rules. This system did not seem to work well at first, so Rachel re-evaluated it and talked with James. Fortunately, James, like most other teens, had learned English in school, so communicating with him was not a problem. James was actually multi-cultural; his mother was white and his father was from India. Although he identified as white, he spoke Xhosa fluently, was well accepted by Xhosa people, and participated in Xhosa cultural songs and dances, which was a real strength in an environment where there was still separation between white and black people, even among the staff of the center. James stated forcibly that he did not think he was being evaluated fairly. So Rachel and James together designed a checklist for the staff to evaluate James's chores and behavior. As the staff began to work with this checklist, they found that James was actually doing better than they first thought he was. Having decided on his own goals and helped in creating the checklist, James became increasingly motivated to do well.

The next hurdle was transitioning James back into school. After many phone calls, a private school was finally found that was willing to take James as long as he followed strict rules. James was a likeable child and the teachers enjoyed having him right away. James was easy to get along with, but Rachel understood that he could push the limits. Early on, Rachel talked with the principal to ensure that there would be open communication about James's progress. The principal and the teachers found it difficult to believe that such a likeable kid would cause any problems. After the school encountered some behavior problems, however, the communication between the school and the center became better. Improved communication between the school and the center made it easier for the center's staff to encourage James with his homework and extracurricular activities at school. James's overall behavior and attitude changed gradually. James was able to establish friendships with roommates, and he began to take pride in the change that he was making in his life.

Then James began to express a desire to live with his mom again. His mother had given up her parental rights, but she was still allowed to continue to be part of his life through visits. It was decided that it might be best for James if he was moved to a child care center that was closer to where his mother lived so that she could visit James more often. Because of the progress that James made, Rachel and the staff were able to find a child care center that was in the same city where his mother lived and that was willing to accept him.

Rachel had developed a close relationship with James, and she missed him. Just before it was time to return to the United States, Rachel was gladdened when she received information that James had made a good adjustment and was doing well.

Although Rachel and her friend, Emma, had told the children and families of their agency at the very beginning that they would be leaving in early December, when that time came, the separation was very difficult. It seemed that they had just arrived and now they would be leaving. It seemed that they were doing everything with much greater intensity. They were in a countdown to the very last day, and everything seemed more dramatic. The day had come, however, and they did say their good-byes, tearfully, of course.

Now, on her return flight to the United States, Rachel looked out the window of the airplane over the Atlantic Ocean and thought back over her amazing experience. How could she ever explain this experience to anyone else? Only two words came to mind: *life changing*!

SOCIAL WORK: A PROFESSION AT THE EDGE OF CHANGE

This chapter's case study features Rachel Fox. She is not a fictitious person as are the other social workers in previous chapter case studies. Instead, she is a very real person who gave us permission to share the story of her South African fieldwork learning experience. Rachel is a compassionate, ethical, student social worker. She is also attuned to change, adventuresome, willing to take risks, and ready to use promising opportunities when they emerge. She cares deeply about the children of the world and their families.

As a student social worker, Rachel is building confidence in her social work knowledge and skills. The profession's values are her values. She is also very committed to a lifetime of learning and humble in her awareness that she has much to learn. She is fully aware that her efforts to help people will not always work; when they don't, she is ready to look for new interventions. As a generalist social worker, Rachel may begin her work with individuals and their families. As a result of her experience in a South African child care center, she has discovered that in her future practice, she may need to seek change within organizations, sometimes the very organization that may be her employer. She has realized that in the United States, just as in South Africa, organizations have problems that need to be overcome in order to best serve the needs of families and children. Because she is a generalist, Rachel has recognized that in her career, she may need to work not only at the individual or family level but also within her own field placement agency as that organization experiences change, and possibly at the community or governmental level as well. This would probably be true whether she held a social work position in South Africa, the United States, or anywhere else in the world. Change that will truly help people, she has come to realize, often needs to be made at the larger social system level. Today, as she begins her career as a social worker, Rachel is committed to helping people, and she is ready to work where change is needed, even if this is not within her own familiar local environment or her own country. Social work is, at its core, a change profession wherever it exists.

Chapter 13 concludes this book by engaging our readers in an exploration of the future. We chose the Rachel Fox international social work case study to provide a global perspective for this endeavor. Our study of the future will begin by looking at how the United States and the United Nations do strategic planning. The chapter will then introduce the major forces that are driving transformation within the world. We will delve into demographic, political, economic, technological, and biomedical trends as well as global issues of environmental sustainability. The chapter and this text will end with a consideration of the future of the social work profession.

In the case study, Rachel saw change taking place rapidly all around her in South Africa. On returning to the United States, she became aware that the entire world is alive with change, and she has begun to realize that change is at the heart of the profession of social work. Ann Fadiman, author of *The Spirit Catches You and You Fall Down*, once described her position as a storyteller in a way that resembles that of the social worker. She found fascination in the edges of life—places like shorelines, storm fronts, and borders between countries. She could sense frictions and tensions in those places as well as energy (1997). What she described is a microcosm of the world. Indeed, a stream of exciting, sometimes frightening, highly energized forces that are rapidly reshaping our world today. Perhaps Rachel Fox, the student social worker, represents the social work profession at this confluence of change. Like Rachel, social workers live with change every day. Social workers also create change. Key to much of the change taking place in the world today is cultural transformation and globalization.

In the next 10 years, the United States will become far more culturally diverse than it is today, and social work practice will be at that confluence of change. The profession of social work will be challenged by a society that still does not understand it or its clients well. The old stereotype of the welfare worker (social worker) dispensing "the dole" to lazy, fraudulent recipients (clients) truly needs to change. This book has attempted to destroy such stereotypes by providing extensive case studies that illustrate the true nature of social work practice and the people social workers work with. The people in the case studies—the clients as well as the social workers—were drawn from real-life situations. These are people of dignity. They do not fit into stereotypes. Instead, the varying circumstances of their lives lead naturally into an exploration of the values, social policy issues, research findings, practice, and history of the profession of social work.

Many persons considering a career in social work will find that the value base of the profession is inconsistent with their own values, and they will need to look for another career. Those who enter social work will find that the profession is strongly influenced by various outside forces: demographic trends, political trends, economic conditions, technological advances in science and health care, and environmental concerns, just to name a few. These forces contain energy that drives change. When these forces overlap and intermingle, they sometimes build momentum that speeds change. Increasingly, they are not contained within national borders but, instead, operate globally. They are among the forces that futurists analyze when they seek to forecast change that will take place in the next 5 to 25 years on this planet.

This chapter, then, is about change. It cites the work of social workers, of other researchers, and of **futurists**. Futurists are people who study global trends to predict the nature of life in the future. They do not predict specific future events but instead provide alternative scenarios. True futurists are exceptionally well educated, often holding several PhD degrees; they are fluent in multiple languages; and they often live and work in several countries. This chapter uses the work of futurists, international organizations, U.S. government offices, and other sources to examine trends in the United States and other parts of the world and to generate thinking about the implications of these trends for the profession of social work.

The term **globalization** has come to have different meanings within different contexts. Many futurists believe that this concept is evolving over time. Initially, international commerce dominated discussion and thinking about globalization, but today financial aspects are considered to be just one component of this concept. Newer thinking incorporates recognition of the increasingly borderless world that is characterized not only by mobility of people, ideas, cultures, talent, and collaboration but also by threats such as terrorism, movement of dangerous addictive drugs, and human trafficking.

But futurists, other researchers, and the media have not yet agreed on a single definition of globalization. The absence of a precise definition could, perhaps, be attributed to the multiplicity of forces driving global change as well as the fact that globalization is itself a process that is ever evolving. So, where did globalization actually begin? Two sociologists, Hewa and Stapleton, note that from early human history forward, people have changed locations, often crossing geographic as well as tribal or national borders. Human movement, communication, and development of social relations, however, increased markedly during the twentieth century, setting the stage for a new burst of international collaboration. Hewa and Stapleton see the growing awareness of global human interconnectedness to be the heart of the way we think about globalization (2006). Critical to their definition is the concept of an exchange of ideas and values that crosses national borders and creates global communities.

Instead of letting ourselves think of globalization as merely a form of modernization or just from the perspective of commerce and trade, a more informed understanding of globalization considers four central themes:

1. Globalization is, in fact, a sustained process that has been underway throughout human history.
2. Globalization includes economics, but, perhaps more importantly, it includes the communication of culture, values, technological advances in communication and transportation, and urbanization.
3. Globalization as a process does not move in a single direction (e.g., top-down) but instead is multi-directional.
4. This process has an impact on local and global dimensions alike, not as a clash with one ultimate victor, but in recreating an entirely new version (Grew, 2006).

National and International Strategic Planning

Each country, the United States included, engages in strategic planning to anticipate and guide the direction the future will take. No longer can strategic planning ignore the impact of globalization. In the United States, the U.S. Government Accountability Office (GAO) is responsible for helping Congress to engage in planning within a global context. The GAO's 2014–2019 Strategic Plan was developed around several key trends considered likely to shape the future of the nation and the world. These trends include threats to national security, fiscal sustainability, global interdependence, science and technology, communication and information technology, shifting roles of governance, and demographic and societal change (U.S. Government Accountability Office [GAO], 2014). Four goals were established, with clearly stated objectives, to aid Congress as it oversees federal programs and engages in planning. You will learn much more about the GAO Strategic Plan in the next several sections of this chapter.

Internationally, the strategic plans of other countries often emphasize similar concerns to those of the United States. On a global scale, the United Nations in 2000 articulated a set of millennium development goals (MDGs) with 2015 as the target date for accomplishment. This goal statement was adopted by all member nations. In the years that followed, the world experienced terrorism, wars, earthquakes, and other natural and manmade disasters that could have totally defeated efforts to attain the goals.

By 2015, the United Nations was able to report that amazing progress had been made. Goal 1 of the UN development plan was to eradicate extreme poverty and hunger. Despite the international global financial crisis that began in 2008, extreme hunger and poverty declined by one-half. Goal 2, to achieve universal primary school education, demonstrated remarkable improvement even in the poorest regions. The promotion of gender equality and empowerment of women, Goal 3, also demonstrated improvement in the number of women involved in political activity. Goal 4, the reduction in child mortality was also successful globally with deaths due to child killers such as measles declining most dramatically. Goals that were not achieved included the improvement of maternal health and reversing the spread of HIV/AIDS. Ensuring environmental sustainability, as reflected in deforestation, and providing access to safe drinking water and basic sanitation were slightly improved (Ki-Moon, 2007; United Nations, 2010; United Nations Development Programme, 2016).

In 2015 when world leaders came together to forge the new set of goals, they determined to build upon the successes of the MDGs and address the unachieved goals. They also determined to go well beyond the MDGs, seeking to address root causes of poverty and inequality and put the world on a path to peace, well-being, and environmental sustainability. As reported in 2016, the United Nations Development Programme was delegated primary responsibility within the United Nations for implementation of the newly created Sustainable Development Goals, beginning with the development of guidelines for the achievement reports that nations would be required to submit on a scheduled basis. The 17 Sustainable Development Goals, with a brief listing of some of the many targets for each goal, are depicted in Box 13.1.

The United Nations' Sustainable Development Goals represent an optimistic yet potentially realizable plan to involve all 170 member nations in concerted action to achieve peace and well-being. The United Nations stands alone in our world as the only existing organization that has the capacity, with the cooperation of member nations, to undertake this enormous effort.

Globalization: Relevance to Social Work

The 2001 terrorist attacks on the World Trade Center in New York and the Pentagon in Washington, D.C. awakened people in the United States to globalization in a new and dangerous form. Americans came to realize that even as a world superpower, they were vulnerable to international terrorism even within their own borders. Terrorism has increasingly emerged in the United States as well as locations around the world, posing important questions about why terrorism exists. What nourishes, supports, and sustains it? While social workers don't have answers to all of these questions, social workers do understand that frustrations related to poverty, economic exploitation, differences in religion and in worldview, among other issues, drive much of the unrest and strife in the global environment in which we all live.

Social workers, in concert with other health and human service professionals, play a key role in the healing and transformation of the world. This has been true since the

Box 13.1 The United Nations Sustainable Development Goals for 2020 (with Some Sample Targets)

Goal 1: End Poverty Everywhere
- eradicate extreme poverty
- implement social protection systems within all nations that provide coverage for the poor
- reduce vulnerability to severe climate-related events and other disasters
- create social policies to eradicate poverty that are pro-poor and gender sensitive

Goal 2: End Hunger
- end hunger and ensure access to sufficient, safe, and nutritious food
- double agricultural productivity and incomes of small-scale producers
- ensure sustainable farming production systems with ability to adapt to climate change

Goal 3: Ensure Health and Well-Being
- reduce maternal mortality to less than 70 of 100,000 births
- end preventable deaths of newborn babies and children under age 5
- provide access to sexual and reproductive health services
- ensure universal health coverage

Goal 4: Ensure Quality Education
- provide free, good quality primary and secondary education
- eliminate gender disparity and provide equal access to education for persons with disabilities

Goal 5: Ensure Gender Equality and Empowerment for Women and Girls
- end discrimination of women and girls
- eliminate trafficking and all violence and exploitation of women and girls
- eliminate harmful practices including early and forced child marriage as well as genital mutilation

Goal 6: Ensure Clean Water and Sanitation
- ensure access to safe drinking water, sanitation, and hygiene
- protect rivers, aquifers, lakes, forests, mountains, and other water-related ecosystems

Goal 7: Ensure Affordable and Clean Energy
- ensure access to reliable, modern energy
- in developing and least-developed countries, expand sustainable energy services

Goal 8: Promote Productive, Decent Work and Full Employment
- sustain per capital economic growth of at least seven per cent of gross domestic product
- immediately stop forced labor, modern slavery, and human trafficking

Goal 9: Promote Infrastructure and Sustainable Industrialization
- support economic development and human well-being
- encourage innovation, research, and development
- provide access to the Internet for least-developed countries by 2020

Goal 10: Reduce Inequality Both within and Among Countries

Goal 11: Make Cities and Communities Safe and Sustainable
- upgrade slums; provide safe and affordable housing for all
- protect and safeguard the world's cultural and natural heritage
- adopt policies that help cities mitigate disasters related to climate change

Goal 12: Ensure Responsible and Sustainable Production and Consumption
- achieve sound environmental management of chemicals and waste by 2020
- reduce generation of waste through reduction as well as recycling and reuse

Goal 13: Urgently Combat Climate Change

Goal 14: Conserve and Sustainably Use the Oceans and Seas
- by 2020, end overfishing and unregulated fishing; conserve coastal and marine areas

(continued)

> **Box 13.1 (Continued)**
>
> **Goal 15: Promote Sustainable Use of Land and Forests; Combat Desertification**
> - by 2020, protect and prevent the extinction of threatened species
> - take urgent action to end poaching and trafficking of protected species
>
> **Goal 16: Promote Peace, Justice, Sustainable Development, and Strong Institutions**
> - reduce bribery and corruption
> - ensure legal identity of all, including birth registration
> - strengthen international cooperation to prevent violence, combat terrorism and crime
>
> **Goal 17: Strengthen Global Partnerships to Achieve Sustainable Development**
>
> Source: United Nations Sustainable Development Knowledge Platform, Department of Economic and Social Affairs. (2015). *Sustainable development goals*. Retrieved from https://sustainabledevelopment.un.org/?menu=1300.

days of Jane Addams and the pioneers of the social work profession. Social workers from the United States act internationally as well as domestically. Social workers increasingly recognize that emerging global issues including war, terrorism, environmental devastation, and massive migration all produce new challenges. Social workers now, more than ever, need to think critically about their practice through the lens of global events and diverse perspectives. Increasing numbers of social workers are now working in international settings for at least a part of their careers. All social workers, however, must now be prepared to bring internationalized perspectives into their daily practice (Lyons, Manion, & Carlsen, 2006).

Social work is, indeed, a profession at the edge of change. As the world around us changes, so must our profession. As we prepare for the future, the values of the social work profession—service, social justice, dignity and worth of all persons, and the importance of human relationships—remain as beacons, guiding our actions and our practice. Standard 6 of the NASW Code of Ethics reminds us that social workers have ethical responsibilities, not just to our individual clients, but also to the broader society on local as well as global levels (NASW, 2008).

> **?** Assess your understanding of how social work can be viewed as a profession at the edge of change by taking this brief quiz.

THE MAJOR FORCES DRIVING TRANSFORMATION OF THE WORLD

The Rachel Fox case study initiated an international perspective at the start of this chapter and globalization will remain a theme throughout the remainder of this chapter. It is inherent in the five major forces that are energizing, shaping, and transforming the world. We begin with what is arguably the most significant transforming force: demographic change. Following this, this chapter will consider other forces of change: political trends, economic conditions, biomedical and scientific advances, and environmental sustainability.

Demographic Trends

Demographics, the study of population characteristics and trends, is an area of considerable interest to researchers and futurists who monitor patterns of change from which they develop forecasts of the future. Demographics is one of the most significant forces creating change in the United States today, change that will carry into the next 40 or 50 years. The U.S. Census Bureau, which charts population shifts, predicts that by the year 2044, over half of the people in the country will belong to what is now thought of as a minority group. By 2060, approximately 20 percent of the population is expected to be foreign born (2015). In reality, the "new" multi-cultural world that is predicted may be new for some people, but not for all. Already, in some parts of the country, there is so much diversity that there is no single majority population. With rapidly changing demographics in the next few decades, the social work profession, with a value system that respects diversity, should be well positioned to take on the challenges that lie ahead. Other demographic trends that will influence social work practice are the increase in our elderly population, evolutions in American family structures, and the changing immigrant and refugee population.

A Multi-Cultural America

Although white Americans made up 85 percent of the U.S. population in 1950 (U.S. Bureau of the Census, 1950), non-Hispanic white persons are expected to decline in population and comprise only 44 percent of the 2060 U.S. population (U.S. Census Bureau, 2015). Already anticipating this rapid shift, author Farai Chideya predicted that the coming demographic shift would have considerable impact. Groups that hold power generally do not like to give it up. So, in anticipation of potential political power shifts along racial lines, some states would redraw congressional districts and sustain political power during elections through reapportionment. Concern about job loss to new ethnic groups could increase tension in the workplace and community. She concluded that the worst crisis to be faced would not be in our workplaces or neighborhoods, but it would be in our minds. If we look around our communities, we may see that some of these predictions are emerging. Chideya's belief, however, is that the millennium generation of 15- to 25-year-olds, which is already far more culturally diverse than any previous generation, will create a future that is much less negatively biased on issues of race than previous generations (1999).

Americans have typically thought about race in terms of black and white. This tends to be how race continues to be covered in the media. The reality, though, is that America is already diverse and rapidly becoming more so. The Census Bureau reported that the fastest growing population was the two or more races group, which is expected to increase from 8 million in 2014 to 26 million by 2060. The next fastest growing group, according to the Census Bureau, is the Asian population, which is expected to increase by 128 percent, from 17 million in 2014 to 39 million by 2060. The Hispanic population is projected to increase by 115 percent, from 55 million in 2014 to 119 million in 2060. The population group of Native Hawaiian and other Pacific Islanders is expected to increase

---

Assessment

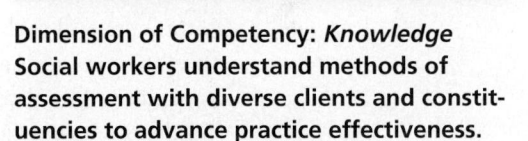

Dimension of Competency: *Knowledge*
Social workers understand methods of assessment with diverse clients and constituencies to advance practice effectiveness.

Critical Thinking Question: If social workers were planning to conduct a needs assessment of their community, why would it be important to determine all of the demographic characteristics of that community?

by 63 percent (from 734,000 to over one million), while the black population has a projected increase of 42 percent (42–60 million). One population group is expected to sustain a nearly stable population: American Indian/Alaska Native people (increases from four million to five million). The non-Hispanic white population is projected to decrease by 8.2 percent between 2014 and 2060, from 198 million to 182 million, and there is an expected decrease in white children of 23 percent (U.S. Census Bureau, 2015).

The social work profession was birthed in a spirit of reform and celebration of multi-culturalism, as revealed in the history sections of past chapters of this book. The Council on Social Work Education has written accreditation standards that ensure inclusion of human diversity content in all baccalaureate and master's degree programs. **Ethnic-sensitive approaches** to social work practice are now taught in schools of social work that link knowledge of culture and ethnicity with understandings of social class differences. In many ways, social work as a profession has meant being an advocate and a supporter of human diversity.

But there is much more for social work to do to create a just society, and the predicted transformation of our nation's ethnic and cultural makeup will challenge the profession to become much more proactive. An **ethnoconscious approach** incorporates ethnic sensitivity with empowerment tactics that build upon appreciation for the strengths already existing in ethnically diverse communities. An ethnoconscious approach would seek to create anti-racism organizations that reflect the ethnic makeup of the community served by the agency from board members to executives, and all levels of staff. Consistent with this approach, social work agencies can feature commitment to diversity in their mission statements and seek to hire as well as empower diverse staff (Miller & Garran, 2009). An ethnoconscious approach also supports social change. Linked not only to its service community, but also to the region, nation, and other countries, the organization and its social workers can take on human problems in the lives of people as they live in families and function within groups, organizations, and entire communities.

The Graying of America

As indicated in Chapter 10, "Social Work with Older Adults," a significant shift in the age of the population is taking place in the United States. During the colonial period of American history, approximately half the population was under the age of 16, and relatively few persons lived to age 65. By 1900, about 4 percent of the population was 65 years of age or older. By 2000, this had increased to 12.4 percent (34,991,733 persons) (Vincent & Velkoff, 2010). The population aged 65 and older is now expected to reach 83.7 million by the year 2050 (Ortman, Velkoff, & Hogan, 2014).

Despite a long history of age discrimination in the United States (unlike most Asian countries, where age is revered), the new and rapidly growing cohort of older adults may produce shifts in ageism attitudes. Today's older adults are quite different from previous generations. They have achieved higher levels of education than their predecessors, they generally have a higher level of income and buying power, and they are politically active. They have fewer disabilities, and if disabilities do occur, they have better designed equipment (e.g., motorized wheelchairs) to enable them to sustain a vigorous, active lifestyle. Today social workers provide financial counseling, recreation and wellness programs, housing assistance, advocacy (especially in relation to health care), adult protective services, counseling, and case management. People who compose the oldest cohort of the

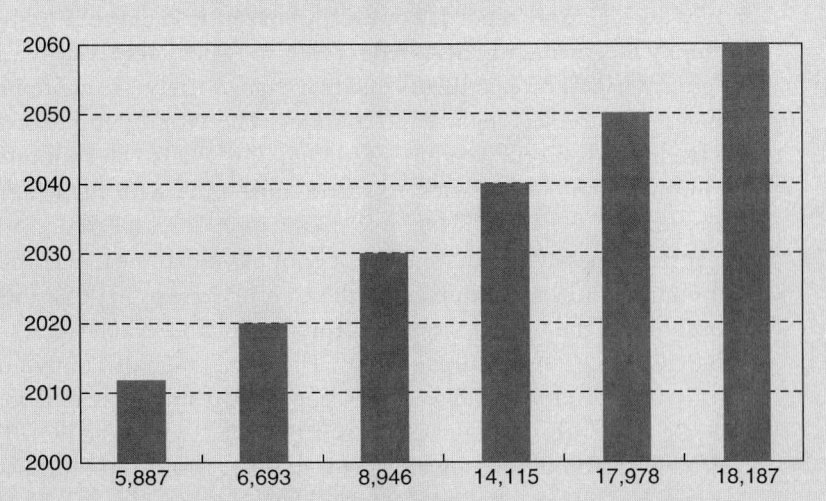

> **Box 13.2 Projected Population 85 Years and Older (in Thousands)**[a]
>
> | Year | Population |
> |------|-----------|
> | 2010 | 5,887 |
> | 2020 | 6,693 |
> | 2030 | 8,946 |
> | 2040 | 14,115 |
> | 2050 | 17,978 |
> | 2060 | 18,187 |
>
> Source: Ortman, J.M., Velkoff, V.A., & Hogan, H. (2014, May). Appendix Table A-2. Projections and distribution of the total population by selected age groups, race, and Hispanic origin for the United States: 2012 to 2060-Con, *An Aging Nation: The Older Population in the United States*, p. 27. U.S. Census Bureau. Retrieved from http://www.census.gov/prod/2014pubs/p25-1140.pdf.
>
> [a]Table used 2012 Population Estimates and 2012 National Projections.

elderly, those 85 years and older, require the greatest number of services. As Box 13.2 indicates, this segment of the elderly population is growing rapidly. Because of advanced age, these people are more likely to have cognitive disorders, such as dementia, as well as physical disabilities, so they require care that is physically and psychologically demanding for caregivers. Intervention, then, would seek to strengthen bonds of intergenerational caregiving as well as economic and social service policies to ensure good quality of life.

A demographic characteristic that influences the planning and delivery of social services to the elderly is the lifespan of women. Women tend to outlive men by several years and they also tend to marry men who are several years older, so it is common for women to outlive their husbands by 10 years or more. Women are more likely than men to have to deal with the complex health, economic, and housing problems of old age, first as caregivers of others and later as receivers of care.

The complex problems of aging require social workers to have both a sound understanding of the aging process and a broad generalist practice background that enables them to work simultaneously with individual clients, families, and community systems. Fortunately, the number of students interested in social work with older adults has increased in recent years. Encouraged by the financial support of organizations like the Hartford Foundation, schools of social work have increased the aging content in required courses, and some have also added elective courses on social work with older adults. More field placements in aging, too, are now available. As a result, it appears that the new generation of social workers will be better prepared for work with older adults, especially when the older adult population is increasing and the number of social work positions in this field is growing substantially.

The Evolving American Family

The American family, too, has undergone considerable change, and it continues to evolve. In the 1980s, some writers predicted the imminent collapse of the traditional American family. Such gloomy reports, however, were replaced in the 1990s by a renewed valuing of family life, including increased interest in issues such as early childhood education, long-term health care, and enriched marriage. Society has continued to place value on families. This trend is expected to continue. The World Future Society predicted that as the twenty-first century continues to unfold, workers will continue to make sacrifices, sometimes of higher salaries, to spend more time with their families (World Future Society, 2007).

Interesting patterns have been developing in families. According to the American Community Survey conducted by the Census Bureau in 2014, there were 123 million households in the United States, up from 105 million in 2000 (U.S. Census Bureau, 2015, Table FG; U.S. Census Bureau, 2010). The percentage of family households with children living at home stood at 52 percent in 1950 and decreased to 43 percent by 2014 (U.S. Census Bureau, 2009; U.S. Census Bureau, 2015, Table FG). This demonstrated a continuing, although relatively small, decline. Also, non-family households reached 34 percent of all households by 2014 (Table FG).

So, as the population increases, the trend has been for families to exist, with relative stability, since the 1990s. What is changing, however, is the size of family households. The average household is shrinking in size. There are an increasing number of households consisting of one person living alone: from 17 percent of all households in 1970 to 27.7 percent in 2014 (U.S. Census Bureau, 2010; U.S. Census Bureau, 2015, Table H1).

As other chapters in this book have reported, there are many grandparents raising children today because drugs and incarceration have left parents unable to care for their children. Approximately 7.4 million children under age 18—nine percent of all children in the United States—lived in a household that included a grandparent in 2014 (U.S. Census Bureau, 2015, Table C4). More than half of these children actually lived in the grandparent's home, and most had a parent living there, too (U.S. Census Bureau, 2008). This is increasingly the face of poverty. Many sacrifices are made by parents and grandparents to try to keep their families intact or to try to help young parents to continue their education.

Since its beginnings, the profession of social work has provided service to the American family. As families and societal conditions changed over time, the profession found that it needed to rethink how it worked with families. In the past two or three decades, for example, the profession switched from strongly encouraging single mothers to place their babies for adoption to helping families to remain together. Federal legislation, much of which was promoted by social workers, also resulted in renewed efforts to keep families together. The 1978 Indian Child Welfare Act, for example, discouraged adoption of Indian children into non-Indian families and gave tribes some limited funds for family support services. The 1980 Adoption Assistance and Child Welfare Act was considered benchmark legislation for its attempt to ensure permanent families for children. The 1997 Adoption and Safe Families Act furthered commitment to adoption rather than long-term foster care by shortening the time limits of foster care and speeding up the adoption process.

This sounds quite wonderful, but there is another perspective on adoption that social workers must consider. Some cultures define family differently from the nuclear family concept that is valued by people of white, European descent. African Americans, for example, have traditionally valued the extended family. The Association for Black Social Workers has articulated clear preference for **kinship care** over adoption. Kinship is a broad concept, incorporating persons related by blood or legal ties, plus persons related by strong affectional ties. Bonding with family members, permanency of care, and uninterrupted cultural identity are all potentially available through kinship care, which often evolves into long-term foster care (Holody, 1999). Social work as a profession has learned to appreciate the strengths of kinship care.

Families clearly are changing. The family of the future is likely to be diverse in culture and ethnicity, in age, and in structure (single-parent households, two-parent households, gay- or lesbian-parent households, blended families, kinship units, or non-marital parenting by either biological parents or non-related couples). Poverty tends to increase the numbers of related and non-related persons occupying the family household as persons attempt to share resources especially on a temporary basis. Nevertheless, social workers understand that how "family" is defined is often much less important than the commitment and caring of those family members.

> In light of the variety of family dynamics shown and described in this video, how do we begin to transform the image of the typical American family?
> https://www.youtube.com/watch?v=UE2Fw2V2jik

Social work research and practice over the past 10 years have provided considerable insight into the remarkable strengths of families. This has led to a new paradigm in which social workers are shifting away from focusing on problems and dysfunction to an acknowledgment of the assets and resilience of families. Out of this new way of thinking has evolved ways of working with families in which collaboration and partnership are emphasized. Caring professional relationships with children and families are paired with high expectations. Social workers today appreciate the potential richness of kin relationships, which offer sustained family connections (McGoldrick, 2009). Similarly, social workers have learned that it is critical to support not only family members but also the people outside the family (teachers, caregivers, mentors, etc.) who nurture, educate, socialize, and often transform the lives of children. Finally, helping families requires lobbying for and even creating programs that ensure the existence of basic social and economic resources to all families.

The Changing Immigrant and Refugee Population

The demographic trends that we have looked at so far include multi-cultural diversity, aging, and evolving patterns in families. Immigration, the final process affecting change, is contributing dramatically to the increasing multi-culturalism of the United States. Immigration is a worldwide phenomenon, and it is yet another way in which regions of the world are increasingly interconnected. Actually, throughout history, patterns of human migration have evolved, often reflecting events such as war, famine, natural disasters, and religious or political persecutions. The early history of the United States is replete with descriptions of waves of immigrations. People arrived on U.S. shores seeking wealth and adventure. They also came as indentured servants, slaves, or promised brides. The mass migration of the past several years, precipitated by war, terrorism, and civil unrest has been unlike any other global migration in recent history. Millions of people around the globe have become displaced; many have died in their desperate effort to escape violence, starvation, war, and total destruction of their home environments.

People, in general, enter another country through three legal means: as an immigrant, asylee, or refugee. An **immigrant** is someone who moves to another country for the purpose of settling there permanently. **Asylum** is a protected status that is granted only on a case-by-case basis to persons who can substantiate serious, possibly life-threatening political persecution. **Refugees** are people who leave their country because of persecution related to their race, nationality, religion, or political activity. Applications for refugee status in the United States are processed by the State Department before entry to the United States. Persons seeking asylum, on the other hand, may already have arrived in the United States, or they may be physically present at a border. Persons who persecuted others are not accepted either as asylees or as refugees. Once they have been admitted and lived in the country for one year, both refugees and persons accepted for asylum may apply for permanent resident status. If granted, they then have a "green card," and, after five years, they may apply for full (naturalized) citizenship.

The U.S. Congress sets the refugee admission ceiling each year, traditionally at 70,000. In 2015, 244 million people lived outside their home countries, according to the United Nations Population Fund (2016), and the refugee population was growing rapidly. In recognition of this worldwide crisis, President Obama requested the U.S. Congress to approve a ceiling of 85,000 refugees for 2016. The United States is one of at least 28 countries that have admitted refugees in recent years (U.S. Department of State et al., 2015). Canada and many European countries have admitted far more refugees than the United States, and they have provided the newcomers with quite generous welfare programs. Germany admitted over one million refugees in 2015 alone!

Hungry child in refugee camp

In addition to the legal forms of entry, there is, of course, illegal immigration. When this occurs, people are considered to be "undocumented," which means that they do not possess legal documentation of citizenship. The United States has implemented border patrols, specialized policing, and considerable legislation to stop illegal immigration. Many people do enter the United States over guarded land or water routes, which is the way illegal immigration is often portrayed in the media, yet others arrive quite legally. They simply overstay the expiration of their employment, student, or other legal visa.

Concern about the significant numbers of persons and goods illegally entering the United States became a volatile issue in the 2016 presidential election when candidate Donald Trump alleged that many Mexicans and others who illegally crossed the southern border were rapists, terrorists, murderers, and drug traffickers. This instantly connected with previously unspoken sentiments of many low income rural and underemployed urban white workers. They joined others who supported Donald Trump's campaign promise to deport undocumented people in the United States and to build a wall, one that Mexico would pay for, that would permanently end illegal immigration. As terrorist acts struck many parts of the world, many Americans also became suspicious of potential immigrants or refugees from Syria, Iraq, Pakistan, and several African countries.

A political climate that views immigration as a threat is not a good fit with the social work profession's values. Instead, from a social work perspective, it is refreshing to see the United Nations Development Programme's view of immigration as a potential positive force for the future development of nations (2016). This is a reminder that one reason Germany admitted over one million refugees in 2015 was that country's realization that its birthrate had slowed, its population was growing older, and the future would depend upon an influx of younger persons. Germany recognized that a significant portion of the world's young refugees were well-educated, professional people: pharmacists, accountants, teachers, and medical personnel. Refugees were eager to find work and secure a good education for their children. Political leaders in Germany saw the refugees as a potential asset to the future well-being of their country.

Like Germany, the United States' population growth has declined. The fertility rate has actually declined below replacement level and is expected to remain so until at least 2060. Based on U.S. Census Bureau data, the current GAO Strategic Plan predicts that by at least 2027, international migration will become the primary source of population growth in our country (U.S. GAO, 2014). Already, employers have begun to recognize the need for more bilingual employees in their shops, schools, and health care services.

Bilingual and culturally sensitive social workers are in even greater demand now than in the recent past. The profession needs to be able to recruit people who reflect the culture of the immigrant newcomers. With the influx of immigrant groups in coming years, existing ethnic communities will likely expand and new ethnic communities emerge. Throughout the United States, social workers are and will be among the first professional persons to advocate for and assist new residents—immigrants, refugees, and asylum-seekers—with resettlement. Social workers will continue to help organizations such as church groups to sponsor new immigrants. In international social service agencies such as the Red Cross, social workers will communicate across borders to keep relatives linked, especially during disasters or in the event that a person becomes a prisoner of war. Program planning will be undertaken, too, to assist communities in providing for the child care, health, and other needs of new immigrants.

Political Forces

Politics is the basis for the second major force that will generate change in the future. Political trends and political balance of power shift over time, and these shifts have enormous impact on the health, welfare, criminal justice, and educational services that are available to people. Of course, these same shifts also determine social work employment opportunities. Looking back over the past several decades, it is apparent that politically conservative forces were gaining power in many countries, including the United States. Legislation favored by liberals was passed in the early years of the Obama Administration, but soon national and global economic crises shifted voter support toward much more conservative policies that threatened newly enacted programs such as health care reform as well as stable, well-institutionalized programs such as Social Security.

When the most volatile presidential U.S. election in recent memory erupted in 2016, existing political party affiliations fell apart. Shrill, vulgar political rhetoric drew enormous crowds at rallies. People who previously voiced no political opinions and had never voted suddenly became lively debaters. "Make government small" and "hate government programs" were slogans along with "build a wall on our southern border to keep the Mexicans out!" Other candidates did run for office who proposed free tuition for students attending public universities, increases in Social Security, and a single-payer national health care system. They, however, did not have sufficient voter support, especially from young voters, to elect pro-human rights leadership.

Welfare Reform and Poverty

Against the backdrop of a shifting political climate lies the need for sound, predictable planning so that the health and well-being of U.S. citizens is ensured. Social workers and other advocates for the poor are especially concerned about the future of welfare reform. The Temporary Assistance for Needy Families (TANF) program, enacted in 1996, was referred to earlier in this book. It remains the nation's current primary financial assistance program for the poor. The TANF program was widely regarded as very successful when a dramatic decline in welfare caseloads and TANF payments to recipients followed its enactment. It is true that many persons became employed and left the TANF program, but other persons left the program because they gave up, were **sanctioned** (penalized) for failure to comply with requirements, or they had reached the five-year lifetime limitation. Following the 2008 national and global recession, TANF cases increased for a time and then began to decline (see Figure 13.1).

Now there is growing concern that a portion of the people receiving assistance has serious, persistent barriers to employment and self-sufficiency and may never have the capacity to be self-supporting. Health conditions often limit the employability of persons and, if they were never able to complete high school, their job prospects remain minimal. Numerous other circumstances affect ability to work: mental health or substance abuse problems, a history of imprisonment, recent exposure to domestic violence, and learning disabilities. TANF is an important financial assistance program that sustains millions of people, but it is affected by changes in the economic cycle of the country. When the economy is "soft," or slowing down, jobs are lost or harder to find and TANF cases increase.

Despite apparent success, the TANF program critics are increasingly concerned about issues such as work requirements that cannot be met, the program's ability to sanction

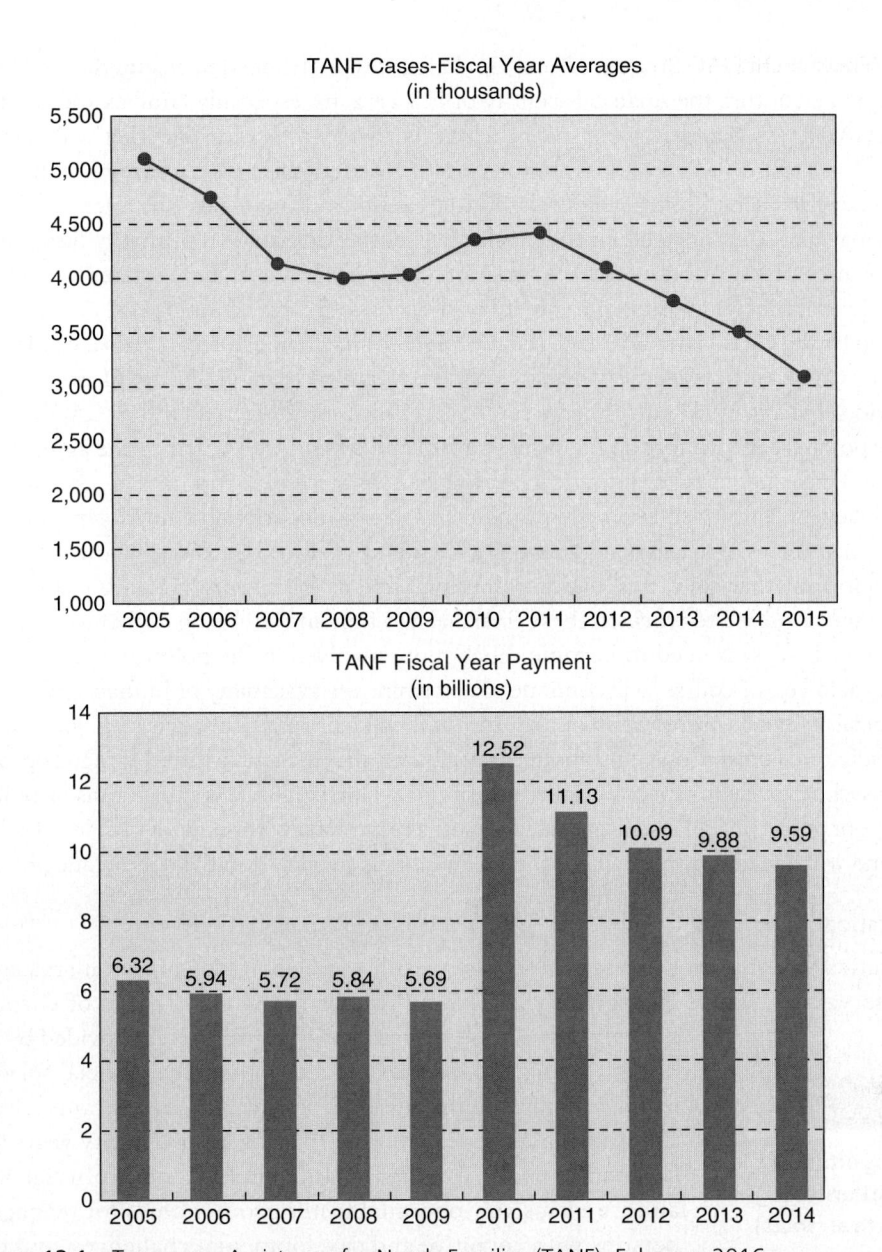

Figure 13.1 Temporary Assistance for Needy Families (TANF): February 2016
Adapted from U.S. Department of Public Health and Human Services Office of Family Assistance. (2016, Feb.). Retrieved from http://www.acf.hhs.gov/programs/ofa/programs/tanf/data-reports.

recipients who fail to comply with regulations, and the five-year lifetime limit. States, having enjoyed power and control in administering the program, are also increasingly concerned about their ability to deal with potentially large numbers of "hard-core poor" families who will not be able to transition from TANF to employment. Issues of social welfare tend to polarize Americans, but it is very likely that the political process will soon need to take on some difficult issues regarding poverty, welfare reform, and TANF.

The current GAO Strategic Plan's Goal 1 focuses on the need to ensure the well-being and, related to this, the financial security of U.S. citizens, especially families and children. The GAO's task is to help Congress achieve this goal by providing data that will help prioritize greatest needs and assess approaches for reaching this goal. Accordingly, the GAO has identified specific strategies related to benefits and financial assistance. The GAO anticipates continuing need for food assistance, currently provided primarily through the Supplemental Nutrition Assistance Program (SNAP). The capacity for states to continue to deliver financial assistance in an equitable, cost-effective manner, is seriously questioned by the GAO. The GAO has, therefore, set for itself a performance goal of identifying for Congress possible ways to improve the effectiveness and integrity of programs to provide economic and nutrition assistance and social services. In addition, GAO's Goal 1 incorporates concern for the financial security and overall well-being of the aging population. Performance goals have been set for the GAO to assist Congress by assessing the adequacy and effectiveness of programs such as Social Security and employer-sponsored retirement plans. Securing the long-term adequacy of Social Security will involve GAO in exploring other countries' national pension systems for insight (U.S. GAO, 2014). The GAO seems poised to work on these financial and human well-being challenges.

Social workers need to become much more involved in the political arena because political forces, of course, will continue to determine the availability of human services and financial assistance programs in our country and in the nations of the world. If social workers truly care about people and about social change, they will not sit idly by, merely providing psychotherapy for the emotional and physical pain suffered by the victims of politics and poor public policy; instead, they will assume responsibility for their own political behavior and will also empower their colleagues and clients to engage in the democratic process.

Privatization of Social Services

Privatization of social services is another result of the shift toward an increasingly conservative political environment. This trend can be seen in the advent of corporation-owned prison systems, child abuse services provided by for-profit organizations, and states contracting for social services instead of sustaining their own social service programs. Group homes are another example of privatization. Twenty years ago, state and county welfare departments or non-profit agencies almost exclusively operated foster group homes for teenagers, persons with cognitive and developmental challenges, and frail older adults. In most communities today, group homes are generally not run by non-profit organizations. Instead, most are owned and operated by private, often for-profit corporations. The same is true of residential treatment centers for emotionally disturbed children. Substance abuse programs—once provided almost exclusively by tax-supported hospitals or denominational facilities—have become big business and are being marketed aggressively.

The entrepreneurial practice of social work has also expanded significantly, especially for MSWs. Social workers in private practice offer their services for a fee in much the same way that physicians or attorneys in private practice do. Many health insurance

Policy Practice

Dimension of Competency: *Cognitive and Affective Reactions* Social workers recognize and understand the historical, social, cultural, economic, organizational, environmental, and global influences that affect social policy.

Critical Thinking Question: What strategies could social workers use to contribute their understanding and critical thinking to political discussion in order to more effectively impact social policy change?

policies cover the cost of counseling through social workers. In social work, **private practice** refers to the provision of services by a social worker with appropriate credentials (e.g., a license to practice clinical social work or psychotherapy) with payment provided by the client or the client's insurance. Service is terminated when the contract is completed, often with no provision for follow-up care, although social work private practitioners who are guided by the NASW Code of Ethics typically refer clients for additional services to other organizations, if needed.

On the surface, this may look like economic efficiency, but when vulnerable populations such as frail older adults or children with serious mental health disorders are involved, such apparent efficiency may actually be detrimental to clients. Neither economic nor human justice interests are served when clients' well-being suffers because of disrupted or prematurely discontinued service. What is needed instead is service that is efficient, effective, humane, and readily available—whether it is delivered through a public or private agency or through a professional person in private practice.

The trend toward privatization in human services, whether prisons or family therapy, breaks with a long tradition of tax-supported public services delivered without the cost and the potential conflicts of interest of the for-profit, entrepreneurial enterprise. This trend raises concerns about the inherent values of some organizations. Is monetary profit the primary goal, or are the best interests of the client the real goal? While moving more and more into for-profit practice, the profession of social work nevertheless maintains a somewhat skeptical stance about it. Of concern is the potential that social workers might lose their traditional commitment to advocacy, to social change, to social and economic justice, and to service to vulnerable populations.

The political drive to shift public health and social services to the private sector remains very strong. Yes, it can save money for taxpayers by reducing personnel costs and fragmenting services, but at a substantial cost of the quality of services. Although professional people may be accused of being self-serving, they will need to become proactive to ensure that the quality of professional services provided in the private sector is not further jeopardized and that public social services continue to exist.

Women's Issues

Because the profession of social work serves many poor and vulnerable women and is comprised of significant numbers of women in its workforce, the field is especially attuned to the needs of women and their struggle for equality. Social work pioneers such as Jane Addams and Florence Kelley of Chicago's Hull House were outstanding leaders in the struggle for the right to vote and for equality for women. Despite public ridicule and imprisonment in the early days of the women's movement, these women and the men who supported them succeeded in 1920 in obtaining passage of the Nineteenth Amendment to the U.S. Constitution—the right to vote for women.

The next effort of women, to pass the **Equal Rights Amendment (ERA)** prohibiting discrimination on the basis of gender, was not as successful. The effort to achieve the ERA was immense, with huge political rallies, statewide and regional conventions, parades, and much demonstration of public support. In 1972, Congress did pass the ERA, but it was defeated when the necessary number of states failed to ratify this proposed amendment to the U.S. Constitution.

Box 13.3 Wage Gap by Gender

Median Annual Earnings of Full-Time Workers by Sex: 1960–2014.

		Earnings in Real Dollars	
Year	Women's Earnings as a % of Men's	Women's Earnings in U.S. Dollars	Men's Earnings in U.S. Dollars
1960	60.7	11,003	18,175
1970	59.4	13,719	23,105
1980	60.2	13,589	22,587
1990	71.6	15,166	21,177
1995	71.4	14,762	20,667
2000	73.0	27,355	37,339
2005	77.0	31,858	41,386
2010	75.5	36,931	47,715
2011	77.0	37,118	48,202
2012	76.5	37,791	49,398
2013	78.3	39,157	50,033
2014	78.6	39,621	50,383

Source: National Committee on Pay Equity. (2015). *Wage Gap Statistically Unchanged*. Retrieved from http://www.pay-equity.org/info-time.html.

A gain for women, although a painfully slow one, has been the narrowing of the wage gap between men and women. Box 13.3 documents the progress that has taken place in narrowing the wage gap between American women and men. Between 1963 and 2014 (most current available data), the wage gap for women working full-time began to close, but only very gradually, and it is not estimated to achieve pay equality until approximately 2059 (National Committee on Pay Equity, 2015).

How does education impact earnings for men and for women? One would expect that completion of additional degrees would provide increased income. Do you think that additional higher education would narrow the gap between income for women and men? Here is the latest available data (based on median weekly income, recalculated as annual income) for persons aged 25 or older:

- No high school diploma: Males earn $26,884; women earn $21,268.
- High school graduates: Males earn $39,364: women earn $30,004.
- Some college or an associate degree: Males earn $45,344; women earn $34,372.
- College graduates: Males earn $64,948; women earn $50,180.
- Bachelor's degree and higher: Males earn $72,020; women earn $54,548.
- Advanced degrees: Males earn $84,760; women earn $61,620 (U.S. Bureau of Labor Statistics, 2016).

The assumption that additional education and credentials narrow the gender wage gap is simply not true. This is quite a shocking realization, especially for many female college students. The shocking difference in income at each level is heightened by a close examination of the growing differentials as women and men complete high school, and then among college graduates, with the most significant difference by far demonstrated between women and men who have earned graduate or professional degrees.

As pronounced as the wage differences are for upper-income women, poor women are actually most at risk of being economically exploited. As the TANF program further tightens work requirements, many recipients (who are largely women) are pushed into low-wage jobs. Not surprisingly, inequality in wages is a political issue that women's organizations in particular target for change. Several years ago, as women's professional groups such as the 70,000-member Business and Professional Women/USA (BPW/USA) joined with labor unions and other politically active women's groups, the pragmatic concept of **pay equity** emerged. The National Committee on Pay Equity explains that pay equity would occur when employers set wages that are completely gender and race neutral ("Questions and Answers on Pay Equity," 1998). With more women than ever in the workplace, pay equity is one political issue that will be on the agenda of women in the future.

Historically and currently, men far outnumber women in legislative offices in the United States, but women are becoming a political force in state legislatures, and they are now challenging men in races for the highest political offices in this country. Today, however, many exciting political races are emerging with high-powered women running effective campaigns for key offices. Social workers of prominence in the U.S. Senate include the longest-serving of current women senators, Barbara Mikulski of Maryland. Senator Debbie Stabenow, from Michigan, is another social worker. Social workers also serve in the U.S. House of Representatives and in state legislatures. The 2016 presidential election saw a high level of political activity from the millennial generation. The increased political awareness and enthusiasm of incoming social work students, too, suggests a promising future for the social work profession.

Economic Trends

The people served by social workers, especially generalist baccalaureate social workers, are often poor people. Of course, social workers work with all sectors of society and the economy affects all people, but poor people and near-poor persons are likely to be most dramatically impacted by economic conditions. Not surprisingly, political forces and economic conditions are strongly interrelated. And now more than ever, events and conditions in other parts of the world affect our lives. From an economic perspective, in the past decade there has been an expansion of industrialization around the globe, especially in third world countries, Eastern Europe, and the former Soviet Union. Some of the industrialization exploited the masses of poor people in emerging countries, luring them into urban areas and leaving their villages and farms bereft of able-bodied workers. In the United States, economic development has increasingly moved from central-city areas to suburbs and from northern states to southern states.

As early as the 1980s in the United States, **underemployment**—employment at or near minimum wage, often part-time and without health insurance or other benefits—began to replace unemployment. The numbers of employed persons receiving financial and medical assistance and food stamps increased, while the unemployment rate decreased dramatically. Food pantries provided groceries, and community feeding programs served meals to the families of employed persons whose income was inadequate to meet their daily needs. When the federal welfare reform law, Temporary Assistance for Needy Families, was passed in 1996, it was heralded as an end to poverty in the United States. TANF caseloads did continue to decrease, but unevenly and at an increasingly slower pace, for years.

Shocks to the U.S. economy began in 2007 and a global economic downturn was underway by 2008, resulting in a recession in the United States that was the most severe downturn since World War II. Between December 2007 and December 2009, 8.8 million people lost their jobs, bank failures occurred, and record-high home foreclosures and bankruptcies took place. By 2017 signs of economic stabilization were apparent. Much of Europe, too, appeared to be slowly coming out of the global recession, but the massive migration to European countries from Syria, Pakistan, and other areas put serious economic strains on the European economy. The United States admitted far fewer immigrants than the European countries; therefore, the U.S. economy did not experience the same impact as that of some European countries.

Occupy Wall Street—a 2011 grassroots movement that looked a lot like earlier labor reform action—spurred by social media, focused the nation's attention on the potent connection between politics and economics. The primary message of Occupy Wall Street was that corporate and political power had become corrupt in America. The issue of income inequality was paired with the political corruption of wealthy corporations, as money was used to purchase political power. Although it occurred years ago, Occupy Wall Street remains significant because it exposed the nation to the income inequality that had been growing for many years. Low-wage workers demanded an increase in the minimum wage and student voices called for action on the student-debt crisis. A New York City strike by fast-food workers in 2012 evolved into a national movement to raise the minimum wage to $15 per hour (Levitin, 2015).

The Occupy Wall Street movement also appears to have energized the simmering environment movement. Huge numbers of protestors poured into the anti-fracking fight and other groups took on the proposed Keystone XL Pipeline. Protection for the environment and issues of climate change brought new groups into the growing movement that, by 2014, had outgrown its identification as Occupy Wall Street. In 2015, 400,000 marchers in New York City called for decrease in emissions and increased investment in renewable energy. The president responded by requiring carbon cuts from power plants and vetoing the legislation for the Keystone Pipeline (Levitin, 2015).

Probably the most notable achievement of Occupy Wall Street was the vastly increased visibility of inequality and the wealth gap. It was no longer possible for candidates in the presidential election in 2016 to avoid this issue. The unavoidable truth of the existence of a wealthy one percent of the population alongside an expansive population of "have-nots" became a painful realization for this democracy. Although both the Democratic and the Republican parties promised to improve access to jobs, the message of billionaire Donald Trump was more persuasive both to low income workers and to corporate America. Trump favored tax cuts for the wealthiest Americans as well as the poor. The politics of the future promises a continuing lively exchange!

Unless income inequality is addressed, the persons with the lowest income will continue to be most vulnerable. Consequently, social workers will continue their support for pro-poor, poverty-reduction programs and other social programs that are so necessary for the well-being, not just of the poor, but of all people.

Technological Trends and Biomedical Advances

The fourth major trend or force influencing and shaping the future is that of technological and biomedical advancement. The evolution in these areas in the past decade has generated energy and knowledge that will continue to produce new products, software, and biomedical options in the near future. The ongoing change in these areas will influence social work practice and challenge the profession in many ways.

Information and Communication Technology

Today's social work students are likely to be among the "native tech users," those who grew up using computer technology in their everyday lives. Their college class assignments anticipate that they will have a higher level of technology competency than previous classes of students. Increasingly, they will be asked to run sophisticated statistical analyses for their research projects and work comfortably with spreadsheet and database programs. Text messaging and the Internet are also commonly used in home visits made by students in their field placements. Before they graduate, students will become proficient with library electronic databases such as **Social Work Abstracts**, which is available in many college and university libraries. Social work education increasingly incorporates emerging technologies including podcasting lectures and the use of webcams in distance education programs. Social work degrees built on computer technology are readily available online at the BSW, MSW, and PhD levels.

Social worker conducts Internet search for housing resources during interview with father and child just evicted from their home

Access to information about social work agencies, services, and social work employment opportunities is readily available on the Internet, and social workers increasingly refer clients to these same sources. While computer access is still not available to all of the people social workers see, this is less problematic as libraries and other public services provide computers for public use. The use of computerized client self-assessments that screen for anxiety, depression, chemical dependency, and other unmet basic needs has enriched social work practice. Several years ago, a survey of the clients of an employee assistance agency found that some people had initially turned to websites for help because they were too embarrassed to expose their situation in a face-to-face encounter (O'Neil, 2002). This poignant description of vulnerability, added to the fact that Internet counseling is rapidly increasing, underscores the importance of social workers adhering to strict ethical guidelines when using electronic technology.

Today's office technology—including computers, fax machines, cell phones, voicemail, digital cameras, and all other electronic equipment—is a potential source of ethical problems. The NASW Code of Ethics holds social workers responsible for protecting confidentiality for clients, which includes accepting responsibility for the careful use of current technology in handling client records. Security systems are available within computer software or agency computer network systems. Social workers need to ensure that they have access to security systems that protect confidential documents.

Increasingly, sophisticated software is being developed that can assist social workers to assess client problems, develop intervention plans based on well-researched evidence of potential outcomes, and evaluate the results of their interventions. Online groups dealing with specific issues such as breast cancer or children who are school-phobic are now being used and are likely to be further developed rapidly. They are inexpensive for clients with computer access, and they usually function within a timeframe that fits today's hectic lifestyles. In other countries, too, technology is increasingly used to improve communication. As early as 2010, Russian social workers, for example, were using the Internet to help incarcerated youths stay in touch with their families (Malamud, 2010).

Social action, advocacy, and policy research also benefit dramatically from the availability of shared databases, from programs that permit statistical analysis of massive amounts of statistical data, and from the ease of computer-assisted international communication. Online databases available through the Internet are rich sources of data for social workers. Technological advances in computers, fax transmissions, and long-distance telephone access will continue to affect the way social workers "do business" each day. These tools are fostering globalization at a rapid rate, and for creative social workers, their potential uses in organizational, community, and even international change efforts are nearly unlimited. Technology resources that help social workers keep connected also help to remedy one of the most serious problems in social work: fragmentation of services.

Biomedical Technology

Technological advances in medicine continue to bring both hope and havoc to the lives of patients and their families. Social workers in health care settings very quickly encounter the joys as well as the ethical and personal dilemmas precipitated by advances in medicine. Across social work settings all social workers can anticipate working with people whose lives are affected by advances in medical technology.

Regenerative medicine is the name given to the promising new field that utilizes the science of chemistry, medicine, engineering, computer science, biology, and other areas (including stem cell research) to restore and even replace damaged tissue and organs. Organ transplantation offered the only hope, for many years, for people with significant disease or injury to vital organs. It remains a vital part of medicine today and continues to involve social workers as key members of the medical team. Social workers help to bridge the communication gap between highly specialized medical professionals and the persons so profoundly affected—such as organ recipients and family members of the organ donor. Social workers help family members understand the medical situation, the decisions that need to be made, and the potential ramifications. Simultaneously, they help people deal with the overwhelming emotions of such health crisis situations. Many lives could be saved today if organ donors could be found, but only a small fraction of donors are found in countries like Canada or the United States, where reluctance to consent to organ donation seems especially strong.

Regenerative medicine, or tissue engineering as it is sometimes called, seems on the brink of revolutionizing the quality of life for people whose previous only hope was the long wait for a transplant to become available. Regenerative medicine does not focus on whole organs, but, instead, it is based on stem cell research. In the late 1990s, scientists learned that certain cells, known as pluripotent cells, had the ability to grow into or regenerate many different human organs. The potential of these cells could be directed. Initially, these cells were only found in embryos. In humans, this meant the use and destruction of a fertilized human egg that was at least nine weeks old and that had the potential of becoming a human child although the cells had not yet differentiated into distinct, separate body organs.

Ethical issues regarding human embryo stem cell research immediately emerged. Scientists argued that these pluripotent, **embryonic stem cells** had enormous potential for research and for future human health and well-being. Then multipotent cells, known as **tissue stem cells**, were discovered. These cells, already differentiated, do not have the unlimited potential for regeneration of embryonic stem cells. They exist in human body tissue such as skin, bone marrow, and the eye. They maintain and repair body tissue throughout life. They have some potential to assist in regeneration in certain organ diseases or injury. Bone marrow transplants are a prime example of how donor tissue stem cells may successfully restore a diseased blood system for the life of the patient. Potential complications exist: The patient's own blood marrow cells must first be killed with chemotherapy, and then there is the possibility that the patient's body will reject the donor transplant cells. Similarly, skin cell transplants are effective; however, they do not have the capacity to grow hair and do not contain sweat glands (EuroStemCell, 2012). Ethical issues, however, remained a significant concern and a deterrent to use of embryonic and, in some cases, tissue stem cells.

Until 2009, the U.S. government did not outlaw stem cell research, but it placed considerable restrictions on it. In 2010, Amendments to the National Academies' Guidelines for Human Embryonic Stem Cell Research were issued. These guidelines permitted federal funding for research but only for the use of embryonic lines that had been created from fertility clinic embryos that were not going to be saved, and only as long as they had been obtained ethically and from couples who had received no financial incentive (Stein, 2009; National Academy of Sciences, 2011). Research remained constrained in some areas of regenerative medicine.

For some time, researchers had been aware of the existence of pluripotent cells in the blood from the umbilical cord that is delivered (and generally discarded) when babies were born. Recently, it has been found that this blood could be preserved for the future use of that child. These pluripotent stem cells have the potential to be used to repair the damaged hearts or other organs of babies and, if stored for future use, these cells may be able to aid regeneration of adult organs without the hazard of rejection as is the case with organ transplants. It is even anticipated that stored pluripotent stem cells could be used to create tissues and organs in the laboratory for transplant into the person's own body. This approach could potentially decrease the need for donor transplants as well as solve the problems of transplant rejection (ScienceDaily, 2015). Reserved cord blood for future use in the same human body would seem to lessen the ethical concerns that emerged with embryonic stem cell use—use that necessitated the destruction of a fertilized human egg, potentially a human child.

Meanwhile, researchers in many other countries, notably the United Kingdom, Spain, and Japan, are aggressively moving ahead with stem cell research aimed at advancing treatment for cancer, Alzheimer's disease, and other human organ malfunctions. Some of the newest research is expanding the diagnostic potential of laboratory-grown stem cells to determine the existence of specific diseases and the potential for successful medical intervention. Additional adult sources and even non-human sources of the equivalent of stem cells are being researched.

Biomedical ethics groups remain engaged in serious and deeply emotional considerations of myriad difficult questions engendered by stem cell research, questions such as when human life begins, when it becomes sacrosanct, and whether one human life can ethically be sacrificed to save the life of another. These are tough questions!

Genetic Research

Significant advances have also been made in genetics, thanks to the **Human Genome Project**. The Human Genome Project was an international effort, initiated in 1990, to create understanding of how human genetics could cure diseases and promote health and longevity. A **genome** is an organism's DNA that contains the genetic instructions responsible for developing and directing the activities of that organism. It is made up of three billion twisted strands of chemicals that exist in the 23 pairs of chromosomes within human cells (National Human Genome Research Institute, 2006). The Human Genome Project was completed in 2003.

Its findings have led to the development of more than 2,000 genetic tests that aid diagnostic studies or reveal specific genetically linked risk factors. There are genetic tests to determine the potential for such conditions as cystic fibrosis, Huntington's disease, sickle-cell anemia, and certain kinds of cancer (including some forms of ovarian, colon, and breast cancer). Genomics can also guide decisions about prescription medication. HIV-infected patients' anti-retroviral medications are now routinely genetically guided prescriptions. Genetic testing is increasingly guiding prescriptions, too, for Plavix (used for anxiety), tamoxifen (cancer treatment), and warfarin (a blood thinner) (Malone, 2011).

Stanford Children's Hospital lists the following uses of genetic testing:

- Diagnostic testing, which usually provides a clear "yes" or "no" answer on the existence of a specific disease.

- Predictive testing, which determines the likelihood that a healthy person without a family history of, for example, a specific type of heart disease or cancer, might develop that disease.
- Pre-symptomatic testing, which determines whether a person with a family history actually has the gene associated with a specific disease.
- Prenatal diagnosis, which determines whether a genetic disease exists in a developing fetus.
- Newborn screening, which detects genetic diseases when early treatment might be needed (often done by the state health department) (Stanford Children's Hospital).

As genetic information becomes increasingly available, it raises difficult spiritual, emotional, and ethical questions, such as whether to terminate a pregnancy or whether to talk with other family members about their possible medical risks. Because the meaning of genetic risk carries such significance and potentially involves multiple generations of family members, social workers often become involved. Social workers also help people understand what genetic testing means, the kinds of tests that are available and the kind of information that can come from the tests, and how it can be used. They help family members resolve the issues that testing results bring: the multi-generational consequences of information suggesting susceptibility to disease. The social worker is not usually the actual genetics counselor—that person is a medical specialist—but social workers provide the supportive relationship, assist with panic or psychological crises that result, and assist families after they receive the information.

The genetic testing that is commercially available is costly but the National Institute of Health predicts that it will decline. Eventually, it is expected to reach the point where, for less than $1,000, it will be possible to obtain the ultimate genetic test—one that provides genetic data for the sequencing of a person's entire genome. With such rich sources of genetic data, a new era of "personalized medicine" is predicted in which genetic data will result in more accurate diagnoses and guide planning for health maintenance as well as for treatment options when injury or disease occurs (National Institute of Health, n.d.).

Human Reproductive Technology

The area of human reproduction continues to evolve through changes in reproductive technology, and future advances may result in quite complex moral and ethical issues. Currently, multiple for-profit organizations exist (many are advertised on Internet websites) that offer infertile persons alternatives for parenthood. Among the alternatives are surrogate parenting, human egg donation (or sale), and embryo transfer. In **surrogate parenting**, a woman agrees to be impregnated and to release the baby that she delivers to the person(s) who contracted with her for this purpose. In human **egg donor programs**, the egg, also called ovum, of a donor is surgically implanted in another woman who is unable to produce her own ovum; she may then be able to conceive a baby through sexual intercourse. **Embryo transfer** involves surgical implantation in a woman of another woman's egg that has been fertilized by her husband's, partner's, or a donor's sperm. Implantation of a genetically tested embryo can enable the parents to select the gender, hair color, eye color, and other traits.

> **Box 13.4 Up-for-Debate**
>
> *Proposal: In the future, humans should be cloned the way animals are now.*
>
> | Yes | No |
> |---|---|
> | Children would not be born with inheritable diseases or defects. | Cloning may not totally prevent defects and may, in fact, result in tragic malformations. |
> | Regulating human reproduction has so many benefits to humankind that it should be mandatory. | Moral and spiritual values that view God as the creator should prevail over procedures that science makes possible. |
> | Cloning should be allowed in order to obtain the most perfect human specimen. | Who is to determine the "perfect" human? Is the perfect human a mighty warrior or a peacemaker, an intellectual giant, or a nurturer? |
> | The health, longevity, and economic benefits of cloning are obvious. | Human variety and diversity are such valuable traits that they should be cherished, not obliterated. |

Most infertility is successfully treated with medication or surgery; therefore, people seeking more involved procedures, such as in vitro fertilization using sperm banks or human egg donors, are likely to have to pay large fees (generally not covered by insurance). Fees in excess of $5,000 for an egg (oocyte) donor are not uncommon. Often people are not aware that egg donation is painful and risky for a woman. It involves repeated injections of hormones over several weeks, followed by surgery and the possibility of severe pelvic pain, bleeding, cysts, and some forms of cancer. Low-income women are at greatest risk of exploitation, especially in the United States, where this procedure is not legally regulated.

Cloning is an asexual, as compared with a sexual, form of reproduction. Animals have been cloned, so why not humans? That, at least, is a question asked by futurists. In human cloning, an embryo grows from either a male or a female stem cell and then is implanted in a woman so that it can be brought to term and delivered as a newborn infant. This "clonal embryo" does not carry the genetic makeup of two persons; it consists of the genes of only the person who donated the stem cell. Obviously, these genes could also be scientifically engineered or altered so that the child will not carry a predisposition to known diseases. There could potentially also be alterations to determine the sex of the child, hair color, intelligence, body type, and numerous other traits. Or the child might be a true clone, identical to the "parent." Therapeutic cloning occurs when stem cell tissue is used to replace organs or held indefinitely to permit future creation of future organs, should there be a need. Box 13.4 suggests some of the arguments that are inevitable as cloning possibilities draw near. What a strange and fascinating future awaits us!

Environmental Sustainability

Environmental sustainability is now recognized as a global concern. Americans better understand today that damage to the environment has the potential to threaten not only America's future but also the health and well-being of the entire world. Pollutants of various kinds are increasingly overwhelming the earth, even today. Around the world, carbon is being produced in twice the amount that oceans and forests can absorb. Global climate change is likely to threaten both coasts of the United States as well as coastlines in many other countries with major flooding. Small, low-lying islands with significant human populations could be lost entirely.

The earth's inherent self-regulating mechanisms, however, do not have to be totally overwhelmed by pollutants and chemicals of modern living. Efforts are increasing worldwide to save the planet. The European Union has assumed a remarkable leadership role with its precautionary principle that holds all nation-members of the EU to regulations that will not permit economic activity, no matter how lucrative, to compromise the integrity of the biosphere that must support human dwellings and human sustenance (Rifkin, 2004). Nations that wish to become EU members, too, must clean up their environments and initiate earth-friendly ecological practices.

The Paris Agreement on Climate Change, signed in 2016 by 195 countries, was an amazing feat. The agreement pledged these nations to curb greenhouse gas emissions sufficiently to limit the increase of global warming to two degrees Fahrenheit. Considerable scientific research prior to the agreement supported the belief that not only could this be accomplished but that it would stave off massive damage that would result from a two-degree increase in global warming. Since burning of oil is probably the major contributor to greenhouse emissions, industries that depend on oil (trucking, automobiles, airlines, among others) will be most impacted. There will be challenges to meeting this goal. In some cases, the technology to make it possible has not yet been developed (Bradsher, 2016). While President Obama signed the agreement on behalf of the United States, President Trump has suggested that he may remove the United States as a signator.

Both the United Nations, through its new Sustainable Development Goals for 2030, and the GAO Strategic Plan of the United States forcibly address environmental needs for the future of humankind. The United Nations' Sustainable Development Goals seek to achieve an end to poverty and hunger by 2030 but to do so in a manner that protects the environment. Every one of the 17 goals incorporates dimensions related to environmental threats or protection. Goal 1, for example, relates to ending poverty, but one of its targets seeks to protect the poor and especially vulnerable people from extreme climate-related events and environmental disasters. Some of the goals directly address environmental issues. For example, Goal 2 promotes sustainable agriculture; Goal 6 ensures clean water and sanitation; Goal 7 ensures access to sustainable energy; Goal 11 promises safe and sustainable housing (including upgrading slums); Goal 14 conserves oceans, seas, and marine life; and Goal 15 protects forests and combats land degradation. The final goal, Goal 17, calls for revitalizing global partnerships that will ensure a sustainable future (United Nations Sustainable Development Knowledge Platform, 2015).

The GAO Strategic Plan of the United States recognizes that some of the nation's natural resources are increasingly stressed. Energy is of special concern since the citizens of the United States, which comprise 4.5 percent of the world population, are currently consuming approximately 19 percent of the world's energy resources. The nation has invested in production of energy, but the transmission pipelines are aging and need updating to remain secure. A competing demand is the preservation of natural resources and wildlife habitat. Already over 53 percent of rivers and streams are polluted. The GAO Strategic Plan contains Objective 1.8 Responsible Stewardship of Natural Resources and the Environment, which seeks to assist the U.S. Congress to ensure environmentally sound energy, manage land and water resources, clean up hazardous waste, and ensure a safe food supply while minimizing agricultural environmental damage (U.S. Government Accountability Office, 2014).

The social work profession is awakening to the enormous impact of current and past environmental degradation on humanity. Increasingly, there are calls for a fresh generation of leaders who will revitalize the social work literature and enrich social work practice with a holistic, planetary view of practice (Besthorn & Canda, 2002; Dominelli, 2012; Holland, 2005; Mary, 2008). A future for the profession is envisioned where the ecological, social, and spiritual dimensions of practice will be merged and strengthened. Increased involvement with the environment, possibly including planned experiences with natural and wilderness areas, will be built into social work education and practice.

Today social work environmental advocates believe that as an interdependent planet, we all must learn to value and share responsibility for our human habitat. In acknowledging the interdependence of all living things, people are viewed as connected to each other and to the life of the planet. When people or the environment is endangered, nurturing and care are needed. Social workers can help others develop capacity to care for other people and other living things. As social workers help their clients and communities to assume greater responsibility in nurturing the environment so, too, can social workers experience a new emergence as we become actors in the work of creating an environment that truly respects and nurtures all people and all living beings.

> **?** Assess your understanding of the major forces that are driving transformation of the world by taking this brief quiz.

THE FUTURE OF THE SOCIAL WORK PROFESSION

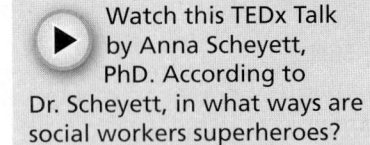

> ▶ Watch this TEDx Talk by Anna Scheyett, PhD. According to Dr. Scheyett, in what ways are social workers superheroes?
> https://www.youtube.com/watch?v=A27QjpQ_Ieo

Throughout this chapter, we have explored several powerful forces—demographic, political, and economic trends, technological and biomedical advances, and issues of environmental sustainability—that will affect life on the planet in the next 5, 10, 20 years, or longer. We now narrow our focus and briefly look at the future for the social work profession in terms of employment opportunities and projections. We conclude this section with a glimpse of the grand challenges and contributions of the social work profession.

The Social Work Workforce: Employment Projections, Social Worker Shortages

The organization that undoubtedly has the greatest amount of data on which to build future employment projections for social work or any other profession or occupation is the U.S. Department of Labor's Bureau of Labor Statistics (BLS). If BLS Statistics is one criterion of predictability, then the profession of social work is likely to remain healthy and in existence for a long time. In its most recent report, the BLS reported its expectation that employment for social workers would grow *faster* than that of the average for all U.S. occupations through the year 2024 (U.S. Bureau of Labor Statistics, 2016). The BLS publication, the *Occupational Outlook Handbook*, is a good source of information on trends in employment.

According to this publication, changing demographics in the United States and technological advances will create new and expanding opportunities for social work employment. The demand will be driven, to a considerable degree, by growing needs for social workers in the health care field. Some of this will be a response to a need to serve the expanding population of older adults, creating employment opportunities in home health care, assisted living, and within nursing homes and hospice programs. The BLS projects demand for health care social workers to increase at the very high level of 19 percent, with mental health and substance abuse social workers to also increase by 19 percent. The combined area of child/family/school social work is expected to increase by 6 percent, which may seem low, but 6 percent is the approximate increase anticipated across all occupations (U.S. Bureau of Labor Statistics, 2016).

A recent study examined the future social work workforce and predicted nationwide shortages of social workers. This study examined data related to the future supply of potential social workers with data depicting the future demand. The states of Florida, California, Texas, Georgia, and Arizona were clearly projected to have the most severe social work shortages across the country. The United States as a whole was found to have a total projected shortfall of 195,850 social workers. In the Midwest, the states of Kansas, Wisconsin, and Indiana are projected to have the most serious shortage by 2030. New Hampshire, New Jersey, and Delaware were the northeastern states projected to have the most significant shortages. In the southern region, Florida, Georgia, Texas, and Alabama had seriously high shortfall data, but a number of additional southern states were nearly in the same range. States in the West with high shortfall data included Arizona, Utah, California, Idaho, and Nevada (Lin, Lin, & Zhang, 2016).

The study described above provides some perspectives on the social work populations most in need of services by 2030. Like the GAO, this study discussed the growing need of older adults for services. Lin, Lin, and Zhang, the researchers for the study described above, noted that in the southern and western states, the older adult population has grown faster than in other regions of the United States. The older adult population's need for social work services reflects the more frequent development of chronic health problems than in younger age cohorts. The older population is increasingly diverse, with the minority population increasing. The increasing minority population is even greater among children (aged 17 and younger). By 2030, the minority elderly population is expected to rise to 25 percent, but the child minority population is expected to rise to 60 percent. Children, as we know, are vulnerable to neglect, abuse, and poverty, but they are also projected to have very high levels of need for mental health services. Child welfare social work positions will continue to be in demand well into the foreseeable future and, since social workers provide the majority of mental health services in the United States, this will clearly continue to be an area of demand (Lin, Lin, & Zhang, 2016).

The Grand Challenges and Contributions of Social Work

The notion of "grand challenges" seemed to be an inspiring and perhaps even a fun way to end this text. Within a number of professions, **grand challenges** refer to thoughtful, critical, focused, and structured efforts to identify potentially efficient and effective strategies for solving some of society's most compelling needs.

Although the concept of grand challenges originated within the field of mathematics as early as 1900, it gained impetus across many professions in the recent past. The American Academy of Social Work and Social Welfare (AASWSW), an organization primarily comprised of educators but with some practitioners as well, launched a grand challenges project for social work in 2013. In social work, right from the start, the intent was to utilize well-researched interventions that held promise for delivering results within 10 years (American Academy, 2015).

The AASWSW executive committee that initiated the Grand Challenges Project was comprised of respected, well-published, leading academics, researchers, and policy experts in social work. Through their partnership with social work national professional organizations, universities, and other social work interest groups, the committee issued a call for ideas that would spark development of the project. From the 80 concept papers received, the committee ultimately narrowed the focus to 12. Thus began what we know today as the 12 Grand Challenges. They represent the profession well as they incorporate strong research with clear connection to intervention strategies that project a path to delivery of solutions. This effort seeks to help create a more just society through focusing on challenges relating to individuals, families, and the larger society. The 12 Grand Challenges include the following:

- Ensuring healthy development of youths
- Closing the health gap
- Advancing healthy and productive lives
- Eradicating social isolation
- Ending homelessness
- Creating responses to the changing environment
- Harnessing technology for the social good
- Promoting smart incarceration
- Reducing extreme economic inequality
- Building financial capability
- Achieving equal opportunities and justice (American Academy, 2015)

Extensive papers have been prepared on the 12 Grand Challenges. The Grand Challenges Committee invites you to peruse the information that is available about the committee as well as the challenges at the AASWSW website. You are also encouraged to click the video link below.

At the AASWSW location, you will also find the remarkable paper entitled *The Grand Accomplishments in Social Work*. The 23 accomplishments described in this paper represent social work's important contributions to social justice and human rights over time. Because they are organized chronologically, they provide a developmental and growing sense of pride in social work for the often unrecognized achievements and contributions made by this profession. A sampling of the **grand accomplishments** include the protection of dependent children and their removal from orphanages (efforts began just before 1900); the development of foster care and adoption (early 1900s through today); child labor reform (early 1900s); development of social insurance: Medicare, Medicaid, unemployment insurance (1930s to today); human

> ▶ After watching this video by the American Academy of Social Work and Social Welfare, explain the purpose of the 12 Grand Challenges in the coming decades.
> https://www.youtube.com/watch?v=oKbj3y-LUbw

rights including women's rights and civil rights (1930s to today); child protection services leading to a decline in child abuse (1970s to today); and services for older adults including long-term care, end-of-life care, and healthy aging initiatives (1960s to the present). *The Grand Accomplishments* paper describes many additional achievements that were spearheaded by social work leaders or where social workers collaborated with others to accomplish change that advanced the quality of life for individuals, families, and communities (American Academy, 2013).

We know that American social work practice benefitted from the work of practitioners in other countries, but U.S. social workers have impacted practice in other countries, too. Persons from other countries, more recently from African and Asian countries, have completed their professional education in the United States before returning to apply that knowledge and skill in their home nations. The international work of the renowned U.S. social worker Katherine Kendall led to the United Nations resolution in 1950 affirming that, as a profession, social work required professional training. Kendall went on to develop the field of international social work practice that has contributed to the development of social work practice and professional education globally (American Academy, 2015). Yes, social work faces challenges, but as a profession, it has amazing, even *grand* accomplishments from which to construct the future.

Evaluation

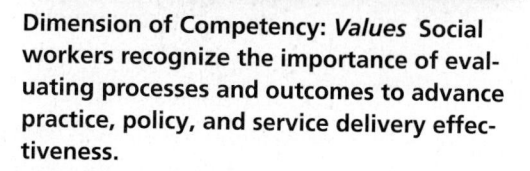

Dimension of Competency: *Values* Social workers recognize the importance of evaluating processes and outcomes to advance practice, policy, and service delivery effectiveness.

Critical Thinking Question: How does evaluating the "grand accomplishments" of the profession help social workers to acknowledge and sustain the values of the social work profession?

Assess your understanding of the future of the social work profession relative to employment projections and the grand challenges by taking this brief quiz.

SUMMARY

- Globalization and its affects on social workers and social work practice are explained. Chapter 13's case study gives readers the opportunity to share portions of the international social work field placement of a BSW student from the United States in the fascinating country of South Africa. The case study draws the reader into the thinking and feelings of the social work student as she interacts with a child who is lonely for his mother, angry, and in much trouble at school. Despite great differences in child welfare policy between the United States and South Africa, the student's successful intervention may forever change the life of the child, while this field placement will leave an indelible impact on the student. The international field placement of the case study leads readily to a consideration of globalization, its relevance to social work, and strategic planning for the future by the United Nations and by the United States.
- The major social forces that are transforming the world are identified. Five major forces transforming the world are explored: demographic trends, political forces, economic trends, technological and biomedical advances, and environmental sustainability.
- The future of the social work profession in terms of employment opportunities and future challenges is described. The employment projections we provided

were tailored to students' legitimate interest in learning about jobs that will be available to them when they graduate. The chapter and the text conclude with a review of the 12 Grand Challenges facing social work, and we, the text authors, send you forward with the gift of the Grand Contributions in Social Work.

Recall what you learned from this chapter by completing the Chapter Review.

Glossary

ableism A practice in which people without disabilities exclude and/or oppress those who do.

abuse The infliction of physical or emotional injury through beatings, corporal punishment, persistent ridicule and degradation, or sexual maltreatment.

accommodation Making environmental modifications in architecture, equipment, commercial structures, employment facilities, and so forth, to make them accessible to persons with disabilities.

ACSW This acronym designates membership in the Academy of Certified Social Workers. Available to members of NASW who have an MSW degree, have 2 years of additional supervised social work practice, and have passed the ACSW examination.

active treatment Training, therapy, and services provided to people with disabilities to address any social, intellectual, or behavioral deficits and achieve the highest possible level of functioning.

activities of daily living (ADLs) Those daily activities such as dressing, eating, and bathing that a person must be able to perform to maintain independence.

activity center A place in which persons with disabilities can gather in groups to perform various activities for the purpose of socialization, recreation, and the like.

acute care Health care facilities such as hospitals, outpatient clinics, and emergency rooms that provide immediate, short-term care.

acute traumatic stress Overwhelming physical and psychological distress that occurs during and immediately following life-threatening or overwhelming personal, family, or community events.

adjudication Decisions made by the juvenile court judge when a charge against a youth is reviewed. The court may decide to drop all charges, but if instead the youth is found guilty, sentencing follows.

adversarial court A court setting in which there is opportunity for cross-examination by a prosecutor and a defense attorney. Although this procedure has been adopted in juvenile courts since the 1967 *Gault* decision, a much less formal court was envisioned when children's courts were first established.

advocacy Representing and defending the rights of individuals, groups, or communities through direct intervention.

affirmative action Procedures used to ensure opportunities such as employment, advancement, or admission to professional programs to people who have been discriminated against, such as women and members of minority groups.

Affordable Health Care for America Act (ACA) Health, mental health, and substance abuse health insurance reform legislation passed in 2010.

ageism The practice of stereotyping people according to their age; frequently refers to prejudice against older adults.

Aid to Families with Dependent Children (AFDC) A government program authorized under the Social Security Act to provide income for dependent children of poor families and sometimes their parents. A means test and other eligibility criteria were required. Programs were administered by each state, and benefits varied by state. AFDC was eliminated in 1996.

alcoholism A substance use disorder characterized by diminished control of drinking, inability to sustain social responsibilities, use despite hazards to personal or others' wellbeing, and increasing use despite resulting physical symptoms. Alcohol is recognized as the most abused drug.

almshouse An institution or shelter, common before the twentieth century, to house and feed certain categories of poor people, usually the aged, blind, or disabled.

ALS (Amyotrophic lateral sclerosis) A progressive, degenerative disease that damages the brain and spinal cord.

alternative schools Schools that operate outside the regular public school system.

Alzheimer's disease Affecting more than five million older Americans today, this disease causes irreversible damage to one's brain, including memory loss, behavioral and psychological disorders, and inability to carry on self-care functions. Symptoms of Alzheimer's disease are progressive; eventually, the afflicted person loses use of both body and mind.

anxiety disorder The term used by the *DSM–V* to describe a large number of anxiety-related states; these tend to be chronic or recurring experiences arising from unknown or unrecognized perceptions of danger or conflict.

anxiolytics Drugs that reduce anxiety.

assisted living Programs that provide accommodation for people who need help with activities of daily living such as dressing and bathing but do not need the high level of nursing care provided in a nursing home. Assisted living environments tend to provide comfortable, apartment-like units with private bedrooms and small kitchens. Many also provide restaurant-like dining rooms for those who no longer wish to prepare their own meals. Unfortunately, usually only older persons with ample means can afford these accommodations.

asylum The protected legal status that is granted by the government on a case-by-case basis to persons who can substantiate serious, possibly life-threatening, political persecution. This status permits people to remain in the country for a specified period of time, but it may not afford them rights to citizenship.

basic professional level The BSW social worker who has been prepared as a generalist and is able to intervene in practice with individuals, families, groups, organizations, and communities.

behavioral health care A broad area of health care services often involving a combination of medication, various forms of psychotherapy or counseling, and patient education.

bilingual education Education provided in two languages, usually including the language spoken by the majority culture and one spoken by a minority group.

binge drinking Five or more drinks in 1 day within a 30-day period.

bipolar disorder A mental disorder characterized by episodes of excessive mood highs and lows.

BSW A social worker who has completed a baccalaureate degree from a CSWE-accredited school.

bullying Unwanted aggressive behavior directed toward another that involves a power imbalance and a high likelihood of repetition. Bullying can take many forms, including physical, verbal, social, and via use of digital technologies such as the Internet, texting, or email.

cannabis A plant which produces the chemical, tetrahydrocannabinol, that provides mild euphoria when ingested or smoked; marijuana is its most common form.

capital punishment A sentence of execution; the death penalty.

career ladder The imaginary upward-directed steps that must be taken, as on a ladder, to advance in a profession or occupation. In some fields, career advancement is based on performance, while in others additional academic credentials must be completed.

case advocacy Advocacy strategies used to attain social and economic justice on an individual basis.

case manager In social work, the combination of counselor/enabler, advocate, and broker roles plus responsibility for planning, locating, securing, and monitoring services for people who are unable to do this for themselves because of ill health or other frailties. Should not be confused with the term *case management* as used by insurance companies primarily to restrict access to care.

cause advocacy Advocacy strategies used to attain social and economic justice for whole groups of people.

certification A form of state legal regulation that protects use of the title "social worker"; however, it does not prohibit people without the title from practicing social work.

charity The donation of goods and services to those in need.

charter schools Independent, tuition-free public schools that can be more innovative than regular public schools and have more flexibility in staffing. They are accountable to the public to advance student achievement.

child trafficking The recruitment, transpiration, harboring and/or receipt of a child in order to exploit that child for his or her labor, sexual availability, etc.

children at risk Children born to or residing with families suffering significant problems—such as poverty, disability or absence of a parent, and substance abuse—that tend to increase the probability of abuse or neglect.

clinical social worker An MSW social worker qualified and state licensed to engage in psychotherapy; formerly referred to as a *psychiatric social worker*.

cloning The procedure whereby the nucleus of a single cell is used to reproduce an entirely new organism with identically the same genetic makeup as the organism that provided the original parent cell.

co-insurance The percentage of an overall medical bill that a person must pay in addition to what his or her health insurance pays.

community placement Arranging supervised care for children and adults with special needs in small-group and family care homes rather than in large custodial institutions.

community-based corrections Programs, such as probation and parole, that provide an alternative to incarceration.

community-service sentence An alternative to imprisonment that requires work without pay in a human service organization for a specified period of time.

competency The ability to integrate and apply social work knowledge, values, and skills in a purposeful, intentional, and professional manner to promote human and community well-being.

compulsory health insurance program A government's program that ensures access to health care by requiring all citizens to purchase health insurance.

conservative A political perspective that is influenced by a desire to maintain the status quo and avoid change. The conservative view of human nature is pessimistic: People will not work without economic insecurity and inequality to motivate them. Thus, conservatives tend to oppose government intervention in the economic market to aid poor people and, instead, may support tax breaks for the rich as incentives for investment.

continuum of care Caregiving services that are coordinated to provide for a variety of client needs with minimal duplication or gaps in service.

conversion therapy Psychotherapy designed to change a person who has homosexual orientation to heterosexual orientation. It may involve painful electric shocks. Research indicates conversion therapy is ineffective in its goals.

cost containment Policies and procedures that seek to control rising costs. Health care organizations have been under considerable pressure from government and citizen groups to cut or at least stabilize health care costs.

cross-addiction Addiction to two or more drugs. The combination of two or more drugs often results in more serious consequences than either drug would if used alone.

cultural competency The skill of communicating and working competently and effectively with people of contrasting cultures.

cultural conservatism A political perspective in which single parenthood, sex outside of marriage, homosexuality, gay marriage, etc., are disapproved. Cultural conservatives favor government intervention restricting life choices such as these.

cultural pluralism A model for understanding ethnic and racial diversity in which difference is expected and respected.

culture The customs, habits, values, beliefs, skills, technology, arts, science, and religious and political behavior of a group of people in a specific time period.

deinstitutionalization A policy promoting the use of alternatives to institutional care. The process of releasing people who are dependent for their physical and mental care from residential-custodial facilities, presumably with the understanding that they no longer need such care or can receive it through community-based services.

delusions Inaccurate but strongly held beliefs about reality, often with elements of persecution; delusional thinking suggests the presence of a form of serious mental illness.

dementia A mental condition involving loss of cognitive or intellectual capacity, occurring most often in older adults. It may be mild, moderate, or severe.

demographics The study of population trends and statistics.

depressive disorder Disorders of persistent low mood (depression) with symptoms of low energy, insomnia, recurrent thoughts of suicide; range from mild to severe with high risk of self-harm.

detoxification The medical removal of harmful substances from the body.

developmental disability A condition that occurs as a result of disease, genetic disorder, or impaired growth pattern that is evidenced before adulthood. Such conditions include intellectual or cognitive disabilities, cerebral palsy, autism, orthopedic problems, hearing problems, epilepsy, traumatic brain injury, learning disabilities, fetal alcohol syndrome, cocaine exposed babies, and co-occurrence of disabilities.

Diplomate in Clinical Social Work (DCSW) An advanced practice credential awarded by the NASW to social workers who have completed the MSW degree as well as 4,500 hours of clinical practice plus an additional three or more years of post-MSW or post-doctorate clinical practice, and 30 hours of continuing education specific to clinical practice in the past 2 years.

discrimination In the context of social work practice, this term refers to the negative prejudgment of a person due to an identifiable characteristic such as race, gender, or disability.

disposition Within the justice system, the carrying out of the court order; sentencing.

domiciliaries Homes, such as those offered by the Veterans Administration, that provide ongoing 24-hour care for special populations.

DSM-V The fifth edition of the *Diagnostic and Statistical Manual of Mental Disorders* (American Psychiatric Association), a book providing comprehensive descriptions and classifications of various mental disorders, often used as a reference tool for diagnostic purposes.

dual diagnosis The co-existence of mental illness and chemical dependence; this situation requires careful assessment and well-coordinated treatment between the substance abuse and mental health programs.

earned income tax credit (EITC) A government program in which low-income workers can receive refunds through their annual tax returns even without paying any taxes. The EITC is an income supplement that can encourage low-wage workers to remain in the workforce.

ecosystems perspective A perspective that maintains simultaneous focus on person and environment and is attentive to their interactions and adaptations.

egg donor programs Medical programs that provide for the ovum (a human egg) of a donor to be surgically implanted in another woman who is unable to produce her own ovum; the recipient may then be able to conceive a baby through sexual intercourse.

embryo transfer The surgical implantation in a woman of another woman's egg that has already been fertilized by her husband's, her partner's, or a donor's sperm.

embryonic stem cells The undifferentiated cells from a fertilized human egg that are considered to have potential for research related to advancing treatment for certain kinds of cancer, Alzheimer's disease, and other human organ malfunctions. Because these cells have the potential to differentiate and become a human embryo, there is considerable controversy over their use for research purposes.

emotional or behavioral disturbance A condition characterized by inappropriate or harmful behavior. In children, this diagnosis may lead to eligibility for special education services in a school setting. Eligible children demonstrate disturbed behavior in at least two of three environments: the school, the home, and/or the community.

empowerment A process through which people gain the strength to significantly alter the institutions that affect their lives.

English as a Second Language A special method of instruction in public schools used to teach children who do not speak English. The goal is to bring children up to grade level in English and into regular classrooms as soon as possible.

entitlement The legal obligation of the government to provide services, goods, cash, or other benefits to persons who meet certain eligibility criteria established by law, for example, as under the Social Security Act.

entitlement program A program providing services, goods, or money due to an individual by virtue of a specific status.

Equal Rights Amendment (ERA) An amendment to the U.S. Constitution prohibiting discrimination on the basis of gender and providing equal protection of all constitutional rights to women. Although Congress passed it in 1972, the amendment failed to achieve the ratification of a sufficient number of states and, hence, did not become law.

ethnic group A population group that shares certain cultural characteristics that distinguish it from others, characteristics such as customs, values, language, and a common history.

ethnic sensitive approaches Strategies in social work practice that link knowledge of culture and ethnicity with understandings of social class differences; these approaches to practice reflect respect for and valuing of differences in people and communities.

ethnoconscious approach A theoretical construct that links ethnic sensitive approaches with empowerment tactics that build upon appreciation for the strengths already existing in ethnically diverse communities.

Fair Sentencing Act of 2010 Legislation that reduced racially discriminatory sentencing for crack vs. powder cocaine possession.

faith-based organization An organization that provides social services to people in need in accord with its religious mission or as part of its affiliation with a religious group.

family care home A foster care home where unrelated persons are cared for in a family-like setting.

felony A serious criminal offense, generally punishable by a prison sentence. Murder, rape, and armed burglary are examples of felonies.

feminization of poverty The increasing incidence of poverty among women, due to lower average wages than men and limited access to high-paying positions.

fetal alcohol syndrome (FAS) A condition in which the fetus is damaged by the mother's excessive drinking.

First Nations People Also known as Native Americans, these were the first people to inhabit America.

food insecurity A condition in which people do not have sufficient access to the quantity and quality of food needed to achieve a reasonably healthy life; the term used by the U.S. Department of Agriculture to denote insufficient access to enough food to sustain an active, healthy life.

food stamps The principal food assistance program in the United States, commencing in 1964. The "stamps" are currently issued as part of the Supplemental Nutrition Assistance Program (SNAP). Since 1996, with the passage of the Personal Responsibility and Work Opportunity Act, states may place serious restrictions on the program; many states require a work history to receive them. Today debit cards are the primary means of transaction, and a payment or deductible is usually required.

forensic social work An area of specialization in social work that is characterized by expertise in legal matters related to child welfare, juvenile offenses, divorce and child custody issues, and various areas of dispute negotiation.

frail elderly Aged men and women who suffer from, or are vulnerable to, physical or emotional impairments and require services to ensure their well-being.

futurists Persons who engage in serious, in-depth study of global trends to predict the nature of life in the future; they generally do not predict specific future events but instead provide alternate scenarios.

gay A person whose sexual orientation is homosexual. This term usually refers to homosexual men.

generalist approach An approach to social work practice requiring the ability of the practitioner to intervene on multiple levels of intervention according to assessed need: individual, family, group, organization and/or community. The generalist approach is strongly rooted in systems theory and its descendent, the ecosystems perspective.

genetic counseling A service to help people translate scientific genetic findings into practical information. A genetic counselor works with individuals and/or families who may be at risk for an inherited disease or abnormal pregnancy, discussing the chances of having children who will be affected.

genome An organism's DNA, which contains the genetic instructions needed to develop and direct the activities of that organism; the DNA of humans exists within the 23 pairs of chromosomes within human cells.

globalization The interconnectedness of all regions and people of the world as a result of technological advances in communication and transportation. Often thought of in terms of international commerce, this term also encompasses issues such as poverty and exploitation, religious movements, and terrorism.

grand accomplishments An effort undertaken by some professions including social work to identify the profession's contributions to society over time.

grand challenges A focused effort by many professions including social work to identify strategies for solving some of society's most compelling needs.

group home A home-like facility providing room, board, and staff helping meet the needs of more than a single individual but usually 8 or fewer who require a supportive living environment.

habilitation Services designed to help a person achieve and maintain his or her maximum level of functioning.

hallucinations False perceptions of reality that result from mental illness, abuse of chemical substances, or damage to the brain. People who hallucinate sometimes respond to voices that they believe they hear; their behavior may be very inappropriate.

hallucinogens A category of drugs that produce dreamlike experiences and hallucinations involving visual and/or auditory effects. The effects of such drugs are not always predictable; they sometimes include gross distortions of reality, frightening visualizations, and mental confusion. Heavy use can intensify underlying mental disorders.

harm reduction model A variety of alternative substance abuse treatment programs that seek to limit the hazards (such as overdose deaths, spread of disease, car accidents) that can occur while people are using chemical substances. It is based on the philosophy that people can discontinue substance use more safely, effectively, and humanely if this process is done slowly.

heavy drinking Five or more drinks on five or more days within 30 days.

hemodialysis A medical procedure in which the blood of a person with renal (kidney) disease is cleansed of toxins and impurities.

heterosexism The belief that people who are heterosexual are better in some way than people who are homosexual.

home health care The provision of health care services, including social services, to people in their own homes.

homophobia The fear, dread, or hatred of people who are homosexual those who are attracted to members of their own gender.

homosexual A person whose sexual orientation is toward members of that person's own gender.

hospice A program that cares for terminally ill people in an environment that is less restrictive than a hospital.

Human Genome Project A research effort coordinated by the U.S. Department of Energy and the National Institute of Health to determine the makeup of human DNA. The data produced will continue to have implications for health care and disease prevention, potentially through genetic engineering.

human service aide A preprofessional (or paraprofessional) who may have a bachelor's degree in an area related to social work, or may have specialized knowledge or skill but no degree, and assists persons in accessing resources or with complicated paperwork.

humanitarianism The belief or philosophy that people are obliged to assist in achieving the welfare of humankind; the practice of assisting other people in meeting pressing needs.

hypnotic medication Various types of prescribed medication that produce a sleep-like state during which a person becomes increasingly responsive to suggestions.

hypothermia Extreme loss of body temperature; this condition can result in death if not treated immediately.

immigrant   Someone who moves to another country for the purpose of settling there permanently.

impairment   A condition in which mental health issues, substance use, or other personal problems interfere with a person's ability to practice their profession competently.

in-home services   Services provided to assist families that have special needs to remain living together in their own homes. Services include homemaker aides, home health care, day care services, and the like.

income maintenance   Social welfare programs designed to provide individuals with enough money or goods and services to maintain a pre-determined standard of living.

individualized Education Program (IEP)   A formal, written document developed by a multi-disciplinary team for each public school child eligible for special education services.

indoor relief   A practice under the Elizabethan Poor Law in which certain categories of poor people (old, blind, disabled) were to be provided relief in an institution such as an almshouse.

insurance   A program designed to protect people from the full consequences of the risks to which they are vulnerable, such as disability, death of a breadwinner, medical needs, and financial problems in old age. Covered individuals may be required to make regular contributions to a fund set aside to pay for the claims of those insured.

intensive probation   A specialized category of probation in which monitoring contacts occur very frequently and consistently, sometimes daily or at least several times a week. This form of probation is more cost-effective than imprisonment. It provides a relatively high level of community protection when used with discretion.

interprofessional collaboration   The effective, well functioning communication and teamwork with other professionals undertaken to enhance the quality of service to people.

intersectionality   The quality of various factors interweaving and becoming entangled such that each affects the other significantly. For example, the intersectionality of multiple factors impacting poverty such as race, gender, and age can greatly increase the overall risk of poverty.

intervention process   A systematic process used by social workers to help create desired change involving four major steps: engaging the client system, assessing information, implementing plans of action, and evaluating outcomes.

isms   Prejudices common to large segments of society.

jail   A correctional facility generally used for short sentences or for detaining persons while they await a court hearing. Prisons, by contrast, are used for lengthier sentences.

job coach   An employment specialist who helps people learn to do their jobs appropriately, often in an employment setting that hires people with disabilities.

juvenilization of poverty   The increasing incidence of poverty among children, related to the feminization of poverty.

kinship care   Care provided beyond the nuclear family to an inclusive family system of extended family members that also incorporates persons unrelated by blood or legal ties (in other words, persons related instead by strong affectional ties).

lady almoner   A forerunner of today's health care social worker. The original lady almoners were social workers from London's Charity Organization Society, who in the late 1800s interviewed patients at the Royal Free Hospital to determine who was eligible to receive free medical care. Lady almoners soon broadened their services to include advocacy, referral to other community resources, and patient education and counseling.

laissez faire   A term that in French literally means "leave to be" or "let be." It refers to the idea that government should not regulate the economic market, but allow it to function entirely according to the influences of supply and demand.

law enforcement   The police component of the criminal justice system.

least restrictive environment   The setting that provides the least interference with normal life patterns and yet provides the most important and most needed services to a given client.

legal regulation The control of certain activities, such as professional conduct, by government rule and enforcement; governmental controls that limit access to use of professional titles such as *social worker* or *psychologist*.

lesbian A female whose sexual orientation is toward other females.

less eligibility The concept, based on the belief that pauperism is voluntary, that the condition of a poor person receiving "relief" should be worse than the condition of the poorest self-supporting worker in the community.

levels of intervention The systems with which social workers intervene or work: individual, family, group, organization, and community.

liberal or progressive A political perspective that supports government intervention in the economic market to help "level the playing field" for disadvantaged groups such as women or minorities. Persons of this perspective tend to believe that people are inherently good, are naturally industrious, and will work hard if conditions are humane. Liberals or progressives believe that it is conditions in the social environment that keep many poor people from achieving a decent standard of living.

licensure Considered to be a strong form of legal regulation as only persons with defined credentials (usually degrees from CSWE-accredited schools) are permitted to take the required state social work examination.

long-term care Any combination of nursing, personal care, volunteer, and social services provided intermittently or on a sustained basis over a span of time to help persons with chronic illness or disability to maintain maximum quality of life.

mainstreaming In the context of educational policy, the term refers to a philosophy and practice in which children with disabilities—or children who are different from the majority in some special characteristic such as native language—are educated in regular classrooms as much as possible.

means test Evaluation of a client's financial resources, using the result as the criterion to determine eligibility to receive a benefit.

Medicaid Title XIX of the Social Security Act, Medicaid is a federal program designed to provide health care for poor people of all ages.

Medicare Title XVIII of the Social Security Act, Medicare is a federal program designed to provide health care for the elderly and for long-term disabled persons. Recent legislation has decreased Medicare coverage substantially, and older people especially are often surprised to learn how few hospital and nursing home bills are actually covered by Medicare.

mental disorder Impaired or dysfunctional cognitive or behavioral patterns that occur in individuals and that cause suffering, pain, or some level of disability.

minority group A group that has less power than the majority group so that members are relatively vulnerable to poverty and discrimination.

misdemeanor An offense that is considered to be relatively minor by the judicial system. Misdemeanors are generally punishable by fines, probation, or a short jail sentence; misdemeanors are contrasted with felonies, which are more serious offenses.

moderate drinking Consumption of one drink a day for women or two for men.

MSW A social worker at the master's degree level of the profession.

multidisciplinary team (M-team) A small, organized group of persons—each trained in different professional disciplines (e.g., teaching, social work, psychology) and each possessing his or her own skills—working together to achieve a common goal.

mutual aid Reciprocal aid among members of a family, ethnic group, organization, or some such community.

National Alliance on Mental Illness (NAMI) A mental health services consumer organization founded in 1979 to support research, education, social policy, and political activity that will enhance access to community-based mental health services.

national health insurance plan A system that provides participation in comprehensive health care insurance for all citizens.

national health service A nation's ownership and administration of health care facilities and services that provide the complete range of health care to all citizens.

neglect The failure of responsible persons to provide for the appropriate care of a dependent, including inadequate nutrition, improper supervision, and deficient health care.

neoconservative A political perspective that arose in the mid-1970s that opposed government welfare programs for the poor and advocated ending entitlements to assistance under the Social Security Act for poor children and their parents. People of this perspective believe that public social welfare programs should be privatized.

neoliberal A political perspective held by some liberals involving a more favorable attitude toward big business and more caution about the role of big government. This perspective was developed in hopes of improving chances for election.

nondiscrimination Practices that avoid discrimination against minorities; laws that ban bias and require equal access to resources such as education and jobs.

normalization Making available to persons with disabilities those conditions of everyday life that are as close as possible to the norms and patterns of mainstream society.

norms Rules of behavior, both formal and informal, and expectations held collectively by a culture, group, organization, or society.

opiods Drugs used to deaden pain; may produce addiction and overdose can be fatal.

osteoporosis A bone-thinning disease most commonly found in women over 50 years of age. Osteoporosis is a frequent cause of fractures in older persons.

out-of-home services Services provided to assist needy children and their families when families are no longer able to care for their children in the home. Such services include foster care (both short-term and long-term) and institutional care.

outdoor relief A practice under the Elizabethan Poor Law in which some categories of poor people (old, blind, disabled) could be provided aid in their own homes if permitted by local authorities.

palliative care An active form of treatment to relieve pain and provide the best quality of life possible to persons who are terminally ill.

parole The release of a prisoner by corrections officials before completion of the full sentence; supervision by persons designated by the court (often social workers) is generally required until the full sentence has been completed. Any violation of the terms of the parole agreement can result in return to prison for the remainder of the sentence (revocation).

pay equity The policies and procedures used to ensure that sex and race discrimination are eliminated from wage-setting systems used by employers.

pension A payment made regularly to an individual because of retirement, age, loss, or incapacitating injury or to dependents in the event of the holder's death.

pension plan A plan or program designed to provide financial support for older adults who have retired from their former occupations.

permanency placement Placement of children who, for whatever reason, cannot live with their biological parents, in permanent adoptive homes.

personal care home A residential facility providing custodial care and supportive services such as assistance with meals, bathing, and dressing for elderly people. Nursing care provisions are limited or absent.

PhD A doctorate degree that may be earned in social work as well as numerous other professions and academic disciplines.

police social work The practice of social work within police departments. Direct services are provided to persons accused of crime and to family members; some services may also be provided to victims and witnesses of crime and to police personnel to help them deal with crises, trauma, and stress. Community education and crime prevention work are frequently an additional responsibility.

policy practice Social work practice that involves participating in the political system to influence the direction and substance of social welfare policy to bring about systems change on behalf of people who are marginalized and disadvantaged.

post-traumatic stress disorder (PTSD) Acute and overwhelming physical and psychological distress lasting for a prolonged time (generally beyond 1 month) following a traumatic life event. Unless entity to carry forward a plan or an action (thus, it can be said that social work is sanctioned by society); or (2) a response that penalizes an individual for failure to conform to established policies or procedures; NASW, for example, can sanction a member who is found to have violated the NASW Code of Ethics.

sandwich generation Adults who provide unpaid caregiving to older adults, usually parents or other relatives, who must also provide care for their own children. Many members of the sandwich generation also must hold paying jobs to make ends meet.

schizophrenia A serious form of mental disorder in which the person has lost the capacity to function normally; disturbances in communication, perception, and affect are common, although the disease has several different forms.

secondary social work setting A setting in which social work services support the primary purpose of the setting. For example, the primary purpose of a school system is educational; the primary professionals who carry out that purpose are teachers.

sedative Drugs that reduce anxiety or calm excessive activity or excitement.

seizure A short change in normal brain activity. Generalized seizures affect both sides of the brain. Focal or partial seizures affect just one area of the brain. Seizures manifest in many ways, sometimes causing a person to appear to be staring into space sometimes causing a person to fall to the ground and shake violently.

self-determination An ethical principle of the social work profession that recognizes the right and need of clients to make their own choices and decisions.

sexism The belief that one sex is superior to the other, usually that males are superior to females.

sexual orientation An individual's orientation toward heterosexual, homosexual, or bisexual behavior.

Sheltered English Immersion (SEI) An educational model in which children who do not speak English are placed in classrooms where only English is spoken. Their teachers have training in working with non-English-speaking students.

sheltered workshop A work environment that hires people with disabilities and provides special services enabling persons with handicaps to perform their work successfully.

single-payer system A government's health care system where either the government or a single selected corporation administers the health insurance program.

social and economic justice Fairness among people so that members of diverse population groups have an equal chance to achieve a reasonably comfortable standard of living.

Social Emotional Learning (SEL) Learning how to recognize one's emotions and to use a variety of methods to regulate one's responses to stress, such as contemplative practice, meditation, and/or breathing exercises.

social insurance Government programs to protect citizens from the full consequences of the risks to which they are vulnerable, such as unemployment, disability, death of a breadwinner, and catastrophic medical care needs. Typically, the government requires covered individuals to make regular contributions to a fund that, theoretically, is set aside and used to reimburse those who are covered by the plan for any losses they suffer as a result of covered risks.

social justice A state of affairs desired by most persons of liberal or progressive persuasion in which all members of society would have the same basic opportunities, protections, rights, obligations, and social benefits.

social welfare A system, sometimes referred to as an institution, comprising a wide variety of policies, programs, and services that help people meet their basic needs.

social work The major profession worldwide that helps individual people, families, groups, organizations, and communities to prevent or resolve problems in social and psychological functioning, meet basic human needs, achieve life-enhancing goals, and create a just society.

special education Educational services and programs designed to meet the needs of children with special needs, such as physical disabilities, learning disabilities, emotional or behavioral disturbances, speech and language problems, or pregnancy.

spinal cord injuries Damage to the disks or the spinal cord itself that result most frequently from a traumatic blow to the spine, gunshot wound, car accident, sports injury, or a fall.

spirituality A personal quality or characteristic pertaining to the search for meaning. Spirituality may or may not involve religious practices or beliefs.

State Supplementary Payment (SSP) A cash payment provided in some states to supplement the small income provided by Supplemental Security Income (SSI) to aged and blind persons, and persons with disabilities.

stigma Negative attitudes and behaviors directed toward people based on their perceived race, socioeconomic status, mental illness, sexual identification, etc.

stimulants Drugs that produce energy, increase alertness, and provide a sense of strength and well-being; one example is amphetamines.

strengths perspective The idea or view that identifying and assessing a client's assets and abilities is essential to successful problem solving, rather than merely identifying and assessing a client's problems.

subculture A smaller variant of a particular culture.

subpoena An order to appear in court on a specified date; failure to appear may result in a penalty.

substance-induced disorder A condition in which intoxication or withdrawal symptoms that are reversible occur during or following substance specific use.

substance-related disorders A general diagnostic category denoting excessive and problematic use, intoxication, and/or withdrawal of one or more of the 10 substances identified by DSM-V which include, among others: alcohol, hallucinogens, opioids, and sedatives.

Supplemental Security Income (SSI) The public assistance program providing assistance for the elderly, the blind, and persons with disabilities who meet a means test (have very low income). It was established in 1974 to reduce the stigma of "welfare," and is administered by Social Security Administration. However, SSI omits entitlement to aid for poor children and their families.

supported employment A vocational option providing individualized supports to people with disabilities so that they can achieve their goals in the workplace.

surrogate parent Women who agree to be impregnated and to release the baby that they deliver to the person(s) who contracted with them for this purpose.

system A whole consisting of interacting parts such that a change in one part affects all others.

tax-sheltered annuity A government program with the purpose of assisting workers to have a source of income in retirement. Workers may have money deducted from their paychecks during their working years and deposited, tax-free, in a special account. Some employers match employee contributions. Money may be withdrawn in retirement (and in other special circumstances such as medical emergency) and is taxed at the time of withdrawal. Tax-sheltered annuity programs are becoming more important as retirement benefits from private employers become increasingly scarce.

telemedicine The remote provision of health care by means of electronic communication and information technology.

Temporary Assistance for Needy Families (TANF) The program replacing Aid to Families with Dependent Children. It is not an entitlement, but may provide limited assistance for a limited time to families that meet strict eligibility criteria if a state has allocated sufficient funds.

third-party payment system A program in which insurance companies reimburse some insured members' health care costs.

tissue stem cells Cells within the human body that routinely repair and maintain tissues such as the skin, bone marrow, and eye.

tolerance The continuing need to use increasing amounts of a substance to achieve a desired effect.

trafficking The use of physical or psychological coercion to transport persons, often for financial gain;

women may be trafficked for commercial sex or domestic labor purposes, while children may be transported for sexual purposes, low cost labor, or illicit adoption.

transphobia The fear, dread, or hatred of people who are transsexual—people who believe they have been born into the body of the wrong gender.

trauma- and stressor-related disorders Intense fear and stress response related to a personally experienced or witnessed event that was perceived to be life-threatening; may be a brief reaction or may last for years and be debilitating.

truancy The failure to attend school as required by law.

underemployment Employment at or near minimum wage, often part-time and without health insurance or other benefits.

universal coverage The assurance of health care for all people in need.

universal health care system A government's policies and provisions that ensure health care benefits for all citizens at the same rate and without regard to their economic status.

vagrants People who wander from place to place with no permanent home or job; or persons who cannot prove residency in a particular community.

values Preferred ways of believing; the philosophical concepts that we cherish as individuals, within our families, as a profession, and as a nation.

voucher A coupon or stamp worth a certain amount of money only if spent on specified services or products.

workhouse An "indoor relief" form of assistance in which poor people who received help had to live and work in an institutional setting.

worldview A comprehensive conception of the world especially from a specific standpoint (e.g., as shaped by a particular culture).

zero tolerance A government policy requiring schools to expel any student caught carrying a weapon. Some schools have adopted zero-tolerance policies for other types of infractions as well.

References

Chapter 1

Association of Social Work Boards. (2013). *About licensing and regulation.* Retrieved from https://www.aswb.org/licensees/about-licensing-and-regulation/

Buchan, V., Hamilton, T. D., Christenson, B., Rodenhiser, R., Gerritsen-McKane, R., & Smith, M. (2010). *The annual BEAP report*, 28th Annual BPD Conference, Cincinnati, OH.

Bureau of Labor Statistics, U.S. Department of Labor. (2015a). *Occupational outlook handbook, 2014-2024 edition.* Psychologists: Job outlook. Retrieved from http://www.bls.gov/ooh/life-physical-and-social-science/psychologists.htm#tab6

Bureau of Labor Statistics, U.S. Department of Labor. (2015b). *Occupational outlook handbook, 2016-2017 edition.* School and career counselors. Retrieved from http://www.bls.gov/ooh/community-and-social-service/school-and-career-counselors.htm

Bureau of Labor Statistics, U.S. Department of Labor. (2015c). *Occupational outlook handbook, 2016-2017 edition.* Social workers. Retrieved from http://www.bls.gov/ooh/community-and-social-service/social-workers.htm

Bureau of Labor Statistics, U.S. Department of Labor. (2015d). *Occupational employment statistics:* Occupational employment and wages, May 2015: 21-1021 Child, family, and school social workers; 21-1022 Healthcare social workers; 21-1025 Mental health and substance abuse social workers; and 21-1029 Social workers, all others. Retrieved from http://www.bls.gov/ooh/community-and-social-service/print/school-and-career-counselors.htm

Council on Social Work Education. (2015). *Accreditation.* Retrieved from http:cswe.org/Accreditation.aspx

Council on Social Work Education. (n.d.) *Annual statistics on social work education in the United States* (Tables 29 & 36, pgs. 26 & 32). Retrieved from the Council on Social Work Education website: http://www.cswe.org/File.aspx?id=82845

Hooyman, N. (Ed.). (2009). *Transforming social work education: The first decade of the Hartford Geriatric Social Work Initiative.* Alexandria, VA: Council on Social Work Education.

International Federation of Social Workers [IFSW]. (2015). *What we do.* Retrieved from the International Federation of Social Workers website: http://ifsw.org/what-we-do/

National Association of Black Social Workers [NABSW]. (n.d.) *History.* Retrieved from http://nabsw.org/?page=History

National Association of Puerto Rican/Hispanic Social Workers [NAPRHSW]. (2015). *Mission.* Retrieved from http://www.naprhsw.com/info/naprhsw-mission

National Association of Social Workers [NASW]. (2009). Environment: Policy statement. In J. J. Kelley & E. J. Clark (Eds.), *Social work speaks: National Association of Social Workers policy statements 2009-2012* (8th ed., pp. 121–126). Washington, DC: NASW Press.

National Association of Social Workers [NASW]. (2015a). *About NASW.* Retrieved from https://www.naswdc.org/nasw/default.asp

National Association of Social Workers [NASW]. (2015b). *Academy of certified social workers (ACSW).* Retrieved from https://www.socialworkers.org/credentials/credentials/acsw.asp

National Association of Social Workers [NASW]. (2015c). *Code of ethics of the National Association of Social Workers.* Retrieved from https://www.socialworkers.org/pubs/code/code.asp

National Association of Social Workers [NASW]. (2015d). *The diplomate in clinical social work (DCSW).* Retrieved from https://www.socialworkers.org/credentials/credentials/dcsw.asp

National Association of Social Workers [NASW]. (2015e). *NASW professional social work credentials and advanced practice specialty credentials.* Retrieved from https://www.socialworkers.org/credentials/list.asp

Morales, A. T., & Sheafor, B. W. (2002). *The many faces of social workers.* Boston, MA: Allyn & Bacon.

Thyer, B. A., & Biggerstaff, M. A. (1989). *Professional social work credentialing and legal regulation: A review of critical issues and an annotated bibliography.* Springfield, IL: Charles C. Thomas.

Whitaker, T., & Wilson, M. (2010). *National Association of Social Workers 2009 compensation and benefits study: Summary of key compensation findings prepared for the 2010 Social Work Congress, April 2010.* Washington, DC: National Association of Social Workers.

Whitaker, T., Wilson, M., & Arrington, P. (2009). *The results are in: What social workers say about social work.* Washington, DC: NASW Press.

Chapter 2

Abbott, A. (1999, October). Measuring social work values. *International Social Work, 42*(4), 455–470.

Abramovitz, M. (2000). *Under attack, fighting back: Women and welfare in the United States.* New York: Monthly Review Press.

Berg-Weger, M. (2005). *Social work and social welfare: An invitation.* Boston, MA: McGraw-Hill.

Compton, B., & Galaway, B. (1999). *Social work processes* (6th ed.). Pacific Grove, CA: Brooks/Cole.

Council on Social Work Education. (2015). *Council on social work education: Educational policy and accreditation standards.* Alexandria, VA: Author.

Davenport, C. (2014, November 13). Deal on Carbon Emissions by Obama and Xi Jinping Raises Hopes for Upcoming Paris Talks. *The New York Times.* Retrieved from http://www.nytimes.com

Dubois, B., & Miley, K. K. (2011). *Social work, an empowering profession* (7th ed.). Boston, MA: Allyn & Bacon.

Figuera-McDonough, J. (2007). *The welfare state and social work.* Thousand Oaks, CA: Sage Publications Inc.

Franklin, C., & Warren, K. (1999). Advances in systems theory. In C. Franklin & C. Jordan (Eds.), *Family practice: Brief systems methods for social work* (pp. 397–425). Pacific Grove, CA: Brooks/Cole.

Germain, C. B., & Gitterman, A. (1995). Ecological perspective. In R. Edwards (Ed.), *Encyclopedia of social work* (19th ed., pp. 816–822). Washington, DC: NASW Press.

Ginsberg, L. (1998). *Conservative social welfare policy, a description and analysis.* Chicago, IL: Nelson-Hall.

Glicken, M. D. (2004). *Using the strengths perspective in social work practice.* Boston, MA: Allyn & Bacon.

Guralnik, D. (Ed.). (1984). *Webster's new world dictionary of the American language* (2nd ed.). New York: Simon and Schuster.

Johnson, M. J., & Rhodes, R. (2005). *Human behavior and the larger social environment.* Boston, MA: Pearson.

Karger, J. K., & Stoesz, D. (2005). *American social welfare policy: A pluralist approach* (4th ed.). Boston, MA: Allyn & Bacon.

Karger, J. K., & Stoesz, D. (2010). *American social welfare policy* (6th ed.). Boston, MA: Allyn & Bacon.

Kiefer, F. (2016, November 7). Where 'Obamacare' stands in 2016. *The Christian Science Monitor,* p.17.

Kirst-Ashman, K., & Hull, G. (2006). *Understanding generalist practice* (4th ed.). Pacific Grove, CA: Wadsworth.

Lampman, J. (2006, November 9). New sermon from evangelical pulpit: Global warming. *The Christian Science Monitor,* pp. 13, 14.

Lerner, M. (2006). Surviving the great dying. In M. Schlitz, T. Amorok, & M. S. Micozzi (Eds.), *Consciousness and healing.* St. Louis, MO: Elsevier.

Lum, D. (2007). *Culturally competent practice, a framework for understanding diverse groups and justice issues* (3rd ed.). Pacific Grove, CA: Wadsworth.

Nadakavukaren, A. (2006). *Our global environment.* Long Grove, IL: Waveland Press, Inc.

Naughton, M. (2014, November 10). Harvard Divinity School, *Spiritual and Sustainable.* Retrieved from http://hds.harvard.edu/news

Norlin, J., Chess, W., Dale, O., & Smith, R. (2006). *Human behavior and the social environment: Social systems theory* (5th ed.). Boston, MA: Allyn & Bacon.

Popple, P. R., & Leighninger, L. (2008). *Social work, social welfare and American society* (7th ed.). Boston, MA: Allyn & Bacon.

Popple, P. R., & Leighninger, L. (2011). *The policy based profession: An introduction to social welfare policy analysis for social workers* (5th ed.). Boston, MA: Allyn & Bacon.

Poulin, J. (2005). *Strengths-based generalist practice* (2nd ed.). Pacific Grove, CA: Wadsworth.

Robbins, P., Chaterjee, P., & Canda, E. (2006). *Systems theory. Contemporary human behavior theory: A critical perspective for social work* (2nd ed.). Boston, MA: Allyn & Bacon.

Rothman, J. C. (2005). *From the front lines, student cases in social work ethics* (2nd ed.). Boston, MA: Allyn & Bacon.

Saleebey, D. (2006). *The strengths perspective in social work practice* (4th ed.). Boston, MA: Allyn & Bacon.

Schriver, J. M. (2004a). Global perspectives and theories. *Human behavior in the social environment, shifting paradigms* (4th ed., pp. 542–567). Boston, MA: Allyn & Bacon.

Schriver, J. M. (2004b). Paradigm thinking and social work knowledge for practice. *Human behavior in the social environment, shifting paradigms* (4th ed., pp. 105–166). Boston, MA: Allyn & Bacon.

Segal, E., & Brzuzy, S. (1998). *Social welfare policies, programs, and practice.* Itasca, IL: Peacock.

Shaefor, B. W., Horejsi, C. R., & Horejsi, G. A. (2000). *Tactics and guidelines for social work practice* (5th ed.). Boston, MA: Allyn & Bacon.

Sommer, V. L. (1995). The ecological perspective. In M. J. Macy, N. Flax, V. L. Sommer, & R. Stoessen (2004, July). Collaborating with faith-based services. *NASW News,* p. 4.

Talking financial reform to death. (2010, March 1). *The Washington Spectator, 36*(4), 1, 2.

Trumbull, M. (2007, May 16). Corporate concern on climate rises. *The Christian Science Monitor,* pp. 1, 10.

Tucker, M. E., & Grim, J. (2009). *Overview of world religions and ecology.* Retrieved from http://fore.research.yale.edu/religion/

Tyuse, S. W. (2003). Social justice and welfare reform: A shift in policy. In J. Stretch, E. Burkemper, W. Hutchinson, & J. Wilson (Eds.), *Practicing social justice.* New York: Hayworth Press.

United Nation's Intergovernmental Panel on Climate Change. (2014). *Climate Change 2014: Synthesis Report and Summary for Policy Makers.* Retrieved from http://www.ipcc.ch/

Weissman, R. (2010, January/February). Shed a tear for democracy. *Public Citizen News,* p. 3.

Wells, C. (1998). *Stepping to the dance: The training of a family therapist.* Pacific Grove, CA: Brooks/Cole.

Wernick, A. (2016, September 25). *The US and China have now officially ratified the Paris climate agreement.* Retrieved from http://www.pri.org/stories/2016-09-25/us-and-china-have-now-officially-ratified-paris-climate-agreement

Wheatley, M. (2009). *Leadership and the new science.* San Francisco, CA: Berrett-Koehler Publishers, Inc.

Wheatley, M. (2010, January). *Community leadership.* Paper presented at the Milwaukee Community Leadership Conference, Marquette University, Milwaukee, WI.

Zastrow, C. H. (2007). *The practice of social work, applications of generalist and advanced content* (8th ed.). Pacific Grove, CA: Brooks/Cole.

Chapter 3

Anti-torture efforts on Capitol Hill. (2006, June). *FCNL Washington Newsletter, 708,* pp. 6, 8.

Amadeo, K. (2014, February 14). *Income inequality in America.* Retrieved from http://useconomy.about.com/od/suppl1/a/income-inequal.htm

References

Baxter, E. (2015, April). *What occupational data show about the causes of the gender wage gap*. Retrieved from https://americanprogress.org/issues/women/news/2015

Butler, R. (1994). Dispelling ageism: The cross-cutting intervention. In R. D. Enright Jr. (Ed.), *Perspectives in social gerontology* (p. 5). Boston, MA: Allyn & Bacon.

Caldera, S. (2009). Social security: Ten facts that matter. *AARP Public Policy Institute*. Retrieved from www.aarp.org/ppi

Civil liberties and human rights. (2004, September). *FNCL Washington Newsletter*, 8.

Crary, D., & Swanson, E. (2015, July 18). *Americans are still divided over gay marriage after Supreme Court decision*. Retrieved from http://www.huffingtonpost.com

Davis, J. D. (2016, May 17). *Obama defends transgender directive for school bathrooms*. Retrieved from http://www.nytimes.com/2016/05/17/us/politics/obama-defends-transgender-directive-for-school-bathrooms.html?_r=0

Dumesnil, C. (2016, Summer). LGBT parenting progress. *Stand*, p. 8.

Dumhoff, G. W. (2009, October). *Who rules America? Wealth, income, and power*. Retrieved from http://sociology.ucsc.edu/whorulesamerica/power/wealth.html

Eisler, R. (1987). *The chalice and the blade*. San Francisco, CA: Harper.

Ending Child Poverty Now. (2015). Retrieved from http://childrensdefense.org/

Fact sheet, Social Security (2013, December). Retrieved from http://www.ssa.gov/news/press/factsheets/

Farrell, M. B. (2010, January 24). Trial raises stakes in gay-marriage debate. *The Christian Science Monitor*, pp. 19, 20.

Federal minimum wage increase for 2007. Retrieved from www.laborlawcenter.com/federal-minimum-wage.asp

Feldmann, L. (2006, June 6). GOP targets gay marriage. *The Christian Science Monitor*, pp. 1, 10.

Fisher, G. M. (1998, Spring). Setting American standards of poverty: A look back. *Focus*, 19(2), 47–51.

Gabriel, P., & Schmitz, S. (2007, June). Gender differences in occupational distributions among workers. *Monthly Labor Review*, 19–23.

General information on social security. (2005, April). Retrieved from http://www.aarp/research/socialsecurity/general/aresearch-import-352-FS39R.html

Goldberg, G. (2002). More than reluctant: The United States of America. In G. Goldberg & M. Rosenthal (Eds.), *Diminishing welfare, a cross-national study of social provision* (pp. 33–71). Westport, CT: Auburn House.

Grier, P. (2001, December 13). Fragile freedoms, which civil liberties, and whose, can be abridged to create a safer America? *The Christian Science Monitor*, pp. 1, 8, 9.

Hill, C. (2015, Spring). *The simple truth about the gender pay gap*. Retrieved from http://www.aaup.org/research/the-simple-truth-about-the-gender-pay-gap/

Heining, A. (2010, August 16 & 23). Gay marriage, to a national stage? *The Christian Science Monitor*, p. 19.

Hidden pockets of elderly said to be in poverty. (2009, September 4). *AARP Bulletin Today*. Retrieved from http://bulletin.aaro/org/yourmoney/personalfinance/articles/hidden_pockets_of_eelderly_said_to_be_in_poverty.html

Hodge, D. R. (2007, April). Social justice and people of faith: A transnational experience. *Social Work*, 52(2), 139–147.

Huang, C. (2007, April 19). The House of Representatives in Oregon passed a bill Tuesday to recognize same sex couples. *The Christian Science Monitor*, p. 3.

Hunger and Poverty Fact Sheet. (2013). Retrieved from http://www.feedingamerica.org/hunger-in-america/impact-of-hunger/

Income, poverty and health insurance in the United States 2009: Highlights. (2009). Retrieved from http://www.census.gov/newsroom/releases/archives/income_wealth/

Irons, J. S. (2009, September 30). *Economic scarring: The long term impacts of the recession*. Retrieved from http://www.epi/publications/entry/bp243/

Karger, H. J., & Stoesz, D. (2010). *American social welfare policy, a pluralist approach*. Boston, MA: Allyn & Bacon.

Karimi, F. (2015, January 19). Wealthiest 1% will soon own more than the rest of us combined, Oxfam says. Retrieved from http://www.cnn.com/2015/01/19/world/wealth-inequality

Kavoussi, B. (2012, September 11). *The one percent is 288 times wealthier than the median U.S. household*. Retrieved from http://www.huffingtonpost.com/2012/09/11/one-percent-vs-median-household/

Key facts about the uninsured population. (2014, October 29). Retrieved from http://kff.org/uninsured/fact-sheet/key-facts-about-the-uninsured-population/

Krogstad, J. M. (2014, June 13). *One-in-four Native Americans and Alaska Natives are living in poverty*. Retrieved from http://www.pewresearch.org/author/jkrogstad/

Kramer, S. (2004, August 5). Same sex marriage takes a hit. *The Christian Science Monitor*, pp. 1, 10.

Lilly Ledbetter Fair Pay Act. (2009). Retrieved from 'http://www.nwlc.org/fairpay/ledbetterfairpayact.html

Liptak, A. (2016, June 23). *Supreme Court upholds affirmative action program at University of Texas*. Retrieved from http://www.nytimes.com/2016/06/24/us/politics/supreme-court-affirmative-action-university-of-texas.html?_r=0

Lum, D. (2007). *Culturally competent practice, a framework for understanding diverse groups and justice issues* (3rd ed.). Pacific Grove, CA: Wadsworth.

Marks, A. (2000, April 27). Vermont launches revolution by allowing same-sex unions. *The Christian Science Monitor*, p. 2.

May-Chahal, C., Katz, I., & Cooper, L. (2003). Social exclusion, family support and evaluation. In I. Katz & J. Pinkerton (Eds.), *Evaluating family support, thinking internationally, thinking critically* (pp. 45–65). West Sussex, UK: John Wiley.

Mishel, L., & Bivens, J. (2011, October 26). Occupy wall streeters are right about skewed economic rewards in the United States. Retrieved from http://www.epi.rg/publication/bp331-occupy-wall-street/

Native Americans still poorest in United States. (2006, August 30). Retrieved from http://64.38.12.138/News/2006/015687.asp

Navetta, J. M. (2005, Spring). Gains in learning, gaps in earning. *Outlook*, 99(1), 11–13.

Nine million uninsured children need a solution now. (2007). Retrieved from http://childrensdefense.org/site/PageServer

Pagels, E. (1979). *The gnostic gospels*. New York: Random House.

Pagels, E. (2003). *Beyond belief*. New York: Random House.

Palazzolo, J. (2014, April 22). *Affirmative-action rulings at the Supreme Court: A timeline*. Retrieved from http://blogs.wsj.com/law/affirmative-action-rulings-a-timeline/

Paulson, A., & Stern, S. (2003, November 19). Landmark ruling on gay marriage. *The Christian Science Monitor*, pp. 1, 10.

People quick facts. (2015, June). Retrieved from http://quickfacts.census.gov/qfd/states/00000.html

Poverty in the United States: a snapshot. (2013). Retrieved from http://www.nclej.org/poverty-in-the-us.php

Poverty thresholds for 2013 by size of family and number of related children under 18 years. (2015). Retrieved from http://www.census.gov/search-results-html?q=poverty+thresholds&page

Poverty thresholds for 2015 by size of family and number of related children under 18 years. (2016, September 1). Retrieved from http://www.census.gov/data/tables/time-series/demo/income-poverty/historical-poverty-thresholds.html

Racist hate crimes. (2015, Summer). *Intelligence Report*, p. 13.

Richey, W. (2007, June 29). Court rejects diversity plans. *The Christian Science Monitor*, pp. 1, 10.

Richey, W., & Feldman, L. (2006, June 12). Many perils at Guantanamo—for Bush, too. *The Christian Science Monitor*, pp. 1, 10.

Rocha, C. J., & McCarter, A. K. (2003/2004, Fall/Winter). Strengthening economic justice content in social work education. *Arete*, *27*(2), 4–14.

Restrepo, D., & Garcia, A. (2014, July 24). *The Surge of Unaccompanied Children from Central America*. Retrieved from https://www.americanprogress.org/issues/immigration/report2014/

Scherer, R. (2006, July 7). Two states say "no" to gay marriage. *The Christian Science Monitor*, p. 3.

Scherer, M. (2015, July 20). Up with people. *Time*, p. 42.

Schekhtman, L. (2016, September 26). Has US economy turned a corner? *The Christian Science Monitor*, pp. 18 & 20.

Segal, E., & Brzuzy, S. (1998). *Social welfare policies, programs, and practice*. Itasca, IL: Peacock Publishers.

Sorcher, S. (2015, June 22). How an unlikely coalition curtailed federal surveillance. *The Christian Science Monitor*, p. 14.

Sheirholz, H. (2009, September 10). *New 2008 poverty, income data reveal only tip of the recession iceberg*. Retrieved from http://www.epi.org/publications/entry/income_picture_20090910

State by state: *The legal battle over gay marriage*. (2009, December 15). Retrieved from http://www.npr.org/templates/story/story.php?storyId=112448663

Terry, D. In the crosshairs. (2015, Summer). *Intelligence Report*, pp. 27–33.

Temporary cash assistance for the poor. (2015, May 13). Retrieved from https://singlemotherguide.com/temporary-cash-assistance-for-the-poor/

Terzieff, J. (2007, June 1). *Maloney and Ginsberg parry high court ruling*. Retrieved from http://www.womensnews.org/article/cfm?aid=3190

The defense of marriage act. (2015, June). Retrieved from http://www.freedomtomarry.org/states/entry/c/doma

The Obama Administration's Deferred Action for Childhood Arrivals (DACA). (2015, March). Retrieved from http://www.nilc.org/FAQdeferredactionyouth.html

Thirty seven states have legal same-sex marriage. (2015). Retrieved from http://gaymarriage.procon.org/view.resource.php?resourceID=004857

United Nations. (1948). *Declaration of human rights*. Retrieved from http://www.un.org/overview/rights/html

Wilson, C. (2016, March 14). How the pay gap hurts women's financial security. *Time*, p. 14.

Whitehead, J. W. (2012, June 25). *In a Police State, Everyone Loses: The Supreme Court's Ruling in Arizona v. United States Endangers Us All*. Retrieved from http://www.huffingtonpost.com/john-w-whitehead/supremer-court-arizona-immigration-law

You can't save what you don't earn. (2008). *Older Women's League*. Retrieved from http://www.owl-national.org.Policy_Issues_files/Equal%20Pay%Day202008.doc

Chapter 4

Alfredsson, S. (2013, January 30). *Even in Sweden, the social security system is failing people*. Retrieved from http://www.theguardian.com/commentisfree/2013/jan/30/sweden-social-security-system

Association joins global coalition. (2005, February 1). *NASW News*, *50*(2), 1.

Bane, M. J. (2003). A Catholic policy analyst looks at poverty. In M. J. Bane & L. M. Mead (Eds.), *Lifting up the poor* (pp. 12–52). Washington, DC: Brookings Institution Press.

Bartkowski, J. P., & Regis, H. A. (2003). *Charitable choices: Religion, race and poverty in the post-welfare era*. New York: New York University Press.

Bishaw, A., & Glassman, B. (2016, September). *Poverty: 2014 and 2015*. Retrieved from http://www.census.gov/content/dam/Census/library/publications/2016/demo/acsbr15-01.pdf

Brieland, D. (1995). Social work practice: History and evolution. In R. L. Edwards (Ed.), *Encyclopedia of social work* (19th ed., Vol. 3, pp. 2250–2255). Silver Spring, MD: NASW Press.

Bryner, G. (1998). *The great American welfare reform debate, politics and public morality*. New York: W. W. Norton.

Champagne, A., & Harpham, E. (1984). *The attack on the welfare state* (pp. 97–105). Prospect Heights, IL: Waveland.

Democracy and the death tax. (2006, June 12). *The Christian Science Monitor*, p. 17.

Earned income and AGI limits. (2015, July). Retrieved from www.irs.gov/Credits-&-Deductions/Individuals/Earned-Income-Tax-Credit

Federico, R. (1984). *The social welfare institution* (4th ed.). Lexington, MA: Heath.

Floyd, I., & Schott, L. (2014, October 30). *TANF cash benefits have fallen by more than 20 percent in most states and continue to erode*. Retrieved from http://www.cbpp.org/research/tanf-cash-benefits-have-fallen-by-more-than-20-percent-in-most-states-and-continue-to-erode?fa=view&id=4222

Frequently asked questions about WIC. (2015). Retrieved from http://www.fns.usda.gov/frequently-asked-questions-about-wic#3

General information on social security. (2005, April). Retrieved from http://www.aarp/research/socialsecurity/general/aresearch-import-352-FS39R.html

Goldberg, G. (2002a). Diminishing welfare: Convergence toward a liberal model? In G. Goldberg & M. Rosenthal (Eds.), *Diminishing welfare, a cross-national study of social provision* (pp. 320–372). Westport, CT: Auburn House.

Goldberg, G. (2002b). More than reluctant: The United States of America. In G. Goldberg & M. Rosenthal (Eds.), *Diminishing* welfare: A cross-national study of social provision (pp. 33–71). Westport, CT: Auburn House.

Goldberg, G., & Rosenthal, M. (Eds.). (2002). *Diminishing welfare: A cross-national study of social provision*. Westport, CT: Auburn House.

Harrington, M. (1962). *The other America: Poverty in the United States*. New York: MacMillan.

Heilprin, J. (2009, June 22). *Obama administration seeks to join U.N. Rights of the Child Convention*. Retrieved from http://www.huffingtonpost.com/2009/06/23/obama-admininstration-seek_n_219511.html

How America ranks among industrialized countries. (2015). Retrieved from http://www.childrensdefense.org/libraryJapan and the poor, on yer bike (2013, November 23). Retrieved from http://www.economist.com/news/asia/2159099-public-approves-government-taking-aim-welfare-recipients-yer-bike

Johnson, N. (2000, November 2). *A hand up, how state earned income tax credits help working families escape poverty in 2000: An overview*. Retrieved from http://www.cbpp.org/11-2-00sfp.htm

Karger, H. J., & Stoesz, D. (2010). *American social welfare policy: A pluralist approach* (6th ed.). Boston, MA: Allyn & Bacon.

Kayama, S. (2011, July 5). *Welfare rise: Sign of economic, aging times*. Retrieved from http://search.japantimes.co.jp/news/2011/07/05/news/welfare-rise-sign-of-econic-aging-times

Kim, R. Y. (2001). The effects of the earned income tax credit on children's income and poverty: Who fares better? *Journal of Poverty*, 5(1), 1–22.

Lieby, J. (1987). History of social welfare. In R. L. Edwards (Ed.), *Encyclopedia of social work* (18th ed., Vol. 1, pp. 761–765). Silver Spring, MD: NASW Press.

McSteen, M. (1989). Fifty years of social security. In I. Colby (Ed.), *Social welfare policy: Perspectives, patterns, insights* (pp. 172–174). Chicago, IL: Dorsey.

National Coalition on Health Care. (2007). *Facts on health insurance coverage*. Retrieved from http://www.nchc.org/facts/coverage.html

NASW. (2015). *Collaborative Partners*. Retrieved from http://socialworkers.org/practice/intl/patners.asp#

NASW. (2015). *Issue Areas*. Retrieved from http://socialworkers.org/practice/intl/issues/defalut.asp

Nomura, M., & Kimoto, K. (2002). Is the Japanese style welfare society sustainable? In G. Goldberg & M. Rosenthal (Eds.), *Diminishing welfare: A cross-national study of social provision* (pp. 295–320). Westport, CT: Auburn House.

Osaki, T. (2014, July 19). *Welfare ruling stuns foreigners*. Retrieved from http://www.japantimes.co.jp/news/2014/19/national/social-issues/welfare-ruling-stuns-foreigners/#Vcu-jvlVikp

Picchi, A. (2015, September) *The shocking reach of U.S. child poverty*. Retrieved from http://www.cbsnews.com/news/the-shocking-reach-of-us-child-poverty/

Sweden corporate tax rate. (2015, September 8). Retrieved from http://www.tradingeconomics.com/sweden/corporate-tax-rate

Taro M. (2015, May 20). *Work centered welfare for the twenty-first century*. Retrieved from http://www.nipon.com/en/in-depth/a04203/

Tropman, J. (1989). *American values and social welfare*. Boston: Pearson.

W. Gertrude Brown placed a premium on education. (1993). Retrieved from http://www.aaregistry.org/historic_events/view/w-gertrude-brown-placed-premium-education

Welfare payments to be slashed Y74 billion to root out the comfortably poor. (2013, January 28). Retrieved from http://www.japantimes.co.jp/news/2013/01/28/business/economy-business/welfare-payments-to-be-slashed-%C2%A574-billion-to-root-out-the-comfortably-poor

Where do our Income Tax Dollars Go? (2015). Retrieved from www.fcnl.org/12taxchart

World hunger falls to under 800 million, eradication is next goal. (2015, May 27). Retrieved from www.fao.org

Nomura, M., & Kimoto, K. (2002). Is Japanese-style welfare society sustainable? In G. Goldberg & M. Rosenthal (Eds.), *Diminishing welfare: A cross-national study of social provision* (pp. 296–319). Westport, CT: Auburn Press.

Paulson, A. (2006, June 12). A tighter rein on faith-based initiatives. *The Christian Science Monitor*, p. 3.

Popple, P. R. (1995). Social work profession: History. In R. L. Edwards (Ed.), *Encyclopedia of social work* (19th ed., Vol. 3, pp. 2250–2255). Silver Spring, MD: NASW Press.

Poverty in the Unites States: A Snapshot. Retrieved from http://www.nclej.org/poverty-in-the-us-php

Press conference by world food programme on hunger and financial food crises. (2009, May 28). Retrieved from http://www.un.org.News/briefings/docs/2009/090528_WFP.doc.htm

Quadagno, J. (1982). *Aging in early industrial society: Work, family and social policy in 19th century England* (p. 95). New York: Academic Press.

Rocha, C. J., & McCarter, A. K. (2003/2004, Fall/Winter). Strengthening economic justice content in social work education. *Arete*, 27(2), 4–14.

Segal, E., & Brzuzy, S. (1998). *Social welfare policies, programs, and practice*. Itasca, IL: Peacock Publishers.

Stoessen, L. (2004, July). Collaborating with faith-based services. *NASW News*, p. 4.

Supplemental Nutrition Assistance Program and Costs. (2015, September 4). Retrieved from www.fns.usda.gov

Temporary Cash Assistance for the Poor. (2015, May). Retrieved from the Single Mother Guide website: https://singlemotherguide.com/temporery-cash-assistance-for-the-poor/

The state of America's children 2008, key data findings. (2008). Retrieved from http://www.childrensdefense.org/child-research-data-publications/data/state-of-America's-children-2008-report-key-data-findings-pdf

Thompson, R. A., & Raikes, H. A. (2003). Children and welfare reform. In R. Gordon & H. Walberg (Eds.), *Changing welfare*. New York: Kluwer Academic/Plenum.

Trattner, W. I. (1999). *From poor law to welfare state* (6th ed.). New York: The Free Press.

Trumbull, M. (2007, July 24). Rising food prices curb aid to global poor. *The Christian Science Monitor*, pp. 1, 2.

Tyuse, S. W. (2003). Social justice and welfare reform: A shift in policy. In J. Stretch, E. Burkemper, W. Hutchison, & J. Wilson (Eds.), *Practicing social justice*. New York: Hayworth Press.

Whitaker, W., & Federico, R. (1997). *Social welfare in today's world* (2nd ed.). New York: McGraw-Hill.

Whittle, D., & Kuraishi, M. (2009, August 16). Small doners, big impact. *The Christian Science Monitor*, p. 27.

WIC program participation and costs, 2009. (2010, January 8). Retrieved from http://www.fns.usda.gov/pd/wisummary.htm

Wilensky, H., & Lebeaux, C. (1965). *Industrial society and social welfare* (pp. 138–139). New York: Free Press.

Wyers, N. (1987). Income maintenance system. In R. Edwards (Ed.), *Encyclopedia of social work* (18th ed., p. 888). Silver Spring, MD: NASW Press.

Chapter 5

About poverty—2014 highlights. Retrieved from http://www.census.gov/hhes/www/poverty/about/overview/index.html

Adoption and Safe Families Act clarifies child welfare commitments. (1998, February). *Partnerships for Child Welfare, 5*(5), 3.

Adoption subsidy definitions. (n.d.). Retrieved from http://www.nacac.org/adoptionsubsidy/definitions.html

Allen, M., Kakavas, A., & Zalenski, J. (1994, Spring). Family preservation and support services. *The prevention report* (p. 2). Iowa City, IA: National Resource Center on Family Based Services, University of Iowa School of Social Work.

Appleby, G., Colon, E., & Hamilton, J. (2001). *Diversity, oppression and social functioning.* Boston, MA: Allyn & Bacon.

Axinn, M., & Levin, H. (1992). *Social welfare: A history of the American response to need* (3rd ed.). New York: Longman.

Bump, P. (2016, January 2). *The CEO of your company has probably already earned your 2016 salary this year.* Retrieved from https://www.washingtonpost.com/news/the-fix/wp/2016/01/05/the-ceo-of-your-company-has-probably-already-earned-your-2016-salary-this-year/

Campbell, K. (2004, June 23). Welfare reform hasn't led to more marriage—yet. *The Christian Science Monitor,* p. 11.

Carter, B., & McGoldrick, M. (2005). *The expanded life cycle, individual, family, and social perspectives.* Boston, MA: Allyn & Bacon.

Carter, R. (2014, May 31). *In military families, caregivers need help.* Retrieved from http://www.huffingtonpost.com/former-first-lady-rosalynn-carter/in-military-families-care_b_5063165.html

Casey, T. (2009, December 9). *New data reveals TANF caseload declines in twenty two states over the first sixteen months of the recession.* Retrieved from http://www.legalmomentum.org/assets/pdfs/tanf-caseload-down-in-over-22.pdf

Census 2010 shows interracial and interethnic married couples grew by 28% over decade. (2012, April 25). Retrieved from http://www.census.gov/newsroom/releases/archives/2010_census/cb12-68.html

Chappell, B. (2015, March 4). *For U.S. children, minorities will be the majority by 2020, census says.* Retrieved from http://www.npr.org/sections/thetwo-way/2015/03/04/390672196/for-u-s-children-minorities-will-be-the-majority-by-2020-census-says

Climate change facts; answers to common questions. (2015). Retrieved from http://www3.epa.gov/climatechange/basics/facts.html

Collins, C. (2005, January). N.H. adoptees gain access to records. *The Christian Science Monitor,* p. 14.

Crary, D., & Swanson, E. (2015, July 18). *Americans are still divided over gay marriage after Supreme Court decision.* Retrieved from http://www.huffingtonpost.com/entry/gay-marriage-public-opinion

Davenport, C. (2016, November 10). *Donald Trump could put climate change on course for "danger zone."* Retrieved from http://www.nytimes.com/2016/11/11/us/politics/donald-trump-climate-change.html?_r=1

Delgado, M., Jones, K., & Rohani, M. (2005). *Social work practice with refugee and immigrant youth in the United States.* Boston, MA: Allyn & Bacon.

Diller, J. V. (1999). *Cultural diversity: A primer for the human services.* Pacific Grove, CA: Brooks/Cole.

Dossey, L. (1989). *Recovering the soul: A scientific and spiritual search.* New York: Bantam Books.

Dossey, L. (2003). *Healing beyond the body: Medicine and the infinite reach of the mind.* Boston: Shambhala.

Dossey, L. (2008). Compassion and healing. In D. Goleman (Ed.), *Measuring the immeasurable: The scientific case for spirituality* (pp. 47–60). Boulder, CO: Sounds True, Inc.

Dossey, L. (2013). *One mind: How our individual mind is part of a greater consciousness and why it matters.* New York: Hay House, Inc.

Early immigration in the U.S.—the north: 1800s to 1850s. (n.d.). Retrieved from http://sites.google.com/site/thenorthsite/

Eighty-one years of paving the way, a history of family planning in America. (1997, Fall/Winter). *Planned Parenthood Today, 4,* 5.

Engbur, A., & Klungness, L. (2000). *The complete single mother.* Holbrook, MA: Adams Media Corporation.

Erickson, J. (2006a, Fall). FDA finally acts on emergency contraception with plan B approval. *National NOW Times,* p. 16.

Erickson, J. (2006b, Fall). NOW scores with U.N. Human Rights Report. *National NOW Times,* p. 17.

Frequently asked questions. (2015). Retrieved from http://www.endhomelessness.org/pages/faqs#youth

Ford, P. (2005, June 2). Europe's balancing act. *The Christian Science Monitor,* pp. 1, 10.

FY 2016 Childrens Bureau discretionary grant awards. (2016, October 11). Retrieved from http://www.acf.hhs.gov/cb/resource/discretionary-grant-awards-2016

Gardner, M. (2006, July 31). The problem of a pregnant pause. *The Christian Science Monitor,* pp. 13-14

Grieg, A. (2013, August). *Seven essential facts about multiracial youth.* Retrieved from http://www.apa.org/pi/families/resources/newsletter/2013/08/multiracial-youth.aspx

Guarino, M. (2010, February 14). Poverty's new face: Suburbs. *The Christian Science Monitor,* p. 18.

Gustavsson, N. S., & Segal, E. A. (1994). *Critical issues in child welfare.* Thousand Oaks, CA: Sage Publications.

Hanes, S. (2015, April 6). How working parent's manage. *The Christian Science Monitor,* pp. 26–32.

Home at last. (2007). Retrieved from http://www.pbs.org/now/shows/305/index.html

Hunger and poverty fact sheet. (2015). Retrieved from http://www.feedingamerica.org/hunger-in-america/

Immigrant families. (2014). Retrieved from http://www.nccp.org/topics/immigrantfamilies.html

International migration 2013. (2013). Retrieved from http://www.unfpa.org/resources/international-migration-2013-wall-chart

International migration outlook 2016, facts and figures. (2016). Retrieved from http://www.oecd.org/migration/international-migration-outlook-1999124x.htm

Indian child welfare act of 1977. (n.d.). Retrieved from http://www.nicwa.org/Indian_Child_Welfare_Act/

Kadushin, A., & Martin, J. (1988). *Child welfare services* (4th ed.). New York: Macmillan.

Karger, J., & Stoesz, D. (1998). *American social welfare policy: A pluralist approach* (3rd ed.). New York: Addison Wesley Longman.

Karger, J., & Stoesz, D. (2010). *American social welfare policy: A pluralist approach* (6th ed.). Boston, MA: Allyn & Bacon.

Key data findings. (2008). Retrieved from http://www.childrensdefense.org/child-research-data-publications/data/state-of-america's-children-2008-report-key-data-findings.pdf

Ki-moon, B. (2009). *Forward, Millennium Development Goals Report*. Retrieved from http://un.org/millenniumgoals/pdf/MDG_Report_2009_ENG.pdf

Kirchheimer, S. (2005, April). *The credit card sinkhole*. Retrieved from http://www.aarp.org/bulletin/consumer/ec_sinkhole.html

Kochanek, K. D., Murphy, S. L., Xu, J., & Arias, E. *Mortality in the United States, 2013*. Retrieved from http://www.cdc.gov/nchs/data/databriefs/db178.htm

LeShawn, L. (2009). *A new science of the paranormal, the promise of psychical research*. Wheaton, IL: Theosophical Publishing House.

Levin, J. (2001). *God, faith, and health, exploring the spirituality-healing connection*. New York: John Wiley & Sons, Inc.

Lindsay, R. (2002). *Recognizing spirituality: The interface between faith and social work*. Crawley, Western Australia: Western Australia Press.

Llana, S. M. (2010, February 7). Women leaders on rise in Latin America. *The Christian Science Monitor*, p. 7.

Loeb, P. R. (1999). *Soul of a citizen, living with conviction in a cynical time*. New York: St. Martin's Griffin.

Logan, S. M. L., Freeman, E. M., & McRoy, R. G. (1990). *Social work perspective with black families: A culturally specific perspective*. New York: Longman.

Lum, D. (1992). *Social work with people of color: A process-stage approach* (2nd ed.). Pacific Grove, CA: Brooks/Cole.

Macdonald, G. (2004, February 4). Is having a home a right? *The Christian Science Monitor*, pp. 15–16.

MacDorman, M., Mathews, T. J., Mohangoo, A. D., & Zeitlin, J. (2014, September 24). *International comparisons of infant mortality and related factors: United States and Europe, 2010*. Retrieved from http://www.cdc.gov/nchs/data/nvsr/nvsr63/nvsr63_05.pdf

McKenzie, J. K., & Lewis, R. (1998). Keeping the promise of adoption and safe families act. *The Roundtable, 12*(1), 1–9.

McNally, J. (2015, March 26). The war on eating. *The Shepherd Express*, p. 11.

Mehta, S. (2015, November 20). *There is only one country that hasn't ratified the convention on children's rights: US*. Retrieved from https://www.aclu.org/blog/speak-freely/theres-only-one-country-hasnt-ratified-convention-childrens-rights-us

Meyers, M., Han, W., Waldfogel, J., & Garfinkel, I. (2001, March). Child care in the wake of welfare reform: The impact of government subsidies on the economic well-being of single-mother families. *Social Service Review, 75*(1), 30–59.

Miks, J. (2006, December 20). Growing income inequality troubles Japanese. *The Christian Science Monitor*, p. 4.

Miller, S. (2005, August 22). Rise in homes with multiple generations. *The Christian Science Monitor*, p. 2.

Mink, G. (1998). *Welfare's end*. Ithaca, NY: Cornell University Press.

Myers, J. E. B. (2008). *A short history of child protection in America*. Retrieved from https://www.americanbar.org/content/dam/aba/publishing/insights_law_society/ChildProtectionHistory.authcheckdam.pdf

Nadakavukaren, A. (2006). *Our global environment* (6th ed.). Long Grove, IL: Waveland Press.

NASW professional social work credentials and advanced practice specialty credentials. (n.d.). Retrieved from http://www.naswdc.org/credentials/list.asp

NASW backs court's abortion clinic ruling. (2016, September). *NASW News, 61*(8), pp. 1 & 5.

National Association of Social Workers. (2015). *Social work and service members: Joining forces to support veterans and military families*. Retrieved from http://socialworkers.org/military.asp

National Coalition on Health Care. (2007). *Facts on health insurance coverage*. Retrieved from http://www.nchc.org/facts/coverage.shtml

New American community survey statistics for income, poverty, and health insurance available for states and local areas. (2016, September 15). Retrieved from http://www.census.gov/newsroom/press-releases/2016-cb16-159.html

Novotney, A. (2014, May). Who me? Marry? Retrieved from http://www.apa.org/monitor/2014/05/marriage.aspx

Ornes, S. (2007, February). The hole story. *Discover, Science, Technology and the Future*, 60–65.

Pardess, E. (2005). Pride and prejudice with gay and lesbian individuals. In C. L. Rabin (Ed.), *Understanding gender and culture in the helping process* (pp. 109–128). Belmont, CA: Thompson Wadsworth.

Quarles, B. (1987). *The Negro in the making of America* (3rd ed.). New York: Macmillan.

QuickFacts, United States. (2015). Retrieved from https://www.census.gov/quickfacts/table/PST045215/00

Radin, D. (2006). *Entangled minds: Extrasensory experiences in a quantum reality*. New York: Simon & Schuster.

Radin, D. (2013). *Supernormal, science, yoga, and the evidence for extraordinary psychic abilities*. New York: Random House.

Racial and ethnic diversity in the U.S. (2015, July 21). Retrieved from https://www.boundless.com/political-science/textbooks/boundless-political-science-textbook/american-politics-1/who-is-american-21/racial-and-ethnic-diversity-in-the-u-s-123-11224/

Ramanathan, C. S., & Link, R. J. (1999). *All our futures: Principles and resources for social work practice in a global era*. Belmont, CA: Science and Behavior Books.

Reich, J. (2005). *Fixing families, parents, power, and the child welfare system*. New York: Routledge.

Richey, W. (2007, April 19). Court allows late-term abortion ban. *The Christian Science Monitor*, pp. 1, 2.

Ross, J. (2006, September 12). In Chile, free morning-after pills to teens. *The Christian Science Monitor*, pp. 1, 10.

Roth, C. (2006, Summer). War against reproductive rights surges through states. *National NOW Times*, pp. 1, 3.

Samantrai, K. (2004). *Culturally competent public child welfare practice*. Pacific Grove, CA: Brooks/Cole-Thompson Learning.

Sanctuary mayors revolt against Trump immigration reform. (2016, November 11). Retrieved from http://www.trunews.com/article/sanctuary-mayors-revolt-against-trump-immigration-reform

Signorile, M. (2016, November 12). *The Mike Pence (Donald Trump) assault on LGBTQ equality is already underway*. Retrieved from http://www.huffingtonpost.com/entry/mike-pence-assault-lgbtq-equality_us_58275a17e4b02d21bbc8ff9b

Same-sex marriage and children's well-being: Research roundup. (2015, June 26). Retrieved from http://journalistsresource.org/studies/society/gender-society/same-sex-marriage-children-well-being-research-roundup

Savin-Williams, R., & Esterberg, K. G. (2000). Lesbian, gay, and bisexual families. In D. Demo, K. Allen, & M. A. Fine (Eds.), *Handbook of family diversity* (pp. 197–215). New York: Oxford University Press.

Schlitz, M. (2005). Consciousness beyond death. In M. Schliz, T. Amorok, & M. Micozzi (Eds.), *Consciousness and healing: Integral approaches to mind body medicine* (pp. 221–223). St. Louis, MO: Elsevier.

Schwartz, G., Simon, W., & Chopra, D. (2002). *The afterlife experiments*. New York: Atria Books.

Segal, E., & Brzuzy, S. (1998). *Social welfare policy, programs, and practice*. Itasca, IL: F. E. Peacock Publishers.

de Silva, E. C. (2006, June). Human rights and human needs. *NASW News*, p. 3.

Smith, E. B., & Kuntz, P. (2013, April 29). CEO pay 1,705-to-1 multiple of wages skirts U.S. law. Retrieved from http://www.bloomberg.com/news/articles/2013-04-30/ceo-pay-1-795-to-1-multiple-of-workers-skirts-law-as-sec-delays

Smith, M. K. (1998, January). Utilization-focused evaluation of a family preservation program. *Families in Society: The Journal of Contemporary Human Services, 76*(1), 11–19.

Soss, J., Schram, S., Vartanian, T., & Obrien, E. (2004, Winter). Welfare policy choices in the states: Does the hard line follow the color line? *Focus, UW Madison Institute for Research on Poverty, 23*(1), 9–15.

State and family medical leave laws. (2014). Retrieved from http://www.ncsl.org/research/labor-and-employment/state-family-and-medical-leave-laws.asp

Steinberg, D. (2006, November 17). When war and children collide. *The Christian Science Monitor*, p. 9.

Stoessen, L. (2005, March). Court reverses foster care decision. *NASW News*, p. 6.

Stoessen, L. (2007, March). Children said at higher risk in red states. *NASW News*, p. 11.

Tart, C. T. (2009). *The end of materialism: How evidence of the paranormal is bringing science and spirit together*. Oakland, CA: New Harbinger Publications, Inc.

The millennium development goals report, 2015, summary. (2015). Retrieved from http://www.un.org/millenniumgoals/2015_MDG_Report/pdf/MDG%202015%20Summary%20web_english.pdf

The Orphan Trains. (n.d.). Retrieved from www.childrensaidsociety.org/about/history

The 1951 Convention Relating to the Status of Refugees and its 1967 Protocol. (n.d.). Retrieved from http://www.unhcr.org/4ec262df9.html

Trattner, W. I. (1999). *From poor law to welfare state: A history of social welfare in America* (6th ed.). New York: The Free Press.

Trumbull, M. (2015, November 2). Life in the squeezed middle. *The Christian Science Monitor*, pp. 27–32.

UNICEF. (n.d). Fact sheet: UN Convention on the Rights of the Child. Retrieved from http://www.unicef.org/crc/files/Rights_overview.pdf

United States fails to meet key health goals for infants and mothers. (2006, May 17). Retrieved from http://www.childrensdefense.org/site/News2?page=NewsArticle&id=6669

US & world population clock. (2016, November 8). Retrieved from http://www.census.gov/pop/clock/

U.S.-China joint presidential statement on climate change. (2015, September 25). Retrieved from http://www.whitehouse.gov/the-press-office/2015/09/25/us-china-joint-presidential-tatement-climate-change

USA news in brief. (2006, November 17). *The Christian Science Monitor*, p. 3.

Wallace G., & Yoon, R. (2016, November 11). *Voter turnout at 20-year low in 2016*. Retrieved from http://edition.cnn.com/2016/11/11/politics/popular-vote-turnout-2016/

Wernick, A. (2016, September 25). *The US and China have now officially ratified the Paris climate agreement*. Retrieved from http://www.pri.org/stories/2016-09-25/us-and-china-have-now-officially-ratified-paris-climate-agreement

Van Gelder, S. (2010, Spring). America: The remix. *Yes, 53*, 18–23.

Van Wormer, K. (1997). *Social welfare: A world view*. Chicago, IL: Nelson Hall Publishers.

Vick, K. (2015, October 19). The great migration. *Time*, pp. 40–47.

Vick, K. (2015, December 21). 2015 person of the year, Angela Merkel, chancellor of the world. *Time*, pp. 54–96.

Walton, B. (2015, January 11). *NC woman battles for the right to work while pregnant*. Retrieved from http://www.usatoday.com/story/news/nation/2015/01/11/nc-aclu-pregnancy-discrimination-case/21596617/

Weissmann, J. (2014, June 23). *For millennials, out-of-wedlock childbirth is the norm*. Retrieved from http://www.slate.com/articles/business/moneybox/2014/06/for_millennials_out_of_wedlock_childbirth_is_the_norm_now_what.html

Watkins, S. A. (1990, November). The Mary Ellen myth: Correcting child welfare history. *Social Work, 35*(6), 501–503.

Why won't America ratify the UN convention on children's rights ? (2013). Retrieved from http://www.economist.com/blogs/economist-explains/2013/10/economist-explains-2

Yen, H. (2012, April 17). *Interracial marriage in the U.S. climbs to new high, study finds*. Retrieved from http://www.apa.org/pi/families/resources/newsletter/2013/08/multiracial-youth.aspx

Yule, R. (2006, May/June). Super-wealthy families try to repeal estate tax. *Public Citizen News*, pp. 1, 11.

Chapter 6

American Psychiatric Association. (2013). *Diagnostic and statistical manual of mental disorders* (5th ed.). Arlington, VA: Author.

Beers, C. (1908). *A mind that found itself*. New York: Longmans, Green, & Co.

Brave Heart, M. Y. H. (2004). Incorporating native historical trauma content. In L. Gutierrez, M. Zuniga, & D. Lum (Eds.), *Education for multicultural social work practice:*

Critical viewpoints and future directions (pp. 201–211). Alexandria, VA: Council on Social Work Education.

Dominelli, L. (2012). *Green social work: From environmental crises to environmental justice.* Cambridge, UK: Polity Press.

Eng, A., & Balancio, E. F. (1997). Clinical case management with Asian Americans. In E. Lee (Ed.), *Working with Asian Americans: A guide for clinicians* (pp. 400–407). New York: The Guilford Press.

Federal Register. (2016, March 30). Medicaid and Children's Health Insurance Programs; Mental Health Parity and Addiction Equity Act of 2008; the application of Mental Health Parity requirements of coverage offered by Medicaid Managed Care Organizations, the Children's Health Insurance Program (CHIP), and Alternative Benefit Plans. Retrieved from: https://www.federalregister.gov/Id/2016-876/page.18390

Hollis, F. (1964). *Casework: A psychosocial therapy.* New York: Random House.

Johnstone, M. (2007). Disaster response and group self-care. *Perspectives in Psychiatric Care, 43*(1), 38–40.

KEN Publications/Catalog. (n.d.). *Final report: Consumer bill of rights and responsibilities.* Retrieved from http://www.mentalhealth.org/consumersurvivor/billofrights.htm

Kirst-Ashman, K. K., & Hull, G. H. (2015). *Understanding generalist practice* (7th ed.). Stamford, CT: Cengage Learning.

Lum, D. (1992). *Social work with people of color: A process-stage approach* (2nd ed.). Pacific Grove, CA: Brooks/Cole.

Mankiller, W., & Wallis, M. (1993). *Mankiller: A chief and her people.* New York: St. Martin's Press.

Martin, M. E. (2016). *Introduction to social work: Through the eyes of practice settings.* Boston: Pearson.

Meyer, C. (1987). Direct practice in social work: Overview. In A. Minahan (Ed.), *Encyclopedia of social work* (19th ed., Vol. 1, pp. 409–422). Silver Spring, MD: National Association of Social Workers.

National Alliance on Mental Illness. (2010). *About NAMI.* Retrieved from http:www.nami.org

National Association of Social Workers. (2015). *NASW credentialing center.* Retrieved from www.socialworkers.org/credentials/credentials/mkf-sw.asp

Norris, L. (2016, February 16). *How Obamacare improved mental health coverage.* Retrieved from the healthinsurance.org website: https://www.healthinsurance.org/blog/2016/02/16/how-obamacare-improved-mental-health-coverage/

O'Hare, T. (2016). *Essential skills of social work practice: Assessment, intervention, and evaluation.* Chicago: Lyceum Books.

Pace, P. R. (2014, April). Social work efforts aim to prevent suicide deaths: Walking out of the darkness. *NASW News, 59*(4), 8.

Perlman, H. H. (1957). *Social casework: A problem-solving process.* Chicago, IL: University of Chicago Press.

Red Horse, J. (1988). Cultural evolution of American Indian families. In C. Jacobs & D. D. Bowles (Eds.), *Ethnicity and race: Critical concepts in social work* (pp. 86–102). Silver Spring, MD: National Association of Social Workers.

Reynolds, B. C. (1934). *Between client and community.* Silver Spring, MD: National Association of Social Workers.

Reynolds, B. C. (1935). *Social work and social living: Explorations in philosophy and practice.* New York: Citadel Press.

Reynolds, B. C. (1942). *Learning and teaching in the practice of social work.* Silver Spring, MD: National Association of Social Workers.

Richmond, M. E. (1917). *Social diagnosis.* New York: Russell Sage Foundation.

Richmond, M. E. (1922). *What is social casework? An introductory description.* New York: Russell Sage Foundation.

Sickel, A. E., Nabors, N. A., & Seacast, J. D. (2014). Mental health stigma update: A review of consequences. *Advances in Mental Health, 12*(3), 202–215.

Social work in the public eye. (2002). *NASW News, 47*(1), 15.

Social work in the public eye. (2006). *NASW News, 51*(9), 11.

Social work in the public eye. (2015). *NASW News, 60*(1), 9.

Taft, J. (1933). *The dynamics of therapy in a controlled relationship.* New York: The Macmillan Co.

Wilson, D. C. (1975). *Stranger and traveler: The story of Dorothea Dix, American reformer.* Boston, MA: Little, Brown & Co.

World Health Organization. (2007). *Quantifying environmental health impacts.* Retrieved from http://www.who.int/quantifying_ehimpacts/global/en/

World Health Organization. (2013). *Mental health action plan 2013–2020.* Retrieved from http://apps.who.int/iris/bitstream/10665/89966/1/978924/506021_eng.pdf?ua=1

Chapter 7

Bab, I. A., & Yirmiya, R. (2010). Depression and bone mass. *Annals of the New York Academy of Sciences, 1192*(1), 170–175.

Barnes, F. (1994, August 15). A White House watch: Left out. *New Republic, 211*(7), 15–17.

Battista-Frazee, K. (2015). Rural social workers face own set of challenges. *NASW News, 60*(7), 7–8.

Cannon, I. M. (1952). *On the social frontier of medicine: Pioneering in medical social service.* Cambridge, MA: Harvard University Press.

Cizza, G., Primma, S., Coyle, M., Gourgiotis, L., & Csaka, G. (2010). Depression and osteoporosis: A research synthesis with meta-analysis. *Hormone and Metabolic Research, 42*(7), 467–482.

Commission on Social Determinants of Health, World Health Organization. (2008). *Closing the gap in a generation.* Retrieved from http://wholibdoc.who.int/pblications/2008/97892415637

Csikai, E. L., & Chaitin, E. (2006). *Ethics in end-of-life decisions in social work practice.* Chicago, IL: Lyceum Books.

Department of Veterans Affairs. (n.d.). *About VA: History—Department of Veterans Affairs (VA).* Retrieved from http://www.va.gov/about_va/vahistory.asp

Donaldjtrump.com. (2016). *Healthcare reform to make America great again.* Retrieved from https://www.donaltjtrump.com/positions/healthcare-reform/

Dziegielewski, S. F. (2004). *The changing face of health care social work: Professional practice in managed behavioral health care* (2nd ed.). New York: Springer.

HealthCare.gov. (2010). *The Affordable Care Act: Overview; Affordable Health Care for America: Health insurance reform at a glance, implementation timeline.* Retrieved from http:www/healthcare.gov/law/introduction/index.html

Health Care in Canada. (2015). Retrieved from https://en.wikipedia.org/Wiki/Health_care_in_Canada

Henry, H., & Kaiser Family Foundation. (2010). *Kaiser health tracking poll—June 2010* (Publication Report No. 8082). Retrieved from http:www/kff.org/kaiserpols/8082.cfm

HHS.gov/HealthCare: *Key features of the Affordable Care Act by year.* (2014). Retrieved from http://www.hhs.gov/healthcare/facts/timeline/timeline-text.html#2014

Karger, H. J., & Stoez, D. (2010). *American social welfare policy: A pluralistic approach* (6th ed.). Boston: Pearson Education.

Khazan, O. (2014, October 21). *Health: What if America had Canada's healthcare system?* Retrieved from http://www.theatlantic.com/health/archive/2014/10/what_if_america_had_canadas_healthcare_system/381662

Kelly, J. J., Clark, E. J., & National Association of Social Workers [NASW]. (2009). Hospice care: Policy statement. J. J. Kelly & E. C. Clark (Eds.), *Social work speaks: National Association of Social Workers policy statements 2009–2012* (8th ed., pp. 180–191). Washington, DC: NASW Press.

Lawrence, S. A., & Azhar, A. (2010). Osteoporosis: Prevention and implications for social work practice and policy. *Social Work in Public Health*, 25(1), 511–526.

Lee, C. W. (2015). Increased risk of osteoporosis in patients with depression: A population-based retrospective cohort study. *Mayo Clinic Proceedings*, 92(1), 63–70.

Mayo Clinic. (2015). *Spinal cord injury causes.* Retrieved from http://www.mayoclinic.org/diseases-conditions/spinal-cord-injury/basics/causes/con-20023837

Medicaid.gov. (2015). *Keeping America healthy.* Retrieved from https:www.medicaid.gov/affordable-care-act/eligibility/index.html

Medicare Blog. (2015). *Medicare and Medicaid: Keeping Americans healthy for 50 years.* Retrieved from http://blog.medicare.gov/2015/07/27/medicare-and-medicaid-50-year-anniversary

Medicare.gov. (2015). *Costs for Medicare drug coverage.* Retrieved from https://www.medicare.gov/part-d/costs/part-d-costs.html

Medicare.gov. (2016). *Your Medicare costs: Part B.* Retrieved from https://www.medicare.gov/your-medicare-costs/part-b-costs-part-b-costs.html; *Part D* retrieved from https://www.medicare.gov/part-d-costs/part-d-costs.html; Costs in the Coverage Gap retrieved from https:www.medicare.gov/part-d-costs/costs/coverage-gap/part-d-coverage-gap.html

Mizrahi, T., Fasano, R., & Dooha, S. N. (1993). National health line: Canadian and American health care: Myths and realities. *Health & Social Work*, 18(1), 7–8.

Moniz, C., & Gorin, S. (2010). *Health and mental health care policy: A biopsychosocial perspective* (3rd ed.). Boston: Allyn & Bacon.

National Institute of Mental Health. (n.d.). *Depression and osteoporosis* (NIH Publication No. 11-7743). Retrieved from http://www.nimh.nih.vov/health/publications/depression-and-osteoporosis/index.shtml

National Osteoporosis Foundation. (n.d.). *Emotional aspects of osteoporosis.* Retrieved from http://nof.org/articles/11

New Rules Project. (n.d.). *Canadian healthcare system.* Retrieved from http://www.newrules.org/equity/rules/singlepayer-and-universal-health-care/cnandian-healthcare-system

Obamacare Facts. (2016, July 27). *Obamacare enrollment hits 20 million as of March 2016.* Retrieved from http://obamacarefacts.com/2016/o7/27/obama-care-enrollment-hits-20-million-as-of-March-2016/

Organisation for Economic Co-Operation and Development. (2016). *OECD health statistics 2016: Life expectancy at birth.* Retrieved from https://data.oecd.org/healthstat/life-expectancy-at-birth.htm

Pace, P. R. (2013). Meeting focuses on social work health care. *NASW News*, 58(4), 1, 5.

Rehr, H. (Ed.). (1994). *Medicine and social work: An exploration in interprofessionalism.* New York: Prodist Press.

Rehr, H., & Rosenberg, G. (1982). *Advancing social work practice in the health care field.* New York: Haworth Press.

Rehr, H., & Rosenberg, G. (2006). *The social work-medicine relationship: 100 years at Mount Sinai.* New York: Haworth Press.

Richman, J. M. (1995). Hospice. In R. L. Edwards (Ed.), *Encyclopedia of social work* (19th ed., pp. 1358–1365). Washington, DC: NASW Press.

Rubenstein, G. (2013, January 10). *New health rankings: Of 17 nations, U.S. is dead last.* Retrieved from http://www.theatlantic.com/health/archive/2013/new-health-rankings-of-17-nations-us-is-dead-last/267045

Sable, M. R., Schild, D. R., & Hipp, J. A. (2012). Public health and social work. In S. Gehlert & T. Browne (Eds.), *Handbook of health social work* (2nd ed.), pp. 64–99. Hoboken, NJ: Wiley.

Susser, E., & Morabia, A. (2006). The arc of epidemiology. In E. Susser, S. Schwartz, A. Morabia, & E. V. Bromet (Eds.), *Psychiatric epidemiology: Searching for the causes of mental disorders* (Ch. 2). New York: Oxford University Press.

Turner, G. (2015, June 9). *Health policy matters posts: 51 changes to ObanaCare ... so far.* Retrieved from http://www.galen.org/newsletters/changes-toobamacare-so-far/

United Nations, Sustainable Knowledge Platform. (2015). *Transforming our world: The 2030 agenda for sustainable development.* Retrieved from https://sustainabledevelopment.un.org/Post2015/transformingourworld

United States Census Bureau. (2015, September 16). *Income, poverty and health insurance coverage in the United States: 2014* (Release No. CB 15–157). Retrieved from http://census.Gov/newsroom/press-releases/205/cb15-157.html?cid=CB1515701

Veterans Health Administration, Office of Patient Care Services. (n.d.). *Spinal cord injury/disorders services.* Retrieved from http://www.sci.va.gov/docs/VA_Spinal_Cord_Injury_Patient_Brochure.pdf

Weiss, L. (1997). *Private medicine and public health: Profit, politics, and prejudice in the American health care enterprise.* Boulder, CO: Westview Press.

Wolfe, S. M. (2006). Outrage of the month: Massachusetts' mistake. *Public Citizen Health Research Group Health Letter*, 22(5), 10, 12.

World Health Organization. (2015). Ch.1 Bringing UHC into focus and Ch. 7 Health expenditure. In *Tracking universal health coverage: First global monitoring report.* Geneva, Switzerland: WHO Press.

World Health Organization, Media Centre. (2015, September 25). *WHO Statement: Ensure healthy lives and promote well-being for all at all ages.* Retrieved from http://www.who/int/mediacentre/news/statements/2015/healthy-lives/en

Chapter 8

After decades of action, Supreme Court cools on school cases. (2014, September 30). Retrieved from http://www.edweek.org/ew/articles/2014/10/01/06scotus.h34.html

Baumel, J. (2010, February). *What is an IEP?* Retrieved from http://www.greatschools.org/gk/category/special-needs/

Bernstein, R. (2007, May 17). *Minority population tops 100 million.* Retrieved from http://www.census.gov/Press-Release/www/releases/archives/population/010048.html

Bishop, K. (2006). Family-centered services to infants and toddlers with or at risk for disabilities: IDEA 2004, Part c. In R. Constable, C. Massat, S. McDonald, & J. Flynn (Eds.), *School social work* (6th ed., pp. 189–204). Chicago, IL: Lyceum Books.

Boyle-Del Rio, S., Carlson, R., & Haibeck, L. (2000, Fall). School personnel's perception of the school social worker's role. *School Social Work Journal, 25*(1), 59–75.

Brody, R. (2014, July 7). *Should unaccompanied immigrant children be sent home?* Retrieved from http://www.usnews.com/opinion/articles/2014/07/07should-undocumented-immigrant-children-be-sent-home-from-the-border

Brown, A., & Lopez, G. H. (2013, August 29). *Ranking Latino populations in the states.* Retrieved from http://www.pewhispanic.org/2013/08/29/ii-ranking-latino-populations-in-the-states/

Brown, A. (2015, November 12). *The unique challenges of surveying U.S. Latinos.* Retrieved from http://www.pewresearch.org/2015/11/12/the-unique-challenges-of-surveying-u-s-lations/

Brown, R. L. (2015, December 15). A less bitter cocoa harvest. *The Christian Science Monitor*, pp. 30–31.

Burt, M., Resnick, G., & Novick, E. R. (1998). *Building supportive communities for at-risk adolescents.* Washington, DC: American Psychological Association.

Button, J., & Rienzo, B. (2002). *The politics of youth, sex, and health care in American schools.* New York: The Hayworth Press.

Caple, F. S., & Salcido, R. M. (2006). A framework for cross-cultural practice in school settings. In R. Constable, C. Massat, S. McDonald, & J. Flynn (Eds.), *School social work* (6th ed., pp. 299–320). Chicago, IL: Lyceum Books.

Constable, R. (2006). The role of the school social worker. In R. Constable, C. Massat, S. McDonald, & J. Flynn (Eds.), *School social work, practice, policy, and research* (6th ed., pp. 3–27). Chicago, IL: Lyceum Books.

Constable, R., & Kordesh, R. (2006). Policies, programs, and mandates for developing social services in the schools. In R. Constable, C. Massat, S. McDonald, & J. Flynn (Eds.), *School social work, practice, policy, and research* (6th ed., pp. 123–144). Chicago, IL: Lyceum Books.

Constable, R., & Thomas, G. (2006). Assessment, multidisciplinary teamwork, and consultation: Foundations for role development. In R. Constable, C. Massat, S. McDonald, & J. Flynn (Eds.), *School social work, practice, policy, and research* (6th ed., pp. 283–320). Chicago, IL: Lyceum Books.

Constable, R. (2009). The role of the social worker. In R. Constable, C. Massat, S. McDonald, & J. Flynn (Eds.). *School social work, practice, policy, and research* (7th ed., pp. 1–29). Chicago, IL: Lyceum Books.

Costin, L. (1987). School social work. In A. Minahan (Ed.), *Encyclopedia of social work* (18th ed., pp. 536–539). Silver Spring, MD: National Association of Social Workers.

Current population trends in the Hispanic population. (2006). Retrieved from http://www.census.gov/population/www/socdemo/hispanic/files/Internet_Hispanic_in_US_2006.ppt#11

Dayton, L. (2014, January 15). *Trend towards early puberty in girls continues, researchers ask why.* Retrieved from https://www.cygnet-study.com/news/newsmedia/2-uncategorized/44-chrstory

De Silver, D. (2015, February 2). *U.S. students improving-slowly in math and science, but still lagging internationally.* Retrieved from http://pewresearch.org/fact-tank/2015/02/02/u-s-students-improving-slowly-in-math-and-science-but-still-lagging-internationally/

Dupper, D. R. (2000). The design of social work services. In P. Allen-Meares, R. O. Washington, & B. L. Welsh (Eds.), *Social work services in schools* (3rd ed., pp. 243–272). Boston, MA: Allyn & Bacon.

Dupper, D. R. (2003). *School social work, skills and interventions for effective practice.* Hoboken, NJ: John Wiley & Sons.

Elias, M. J. (2003). *Academic and social-emotional learning.* Brussels, Belgium: International Academy of Education.

Every student succeeds act. (2016, January 9). Retrieved from http://www.ed.gov/essa

Foroohar, R. (2016, February 1). In Davos, taking bets on when the technology revolution will finally deliver enough jobs. *Time*, p. 26.

Fast facts. (2009). Retrieved from http://nces/gov/FastFacts/display.asp?id=16

Finishing school. (2015, December 28–2016, January 4). *Time*, p. 21.

Franklin, C. (2000). The delivery of school social work services. In P. Allen-Meares, R. O. Washington, & B. L. Welsh (Eds.), *Social work services in schools* (3rd ed., pp. 273–298). Boston, MA: Allyn & Bacon.

Freeman, E. M. (1995). School social work overview. In R. L. Edwards (Ed.), *Encyclopedia of social work* (19th ed., pp. 2087–2097). Washington, DC: NASW Press.

Freeman, E. M., Halim, M., & Peterson, K. J. (1998). HIV/AIDS policy development and reform: Lessons from practice, research, and education. In E. M. Freeman, C. G. Franklin, R. Fong, S. G. Shaffer, & E. M. Timberlake (Eds.), *Multisystem skills and interventions in school social work practice* (pp. 371–377). Washington, DC: NASW Press.

Gardner, W. (2009, August 30). Grade for charter schools? "Needs improvement." *The Christian Science Monitor*, p. 27.

Ghana data. (2014). Retrieved from http://data.worldbank.org/country/ghana

Ghana: median age of the population from 1950 to 2020. (2015). Retrieved from http://www.statista.com/statistics/447568/average-age-of-the-population-in-ghana/

Ginorio, A., & Huston, M. (2001). *Si, se puede! Yes, we can, Latinas in school.* Washington, DC: AAUW Educational Foundation.

Hancock, B. (1982). *School social work.* Englewood Cliffs, NJ: Prentice Hall.

Hanes, S. (2014, October 20). To spank or not to spank. *The Christian Science Monitor*, pp. 26–32.

Hanes, S. (2015, December 28 & 2016, January 4). Out of the dark, labor trafficking is entwined in consumer habits. *The Christian Science Monitor*, pp. 25–31.

Hare, I., Rome, S., & Massat, C. (2006). The developing social, political, and economic context for school social work. In R. Constable, C. Massat, S. McDonald, & J. Flynn (Eds.),

School social work, practice, policy, and research (6th ed., pp. 145–170). Chicago, IL: Lyceum Books.

Harris Interactive. (2001). *Hostile hallways, bullying, teasing, and sexual harrassment in school*. Washington, DC: AAUW Educational Foundation.

Heasley, S. (2016, May 23). *Senator calls for full funding of IDEA*. Retrieved from https://www.disabilityscoop.com/2016/05/23/senator-calls-full-funding-idea/22343/

Hinkelman, J. M. (2005). Triple oppression. In C. L. Rabin (Ed.), *Understanding gender and culture in the helping process* (pp. 167–185). Belmont, CA: Thompson Wadsworth.

Hinkley, S. (2015, November 16). Rise in high school graduation rates. *The Christian Science Monitor*, pp. 18 & 20.

Ianzito, C. (2016, January-February). The new face of hunger. *AARP Bulletin*, p. 20.

Idea Funding Gap. (2010, February 1). Retrieved from http:www.nea.org.specialed

Jacobs, T. (2008, September 15). *10 Supreme Court cases every teen should know*. Retrieved from http://www.nytimes.com/learning/teachers/featured_articles/20080915monday.html

Jayson, S. (2009, January 1). Teen birth rates up in 26 states. *USA TODAY*. Retrieved from http://www.usatoday.com/news/health/2009-01-07-teenbirths_N.htm

Jolly, E. J. (2004, Spring). *Mosaic, an EDC report series*. Retrieved from http://main.edc.org/Mosaic/Mosaic9/beneath.asp

Khadaroo, S. (2009, April 19). Schools are learning how to foil attacks. *The Christian Science Monitor*, p. 21.

Khadaroo, S. (2009, August 23). Online school is cheaper than a bricks-and-mortar one. *The Christian Science Monitor*, p. 18.

Koch, K. (2000). School violence, are American schools safe? In D. Bonilla (Ed.), *School violence* (pp. 5–33). New York: H. W. Wilson.

Kopels, S. (2000). Securing equal educational opportunity: Language, race, and sex. In P. Allen-Meares, R. O. Washington, & B. L. Welsh (Eds.), *Social work services in schools* (3rd ed., p. 216). Boston, MA: Allyn & Bacon.

Kronick, R. F. (2005). *Full service community schools*. Springfield, IL: Charles C. Thomas.

Llana, S. M., & Paulson, A. (2006, June 13). Bilingualism issue rises again. *The Christian Science Monitor*, pp. 1, 11.

Lum, D. (1992). *Social work with people of color: A process-stage approach*. Pacific Grove, CA: Brooks/Cole.

Mann, E., & Reynolds, A. (2006, September). Early intervention and juvenile delinquency prevention: Evidence from the Chicago longitudinal study. *Social Work Research*, 30(3), 153–167.

Martin, J. A., Hamilton, B. E., Sutton, P. D., Ventura, S. J., Menacker, F., Kirmeyer, S., et al. (2009, January 7). Births: Final data for 2006. *National Vital Statistics Reports*, 57(7), 1–6.

Matuszek, T., & Rycraft, J. (2003). Using biofeedback to enhance interventions in schools. In B. Pahwa (Ed.), *Technology-assisted delivery of school based mental health services* (pp. 31–56). New York: Hayworth Press.

Mercola, J. (2001, January 21). *Chemical contamination linked to early puberty*. Retrieved from http://cmsadmin.mercola.com/2001/jan/21/chemicalspuberty.htm

More Mexicans Leaving Than Coming to the U.S. (2015, November 19). Retrieved from http://www.pewhispanic.org/

NASW standards for school social work services. (2012). Retrieved from http://www.socialworkers.org/practice/standards/NASWSchoolSocialWorkStandards.pdf

National Campaign to Prevent Teen Pregnancy. (2007). *New survey of Latino teens shows that there is still work to do and foster care youth*. Retrieved from http://www.teenpregnancy.org

O'Driscoll, P. (2007, April 20–22). Teen rant reminiscent of Columbine: Shooters in both spewed contempt in recordings. *USA Today*, p. 1.

Openshaw, L. (2008). *Social work in schools: Principles and practice*. New York: The Guilford Press.

Our special needs school. (2014, May). Retrieved from www.reyoschool.com

Paulson, A. (2005, March 25). Schools using many lessons from Columbine. *The Christian Science Monitor*, pp. 1, 10.

Paulson, A. (2006, September 5). Push to win back dropouts. *The Christian Science Monitor*, pp. 1, 11.

Paulson, A. (2007, January 8). Next round begins for No Child Left Behind Law. *The Christian Science Monitor*, pp. 1, 10.

Paulson, A. (2009, November 1). Why Johnny stays in school till 5 p.m. *The Christian Science Monitor*, p. 23.

Paulson, A. (2010, January 10). At US high schools, good news is scarce. *The Christian Science Monitor*, p. 22.

Pawlak, E., Wozniak, D., & McGowen, M. (2006). Perspectives on groups for school social workers. In R. Constable, C. Massat, S. McDonald, & J. Flynn (Eds.), *School social work: Practice, policy, and reseach* (6th ed., pp. 559–578). Chicago, IL: Lyceum Books.

People in poverty by selected characteristics: 2014 and 2015. (2016). Retrieved from https://www.census.gov/content/dam/Census/library/publications/2016/demo/p60-256.pdf

Picchi, A. (2015, September 11). *The shocking research of U.S. child poverty*. Retrieved from http://www.cbsnews.com/news/the-shocking-reach-of-us-child-poverty/

Politics & Opinion. (2002). *National survey of Latinos*. Retrieved from http://www.hispaniconline.com/pol&opi/02_nat_survey_latinos.html

Post-Trump victory bullying, harassment reported in schools. (2016, November 13). Retrieved from http://www.cbsnews.com/news/post-trump-victory-bullying-harassment-reported-schools/

Poverty rate among Hispanic origin groups, 2013. (2015, September 11). Retrieved from http://www.pewhispanic.org/2015/09/15/the-impact-of-slowing-immigration-foreign-born

Prevention at School. (n.d.). Retrieved from https://www.stopbullying.gov/prevention/at-school/index.html

Reed, C. (2015, November 24). *UNO study: Fertility rate gap between races, ethnicities is shrinking*. Retrieved from http://www.unomaha.edu/news/2015/01/fertility.php

Respect for charter schools. (2009, October 11). *The Christian Science Monitor*, p. 26.

Rottmann, A. (2015–16, Winter). God loves them as they are. *The Wisconsin Magazine of History*, p. 213.

Sanburn, J. (2016, November 21). States lean left on local votes. *Time*, p. 16.

Sappenfield, M. (2001, June 22). For more students, summer means–more school. *The Christian Science Monitor*, pp. 1, 9.

School social work association of Ghana. (2015). Retrieved from https://me-kono-eu/institutions;school-social-work-association-of-ghaha-sswag

Sossou, M., & Daniels, T. (2002). School social work practice in Ghana: A hope for the future. In M. Huxtable & E. Blyth (Eds.), *School social work worldwide* (pp. 93–108). Washington, DC: National Association of Social Workers.

Special education and the Individuals with Disabilities Education Act. (2007). Retrieved from http://www.nea.org/specialed/index.html?mode=print

Stoessen, L. (2006, July). Health focus of LGBQ workshop. *NASW News*, p. 5.

Students who serve, graduate. (2009, November 15). *The Christian Science Monitor*, p. 26.

Study: Safe-sex programs don't increase sexual activity [West Bend, WI]. (2001, May 30). *The Daily News, West Bend, WI*, p. A 10.

Sunderman, G. L., Kim, J. S., & Orfield, G. (2005). *NCLB meets school realities: Lessons from the field*. Thousand Oaks, CA: Corwin Press.

Teen pregnancy in the United States. (2015, May 19). Retrieved from http://www.cdc.gov/teenpregnancy/about/index.htm

Thomas. (2009, January 5). *Abstinence-only sex education statistics–final nail in the coffin*. Retrieved from http://www.openeducation.net/2009/01/05/abstinence-only-sex-education-statistics-final-nail-in-the-coffin

Twemlow, S. W., & Sacco, F. C. (2008). *Why school antibullying programs don't work*. New York: Jason Aronson.

Tyre, P. (2006, January). *The trouble with boys*. Retrieved from http://www.msnbc.msn.com/id/10965522/site/newsweek/

Understanding school violence, fact sheet. (2015). Retrieved from www.cdc.gov/violenceprevention

United States data. (2014). Retrieved from http://data.worldbank.org/contry/united-states

Vaughn, B., & Princiotta, D. (2013, September 24). *What the Affordable Care Act means for K-12 schools*. Retrieved from http://www.childtrends.org/what-the-affordable-care-act-means-for-k-12-schools/#more-11528

Vega, V. (2015, December 15). *Social and emotional learning research review*. Retrieved from http://www.edutopia.org/sel-research-learning-outcomes

What are charter schools? (2015, December 9). Retrieved from http://www.publiccharters.org/get-the-facts/

Chapter 9

The A.A. Grapevine. (n.d.). *Information on A.A., Alcoholics Anonymous*. Retrieved from http://www.aa.org/lang/en/subpage.cfm?pa

Alcoholics Anonymous, General Service Office. (2015). *Estimated worldwide A.A. individual and group membership* (Report No. SM F-132). Retrieved from http://www.aa.org/assets/en_US/smf-132_en.pdf

American Psychiatric Association. (2013). *Diagnostic and statistical Manual of Mental Disorders DSM-5* (5th ed.). Washington, DC: American Psychiatric Publishing.

Anderson, S. C. (1995). Alcohol abuse. In R. L. Edwards (Ed.), *Encyclopedia of social work* (19th ed., pp. 203–215). Washington, DC: NASW Press.

Angell, T. (2015, November 28). Canada's health minister studying marijuana legalization models. *International News, Law & Politics*. Retrieved from http://www.marijuana.com/blog/news/2015/11/canadas-health-minister-studying-marijuana-legalization-models/

The Associated Press. (2015, October 15). *Early release: Who the drug felons are and where they'll go*. Retrieved from http://bigstory.ap.org/article/25293bcb4e3f4c1f9413054028af1fea/early-release-who-drug-felons-are-and-where-they'll-go

Babor, T. F., Higgins-Biddle, J. C., Saunders, J. B., & Monteiro, M. G. (2001). *AUDIT, The Alcohol Use Disorders Identification Test: Guidelines for use in primary care* (2nd ed.). World Health Organization (WHO/MSD/MSB/01.6a). Retrieved from http://whqlibdoc.who/int/hq/2001/WHO_MSB_01.6a.pdf

Butcher, J. N., Mineka, S., & Hooley, J. M. (2008). *Abnormal psychology: Core concepts*. Boston, MA: Pearson Allyn & Bacon.

Centers for Disease Control and Prevention (CDC). (2015). *Substance abuse*. Retrieved from http://www.cdc.gov/msmhealth/substance-abuse.htm

Hannon, L., & Cuddy, M. M. (2006). Neighborhood ecology and drug dependence mortality: An analysis of New York City census tracts. *American Journal of Drug and Alcohol Abuse, 32*, 453–463.

Hazelden Betty Ford Foundation. (2015, May 11). *Substance abuse among the elderly: A growing problem*. Retrieved from http://www.hazeldenbettyford.org/articles/substance-abse-among-the-elderly-a-growing-problem

Johnson, J. A., Lee, A., Vinson, D., & Seale, J. P. (2013, January). Use of AUDIT-based measures to identify unhealthy alcohol use and alcohol dependence in primary care: A validation study. *Alcoholism: Clinical and Experiential Research, 37*(1), E253-E259. doi:10.1111/j.1530-0277.2012.01898.x

King, A. C., McNamara, P. J., Hasin, D. S., & Cao, D. (2014, May). Alcohol challenge responses predict future alcohol use disorder symptoms: A 6-year prospective study. *Biological Psychiatry, 17*(10), 798–806.

Kinney, J., & Leaton, G. (1995). *Loosening the grip: A handbook of alcohol information* (5th ed.). St. Louis, MO: Mosby.

Kisthardt, W. E. (2009). The opportunities and challenges of strengths-based, person-centered practice. In D. Saleebey (Ed.), *The strengths perspective in social work practice* (5th ed.). Boston, MA: Pearson Allyn & Bacon.

de Koning, P., & de Kwant, A. (2002). Dutch drug policy and the role of social workers. In L. A. Straussner & L. Harrison (Eds.), *International aspects of social work practice in the addictions* (pp. 49–68). New York: Haworth Press.

Krimmel, H. (1971). *Alcoholism: Challenge for social work education*. New York: Council on Social Work Education.

Lacerte, J., & Harris, D. L. (1986). Alcoholism: A catalyst for women to organize: 1850–1980. *Affilia, 1*(2), 41–52.

Loebig, B. J. (2000). *European alcoholism and drug abuse perceptions*. Retrieved from http://www.geocities.com/bourbonstreet/2640/topic.htm

Logan, S., McRoy, R. G., & Freeman, E. M. (1987). Current practice approaches for treating the alcoholic client. *Health and Social Work, 12*(3), 176–186.

McNeece, C. A., & DiNitto, D. M. (2005). *Chemical dependency: A systems approach* (3rd ed.). Boston, MA: Pearson Allyn & Bacon.

Murphy, B. C., & Dillon, C. (2011). *Interviewing in action in a multicultural world* (4th ed.). Belmont, CA: Brooks/Cole.

National Association of Social Workers [NASW]. (2015). *Code of ethics of the national association of social workers*. Washington, DC: NASW Press.

National Institute on Drug Abuse. (n.d.). *Commonly abused drugs*. Retrieved from http://www.drugabuse.gov/DrugPages/DrugsofAbuse.html

National Institute on Drug Abuse (NIDA). (2014). *Drugs, brains, and behavior: The science of addiction*. Retrieved from http://www.drugabuse.gov/publications/drugs-brains-behavior-science-addiction/drugs-brain

O'Connor, M. J., & Whaley, S. E. (2007). Brief intervention for alcohol use by pregnant women. *American Journal of Public Health, 97*(2), 252–258.

O'Hare, T. (2016). *Essential skills of social work practice: Assessment, intervention, and evaluation* (2nd ed.). Chicago: Lyceum Books, Inc.

Osman, M. M. (2002). Drug and alcohol addiction in Singapore: Issues and challenges in control and treatment strategies. In L. A. Straussner & L. Harrison (Eds.), *International aspects of social work practice in the addictions* (pp. 97–117). New York: Haworth Press.

Peltenberg, C. (1956). Casework with the alcoholic patient. *Social Casework, 37*(2), 81–85.

Rapp, R. (1997). The strengths perspective and persons with substance abuse problems. In D. Saleebey (Ed.), *The strengths perspective in social work practice* (2nd ed., pp. 77–96). New York: Longman.

Rapp, R. C., & Lane, D. T. (2009). Implementation of brief strengths-based case management. In D. Saleebey (Ed.), *The strengths perspective in social work practice* (5th ed., pp. 147–160). Boston, MA: Pearson Allyn & Bacon.

Rhodes, R., & Johnson, A. D. (1994). Women and alcoholism: A psychosocial approach. *Affilia, 9*(2), 145–154.

Richmond, M. E. (1917). *Social diagnosis*. New York: Russell Sage Foundation.

Robertson, N. (1988). *Getting better: Inside alcoholics anonymous*. New York: Ballantine.

Rubinsky, A. D., Dawson, D. A., Williams, E. C., Kiviahan, D. R., & Bradley, K. A. (2013, August). AUDIT Scores as a scaled marker of mean daily drinking, alcohol use disorder severity, and probability of alcohol dependence in a US general population sample of drinkers. *Alcoholism: Clinical and Experimental Research, 37*(8), 1380–1390. doi:10.1111/acer.12092

Sapir, J. V. (1957). The alcoholic as an agency client. *Social Casework, 38*(7), 355–361.

Singapore Anti-Narcotics Association (SANA). (2008). *Services: Preventive education*. Retrieved from http://www.sana.org.sg/ourservices.shtml

Smith, M. J. W., Whitaker, T., & Weismiller, T. (2006). Social workers in the substance abuse treatment field: A snapshot of service activities. *Health & Social Work, 31*(2), 109–115.

Steiker, L. K. H., & MacMaster, S. A. (2008). Substance abuse. In K. M. Sowers & C. N. Dulmus (Eds.), *Comprehensive handbook of social work and social welfare: The profession of social work* (Ch. 11, pp. 227–252). Hoboken, NJ: John Wiley & Sons, Inc.

Substance Abuse and Mental Health Services Administration. (1998). *Table 11: Percentages reporting past month use of any illicit drug, by age group, race/ethnicity, and sex: 1979–1997* [Online]. Retrieved from http://www.samhsa.gov/oas/nhsda/hnsda97/97tab.htm

Substance Abuse and Mental Health Services Administration. (2006). *Results from the 2005 National Survey on Drug Use and Health: National findings. Office of Applied Studies* (NSDUH Series H-30, DHHS Publication No. SMA 06–4194). Rockville, MD.

Substance Abuse and Mental Health Services Administration. (2015a). *Age- and gender-based populations*. Retrieved from http://samhsa.gov/specific-populations/age-gender-based

Substance Abuse and Mental Health Services Administration. (2015b). *Substance use disorders*. Retrieved from http://samhsa.gov/disorders/substance-use

Substance Abuse and Mental Health Services Administration, Center for Behavioral Health Statistics and Quality. (2012, November 7). *Data spotlight*. Retrieved from http://www.store.samshsa.gov/sites/default/files/Spot107AINAuditCUAdmission/Spot107AIANAdultCUAdmssions.pdf

Substance Abuse and Mental Health Services Administration, Center for Behavioral Health Statistics and Quality. (2015, September 10). *National survey on drug use and health, 2013 and 2014* (Table 1.11A, 1.198, 2.37B, 7.1B). Retrieved from http://www.samhsa.gov/data/sites/default/files/NSDUH-DetTabs2014/NSDUH-DetTabs2014.pdf

Substance Abuse and Mental Health Services Administration, Center for Substance Abuse Prevention. (n.d.). *Fetal alcohol spectrum disorders among Native Americans*. Retrieved from http://www.store.samshsa.gov/shin/content/SMA06-4245/SMA06-425.pdf

Teo, M. (2010, June 5). Singapore's policy keeps drugs at bay. *Guardian*. Retrieved from http://www.guardian.co.uk/commentisfree/2010/jun/05/Singapore-policy-drugs-bay/print

Traub, J. (2010, April 9). Africa's drug problem. *New York Times*. Retrieved from http://www.nytimes.com/2007/10/21/magazine/21wwln-idealab-t.html

U.S. Department of Health and Human Services, National Institute on Drug Abuse. (n.d.). *Commonly abused drugs*. Retrieved from http://www.drugabuse.gov/DrugPages/DrugsofAbuse.html

U.S. Sentencing Commission. (2010, November 1). *Supplement to the 2010 guidelines manual*. Retrieved from http://www.ussc.gov/2010guid/PDF_Supplement_2010_guidelines_Manual.pdf

van Wormer, K. (1995). *Alcoholism treatment: A social work perspective*. Chicago, IL: Nelson-Hall Publishers.

van Wormer, K., & Davis, D. R. (2008). *Addiction treatment: A strengths perspective* (2nd ed.). Belmont, CA: Thomson, Brooks/Cole.

Vogt, I. (2002). Substance use and abuse and the role of social workers in Germany. In L. A. Straussner & L. Harrison (Eds.), *International aspects of social work practice in the addictions* (pp. 69–83). New York: Haworth Press.

World Health Organization. (2010). *HIV/AIDS: Injecting drug use and prisons*. Retrieved from http://www.who.int/hiv/topics/idu/en/index.html

Wozniak, A. (2014, December 11). Feds: Native American tribes can make their own marijuana laws. *Huff Post: Politics*. Retrieved from http:www/huffingtonpost.com/2014/12/11/native-american-tribes_marijuanan_n_6311738.html

Chapter 10

A profile of older Americans. (2015). Retrieved from http://www.aoa.acl.gov/aging_statistics/profile/2015/docs/2015-Profile.pdf

About ALFA. (2007). Retrieved from http://www.alfa.org/alfa/About_ALFA.asp

About Bernard Nash. (2006). Retrieved from http://www.aarp.org/money/careers/employerresourcecenter/bestemployers/bernardnash

About us. (n.d.). Retrieved from www.raginggrannies.com

Abuse of residents in long-term care facilities. (n.d.). Retrieved from http://www.ncea.aoa.gov/Resources/Publication/docs/LTCF_ResearchBrief_web508.pdf

Administration on Aging. (2010, May 11). *Frequently asked questions (FAQs)*. Retrieved from http://www.aoa.gov/aoaroot/aoa_programs/oaa/resources/Faqs.aspx#Resource

Aging in 2015: HHS and the White House Conference on Aging. (2015, July 13). Retrieved from http://hhs.gov/about/news/2015/07/13/aging-in-2015-hhs-and-the-white-house-conference-on-aging.html#

Alzheimer's disease and related dementias. (2015). Retrieved from https://aspe/hhs.gov/national-plan-to-address-alzheimer%E2%80%99s-disease-2015-update

Alzheimer's facts and figures. (2010, December 6). Retrieved from http://www.alz.org/alzheimers_disease_facts_and_figures.asp

Austin, C. D., & McClelland, R. W. (2003). Case management practice with the elderly. In M. J. Holosko & M. D. Feid (Eds.), *Social work practice with the elderly* (3rd ed., pp. 175–202). Toronto, ON: Canadian Scholars Press.

Barry, P. (2006, June). Medicare Part D: In and out of the doughnut hole. *AARP Bulletin*, 16–18.

Bellos, N. S., & Ruffalo, M. S. (1995). Aging: Services. In R. L. Edwards (Ed.), *Encyclopedia of social work* (19th ed., Vol. 1, pp. 165–171). Washington, DC: NASW Press.

Blancato, B. (2015, January 9). *6 ways to nudge Congress to help older Americans*. Retrieved from http://www.nextavenue.org/6-ways-to-nudge-congress-help-older-americans/

Blanchard, J. (2014, February 4). *Aging in community: The communitarian alternative to aging in place, alone*. Retrieved from http://www.asaging.org/blog/aging-community-communitarian-alternative-aging-place-alone

Breytspraak, L. (2016, January 6). *How many seniors really end up in nursing homes?* Retrieved from http://nursinghomediaries.com/tag/how-many-seniors-in-nursing-homes

Butler, S., & Kaye, L. W. (2004). Rurality, aging, and social work: Setting the context. In S. Butler & L. W. Kaye (Eds.), *Geronological social work in small towns and rural communities* (pp. 1–18). New York: The Haworth Press.

Caregiving in the U.S., 2009. (2009). Retrieved from http://www.aarp.org/research/surveys/care/ltc/hc/articles/caregiving_09.html

Chetty, R., Stapner, M., Abraham, S., et al. (2016, April 26). *The association between income and life expectancy in the United States, 2001-2014*. Retrieved from http://jamanetwork.com/journals/jama/article-abstract/2513561

Combating Alzheimer's and other dementias. (2015, July 13). Retrieved from http://www.hhs.gov.about/news/2015/07/13/white-house-conference-on-aging-combating-alzheimers-and-other-dementias.html

Combating food insecurity: Tools for helping older adults access SNAP. (2015). Retrieved from http://frac.org/pdf/senior_snap_toolkit_aarp_frac.pdf#page=6

Congress renews law aimed at helping Americans over 60. (2016, April). *AARP Bulletin*, 6.

Conner, K. A. (2000). *Continuing to care*. New York: Palmer Press.

Cox, C. B. (2005). *Community care for an aging society*. New York: Springer.

Cox, E., & Parsons, R. (1994). *Empowerment-oriented social work practice with the elderly*. Pacific Grove, CA: Brooks/Cole.

Demko, D. (2016, January 6). *How many seniors really end up in nursing homes?* Retrieved from http://nursinghomediaries.com/tag/how-many-seniors-in-nursing-homes/

Dunkel, R. E. (1987). Protective services for the aged. In A. Minahan (Ed.), *Encyclopedia of social work* (18th ed., Vol. 2, pp. 393–395). Silver Spring, MD: NASW Press.

EASI does it! (n.d.). Retrieved from http://www.easi.org/

Edwards, M. (2004, November/December). As good as it gets; what country takes the best care of its older citizens? *AARP Magazine*, 47–53.

Elderly poverty. (2016). Retrieved from http://www.conference-board.ca/hcp/details/society/elderly-poverty.aspx

End of life care. (2006). Retrieved from https://www.socialworkers.org/practice/children/statements/129-135%20End-of-Life%20Care.pdf

Eustis, N., Greenberg, J., & Patton, S. (1984). *Long term care for older persons: A policy perspective*. Monterey, CA: Brooks/Cole.

Ex, C., Gorter, K., & Janssen, U. (2004). Providing integrated health and social care for older persons in the Netherlands. In K. Leichsenring & A. Alaszewski (Eds.), *Providing integrated health and social care for older persons* (pp. 415–445). Burlington, VT: Ashgate.

Feinberg, L. F. (2014, June 23). *States move to support working family caregivers*. Retrieved from http://blog.aarp.org/2014/06/23/states-move-to-osupport-working-family-caregivers/

Fischer, M. (2010, March & April). Love is (not) all you need. *AARP Magazine*, 29–33.

Freeman, M. S. (1998, December 2). Sharing a roof and a way of life. *The Christian Science Monitor*, pp. 11, 14–15.

Gardner, G. (2006, June 21). Independent but alone. *The Christian Science Monitor*, pp. 13–14.

Generations United. (n.d.). *About Us*. Retrieved from http://gu.org/ABOUTUS.aspx

Genworth 2015 cost of care survey. (2016). Retrieved from https://www.genworth.com/dam/Americas/US/PDFs/Consumer/corporate/130568_040115_gnw.pdf

Get palliative care. (2012). Retrieved from https://getpalliativecare.org/whatis/faq/#what-is-the-difference-between-hospice-and-palliative-care

Green, A. (2006, December 26). A flap over recouping costs of Medicaid. *The Christian Science Monitor*, p. 3.

Green, R. R. (1986). *Social work with the aged and their families*. New York: Aldine de Gruyter.

Greene, R. R. (2000). *Social work with the aged and their families* (2nd ed.). New York: Aldine de Gruyter.

Hager, M. (2015). *What is aging in place?* Retrieved from http://ageinplace.com/aging-in-place/what-is-aging-in-place/

Healy, T. C. (2003). Ethical practice issues in rural perspective. In S. Butler & L. Kay (Eds.), *Gerontological social work in small* towns and rural communities (pp. 265–285). New York: The Hayworth Social Work Practice Press.

Helliwell, J., Layard, R., & Sachs, J. (2015). *World happiness report, 2015.* Retrieved from http://worldhappiness.report/wp-content/uploads/sites/2/2015/04/WHR-2015-summary_final.pdf

HHS proposes to improve care and safety for nursing homes residents. (2015, July 13). Retrieved from http://www.hhs.gov/about/news/2015/07/13/hhs-proposes-to-improve-care-and-safety-for-nursing-homes-resideents.html

Hinden, S. (2010, December). Top questions and answers on Social Security. *AARP Bulletin, 51*(10), 21–24.

Hodge, G. (2008). *The geography of aging: Preparing communities for the surge of seniors.* Quebec, CA: McGill-Queen's University Press.

Hong, L. (2006, June). Rural older adults' access barriers to in-home and community-based services. *Social Work Research, 30*(2), 109–118.

Hopkins led nation's relief effort. (1998). Retrieved from http://www.socialworkers.org/profession/centennial/hopkins.htm

Hospice Services of America. (2006). *Hospice services and expenses.* Retrieved from http://www.hospicefoundation.org/hospiceInfo/services.asp

Housing choice vouchers fact sheet. (2016, February 5). Retrieved from http://portal.hud.gov/hudportal/HUD?src=/topics/housing_choice_voucher_program_section_8

Huttman, E. (1985). *Social services for the elderly.* New York: Free Press.

Income, poverty and health insurance coverage in the United States. (2010, September 20). Retrieved from http://www.census.gov/newsroom/releases/archives/income_wealth/cb10-144.html

Karger, H. J., & Stoesz, D. (1998). *American social welfare policy: A pluralist approach* (3rd ed.). New York: Addison Wesley Longman.

Karger, H. J., & Stoesz, D. (2010). *American social welfare policy: A pluralist approach* (6th ed.). Boston, MA: Allyn & Bacon.

Kirkham, E. (2016, March 14). *1 in 3 Americans has saved $0 for retirement.* Retrieved from http://time.com/money/4258451/retirement-savings-survey/

Kochman, A. (1997). Gay and lesbian elderly: Historical overview and implications for social work practice. In J. K. Quam (Ed.), *Social services for senior gay men and lesbians* (pp. 1–10). New York: Haworth Press.

Kosberg, J. I., & Nahmiash, D. (1996). Characteristics of victims and perpetrators and milieus of abuse and neglect. In L. A. Baumhover & S. C. Beall (Eds.), *Abuse, neglect, and exploitation of older person* (pp. 31–45). Baltimore, MD: Health Professions Press.

Kropf, N. P., & Wilks, S. (2003). Grandparents raising grandchildren. In B. Berkman (Ed.), *Social work and healthcare in an aging society* (pp. 177–200). New York: Springer.

Kubler-Ross, E. (1969). *On death and dying.* New York: Macmillan.

Lamb, G. M. (2004, November 9). In some nations, the rise of "shortgevity." *The Christian Science Monitor,* pp. 13, 14.

Life expectancy at birth. (2015). Retrieved from https://www.cia.gov/library/publications/the-world-factbook/rankorder/2102rank.html

Llana, S. M. (2006, September 8). Seniors raising their grandkids get a new boost. *The Christian Science Monitor,* pp. 1, 2.

Mackelprang, R. W., & Mackelprang, R. D. (2005, October). Historical and contemporary issues in end-of-life decisions: Implications for social work. *Social Work, 50*(4), 315–323.

Magnusson, P. (2006, June). Today's do-it-yourself pension. *AARP Bulletin,* 22–23.

Malamud, M. (2010, November). NASW board approves family caregiver standards. *NASW News,* p. 9.

Marsh, J. C. (2005, April). Bush plan takes security out of social security. *Social Work, 50*(2), 99.

Medicare and Medicaid Programs: Reform of requirements for long-term care facilities. (2016, October 4). Retrieved from https://www.federalregister.gov/documents/2016/10/04/2016-23503/medicare-and-medicaid-programs-reform-of-requirements-for-long-term-care-facilities

Metz, P. (1997). Staff development for working with lesbian and gay elders. In J. K. Quam (Ed.), *Social services for senior gay men and lesbians* (pp. 35–45). New York: Hawthorn Press.

Miller, K. (2010, August 6). *Ten things you should know about social security.* Retrieved from http://aarp.org/work/social-security-info-08-2010-/10-things-you-need-to-know-about-social-security.html

Miller, S. G. (2015, September 9). *The best countries for older people, ranked.* Retrieved from http://www.livescience.com/52115-best-countries-older-people-ranking.html

Moody, R. A. (1976). *Life after life: The investigation of a phenomenon—survival of bodily death.* Harrisburg, PA: Stackpole Books.

Mui, A. C., Choi, N. C., & Monk, A. (1998). *Long term care and ethnicity.* Westport, CT: Auburn House.

Mullin, E. (2013, February 26). *How to pay for nursing home costs.* Retrieved from http://health.usnews.com/health-news/best-nursing-homes/articles/2013/0226/how-to-pay-for-nursing-home-costs

Nadelhaft, A. (2005). *NASW launches "Understanding aging, the social worker's role."* Retrieved from www.socialworkers.org

Nadelhaft, A. (2006). *NASW launches new aging credential for social workers.* Retrieved from www.socialworkers.org

Naleppa, M. J., & Reid, W. J. (2003). *Gerontological social work: A task centered approach.* New York: Columbia University Press.

Nathanson, I. L., & Tirrito, T. T. (1998). *Gerontological social work: Theory into practice.* New York: Springer.

National Association of Social Workers. (2016). *New aging specialty credentials.* Retrieved from http://socialworkers.org/credetials/specialty/aging/asp

National Shared Housing Resource Center. (2006). *Shared housing, more than just a place to live.* Retrieved from http://www.nationalsharedhousing.org/index.html

NHPCO facts and figures: Hospice care in America. (2009). Retrieved from http://www.nhpco.org/files/public/Statistics_Research/NHPCO_facts_and_figures.pdf

Nursing homes, business as usual. (2006, September). *Consumer Reports,* 38–41.

Older Americans Act. (n.d.) Retrieved from http://www.aoa.gov/about/legbudg/oaa/legbudg_oss.asp

Olson, L. K. (2003). *The not so golden years: Caregiving, the frail elderly, and the long term care establishment.* Lanham, MD: Rowman & Littlefield.

Overview of nursing facility capacity, financing and ownership. (2013, June 28). Retrieved from http://kff.org/

medicaid/fact-sheet/overview-of-nursing-facility-capacity-financing-and-ownership-in-the-united-states-in-2011/

Park, A. (2015, November 23). New hope for the treatment and prevention of Alzheimer's. *Time*, 38.

Policy basics: The housing choice voucher program. (2015, September 29). Retrieved from http://www.cbpp.org/research/housing/policy-basics-the-housing-choice-voucher-program

Policy basics: Introduction to public housing. (2015, December 21). Retrieved from http://www.cbpp.org/research/policy-basics-introduction-to-public-housing

Policy basics: Section 8 project-based rental assistance. (2015, June 1). Retrieved from http://www.cpbb.org/research/housing/policy-basics-section-8-project-based-rental-assistance

Policy Basics: Top ten facts about social security. (2016, August 12). Retrieved from http://www.cbpp.org/research/social-security/policy-basics-top-ten-facts-about-social-security

Popple, P. R., & Leighninger, L. L. (1999). *Social work, social welfare, and American society*. Boston, MA: Allyn & Bacon.

Providing care for another adult a second job for many, National Alliance for Caregiving/AARP study shows. (2004, April 6). Retrieved from http://www.aarp.org/research/press-center/presscurrentnews/2004–03–30-caregiving.html

Radin, D. (2006, September–November). Becoming mindful of consciousness. *Shift: At the Frontiers of Consciousness*, *12*, 40–41.

Reinhard, S., Friss, L., Choula, R., & Hauser, A. (2015, July 16). *Valuing the invaluable 2015 update*. Retrieved from http://www.aarp.org/ppi/info-2015/valuing-the-invaluable-2015-update.html

Rose Dobrof, DSW. (2001). Retrieved from http://nextagespeakers.com/rdobrof.htm

Rosengarten, L. (2000). *Social work in geriatric home health care*. New York: Hayworth Press.

Salamon, M. (1986). Mind/body health in practice, taking care of the caregivers. *Mindbody Health Newsletter*, *7*(3), 3.

Sandwich generation moms feeling the squeeze. (2016). Retrieved from http://www.apa.org/helpcenter/sandwich-generation.aspx

Schlesinger, R. (2006, June). An expert's view of ageism: Things aren't any better. *AARP Bulletin*, 6.

Schroeder-Sheker, T. (2001). *Transitus: A blessed death in the modern world*. Missoula, MT: St. Dunstan's Press.

Schwartz, K. (2010, October 12). *Unemployment among older adults stuck near record highs*. Retrieved from http://www.ncoa.org/press-room/press-release/unemployment-among-older.html

Schwartz, S. A. (2016, January/February). Science, death, and consciousness. *Explore*, *12*(1), 15.

Sebelius, K. (2010). *Medicare and the new health care law—what it means for you*. Washington, DC: Centers for Medicare and Medicaid Services, Department of Health and Human Services.

Seeber, J. (1995). Congregational models. In M. Kimble, S. McFadden, J. Eilor, & J. Seeber (Eds.), *Aging, spirituality, and religion* (pp. 253–269). Minneapolis, MN: Fortress Press.

Segal, E., & Brzuzy, S. (1998). *Social welfare policy, programs, and practice*. Itasca, IL: Peacock Publishers.

Sherter, A. (2014, March 31). *Danger zone: America's retirement system is breaking down*. Retrieved from http://www.cbsnews.com/news/danger-zone-americas-retirement-system-is-breaking-down/

Small, G.W., Rabins, P. V. B., Patricia, P. B., Neil, S. D., Steven, T. F., Steven, H. F., et al. (1997, October 22). Diagnosis and treatment of Alzheimer's disease and related disorders: Consensus statement of the American Association for Geriatric psychiatry, the Alzheimer's Association, and the American Geriatrics Society. *Journal of the American Medical Association*, *278*(6) (electronic version). Retrieved from http://www.alz.org/Resources/FactSheets/Diagnosistreatment.pdf

Smits, C., Van den Beld, H., Aartsen, M., & Schroots, J. (2013, September 2). *Aging in the Netherlands: State of the art and science*. Retrieved from http://gerontologist.oxfordjournals.org/content/early/2013/08/31/geront.gnt096.full

Smoothing the way to retirement pay. (2006, July 28). *The Christian Science Monitor*, p. 8.

SNAP/Food Stamps. (2010). Retrieved from http://frac.org/federal-foodnutrition-programs/snapfood-stamps/

Social Security basic facts. (2016). Retrieved from http://www.cbpp.org/research/social-security/policy-basics-top-ten-facts-about-social-security

Social services block grants. (2016). Retrieved from http://www.acf.hhs.gov/programs/ocs/programs/ssbg/about

State of affairs of social security, January 2014. (2014, January). Retrieved from file:///C:/Users/Carolyn/Downloads/stand-van-zaken-januari-2014-engels-def%20(3).pdf

Statistics/Data. (n.d.). Retrieved from http://www.ncea.aoa.gov/Library/Data/index.aspx#problem

Status of the Social Security and Medicare Programs. (2015). Retrieved from https://www.ssa.gov/OACT/TRSUM/index.html

Stevens, D. G. (2001, May 23). Elderly help fill adoption gap. *The Daily News*, West Bend, WI, p. A5.

Stoessen, L. (2006, June). Legal articles cover CIGNA case, end-of-life choices. *NASW News*, p. 10.

Stoessen, L. (2007, January). Stress on women studied. *NASW News*, pp. 1, 8.

The national movement. (2009). Retrieved from http://villagesnw.org/the-national-movement/

The new Medicare (Part D) drug "benefit." (2006, January). *Health Letter, Public Citizen Research Group*, pp. 14–16.

The Social Services Block Grant Plan. (2009–2010). Retrieved from http://www.ncdhhs.gov/dss/publications/docs/SSBG_2010.pdf

Toedtman, J. (2010, October). The great recession's next wave. *AARP Bulletin*, *51*(8), 3.

Torres-Gil, F. M., & Puccinelli, M. A. (1995). Aging: Public policy issues and trends. In R. L. Edwards (Ed.), *Encyclopedia of social work* (19th ed., Vol. 1, pp. 159–164). Washington, DC: NASW Press.

Trumbull, M. (2006, August 18). Reform erodes future of pensions. *The Christian Science Monitor*, p. 2.

Van de Water, P., Sherman, A., & Ruffing, K. (2013, October 25). *Social Security keeps 22 million Americans out of poverty: A state by state analysis*. Retrieved from http://www.cbpp.org/research/social-security-keeps-22-million-americans-out-of-poverty-a-state-by-state-analysis

What is Alzheimers? (2007). Retrieved from http://www.alz.org/alzheimers_disease_what_is_alzheimers.asp

What is the EPA Aging Initiative? (n.d.). Retrieved from http://archive.epa.gov/ordntrnt/ord/archive-aging/web/pdf/factsheet.pdf

Women and caregiving: Facts and figures. (2015, February). Retrieved from https://www.caregiver.org/women-and-caregiver-facts-and-figures

Yeoman, B. (2010, March, April). Living on the edge. *AARP Magazine*, 45–75.

Chapter 11

ACLU, American Civil Liberties Union. (2014, January 30). *Major sentencing reform bill moves to Senate floor*. Retrieved from https://aclu.org/news/major-sentencing-reform-bill-moves-senate-floor

ACLU, American Civil Liberties Union. (2015, December 15). *ACLU comment on President Obama's commutations and pardons*. Retrieved from https://aclu.org/news/aclu-comment-president-obama-commutations-and-pardons

Aging inmates prompt creation of assisted living center at Washington prison. (2010, August 16). *FOX News.com*. Retrieved from http://www.foxnews.com/us/2010/08/16/aging-inmates-prompt-creation-assisted-living-center-washington-prison-FoxNews.com

Amnesty International. (2000, May). *A briefing for the UN Committee Against Torture*. Retrieved from http://www.web.amnesty.org/ai.nsf/indes/AMR510562000

Amnesty International USA. (2010). *Lesbian, gay, bisexual and transgender human rights*. Retrieved from http://www.amnestyusa.org/print/php

Ashford, J. B. (2009). Overview of forensic social work: Broad and narrow definitions. In A. R. Roberts (Ed.), *Social workers' desk reference* (pp. 1055–1060). New York: Oxford University Press.

Associated Press. (2015, October 25). *Early release: Who the drug felons are and where they'll go*. Retrieved from http://bigstory.ap.org/article/25293bcb4e3f4c1f9413054028afl1fea/early-release-who-drug-felons-are-and-where-they'll-go

Barker, R. L., & Branson, D. M. (2000). *Forensic social work: Legal aspects of professional practice* (2nd ed.). New York: Haworth Press.

Bernstein, N. (2014). *Burning down the house: The end of juvenile prison*. New York: The New Press.

Black Lives Matter Network. (n.d.). *About the Black Lives Matter Network*. Retrieved from http://blacklivesmatter.com/about/

Bonczar, T. P., Kaeble, D., & Maruschak, L. (2015, November 19). *Correctional populations in the United States, 2014* (NCJ 249513). Retrieved from http://www.bjs.gov/index.cfm?ty=pbdetail&iid=5415

Brown, G. (2010). *The intersectionality of race, gender, and reentry: Challenges for African-American women*. Washington, DC: American Constitution Society.

Carson, E. A. (2015, September 17). *Prisoners in 2014* (NCJ Publication No. 248955). Retrieved from http://www.bjs.gov/content/pub/pdf/p14.pdf

Children in prison. (2016). Retrieved from http://www.eji.org/childrenprison

Chiu, T. (2010). *It's about time: Aging prisoners, increasing costs, and geriatric release*. New York: Vera Institute of Justice.

Cohen, B., & Smith, R. (2010). *The racial geography of the federal death penalty*. Retrieved from http://www.sentencingproject.org/detail/clearinghouse.cfm?clearinghouse_id=529

Death Penalty Statistics. (2016, September 7). Retrieved from the StatisticBrain website: http://www.statisticbrain.com/death-penalty-statistics/

Dickerson, J. G. (2001). Margaret Murray Washington: Organizer of rural African American women. In I. B. Carlton-LaNey (Ed.). *African American leadership: An empowerment tradition in social welfare history*. Washington, DC: NASW Press.

EJI: Equal Justice Initiative. (2016, January 26). *President Obama bans solitary confinement for juveniles in federal prisons*. Retrieved from http://www.eji.org/node1211

FAMM, Families Against Mandatory Minimums. (2015). *S. 502/H.R. 920, The Smarter Sentencing Act*. Retrieved from http://famm.org/s-502-the-smarter-sentencing-act/

Farr, K. A. (2000). Classification for female inmates: Moving forward. *Crime & Delinquency, 46*(1), 3–15.

FBI, Federal Bureau of Investigation. (2014). *Uniform crime reports: Crime in the United States* (Tables 39 & 40). Retrieved from https://www.fbi.gov/about-us/cjis/ucr/crime-in-the.u.s./2013crime-in-the.u.s.-2013//tables/table-40/table_40_arrests_males_by_age_2013.xls and https://www.fbi.gov/about-us/cjis/ucr/crime-in-the.u.s./2013crime-in-the.u.s.-2013//tables/table-40/table_40_arrests_females_by_age_2014.xls

FBI, Federal Bureau of Investigation. (2015). *Uniform crime reports: Crime in the United States* (Tables 39 & 40). Retrieved from https://www.fbi.gov/about-us/cjis/ucr/crime-in-the.u.s./2014crime-in-the.u.s.-2014//tables/table-40/table_40_arrests_males_by_age_2014.xls and https://www.fbi.gov/about-us/cjis/ucr/crime-in-the.u.s./2014crime-in-the.u.s.-2014//tables/table-40/table_40_arrests_females_by_age_2014.xls

Federal Bureau of Prisons, *BOP Statistics: Inmate Offenses*. (2015, December 26). Retrieved from https:www.bop.gov/about/statistics_inmate_offenses.jsp

Friends Committee on National Legislation. (2015, April). Mass incarceration: Massively wrong. *Washington FCNL Newsletter* (No. 769). Washington, DC: Friends Committee on National Legislation.

GovTrack.us. (2015, November 25). *Summaries for the Sentencing Reform and Corrections Act of 2015*. Retrieved from https://www.govtrack.us/congress/billos/114/s2123/summary

Greene, J., & Mauer, M. (2010). *Downscaling prisons: Lessons from four states*. Washington, DC: The Sentencing Project.

Human Rights Watch. (n.d.). *Did you know?* Retrieved from http://www.hrw.org

Institute for Criminal Policy Research. (2016). *World prison brief: Highest to lowest prison population rate*. Retrieved from http://prisonstudies.org/highest-to-lowest/prisonpopulaton_rate?field_Region_taxonomy_tied=All

International Centre for Prison Studies. (2001, July 17). *World prison brief of the International Centre for Prison Studies*. Retrieved from http://www.kcl.ac.uk/depsta/rel/icps/home.html

Jensen, J. M., & Howard, M. O. (1998). Youth crime, public policy, and practice in the juvenile justice system: Recent trends and needed reforms. *Social Work, 43*(4), 324–334.

Johnson, K. (2016, November 18). *FBI investigating suspected post-election hate crimes*. Retrieved from the USA Today website: http://www.usatoday.com/story/news/2016/11/18/

fbi-investigating-post-election-hate-incidents-ag-lynchays/9407332/

Knox, K. S., & Roberts, A. R. (2009). The social worker in a police department. In A. R. Roberts (Ed.), *Social workers' desk reference* (pp. 85–94). New York: Oxford University Press.

Maschi, T., Hatcher, S. S., Schwalbe, C. S., & Rosato, N. S. (2008). Mapping the social service pathways of youth to and through the juvenile justice system: A comprehensive review. *Children and Youth Services Review, 30*(12), 1376–1385. doi:10.1016/jchildyouth.2008.04.006

Mauer, M. (1994). *Americans behind bars: U.S. and international use of incarceration, 1992–1993*. Washington, DC: The Sentencing Project.

Moon, M. M., Sundt, J. L., Cullen, F. T., & Wright, J. P. (2000). Is child saving dead? Public support for juvenile rehabilitation. *Crime & Delinquency, 46*(1), 38–60.

National Association of Social Workers. (2008). *Code of ethics of the National Association of Social Workers*. Washington, DC: Author. Retrieved from http://www.naswdc.org/pubs/code/code.asp?

Pinard, M. (2010). Collateral consequences of criminal convictions: Confronting issues of race and dignity. *New York University Law Review, 84*, 457–534.

Pray, K. (1945). Place of social casework in the treatment of delinquency. *Social Service Review, 19*(2), 235–248.

President Obama bans solitary confinement for juveniles in federal prisons. (2016). Retrieved from http://www.eji.org/node/1211

Ritter, J. A., Vakalahi, H. F. O., & Kiernan-Stern, M. (2009). *101 careers in social work*. New York: Springer Publishing Company.

Rogers, D. (2015, November 11). *Black Lives Matter supporters in Oregon targeted by state surveil-lance*. Retrieved from https://www.aclu.org/blog/speak-freely/black-lives-matter-supporters-oregon-targeted-state-surveillance

Saleebey, D. (Ed.). (2006). *The strengths perspective in social work practice* (4th ed.). Boston, MA: Pearson Allyn & Bacon.

Schiller, L. Y., & Zimmer, B. (2005). Sharing the secrets: The power of women's groups for sexual abuse survivors. In A. Gitterman & L. Shulman (Eds.), *Mutual aid groups, vulnerable & resilient populations, and the life cycle* (pp. 290–319). New York: Columbia University Press.

Schuppe, J. (2016, November 10). *With Trump in White House, criminal justice reformers will look elsewhere*. Retrieved from http://www.nbcnews.com/storyline/2016-election-day/trump-white-house-criminal-justice-reformers-will-look-elsewhere-in681536

Scott, E. S., & Grisso, T. (1998). The evolution of adolescence: A developmental perspective on juvenile justice reform. *Journal of Criminal Law and Criminology, 88*(1), 137–189.

Sickmund, M., & Puzzanchera, C. (Eds.). (2014). *Juvenile offenders and victims: 2014 national report*. Retrieved from http://www.ojjdp.gov/ojstatbb/nr2014/downloads/NR2014.pdf

Siefert, K., & Pimlott, S. (2001). Improving pregnancy outcome during imprisonment: A model residential care program. *Social Work, 46*(2), 125–134.

Snell, T. L. (2014, December 19). *Capital punishment, 2013: Statistical tables*. Retrieved from http://www.bjs.gov/content/pub/pdf/cp13st.pdf

State of Wisconsin Department of Corrections. (2007). Form DOC-10 (Rev. 12/2006): Rules of community supervision. Form DOC-10SO (Rev. 12/2006): Standard sex offender rules. Form DOC-502 (Rev. 1/03): Admission to adult field caseload: Assessment of offender risk. Wisconsin Administrative Code. Madison, WI: Author.

Travis, J. (2004). Building from the ground up: Strategies for creating safe and just communities. In E. H. Judah & M. Bryant (Eds.), *Criminal justice: Retribution vs. restoration* (pp. 173–195). New York: Haworth Press.

Trenticosta, C., & Collins, W. (2011). *Death and Dixie: How the courthouse Confederate flag influences capital cases in Louisiana*. Retrieved from http://www.sentencingproject.org/detail/clearinghouse.cfm?clearinghouse_id=549

Trimble, D. (2005). Uncovering kindness and respect: Men who have practiced violence in intimate relationships. In A. Gitterman & L. Shulman (Eds.), *Mutual aid groups, vulnerable and resilient populations, and the life cycle* (pp. 352–372). New York: Columbia University Press.

U.S. Census Bureau. (2015). *USA quickfacts from the US Census Bureau*. Retrieved from http:quickfacts.census.gov/qfd/states/00000.html

U.S. Conference of Catholic Bishops. (1999, April 2). *A Good Friday appeal to end the death penalty: A statement of the Administrative Board of the United States Conference of Catholic Bishops*. Retrieved from http://www.usccb.org/isues-and-action/human-life-and-dignity/death-penalty-capital-punishment

U.S. Conference of Mayors. (2015, January 22). *Strengthening police-community relations in America's cities: A report of The U.S. Conference of Mayors Working Group of Mayors and Police Chiefs*. Retrieved from http://www.usmayors.org/83rdWinter/Meeting/media/012215-report-policing.pdf

U.S. Department of Justice, Bureau of Justice Statistics. (2013a). *Sourcebook of Criminal Justice Statistics Online*. Table 6.1.2011, Adults on probation, in jail or prison, and on parole, United States, 1980–2011. Retrieved from ttp:www.albany.edu/sourcebook/tost_6.html/#6_f

U.S. Department of Justice, Bureau of Justice Statistics. (2013b). *Sourcebook of Criminal Justice Statistics Online*. Table 6.28.2012, Number and rate (per 100,000 U.S. residents population in each group) of sentenced prisoners under jurisdiction of State and Federal correctional authorities on December 31. Retrieved from http://www.albany.edu/sourcebook

U.S. Department of Justice, Office of Justice Programs. (2015, December 13). *Statistical briefing book: Juvenile arrest rate trends*. Retrieved from http://www.ojjdp.gov/ojstatbb/crime/JAR_Display.asp?ID=qa05200

van Wormer, K. (2010). *Working with female offenders: A gender-sensitive approach*. Hoboken, NJ: John Wiley & Sons, Inc.

van Wormer, K., Roberts, A., Springer, D. W., & Brownell, P. (2008). Forensic social work: Current and emerging developments. In K. M. Sowers & C. N. Dulmus (Eds.), *Comprehensive handbook of social work and social welfare: The profession of social work* (pp. 315–342). Hoboken, NJ: John Wiley & Sons.

Walmsley, R. (2001). *An overview of world imprisonment: Global prison populations, trends, and solutions*. Paper presented at the United Nations Programme Network Institutes Technical Assistance Workshop, Vienna, Austria. Retrieved from http://www.kcl.ac.uk/depsta/rel/icps/worldbrief/north_Records_php?code=4.

Walmsley, R. (n.d.). *World prison population list* (11th ed.). Retrieved from http://www.prisonstudies.org/sites/default/files/resources/downloads/world_prison_population_list_11th_edition.pdf

Chapter 12

About epilepsy. (2016, February 2). Retrieved from www.cdc.gov/epilepsy/basics

About us. (2015, July 9). Retrieved from http://www.cdc.gov/ncbddd/developmentaldisabilities/about.html

Advisory committee on increasing competitive integrated employment for individuals with disabilities. (2015, January 22). Retrieved from http://www.dol.gov/odep/topics/WIOA.htm

Americans with Disabilities Act of 1990. Section 2, Findings and Purposes. Public Law 101–336. (n.d.). Retrieved from http://www.eeoc.gov/eeoc/history/35th/thelaw/ada.html

Asch, A., & Mudrick, N. R. (1995). Disability. In R. L. Edwards (Ed.), *Encyclopedia of social work* (19th ed., Vol. 1, pp. 752–760). Washington, DC: NASW Press.

Beaulaurier., R. L, & Taylor, S. H. (2001). Social Work practice with people with disabilities in the era of disability rights. *Social Work in Health Care, 32*(4), 67–91.

Bagenstos, S. R. (2009). *Law and the contradictions of the disability rights movement*. New Haven, CT: Yale University Press.

Barnwell, D. A., & Day, M. (1996). Providing support to diverse families. In P. Beckman (Ed.), *Strategies for working with families with disabilities* (pp. 47–65). Baltimore, MD: Paul H. Brookes.

Baroff, G. S. (1991). *Developmental disabilities: Psychosocial aspects*. Austin, TX: ProEd.

Bishop, K. (2006). Family-centered services to infants and toddlers with or at risk for disabilities: IDEA 2004, Part C. In R. Constable, C. Massat, S. McDonald, & J. Flynn (Eds.), *School social work* (6th ed., pp. 189–204). Chicago, IL: Lyceum Books.

Casey, M. (2015, June 11). *The necessity of technology: Equal access and the law*. Retrieved from http://www.ncld.org/archives/action-center/what-we-ve-done/the-necessity-of-technology-equal-access-and-the-law

CCD response to the President's FY 2017 budget request. (2016). Retrieved from https://www.c-c-d.org/fichiers/CCD-Budget-Response.pdf

Christensen, C. (1996). Disabled, handicapped, or disordered: What's in a name? In C. Christensen & F. Rizvi (Eds.), *Disability and the dilemmas of education and justice* (pp. 63–78). Buckingham, UK: Open University Press.

Cocaine. (2010, September). Retrieved from https://www.drugabuse.gov/publications/research-reports/cocaine/what-are-effects-maternal-cocaine-use

Communities of L'Arche, USA. (2016). Retrieved from http://www.larcheusa.org/who-we-are/communities/

Convention on the rights of persons with disabilities. (2007, June 7). Retrieved from http://www.aamr.org/unresolution.shtml

Council on Social Work Education. (2001). *Educational policy and accreditation standards*. Alexandria, VA: Author.

Council on Social Work Education. (2015, March). *Final 2015 educational policy*. Alexandria, VA: Author

Data and statistics. (2015, August 12). Retrieved from http://www.cdc.gov/ncbddd/autism/data.html

Definition of genetic counseling. (2016). Retrieved from http://www.medicinenet.com/script/main/art.asp?articlekey=13548

Definition of intellectual disability. (2013). Retrieved from https://aaidd.org/intellectual-disability/definition#.VsOidfkrldU

Dennis, B., & Cha, A. E. (2016, February 26). *U.S. details 9 Zika pregnancies: 2 abortions, 2 miscarriages, 1 baby with "severe microcephaly"*. Retrieved from https://www.washingtonpost.com/news/to-your-health/wp/2016/02/26/after-zika-diagnosis-at-least-two-u-s-women-chose-to-have-abortions-cdc-says/

Devitt, T. (2010, August 3/Fall). Study by Sigan Hartley, PhD, and Marsha Mailick Seltzer, PhD, details autism's heavy toll beyond childhood on marriages. *Autism Society Wisconsin, 10*(3), 2.

DeWeaver, K., & Kropf, N. (1992, Winter). Persons with mental retardation: A forgotten minority in education. *Journal of Social Work Education, 28*(1), 38–40.

Dickerson, M. U. (1981). *Social work practice with the mentally retarded*. New York: Free Press.

Disability statistics. (2016, January). Retrieved from http://www.dol.gov/odep/

Dossey, L. (2003). *Healing beyond the body, medicine and the infinite reach of the mind*. Boston, MA: Shambala.

Drug facts: Cigarettes and other tobacco products. (2015, August). Retrieved from http://www.drugabuse.gov/publications/drugfacts/cigarettes-other-tobacco-products

Emotional disturbance. (2015, March). Retrieved from http://www.parentcenterhub.org/repository/emotionaldisturbance/#

Epilepsy basics. (2015, March 8). Retrieved from www.cdc.gov/epilepsy/basics

Facts about ASD. (2015, February 14). Retrieved from www.cdc.gov/ncbddd/autism/facts.html

Facts about cerebral palsy. (2015, July 13). Retrieved from www.cdc.gov/ncbddd/cp/facts.html

Facts about FASDs. (2015, April 16). Retrieved from www.cdc.gov/ncbddd/fasd/facts.html

Facts for features: Asian/Pacific Heritage Month: May 2015. (2015, April 29). Retrieved from https://www.census.gov/newsroom/facts-for-features/2015/cb15-ff07.html

Flagel, R. (2007). *Raven's guide to special education, summary*. Retrieved from http://www.seformmatrix.com/raven/raven2.htm

Freedman, R. (1995). Developmental disabilities: Direct practice. In R. L. Edwards (Ed.), *Encyclopedia of social work* (19th ed., Vol. 1, pp. 721–728). Washington, DC: NASW Press.

Genetic counseling. (2007). Retrieved from http://www.marchofdimes.com/printableArticles/4439_15008.asp

Gilson, S. F. (1998). Choice and self-advocacy: A consumer's perspective. In P. Wehman & J. Kregel (Eds.), *More than a job: Satisfying careers for people with disabilities* (pp. 3–23). Baltimore, MD: P. H. Brookes.

Gold, S. (2005, February 20). *2003 census data for persons with disabilities*. Retrieved from http://namiscc.org/Research/2004/2003-CensusData.htm

References

Hall, J., & Parker, K. (2010, September 10). *Federal programs to assist the unemployed are failing job seekers with disabilities*. Center for Research on Learning, University of Kansas. Retrieved from http://www.disabled-world.com/disability/employment/unemployment-programs.php

Hearing loss. (2014). Retrieved from http://www.marchofdimes.org/complications/hearing-impairment.aspx

Hearing loss in children. (2015, October 23). Retrieved from http://www.cdc.gov/ncbddd/hearingloss/facts.html

Hooyman, N. R., & Gonyea, J. G. (1995). Family caregiving. In R. L. Edwards (Ed.), *Encyclopedia of social work* (19th ed., Vol. 1, pp. 951–957). Washington, DC: NASW Press.

HUD's 2015 annual homeless assessment report to Congress. (2015). Retrieved from http://portal.hud.gov/hudportal/HUD%3Fsrc%3D/press/press_releases_media_advisories/2015/HUDNo_15-149

Illicit drug use during pregnancy. (2006, November). Retrieved from http://search.marchofdimes.com/cgi-bin/MsmGo.exe?grab_id=0&page_id=480&query=coc

Issue brief: Self advocacy by people with IDD. (2015, December). Retrieved from http://www.aamr.org/Policies/fac_movements.html

Johnson, A. B., & Surles, R. C. (1994). Has deinstitutionalization failed? In S. A. Kirk & S. D. Einbinder (Eds.), *Controversial issues in mental health* (pp. 213–216). Boston, MA: Allyn & Bacon.

Learning disabilities. (2010, August 11). Retrieved from http://www.medicinenet.com/learning_disability/article.htm

Liu, G. Z. (2005). Best practices: Developing cross-cultural competence from a Chinese perspective. In J. Stone (Ed.), *Culture and disability: Providing culturally competent services* (pp. 65–85). Thousand Oaks, CA: Sage.

Lum, D. (1992). *Social work with people of color: A process-stage approach* (2nd ed.). Pacific Grove, CA: Brooks/Cole.

Mackelprang, M., & Saisgiver, R. (1999). *Disability: A diversity model approach in human service practice*. Pacific Grove, CA: Brooks/Cole.

May, G. E. (2005). Changing the future of disability: The disability discrimination model. In G. May & M. B. Raske (Eds.), *Ending disability discrimination: Strategies for social workers* (pp. 82–98). Boston, MA: Allyn & Bacon.

May, G. E., & Raske, M. (Eds.). (2005). *Ending disability discrimination: Strategies for social workers*. Boston, MA: Allyn & Bacon.

McDonald-Wikler, L. (1987). Disabilities: Developmental. In A. Minahan (Ed.), *Encyclopedia of social work* (18th ed., Vol. 1, pp. 423–431). Silver Spring, MD: NASW Press.

Meekosha, H., & Jakubowicz, A. (1996). Disability, participation, representation and social justice. In C. Christensen & F. Rizvi (Eds.), *Disability and the dilemmas of education and justice* (pp. 9–95). Buckingham, UK: Open University Press.

Morrison-Orton, D. J. (2005). The use of religion and spiritual strategies in rehabilitation. In J. Murphy & J. Pardeck (Eds.), *Disability issues for social workers and human services professionals in the twenty-first century* (pp. 5–41). New York: Haworth Press.

Murphy, J. W., & Pardeck, J. T. (Eds.). (2005). *Disability issues for social workers and human service professionals in the twenty-first century*. New York: Haworth Press.

National Association of Social Workers. (1999). *NASW code of ethics*. Washington, DC: NASW Press.

NINDS traumatic brain injury information page. (2010, November 19). Retrieved from http://www.ninds.nih.gov/disorders/

Oliver, M., & Sapey, B. (2006). *Social work with disabled people* (3rd ed.). New York: Palgrave Macmillan.

Pardeck, J. T. (1998). *Social work after the Americans with Disabilities Act*. Westport, CT: Auburn House.

Pardeck, J. T. (2005). An analysis of the Americans with Disabilities Act (ADA) in the twenty-first century. In J. Murphy & J. Pardeck (Eds.), *Disability issues for social workers and human service professionals in the twenty-first century* (pp. 121–151). New York: Haworth Press.

Parent, W. S., Cone, A. A., Turner, E., & Wehman, P. (1998). Supported employment: Consumers leading the way. In P. Wehman & J. Kregel (Eds.), *More than a job: Securing satisfying careers for people with disabilities* (pp. 149–166). Baltimore, MD: P. H. Brooks.

Parkinson, C. B., & Howard, M. (1996). Older persons with mental retardation/developmental disabilities. In M. J. Mellor (Ed.), *Special populations and systems linkages* (pp. 91–101). New York: Haworth Press.

Patton, J. R., Blackbourn, J. M., & Fad, K. (1996). *Exceptional individuals in focus* (6th ed.). Englewood Cliff, NJ: Prentice Hall.

Poverty in the United States. (2013). Retrieved from http://www.nclej.org/poverty-in-the-us-php

Prevalence of FASDs. (2015, November 17). Retrieved from www.cdc.gov/ncbddd/fasd/data.html

Putnam, M. (2007). Moving from separate to crossing aging and disability service networks. In M. Putnam (Ed.), *Aging and disability: Crossing network lines* (pp. 5–17). New York: Springer.

Raske, M. (2005). The disability discrimination model in social work practice. In G. May & M. Raske (Eds.), *Ending disability discrimination strategies for social workers* (pp. 106–107). Boston, MA: Allyn & Bacon.

Richey, W. (2002, January 9). In workplace, tougher standards on job-related injuries. *Christian Science Monitor*, p. 2.

Richey, W. (2004, May 18). Court boosts civil rights law for disabled. *The Christian Science Monitor*, pp. 1, 10.

Richmond, M. (1917). *Social diagnosis*. Philadelphia, PA: Russel Sage Foundation.

Rothman, J. C. (2003). *Social work practice across disability*. Boston, MA: Allyn & Bacon.

Rothman, L. (2015, November 23). Ugliness: A cultural history. *Time*, p. 30.

Schlitz, M., & Amorok, T. (2005). *Consciousness and healing, integral approaches to mind-body medicine*. St. Louis, MO: Elsevier.

Segal, S. P. (1995). Deinstitutionalization. In R. L. Edwards (Ed.), *Encyclopedia of social work* (19th ed., Vol. 1, pp. 704–711). Washington, DC: NASW Press.

Segregated and exploited. (2012). Retrieved from http://www.ndrn.org/en/issues/employment.html

Self advocates becoming empowered. (2015). Retrieved from http://www.sabeusa.org

Smart, J. (2001). *Disability, society, and the individual*. Gaithersburg, MD: Aspen.

Snyder, R., & Ne'eman, A. (2007, July 10). *Autism from autistics*. Retrieved from http://www.autisticadvocacy.org

Special education and the Individuals with Disabilities Education Act. (2007). Retrieved from http://www.nea.org/specialed/index.html?mode=print

Stites, S. (2001). *Allyse*. Unpublished paper, Smith College, Northampton, MA.

Stoessen, L. (2005, March). Children with disabilities: A family affair. *NASW News*, p. 4.

Stone, J. H. (Ed.). (2005). *Culture and disability: Providing culturally competent services*. Thousand Oaks, CA: Sage.

Switzky, H., Dudzinski, M., Van Acker, R., & Gambro, J. (1988). Historical foundations of out-of-home residential alternatives for mentally retarded persons. In L. Heal, J. Haney, & Amado A (Eds.), *Integration of developmentally disabled individuals into the community* (2nd ed., pp. 19–35). Baltimore, MD: P. H. Brooks.

Talbott, R. E. (1992). Communication disorders. In P. J. McLaughlin & P. Wehman (Eds.), *Developmental disabilities: A handbook for best practices* (pp. 98–100). Boston, MA: Andover Medical.

The 2015 Annual Homeless Assessment Report to Congress. (2015, November). Retrieved from https://www.hudexchange.info/resources/documents/2015-AHAR-Part-1.pdf

Torres-Gill, F. (2007). Translating research into program and policy changes. In M. Putnam (Ed.), *Aging and disability* (pp. 245–262). New York: Springer.

United Nations Treaty Collection: Convention on the Rights of People with Disabilities. (2016, February 22). Retrieved from https://treaties.un.org/Pages/ViewDetails.aspx?src=IND&mtdsg_no=IV-15&chapter=4&lang=en

U.S. Census Bureau. (2007, May). *Asian/Pacific American Heritage Month*. Retrieved from http://www.imdiversity.com/Villages/Asian/reference/census_asian_pacific_american_heritage_2007.asp

Walsh, B. (2015, November 16) It may be too late to reverse the damage of China's on-child policy. *Time*, p. 23.

Weathers, R. R. II. (2005). *A guide to disability statistics from the American Community Survey*. Retrieved from http://digitalcommons.ilt.cornell.edu/edicollect/129

Wehman, P. (2006). *Life beyond the classroom*. Baltimore, MD: Paul H. Brookes.

Wehman, P., Inge, K., Revell, W. G., Jr., & Brooke, V. (2007). *Real work for real pay: Inclusive employment for people with disabilities*. Baltimore, MD: Paul. H. Brookes.

What are learning disabilities. (2015, July). Retrieved from http://www.parentcenterhub.org/repository/ld#def

What is traumatic brain injury. (2016, February 11). Retrieved from http://www.ninds.nih.gov/disorders/

What we know and what we don't know. (2016). Retrieved from http://www.cdc.gov/zika/pdfs/Zika-What-We-Know-Infographic.pdf

What you need to know about cerebral palsy. (2014, March 3). Retrieved from http.cdc.gov/ncbddd/cp/index.html

Who we are. (2016). Retrieved from http://www.larcheusa.org/who-we-are/

Willer, B., & Itagliata, J. (1984). *Promises and realities for mentally retarded citizens*. Baltimore, MD: University Park Press.

Wolfe, P. S. (1992). Challenges for service providers. In P. J. McLaughlin & P. Wehman (Eds.), *Developmental disabilities: A handbook for best practices* (pp. 125–130). Boston, MA: Andover Medical.

Wraparound services. (2015, September). Retrieved from http://dlcv.org/aboutus/

Chapter 13

American Academy of Social Work & Social Welfare. (2013). *Grand accomplishments in social work* (Working Paper No. 2). Retrieved from http://aaswsw.org/grand-accomplishments-in-social-work-working-paper-no-2/

American Academy of Social Work & Social Welfare. (2015). *Grand challenges for social work initiative*. Retrieved from http://aaswsw.org/grand-challenges-initiative/12-challenges/

Besthorn, F., & Canda, E. R. (2002). Revisioning environment: Deep ecology for education and teaching in social work. *Journal of Teaching in Social Work*, 22(1/2), 79–101.

Bradsher, B. (2016, November 3). The Paris Agreement on Climate Change is official: Now what? *The New York Times*. Retrieved from http://www.nytimes.com/2016/11/04/business/energy-environment/paris-climate-change-agreement-official-now-what.html?_r=0

Bureau of Labor Statistics. U.S. Department of Labor. (2015). Median weekly earnings by educational attainment in 2014, *The Economics Daily*. Retrieved from www.bls.gov/opub/ted/2015/median-weekly-earnings-by-education-gender-race-and-ethnicity-in-2014.htm

Chideya, F. (1999). *The color of our future*. New York: William Morrow.

Dominelli, L. (2012). *Green social work: From environmental crises to environmental justice*. Malden, MA: Polity Press.

EuroStemCell. (2012). *Types of stem cells and their current uses*. Retrieved from http://www.eurostemcell.org/factsheet/stem-cell-research-therapy-types-stem-cells-and-their-current-uses

Fadiman, A. (1997). *The spirit catches you and you fall down: A Hmong child, her American doctors, and the collision of two cultures*. New York: Farrar, Straus and Giroux.

Grew, R. (2006). Global history and globalization. In S. Hewa & D. Stapleton (Eds.), *Globalization, philanthropy, and civil society: Toward a new political culture in the 21st century* (pp. 15–32). New York: Springer.

Hewa, S., & Stapleton, D. H. (2006). Structure and process of global integration. In S. Hewa & D. Stapleton (Eds.), *Globalization, philanthropy, and civil society: Toward a new political culture in the 21st century* (pp. 3–13). New York: Springer.

Holland, J. (2005). The regeneration of ecological, societal, and spiritual life: The holistic post modern mission of humanity in the newly emerging planetary civilization. *Journal of Religion and Spirituality in Social Work*, 24(1/2), 7–25.

Holody, R. (1999). Toward a new permanency planning: How kinship care can revitalize the foster care system. *Areté*, 23(1), 1–10.

Ki-Moon, B. (2007). *The millennium development goals report 2007*. New York: United Nations.

Levitin, M. (2015, June 10). The triumph of Occupy Wall Street, *The Atlantic*. Retrieved from http://www.theatlantic.com/politics/archive/2015/06/the-triumph-of-occupy-wall-street/395408/

Lin, V., Lin, J., & Zhang, X. (2016). U.S. social worker workforce report card: Forecasting nationwide shortages. *Social Work, 61*(1), 7–15.

Lyons, K., Manion, K., & Carlsen, M. (2006). *International perspectives on social work: Global conditions and local practice.* New York: Palgrave Macmillan.

Malamud, M. (2010, November). In Russia, discovering a new view of social work. *NASW News, 55*(10), 1, 12.

Malone, B. (2011). 10 years after the human genome project: Will the DTC genetic test debate shape the future of genomics? *Clinical Laboratory News, 37*(4). Retrieved from http://www.Aacc.org/publications/cln/2011/April/Pages/10YearsAftertheHumanGenomeProject.aspx

Mary, N. L. (2008). *Social work in a sustainable world.* Chicago: Lyceum Books.

McGoldrick, M. (2009). Using genograms to map family patterns. In R. Roberts (Ed.), *Social workers' desk reference* (2nd ed., pp. 409–423). New York: Oxford University Press.

Miller, J., & Garran, A. M. (2009). The legacy of racism for social work practice today and what to do about it. In A. R. Roberts (Ed.), *Social workers' desk reference* (2nd ed., pp. 928–933). New York: Oxford University Press.

National Academy of Sciences. (2011). *Appendix A: National institutes of health guidelines for research using human embryonic stem cell research (2010).* Retrieved from http://search.nap.edu/nap-cgi/skimchap.cgi?recid=12923&chap=9-16&act=nap

National Association of Social Workers. (2008). *Code of ethics of the National Association of Social Workers.* Washington, DC: NASW Press.

National Committee on Pay Equity. (2015). *Wage gap statistically unchanged.* Retrieved from http://www.pay-equity.org

National Human Genome Research Institute. (2006, December). *The Human Genome Project completion: Frequently asked questions.* Retrieved from http://www.genome.gov/11006943

National Institute of Health, U.S. Department of Health & Human Services. (n.d.). *Fact sheet: Genetic testing: How it is used for healthcare.* Retrieved from https://report.nih.gov/nihfactSheets/ViewFactSheet.aspx?csid=43

O'Neil, J. V. (2002). EAPs offer multitude of internet services. *NASW News, 47*(1), 14.

Ortman, J. M., Velkoff, V. A., & Hogan, H. (2014, May). *An aging nation: The older population in the United States.* U. S. Census Bureau. Retrieved from https:www.census.gov/prod/2014pubs/p25-1140.pdf

Questions and answers on pay equity. (1998). Retrieved from http://www.Feminist.com/fairpay.htm

Rifkin, J. (2004). *The European dream: How Europe's vision of the future is quietly eclipsing the American dream.* New York: Jeremy P. Tarcher/Penguin.

ScienceDaily. (2015). Embryonic stem cell. Retrieved from https://www.sciencedaily.com/terms/embryonic_stem_cell.htm

Stanford Children's Hospital. (n.d.). *Uses of genetic testing.* Retrieved from http://www.stanfordchildrens.org/en/topic/default?id=uses-of-genetic-testing-90-P02160

Stein, R. (2009). U.S. set to fund more stem cell study. *The Washington Post.* Retrieved from http://www.washingtonpost.com/wp-dyn/content/article/2009/12/02/AR2009120201955_pf.html

United Nations. (2010). *The millennium development goals report 2010.* New York: United Nations.

United Nations Development Programme. (2016). *Sustainable development goals booklet.* Retrieved from http://www.undp.org/content/undp/en/home/librarypage/corporate/sustainable-development-goals-booklet.html

United Nations Population Fund. (2016). *Migration.* Retrieved from http://www.unfpa.org/Migration

United Nations Sustainable Development Knowledge Platform, Department of Economic and Social Affairs. (2015). *Sustainable development goals.* Retrieved from https://sustainabledevelopment.un.org/?menu=1300

United States Department of State, U. S. Department of Homeland Security, & U.S. Department of Health and Human Services. (2015). *Proposed refugee admissions for fiscal year 2016: Report to the Congress.* Retrieved from http://www.state.gov/documents/organization/247982.pdf

U.S. Bureau of Labor Statistics, U.S. Department of Labor. (2016). Social workers, *Occupational Outlook Handbook, 2016–2017 Edition.* Retrieved from http://www.data.bls.gov/ooh/community-and-social-service/social-workers.htm

U.S. Bureau of the Census. (1950). *Census of population: 1950* (Vol. II, Pt. 1, U.S. Summary, Table 38, pp. 90–91 & Table 61, pp. 109–111) and *U.S. census of population: 1950* (Special Reports: Nonwhite Population by Race, Table 2, p. 16, Table 3, p. 17, Table 4, p. 18, and Table 5, p. 19).

U.S. Census Bureau. (2008). *Newsroom: An older and more diverse nation by midcentury.* Retrieved from http://www.census.gov/newsroom/releases/archives/population/cb08-123.html

U.S. Census Bureau. (2009). *Newsroom: As baby boomers age, fewer families have children under 18 at home.* Retrieved from http://www.census.gov/newsroom/releases/archives/families/_households/cb09-29.html

U.S. Census Bureau. (2010). *United States S2501 occupancy characteristics, American factfinder.* Retrieved from http://factfinder.census.gov/servlet/STTable?bm=y&-geo_id=01000US&-qr_name=ACS

U.S. Census Bureau, U.S. Department of Commerce. (2015, March). *Projections of the size and composition of the U.S. population: 2014 to 2060.* Retrieved from https://census.gov/content/dam/Census/library/publications/2015/demo/p25-1143.pdf

U.S. Government Accountability Office. (2014). *Serving the Congress and the nation: Strategic plan 2014-2019* (GAO No. GAO-14-1SP). Retrieved from http://www.gao.gov/assets/670/661281.pdf

Vincent, G. K., & Velkoff, V. A. (2010, May). Appendix Table A-1. Projections and distribution of the total population by age for the United States: 2010 to 2050, The next four decades: The older population in the United States: 2010 to 2050, p. 10. U.S. Census Bureau. Retrieved from http://www.census.gov/prod/2010pubs/p25-1138.pdf

World Future Society. (2007). *Forecasts: Top 10 forecasts from Outlook 2007; World trends & forecasts.* Retrieved from http://www.wfs.org/forecasts.htm

Photo Credits

p. 1: Warren Goldswain/Shutterstock;

p. 27: Mangostock/Fotolia;

p. 34: Halfpoint/Shutterstock;

p. 45: Alexey Kokoulin/123 RF;

p. 50: Auremar/Shutterstock;

p. 59: Sascha Burkard/Shutterstock;

p. 65: Federico/Fotolia;

p. 71: Halfpoint/Shutterstock;

p. 88: Phils Photography/Fotolia;

p. 102: Michaeljung/Fotolia;

p. 118: ChameleonsEye/Shutterstock;

p. 143: Barnaby Chambers/Shutterstock;

p. 147: JHogan/Shutterstock;

p. 160: Dean bertoncelj/Shutterstock;

p. 175: Kuttelvaserova Stuchelova/Shutterstock;

p. 190: Wavebreakmedia/Shutterstock;

p. 207: Monkey Business Images/Shutterstock;

p. 223: Jules Selmes/Pearson Education;

p. 242: Mangostock/Shutterstock;

p. 250: Dawn Shearer-Simonetti/Shutterstock;

p. 261: Thaumatrope/Shutterstock;

p. 284: Ejwhite/Shutterstock;

p. 294: Noam Armonn/Shutterstock;

p. 311: Monkey Business Images/Shutterstock;

p. 326: Dennis Sabo/Shutterstock;

p. 336: Spirit of america/Shutterstock;

p. 353: Lisa F. Young/Shutterstock;

p. 363: Cameron Whitman/Shutterstock;

p. 373: Jaren Jai Wicklund/Shutterstock;

p. 383: Lisa F. Young/Shutterstock;

p. 389: Jenny Sturm/Shutterstock;

p. 411: Cathy Yeulet/123RF;

p. 426: ZouZou/Shutterstock;

p. 435: Lakov Filimonov/Shutterstock;

Cover: Rory McDonald/Moment/Getty Images.

Index

A

AAMSW. *See* American Association of Medical Social Workers (AAMSW)
Abbott, E., 340
Abbott, Grace, 210
Ableism, 49
Abortion
    access to, 140
    clinics, 134, 140
Abuse, 120
    domestic, 5
    elder, 315–316
ACA. *See* Affordable Health Care for America Act (ACA)
Academic credentials, 16
    state licensing and, 25
Academy of Certified Social Workers (ACSW), 25, 165
Accommodation, 401
    lack of, 403
Acculturated family, Native American, 178
ACSW. *See* Academy of Certified Social workers (ACSW)
Active treatment, 35–36, 38
Activities of daily living (ADLs), 307, 314, 327
Activity center, 397
Acute care, health care, 197–198
Acute traumatic stress, 177
Addams, J., 9, 97, 420
    correctional social work and, 340
    juvenile justice system and, 351
Addiction Equity Act, 187
Adjudication, in juvenile justice, 353
ADLs. *See* Activities of daily living (ADLs)
Administrative barriers to aid, 86
Adoption, 131–132, 134–135, 145
    by gays and lesbians, 144–146
    intercultural, 147
    interracial, 146
    kinship care vs., 425
    perspectives on, 425
Adoption and Safe Families Act, 131–132, 134, 136, 313, 424
Adoption Assistance and Child Welfare Act (1980), 128, 132, 135, 424
Adult criminal justice systems, 367–372
Advanced generalist practice, 18, 25
Advanced practice, 11, 33
    NASW credentials and, 25–26
Advanced specialist practice, 18, 25

Adversarial court, 352
Advocacy, 296
    for disabled persons, 395–398
AFDC. *See* Aid to Families with Dependent Children (AFDC)
AFDC-UP (Unemployed Parent) program, 104
Affirmative action approach, 83
Affirmative action programs, 83–84
    attacks on, 83
    liberal support for, 54
Affordable Care Act, 214, 216, 218, 328
Affordable Health Care Act, 56, 82, 86
Affordable Health Care for America Act (ACA), 187
African American alcohol consumption rate, 280
African Americans
    alcohol and substance use disorder, 280
    aid to, 128
    challenges of, 127–128
    family structure of, 128
    mutual aid and self-help for, 128
    orphans, 127
    as slaves, 127
    social security benefits to, 102
    social welfare agencies for, 127
    substance abuse, 281
Ageism, 79
Aging population, 408. *See also* Older adults
    increase in, 423
    social work positions with, 24
Aides, professional social work or human service, 16
Aid to Families with Dependent Children (AFDC), 102, 106, 130
AIDS, social work and, 412–413
Ainsworth, M., 140
Al-Anon/Ateen, 287
Alcohol abuse, 269
Alcohol dependence, 269
Alcoholics Anonymous (AA), 273, 287–288
Alcoholism, 265
Alcoholism: Challenge for Social Work Education (Krimmel), 265
Alcohol use disorder. *See* Substance use disorder
Alcohol Use Disorders Identification Test (AUDIT), 268
Almshouses (indoor relief), 94, 123
ALS (Amyotrophic lateral sclerosis), 204
Alternative schools, 239–240
Alzheimer, Alois, 309
Alzheimer's disease, 308–309
Ambivalent attachment, 140
Amendments, equal rights, 431

American Academy of Social Work and Social Welfare (AASWSW), 444
American Association for the Mentally Retarded (AAMR), 385
American Association of Medical Social Workers (AAMSW), 26, 209
American Association of Psychiatric Social Workers, 184–185
American Association of Retired Persons (AARP), 299
American Association on Intellectual and Developmental Disabilities (AAIDD), 382, 385
American Bar Association, 365
American Cancer Society, 101
American Civil Liberties Union (ACLU), 365
American Community Survey, 424
American Council for Voluntary International Action, 116
American private pensions, trends in, 317
American Psychiatric Association, 168
American Red Cross, 8, 177
American social welfare policy, 88–91
American social workers, 29
Americans with Disabilities Act (1990), 74, 398, 404–407
Amnesty International on U.S. treatment of prisoners, 362
Amniocentesis, 406
Amodeo, Mary Ann, 265
Amorok, T., 397
Anderson, S. C., 281
Anger management, 358
Antabuse, 272, 291
Anti-Drug Abuse Act (1986), 292
Anxiety disorder, 170
Anxiolytics, 285
Arias, E., 153
Arrington, P., 20
Asch, A., 403
Ashford, J. B., 341
Asian Americans, 400–401
  social workers, 29
Asian clients, case management with, 172
Asperger syndrome, 386–387
Assessment
  criminal justice, 343, 350, 352, 353
  disabilities related, 375–377, 384, 393, 396
  family issues, 132
  licensing related, 275–276, 421
  of mental disorders, 170, 192, 195, 264, 268–271
  older adult needs, 322
  school related, 234
  in social work, 18, 63, 110, 163,193,198–199, 202, 208, 264, 436
  of substance use disorders, 268–274
Assistance programs, TANF and, 107
Assisted living, 327
Assisting families around the world, 156–157
Association for Black Social Workers, 425
Association for Medical Educators and Researchers in Substance Abuse, 265
Association Joins Global Coalition, 116
Association of Baccaluareate Social Work Program Directors (BPD), 19
Association of Retired Persons (AARP), 299
Association of Social Work Boards (ASWB), 25
ASWB. *See* Association of Social Work Boards (ASWB)

Asylee (political), for people from other countries, 426
Asylums, 379–380, 426
  for abandoned infants, 122
  for mentally ill, 183
  protected admission status for entry into the U.S., 426, 427
Ataxic cerebral palsy, 36
Attachment theory, 139–140
  ambivalent attachment, 140
  avoidant attachment, 140
Attention-deficit/hyperactivity disorder (ADHD), medications for children with, 171
Augustus, J., 340
Australian Association of Social Workers, 29
Avoidant attachment, 140
Axinn, M., 128

B

Baby boomers, 24, 277
Baccalaureate-degree program, 196
Baccalaureate Education Assessment Project (BEAP), 19
Bachelet, M., 141
Bagenstos, S. R., 405
Balancio, E. F., 174
Bane, M. J., 105
Barbiturates (downers), 285
Barker, R. L., 340, 355
Barnwell, D. A., 399
Barriers
  to aid, 86
  to persons with disabilities, 74
Bartkowski, J. P., 101, 103
Barton, C., 8
Basic professional level, 17
Battered women, 134, 344
  shelters for, 134
BEAP. *See* Baccalaureate Education Assessment Project (BEAP)
Beaulaurier, R. L., 396, 403
Beers, C., 184
Behavioral disturbance. *See* Emotional disturbance
Behavioral health care, 171
Berg-Weger, 49
Besthorn, F. H., 442
Between Client and Community (Reynolds), 185
Beyond Belief, 78
Bicêtre asylum, 183
Biggerstaff, M. A., 25
Bilingual education, 237–238
"Bill W.", legacy of, 288
Binet, A., 380
Binge drinking, 269
Biomedical ethics, stem cell research and, 438
Biomedical technology
  genetic research, 438–439
  human reproduction and, 439–440
  organ transplantation, 437–438
  regenerative medicine, 437–438
Bipolar disorder, 169
Blackbourn, J. M., 379

Black Codes, 128
Black Death (bubonic plague), 93
Black Lives Matter, 370–371
Block grants
    for child abuse programs, 125
    TANF funding by, 106
Bone marrow transplants, 437
Boundary work, 396
Bowlby, J., 139
Boy Scouts, 101
BPD. *See* Association of Social Worker Program Directors
Brace, C.L., 123, 124
Branson, D. M., 340, 355
Breckinridge, S., 340
"Broken Windows" theory, 360
Brooke, V., 397
Brownell, P., 341
Brzuzy, S., 94, 101, 105, 125
BSW, 10
BSW social worker, 5, 17
    competence and expertise of, 14–15
    curriculum for, 14–15
    employment for, 18–20
    in mental health work, 163–165
    practice behavior of, 12
    primary practice areas, 19
    as probation or parole agent, 349–350
Buchan, V., 20
Budget deficit, Reagan and, 105
Budget, welfare programs in, 112
Bullying, 176, 239
    risk factors and signs, 250
Bullying and violence, school, 249–250
Bureaucracy, health care, 214, 218
Bureau of Labor Statistics, 16, 20–23, 432, 442–443
    employment projections from, 23–24
    Occupational Outlook Handbook, 16, 442
    social work employment and mean annual wages, 21
Bureau of Prisons, 345
Bush, G. H. W., 53
Bush, G. W., 53, 70, 73–74, 76, 85, 107, 109, 111–112, 142, 154, 158, 320
    on abortion rights, 142
    Afghanistan and Iraq wars and, 73
    attack on poor by, 99
    on death penalty, 365
    on faith-based organizations, 110
    on gay marriage ban, 76
    TANF and, 107
    tax cut by, 111, 158
Business and Professional Women/USA (BPW/USA), 433
Butcher, J. N., 275
Butler, R., 79

C

Caffeine, 282
Cambodian people, 401
Campbell, K., 142
Canada, capital punishment and, 365
Canadian Association of Social Workers, 29
Canda, E. R., 442
Cannabis, 282
Cannon, Ida, 208, 209
Cannon, M. A., 184
Capital punishment, 365–367
CARE, 116
Career choice, social work in, 16–18
Career ladder, 16–18
Caregiver stress, 314–315
Caring and helping, 57
Carlsen, M., 420
Carter, B., 151
Carter, J., 54
Case advocacy, 15
Case management, 273, 302
    BSW social worker in, 174
    case study in, 173
    generalist practice in, 172–174
    MSW social worker in, 174
    social worker educational levels in, 174
Case manager, 165, 296
Casework: A Psychosocial Therapy (Hollis), 185
Categorical versus functional definitions of developmental disability, 384
Cause advocacy, 15
Cayuga Indians, 180
Center for Disease Control and Prevention, 249, 386
Center for WorkLife Law, 155
Center on Child Abuse, 125
Centers for Independent Living (CILs), 382
Cerebral palsy, 386
Certification, 24–25
    of nursing homes, 35
Certification and licensure difference, 25
Certified Advanced Clinical Social Worker in Gerontology (CACSW-G), 300
Certified Advanced Social Worker in Gerontology (CASW-G), 300
Certified Social Worker in Gerontology (CSW-G), 300
Champagne, A., 104
Change model, stages of, 272
Change, planned, 47
Charitable choice, 109
Charity, 92, 122, 321
    protestant ethic and, 96
Charity Organization Society (COS), 9, 97–98, 123–125, 184, 395
    and settlement house movement, 97–98
    settlement movement compared with, 100–101
Charter schools, 239–240
Chavez, J., 59
Cherokees, 179–181
    development, 179
    history of, 180
    school system in, 180
Cherry, 140
Chideya, F., 421
Child abuse, block grants for, 125

Child Abuse Prevention, Adoption and Family Services Act (1988), 131
Child Abuse Prevention and Treatment Act (1974), 125
Child Care Center, social work and, 413–414
Child care conundrum, 144
Child labor laws, 340
Child maltreatment, 131
Child mortality, 122
    UN development plan and, 418
Children
    with AIDS, 413
    bilingual education, 237–238
    with cerebral palsy, 386
    child poverty rate, 66
    conduct disorder in, 140
    criminal justice for, 339–340
    developmental history, 242
    with disabilities, 378, 407
    federal aid to, 103
    group work with mothers of sexually abused, 357
    in immigrant families, 148
    with intellectual disability, 385
    limited or no English, 237
    loss of aid for, 107
    in multi-racial families, 146–147
    NCLB, 253
    oppositional defiant disorder in, 140
    poverty, diversity and intersectionality of multiple factors, 67–68
    post-traumatic stress disorder in, 140
    poverty and homelessness, costs of, 254
    protective services for, 124
    public assistance for, 137
    raised by grandparents, 242
    shipped to West, 123
    special-needs, 243–247
    in Sweden, 113
    trafficking, 220
Children and family services
    as continuum of care, 128–136
    history of, 121–127
    in-home, 129–133
    out-of-home, 133–136
Children at risk, 131
Children's Aid Society, 9, 123–125, 185
Children's Bureau, 101, 340
Children's Defense Fund, 107, 110
Children's rights, as international law, 126–127
Child savers movement, 351
Child trafficking, 257
Child welfare movement, 124–126
Chinese Association of Social Workers, 29
Chinese people, 400
    perceptions of disability and, 399
CHIPS petition, 373
Christensen, C., 403
Christenson, B., 20
Churches, community health and, 360
Civil Rights Act of 1964, 83
Civil Rights Act of 1991, 405, 407, 410

Civil rights movement, 78, 104
    disabled and, 74
Civil rights, of gay and lesbian persons, 75
Civil War, Cherokees in, 179
Cizik, R., 46
Clairvoyance, 152
Clark, E. J., 201
Climate change, 142, 441
Clinical social worker, 165
Clinical Social Worker in Gerontology (CSW-G), 26
Clinton, B., 106, 132, 187
    health care financing and, 187
    Mental Health Bill of Rights and, 187
    neoliberal movement and, 55
Cloning, 440
Clubhouse model, 175–176
Cocaine, 285
Code of Ethics, 69, 28, 296
Code of Ethics (NABSW), 28
Code of Ethics (NASW), 354, 362, 407, 420, 436
    confidentially of clients and, 436
    on cultural competence, 150
    human rights and, 362
    self-determination in, 136
Coercion, criminal justice social work and, 354
Cognitive disorders, 423
Co-insurance, 307
Cold turkey detoxification, 286
College work-study programs, 104
Collins, C., 135
Colonies and colonization, poor laws in, 96
Columbia University School of Social Work, 9, 97
"Common Core" curriculum, 254
Communication technology, 435–436
Communities
    disabled persons in, 396–397
    generalist practice with, 172–181
    at risk, crime and, 359
    strengths, restoration, spirituality, and resilience in, 359–360
Community-based arrangements, for disabled, 34–38
Community-based corrections, 349–351, 358
Community-based homes, for adolescents, 358
Community level, intervention at, 43
Community Mental Health Centers Construction Act (1963), 185
Community mental health programs, 186
Community organization work, by police, 344
Community outreach, 274
Community placement, 36
    of disabled people, 382
Community practice, 176
Community services
    older adults, 325
    as punishment for crimes, 345, 353
Community-service sentencing, 345
Competency, 47
Complementary therapies, 333
Comprehensive Alcohol Abuse and Alcoholism Prevention, Treatment, and Rehabilitation Law, 265
Comprehensive Drug Abuse Prevention and Control Act (1970), 291

Compulsory health insurance program, 210
Computers, 435–436
Conditional release, for prisoners, 340
Conductive hearing loss, 389
Confidentiality of clients, NASW Code of Ethics and, 436
Connecticut Society for Mental Hygiene, 184
Conservatism, cultural, 53
Conservative, 51
Conservative evangelical Christian movement, 46
Conservative(s), 51–52
    community placement of disabled people and, 383
    perspective of, 52–53
    political spectrum of, 54
Constitution (U.S.), assistance to the poor as state prerogative, 96
Consumer movement, for mental health services, 186
Continuum of care, 128–136, 324–330
    for disabled persons, 394–395
    older adults, 394–395
Contraception pill, 141
Convention on the Rights of Persons with Disabilities (2007), 406
Convention on the Rights of the Child, 116, 126–127
Conversion therapy, 146
Convulsion, 36
Co-occurrence, of disabilities, 393–394
Corporations, diminishing welfare and, 112
Correctional system, 345–351
COS. *See* Charity Organization Society (COS)
Cost–benefit analysis, health care, 215–218
Cost containment, 198
Cost-cutting, 56
Council on Social Work Education (CSWE), 10, 24–25, 27–28, 300, 395, 422
    accreditation by, 10, 17, 27–28
    Educational Policy and Accreditation Standards, 47
    other activities, 28
Counseling, 164
    for prisoners, 341
    in police social work, 343–344
    disabled persons and, 397
    genetic, 397, 406
    Internet, 436
    social work compared with, 30–31
Courts, in criminal justice system, 344–345
Cox, C. B., 312
Crack, 285, 292
Credentials, academic, 16
Cretinism, 379
Criminal justice system, 336–372
    correctional system in, 345–351
    courts in, 344–345
    groups and organizations social work in, 357–358
    history of social work in, 339–341
    juvenile, 336, 340
    juvenile justice system in, 351–354
    law enforcement and, 342–344
    misdemeanors and felonies in, 342
    NASW Code of Ethics and, 362
    person-in-environment perspective and, 359
    police social work and, 340, 343–344
    probation and parole in, 342
    reforms and, 341
    social justice and, 362–364
    social work in, 354–358
    UN Universal Declaration of Human Rights and, 362
    value dilemmas in, 354–355
Cross-addiction, 285
Cross-cultural competence, 400
CSWE. *See* Council on Social Work Education (CSWE)
CSWE Educational Policy, 395
CSW-G. *See* Clinical Social Worker in Gerontology (CSW-G)
Cullen, F. T., 351
Cultural competence, 71, 150–153, 178
    diverse family structures, 150–151
    spirituality and religion, 151–153
Cultural competency, 71
Cultural conservatism, 53
Cultural diversity
    families of disabled people and, 399–400
    in schools, 236–247
    in U.S., 416
Cultural groups, cultural competence and, 178
Cultural pluralism, 71
Culture, 224
    family expectations by, 150
    Native American, 179–181
Curriculum, for BSW social workers, 14–15
Currie, Charles, 265
Curtis act (1898), 180
Custodial care, for disabled people, 380

D

Darwin, Charles, 96–97, 380
Databases, 435–436
Davis, D. R., 273, 287, 292
Dawes Act (1887), 180
Day care, 131
Day, M., 399
DCSW. *See* Diplomate in Clinical Social Work (DCSW)
DD. *See* Developmental disabilities (DD)
Death, of older adults, 331
Death penalty, 365–367
Decision making, professional, 136–137
Declaration of Human Rights, 115
Declaration on the Rights of the Child, 126–127
Deerinwater, D., 160–163
Defense Department, military prisons of, 345
Defense of Marriage Act of 1996, 75
Deinstitutionalization, 382–383, 403
Delgado, M., 148
Delusions, 169
Demand, for social workers, 20–22
Dementia, 308
Democratic Carter administration, 104–105
Democratic Party, 52, 54
Demographic Programs, U.S. Bureau of the Census, 421
Demographics, defined, 421

Demographic trends, 421
    of families, 424–425
    of immigrants, 425–427
    multi-culturalism, 421–422
    older adults, 423
Department of Health and Social Services (DHSS), 34–35, 38, 42
Department of Social Services, 38
Depressive disorder, 169
Depressive state, 169
Designer drugs, 285
De Silva, E. C., 155
Detention, in juvenile justice, 352
Detoxification, 269
Developmental Disabilities Act (1969), 382, 398, 403
Developmental Disabilities Assistance Bill of Rights, 403
Developmental disabilities (DD), 34–35, 48–49, 384
Developmental disability, 384
Developmentally disabled people, 395. *See also* Disabled persons
    autism/autism spectrum disorder, 386–387, 399
    categorical versus functional definitions of, 384
    cerebral palsy, 386
    community-based arrangements, 34–38
    continuum of care for, 394–395
    co-occurrence and, 393–394
    emotional disturbance, 392
    epilepsy, 390
    fetal alcohol syndrome, 392–393
    hearing problems, 389–390
    institutionalization of, 36–38
    intellectual disability, 384–386
    learning disabilities, 391
    orthopedic problems, 388–389
    traumatic brain injury, 390–391
    types of disabilities, 384–395
Developmental, psychology, 30
DHSS. *See* Department of Health and Social Services (DHSS)
Diagnostic and Statistical Manual of Mental Disorders (DSM), 168
Diagnostic and Statistical Manual of Mental Disorders (DSM-5), 168–169
Diagnostic labels, mental health and, 181
Dickerson, J. G., 352
Dickerson, M. U., 378
Diminishing Welfare (Goldberg and Rosenthal), 112
Diplomate in Clinical Social Work (DCSW), 17, 26, 165
Disability paradigm, 404
Disability rights movement, 403–404
Disabled persons
    ableism and, 49
    community settings, 396–397
    CSWE Educational Policy, 395
    defined, 384
    deinstitutionalization and, 382–383
    disability rights movement, 404
    education for work with, 395
    empowerment of, 402
    federal aid for, 103
    genetic counseling and, 397, 406
    history of services for, 378–383
    institutional settings, 396
    lifespan of, 409

    NASW Code of Ethics, 395–396
    need for care, 49
    normalization and, 382
    population at risk, 49
    prevalence of disabilities, 393–394
    risk of poverty and discrimination, 51
    social policy and, 403–406
    social work practice with, 395–398
    strengths perspective for, 50
    values issues and ethical implications, 406–409
Disaster services, 176–177
Disasters, social workers for, 12
Disciplinary action, school social work, 249
Discrimination, 64, 395
    affirmative action and, 83
    by age, 79, 422
    Americans with Disabilities Act and, 404
    against disabled persons, 398, 403, 405
    against gay and lesbian persons, 75–76
    heterosexism and homophobia as, 79–80
    against minorities, 71
    poverty from, 87
    racism as, 78
    sexism as, 78–79
    against women, 69, 156
Disposition, 353
    in juvenile justice, 352
Diversity
    social work practice and, 178–179
    values, ethics, and, 49, 150–151
Dix, D. L., 183–184
    investigation on mentally ill by, 183
Dobroff, Rose, 299
Doctorate degrees, 11, 18
Domestic abuse, 5
    case study, 1–5
Domestic violence services, 341
Domiciliaries, 203
Donut hole, Medicare, 212, 216
Dossey, L., 152, 397
Doughnut hole, Medicare, 308
Drugs
    appropriate uses of, 171
    psychotropic, 170
    use in children, 171
DSM. *See* Diagnostic and Statistical Manual of Mental Disorders (DSM)
DSW social workers, 11
Dual diagnosis, 281
Dubois, B., 51
Dudzinski, M., 379
Dunn, Susan, 1–5
Dynamics of Therapy in a Controlled Relationship (Taft), 185

E

Earned Income Tax Credit (EITC), 95–96, 104–107
    issues with, 105
EASI. *See* Environmental Alliance of Senior Involvement (EASI)

Ecological concerns, 142–144
Ecological concerns, population growth and, 142–144
Ecological sanity, 47
Ecology. *See also* Environment
    human social welfare and, 13
Economic inequality, 158
Economic market, intervention in, 53
Economic Opportunity Act (1964), 232
Economics, social welfare values and, 96
Economic system, trends in, 433–435
Economic values, 56–57
Ecosystem perspective, 40–41
Education
    for African Americans, 127
    importance of, 143
    social work career ladder and, 16–18, 17f
    for work with disabled people, 395
Educational opportunity programs, 104
Educational Policy and Accreditation Standards, 395
Education for All Handicapped Children Act (1975), 232, 240, 403
Edward II (England), 378
Egg donor programs, human, 439
Eisler, R., 78
EITC. *See* Earned Income Tax Credit (EITC)
Elder abuse, 315–316
Elementary and Secondary Education Act, 232–253
Elizabethan Poor Law (England, 1601), 94–95, 378
Elmira Reformatory (New York), 340
Embryonic stem cells, 437
Embryo transfer, 439
Emergency department, 201–203
Emotional bonding, 139–140
Emotional disturbance, 241, 377, 392
Emotional or behavioral disturbance, 234
Employee assistance program (EAP), 265
Employment
    for disabled people, 74, 382–383, 394, 396
    for MSWs, 20
    opportunities in, 18–24
    private sector, 20
    Roosevelt, Franklin D., and, 101
    underemployment and, 433
Empowerment, 50–51
    disabled people and, 396, 402
    school social work, 255–256
    of women, 418
Eng, A., 174
Engagement processes, 48
England
    social welfare model from, 93
    transporting of convicts, 340
English as a Second Language (ESL) course, 237
Entitlement, 101
Entitlement program, 317
Environment. *See also* Global warming
    context and work, 12–13
    crime and communities at risk, 359
    danger to, 142
    degradation, 46
    global physical, 13
    issues, 44–47
    strengths, restoration, spirituality, and resilience, 359–360
Environmental Alliance of Senior Involvement (EASI), 310
Environmental degradation, 442
    impact on humans, 442
Environmental Protection Agency (EPA), 310
Environmental sustainability, 54, 440–442
    UN development plan and, 418
EPA. *See* Environmental Protection Agency (EPA)
Epidemiologists, 206
Epilepsy, 390
Equal Rights Amendment (ERA), 431
Erickson, J., 155
ESSA. *See* Every Student Succeeds Act (ESSA)
Essay on the Principle of Population, An (Malthus), 96
Ethical issues
    genetic testing and, 438–439
    selling human organs, 437
    stem cell research, 437
Ethics, 49
    disabled persons and, 406–409
    in mental health work, 166–167
    psychotropic medication uses and, 171
Ethnic groups, 71
    change in, 422
Ethnicity, 309–310
Ethnic minority, 70–71
Ethnic sensitive approaches, 422
Ethnoconscious approach, 422
Eugenics movement, 380–381
European prevention and treatment approach, 286–287
Europeans, Native American history with, 179–181
European Union, environmental protection and, 441
Europe, children's rights in, 122
Every Student Succeeds Act (ESSA), 253, 257
Experimental or research psychology, 30
Extended families, 425
Extraordinary rendition, 73

F

Fadiman, A., 416
Fad, K., 379
Fair Sentencing Act (2010), 292, 369–370
Faith-based organization, 93, 110
Families. *See also* Children and family services
    assisting, 156–157
    of Chinese people, 400
    cultural expectations by, 150
    demographics of, 424–425
    of disabled persons, 396, 399–400, 407–408
    diverse structures of, 150–151
    extended, 425
    gay and lesbian, 144–146
    immigrant, 147–148
    issues and types, 137–150
    in Japan, 114

Families (*Continued*)
   military, 148–150
   of older adults, 311–316
   of prisoners, 348
   slavery and, 127–128
Family and Medical Leave Act, 156
Family-based services, 132–133
   at-risk families, 133
Family care, 316
Family care homes, 36
   for disabled people, 381, 394
Family leave, 155
Family level, intervention at, 43
Family life education, 130
Family planning services, 143
Family policy, 153–158
   assisting families around the world, 156–157
   current trends in the United States, 157–158
   Family and Medical Leave Act, 156
   workplace, family-friendly nature of, 154–156
Family Preservation and Support Services Act (1993), 126, 132
Family preservation services, 133
Family Support Act (1988), 106
Family therapy, 148
Family work, school social work, 234
Farrell, M. B., 76
Farr, K. A., 348
Federal government, 38
   policy changes by, 51
   poverty assistance from, 51
Federal Health Care Administration, 34
Federal Housing Assistance Program, 319–320
Federal Initiatives (1930–1968), 101–104
Federal Mental Health Parity, 187
Federico, R., 93, 94
Feldman, L., 73
Felony, 342
Females. *See* Women
Feminization of poverty, 69
Fernald, W. E., 381
Fetal alcohol syndrome (FAS), 277–278, 384, 393
FICA, 101
Field education, 15
Field placement, 15, 13, 24
Final 2015 Educational Policy, 395
Financial aid, 130
Financial crisis, 56
First Nations Peoples, 179
Food and Agricultural Organization, 116
Food and Drug Administration (FDA), 141
Food insecurity, 65–66
Food, population and, 142
Food stamps, 95–96, 103–104, 130, 321
Ford, G., 105
Forensic social work, 341, 355
   case study, 356
Foster care, 38, 123–124, 133
   for children of female prisoners, 348
   social worker in, 133

Foster homes, 133
   for disabled persons, 394
Foster parents, 133
Frail elderly, 297
France, education of disabled persons in, 378–379
Franklin, C., 236
Freedman, R., 398
Freedmen's Bureau, 96
Freeman, E. M., 127, 230, 232, 233
Freudian theory, 9
Freud, Sigmund, 299
"Full-service" schools, 236
Funding
   for public assistance, 102–103
   for TANF, 106
Future issues, policy and practice, 187–188
Futurists, 416
   environmental sustainability and, 440–442
   globalization perspectives of, 416–417
   stem cell technology and, 437

G

Gag rule, 158
Galton, F., 380
Gambro, J., 379
GAO Strategic Plan, 441–442
Gap, rich-poor, 84–85
Gardner, G., 155
Garran, A. M., 422
Gay and lesbian older adults, 313
   family structures, 425
   and hate crimes, 371
   promoting human rights and social justice, 362
Gay and lesbian persons, 75–76, 144–146
Gays, 144–146, 280–281
Gay youth, challenges of, 248
Gender equality, UN development plan and, 418
Gender Shadow Report, 155
General Allotment Act (Dawes Act, 1887), 180
General assistance, 103
Generalist approach, to social work practice, 41–48
Generalist practice in case management, 172–174
Generalist practice, in mental health, 172–181
   case management, 172–174
   Cherokee experience, 179–181
   community practice, 176
   disaster services, 176–177
   with diverse populations, 178–179
   Native American history, 179–181
   working with groups, 174–176
General Motors, pollution and, 46
Genetic counseling, 12, 397, 406
Genetic research, 438–439
Genetic testing, 439
   ethical and social issues in, 438–439
Genome, 438–439
Genomics, 438
Gerontological social work, 19
Germain, C. B., 40

Gerritsen-McKane, R., 20
Ghana, 29
 school social work in, 257–260
Gilson, S. F., 402
Ginsburg, R. B., 68, 140
Girl Scouts, 101
Gitterman, A., 40
Glicken, M. D., 50
Global climate change, 441
Global crisis, 56
Global issues, environmental, 50–53
Globalization, 416
 definitions and themes, 417
 futurists' perspectives of, 416–417
 national and international strategic planning and, 417–418
 relevancy to social work and, 418, 420
Global physical environment, 13
Global warming, 46
Goldberg, G., 107, 112, 113, 114, 116
Good Housekeeping (Magazines), 100
Gould, Allison, 176
Government
 economic involvement of, 101
 federal, 51
 fuel assistance, 104
 infant nutritional supplements, 104
 poverty assistance from, 51
 rent subsidies, 104
Government Accountability Office (GAO), Strategic Plan, globalization and, 417
Government social policy *vs.* social work values, 117
Grand accomplishments, 444–445
Grand challenges, 443
Grandparents, children raised by, 242
Graves, Dan, 261–264
Great Depression, 92, 231
 social welfare after, 104
Greene, R. R., 312
Green Party, The, 54
Greenwich House, 230
Grew, R., 417
Grier, P., 74
Group homes, 133–134, 297
 for disabled people, 382
 for juveniles recently released from prison, 358
 privatization of, 430
Group level, intervention at, 43
Group(s)
 generalist practice with, 172–181
 mental health work with, 174–176
 in prisons, 358
 sexual abuse and domestic violence, 357
Group treatment
 for disaster survivors and volunteers, 177
 substance abuse, 272
Group work, 48
Group work, school social work, 234
Guggenbuhl, J., 379
Guilds, for family needs, 122
Gun-Free Schools Act, 249

"Guns *vs.* butter" debate, 153–154
Gustavsson, N. S., 131, 135

H

Habilitation, 379
Habilitation services, 382
Haines, Frank, 229, 238
Haines, Helen, 300, 302
Hallucinations, 169
Hallucinogens, 282–284
Hamil, S., 176
Hamilton, T. D., 20
Harm reduction model, 286–287
Harpham, E., 104
Harrington, M., 104
Harrison Narcotics Act (1914), 291
Hartford Foundation, 24
Hartley House, 230
Hatcher, S. S., 352
Haves, 52
Head Start program, 104, 232
Health and welfare services, 101
Health care
 access, 218
 acute care, 197–198
 behavioral, 171
 case study, 190–193
 changes in, 213–214
 community and populations at risk, 195–196
 competence for practice, 196–197
 emergency department, 201–203
 historical perspectives, 208–209
 home, 200
 hospice care, 200–201
 insurance companies, 210
 long-term care, 198–200
 medicaid, 212–213
 medicare, 211–212
 palliative care, 200–201
 politics and economics in, 209–221
 public health and health departments, 206–208
 in rural areas, 205
 settings for, 197
 services, 205–211
 social work competencies in, 193–197
 values and ethics in, 194–195
 for veterans, 203
Health care reform, 213–214
Health care systems, 178, 203, 413
Health insurance. *See also* Insurance
 accessibility to, 85–86
 in Japan, 114
Health maintenance organizations (HMOs), 197
Hearing problems, 389–390
Heavy drinking, 269
Heinrich, Abbie, 294–299, 320
Help Starts Here (NASW Web resource), 27
Hemodialysis, 205
Hermann, Stephanie, roles of, 34–38

Heroin, 291
Heterosexism, 79–80, 145
Heterosexist, 248
Hewa, S., 417
Higher learning, for African Americans, 127
Hippocrates, 339
Hispanics, 227–229, 238
    alcohol and substance use disorder, 279–280
Hispanic social workers, NAPRHSW and, 28–29
History. *See also* specific groups and issues
    events in social welfare and social work, 99–100
    of family and children's services, 121–127
    Native American, 179–181
    of social welfare policy, 91–96
History of social work, 8–10
Hitler, A., 380
HIV/AIDS, 280, 418
    UN development plan and, 418
Hoakley, Z. P., 381
Hodge, D. R., 65
Holland, J., 442
Hollis, F., 185
Holody, R., 425
Home health care, 200
    for disabled people, 394
Homelessness, 154
Homemaker services, 130–131
Homophobia, 79–80, 145
Homophobic, 248
Homosexual, 243
Hooley, J. M., 275
Hoover, H., 101
Hopkins, Harry, 299
Horejsi, C. R., 39
Horejsi, G. A., 39
Hospice, 200
Hospice care, 200–201, 211
Hospice services, 333, 443
Hospitalization, for mental health disorders, 171
Households, decline of family, 424
Housing, for disabled people, 408
How America Ranks Among Industrialized Countries, 110
Howard, M., 367, 382
Howe, S. G., 379, 380
Hull, G. H., 176
Hull House, 97, 123, 340, 351, 431
Human diversity. *See* Diversity
Human Genome Project, 438–439
Humanitarianism, 96
Human reproduction, biomedical technology and, 439–440
Human Rights
    commission, 155
    human rights covenants of, 155
    NASW and, 116, 362
    and social justice, 362–364
    in United States, 362
Human Rights and International Affairs Department, of NASW, 116
Human Rights Commission (UN), 155
Human rights covenants, of UN, 155
Human service aide, 16

Human service professions, social workers as, 266, 418
Human services, social work compared with, 31
Hunger, 154
    UN development plan and, 418
Hyde Amendment (1976), 140
Hypnotic medication, 285
Hypothermia, 262

I

ICF/CD, 35
IFSW. *See* International Federation of Social Workers (IFSW)
Illegal immigrants, 427
Immigrant, 426
Immigrants and immigration
    African American slaves as, 127
    demographic trends and, 425–427
    families of, 147–148
    illegal, 427
Immigration Act (1965), 400
Impairment, 267
Incarceration
    international comparison of, 360–361
    levels of, 359
Income maintenance, 101
Income tax, EITC and, 104–106
Independent living, 403
    for disabled people, 402
Indian Child Welfare Act (1978), 424
Indian Reorganization Act (1934), 180
Individualized Education Program (IEP), 232, 241
Individual level, intervention at, 42–43
Individuals with Disabilities Education Act (IDEA), 232, 240, 403
    emotional disturbance defined in, 392
Indoor relief, 94
Industrial-organizational psychology, 30
Industrial Revolution, 97
Infanticide, in China, 143
Infant mortality, 111, 153, 157, 210, 217
Informal diversion, 351
Information technology, 435–436
Inge, K., 397
In-home services, 129–133
In-home services, older adults, 325
Innovative programs, 328–329
In re: Gault, 352
Institute of Noetic Sciences, 332
Institutional care, 135
Institutionalization
    case study on, 36–38
    disabled persons and, 398
Institutional racism, 78
Institutional services
    for disabled people, 380
    older adults, 325–328
Institutional social welfare, 91–92
Institutions, 395
    social work with disabled persons in, 395
Insurance, 295. *See also* Medicaid; Medicare
Intagliata, J., 382

Intake process, in juvenile justice, 352
Integrity, in mental health work, 166
Intellectual disability, 375–377, 384–386, 394
Intensive probation, 351
InterAction, 116
Interprofessional collaboration, 167
Inter-professional collaboration, social work compared with, 31–32
International Covenant on Civil and Political Rights, 360
International Federation of Social Workers (IFSW), 29–30, 126–127
International law, children's rights as, 126–127
International Perspective, 110–117
International social work, 411–415
International Social Work Organizations, 29–30
Internet, 435–436
    mental health care and, 188
Interracial children, 146
Interracial couples, 146
Intersectionality, 49
Intersectionality of multiple factors, 49
    diversity and, 66–67
Intervention, 47
    aging population and, 423
    case management as, 172–174
    contract, 376
    in disasters, 176–177
    in-home, 374
    levels of, 41–44
    in mental health settings, 164–165
    process, 47–48
In vitro fertilization, 440
Involuntary abortion, 143
IQ tests, 380
    diagnosing mental retardation with, 384–385
Isms, 77
Israel, 29
Itard, J.-M.-G., 378

J

Jackson, A., Cherokee removal and, 179
Jackson Sun (article), 176
Jail, 345. *See also* Prisons
Jakubowicz, A., 403
Jane Addams School of Social Work (University of Illinois), 360
Japan, 114–115
    families, 114
    government assistance, 114
    health care, 114
    pension system in, 114
    social welfare system in, 114–115
    tax policy in, 114
    unemployment in, 115
    women in, 114
Japanese people, 400
Jenkins, Janine, 108
Jensen, J. M., 367
Job coach, 388, 397
Job training programs, 104
Johns Hopkins School of Public Health, 252
Johnson, A. B., 383

Johnson, A. D., 276
Johnson, K., 371
Johnson, L. B., 54
Johnson, Madeleine, 262, 266
Johnson, M. J., 41
Johnstone, M., 177
Jones, K., 148
Journal of Social Work Education, 28
Judicial system, children and, 135–136
Juvenile court system, 340
Juvenile criminal justice systems, 367–372
Juvenile Justice and Delinquency Prevention Act (1974), 352
Juvenile justice system, 351–354
    adjudication in, 353
    arrest in, 351–352
    death penalty and, 365
    due process in, 352
    group work in, 358
    history of, 351–352
    informal diversion in, 351
    intake process in, 352
    police dispositions in, 343
Juvenilization of poverty, 67

K

Kadushin, A., 122
Kaiser, Henry J., 215
Karger, H. J., 52, 53–55, 93, 96, 104, 106, 124, 125
Kelley, F., Children's Bureau of, 340
Kelly, J. J., 201
Kennedy, J. F., 54, 104, 185
Kiernan-Stern, M., 355
Ki-Moon, B., 157, 418
Kimoto, K., 114
Kinship care, vs. adoption, 425
Knowledge base
    for health care work, 193–194
    for mental health, 167–172
Knowledge, to mental health work, 167–172
Knox, K. S., 343
Kochanek, K. D., 153
Korean people, 401
Krimmel, H., 265
Kubler-Ross, Elisabeth, 333
Kuraishi, M., 110

L

Labels, mental health and, 181
Labor Department, Children's Bureau in, 101
Lady almoners, 208
Laissez-faire, 53, 96
Laissez-faire, social welfare values and, 96
Lampman, J., 46
Laotian people, 401
Larkin case, 248–249
LaTanya Tracy, 124
Latchkey children, 131
Lathrop, Julia, 210

Latinos, 227–229
Latino social workers, NAPRHSW and, 29
Latino Social Workers Organization, 29
Law enforcement, 342–344
Law Enforcement Assistance Administration, 341
Law(s). *See also* specific laws
    charity and, 122
    children's rights and, 126–127
    for poor, 94–96
Learning and Teaching in the Practice of Social Work (Reynolds), 185
Learning disabilities, 384, 391
Learning, intellectual disability and, 3
Least restrictive environment, 128–129, 324
Lebeaux, C., 92
Ledbetter, L., 68
Lee, K., 173, 176–177
Left (political), 51
Legal regulation, 24–25
Legislation. *See also* Law(s); specific laws
    mental health, 185
Leighninger, L., 52
Lesbian, 144–146, 244
Lesbian social workers, professional organizations for, 29
Less eligibility, 95
Levels of intervention, 41–43
    by social worker, 48
Levin, H, 127
Lewandowski, Katherine, 190–193
Lewis, R., 132
LGBTQ, 77
Liberal arts base of social work education, 14
Liberal or progressive, 51
    community placement of disabled people and, 383
    political spectrum of, 54
    world view of, 53–54
Libertarian party, 53
Licensing, categories of, 25
Licensure, 25
Licensure and professional credentialing, of social work profession, 10, 24–26
Lieby, J., 96, 98
Life-cycle transition, importance of, 150
Life span, 122
    of women, 423
Life stressors, 41
Lilly Ledbetter Fair Pay Act, 69
Lilly Ledbetter Law, 158
Lin, J., 443
Lin, V., 443
Lindsay, R., 151
Listening skills, 268
Liu, G. Z., 399, 407–408
Llana, S. M., 141
Local level, correctional systems at, 345
Logan, S. M. L., 124, 128, 275
Long-term care
    health care, 198–200
    older adults, 331
Louis XV (France), 378

Lum, D., 127, 179, 400
Lunatic asylum, 183

M

MacDorman, M., 153
Maconochie, A., 340
Mainstreaming, 242
Malamud, M., 436
Malone, B., 438
Malthus, T., 96
Managed care, mental health care and, 188
Mandated reporting, 125
Manion, K., 420
Mankiller, W., 179
Manor, Brockton, 35–38
Marijuana, 282, 292
Marks, A., 75–76
Marot, Mary, 230
Martin, M. E., 175
Marriage for gay, lesbian, and bisexual, 75–76
Marsh, J. C., 319
Martin, Alan, 336–339
Martin, J., 122
Maschi, T., 352
Massachusetts, same-sex civil unions in, 75–76
Master's degree. *See* MSW social worker
Maternal health, UN development plan and, 418
Mathews, T. J, 153
Mauer, M., 361
McCarter, A. K., 65, 85
McCulsky, B., 314
McGoldrick, M., 150, 425
McKenzie, J. K., 132
McNeece, C. A., 292
McRoy, R. G., 127, 275
McSteen, M., 102
Means test, 101–103
Medicaid, 62, 87, 102, 104, 130, 212, 307, 320
    health care, 212–213
    ICF/MR, 35
    in nursing homes, 34–38
    TANF and, 106
Medicare, 69, 102, 104, 130, 211, 307, 320
    health care, 211–212
    hospice care, 211
    in Sweden, 113–114
Medicare advantage plan, 211–212
Medication
    for ADHD children, 171
    for mental health disorders, 171
    psychotropic, 170
Meekosha, H., 403
Men. *See also* Gay and lesbian persons
Mental disorders, 164
    DSM diagnostic categories, 168–172
    impact of environment, 182
    stigma, prejudicial attitudes toward, 166
Mental Health Bill of Rights, 187

Mental health care
    acute and posttraumatic stress, 176–177
    case study, 160–163
    clubhouse model of service, 175–176
    in community practice, 176
    crises and, 164–165
    funding for, 186
    future issues in, 187–188
    generalist practice in case management, 172–174
    historical perspectives on, 183–184
    knowledge and skill for, 160–163
    professional team in, 167
    social justice issues in, 181–182
    social policy affect on, 185–187
    and social policy, 182–188
    working with groups in, 174, 185–187
Mental Health Parity Act, 187
Mental health programs
    care for mentally ill patients, 186
    deinstitutionalization of patients, 185–186
Mental health services, 167–168
Mental health, social policy and, 182–188
    future issues, 187–188
    history, 183–184
    in mental health service, 185–188
    social work profession, emergence of, 184–185
Mental Health Systems Act (1980), 186
Mentally ill, capital punishment for, 366
Mental retardation, 375, 378, 384–385
Methadone, 272, 287, 291
Meyer, C., 185
Michigan, WIAR (Women and Infants at Risk) program in, 363
Middle East, suspicion of people from, 73–74
Mikulski, Barbara, 313, 314
Miley, K. K., 51
Milieu therapy, 135
Military, 148–150
    health care for, 203–205
Military prisons, 365, 345–349
Military, psychiatric social services for, 185
Millennium Development Goals (2015), 221
Mind That Found Itself, A (Beers), 184
Mineka, S., 275
Minimum wage law, 95
Minorities. *See also* specific groups
    affirmative action and, 83
    incarceration rates of, 346, 361
    family issues and types, 137–150
    poverty, diversity and intersectionality, 66–77
    racial and ethnic, 70–74
Minority group, 70
Misdemeanor, 342
Moderate drinking, 269
Mohangoo, A. D, 153
Moody, Raymond, 332
Moon, M. M., 351
Morabia, A., 206
Morales, A. T., 8
Morning after, The, 141

Morrison-Orton, D. J., 397, 398
Mothers
    in Japan, 114
    work outside home, 138
MSW, 10
MSW social worker
    employment opportunities and patterns for, 18–20
    in mental health, 20
    in mental health work, 160–163
    as probation or parole agent, 349–350
M-team. *See* Multidisciplinary team
Mt. Meigs Reformatory for Juvenile Law-Breakers, 351–352
Mt. Meigs Rescue Home for Girls, 351–352
Mudrick, N. R., 403
Multi-culturalism, in U.S., 421–422
Multidisciplinary team, 241
Murphy, S. L., 153
Mutual aid, 98
    for African Americans, 128
Mutual Aid Groups (Gitterman and Shulman), 287, 357

N

NABSW. *See* National Association of Black Social Workers (NABSW)
Nadelhaft, A., 300
Naleppa, M. J., 309, 315
NAMI. *See* National Alliance on Mental Illness (NAMI)
Napoleon III (France), 379
Napoleonic Code, criminal justice for children in, 339
NAPRHSW. *See* National Association of Puerto Rican & Hispanic Social Workers (NAPRHSW)
Narcotics Anonymous (NA), 273–274
Nash, Bernard E., 299
NASW. *See* National Association of Social Workers (NASW)
NASW Credentialing, 25–26
NASW Code of Ethics, 27, 395–396
    social work with disabled people, 395–396
NASW News, 27, 176
NASW policy statement, 201
Nathanson, I. L., 299
National Alliance on Mental Illness (NAMI), 186
National Association for the Advancement of Colored People (NAACP), 101
National Association of Black Social Workers (NABSW), 28
National Association of Evangelicals, 46
National Association of Oncology Social Workers, 29
National Association of Puerto Rican & Hispanic Social Workers (NAPRHSW), 28–29
National Association of Social Workers (NASW), 25–28, 49, 107, 184–185, 232, 296, 300, 337
    advocacy by, 116
    capital punishment and, 365
    Code of Ethics, 362, 395–396, 407, 420
    credentialing of advanced professional practice, 25–26
    criminal justice and, 354
    human rights efforts of, 116

National Association of Social Workers (NASW) (*Continued*)
   ongoing Human Rights Effort, 116
   on self-determination for client systems, 407
   welfare reform principles, 116
National Center for Crime and Delinquency, 350
National Coalition for the Homeless, 154
National Coalition of Anti-Violence Program, 77
National Committee of Visiting Teachers (1921), 230
National Committee on Pay Equity, 433
National Conference of Charities and Correction, 230
National Federation of Societies of Clinical Social Workers, 29
National health insurance, 210
National health insurance plan, 213
National health service, 214
National Human Genome Research Institute, 438
National Indian Social Workers Association, 29
National Institute on Drug Abuse (NIDA), 269
National Institute of Mental Health (NIMH), 185
National Mental Health Act (1946), 185
National Organization of Women (NOW), 155
National Osteoporosis Foundation (n.d.), 192
National Urban League, and the Red Cross, 101
Native Americans
   and Cherokee experience, 179–181
   Dawes Act and, 180
   Europeans and, 179–180
   history and, 179–181
   history of, 179–181
   alcohol and substance disorder, 278–279
Navetta, J. M., 79
Nazi Germany
   Holocaust and, 72–73
   people with disabilities in, 74
Nederlands Instituut voor Zorg en Welzijn, 29
Neglect, 119
Neoconservatism, 54–55
Neoconservative, 51
Neoliberal, 51
Neoliberalism, 54–55
Neo-traditional families, Native American, 178
Neuropsychiatric disorders, 185
New Deal, 101
New Mexico, death penalty in, 366
New Poor Law (England, 1834), 95
New York Children's Aid Society, 123–124
New York School of Philanthropy, 9, 97
NIDA. *See* National Institute on Drug Abuse (NIDA)
Nigeria, 29
Nineteenth Amendment, 431
Nixon, R., 53
No Child Left Behind (NCLB) Law, 253
Nomura, M., 114
Nondiscrimination approach, 83
Nonprofit private agencies, social workers employed by, 12
Norfolk Island, British penal colony on, 340
Normalization, 382
Norms, 239
North American Association of Christians in Social Work, 29
NOW. *See* National Organization of Women (NOW)

Nursing home
   community-based arrangements, 34–38
   disabled persons in, 382–383, 394–396

O

OASI. *See* Old Age and Survivors Insurance (OASI)
Obama, B., 42, 46, 56, 67, 69, 76, 77, 85, 86, 112, 126, 158, 229, 347, 371, 384, 408
   Affordable Health Care Act and, 56, 158
   assist homebuyers, 56
   child care subsidies increased by, 158
   and Democartic congress, 56
   gag rule removed by, 158
   health care legislation (2010), 154
   health care reform and, 187
   increase in college student loans, 56
   more opportunities to Americans, 56
   pay discrimination against women, 56
   restoration of family planning funds, 56
   retain and restore jobs, 56
   spending on war, 158
Occupational Outlook Handbook, 16, 442
O'Connor, M. J., 277
O'Connor, S. D., 83
O'Connor v. Donaldson, 186
Oklahoma, Indians in, 180
Old Age and Survivors Insurance (OASI), 102
Older adults, 13–14, 24, 26–28, 69–70, 294–299
   Alzheimer's disease, 308–309
   education, 304
   environment and, 310
   ethnic and cultural minorities, 312
   gay and lesbian, 313
   lifestyle trends and innovative programs, 328–329
   population at risk, 69
   in poverty, 69
   as caregivers, 313–314
   case study, 294–299
   continuum of care, 324–328
   death, 331
   economic status of, 305–306
   employment of, 304–305
   empowerment model used with, 303
   ethnic and cultural minorities of, 312
   ethnicity, 309–310
   families of, 311–316
   gay and lesbian older adults, 313
   geographical distribution, 303–304
   gerontological or geriatric social work, 302
   hospice services, 333
   housing for, 306–307
   importance of generalist social work, 300–301
   long-term care, 331
   marital status of, 304
   mental health challenges, 308
   in Netherlands, 329–330
   physical and mental health, 307–308
   social policy and, 316–300

social work with, 299–300, 333–334
    spirituality and religion, 331–333
    values and public policy, 323
Older Americans Act (1965), 322–323
Olmstead decision, 398
Omnibus Budget Reconciliation Act of 1981, 105, 186, 323
Omnibus Budget Reconciliation Act of 1993, 126
On Death and Dying (1969) (Kubler-Ross), 333
O'Neil, J. V., 361, 436
One-on-one counseling, 48
On the Origin of Species (Darwin), 57, 96
Open-ended therapies, 188
Opioids, 284
Organization level, intervention at, 43
Organization(s)
    in criminal justice, group work with, 357–358
    professional, 26–30
Organ transplantation, 437–438
Orphanages, 122, 124, 135
Orphan trains, 123
Orthopedic problems, 388–389
Osteoporosis, 190, 194
Other America, The (Harrington), 104
Outdoor relief, 94, 129
Out-of-home services, 133–136
Oxfam America, 116

P

Pace, P. R., 176, 203
Pagels, E., 78
Palliative care, 200–201
Panrenaissance family, Native America, 178
Paraprofessional social work. *See* Human service aide;
    Preprofessional social work
Parapsychology, 151
Pardeck, J. T., 403, 405
Parental leave, in Sweden, 113–114
Parents, gays and lesbians as, 144–146
Parkinson, C. B., 382
Parks, R., 78, 104
Parole, 340–342, 349–351
Parole contract, 337–338
Patient Protection and Affordable Care Act, 214–215
Patterson, K., 366–367
Patton, J. R., 379, 380
Paulson, A., 76, 110
Pauperism, 95
Pay equity, defined, 433
Peace Corps, 104, 112
Peltenberg, Catherine M., 265
Pension Benefit Guarantee Corporation, 317
Pension, 316
Pension plans, 316–317
Pension Protection Act, 317
People of color, intercultural adoptions and, 147
People with disabilities, 74–75
Pereira, J. R., 378
Perlman, H. H., 185

Permanency placement, 132
Personal care homes, 326–327
Personal empowerment, 51
Personal Responsibility and Work Opportunity Act (PRWOA, 1996),
    55, 99, 103, 106, 108–109, 130, 138
Person/environment fit, 41
Persons with disabilities, alcohol and substance use disorder,
    281–282
PhD social workers, 12
Philosophy, social welfare values and, 96–97
Pimlott, S., 364
Pinel, P., 183
Placebo effect, 152
Planned change process, 47
Plan of action, 48
Plymouth Colony, poor law in, 96
Police social work, 341, 343–344
Policy practice, 15
Political Action for Candidate Election (PACE),
    of NASW, 27
Political empowerment, 51
Political parties, 51
Political perspectives, 51–56
    conservative, 52–53
    liberal or progressive, 53–54
    neoliberal and neoconservative perspectives, 54–55
    radical perspectives, 55–56
    spectrum of, 51–52
Political power, of women, 433
Political spectrum, 51–52, 55
Pollutants, 440–441
Poole, Florence, 232
Poor laws
    in England, 94–96, 123
    new concepts in, 94–96
    U.S. values and, 96–98
Poor people. *See also* Poverty
    dependent children, 94
    food pantries for, 433–434
    history in England, 94–96
    impotent poor, 94
    underemployment of, 457–458
Popple, P. R., 52, 53, 55, 97
Population
    African Americans in, 128
    family planning services and, 143
    growth of, 143
    of Indians, 179
    population trends, 421–423
Populations at risk, 49, 51
    African Americans, 280
    children as, 67–68, 275–276
    disabled, 74
    economic hardships, 83
    environmental issues and, 44–47, 359
    gay, lesbian, and bisexual persons, 75–76
    Hispanic Americans, 279–280
    lesbian, gay, bisexual or transgender, 280–281
    Native Americans, 278–279

Populations at risk (*Continued*)
    older adults, 69–70, 277–278
    persons with disabilities, 281–282
    racial and ethnic minority groups, 70–74
    in United States, 67–68
    women as, 68–69, 275–276
Post-Depression Trends, 104
Post traumatic stress disorder (PTSD), 149–150, 177
Potentiation, 285
Poverty, 64
    among disabled, 74
    among gay, lesbian, and bisexual persons, 75–76
    among older adults, 69–70
    among racial and ethnic minority groups, 70–74
    among women, 68–69
    Charity Organization Society and, 123–124
    childhood, 66
    families and, 424
    federal assistance for, 51
    feminization of, 69
    impact of, 66
    juvenilization of, 67
    maintained by poverty programs, 80–81
    minimum wage and, 81–83
    in Sweden, 113–114
    UN development plan and, 418
    War on, 104, 153
Poverty level income, 8
Poverty line, 70
    determination of, 81
Power of attorney, 295
Practice theory, 15
Pray, K., 341
Precognition, 152
Preferred practices, 188
Pregnancy
    substance abuse during, 392–393
    termination of, 134
    UN development plan and, 418
Pregnancy discrimination lawsuits, 155
Prejudice, 64
Premium, 307
Preprofessional social work, 16–17
Presentence investigation, 344
Primary social work setting, 235
Prisons, 345–349
    conditions in, 341
    overcrowding and riots in, 348
    privatization of, 341, 431
    women in, 347
Prison social workers, 348
Private practice, social workers in, 431
Private trouble, 101
Privatization, 109
    of prisons, 341
    of social services, 430–431
Privatization of social services, 430
Probation, 340, 342, 349–350, 377
    federal system of, 345
    innovations in, 341
    intensive, 351
    in juvenile justice, 352
Probation and parole agents, 340, 349
Problem-solving process, 47–48. *See also* Intervention
Professional development, BSW social work curriculum and, 14–15
Professional education, career ladder and, 16–18
Progressive era, reforms during (1900–1930), 100–101
Progressive worldview, 53–54
Promoting Safe and Stable Families Program, 136
Property, African Americans as, 127
Protective Services, 60, 124–126, 131–132
Protestant ethic, poor laws and values of, 96
PRWOA. *See* Personal Responsibility and Work Opportunity Act (PRWOA, 1996)
Psychiatric labels, 181
Psychiatric nurses, in mental health team, 167
Psychiatric social worker, origins of term, 184
Psychiatrists, in mental health team, 167
Psychiatry, social work compared with, 31
Psychic healing, 152
Psychic phenomena, 151
Psychoanalytic theory, 184
Psychokinesis, 152
Psychologists, in mental health team, 167
Psychology, 30
    employment in, 24
    social work compared with, 31
Psychology, social work compared with, 30
Psychosis, 309
Psychotherapy, 164, 171
    crises and, 164–165
Psychotropic medication, 170–172, 186
    treatment, 170–171
PTSD. *See* Post traumatic stress disorder (PTSD)
Public assistance, 101–102
    for poor children, 137
Public Education Association of New York, 230
Public issue, 101
Public Law 94-142, 240
Pupil planning team. *See* Multidisciplinary team
Putnam, M., 382
Puzzanchera, C., 368

Q

QCSW. *See* Qualified Clinical Social Worker (QCSW)
Quadagno, J., 94, 95
Quakers, penitentiaries and, 339
Qualified Clinical Social Worker (QCSW), 26, 165
Qualitative research, 15
Quality Housing and Work Responsibility Act, 319
Quantifying Environmental Health Impacts (WHO), 181
Quantitative research, 15
Quarles, B., 127

R

Race, census and, 421–422
Racial and ethnic minority groups, 70
Racial diversity, 150

Racial group, 237
Racial minority, 70
Racial profiling, 371
Racism, 78
Radical, 51
Radical perspective, 55–56
Radin, Dean, 152, 332
Rapp, R., 273
Raske, M., 395
Reagan, R., 53, 105, 186
Recession, 56
Recidivism, 350
Red Cross, 101
Red Horse, J., 178
Reform(s)
 in criminal justice system, 341
  by Dix, Dorothea, 183–184
  juvenile justice and, 367–372
  in United States (1900–1930), 100–101
  welfare, 142
Refugee status, 426
Regenerative medicine, 437–438
Regis, H. A., 101, 103
Regulation, of social work profession, 24–26
Rehabilitation, 379
 for disabled people, 380–381
 of parents, 132
Rehabilitation Act (1973), 382, 403–404
Rehr, Helen, 209
Reich, J., 132
Reid, W. J., 309, 315
Reinstitutionalization, 383
Relationships importance, 57
Relief
 in England, 94–96
 in United States, 96–98
 welfare, 105
Religion, 331–332
 on caring for needy children, 122
 faith-based initiatives and, 110
 spirituality and, 151–153
Removal, of Cherokees, 179
Reproductive rights, single parenting and, 140–142
Republican Party, 51–53
Research
 on family policy, 153–154
 in mental health, 183–184
Residential treatment center, 135
Residual social welfare, 92
Resilience, 50
Respite care, 315, 325, 394
Restitution, 345, 351, 353
Revell, W. G., Jr., 397
Reverse discrimination, 83
Revocation, of probation or parole, 349
Reynolds, B. C., 185
Rhodes, R., 41, 276
Richey, W., 73, 83, 140, 405
Richmond, M., 9, 97, 123–124, 184, 264
Rich-poor gap, 84–85

Right (political), 51
Rights, of children, 122
Riots, in prisons, 348
Risk rating, for recidivism, 350
Ritter, J. A., 355
Roberts, A., 341
Roberts, A. R., 343
Robinson, V., 185
Rocha, C. J., 65, 85
Rodenhiser, R., 20
Roe v. Wade, 140
Rohani, M., 148
Role-playing, 273
Roosevelt, F.D., 101
Rosato, N. S., 352
Rosengarten, L., 302
Rosenthal, M., 112, 116
Ross, J., 141
Roth, C., 134, 140
Rothman, J. C., 380, 398, 403, 408
Rudnitski, D., 88–89
 case study, 89–91
Runaways, shelters for, 134
Rural poverty, case study in, 82
Rural *vs.* urban area, older adults, 328
Rush, B., 183
Russell Sage Foundation's Charity Organization, 264

S

Sacco, F. C., 249
Safety net approach, 105
Salary, for social workers, 20–22
Saleebey, D., 50, 359–360
Salvation Army, 110
Samantrai, K., 125, 132
Same-sex civil unions, 75–76
Same-sex relationships, in prisons, 348
SAMHSA. *See* Substance Abuse and Mental Health Services Administration (SAMHSA)
Sanction, 139
Sanders, Linda, 190, 194, 197
Sandwich generation, 314–315
Santiago, Lisa, 223
Santiago, Loretta, 223
Sapir, Jean, 265
Saunders, Cicely, 201
Schiller, L. Y., 357
Schizophrenia, 168–169
Schlitz, M., 397
School-linked, integrated services, 235–236
School psychology, 30
School social work
 bullying and violence, 249–250
 case study, 223–227
 certification, 233
 cultural diversity and, 236–239
 current trends, 256–257
 educational evaluations, applied research, 242–243
 environment and early sexual development, 250–252

School social work (Continued)
  family work, 234
  in Ghana, 257–260
  group work, 234
  Hispanic heritage, 227–229
  history of, 229–233
  Latino, people of, 227–229
  roles in, 233–236
  school-linked, integrated services, 235–236
  sex education, 251
  special needs, 240–247
  special-needs children, 243–246
  spiritual development and empowerment, 255–256
  student rights and the law, 246–247
  teamwork, 235
  Truancy, 223, 227, 233, 245, 247, 258
  working with individuals, 233–234
  working with organizations and communities, 234
School-to-prison pipeline, 369
Schwalbe, C. S., 352
Sebelius, K., 328
Secondary setting, 166
Secondary social work setting, 235
Segal, E., 94, 101, 105, 125, 131, 135
Segal, S., 403
Seguin, E., 379
Seizures, in epilepsy, 390
Self-advocacy, by disabled people, 402
Self-Advocates Becoming Empowered, 403
Self-determination, 136
  of disabled people, 402, 407
Self-help, for African Americans, 128
Sensorineural hearing loss, 389–390
Sentencing, in juvenile justice, 353
Sentencing Reform and Corrections Act, 369–370
September 11, 2001, terrorist attacks, 418–420
Settlement Act (England, 1662), 94
Settlement houses, 230, 236
Settlement movement, 97, 100–101, 123
  Charity Organization Society compared with, 97–98
Sexism, 78–79
Sexual abuse
  group work and, 357
  of female prisoners, 348
Sexual orientation, 79–80. *See also* Gay and lesbian persons
  discrimination by, 75–76
Sheafor, B. W., 8, 39
Shell shock, 184
Sheltered English Immersion (SEI), 237–238
Sheltered workshops, 394
Shelters, 134
Sickmund, M., 368
Siefert, K., 364
Simon, T., 380
Single child policy (China), 143
Single mothers, 140
Single parenting, 373–378
  reproductive rights and, 140–142
Single-payer system, 213, 217–219

Slaves, African Americans as, 127
Smart, J., 402
Smarter Sentencing Act, 370
Smiar, Nicholas P., 411
Smith, A., 96
Smith, M., 20
Smith, M. K., 132
Smith College School for Social Work, 184
Smythe, Pat, 300, 302
Social activism, of 1960s, 104
Social and economic justice, 64
Social casework, 184
Social Casework: A Problem-Solving Process (Perlman), 185
Social Darwinism, 57, 96, 380
Social Diagnosis (Richmond), 184, 395
Social-emotional learning (SEL), 255
Social engineering, TANF as, 106
Social insurance, 101
Socialist party, 55
Socialized medicine, 210
Social justice, 9, 49, 64
  Amnesty International on prisoner treatment and, 362–363
  commitment to, 178
  in criminal justice, 362–372
  human diversity and, 398–403
  issues in mental health field, 181–182
  poverty, diversity and intersectionality of multiple factors, 66–77
  progress of, 115–116
Social Justice Issues in the twenty-first Century, 80–87
"Social menace" theory, 381
Social policy
  disabled persons and, 403–406
  mental health services and, 185–187
  rich-poor gap and, 84–85
Social Security, 317–319
  benefits of, 79
  mental health and, 182–188
  older adult poverty and, 69
Social Security Act (1935), 9, 101, 106, 110, 210, 306, 317
Social Services Block Grant, 322–323
Social services, privatization of, 430–431
Social welfare. *See also* Social welfare policy
  concepts of, 93
  defined, 91–92
  Freedmen's Bureau for, 96
  historical events in, 99–100
  international perspective on, 110–116
  liberal support for, 53–54
  in United States in twentieth century, 98–106
  in United States in twenty-first century, 107–110
Social welfare agencies, Freedmen's Bureau as, 127
Social welfare policy
  criminal justice and human rights, 362–372
  health care and, 209–220
  historical roots of, 92–94
  mental health services and, 182–188
  privatization of social services, 430–431
  residual *vs.* institutional, 91–92

Index

social justice and, 86–87
social work practice and (case studies), 34–38
societal response to social justice issues, 80–87
substance use disorders and criminalization, 290–293
in twenty-first century, 107–110
in United States, 86–87
Social work, 5
aging population and, 422–423
class field trip to VA hospital, 204
competencies in health care, 193–197
competency, 47
in criminal justice system, 354–358
defined, 5
education for, 14–24
forensic, 355
grand challenges and contributions of, 443–445
economic trends and, 433–435
environmental sustainability and, 440–442
family trends and, 424–425
future of, 442–445
globalization and, 418–420
history of, 34–36, 188–189
licensure and professional credentialing, 24–26
political forces and, 428–433
practice environment, 12–13
private practice, 430–431
a profession, 5
salary, 20–22
selecting a career in, 16–18
technological and biomedical advances and, 435–440
workforce, 442–443
Social Work and Social Living (Reynolds), 185
Social work degree, 10–11
Social Worker in Gerontology (SW-G), 26
Social workers
acute and posttraumatic stress, 176–177
BSWs and MSWs compared, 10–11
child and family services offered by, 128–136
computer-assisted therapy by, 188
demand for, 20–22, 442–443
ecosystems perspective used by, 40–41
employment with older adults, 334
future employment opportunities, 23–24, 442–443
generalist BSW, 10
in Ghana, Nigeria, and Israel, 29
license of, 25
to maintain ecological sanity, 47
in mental health team, 167
misconception about, 12
monitor medication use, 170–171
professional, 10–12
resolving issues, 48
salaries for, 20–22
social justice needed in, 15
social work and, 10–11
use internet groups, 188
Social Work Imperatives for the Next Decade (NASW), 116–117
Social Work (NASW journal), 27

Social work profession, 5–11
emergence of, 184–185
future of, 442–445
history of, 8–10
and social workers, 10–11
values and ethics, 6–8
Social Work Speaks, 13
Social work students
curriculum, 15
field education, 15
learning phase, 15
problem-solving process, 15
social work practice in, 15
Society, social justice issues and social workers, 90–91
Society for the Prevention of Cruelty to Animals (SPCA), 125
Society for the Prevention of Cruelty to Children (SPCC), 9
Sommer, V. L., 40
Special education, 234, 375, 377
for developmentally disabled, 384
services, 1385
Special Relief Department, of U.S. Sanitary Commission, 8
Speenhamland Act (England), 94–95, 105
Spencer, H., 96
Spending, on war, 158
Sperm banks, 145
Sperm donors, 145
Spinal cord injuries, 204
Spiritual development, school social work, 255–256
Spiritual responses, 44–47
Spirituality, 151–153, 331–333
disabled persons and, 397–398
Springer, D. W., 341
SSI. *See* Supplemental Security Income (SSI)
SSP. *See* State Supplementary Payment (SSP)
Standardized intelligence test, 380
Standardized protocols, in mental health care, 188
Standard of living, 64
Stapleton, D. H., 417
State hospitals, for mentally ill, 183–184
State Licensure, 24–25
State(s)
block grants to, 106
correctional systems in, 345
gay marriages in, 75–76
licensing by, 25
TANF funding by, 106
State Supplementary Payment (SSP), 103
Statute of Laborers, 93
Stein, R., 437
Stem cell research, 437–438
Stern, S., 76
Stigma, 166
Stimulants, 285
Stoessen, L., 109–110
Stoesz, D., 93, 96, 104, 106, 124, 125
Stone, J., 400
Storrs, H. C., 381
Strategic (solution-oriented) approaches, to mental health care, 188

Strengths-based case management, 377
Strengths perspective, 50–51, 359–361
Stress
    acute traumatic, 177
    post traumatic stress disorder and, 176–177
Subculture, 239
Subpoena, 344
Subsidies, for adoption, 135
Substance Abuse and Mental Health Services Administration (SAMHSA), 177, 265, 269, 279–280, 282
Substance-induced disorder, 270
Substance-related disorder, 285
Substance use disorder
    Alcoholics Anonymous (AA), 287–288
    assessment, 268–271
    diversity, 275–282
    case study, 261–264
    classes of substances, 282–286
    criteria/symptoms, 270
    diversity, 275–282
    engagement, 267–268
    evaluation, 274–275
    group treatment, 273–274
    harm reduction model, 286–287
    history of social work, 264–266
    human rights, 293
    individuals and families, 272–273
    intervention, 271–272
    organizations and communities, 274
    prevention and treatment, global differences models, 286
    probation/parole agents for, 349–350
    problem solving, 267–275
    privatization of programs, 430
    social welfare policy, 290–293
    social work contributions and leadership, 265–266
    U.S. social welfare policy, 290–293
    values and ethical issues, 266–267
Subsystems, 39
Suicide
    alcohol and substance use disorders and, 267, 275, 282, 283
    cocaine and, 285
    environmental factors, 181
    Native Americans, substance use disorder and, 278
    opioid use and, 283
    sedatives and, 285
    steps to reduce, 181–182
    women, depression, substance use and, 275
Sundt, J. L., 351
Supplemental Nutrition Assistance Program (SNAP), 130, 252, 321
Supplemental Security Income (SSI), 62, 74, 87, 102–103
    for persons with disabilities, 74–75
Supply-side economics, 53
Supported employment, 397
Suprasystem, 39
Supreme Court (U.S.), 344
    abortion rights and, 140–142
    ADA and, 405
    mental health and developmental disability rulings by, 186
Surles, R. C., 383

Surrogate mothers, 145
Surrogate parenting, 439
Surveillance measures, school social work, 249
Susser, E., 206
Sweden
    children's allowance, 113
    health care, 113
    parental leave, in, 113
    social welfare system in, 113–114
SW-G. *See* Social Worker in Gerontology (SW-G)
Switzky, H., 379, 381, 382
System, 39
Systems theory
    ecosystems perspective and, 40–41
    social work and, 38–40

T

Taft, J., 185
TANF. *See* Temporary Assistance for Needy Families (TANF)
TANF caseloads, 434
Tart, C.T., 151, 152
Taxation
    EITC and, 104–106
    for faith-based programs, 110
Tax-sheltered annuities, 318
Taylor, S. H., 396, 403
Teamwork relationships, 167–168
Teamwork, school social work, 235
Tea Party, the, 53
Technology
    biomedical, 436–439
    information and communication, 435–436
    for probation and parole agents, 349
Telemedicine, 204
Telepathy, 152
Temporary Assistance for Needy Families (TANF), 32, 106–107, 130, 138–139, 144, 428–430, 434
    child care needs and, 60–61
Termination of pregnancy, 134
Terrorism. *See also* September 11, 2001, terrorist attacks
    globalization and, 418–420
    minority ethnic groups and, 73
    terrorist attacks, 73, 418–420
Terzieff, J., 68
The Chalice and the Blade, 78
The Gnostic Gospels, 78
Therapeutic cloning, 440
Therapy, family, 131
Therapy groups, 174
Thyer, B. A., 25
Third-party payment system, 210
Time-limited family and group interventions, 188
Tirrito, T. T., 299
Tissue stem cells, 437
Title VII, of Civil Rights Act, 83
Title XIX, 102
Title XVIII, 211
Title XX, of Social Security Act (1974), 125

Tolerance, 269
Traditional families, Native American, 178
Traditionalist party, 53
Trafficking, 220, 417, 419–420
    of drugs, 286, 290–291
Trail of Tears, 179–180
Training schools for disabled persons, 379
Training, specialized, 10
Tranquilizers, 170–171
Transgender persons, 76–77
Transitional family, Native American, 178
Transphobia, 79
Trattner, W. I., 94, 123
Trauma
    of Native people, 180–181
    psychological, 176–181
Trauma and Crisis Amid Human Diversity, 201–203
Trauma-and stressor-related disorders, 170
Traumatic brain injury, 390–391
Travis, J., 359
Treger, H., 341
Trickle down theory, 53
Trimble, D., 357
Tropman, J., 96
Truancy, 223, 247, 258
Trumbull, M., 46, 154, 157, 158, 317
Trump, Donald
    criminal justice sentencing and, 372
    election, 2016, 46, 434
    environment and, 100, 109, 441
    family and, 141–143, 145, 148
    health care and, 217, 219–220
    immigration and, 67, 427
    mental health care and, 217, 219–220
    older adults and, 308
    school and, 228–229
The Truth about Alex (movie), 243
Turning to each other, 56–57
Twemlow, S. W., 249–250
Tyuse, S. W., 102, 106

U

Underemployment, 433–434
Unemployment
    in Japan, 115
    insurance, 102
UNICEF, 29
United Nations
    Convention against Torture and Other Cruel, Inhuman or Degrading Treatment or Punishment, 362–363
    development plan of, 418–420
United Nations Climate Change Conference, 45
United Nations Sustainable Development Goals, 419–420
United Nations' Universal Declaration of Human Rights, 65
United States
    child poverty rate in, 66
    Convention on the Rights of the Child and, 116
    criminal justice systems in, 340
    current trends, 157–158
    GAO Strategic Plan and, 417–418
    future health care policy in, 218–220
    international social welfare rank of, 110–113
    meeting needs of children and families in, 153–154
    minority groups in, 70–71
    multiculturalism in, 421–422
    people with disabilities in, 74–75
    poverty in, 64
    racism in, 78
    social welfare in, 92, 98–99
    social welfare policy, 86–87
United States Census, 150
Universal coverage, 214
Universal health care system, 214
Universal primary school education, UN development plan and, 418
University of Illinois, Jane Addams School of Social Work at, 341
UN Millennium Declaration, 156
    goals of, 156
Urban Institute, analysis of TANF, 428
Urban Neighborhood Center, 59
USA Patriot Act, 73
US and World Population Clock (2016), 142
U.S. Department of Agriculture, 103
U.S. Department of Housing and Urban Development, 130
U.S. Department of Labor, 101
U.S. social welfare policy, 290–293

V

Vagrants, in England, 94
Values, 6, 49
    criminal justice social work and, 354–355
    disabled persons and, 406–409
    in mental health work, 166–167
    poor law and, 96–97
Van Acker, R., 379
Van Wormer, K., 153, 269, 273, 287, 348, 358
Velkoff, V. A., 422, 423
Vermont, same-sex civil unions in, 75–76
Veterans Administration, 185
Veterans Health Administration (VHA), 203
Veterans, health care for, 203
Victim-offender mediation, 351
Victim/witness programs, 341, 344
Vietnamese people, 401
Vincent, G. K., 422
Violence, in prisons, 348
Violent crime, 353
Vista (Volunteers in Service to America), 104
Volstead Act, 290
Voluntary organizations, 101
    for African Americans, 123
    for child welfare, 124–126
Volunteers in religious groups, 359–360
Von Bertalanffy, L., 40, 41
Voucher programs, 103–104

W

Wage gap, women and, 432–433
Wallis, M., 179
War on Drugs, 291–292
War on Poverty, 104, 153
Washington, B. T., 351
Washington, M. M., 351, 352
Wealth of Nations, The (Smith), 96
Wehman, P., 397
Weismiller, T., 266
Welfare reform, 105–106, 428–430
    NASW and, 116
Welfare state, cutting back of, 104–106
Whaley, S. E., 277
What Is Social Casework? (Richmond), 184
Wheatley, M., 56
    importance of relationships, 56–57
Whitaker, T., 22
Whitaker, W., 93
White House Conference on Children, 124
Whittle, D., 110
WIAR. *See* Women and Infants at Risk (WIAR) program
WIC. *See* Women, Infants, and Children program (WIC)
Wild Boy of Aveyron, The (Itard), 379
Wilensky, H., 92
Willer, B., 381, 382
Wilson, M., 20
Wilson, M. E., 124
WIN. *See* Work Incentive Program (WIN)
Wolfe, P. S., 383
Women. *See also* Females; Gay and lesbian persons; Mothers
    depression, substance use, and suicide, 275
    discrimination against, 69
    egg donation and low income, 439–440
    empowerment of, 418
    ERA and, 431
    group work with sexually abused, 357
    lifespan of, 423
    as minority group, 71–72
    as population at risk, 68, 137–150
    poverty among, 69
    in prisons, 348–349
    trafficking, 220
    voting rights for, 431
    wage gap and, 431–433
Women and Infants at Risk (WIAR) program, 363–364
Women, Infants, and Children program (WIC), 104
Woman's Christian Temperance Union (WCTU), 290
Women's Education Association (in Boston), 230
Worker compensation, laws for, 101
Workhouse, in England, 94–96
Work Incentive Program (WIN), 104, 105
Work requirements, of TANF, 138–139, 428–429, 433–434
Working poor, 105, 107
Workplace, family-friendly nature of, 154–156
World Health Organization (WHO), 181, 220
World Future Society, 424
Worldview, 53
World War I, 184
Wright, J. P., 351
Wright, Pamela, 2–5, 10, 11, 18
Wyatt v. Stickney, 186, 382

X

Xu, J., 153

Y

Yellow Horse Brave Heart, M., 180
Yeoman, B., 305
Youth Correctional Services, 337
Yule, R., 158

Z

Zastrow, C. H., 43
Zeitlin, J., 153
Zero-tolerance policies, 249
Zhang, X., 443
Zimmer, B., 357